THE COMPLETE ART OF WORLD BUILDING

VOLUMES 1-3 OF

THE ART OF WORLD BUILDING SERIES

RANDY ELLEFSON

Evermore Press
GAITHERSBURG, MARYLAND

Evermore Press, LLC
Gaithersburg, Maryland
www.evermorepress.org

Publisher's Note: This book includes fictional passages. All names, charac-ters, locations, and incidents are products of the author's imagination, or have been used fictitiously. Any semblance to actual persons living or dead, locales, or events is coincidental and not intended by the author.

Publisher's Cataloging-In-Publication Data
(Prepared by The Donohue Group, Inc.)

Names: Ellefson, Randy, author.
Title: The complete art of world building / Randy Ellefson.
Description: 1st ed. | Gaithersburg, Maryland : Evermore Press, [2020] |
    Series: The art of world building series ; volumes 1-3 | Includes
    bibliographical references. | Content: Volume 1. Creating life -- Volume 2.
    Creating places -- Volume 3. Cultures and beyond.
Identifiers: ISBN 9781946995414 (Amazon paperback) |
    ISBN 9781946995407 (IngramSpark paperback) |
    ISBN 9781946995421 (IngramSpark hardcover) |
    ISBN 9781946995490 (ePub)
Subjects: LCSH: Fantasy fiction--Authorship. | Imaginary societies. |
    Imaginary places. | Fictitious characters. | Animals, Mythical. |
    Creative writing. | Storytelling.
Classification: LCC PN3377.5.F34 E454 2020 (print) | LCC PN3377.5.F34
    (ebook) | DDC 808.38766--dc23

Creating Life is exhaustive, well written, and knowledgeable...I, as a successful science fiction and fantasy writer, have generated many worlds, so this material is familiar, but it would have been easier and probably better had I had a reference like this. Creating Places...will upgrade you from a mediocre speculative fiction writer to a superior one.

—BESTSELLING AUTHOR PIERS ANTHONY

Creating Life ...is THOROUGH. This book raises ALL the points, and asks all the questions. Not just recommended: essential! Creating Places is one of that rare breed: an essential reference work. Unlike most references, this one is fun to read. Not to mention a goad and spark for the imagination!

—ED GREENWOOD INVENTOR OF THE FORGOTTEN REALMS®
AND DOZENS OF IMAGINARY WORLDS

CONTENTS

FIGURES

I created many images in volume two, but the following individuals created other figures in volume :

Figure 16: KDVP (Wikipedia User)
Figures 20-22: domdomegg (Wikipedia User)
Figure 24: Dustin M. Ramsey
Figure 28: P199 (Wikipedia User)
Figure 29: Ivo Kruusamägi (Wikipedia User)
Figure 48: Stan Shebs
Figure 51: Rama
Figure 53: Lance Woodworth

TABLE OF FIGURES

ACKNOWLEDGEMENTS

Special thanks to Raoul Miller, Laura Scroggins, Anne Heiser, Rachel Hoff, Margarita Martinez, Tom Farr, and Vivian Syroyezhkina

Edited by JJ Henke

Cover design by Deranged Doctor Design

SERIES INTRODUCTION

A ll three volumes of the bestselling books on world building, *The Art of World Building* series, are collected here in one comprehensive reference work.

Minor differences between this set and the individual volumes are solely about organization. This series introduction includes sections that were repeated in each volume and have been condensed and combined here. Similarly, the three, separate bibliographies are collected at the end.

ABOUT ME

By profession I'm a software developer, but I've been writing fantasy fiction since 1988 and building worlds just as long, mostly one planet called Llurien. Yes, I am crazy. But I love what I do. I didn't intend to work on it for so long, but when life has prevented me from writing, I've worked on Llurien. I've done everything in these chapters and authored two hundred thousand words of world building in my files. Llurien even has its own website now at http://www.llurien.com. I've written six novels and over a dozen short stories over the years, and have just begun my publishing career with a novella that you can read for free (see below).

I'm also a musician with a degree in classical guitar; I've released three albums of instrumental rock, one classical guitar CD, and a disc of acoustic guitar instrumentals. You can learn more, hear songs, and see videos at my main website, http://www.randyellefson.com.

Free Book

If you'd like to see a sample of my world building efforts in action, anyone who joins my fiction newsletter receives a free eBook. Please note there's also a separate newsletter for *The Art of World Building*.

Figure 1 Free Book

Disclaimers

World building is defined as the act of creating an imaginary world. While that suggests an entire planet, the result is often one continent or less. By world building, I don't mean using pre-existing ideas and putting your own spin on them, such as reimagining Greek gods in modern or ancient times, or writing an alternate reality of Earth. While such approaches are fine, that's not what this series is about, though such creators may find the series useful.

I've omitted the science behind any real or imagined technology (like the warp drive from *Star Trek*) because other books on these subjects exist. While I've included some details to help you create life forms with appropriate features, the information is tailored to world building uses. The guide focuses on being realistic about imagining new worlds while not being overly technical. Something like plate tectonics is discussed in volume two because it impacts the formation of mountains, but the details of subduction zones are seldom relevant for us when drawing mountain ranges, for example.

While some authors prefer the term "races" to "species," I've used the latter term throughout most of the series except for the section in volume one discussing the merits of both terms. This book uses "SF" to abbreviate science fiction. SF is broadly defined herein as a setting with technology far in excess of current capabilities. Fantasy is loosely defined in this book as a setting using magic, knights, and lacking modern technology. As a stylistic point, to avoid writing "he/she," I've also opted for "he" when discussing someone who could be either gender.

Since I am an author, and primarily write fantasy, the series is admittedly weighted in this direction, but whether you're in the gaming industry, a screenwriter, a hobbyist, or write science fiction, much of the three volumes can help you anyway. I just don't claim to have covered every last element despite my attempts to be reasonably comprehensive. If you have suggested topics you feel should be covered, feel free to contact me at mail@randyellefson.com about updates for later editions.

TEMPLATES AND NEWSLETTER

Effective world building requires having written down details about the created world. To help you organize and jumpstart your efforts, each volume in this series includes templates in the appendices. This series includes twenty-two: gods, species, monsters, world figures (heroes, villains, and more), plants, animals, undead, solar systems, sovereign powers, settlements, cultures, organizations, armed forces, religions, supernatural energies, supernatural lands, magic systems, spells, legal systems, monetary systems, education systems, and games.

In addition, volume two provides two Microsoft Excel files for calculating moon orbits and travel times on land, sea, and air. While the formulas are discussed in the book, the files come set with the needed calculations. I recommend that interested world builders download them rather than try to create them.

Rather than typing these up yourself, you can download these templates for free by joining the newsletter for *The Art of World Building* at http://www.artofworldbuilding.com/ newsletter/. As each volume is published, whether you've bought the book or not, subscribers will automatically receive an email with links to download the templates as Microsoft Word files, which you can repeatedly use.

THE PODCAST

The Art of World Building podcast expands on the material within the series. The additional examples offer world builders more insight into ramifications of decisions. You can hear the podcast, read transcripts, and learn more about the episodes at http://www.artofworldbuilding.com/podcasts.

YOUTUBE CHANNEL

The Art of World Building YouTube channel now has videos that also expand on the material within the series. Check out the growing playlists and subscribe. Videos include replays of webinars that feature a Q&A, lessons from the books, previews of WBU courses, and tips from the book, *185 Tips on World Building.*

http://bit.ly/AOWBYouTube.

WORLD BUILDING UNIVERSITY

World Building University (WBU) has online courses that provide step-by-step instruction on creating all aspects of great fantasy and science fiction worlds. Each includes a series of video lessons, quizzes to test your retention of what you've learned, and assignments designed to make your creation a reality instead of a dream. Courses are intended for authors, game designers, and hobbyists. A free course is available to get you started! See the website or mailing list for details:

http://www.worldbuilding.university/.

CREATING LIFE (VOLUME ONE)

Everything we need to know about how to create gods, species/races, plants, animals, monsters, heroes, villains, and even undead is included in *Creating Life (The Art of World Building, #1)*. Some basic techniques are also discussed, such as using analogies and deciding how many worlds to build in a career. As with every volume, it includes reusable templates that can help you build better, faster.

CREATING PLACES (VOLUME TWO)

The life we create needs to originate from somewhere on a planet: an ocean, a continent, in a land feature (like a forest or mountain range), in a kingdom, or in a settlement. *Creating Places (The Art of World Building, #2)* goes into detail about inventing such locations and figuring out how long it takes to travel between them by various forms of locomotion: foot, horse, wagon, dragon, wooden ship, spaceship, and more. The overall rules of our world are also considered, along with inventing time, history, various places of interest, and how to draw maps. We can start our work with any one of those subjects and crisscross between places and life, for one often impacts the other.

CULTURES AND BEYOND (VOLUME THREE)

Everything not covered in the first two volumes lies within the finale, *Cultures and Beyond (The Art of World Building, #3)*. This includes creating culture, organizations, armed forces, religions, the supernatural, magic systems, technological and supernatural items, languages, names, and various systems our world will have, from health, educational, legal, commerce, to information systems. Finally, we look at how to manage our world building projects. Without these subjects, no world building project is complete.

More books in the series are available, including two workbooks, at https://www.randyellefson.com/mywork

VOLUME 1

CREATING LIFE

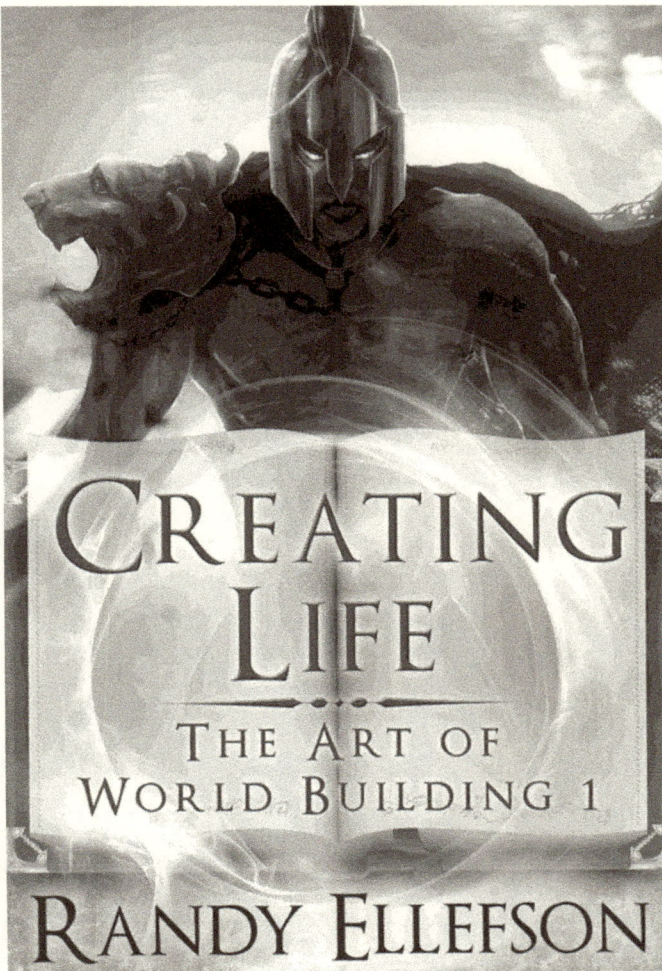

INTRODUCTION

Series like *Harry Potter*, *Star Trek*, *The Lord of the Rings*, and *Star Wars* are beloved for their intricate and detailed worlds. Each has made their creators famous, respected, and fabulously wealthy. They've generated billions in revenue across multiple industries, including books, movies, games, and endless merchandising. They're part of popular culture. How can you emulate such skill? This book series, *The Art of World Building*, will teach you how to create believable, imaginative, and hopefully lucrative worlds to improve your fantasy or science fiction career.

My first goal with this series is to provide you with tools to speed you along in what is often time-consuming work. My second aims to help you realize your dreams and make great choices. Whether you've built many worlds before, are in the middle of your first one now, or have never started, this series can help you achieve your objectives by providing:

- An examination of your goals, options, and how much of your attention each subject needs
- Detailed advice on the pros and cons of every approach and how to balance them
- Extensive research on real-world elements you should understand and utilize
- How and when to use analogues
- Thought-provoking questions to help you make informed decisions and stimulate imagination
- Classification of world building elements into related areas for clarity
- Practical examples illustrating potential results

- Ideas on organizing world building files for quick access and minimized redundancy
- Reusable templates to ensure consistency and thoroughness

The examples included in the text were created specifically for this guide and are not drawn from any setting I've created, except in rare instances. Where possible, well-known books, films, and TV shows have been cited as good examples that illustrate a point. With examples of what to avoid, I've usually avoided naming the work. Many of the examples and discussions herein can trigger ideas.

The book has a website where you can find additional resources and information on other volumes in this series.

Visit http://www.artofworldbuilding.com.

WHERE TO START

The series, and chapters within each volume, can be read in any order but are arranged according to what might come first in a world's timeline. Gods, if real, precede humanoids, which precede undead humanoids, et al. But our creations can be invented in any order. In fact, crisscrossing back and forth between different subjects is part of the work. We might start with inventing gods before working on species, then update our gods based on what we've done with species. It's unusual, even unlikely, to invent something and then never revisit it.

Only you can decide where to begin, but it's recommended to take any idea and run with it, writing down whatever occurs to you. If there are problems with it, they can be fixed later as you update and improve upon it. If you haven't read a chapter in this book and have an idea for something that's covered here, go ahead and write down everything you're thinking. Stopping to read this might make the idea vanish. We can also get it into our heads that we must do something "right." This is a dangerous thought because it inhibits creativity, which is the lifeblood of all art, including world building. It's better to jot down a poor idea and fix it later than to stall, research how it could be done, get overwhelmed, and then forget it or lose interest.

Doing it "right" is itself "wrong" much of the time, as there are seldom rules that cannot be bent and even broken. All advice, whether found in this series or another, is best stated in an open-ended manner and taken as food for thought rather than as a gospel that must be followed. If you disagree with anything written here or elsewhere, good for you. Deciding not to do something, or going about it a different way, still adds clarity to our process and results.

So where do you start? Where your heart lies.

THE CHAPTERS

What follows is a brief summary of what's included in each chapter in volume one, *Creating Life*.

CHAPTER 1 – WHY BUILD A WORLD?

While world building is expected in many genres of fantasy and SF, we must decide how many worlds to build. This will depend on our career plans and goals. Learn the advantages and disadvantages of building one world per story vs. one world for many stories, and when to take each approach. Sometimes doing both is best, allowing for greater depth in one world but the option to step away to keep things fresh. Using analogues can help us create believable societies quickly but has pitfalls that can be avoided. Do you have the ability to create many interesting worlds, and will they have enough depth to make the effort worth it?

CHAPTER 2 – CREATING GODS

Our species will invent gods to believe in even if we don't invent them, so we may need some deities for people to reference in dialogue, whether praying or swearing. In SF, belief in gods may still exist despite, or even because of, advances in science. In fantasy, priests often call on a god to heal someone, and this requires having invented the gods. Pantheons offer advantages over a lone god, including dynamic relationships between them and the species. Half gods and demigods are other options that help us create myths and legends to enrich our world, especially if gods can be born, die, or be visited in their realm.

Myths about how the gods or species came to exist help people understand the purpose of their lives and what awaits them in death. Symbols, appearance, patronage, and willingness to impact the lives of their species all color a pantheon and world. Gods also create places people can visit or items that can fall into the wrong hands, offering possibilities for stories.

CHAPTER 3 – CREATING A SPECIES

Audiences are familiar with using "race" to distinguish between humanoids, especially in fantasy, but species may be a more appropriate term. This chapter explores the meaning and implications of both words, with some examples of which one to use, when, and why.

Creating a species is challenging and time consuming, but the risks and rewards can be navigated and achieved, respectively. This chapter helps us decide on our goals and if the effort is worth it. SF writers might have little choice but to create species because there are no public domain species available like the elves, dwarves, and dragons of fantasy. The benefits of creating something different can outweigh the investment and help our work stand out.

An invented species must compete with legendary ones like elves, dwarves, and dragons; this chapter helps us achieve this. Starting with habitat helps us decide on physical adaptations that affect their minds, outlook, and society, and what a typical settlement might be like and whether or not they live in jointly formed settlements. Their disposition affects their relationships with other species but can also limit their usefulness to us unless steps are taken to avoid this. Characteristics like intelligence, wisdom, and dexterity all play a role in how they can be used in our work, as does their society and world view, both affected by a history we can invent to integrate them with our world. Their familiarity with the supernatural and technology influences their prominence and how they compare to other life in our world.

CHAPTER 4 – CREATING WORLD FIGURES

Villains, heroes, and more give our characters admired or despised individuals who've shaped the world and inspired them. Using Earth analogues can speed the invention of such world figures, though it's best to change some details to obfuscate the similarities. Living figures can provide ongoing usefulness but the deceased can cast a long shadow, too. Their possessions can be just as famous and offer opportunities for our characters to find something helpful or dangerous. Family, friends, and enemies also provide ongoing possibilities for their life to impact our current characters.

CHAPTER 5 – CREATING MONSTERS

The difference between monsters, species, and animals is largely sophistication and numbers. Many monsters are created by accidents that turn an existing species or animal into something else, but sometimes monsters are created on purpose. In the latter case it's especially important to decide who caused this. A monster's habitat has an impact on its usefulness and sets the stage for creating atmosphere and characterization that will largely define our audience's experience with it before the terrifying reveal. Its motivation in life, or in our work, also determines what it does and the sort of trouble it's causing for our species.

CHAPTER 6 – CREATING PLANTS AND ANIMALS

In fantasy, creating plants and animals is optional due to expectations that the world is very Earth-like, but in SF that takes place away from Earth, audiences are more likely to expect new ones. It takes less time to create these than other life in this book, but we'll want to consider our time investment, how often our setting will be used, whether our creations impact our work and the impression it creates, and whether the desire to do something unique and new is worthwhile for both us and our audience.

Plants and animals are classified into categories, such as cycads, conifers, and flowering plants, and amphibians, birds, fish, mammals, and reptiles. The lifecycle of the former and the behavior of the latter help distinguish them and can be used to propel or inhibit stories involving them. While we may have purposes for them as an author, our world's inhabitants have them, too, such as decoration and medicinal uses for plants, and domestication, sports, guards, pets and transportation for animals. Both can be used for food and materials to enrich life and our world.

CHAPTER 7 – CREATING UNDEAD

Many types of undead already exist and are public domain, and it's challenging to invent something new. Undead are often classified by appearance and behavior, but it is also their origins and how they can be destroyed that will help distinguish our undead from pre-existing types. The two basic ones are those with a body, like zombies, and those without, like ghosts. Those with a body might have a soul or not. We can decide on the mental faculties of our undead by deciding if the mind goes with the soul, but there are other factors that can impair the minds and even emotional states of undead. All of these affect behavior, as do their origins, goals, and what they're capable of.

CHAPTER ONE

WHY BUILD A WORLD?

Some people do it for fun, some do it for their stories, and some might do it from a sense of obligation (it's expected in their genre), but world building is always voluntary. We can easily craft a story using standard staples like elves and dragons, castles and wizards, or anything else we've all seen before. But if you wanted to repeat what everyone else has done, this book wouldn't have attracted your attention. We can be creative in more than just storytelling. We can do more than slap together a new species after only a little development time because we aren't going to use it much or dive into details about it.

We've all seen something new that made us wish we'd thought of it. We've all wanted our work to stand out. And who hasn't gotten a little bored with those available, public domain ideas? They're overused because everyone can use them. Why not create something unique, something that makes our world shine brightly?

The answer is that it's not easy. It can be time consuming. They are so many things to consider. And if no one likes what we've built after countless hours of blood, sweat, and tears, we've wasted all of that time and effort. Failure costs us respect. People stop enjoying our work. Maybe they write a snarky review online. The more risk we take, the greater our odds of failure.

And the better our odds of being brilliant.

The Art of World Building series ensures you do the latter. It's designed to help you avoid pitfalls and improve the quality of your ideas so you can create a memorable world that's respected, fascinating, and a huge asset to your works. If you're one of the lucky few, there might even be extensive merchandising opportunities if people are captivated with your world. But let's not get ahead of ourselves or leave all of this to chance.

USING ANALOGUES

Do we need to build a world? Only if our story takes place somewhere other than Earth. But that world can be so Earth-like that it's essentially Earth with another name. This is the easiest approach with the lowest amount of risk. Unfortunately, it's also the least interesting. This is what's referred to as an analogue: something that has a corresponding version on Earth.

For example, maybe we invent a small island country called Xenoi where ritual suicide is accepted, honor is cherished over life, expert swordsman use special swords, women are subservient, everyone has black hair, fish and rice are staples, and there's an emperor. How far did you get through that before you realized Xenoi is Japan? Which elements would you remove so that it's not so obvious?

We should make changes to our analogues so they aren't recognized.

THE RULE OF THREE

When using an analogue, strive to change the source in at least three significant ways. Focus on the most prominent aspects and alter some, or make a longer list and decide what matters to keep and what doesn't. If you have no specific use for a trait that really identifies the analogue, remove it.

For example, an elf lives in the forest, has pointed ears, and disrespects humans. Do we need the pointed ears? Are they serving a purpose we can't live without? Why not ditch the negative attitude? Leaving them in forests might be good, but maybe they should be more wide ranging. This exercise can be done to everything else in this book series. Follow the rule of three and fewer people will recognize your analogues.

WHAT'S IN A NAME?

More than you think.

Let's say I invent a world that features a horse with an extra pair of legs. Next I incorporate a poisonous yellow tomato as well as a lion of superior intelligence. Then I call these objects horse, tomato, and lion. Would you remember the differences or picture the traditional versions?

There's a kind of mental inertia to a known term; it suggests familiarity, which in turn overwrites our memory of a different detail in the book we're reading. For example, if a horse is described as having six legs the first time it's mentioned, but that detail never arises over the next hundred times the creature appears, readers will completely forget it has two more legs.

This issue is less true in a visual medium—we're reminded of the difference every time the creature appears—but in books, we'll have to keep reminding people, which feels like unnecessary exposition and housekeeping (for us and the audience). If we have to keep calling it a "six-legged horse," that encumbrance isn't much better. If we don't call it a horse, but describe it in such a way that people think, "Oh, it's just a horse with two more legs," is that an improvement? More importantly, unless the alteration matters, why do it at all? It does make the world more alien, which is a fine goal.

Another issue we can face is inappropriately using a known term. There are expectations about what a word means, and while we have some creative license to make things our own and put a new spin on something, there's a limit to how much liberty we can take before we cause a negative reaction. An obvious example would be calling a seven-foot-tall humanoid a dwarf (unless all other humanoids are considerably taller than that). In a visual medium, we must be especially careful not to be too obvious with an analogue. I recently saw a movie where characters spoke of goblins. I formed an expectation of what I'd see. Imagine my surprise when the goblin turned out to look like a gorilla with horns and a love of gold. It even moved and behaved like a gorilla. My expectations were defied in a way that jarred me right out of the story.

These factors should be considered when deciding if we should use a different name. A new word also carries some risk. Authors may need to present a longer description to their audience. What we're describing needs to be firmly imprinted on the reader's mind so that little more than the term is needed later. We might use the occasional mention of a characteristic, preferably during action involving that feature so it doesn't seem like a reminder.

World builders can decide based on how many changes we've made to the analogue. The more changes we've made, the more our creation warrants a new name. How to create names is covered in *Cultures and Beyond (The Art of World Building, #3)*.

HOW MANY WORLDS?

ONE VS. MANY

Since world building takes time, we should consider how many worlds we might build over the course of our career and whether it makes sense to build a world per story (twenty worlds for twenty stories), just one world for all [twenty] stories, or a mixture of both. Or neither. Let's look at the pros and cons of each approach.

ONE WORLD FOR ONE STORY

Creating a world for each story has some advantages. We build only what we need for that tale, so it takes less time. We don't have to think through so many items. We're not tied to that world indefinitely; if our audience doesn't like it, or we grow tired of it, or something just doesn't seem to be working, we were done with it anyway. Those creators who aren't sure how much writing they'll do can test the world building waters and learn if it's something they enjoy. If we're a novice at world building and it shows in early work, we can learn and move on rather than having to fix those mistakes. If we have a more experimental concept that takes greater risks with an audience supporting it, we've risked less.

This approach has disadvantages as well. Skimping on world building could cause an under-developed or less interesting world. It can be less unique, too, if we use staples like elves, dwarves, and dragons. It takes considerable work to invent species that favorably compare to those. If we do a lot of work but only use it once, is it worth it? We'll have to repeat much of that work every time we invent another world. This could cause world building fatigue when we're on our twentieth world. The risk of repeating ourselves also rises. If a story becomes very popular and our audience demands more, we might find that our less developed concepts have caused problems we struggle to resolve in later works.

ONE WORLD FOR MANY STORIES

The alternative is to build one world for use on those twenty books. Just doing it once means not repeating ourselves. Greater depth and realism can be created by inventing more detail, which is needed to make new concepts, like species, more believable. This approach becomes worthwhile if we'll use the setting for years. If we invent new life and use only those, we're no longer bound by the expectations that familiar species cause. We have freedom to follow our own rules. Our books will stand out, and if the setting is popular, this alone can draw fans back with each new product released. We might even be able to license the world for product development, from action figures to role-playing spin-offs.

This much attention to detail is a considerable time investment, which *The Art of World Building* will reduce. We need a diverse world to avoid audience boredom over so many tales, and this requires months, even years of development. During that time, we'll benefit from friends who are willing to provide feedback on the world we've created, but this is hard to get. People want to comment on a story, not on our world building. If we know other world building authors, they might help and are our best resource. If we never get published, we never reach an audience and have arguably wasted time, but having multiple stories to set in that world mitigates this, as does the ability to self-publish. Time spent on this is also time not spent on our writing craft. World building fatigue can creep in from inventing so many things, but everything is optional and some elements have higher priorities than others.

On the surface, creating one setting per book may involve less effort at the time, but if we have to create a dozen worlds over the years, is that more or less work than one more detailed, reusable setting?

THE HYBRID

We can split the difference—create one planet that's intended for many stories while also creating less developed ones for single stories. This hybrid approach is the best of both worlds. We might need a break from our "main" world (for lack of a better term) or just want to do something different or new once again. We can utilize a single-use world for more extreme risks, keeping our main world more accessible.

If we create a main world to use many times, a mixed approach will ease the upfront time investment. This is discussed in more detail in volume three, *Cultures and Beyond*, "Getting Started" chapter. What we can do is create our continents in rough form, then the gods of that whole world, and any species, animals, and plants that are found mostly everywhere. Then focus on a continent and some nations on the large scale and some basic history, including wars and animosities. We'll also need a major city or two in every kingdom. At that point, we've created a basic framework for the rest. As needed when writing a story, we can flesh out details of any given city.

At later times, we can develop other continents, cities, and add more monsters and other creatures as we go along. If we have a new book series, we can set it on the world we've created but in another kingdom or continent we haven't used much, or even in another time period. And yet we still have our species, our gods, or a system of magic. We can reuse much of what we've already done.

HOW TO DECIDE

Consider how passionate you are about world building. If you're an author, your primary goal is telling stories. Will you be satisfied with showing your originality in the story more than the setting? Is there a risk you'll get so involved in world building that you'll seldom get around to telling those stories? Authors are well known for finding excuses not to write despite wanting to write. Will this become one? Every minute on this is a minute you could've spent on your writing craft or building an audience. Where does your heart lie?

It's also important to consider how long you intend your career to be. If you're a "lifer" and will write for decades in a genre requiring world building, then expending a lot of effort makes more sense than for someone who wants to give writing a shot and will bow out after failure, or even modest success. If you know that's you, why invest tons of time, even if you love it? Fiction is a speculative field, but writing a book at least produces a product to be sold; building a world seldom does.

Life intrudes on our time to write. This is truer for longer works like a novel. If we don't have time to write a novel this year, because we're in college, or just became a parent, or something else, we can spend time inventing a setting instead. A novel takes months of continuous work to stay involved, but world building can be done in a few minutes here and there. In my case, I spent most of a decade unable to write due to first college and then an injury that made writing difficult; in the meantime, I built an enormous amount for my main world. The younger me gave the older me a great gift.

HOW MANY WORLDS ARE IN YOU?

Do world builders have the ability to create more than one great world? Theoretically, yes. Do you? Creative people try to avoid repeating themselves. The more specific an idea, the more sense it makes to exclude it from a second world. Having dragons on both worlds is okay, but if the first world is dominated by dragons who only breathe fire, cast no magic, and won't let anyone ride them, then repeating that in another world makes us look like we have no imagination; the dreaded "formula" accusation will get hurled at us. With each world created, we further restrict ourselves. Soon we're out of ideas. We could solve that by being generic all the time, but then what's the point of world building?

A CAVEAT

If the first story we publish in a world begins a series, audiences may/will expect subsequent stories set on that planet to have some connection to that initial one. This likely originates from this being what authors frequently do. If we defy this expectation, there may be some backlash. We can avoid this expectation by publishing unrelated stories on that world *before* a series there. One problem with that solution is that if we're self-publishing, it's widely believed that our careers will do best if we publish a series because readers gobble up subsequent books, so perhaps self-publishing a few unrelated short stories or a novella gets us past all of this. Or we can just ignore the issue.

A QUESTION OF DEPTH

A single, detailed world provides a richer, more diverse, immersive experience, but we must remember that they want a story, even in gaming. World building is always subservient to this, and yet when we spend many hours doing it, we're tempted to include more of what we've created than is required for our story. We're too close to our work. It can be prudent to take breaks from world building and remember that it isn't the ultimate goal.

Audiences don't want stories about world building., but about people and conflicts. These should be layered within our setting, not used as an excuse to show off what we've invented. There are ways to achieve this.

For example, when I created the Coiryn Riders, a group of military horsemen distinct from knights, I went overboard. I ended up with a fifteen-thousand-word file of details on their ranks, advancement, training, usages, equipment, and more. I could never get all this across in an average novel even if I wanted to (and I don't). But there are many ways I can use them.

I could have a lead character become a Coiryn Rider and show his rise through the ranks over the course of a novel series, revealing many details about the horsemen and what it's like to be one. As minor characters, they also serve as heralds, so one might be tasked with traveling alone through hostile lands. They are supposed to be given safe passage, which provides an opportunity for a King's Herald to be killed by an enemy power, inciting war. One might use his military skills as part of an adventuring group I'm featuring. I can have my main characters encounter a group of Coiryn Riders on nearing a city, revealing that the riders routinely patrol perimeters, or in their role as heralds, deliver warnings of nearby threats. They are also cavalry in army war scenes.

That's several possible uses. I wouldn't want to try jamming all of this into one story. Instead, I can spread it out across many tales over the course of my career. By having worked out so many details in advance, I run little risk of contradicting myself with later works set on Llurien, a problem that inventing/publishing piece by piece exposes us to.

The Coiryn Riders were not invented for a tale. They were invented for their own sake as something that exists on Llurien, filling a role or need. When I'm assembling a cast or story idea, I include them if they can help achieve my story goals. And when there's no use for them, they don't get a mention. I'm not tempted to include extraneous world building. I know I'm going to write many stories in my career and sooner or later I'll show many facets of these horsemen, collectively painting a broad and a detailed picture. Doing so arguably creates the greatest depth of all. And it prevents me from walloping my audience with a ton of unnecessary info at any given time.

When we create a world to tell a single story, we don't have that option. We might be more tempted to ramble on about our world building. Or we don't invent those things at all because we won't be using them, which predisposes our world to lack depth. But we need to have a well-realized world (just not go too far), for the same reason we invent character backstory—it helps flesh out our depiction of the world, and helps our readers to understand it.

THE PROBLEM OF EXPOSITION

The objection to exposition is that authors cause a loss of momentum when we stop the story to explain a setting or even a character, then resume on the other side. Authors of older books sometimes wrote pages upon pages of exposition; I usually skip over this. Modern audiences expect a story to keep moving. I've had beta-readers give me grief about exposition as short as a four-sentence paragraph. This seems a little harsh to me, and you'll have to use your own judgment. Whether or not an explanation is too much is a personal choice. Keep in mind when inventing something that requires explanation that many readers will skip these passages, or an editor might strike them entirely.

How is an author to get across needed information? That's a writing question more than a world building one, but an old standby is the ignorant character who keeps asking what something means only to have another character explain it. Overusing this is a poor style choice. The technique is especially prominent in films without a narrator, though some shows use heavy voiceovers to explain things. Like it or not, some exposition will always be needed. We just don't want a death certificate for our stories to have "Death by Exposition" on the cause of death line.

SHOW VS. TELL

One way around exposition is to reveal world building details as an integral part of a story. For example, my story "The Garden of Taria" exists so I can reveal an aspect of a humanoid species (querra). However, that's my goal as an author. It's not a reader-centric goal of a story about characters, which is what we want.

So I created a character, Taria, who seeks refuge from a chaotic world in the ordered sanctuary of home. The querra keeps invading her house whilst helping himself to her possessions and food. He makes a mess everywhere and doesn't respect property. All of this is what I wanted to show. Their arguments reveal querran outlook as I'd desired, but this doesn't come as exposition. It's dialogue and behavior. Their conflict causes both characters, and maybe the reader, to question human ideas on property, possession, capitalism, and wealth. In other words, I'm showing this world building element, not telling it. The story is about characters and issues, achieved with world building.

And *that's* what we want.

OTHER METHODS

We can also include more details in a glossary with each published work. Since perusing it is optional, readers with greater curiosity will do so while those who don't care are freed from exposition overkill. Tolkien did something similar with *The Lord of the Rings*, which includes multiple appendices.

A related solution is to create a website all about our world, linking to it from our glossary or even the text of our stories. Each time a new item is mentioned in a tale, the word is a hyperlink to the corresponding page on the website. This is also optional for our readers, who may love being able to do this; they might also be annoyed/distracted by the sight of a hyperlink in a novel unless this sort of thing becomes common.

A website might be overkill unless we're a successful writer, but it can help invest readers in our world and possibly draw in new ones. The size of the website is up to us. It can just be a few pages or a longer glossary associated with our book's page. For me, the online version is the master glossary, the one in a book being far shorter and tailored to that story. For examples, you can see mine at Llurien.com.

THE VALUE OF INFLUENCES

During world building, we can become so focused on inventing something new that we try not to be influenced by anything we've seen before. While this is admirable, we can inadvertently deny ourselves something precisely because someone else done it, which means we're still being influenced. True freedom to invent means not worrying about similarities at all and using every possible good idea, with the caveat that we must avoid copyright infringement.

For example, I avoided inventing an underground species because I figured they'd just be dwarves by another name, because they'd be short. They have to dig most passages and homes, and this will inhibit their vertical growth, or they'll all have stooped backs. I let myself be influenced in the negative, avoiding something useful until I realized that a dwarf is far more than just height and habitat.

Aspire to create a species that looks and lives however you want them to. If a physical adaptation is based on habitat, this is good. If it makes sense for our forest-dwelling species to have pointed ears and slanted eyes, then so be it, even though elves are that way. Incidentally, pointed ears don't have a biological basis and don't improve hearing; such criteria help us eliminate or add features. When you notice that you want to do something that reminds you of someone else's creation, question why theirs is like that. If the feature doesn't make sense, ditch it. The most powerful influences are the ones we don't even realize we have.

Question everything.

CHAPTER TWO

CREATING GODS

Whether we write fantasy or science fiction, chances are sooner or later we'll need a god or gods. At the least, our characters might want to pray, swear, threaten damnation, or utter thanks. And when someone is born, dies, or reaches a milestone, gods are often praised.

Gods are typically credited with the reason for everything existing, but starting our world building with them is optional. Our gods can be real or wishful thinking, but in fantasy and SF, they are typically portrayed as real and taking an active role in the lives of the world's residents. Different religions spring up from different beliefs about even a single shared god, so before we can create religions, decide on deities.

Did the gods create our world on purpose or was it a byproduct of a "big bang" origin, and they stumbled upon it? Did they shape the land or just let it do its thing over millennia? Are they active, causing the seasons, night and day, and the winds, or do they just manipulate these forces?

Appendix 1 is a template for creating a god. It includes more comments and advice, and an editable Microsoft Word file can be downloaded for free by signing up for the newsletter at http://www.artofworldbuilding.com/newsletter/.

IN SCIENCE FICTION

In SF, characters may travel between many worlds, each having a pantheon, which is not to say that we need an extensively developed pantheon for each world. Rather, a general feel for the presence of religion and actual gods appearing can be all that we need, plus few names.

There's an idea that science kills religion, the premise being that the more scientific discoveries are made, the less need we have of religion to explain things. While there's some truth to this, religion shouldn't be ignored. People still often believe in deities. Some might say that less educated, more rural people fall into this category, but many of our greatest scientists believe in God. Writing SF on possibly highly-developed worlds doesn't absolve us from inventing religion, which will never really go away. Our characters can live/arrive on a world dominated by religion despite science.

One way to work religion into SF is to consider world view issues. Planet-hopping characters may believe that gods created the universe and therefore these deities will also rule other planets. Discovering on arrival that no one's heard of those gods will cause distress. They may try to claim the new planet's god X is really their home planet's god Y. Or they may be so incensed that they try to wipe out the inhabitants of this wayward planet. Or convert them. Christian missionaries tried to spread God's word around Earth, so why not do the same on a planetary level?

Whether the gods are real or not is another matter to consider. If real, are they happy with a species gaining so much power that they can leave the world the gods created for them? If they created the universe, maybe they're okay with it because those gods rule the other planets as well. If the gods didn't create the universe and only rule their area of it, maybe they encourage our characters to colonize other worlds and galaxies, or the peaceful lives they live are shattered by alien invaders coming to convert them. Is there a proxy war going on between these gods and those of other worlds? Our gods could provide the technologies being used to travel.

In SF, sometimes the gods are actually advanced aliens masquerading as gods, as in *Stargate SG-1*. This can be useful for having "gods" that can be killed, perhaps to the surprise of the mortals they rule. The discovery of the truth can be psychologically powerful. We'll need to figure out where the aliens came from and why they're doing this.

IN FANTASY

In fantasy, gods often put in appearances that leave little doubt that they exist. In antiquity, there are numerous myths of Norse and Greek gods being jealous of humans, tormenting, killing, and having children with us. The Christian god is the one who keeps quiet. We can choose either approach, but gods who affect events are more useful. Their followers can be the ones impacting life, whether these are your main characters or their enemies. A common use for gods is to have a priest lay hands on wounded people and ask their god to heal them. We need deities for this. A developed pantheon helps us flesh out the priest character's personality as we decide who they pray to.

If our world has multiple humanoid species, do we want each species to have their own gods or to share all of them? The latter reduces the numbers we must create, but the former allows for more variety. Each species can have their own creation and end-of-world myths, for example. We might invent gods that are tailored to a species, rather than all gods being universal and therefore less specific. To minimize the quantity invented, we can decide each species only has a few gods, not twenty each. We might also decide that some gods are universal while others are more tailored to a species. This works well if a subgroup of gods invented that species, their combined attributes influencing the result. That species can worship all the gods but have more allegiance for their creators.

PANTHEONS

A pantheon is a mythological collection of gods. They are often related by familial ties and recognized by the culture that invented them but not usually by others. While creating multiple gods is more work, dynamic relationships among deities is more entertaining and can drive plot. We can start with a list of traits, such as truth, courage, love, hate, patience, curiosity, peace, greed, fear, sloth, deceit, and wrath. We can use phenomena like gods of storms, war, and death. We don't have to choose one approach or the other, but mixing them could make our pantheon seem random and not well thought out. One solution is to decide that traits lead to phenomenon, or vice versa. For example, the god of wrath becomes the god of storms. This is expanded on further in the last section of this chapter.

A pantheon allows characters to show personality by the god(s) they pray to, especially for priests. As our characters investigate catacombs, ancient ruins, or a modern megalopolis, they will see symbols of the gods, encounter overzealous priests, or visit a theocratic society. These elements can affect the decisions they make, such as not entering a given room due to the symbol of the god of torture on it. Even unrecognized symbols from an unknown pantheon can be useful for creating an unsettling feeling.

Our pantheon might have more than one afterlife (covered in *Cultures and Beyond, The Art of World Building, #3)*, whether it's as simple as heaven and hell or more complicated, where different deities have conceived different rewards and punishment and oversee them personally. Deities can have a role in how people are judged, whether they can be redeemed, and if the living can visit the dead, or vice versa. When we assign gods different roles, we can create conflict in how (and if) they choose to do their jobs.

A pantheon is often not organized in any particular way, with the exception of familial relationships, should they exist, but if we assign certain traits to every god, we can group them that way. For example, maybe every god is associated with a season, element, or color. This causes multiple gods of spring, fire, or indigo. This may impact their ability to affect elements, their priests similarly affected. A god or priest of fire might suffer more from water-based attacks. Some people also organize their gods by good and evil.

POWER

Often, the gods of a pantheon are not equally powerful. If one or two are considered the parents of others, this can explain their greater strength. Or a few gods will be affiliated with more powerful subjects, like light and death. If the number of worshippers directly influences a god's power, this can also be used to determine their strength—and give a jealous god reason to kill off a rival's followers.

Some pantheons have gods, demigods, and half gods, the latter usually being human/god, though there's no reason you can't have a half elf/god instead. Or half ogre/god—such a person could wreak additional havoc or be more influential over peers, causing an uprising. Determine if these lesser beings exist, how they come about, and why. These are useful for lesser traits that we might still want a deity of.

CHILDREN

Parental relationships are sometimes cited as the reason for different power levels. This doesn't have to be. Human children, once grown, are no less powerful than their parents, so unless gods become increasingly powerful with time, like vampires, there's little justification for this, unless...

Are children born at full power or did they need to grow into adulthood? The former offers opportunities to create stories of them learning to control their power. Children and adolescents make mistakes and test boundaries. Imagine what problems a budding god can cause. This is a chance to create

THE COMPLETE ART OF WORLD BUILDING | 31

myths, attitudes, grudges, and infamous events or consequences for gods and species alike.

For example, perhaps a god inadvertently created a species that has something wrong with it. Maybe a deity cursed a group of one species, creating a new race. This could've been done to a species that another god admired, either to offend the god or retaliate for another offence.

Older gods may impose limits on younger ones just as parents do for teenagers, which can be a useful metaphor our characters refer to. How do these younger gods chafe at this? Is there an age at which the limits come off? Does something become possible at that age? Are these gods protected from something until then and then they're on their own to save themselves from some force known to harm deities? How long do the child gods take to reach adulthood?

DEMIGODS AND HALF GODS

Demigods can result from mating between gods or a god and a mortal species, though some refer to the latter as half gods, which may live longer than the species but not be immortal. A demigod can be all god and immortal, perhaps just not as strong, but there really are no rules.

A demigod can result from a character who excelled at something in life and became the demigod of that thing in death. A god of music might appoint a skilled singer the demigod/patron of singers after death. Demigods are often depicted as working for one or more gods, such as a messenger. Some might be neutral or they may take sides in godly and earthly disputes; if they did so in the past, maybe now the other side in that dispute doesn't trust them. Decide how much autonomy they enjoy. What happens if a demigod disobeys an order? Such thinking can lead to myths that enrich a pantheon.

RELATIONSHIPS

We can create relationships, familial or not, based on god traits. A god of love and a god of hate can be twins, as can the gods of life and death. The god of winter and demigod of snow can be parent and child. While these are a bit predictable, symmetry is appreciated and easier to remember. Gods can be friends and enemies, too. This often results from conflicts of character and desires, just like with people. If these boil over into arguments that become myths, this helps justify the intensity of bonding or resentment. Not every god in your pantheon needs details worked out, but a few will create the impression of depth we're after.

WHERE DO THEY LIVE?

Deciding where your gods live will have an impact on stories if your characters ever need to visit them. In theory, it shouldn't be easy to reach gods; otherwise, every guy with a cause will beg for help. A useful tradition to follow is that one must prove one's worthiness through an arduous trek to the god.

Do the gods live apart from each other or all together in a city? I recommend avoiding something as obvious as a mountain top because readers will be reminded of Mt. Olympus. On the other hand, the god of the sea living underwater makes too much sense to ignore, but we can still have him do something less common, such as dwell on an island; after all, how is anyone supposed to visit him underwater, or is that what he's trying to avoid?

Are the gods in the mortal world, like our planet, or in a magical realm like an afterlife? What sort of guardians protect the path there? What price must someone pay, literally or figuratively, to get there and back? We can base our decisions on ideas from existing mythologies about travel to other dimensions, such as Charon, but a guy ferrying people across a river for a price is an idea that's too well-known to use without inducing eye rolling.

If the gods are believed to live in the sky, what happens in a world technologically advanced enough to explore the heavens and discover there are no gods up there? They would likely alter their beliefs to compensate for this. But it could be interesting if the gods are real and are indeed up there. Maybe this is the reason advanced technology was sought. There could be important questions the gods must be asked.

LIFESPAN

Where did your gods come from? "Nowhere" is a valid, if not entirely interesting, answer. On Earth, we don't talk much about where God came from so much as where *we* did. We can avoid this question altogether and few will question it. We don't need a reason, but something is usually better than nothing unless the idea doesn't hold up. We may never have a chance to mention it in stories.

Our gods could've come from another world that they've abandoned or destroyed. Is your new planet their second or third chance to get it right? Maybe the gods are fleeing enemies, or they are the terror of the cosmos that other pantheons flee. Did they leave a planet full of life behind? That planet could be the one you're setting up now. If the gods abandoned a world, decide what's happening there now. Is that where Earth's God went? Is He too busy setting up other worlds to drop in?

Consider what the origins of your gods say or imply about them. In Greek mythology, the gods came from the giants before them, but if gods can be born, they can presumably be killed, too. If your gods can die, what happens when one does? Maybe the one who killed them can replace them. A magic or technological weapon might be needed to do it. Perhaps only other gods have the power to destroy one. Maybe they can only become injured. Or imprisoned—and what happens when this occurs? What kind of prison can hold a god? Decide where it is located, how is it guarded and by what. Does their influence over the world stop as long as they're locked up?

Vulnerability

There's an idea that stories about gods who can't be hurt or killed are not interesting because there's no risk to them. This has merit, but there are ways to injure someone other than physically. You can destroy their plans, offend their pride, and cause psychological trauma, all with consequences for god and offender. Don't be afraid to have gods with faults. The one God of Judaism, Islam, and Christianity is supposedly perfect—and uninteresting?

We can make our gods vulnerable to magic items or various kinds of radiation, whether nature or technology causes it. A farmer with a spade shouldn't be able to kill a god unless that spade is magical. Decide what weapons can hurt deities and what the gods have done to find and destroy these, or if some gods are harboring them for eventual use on the others; they likely won't admit to this.

For a god to die of natural causes doesn't fit with our concept of gods, so if you'd like some of them gone forever, you'll need a reason and event that your species are well aware of; a dead god is a powerful idea that might greatly disturb them. It suggests truly frightening foes are out there, unless the culprit was some sort of disease that only affects deities.

In some books, authors have a god sleeping or unconscious instead of dead, the eventual reawakening and possible consequences woven into a prophecy. How did this happen? Failed murder attempt? Poisoning? By who?

What's gone wrong in the meantime? Is this god nefarious or benevolent? Do people long for the return or fear it? What is the god's religion doing to bring it about?

Can the gods hurt our species? Undoubtedly, unless we decide something's preventing them, such as a pact among them, a curse, or a powerful spell. Any of these would give some or all of them something to work against, a story arc that might involve the species, some of whom might be helping or trying to hinder them. Is there an end-of-world doomsday that cannot take place as a result of what's happened? Maybe the species have found a way to thwart the end of all time, and the gods aren't amused.

MYTHOLOGY

A pantheon will have a mythology, whether it's featured in stories or just mentioned by characters or in narration. To avoid exposition, incorporating the myths into a tale is the best way to mention them. This is one area we can stall on inventing, but creation myths and end-of-world myths are among the most important to work out; minor myths can be invented when needed. Even if our world doesn't have gods, these myths will exist, as our awareness of our own mortality has us contemplating the birth and death of everything, not just ourselves. Any story about incidents among the gods, or between gods and their species, can also become a myth people either believe or not.

CREATION MYTHS

Creation myths reveal a species' understanding of where they and the gods who created them originated. The question of "Why are we here?" is fundamental. If we've decided a subgroup of gods who invented this species, why did they do this? What was the purpose? Were they unsatisfied with another species and created this one to solve a problem? Does that mean this new one has a task of wiping out the inferior predecessor? A superiority complex, racism (think white supremacy), and genocide can result.

If the gods jointly created all species, especially at the same time, there may be a single creation myth instead of one per species. But there may be less purpose behind a wholesale invention of life other than to just do it. If there's no real reason, the species might invent stories to explain their existence, as we've done on Earth, where multiple myths exist across one species.

We probably don't want multiple creation myths unless our story heavily features this subject; instead we can focus on just one universal myth.

The gods might have told everyone a story rather than let people invent one. But did the gods tell the truth or a modified version of it? There's more drama and conflict when people discover things are not quite what they believed; the more wrong we were, the more devastated we are. Our world could have a huge secret—the true origins of the gods and species. We can drop hints throughout a collection of stories and eventually have a powerful reveal in a longer work that re-imagines much of our previous work; this sort of thing must be planned to avoid contradicting ourselves.

There are justifications for lying gods. If they originated from the destruction of another being, maybe they don't want the species realizing the gods can be destroyed (under the right circumstances). If they are the ones who destroyed another being, maybe this wasn't as just or honorable as they'd like to believe. Any bad deed can suffice. If different worlds have different gods who war against each other, deity conflicts could result in attempts to protect their species, or themselves, through deceit or ignorance. The word "myth" implies falsehood, but if our gods are real, we can always opt for them to have told the truth. Some characters within a species will believe while others don't, the word myth still being applied.

Myths are imagined early in a civilization's development and have an oral tradition; even uneducated people know them. They often include supernatural beings, which means more than just our gods. The Greek gods had titans they fought, for example. What beings might your gods have battled? Dragons? Any mythical creature from fantasy will do, if it is one of epic power.

The myth may include how the stars, moons, planets, and sun(s) came to be and which one is revolving around the others. Long ago, people thought the Earth was the center of the known universe, with the sun revolving around us. Is your species right about their place in the cosmos? They almost certainly are in SF but maybe not in fantasy. Some fantasy species may know the truth while the more ignorant ones may not.

Some people want to know that their lives are not a mistake, that there's a purpose to their existence and that of all mankind (or another species), and that their efforts to live well will be rewarded in life or death. And those who don't measure up will be punished. In this sense, a creation myth is often tied to an end-of-time myth. A species might be rationalizing their world view with a myth; we might need to invent some species first.

ANALOGUES

Earth provides many examples to leverage. Sometimes a god creates life in a dream or accidentally when something from their body falls to the earth and spawns life, whether this is tears, breast milk, another fluid, or their body somehow being dismembered or otherwise dying. A god can send an animal into a primordial ocean to dredge up enough earth to cause continents. Sometimes they just want to create order from chaos or nothingness. If there are two primeval gods (like earth and sky) who are separated, this sometimes causes life.

Life can be seen as emerging from a previous world, which can be literal or figurative; there's a metamorphosis occurring in which a higher state has been attained, and this current life will pass, too, as beings ascend again to another world in the next life. Sometimes the myth says that people have traveled here from afar, which can be a literal journey; this could be especially true in SF with planet-hopping characters, who might have also been driven from their original world, having an end of world myth to explain what happened.

END OF WORLD MYTHS

Our world also needs an end-of-time myth. This is often depicted as the culmination of many events that inevitably lead to the end of the world. This can be literal in the planet being destroyed, which fits SF very well; maybe everyone is fleeing the planet on spaceships shortly before this foretold event. Or it happened long ago and a new reality is that this species (or many) is without a home; this has been done before but is viable. In fantasy, tremendous magical power can render a world uninhabitable.

The end can be more figurative—life as people know it is over, but the world still physically exists. If the gods are destroyed but were responsible for granting magical or healing power, now no one can do these. If a city is floating in the air thanks to magic, wouldn't it come crashing down? Other forces might be held at bay with magic and now be unleashed. Perhaps horrible creatures have been bound in a supernatural prison and are let loose, with no one able to truly protect themselves. Are these metaphorical hounds being let loose the harbingers of the end time?

It's fun deciding how the gods are going to destroy everyone. A single blast from an asteroid is brutal but maybe less entertaining than letting some-

THE COMPLETE ART OF WORLD BUILDING | 37

thing akin to demons have their way with the evil people, while angel-like beings spare the good. Abandoning the species instead could result in a new world order where technology emerges, dovetailing into a creation myth.

Some people are so devout that they'll remain a true believer (in redemption or any other part of the myth) even as the end of time causes the world to crumble around them. Rather than resisting the destruction, they may welcome it and the new world to follow. This could be quite disappointing when they turn out to have been wrong (if so).

ANALOGUES

On Earth, some myths are tightly focused on Judaism, Islam and Christianity, regarding the one God and Christ, so that if we use them, people may realize this. This includes the second coming of a messiah, resurrection for the good, and damnation of the evil. The trick to using these is to decouple them. Worthy people being resurrected is a good idea, but when paired with a messiah, for example, the origins of our end of time myth become too obvious. It's arguably better to cherry pick from existing mythologies than to use ideas wholesale.

Other myths have focused on a cyclic pattern, with decay (moral, spiritual, or physical) eventually leading to salvation and a rebirth into a new reality. The decay could be an alteration in the sun's cycle, a geological upheaval in the planet, or an asteroid strike; all of these alter life as people know it and cause a new reality. A moral decay can lead the gods to decide the species have gone too far to be saved except by wiping out the evil ones and starting anew with the righteous, which could work in a dystopia.

OTHER STORIES

We can also mirror Earth mythologies of gods doing things to each other and mortals. This includes playing tricks, seducing or falling in love, fathering children, attempting murder, and overthrowing the power structure. Anything we mere mortals do is fair game, and myths are often cautionary tales designed to warn a species against certain behaviors. The myths instruct us and our children how to behave. But on our world, many of these stories will have some truth to them because the gods are real. When inventing each myth, determine what's true about it and what isn't. After inventing the story, revisit it, imagining other options and keeping one a secret to reveal later.

Gods have possessions, like anyone. We can create myths where an item fell into mortal hands through theft, misplacement, or even gambling, and caused havoc, possibly resulting in a physical place where strange things happen. This is a great way to invent areas of interest; I've devoted a chapter to it in *Creating Places* ("Creating Places of Interest"). Our characters can recover these items, often not on purpose or even realizing it at first. What happens when the god learns someone has it?

CHARACTERISTICS

ALIGNMENT

Anyone who's played role playing games is familiar with the concept of alignment, or good vs. evil. This oversimplified view of gods helps classify, organize, and balance them so we don't have too many evil ones, for example. A degree of balance is preferred unless our story requires an imbalance.

We've seen "neutral," but what does this mean? Neither good nor evil? Or does it mean a pacifist position of non-interference in the machinations of gods or species? Such pacifism is less interesting, but it can create resentment among species who call upon a god who won't answer their prayers, possibly resulting in atheists. By contrast, does a neutral god intervene to stop aggressors from upsetting the balance of good and evil? This can be the attitude of species, too, not just gods.

While "good" and "evil" are widely accepted, the words appeal to younger fans. A more sophisticated audience might appreciate other words that mean the same thing without seeming immature. Some options are "benevolent," "kinder," or "helpful" instead of "good," and "nefarious," "sinister," or "feared" instead of "evil." Readers will get the point without feeling talked down to.

Those we consider blatantly evil, like Adolf Hitler, likely didn't view themselves that way. Our evil gods might bristle at such a distinction and smite anyone who says such a thing—an act which suggests they are indeed evil. Like us, these deities may rationalize the worldview that gets them called that. A god of domination might believe others need to be ruled, justifying abuses of tyranny, but a god of hate likely can't justify their outlook and might accept being called evil. Giving thought to this can make our deities more interesting and lead to stories and myths about their interactions.

IDENTIFIERS

Aside from naming our gods, there are other ways to identify them.

TITLES

Deities have titles like "God of War," "Lord of Despair," or "The Weeping God." They can have multiple titles or nicknames, particularly if they oversee more than one area of life. In stories, use only one title at a time to avoid an info dump. One story can reveal one title, another story a different one. We can invent these when needed, skipping this during world building, but always remember to take something invented in a tale and add it to your file on that subject.

PATRONAGE

Gods are sometimes the patron of activities. These can be professions like hunters, farmers, or blacksmiths, or something more general like lovers or children. Who the god patronizes is revealing of their outlook. Look at your god's attributes to decide who they would patronize and who would be praying to them the most. There can be different levels of patronage, such as a god of war favoring all warriors but bestowing greater favors on knights.

SYMBOLS

Symbols are useful for storytelling and gaming. They can be emblazoned on armor, buildings, ships, space stations, and uniforms, or worn as talismans, even branded into flesh. Each tells the audience, and even other characters, something about location or people, allowing easy characterization. Keep symbols, such as a whip suggesting a god of torture, easy to describe in under one sentence. They are usually fairly obvious because residents aren't trying to be creative like us and those with no artistic ability need to draw them. This helps us avoid exposition.

APPEARANCE

We can decide that gods can choose what form they appear in. On Earth, God is sometimes an old man with a long beard and white robe, maybe sandals, but has been portrayed in recent films as female. Do your gods have typical genders they appear as? Do they appear as human or another species? Or do they have an animal form, or even a monstrous one? Make a general decision about all of them and then decide how each one typically manifests. Appearance can help with creating symbols and nicknames like "The Dragon God" for one who takes that form.

OTHER TRAITS

Gods can be identified by other means. The four elements of air, earth, fire, and water can be associated with four gods, each deity only concerned with one element. Or every god in the pantheon can have one or more elements with which they affiliate. A goddess of love might rule fire, but then so might the goddess of hate. In that example, passion has been used to correlate the deities to the element. A simple justification helps our decisions appeal to an audience; the more obvious it is, the less need for exposition, at the risk of being less creative about it. As with symbols, the world's residents need a straightforward association, not something elaborate.

The seasons can be used in a similar manner. If the gods of love and hate are fire gods because of passion, then this affiliation with heat might also make them summer deities. Or one god can be the only summer deity. Cruelty is considered cold, and so this god might be a winter god, and one of ice (i.e., water). A god of agriculture is clearly a god of the earth and either spring (planting) or autumn (the harvest). A goddess of birth can be associated with spring planting.

The seven colors in the spectrum can be associated with deities and subsequently, their symbols and the colors favored by their followers. If your goddess of love favors orange or yellow (going with the fire motif), then perhaps her priests' robes are the same colors. A god of death and/or fear will likely favor black; if we want a less predictable color, we can rationalize that death is not an evil but something natural that happens to everyone.

BEHAVIOR

A god who never does anything might as well not exist from a world building standpoint. For your pantheon, decide what is considered acceptable and unacceptable behavior and whether the gods generally obey this. Each deity will have a different viewpoint, with some being very lawful, others agreeing but not overly caring, some chafing but agreeing, and others outright disdainful and either openly thwarting such rules or doing so secretly, possibly while being amused that they're doing so. We'll need to know our gods to make these decisions.

Do gods punish offending deities? Do guilty gods submit to the punishment (respecting the law they've broken) or resist, possibly by fleeing? We might decide that there's a prison for deities and what its properties are and what, if anything, is preventing other gods, or their followers, from doing a prison break.

How do gods punish their species? Death, a nasty afterlife, misfortune, or removing talent, like one for magic? And for what offenses? Swearing with a god's name is a good one except that so many people might be doing this that the gods would be awfully busy. Failure to undertake a promised mission makes sense for adventurers. Not defending a temple is another. Destroying one is even better. These more serious offenses are more likely to attract divine punishment. Myths about famous people who've suffered a given fate serve as cautionary tales that can be mentioned to spice up our narratives.

REPUTATION

Some gods and their followers have a reputation that comes to mind if they're mentioned. A god of cruelty might force self-mutilation on priests. For a god of love, this might be orgies. A god of wrath might be prone to outbursts of anger, making people afraid to say his name. Does anyone demand sacrifice? Decide how people think of each of your gods (positive/negative) and why that is. Whether or not the god obeys godly rules will come into play. This is where myths can help shape their reputation, too. For some deities, this will be easier than others.

INTERACTION

Do your gods visit the world and peoples they created? Why, how often, and for what? Do they have to be summoned or can they appear wherever they want? Are there restrictions on where they can go? Only other gods are likely to have created a restriction powerful enough that another god must obey. Are there time limits on how long a god can remain here? These limits should have a rationale because we assume gods are without limits.

World builders sometimes decide that the gods will not directly influence events; it's too convenient to have them swoop in and fix things or cause issues when our characters are doing well. One way to avoid this is having the god's behavior be that which caused the story. Past events can also have set something in motion, and this is where myths come into play, with our characters discovering the details or truth of a legend, maybe the hard way.

CREATIONS

Gods are assumed to have invented the world and its life, whether by accident or on purpose. We don't need to give a reason for this, but our world building can be better if we do. We can take some reasons that we have for our own creative work and attribute it to gods, such as a love of doing so. We're curious how our children will turn out while guiding and shaping the result, so the gods can, too.

We can decide which god(s) created what life forms. This really means cherry-picking ones to make decisions about, since no one cares which god invented tomatoes, for example. On the other hand, a plant that devours species might be improved by deciding an evil god invented it, especially if it only eats certain species—namely the ones that god doesn't like.

While a god of war is an obvious choice for the one who invented a weapon, even a god of love could do so if it's reminiscent of Cupid's bow. Look at your god's trait list and imagine what items they might possess for themselves or have given to the world. Decide if there's a limit on what can be created; maybe plants and animals are okay, but the gods must agree to invent a humanoid species. Our god of chaos might be forbidden from creating anything but do it anyway, resulting in some unpredictable monster.

PLACES

Our gods can create special places, which are typically supernatural. These can be on the world, between worlds, or an alternate reality. Prisons, meeting places, means of travel, and hiding places are some possibilities. Explanations are typically better but not needed, as inhabitants often won't know the truth; it's unlikely they'll even learn of these locations, but our characters will or there's no point inventing them.

Temples, whether abandoned or not, are places where gods are likely to visit, and sometimes their religion will build these up extensively. Can the gods be reached here? Is there anything special about the place where they appear? What about the altar where sacrifices to sinister gods were made? Is a church the way to enter a portal to where that god dwells?

The afterlife is a unique place that will be covered in *Cultures and Beyond* (*The Art of World Building, #3*).

WHERE TO START

We can start creating gods by making a list of things we'd like gods of, like love. We can also take existing Earth gods and reimagine them. Both options are delved into below.

STARTING WITH ATTRIBUTES

With a pantheon, each god has areas they oversee, like love or war, which are seldom assigned to more than one god; there's only one god of love. Each deity can be the god of more than one thing, and these lesser concerns are typically related as if one is an outgrowth of another. A god of love might also be the god of marriage and family. The god of cunning might be the god of war, manipulation, bribery, strategy, and deceit. These additional traits can help us understand our god more than assigning a lone trait. Grouping attributes also helps us create fewer gods. Different people will group things differently, which is good. There are no right or wrong answers.

Make a master list of traits and begin grouping them. You'll start realizing who this individual is—personality, interests, and temperament. Traits you overlooked can be added to the master list or an individual god's. Sometimes

a trait might fit more than one god, but that's okay as long as it's not a primary trait, like love.

STARTING WITH ANALOGUES

We can model deities from Earth pantheons or another author, though
this dips perilously close to plagiarism and should be done carefully. Research the gods of a culture and make an attribute list this way. Take note of
how the deity is viewed, what they're the god of, and their relationships with
other ones. When you have a dozen or more gods written down, you can see
all the ideas you like in one place. Make another list that will be *your* deities
and start raiding the first list, combining attributes into new gods.

For example, Zeus is the leader and father figure to other Greek gods and
throws lightning bolts. Most of us would recognize that if you did it verba-
tim, but you can change his appearance and weapon to something else. Zeus
also fathered children with human women (as have other Greek gods). Assign that habit to another god instead. By mixing and matching ideas, you
create something unique. Invent a god of storms and have him be the lightning bolt thrower.

CHAPTER THREE

CREATING A SPECIES

Creating a species is one of the most rewarding but challenging aspects of world building. This chapter focuses on ensuring your species is close to the competition (such as elves and dwarves) in quality and depth. We can feel daunted by all that we could invent, but remember that we can always ditch things that aren't working. Having fun with it and taking it one subject at a time go a long way toward keeping it fun.

Appendix 2 is a template for creating a species. It includes more comments and advice, and an editable Microsoft Word file can be downloaded for free by signing up for the newsletter.

http://www.artofworldbuilding.com/newsletter/

SPECIES OR RACE?

Terminology affects perception and our ability to organize our creations. Fantasy readers are familiar with "race" denoting the difference between an elf and dwarf, for example. These races are very different in physical features, temperament, and society. They seem unrelated except for being humanoid. By contrast, on Earth, we only have humans, a species, and use the word race to distinguish between different biological variations of us. This section explores the difference between "race" and "species" and when we should use each term in our setting, though there's no right or wrong answer.

THE TERMS

What's a race? The answer can be complicated, but on Earth, race has been described as nothing more than a social construct to describe different versions of Homo sapiens (i.e., humans), who are 99.9% the same, having no genetic differences to warrant classification (into races or anything else). In other words, genetics has nothing to do with the term race and more to do with the word species. This means that if two humanoids are genetically different, they'll be considered separate species.

Separate DNA = different species.

Shared DNA = races of a species.

In SF, humanoids originating on different planets will have different genes, so calling them species makes more sense. In fantasy, humanoids are most often from the same world; it's possible for them to share genes and therefore be races of one species. Since elves, dwarves, and others are invented, no genetic material exists to determine if they are, in fact, genetically different. One could assume that the pointed ears of elves must mean there's a genetic difference, but this is superficial. On Earth, human races have different eye shapes, noses, and more while still being genetically the same. Fantasy humanoids could indeed be races, sharing DNA.

Small people, also known as dwarves, exist on Earth, but their distinctive height and other characteristics are caused by a medical or genetic disorder, which is only sometimes passed down from parents (due to genes). It is not a definite outcome, but in fantasy worlds, a dwarf is a different race with a guaranteed passing down of their different genes to children, which suggest they are really a species. We wouldn't expect a fantasy dwarf to give birth to a human, but Earth dwarves have done exactly that.

In some books, authors will say that elves, dwarves, and humans all derive from the same ancestry (same DNA) and they are therefore races, which seems a good term. On the other hand, if we say that the gods created elves, dwarves, and humans separately and that these beings didn't divide themselves during evolution, they probably aren't races. They are different species. Our audience may be indifferent to this and exposition to explain it will bog down our story. They will expect "race" and might balk at "species," so consider this, too.

If our gods are capable of creating one species, why haven't they created two or more? Did some event stop them and they never got around to it? They just did one and let it separate into races on its own? Or did the gods cause those races to develop? Are the gods taking a hands-off approach to the world and not interfering beyond inventing this one species? If they're involved in everyday life, why not create more species?

If races don't exist on a biological level, species is the other obvious term to use, but even biologists struggle with what is known as the "species problem." There are over two dozen definitions of the word "species." If scientists can't define it, how can we? The word is just used to group similar organisms and is what the average person thinks of when considering a cat vs. a dog, for example. Both races and species can interbreed, producing offspring, rendering the distinction between them a moot point, so this shouldn't figure in our thinking.

Bio-Diversity

To decide, consider how diverse your creations are. If they're all humanoid, it suggests shared DNA and they are races. Elves, dwarves, hobbits, orcs, humans, and other fantasy tropes have two arms and legs, one head, and no tail, etc. But if we create one with wings, another with gills and other adaptations for the water, and another with four legs, these suggest different species. Wouldn't a dragon be a different species from Homo sapiens?

On Earth, we distinguish between Caucasians, Asians, and more with the word "race." If such races exist on our world, we should also call them race. But if we also have elves and dwarves and call those races, too, isn't that confusing? Wouldn't humans, elves, and dwarves be species, and Caucasians, Asians, and blacks be races of humans? High elves and drow would be races of elves. This makes more sense than saying they are races of some unnamed parent humanoid species.

A Hierarchy

A hierarchy can illustrate the problems of using race and species poorly. Consider this list where everyone is lumped together as races:
1) Daekais
2) Kadeans
3) Humans
4) Mandeans
5) Morkais
6) Nideans

Can you tell which ones are related? If so, it's only from my naming convention; two of them have "kais" in their name and three of them have "deans" in theirs. This lack of structure results from seeing everything as a race of one species despite their differences. As it turns out, two of those humanoids have wings, and three of the others live in water, having gills and other adaptations. Doesn't the below make more sense?

1) Humans
2) Kais
   a) Daekais
   b) Morkais
3) Mandeans
   a) Kadeans
   b) Nideans

Numbers one, two, and three are species. The differences between them are enough that no one would confuse one for another. Letters a and b are races under their respective species. I refer to daekais as a race of kais, not just a generic "race" of...unspecified. If I want to refer to daekais and morkais simultaneously, I use "kais" to do so.

Let's look at some traditional fantasy races. Ask yourself which is better among these organizations:

1) Drow
2) Humans
3) Hill dwarves
4) Mountain dwarves
5) Wood elves

Or this:

1) Dwarves
   a) Hill dwarves
   b) Mountain dwarves
2) Elves
   a) Drow
   b) Wood elves
3) Humans

You may have little reason to point out such distinctions to your audience; a paragraph of explanation is not advised. Using "species" has an added benefit of pulling readers out of their comfort zone of expectations. Some who feel strongly one way or another will tell you otherwise, but it's your world and you are its ultimate god.

SHOULD WE CREATE A SPECIES?

In SF, we may need to create new species, but in fantasy we have the option not to. This section helps you decide on whether to do it or not.

IN SCIENCE FICTION

Aside from little green aliens, inventors of SF have no public domain species available. We can't use Vulcans from *Star Trek* or Na'-vi from *Avatar* because someone else owns them. We either have only humans or must invent humanoid (or not) species. Do you want your planet-hopping characters to encounter unique lifeforms on different planets or on other spacecraft? That and aliens arriving on Earth are the only scenario where we must create them, as there are plenty of SF stories with only humans, especially those involving explorers from Earth.

In a universe like *Star Trek*, some species are ever-present while others are episodic, only appearing in one or two shows. The latter need far less development time. It might be wise to create a few well-developed species (who are part of a crew we use repeatedly) but then spend less effort on everything else. Some ideas might have limited use anyway; rather than discard them, use them for one story and move on. Riskier ideas are well-suited to this because if our audience doesn't like them, we're not revisiting them anyway.

A caveat here is that the opposite could happen: we might find ourselves using them more than initially intended, in which case we must be careful not to box ourselves into a corner. Don't make unnecessary comments in early uses of them, such as, "They never leave their planet." Unless that's part of that story, this restriction could come back to haunt us when we want them traveling. There are ways around that, like deciding they've been driven from the world, but you get the idea. A side-effect of thinly developed ideas is accidental conflict when we decide to more fully develop them *after* publishing them.

IN FANTASY

Fantasy species are well defined, popular, and mostly public domain. No one can stop us from using them, which is one reason why seemingly everyone does. Does this make them over-used? Are people clamoring for something they haven't seen? Are you? If so, you could skip to the next section, "Creating a Species," right now, but there are a few other points to consider.

Is it okay to present the usual species but with minor or significant changes and still call them the same thing? For minor variations, yes (see "What's In a Name?" in Chapter 1). For more significant alterations, we might want to just strike out farther on purpose and add a new name. Once freed from the original concept via a name, it becomes easier to reimagine an elf or dwarf. Remember the rule of three when using an analogue: at least three changes so people are less likely to realize it's a modified elf.

Sometimes it seems like we can read ten books by ten different authors and get ten slightly different versions of an elf. Is that good or bad? They're on different planets, after all, and might develop differently, but it begs the question of why the humans are usually the same as those on Earth. And the horses. And plants.

There is an important caveat to species that aren't public domain, like Ents and Hobbits from *The Lord of the Rings*. We can create a similar species and then give them a different name. The treants and halflings from *Dungeons & Dragons* come to mind, Tolkien. This has been done for legal reasons, as the original species belong to their creator. We run the risk of legal trouble with this anyway and it goes against the idea of creating something new, but the option remains. It is arguably best to put our own spin on an analogue while renaming it; with enough changes, audiences won't immediately think of a known species.

CREATING SOMETHING DIFFERENT

Inventing unique species can help our work stand out (hopefully in a good way) and even invigorate love of the genre for both us and our audience. With so many people using public domain species, there's probably little we can say about them that hasn't been said before. How many authors have used the long lives of elves to comment on how impatient humans can be? There are constraints on us from these species, possibly making us long for our freedom. But there's also safety there, in the comfort of familiarity, and an assurance that if our audience doesn't like our work, the species won't be their reason. There's risk to invention, but reward, too.

If our species will be alongside public domain ones in our work, comparisons are inevitable. Doing a good job is even more important. The standard species are high quality and set a high bar for us. This chapter is designed to help us get over it.

HOW OFTEN THE SETTING WILL BE USED

It doesn't make sense to spend hours developing a species for a short story. We'll never have a chance to reveal much. If we'd like to develop a detailed species anyway, then we should invent for a setting we'll use repeatedly across multiple works. Creating a thinly developed species for shorter works on a single-use world is another good approach, which can work especially well if the species is bizarre and might face resistance from an audience.

We might invent a species to tell a story, which allows us to tailor our invention to our use. This keeps down unwanted or unneeded invention but might also restrict us, when freedom is one reason we're creating species. Conversely, we might invent a species first and begin to think of story ideas or ways we can use it. This latter approach might yield more material than intended, but having ideas is never a bad thing. We can end up with multiple stories while retaining the freedom to invent. Regardless of our approach, we shouldn't feel that building a species is a waste of time because it can take our work to unexpected and great places. Everyone benefits.

SCOPE

How much effort to expend on creating a species will depend on intentions, but there's a range of possibility from extreme world building to hardly any.

THE MINIMUM

At the least, we must decide on physical appearance and an overall disposition that's shared across members of a species. Such life forms are often used as little more than a beast for characters to overcome in their quests. Ogres, orcs, and other henchmen types from fantasy are good examples. They seldom talk or do much more than get killed by the heroes. A more benevolent species can also have limited use, like Chewbacca from *Star Wars*.

He's a Wookiee, but in the original three films, we never see another Wookiee (George Lucas may have added more in the background when he altered the films later). That we only saw one Wookiee made Chewbacca synonymous with his species. We had no Wookiees to compare him to and his personality traits might as well have been the traits of all of them. That he never spoke a word we could understand eliminated cultural, societal, and other issues that minimized the effort needed to create him. He is useful primarily as a constant physical companion who can fight and do things while Han Solo has conversations without the distraction of doing Chewbacca's tasks.

It is Harrison Ford's acting talents that make Chewy work as a character; his funny responses to Chewy's nonsensical growls are what really characterize the Wookiee. The same can be said of C-3PO's responses to the unintelligible R2-D2. Despite all of this, Chewbacca works, but this approach arguably succeeds onscreen better than on paper, due to the inflections, body language, and tone actors used. In books, a character or species with such limited use is hard to make memorable; our readers may forget the character is there or wonder what they're for. The character is little more than a positive henchman.

Wookiee is capitalized for some reason but your species or races should not be; that's not a title or proper name. You never see "human" capitalized unless it's the start of a sentence. One justification for capitalizing it is when the name is synonymous with a region. For example, Germans are from Germany so we capitalize it. Wookiees are from Kashyyyk so this rule doesn't appear to apply, which just shows you we can get away with things like this.

Continuing with *Star Wars* as an example, there are countless other species shown but never named. They are extras on the set, many with compelling appearances, and that is all we experience of them. This works better onscreen than on paper; a picture really is worth a thousand words, which we don't want to waste on a multitude of characters who have minimal impact on our story.

THE MAXIMUM

At the other extreme is a fully-developed species, including their habitat, climate, settlement preferences, appearance of head, body, and clothing, their gods, society, languages, customs, history, relationships with other species, supernatural and technology talents and attitudes, and combat skills. It can be easy to go overboard inventing things we might never use, but it can also make a great impression of depth and believability.

A major issue with this is not only hours but months, even years of refinement, weeding out the lesser aspects that don't stand the test of time while rounding out and improving the good ideas. As with most things, world building skill grows with practice, making this culling part of the process; this book is designed to give you a head start. As we go on to invent sovereign powers, monsters, animals and plants, we'll continuously update our species, integrating everything and improving realism.

IN MODERATION

If done right, splitting the difference can be a sensible choice. The next section and species template (in the appendix) can help you can make an informed decision about which areas to work on. I recommend deciding on habitat, whether the species lives in joint settlements, overall disposition, appearance, and their relationships with each other and your other creations. Areas to skimp for now can be clothing, gods, characteristics (like agility, intelligence, and morale), language, customs, history, combat, and details on their supernatural and technological level.

"Skimping" ranges from overlooking a subject altogether to jotting down a few words about it. You'll have to decide what is skimped based on your needs, but it's worth it to think about every subject to see if you have any concepts. Sometimes ideas beget ideas, meaning that the act of writing down one subject causes you to think of other details. This happens more often as you develop other aspects of a world, resulting in an integrated setting that could stand out in the crowded marketplace.

HABITAT

Environment is crucial to how a humanoid species develops, just like plants and animals. This may not appear true with humans because it's been eons since we evolved into what we are and we don't remember back that far. We'll also live anywhere, making it seem like habitat has no impact. Our only apparent adaptation is to the sun, changing our skin color near the tropics. If locale affects our invented species, that may depend on how extreme that habitat is and whether they ever leave.

Environment strongly affects a water dwelling species, possibly causing gills, webbed fingers and toes, or making them amphibious. They may have teeth and claws for spearing or holding fish. Their clothes and weapons will be different. Plate mail would likely sink them. Onshore, they might use slings but not bows (the former is less damaged by water, easier to carry beneath the waves, and ammunition might abound near shore). Maybe they take the poisonous spines from fish and use them as blow darts. They probably have less contact with other species that aren't underwater all the time (or ever). Maybe they closely watch ships, attacking them or rescuing those from sinking ships at battle sites. They could be part of the crew. Do they go on land, and how often?

A species that spends most of its time underground will also be affected. They will have much better sight in low light conditions, as there's little or no natural light, except for possible bioluminescence, which could include them. They're probably shorter; this might be a cliché from dwarves, but if you had to tunnel through rock, you wouldn't want to make passages bigger than needed. Having to do this over millennia will influence height downward. An underground species might be less than ideally nourished, becoming shorter in generations. Where are they getting their food? This likely forces them outside and into dealing with other species.

In fantasy, a common trope is for elves to only live in forests. Has this habitat affected them physically? They don't have tails for climbing trees or even strong hands with claws for grasping bark while climbing. They either live on the ground like humans or up in trees so big that they don't need climbing skills, having built stairs, bridges, and whole buildings up there. They're often said to be thin; is that so that can hide behind a tree more easily? The only impact appears to be on their attachment to the woodland plants and animals, which affects personality and culture, but arguably not their bodies.

The idea of elves in a forest and dwarves in a mountain, seldom leaving, is pervasive in fantasy, but is it realistic? Usually the elves are given a haughtiness or contempt for humans (who are everywhere) to explain why they keep to themselves so much. Dwarves are paranoid, distrustful or grumpy and anti-social.

If we're going to create new species, would they be more useful if they not only have a preferred habitat, but are willing to travel and create new settlements elsewhere, or at least be a significant part of them? If so, then we have two choices: they've always been travelers and therefore habitat had no more effect on them than it does on humans, or they kept to their habitat for millennia, long enough to affect their bodies, before venturing out more.

In the latter case, what initially drove them out? War? Famine? A realization that other species have things to offer and are willing to trade? The arrival of settlers from far away? Protection of their assets? Habitat and history are comingled. The inciting incident can be decided later.

ISOLATED SETTLEMENTS

Creating Places (The Art of World Building, #2) covers creating actual settlements, but at a high level, consider what cities created by our new species, and only by them, are like. These are traits most of the towns will share. If the species is short, buildings will reflect this, unless they're welcoming of visitors from other species, in which case they may have some places designated for taller species.

Consider the possible materials that your species builds with; stone, wood, natural cliffs and caves, or a conglomeration of everything. Are they good builders? That implies some sophistication and engineering skills, but if this is a barbaric, violent, uneducated species, they're likely nomadic or living in abandoned, ruined, or conquered settlements built by others. A benevolent and educated species will likely have towering monuments of stone and glass. In SF, the differing technological levels will have a huge impact on not only settlements but warfare, travel, and culture, with those who lack the ability to create advanced things having to steal them from others (or destroy them) to level the playing field.

What influence have outside events caused on the settlement? Is your species peaceful but has learned the value of a wall, moats, and anti-siege engines? How fortified are your species' cities and why? Are there nearby threats of violence? Or are they paranoid that others want what they have, like access to a mountain and its gems, metals, and minerals? Has the forest been cleared around their settlement so an advancing army cannot benefit from its cover? How would that work if the species adores woodland?

Why do they prefer to remain aloof? Have they been at war with others in their area for too long? Are they doing something secret? Did a plague wipe out many of them and now this is how they live generations later? Fear is a powerful motivation. Do they have contempt for the character of other species the way elves are often depicted having contempt for humanity? Is the issue cultural? What's the cost of their isolation? Lack of support in wars with other enemies? Lack of access to resources someone else might control? Or are they the ones depriving others of access to something? And why? All of this figures into the cultural and societal decisions we'll make.

We may decide that our species has isolated settlements in some areas of the world but is more integrated in others, in which case the local events mentioned above are behind the differences. There are many more varieties than the seeming de facto isolation common in fantasy.

JOINT SETTLEMENTS

Enter the joint settlement, one created by multiple species together.

Have you noticed the tendency for all cities to be built by humans for humans? The likely cause is human authors writing for a human audience, featuring mostly human main characters. Other species might live there, but it's mostly a human place. Maybe a species has a quarter, like the French Quarter in New Orleans, but that's about it. Perhaps it's more realistic that a settlement starts off as a village built by one species, but as time passes, a nearby species becomes welcome as visitors, merchants, and allies. As the village becomes a town and then city, isn't it likely that more than one species is involved in calling it home, with all the rights that this entails? Sure, there'd be growing pains as two species with different outlooks clash, but it will become a joint settlement sooner or later.

There can be resistance on the part of those who founded it, but that's a good source of tension and history, making your world richer. When we add more than three species, it becomes harder (in time) for one to be miffed that the community used to be just theirs. It becomes a true melting pot. We can gain inspiration here from the cultural strain in the U.S. between the Europeans who founded the country and minorities or immigrants. This works on a smaller scale like settlements. In SF, visiting aliens may have also influenced the settlement, whether socially, intellectually, or with physical accommodations.

How likely is it that humans are the only ones who've built a city outside of forests and mountains? If we have a bunch of species that are reasonably cooperative, not likely. Animosities can exist and even be more pronounced from sharing a settlement more equally. This can be more interesting than everyone sulking in their preferred habitat and shunning everyone else. This integration is something to revisit as we create multiple cities; when working on maps, which is covered in *Creating Places (The Art of World Building, #2)*, think about which species are in which land features and who is residing in any settlement you draw on the map.

TERRAIN

We've already thought about underground or underwater environments, but what about those on land? The anatomy of a species will impact their terrain preferences. Something that doesn't run well or use horses might not like open land because pursuit and fleeing are both more troublesome; perhaps they've developed an adaptation, like being able to camouflage skin to hide instead. Skin coloring might be greens and browns in a forest setting.

Something with wings likely prefers living in mountains, both because anything that can't fly will have a harder time reaching them and so it's easier to take flight. They could live along forest edges, depending on how big they and the trees are. If they've built cities, towers will dominate, many having open roofs. They're unlikely to live on plains. A desert offers little when they can just go somewhere far more habitable with little trouble.

Their bodies might not be the reason a terrain is preferred, but their lifestyle. A species that enjoys stalking, killing, and consuming other species might prefer woodland for all the opportunity to hide. If the species is smaller and four-legged, plains might be good, too, as tall grass allows hiding (think of lions). A species that excels at jumping and climbing might prefer mountainous terrain, especially if they have great endurance and don't easily tire with the additional exertion; conversely, a species without endurance may avoid mountains or open land (an inability to run for a long time means they get caught by something that can) and prefer forests, for hiding.

CLIMATE

Humans will live anywhere, but what about our species? A water-dwelling one will be influenced by ocean currents, possibly migrating and having more than one settlement. If a land-based species doesn't build settlements, they're outside a lot and likely prefer temperate climates, being found farther from the equator less often. An underground species likely couldn't care less about climate, which doesn't affect them except their crops and livestock; as a result, they might dominate cold regions.

In SF, with interplanetary travel, the shipboard environment will be suited to one species' preferred climate, affecting temperature, humidity, and the brightness and even color of light. Another species might find traveling on such a ship uncomfortable. What if our ship has multiple species working together and some can't handle heat or cold? Might there be areas where they can go to warm up or cool down? Maybe they wear clothing designed to insulate or cool them. Such suits would be needed anyway if landing on a world or in a climate they deem inhospitable, solving the issue but still giving us a detail to comment on. Suit malfunctions raise another issue.

DISPOSITION

Is our species good, evil, or more complicated? Our intended use of them will help in subsequent decisions.

Something violent, uncivilized, and uneducated may not be welcomed in society. Maybe the idea of them is used to frighten children into behaving. They're a danger for travelers, especially non-warriors. Characters might have relatives injured, killed, or even eaten by this species. People go missing, in the wilderness or in space, whether there's a gruesome crime scene or no sign of the body. Its presence causes caravans to be armed and scouting patrols to be around the community's borders. Settlement or space station defenses will take their abilities into consideration when arranging armed forces. Weapons might be designed with them in mind. People can be skilled in tracking and scouting for them. The species will have a reputation that affects the lives of those they threaten.

A pleasant, communicative, and benevolent species will be welcomed by other societies, possibly with reservations. They could be bringing supplies only they have access to, like plants, gems, or special weapons and armor of their creation. They may exchange information on activities by obnoxious species. Our characters might have friends in that species, who could've saved, trained, or befriended a relative. Maybe people aspire to be like them.

The caveat here is the human model—we can't be predicted to be nefarious or benevolent as a whole. Some like to believe mankind is basically good, and while not getting all philosophical about it, this obviously doesn't mean we don't do horrible things to each other and even animals, plants, and the Earth. Is our new species more predictable than us or equally complex?

If they have a uniform disposition, is there a reason for this? Did a set of gods with the same disposition create them? If evil gods created ogres, maybe that explains their attitude. Were they the result of an accident that influenced them? Did they result from breeding sentient life with animals or monsters? Did someone evil or good create them and use magic or something else to ensure their disposition? How strong is that disposition? If they were created ten thousand years ago and something situational at the time made them evil, hasn't that situation likely passed and maybe now they're different, less extreme? Or is it perpetual and they're even more upset?

An evil species might be less useful if shunned by society, effectively relegating them to a smarter monster out in the woods. This places creative limits on us that might be undesirable, particularly if we intend to use our setting for many stories. That species can't do things inside a city without sneaking in, for example, but how many times do we want to use them that way before they become a predictable caricature of themselves? This can be solved by creating two races of similar appearance but with opposing dispositions, such as elves and drow (dark elves).

This can greatly extend the reach of a uniformly good or evil species, allowing new uses for them. It also creates a problem for those on our world: does the person we're looking at belong to the good one or the evil one? Can the person standing before them be trusted? Using elves and drow as an example, the first all good, the second all evil, elves would be trusted, but now people know that drow exist. A drow could pretend to be an elf to gain access to somewhere or something. An elf could pretend to be a drow to infiltrate somewhere under drow control. If you like this idea but also like races that can be physically distinguished from others in the species, just create additional races: one that looks different and one that doesn't; for example, elves and drow looking the same, and a third kind of elf that looks different from both.

APPEARANCE

When creating a species, start with physical traits; bodies influence the minds that develop. Like it or not, appearance plays a crucial role in life, even if no one's likely to draw our species or see it. The overall impression and details combine to add characterization opportunities that shouldn't be overlooked. It's okay to start with envisioning a specific character, but try to get a sense of how the species generally looks, too. This allows us to not only define them all, but then comment on how our character matches or defies expectations, without which, our audience has a limited understanding of how this person fits in (or not) with their own kind or others.

For example, if your species is generally slovenly but this character is neat, maybe he gets more respect from other species. And what does it say about him? Do his kind find him arrogant? Does he care? Why is he like this? Does he aspire to be better? Or does he dress neatly to keep people from suspecting his character is bad? Does this provide him better opportunities?

A neat species but a sloppy character can have the opposite effect. Maybe his own kind think he's a slob in personal and work habits, but other species find him more down to earth. Maybe he's a gambler and wants to fit in with lowlife friends. Or he's disguising himself like an undercover cop. Is he so consumed by his work that he doesn't pay attention to his appearance (a cliché)? He's just clueless or indifferent to the consequences?

ARE THEY HUMANOID?

There's a tendency to create humanoid species like elves and dwarves instead of spider-like ones, for example. This is preferred for most species because otherwise things might get too weird for our audience, or too much like a cartoon. While there's always room for these, non-humanoids have their challenges.

With humanoids, we don't have to decide what they eat, how often they sleep, and other biological basics. They mingle well with humans, being able to live in similar buildings, use horses, and need fewer unusual physical things. By contrast, would a giant spider sleep in a bed, or eat with utensils, or consume the same food? How would one travel if not on foot? Such considerations might be needed if we go this route. It could make things more interesting for both us and the audience.

With a non-humanoid, our ability to quickly and skillfully describe them matters because readers have to imagine them, unless we're in a visual medium. While it's great to have explanations for anatomical features, audiences are used to bizarre things without getting one iota of explanation. Be forewarned that such creations have a tendency to be monsters, or viewed as one, a subject discussed more in Chapter 5, "Creating Monsters."

HEAD

When creating a head, think about every last facial feature, as described next, but when describing a species to an audience, it's often best to comment on the most important features rather than overwhelm with detail. It's even better to do so while describing a character's mood at the moment, as evidenced by the effect of that mood on those features.

HUMANOIDS

Below are some features to write about and the options that are easiest to describe with a word that most will recognize; if we have to explain a facial feature too much, maybe it's better to just go with something easier to envision and convey. An example of this problem is the word "monolid," (listed below in text about eyes) because while we've all seen this, we've likely never heard the word.

Other names can be used in our files but not in our writing because they're of Earth origin, like "Roman nose" or "Cupid's bow," unless Earth figures in our work; we'd need another name, but then no one will know what we're talking about and we'll have to describe it. To see images of many features listed, do an internet search.

Feature	Options
Face/jawline	round, oval, square, heart-shaped
Brow	prominent (often caused by deep set eyes) or shallow (monolid)
Eyebrows	rounded, arched (and to what degree), mono brow
Eyes	round, slanted, deep set, up/down turned (at the outside corner), wide/close set, hooded (as if hidden behind overhanging eyelids all the time), protruding (the opposite of hooded), and monolid (the opposite of deep set, where the brow appears less prominent, as in some Asians)
Iris	shape (vertical/horizontal slit, round, cat's eye, crescent) and typical colors
Cheekbones	sunken/indented or high/prominent. Low is average and not typically mentioned
Nose	straight, long and wide (like blacks), hawkish, snub, thin and pointed, bulbous, upturned, aquiline, broad with large nostrils, and the basic large nose
Mouth	average, wide, small, full or thin lips (sometimes each is different), rounded/pointed/absent Cupid's bow
Teeth	straight, crooked, missing, stained, pointed, serrated, poisonous, tiny, large, and multiple rows (like a shark)
Chin	protruding, cleft, thin and pointing, round, square, jutting, receding (i.e., almost no chin), and long (often points forward)

If you can't draw, then your decisions may look different than you intended when someone like an artist you hire assembles them into a face. There are various games, such as Wii, or online tools that allow you to create a character or avatar that looks like you. You can experiment with these face generators to give you a head start on this. A quick Google search for face avatar generators turned up these free, online programs I experimented with:

Pimp the face: http://www.pimptheface.com/create/

Face your manga: http://www.faceyourmanga.com/editmangatar.php

The second allowed me to generate images in a few fun minutes of poking around. While I wouldn't use it in my work, it gives me a good reference image in my files and can be handed to an artist to draw something similar. Notice some of the different shapes available for eyes, nose, and heads; some of these look similar because I created two races of a species.

NON-HUMANOIDS

The heads of non-humanoids can be based on animals or invented from scratch, but you'll want an understanding of why a feature exists or it might not make sense. In a monster, an explanation isn't necessary; after all, the creepiness of things that don't make sense are part of why it's a monster (the bizarre and nonsensical frightens). The bar is set higher for a species. We needn't ever explain it, but having the species use the feature in a way that makes it clear there's a rationale behind it helps us.

For example, sharks have jaws that can distend for a wider bite, with rows of replaceable, serrated teeth for ripping meat. If our species also eats something (on land?) raw and with high fat content (like a seal), then it might have this as well. If it eats a different prey, then it won't. A crocodile drowns victims by holding them underwater, so it doesn't need shearing teeth. Also, such teeth wouldn't make sense if our species eats plants or cooks all meals.

Predators tend to have eyes facing forward, while prey have them on the sides to see predators coming more easily (from behind). If our species is truly only prey and never predator, consider this option. Prey also tend to have ears that can independently swivel, but a hunter might also have this skill. A wet nose is designed to catch particles for dissolving and smelling, so if we say our species has a great sense of smell but don't say they have a wet nose, that's less believable, though most people won't know that.

BODY

HUMANOIDS

If our species is humanoid, our body design work is largely done. Areas needing description are mostly those of overall size, height, mass, and fitness standards. The prevalence of facial hair on males and average cleanliness of all genders can also characterize them, but these are partly cultural, too, and result from behaviors. A species that does messy work, like farming, might become less careful about cleanliness so that their slovenly appearance characterizes them. Deciding on some bodily issues can come before or after we form an impression of world view.

Females will be different from males in usually minor ways. Human females are more feminine than males, but we can reverse this, making the females brutish and the males delicate; this will benefit from a good reason. Do females wear jewelry or otherwise try to appear more attractive to males, or is the species too brutish for that? Is mating like humans or do females go into heat like animals? Is there a mating season? Much of this is cultural.

Standards of beauty have changed in human history, with larger woman having been seen as better bearers of children long ago, but now thinner women are all the rage, so how are the females? Is it the women who pursue the males, who must try to attract them, and if so, what affect does this have on both genders physically? Making a humanoid body different from those of humans (in more than superficial ways) involves thinking about other aspects of their lives.

Size and mass influence not just strength and endurance, but capabilities. A species with hands that are much larger or smaller than humans will have trouble wielding weapons or using tools designed for us. If they aren't sophisticated enough to invent their own, then is someone creating these for them? Do they just steal the items? Or do they capture people with the know-how to make them, then force these slaves to do that work?

Size also affects relationships with enemies and allies. If our species is three feet tall, do they just run away from something over six feet tall, or do they swarm while attacking? Have they developed great endurance from all that running or are they just faster than everything and then good at hiding? Being encumbered by possessions makes running harder, so do they travel light? Does another, taller species protect them? Is there a flying species who knows this running species will drop everything and flee, so they follow along hoping to pick up the discarded items, like carrion birds circling a battlefield? If they're larger than everyone, are they fearless? Is that overconfidence that can be used against them?

In SF in particular, many aliens have skin like reptiles, not only with scales but similar coloring. This should have a biological basis, such as protection from the elements or predators. Making their skin poisonous is another option, which can introduce some cultural issues. They'd need to avoid touching humans, for example, and might be wearing gloves or other gear to protect others.

NON-HUMANOID

If our species is not humanoid, basing it on an animal can help realize its body and avoid something unintentionally silly. Gigantism is an option but is arguably the least interesting because it's a run of the mill creature except for size. If we also modify our analogue, this is more attractive.

Combining features of animals and humanoids is benefitted by having some understanding why an animal has a feature so we can decide if it makes sense for our species. If our species has a tail, what do they use it for? A weapon is a good answer; that suggests protecting their rear but that they might also be a predator *and* prey. Is the tail is long enough to strike forward? Can that tail sting? How venomous is it? How fast acting is the poison? If it's designed to use against those with weapon skills and not just animals, a poison would be fast acting to neutralize a threat quickly, even if it sedates instead of kills. All of this is true of poisonous teeth and claws.

Research every feature to see why it exists. Why do turtles have shells? Why don't snakes have legs? Tails are often for climbing, but clearly that's not true for a horse. Horns and tusks are used for fighting and even digging in dirt. Coloring may be for camouflage or warning. Wings are obviously for flight, but there are flightless birds, so understand why that happens before inventing one; they typically exist on an island that has no predators, so creating a flightless bird that lives amid many predators doesn't make sense unless it has developed another way of surviving, one that rendered their wings less important. Not only will a little research turn up useful info to make our creations better, but it can give us other ideas and enrich our life as we understand the world around us more.

THE UNIFORMITY ISSUE

Will our fantasy species be able to masquerade as another? A giant spider can't put on a cloak and sneak into a city as if it's a human, unless it can shape shift. A seven-foot species can't pretend they're a three-foot humanoid. The reverse is also true, though two small ones can stand on each other's shoulders and wear a cloak, but you get the idea. Any two species that are similar in appearance, like elves and humans, can try to disguise themselves as the other species, but the more dissimilar they are, the more we deprive ourselves of this option. Decide if you'd like this ability in your work.

Is our species so hostile to others that they aren't allowed in settlements? This reduces them to something few will encounter unless traveling, as our adventurers are likely to do. Would it be more useful if they can be accepted in society, too? If that conflicts with your intention (you like them nasty), we can still achieve this by creating a more benevolent race of them. We'll want a justification for the race, such as the gods created them to counter the existence of the evil species.

The opposite problem can arise: a species so "good" that no one fears or distrusts them. Where's the fun in that? If we create a corrupted race of them that looks the same, people won't always be sure which one they're dealing with. How would this corrupted version originate? A spell, an accident of technology or the supernatural, or they're cursed by someone or something? Does anyone want to "fix" them and how do *they* feel about that?

CLOTHING

Typical clothing helps round out appearance and the impression our species creates. Assuming they can acquire clothes made for them, how do they usually dress? Sloppy or refined? Oversized or tailored? Bright colors or drab? Playfully or seriously? Is there a clothing item associated with them, such as a hat type, scarf, sash, or stylized tunic? How decorated is their attire? Are they inclined to wear symbols of their settlement? Do they have pride in this?

Even if they go naked, that tells us something about habitat and a likely uninhibited world view. They might have free sexuality; while some associate nudity with sex, this isn't really the case and our species might fit or defy that characterization. Nudity might scandalize more prudish species and form part of their view of each other, the prudes thinking these guys are sexed up (even if not) and these guys thinking the prudes need to lighten up. Such things can provide opportunities to comment on human ideas about sexuality and nudity, enriching our world.

Do they make clothing or are they incapable of such industry? The latter suggests stealing clothes from others and might even be one reason they attack. Any clothes probably fit poorly, are worn, mismatched, and create an impression of chaos and vulgarity. But maybe they buy what they need, assuming there are vendors willing to create and sell to them, possibly exposing themselves to dangers if the species is nefarious; a merchant might get a sword in the chest instead of a handful of gold. Do those vendors get hassled by those who don't want products sold to such a species? This is one way in which world building can lead to characters and story ideas.

ACCESSORIES

Our species might be known for various accessories they're often seen possessing. Maybe they smoke pipes. A flying species might be employed as messengers and have a scroll case or a pouch filled with pen, ink, parchment, and sealing wax. An underground species might be interested in appraising and cutting gems and carry a toolset on their waist. Maybe another travels by foot and goes light, carrying a bindle (sack on a stick). If the species is known for a weapon, this can be part of their typical outfit, such as the sheath or quiver. If they're known to enjoy strong drink, maybe they usually have a flagon with them.

SENSES

We don't need to do anything special with senses, but it can be a missed opportunity to differentiate our species from humans and others. We can change the five senses, implement the sixth sense, and leverage others that are less well known. It's arguably best to keep most senses similar to humans and only alter one or two per species to avoid overwhelm and the law of diminishing returns.

THE FIVE SENSES

We can make sight better than humans so that they see much farther, with greater clarity, or read much smaller print. Or perhaps they're all half blind or just poor at recognizing differences between faces of other species.

On Earth, many cannot distinguish between those of different Asian heritages (such as Chinese vs. Japanese) and those who dismissively think all black people look alike are accused of racism. We can leverage this.

Night vision is sensible if they're nocturnal of live underground with little natural light. Since this ability makes everything brighter to them, this could have consequences like being blinded when a close or bright light turns on. Maybe even full sun is like that for them so that they don't venture out. These cons balance the pros. Infrared or heat vision might also develop to assist with nighttime identification, especially in a woodland setting where this helps distinguish predators and prey from foliage.

Supernatural sight could allow seeing active spells and their radius. Maybe they can see spirits without assistance, or into other realms and the doorways to access them. In SF, they see could see energy fields or radiation types. Then there's the infamous x-ray vision of Superman that might allow detection of body issues requiring medical care; it could impact their attitudes about modesty and how those of other species view them. Do we need to wear lead underwear (so they can't see through it) around them or do we just shun them altogether?

Storytellers often want to make a visual indication of eyes with different properties, such as pupil or iris shape and color. Our default is to make a choice that's constant, such as a vertical pupil, but what if this changes when a special ability is used? Such a change suggests that the skill isn't always on or can be intensified, causing a shift that's apparent to onlookers. All of this is especially helpful in TV, film, or games.

Can they hear much fainter sounds or ones farther away? In either case, it's reasonable that louder sounds might bother them. Perhaps the frequency range (high and low sounds) they detect is better or worse, which might be more useful in SF with the machinery producing noises, some of which might indicate an impending mechanical issue. Some animals might also produce sounds outside our range. Their sense of which direction a sound is coming from could be improved, which might help in any labyrinthian setting like a ship's interior or a forest; if worsened, they're more likely to go the wrong way and into danger. Some people have difficulty hearing a given speaker in a noisy room, especially with other voices present as in a crowd; we can make our species prone to this or excel at picking out the words. An underground species might be better at it due to practice dealing with frequent reverberations, but a woodland species might have less need of the skill in their peaceful surroundings.

They might be better at detecting words in other languages. When humans hear a different one we don't speak, it comes across as a series of sounds that have no relation to each other. What if our species can more quickly pick up individual words and their relations? They'd presumably know more languages than us just from exposure more than study. They may also be able to understand inflection or tone better or worse. Or they may be so bad at this that, even with training, they cannot learn others. This could also make their own language simpler.

Regarding feel, our species could have a higher or lower pain threshold, with the latter making them seem tough. They may have a different response to pain, such as enjoying it. This could be useful in battle. Pain serves a vital function to let us know when our body has a problem; on Earth, a little girl who couldn't feel pain once made herself blind because she kept scratching her eyes as a child, so being too extreme with this might be unwise.

They may be more sensitive to pleasure, which could have negative consequences for males who can't perform intimately as long as desired. Imagine how interspecies erotic encounters might go wrong when each finds a different aspect more or less stimulating than the other. Maybe they can sense changes in atmosphere like animals seem to know a storm is coming. They could feel vibrations in the earth ahead of a quake. Maybe temperature changes are easier to feel or go unnoticed. We can have their entire bodies be different from ours this way or just one area. Use their environment to determine what makes sense.

Taste is harder to make interesting in a story unless characters are eating or drinking, as we're unlikely to have them go around licking things. Or people. However, snakes can sniff the air with theirs, so this is a possibility. Tastes can linger longer or shorter for them, be more or less potent, or we could decide that what is sweet for others is sour for them, for example. This can make them hard to live and travel with but it's easy to do because we only need to state it as true without explaining. A more useful skill would be the ability to identify ingredients based on taste. This could be helpful if a poison has been used and they can determine what it was, provided a little doesn't harm them, of course. They could be skilled chefs if all they must do is eat or drink something to reverse engineer how it was prepared, and then duplicate it.

A smell can linger more or less than for us, which can work well if a faint scent aids understanding of a scene they stumble upon, or they'll be the first (or last) to detect smoke and therefore a fire. How long a body has decomposed (a strong scent) can tell them much in the aftermath of battle. Maybe they can identify multiple scents and how many people were present, distinguishing them and able to follow the one that matters, like a bloodhound. More mundane examples would be sensing weather or other changes or how much pollen, for example, is in the air; does such a skill grant the ability to predict changes in the near term? In SF especially, they could be like dogs that are trained to sniff out drugs.

THE SIXTH SENSE

We have several sixth senses we can add to a species.

Telepathy is the ability to communicate with the minds of others through thought instead of talking or body language. Consider their habitat before assigning this. Either their speech or hearing being compromised might lead to an alternate form of communication. An underground species with loud, reverberating halls might resort to this to cut down noise. Predators could inspire it, too, if we can communicate silently while they're around. The skill could also weaken speech or hearing due to lack of use, all of it potentially inhibiting communication with non-telepaths. Decide if they can control who hears their thoughts and how this is achieved. Do we need to look at them, or answer like a phone ringing in our head? Can we shut them out? How far can they be from the person? Remember to include limitations so that they're not all-powerful.

Clairvoyance is the ability to witness future or past people, locations, events, or objects without having interacted or touched them. Distance is seldom portrayed as a limitation, but we should consider it. They're often shown as unable to control what they see, or how much, leading to a poor understanding of the vision. A related version of this is clairaudience, the ability to hear remotely, though this is sometimes implied to be part of clairvoyance. We can split them up to impose limits and decide that two people are needed to gain both visuals and audio, one person specializing in each.

Psychometry is ability to learn information about an object upon contact with it. These objects are thought to have an energy field that can be sensed. The things that can be learned could include who owns or last touched it, its origins or eventual demise, or the role in past or future events. Do practitioners see images in their head, get impressions, hear sound, or feel emotions from the item? It can be useful for different people in the species to have different skills. Maybe someone has perfect understanding but others get limited results.

Precognition is the ability to see events before they occur, while seeing past events is called retrocognition. A species that is likely to cause significant future changes might have some ability to predict how those turn out, but so could a species that's going to be especially affected by such changes.

If a god of fate helped create this species, this can explain why they have some skill. Like most sixth senses, it might benefit us to have the species be capable of them. but few have the talent.

Mediumship is the ability to see, hear and/or feel spirits with or without spells, rituals, drugs or devices like we'd see with necromancy or shamanism (both discussed in *Cultures and Beyond*). If our species has no written language, or a poor one, they cannot pass down information as easily, so perhaps they've resorted to communication with the dead to learn about the past. They might also have a complex afterlife that requires help to navigate to their intended destination. We need to work out the afterlife to understand details of ghosts, such as how frequently they happen, why, and how they can be resolved so the medium no longer sees them.

OTHER SENSES

Our bodies have more than the five senses that Aristotle made famous, and modern scientists think we have more. Some are more pronounced in animals but exist in us, too. The interesting ones are discussed next.

Water conducts electricity well, which is why the ability to sense electrical fields, called electroception, is primarily in aquatic life, where it helps both predators and prey survive. All living beings give off electricity, especially when we move, and the ability comes in two kinds. The passive kind is just the ability to sense it, and it would allow a predator to know we're there even if we're not moving. The active kind, called electrolocation, means that the animal can generate a small electric field that isn't much bigger than they are and then sense what's reflecting it back, like sonar. A rock shows nothing but another fish will, revealing its presence. What if we gave this to a species and extended the field?

Electrocommunication is when animals change the wavelengths they generate to signal other animals for mating, territorial displays, or make themselves appear bigger to intimidate a predator, like the electric eel. The latter can generate a much stronger pulse to stun animals but doesn't hurt humans. But perhaps an animal or species we invent can do better.

The ability to sense pain is called nociception and comes in three types. The mechanical kind is for cutting and crushing pain. Thermal is heat and cold, and chemical is any kind of toxin. We feel much of this on our skin in daily life. It is only injury or something like disease that typically causing internal pain. We may have limited use for this except for a species we want to appear especially tough or wimpy. Others won't understand that a different nociception from us is the cause unless we explain it.

Our sense of time can go awry as we estimate time intervals, duration, and whether events are simultaneous or not. Telescoping is when we recall events as having happened farther in the past than they did. We can also overestimate how short or long an interval is, such as a witness to a crime having trouble remembering how much time has passed. Another temporal illusion is when many things happen in a short span and we recall them as having happened closer to each other than they did, like the expression, "time flies when you're having fun." By contrast, boredom makes time seem to take longer. Little of this is useful for a species to have a very different sense from us, however, and may be relegated to a storytelling issue, such as when warp drive causes time dilation. This means that two observers think a different amount of time has passed due to them being different distances to a gravitational field, or their velocities relative to each other are quite different. We could decide our species is immune to this effect or has programmed their devices to counteract it.

Magnetoception is the ability to detect magnetic fields. It can be used for direction sense, altitude, or location. Both animals and our species might have a much better one than our weak sense. Animals can use this to mentally map a region, which is how birds can fly long distances without using landmarks or having daylight. We use things like the position of the sun, moss growing on the north side of the tree in the northern hemisphere, or an actual compass, but we could give a strong magnetoception to a species so that they're like a living compass. Imagine how valued they would be by traveling companions.

I'm inventing magiception, the ability to sense magical energy. Maybe this is what allows someone to become a wizard (coupled with manipulating it, of course). Perhaps we can tell what spell has been cast, how long ago, or whether it's fading in strength. If we have multiple types of magic in the setting, maybe there's a different sense for each. Can they sense an anti-magic zone before entering it? We should decide how far from them such a sense extends and how the body reacts. Any species could be given this, especially one from a highly magical setting.

GODS

We arguably need to invent gods before deciding which ones influence our species, but we can start with a general sense of a species disposition and then decide which deities are likely on their minds. We can be predictable, such as deciding that a warlike species worships the god of war, and we likely need to do that, but we can also decide they worship less obvious gods. Maybe they love fate and worship that god, too, despite that god also being the god of truth and integrity, good qualities. This can suggest our species values honor in combat and doesn't do things like stab people in the back. Interpretation is where the fun lies. To think more "outside the box," invent gods first and then your species, then assign them gods and find these conflicts you can resolve in ways that enrich a species.

An important consideration is whether the attributes of our gods influenced the resulting species and their outlook. This not only justifies many aspects but ties different creations together. It also allows us to leverage our existing work, such as the deities. If our gods are organized and those deity groups created a species, then perhaps that species is dominated by the character of those gods. The gods of deception, greed, jealousy, and fear might produce a very different species than the gods of truth, vitality, courage, and intuition. Those examples (daekais and karelia, respectively) are from my work on Llurien, a world with seven groups of gods and seven resulting species. A look at my approach with them on Llurien.com can provide ideas for your world.

CHARACTERISTICS

Anyone familiar with gaming has seen a list of characteristics like intelligence, wisdom, charisma, strength, constitution, agility, dexterity, and morale. Each will have a number from one to ten, for example, and a species is rated in each category. The numbering isn't needed for authors, but assigning one can tell us at a glance what we're thinking. We only need a few sentences about each trait and these can be things we never tell our audience. The exercise gets us thinking, and as we write it down, more ideas can occur to us. This example, invented on the fly, demonstrates the kind of work that will be useful to do:

"They aren't the smartest species, having no formal schooling and only learning by word of mouth; their grasp of history is poor. Their street smarts are better, as they can read situations, learning from experience. They lack wisdom, being unable to realize consequences until learning them the hard way. They also don't understand psychology except for how to be menacing, and can be easily lured into traps. They lack charisma, their twisted minds being as repulsive as their bodies, though a certain gleam of excitement does come over them in battle, though only evil people find this attractive.

"Their strength is considerable, allowing them to wield two-handed swords with one hand without fatigue or loss of dexterity. Their constitutions are generally strong in that they have endurance, but they don't heal well and catch sickness easily. Their agility is better than people expect, for they can jump farther and faster than anticipated, but they cannot do acrobatics due to their large size. Dexterity is excellent and they can not only fire all manner of bows with skill but are even gifted musicians, though their music is hideous to other species. Their morale is superior because they have little to no respect for life, whether theirs or someone else's, and feel assured of their place in the afterlife, which is not to say they court death, but dying in battle is an honorable way to go."

WORLD VIEW

One challenge of creating humanoid species is that there's only one on Earth and we tend to conceptualize invented ones that aren't much different from us. This is natural but maybe not ideal. Many aspects of humanity are taken for granted but can be questioned, turned on their head, and varied to create a world view different from all of humanity, not just one human civilization. We can look to different cultures for inspiration and will do so in *Cultures and Beyond, (The Art of World Building, #3)*. If we want to comment on human assumptions, this affords a great opportunity, especially when human characters on our world encounter our species; it's been noted that fantasy in particular tends to be based on a European model of civilization. The humans are seemingly transplanted from Britain.

To create a different world view, we should avoid having characters react in ways that are identical to us. While that's a storytelling issue, its roots lie in species conception, or lack thereof. If we accept that humans are prone to jealousy, and that's how we envision a human character reacting, this can be fine, but if we give an identical reaction to a species that's supposed to be different, this seems like a poor concept. We should question stereotypical reactions of humanity and possibly not give them to our characters, not to mention characters of different species.

A good example of this is Spock from *Star Trek*. He reacts differently than the human crew members to almost everything. It often drives ship mates crazy. He gets misunderstood, some calling him arrogant, cold, or worse. It hurts his badly suppressed feelings. It's as much a species clash as a cultural one. The judgmental aspect of humanity goes on display as they vilify a guy they're trying to make sense of, making the human failing of trying to understand another species in human terms.

Decide what your species is like in broad terms. How do they view themselves vs. other species? What is their imagined place in the world? Do others disagree with it? Are they peaceful or a threat to be reckoned with? Do they keep to themselves or travel extensively, and why? What is their reputation? Do they jump to conclusions? Do they react emotionally? Do they trust emotion more than logic, which is viewed with suspicion? Do they take offense at stupid things or overlook them? For all of these things, are they worse or better about it than us? Try not to just make them the same because you haven't thought about it. Make a list of all the stupid aspects of humanity that you've experienced or witnessed (even if it's just in a story), and then figure out how your species would react instead.

Here's an example of the sort of things you might want to write: Diaden see other species as weak both physically and in ability to pursue and realize goals. This has made them disdainful and snobby. Worse, it makes them routinely conquer other species in a belief that it's their job to lead others to a better life. "An unarmed Diaden is a dead one," they're proud of saying, as they're always prepared for battle and put up a terrible fuss if a city has an ordinance against openly carrying weapons, in which case they'll surrender theirs only because more are hidden on them. They disrespect ideas that go against their own. They practice "a good offense is the best defense." Most other species find them pushy, warlike, and confrontational. They seldom have friends among other species, and humans in particular are thought to be evil, for lack of a better word, if keeping company with Diaden.

SOCIETY

What kinds of government does the species typically have? Monarchies, dictatorships, or republics? These are discussed more in *Creating Places (The Art of World Building, #2)*, but those are three of the big ones that can imply levels of sophistication and concern with what we'd call human rights. A society where people can vote government officials in and out of office is markedly different from one where people are executed for dissention. Get a feel for this now and flesh it out later; each of those sovereign power types has varieties we'll examine in Volume 2.

Do our species marry? Do they divorce? Their religion might forbid or allow this. There was a time on Earth when the former was expected quite young and the latter almost never happened; we can assign one pair of viewpoints to one species and the reverse to another (having a reason is always a plus, and in a world where armed conflict is common, war can be that justification for either). Are big families the norm or does no one care much about their family? Perhaps they're more like animals in that young are born, raised a few years, and then go on their way, never reuniting. Maybe a child is reared by the whole community and they honor their parents but don't live with them for long. Or maybe they never move out and a home and business is passed down generation after generation.

In modern times, some parts of the world allow some gay marriage, but what about our species' typical society? Is it okay, a crime, or somewhere in between? Do they have abortion? Is abortion government sanctioned and paid for by health care? Are weapons allowed or forbidden? How sophisticated are laws and criminals? This list could go on for forever and we needn't invent everything or we'll never have a life, so choose what you might want to comment on. You can always add to it later.

Our species' habitat will affect their society. A forest-preferring one will likely love plants and woodland animals. A sea-dwelling species is the same for sea life. They might have less contact with other species, being more innocent, ignorant of their evils, and trusting; this might be true of an underground species. A flying species likely has more contact with everyone and is very social, maybe acting as messengers or scouts in human society. These will affect society and the overall outlook of a species.

LANGUAGES

Does your species have a written language? Did they invent it, or is it based on another species' language? This will affect how likely it is for two species to share a tongue that has diverged in some way. Is a written language words, symbols, or a combination? Less sophisticated species tend to have symbols. Those without a written language will be less educated, sophisticated, and have less sense of history, being unable to write it down.

We might have little reason to mention this, but is the language written right to left, top to bottom, or something else? There's one plausible theory for why differences exist: earliest writing was chipped into stone, and with most Earth people being right-handed, the chisel was held in the left hand so that it made sense to start on the right. When writing on parchment (or something similar) was introduced, going right to left increased the chance of smudging the writing, so left to right took over. But it's just a theory.

Can they speak, read, and write other languages? Which ones and to what degree of fluency? A flying species might be well traveled and pick up a smattering of many languages. A species that seldom goes anywhere, like elves and mountain dwarves, might not care about becoming bilingual, or they might learn a common tongue in distaste. They could pride themselves on their ignorance. Regionally, one population of a species might be different from another in many ways, including languages.

In SF, the use of universal translators has rendered this subject less important. It's a practical matter for film and TV shows to reduce or eliminate the need for subtitles and invented languages. Authors don't have this issue as much. The "universal" aspect of this doesn't need to be taken literally, as there can and likely should be languages that such a device hasn't been programmed with yet. This is truer for stories where characters are entering seemingly unexplored areas of the cosmos, as anywhere within explored areas is likely included already.

These devices are not typically shown as being able to scan text and translate it, but they would likely have the technology. Our characters may have picked up the ability to read a few key words or symbols in other tongues, but with universal translators abounding, they would have little reason to learn to speak or understand one. Regardless of what we decide, we can always have such a device fail, be lost, or be destroyed so that our characters are reduced to the old-fashioned way of trying to understand an unknown language: with great difficulty.

Is there a common tongue most species can speak if not read and write? If so, where did that language originate? In *Creating Places (The Art of World Building, #2)*, we'll look into creating sovereign powers; that will be a good time to invent an empire, which is a disparate group of sovereign powers united under one power that forces cultural changes on other, previously independent ones. The name of the empire might also be the name of the language that becomes the common tongue, at least in that region or continent. For example, "Antarian" is the common tongue of my Llurien world, named as much for the defunct Empire of Antaria as for the continent Antaria where all life originated; the language is that of the humans.

Cultures and Beyond (The Art of World Building, #3), looks into whether you should create a language and how.

CUSTOMS

Inventing customs, or leveraging Earth analogues, can help bring a species to life. Greetings, farewells, dining, and spiritual habits are all good subjects that will figure in our storytelling. Differences between this species and others can cause a misunderstanding, which has often been done in the *Star Trek* universe to the point of being a cliché, but it still affords us a chance to question human assumptions, which can in turn enlighten our audience. This is an opportunity to explore options other than those we've grown up with.

Actual customs can include shaking hands, holding doors for people, and ceremonies about birth, death, burial, weddings, and divorce. In a warlike story, soldiers might have customs regarding leaving their family, starting service, going into battle, mourning a comrade, and bringing a body home. Religion almost always has a number of customs associated with it.

This subject will be revisited in more depth in *Cultures and Beyond, (The Art of World Building, #3)*.

HISTORY

A history improves world building, but the one for our species doesn't need to be elaborate. An early decision should be where they first appeared. We might have decided this was a forest, but which one? On what continent? If we only have one land mass, the one we're intending to build out and use, that's easier, but we can still name another continent and never (or later) do things like create a map. If they originated from somewhere other than where we intend to tell our story, do we have an idea why they're here? Did all of them migrate, or did only some, resulting in at least two groups that might have biologically diverged over millennia the way humans did on Earth? This gives us races of the species.

It might give us corresponding attitudes, too. After deciding where the original territory was, we can get an idea of how new each additional group is based on geography. For example, Europeans spread around the world only to discover other races, which were then conquered by military might or even disease to which the native races didn't have immunity. If your species did this, it can create conflict with those they live among now, just as Native Americans are in conflict with the society Britain originally brought here. This is a simple justification for your species having issues with others.

Those who haven't left their original location much will have a world view reflecting this. It can manifest as skepticism that places they've heard about are real. It can make them suspicious of outsiders. They could feel abandoned by those among them who left. They might feel the departed are wayward and should be brought back. War may force them out and into a world they're poorly equipped to navigate, literally and figuratively.

Wars are another subject to devote time to as these events are remembered for centuries, causing long lasting attitudes, even when two former foes put aside their differences and become reluctant allies, possibly against another threat. Conquest also causes the conquering species to leave an impact on those they dominate, even long after that dominance ends; a language can become common to both, as can customs. Don't go overboard, however, because we'll likely have little opportunity to use much of it.

Has this species been conquered and/or enslaved in the past? Was it their own species or another? Are they still this way or did they gain their freedom, when, and how? Did others come to their aid or did they do it themselves? What we're after are events to give them attitudes about others.

If you just started creating your first species, you might have to return to this later, when you can think about how you want them to get along. Just make up issues that have boiled over into outright confrontation. Fighting over resources like forests and other land features is a great start because it has more to do with needs than attitude. Depriving others of access to trade routes, or allowing it, can cause animosity or friendliness. Attacks and rescues do the same. Two species can mostly get along, like humans and elves, but still dislike each other over imagined slights, attitudes, and misunderstandings. Look to human history for inspiration. We can google any conflict to learn why it happened, then leverage that idea.

RELATIONSHIPS

Unless this species is the only one, we need to decide how they relate to humans and other species of our invention, or any public domain species we're using. Inventing this tends to be easier when we've created other aspects first, like appearance, habitat, and world view. Ideas can form during those processes. Giving this time and not forcing it can help, as can imagining interactions as if we're writing scenes between them and others. Then think about why you have them acting the way they do. Use various situations that are likely to occur, such as greetings, farewells, dining etiquette, and how they react to various kinds of news that impacts their fortunes.

We must be sure to decide how two invented species interact. Using elves and dwarves as examples, it's easy to fall prey to deciding how humans get along with elves and dwarves but not deciding how elves and dwarves get along with each other. A single paragraph is often enough to get started. We're looking for high level ideas. Anything more detailed can arise while creating stories.

Are they enemies? Friends? Why? Are their legendary battles or animosities? Treaties? Are they allies now but some among them have bad blood? Every species should have opinions and prejudice about others, and humans should feel or think something stereotypical about everything we create (because we do that). There should be classic misunderstandings. Some of our characters should exemplify these ideas while others rise above them. It adds conflict and dimension. We can start with Earth analogues.

Is it normal for one to smash furniture on hearing bad news? Punch a wall? Or react stoically as if nothing has occurred? While these have nothing to do with relationships, the way others perceive them is certainly affected and in turn impacts relationships. If our species literally kills messengers, others aren't going to send them, for example, unless wanting to get rid of someone that way. More to the point, the species would be see as temperamental by others and this will change how people deal with them. Reputations are born of such things.

HUMAN COMMENTARY

A well done species can allow the author to make commentary about humans, which in turn helps our audience relate to our work. We can craft our species to do this. Feel we're dishonest? Make your species honest. Think we jump to conclusions? Make your species slow and deliberate in its evaluations to the point that it bugs humans. If you think humans are faithful to gods, create a species that is quick to turn its back on gods if not answered, making us look good by comparison. Maybe our species doesn't understand the concept of property and just takes other people's stuff like it's no big deal and we accuse them of being thieves. Any social or cultural expectation of ours can be turned on its head, an opposite expectation given to another species to cause conflict with not only humans, but other species.

SUPERNATURAL

If our world has the supernatural, we should decide our species' relationship with it. First, we'll need to decide how prevalent these forces are; this is covered in more detail in *Cultures and Beyond (The Art of World Building, #3)*. In a world where magic is rare, everyone is probably wary of it while also wishing they had such power. In a world where it's common, it might be as unnoticed as electricity is to us. One approach is to decide how much supernatural there is in general, then how much our species is involved with it, and finally how much experience our character has. The reverse method also works, though this is arguably more suited to a world that's invented for a specific tale. The intelligence and morale of our species will greatly impact their relationship with the supernatural, which can be divided into two groups: seemingly natural phenomena and ones caused by people (aka, magic).

PHENOMENA

What does our species think and feel about supernatural places? Are these to be avoided or sought out? The answer might depend on what kind of phenomenon it is. Something that perverts everything or everyone who goes near will naturally repel most people, but maybe we have a species that is unaffected by such things. Or maybe they take it upon themselves to investigate and neutralize them. It adds a great dynamic if everyone else runs away and this species runs toward it.

Imagine how this affects what others think of them. Are they crazy? Suicidal? Evil? Saviors? Honorable? Do they do something unspeakable with whatever they find at the heart of these places? Do they trap something causing it? If so, what do they do with it? Is that thing alive? Are they preventing further horrors? We can have characters who don't fit typical behaviors, but first we'll need to know what that typifies.

Does our species have special protection, weapons, or other devices? This is only likely if they're the ones designing them, unless they've made their willingness to do these things known and others have created things for them. Do those devices fall into the wrong hands and lead to other problems, including foolish people thinking they can now do what this species can, only to wreak havoc?

Our species might be less or more affected by a phenomena than others. We don't need a reason, although in SF, a scientist is probably trying to figure that out. We're talking about imaginary phenomena, which gives us creative license to invent pseudo-science. Sometimes having a mystery is good, however, and if we ever reveal our invented truth, long hidden, it had better be good. Remember the collective groan when the *Star Wars* universe named the thing that gives some people the ability to use the force. A mundane explanation to something that appears mystical and magical is arguably a mistake.

MAGIC

Whether we call them wizards, sorcerers, or something else, decide whether the species is likely to become magicians. This can be influenced by how magic works on our world. There seem to be two varieties of wizards: those who can do magic by force of will like a god, and those who must learn spells, with the requisite words, gestures, and physical materials and preparation needed for each. Our world might have both, giving us some flexibility.

This distinction matters because spells are often depicted as requiring schooling, discipline, and access to materials, which are often exotic and therefore hard to acquire. An uneducated species might have the aptitude for magic but lack the training or materials. Or if they're nefarious, perhaps no one will teach them. Education might come not from schools and guilds but tutors, who can in turn exact brutal requirements from an apprentice, holding the quest for power over their heads and making them earn their trade after performing terrible acts.

The species might not have access to spell materials without dangerous quests to get them or paying exorbitant fees to buy them. A nearby wizard's tower might be a seemingly good source of what they need, except that any magician with half a brain would fortify their dwelling. Rare items are often regarded as allowing for more powerful magic, so our species might be prevented from great power by difficulty attaining what they need.

Is our species disciplined enough to learn spells? Compare their impulsiveness to humanity's and make a decision. Those who easily give in to frustration might not succeed at all in casting spells or might do a poor job of it, causing unintended side effects to themselves, others, or their surroundings. Is this chaos the reason they're feared?

If our species can't read, casting spells seems less likely, given the need for learning from a spell book, for example. If they can read their language or "common," can they read magic words? This is usually considered higher learning and someone would have to teach them, unless there's a simple spell that would allow them to read anything. There are ways around these issues, should we decide we want a character who's an exception. We can also decide that spells can be taught orally and memorized.

By contrast, wielding supernatural power without spells or materials, just by imagining something and drawing power from around us, may require none of these things. A disadvantaged species could have powerful but undisciplined, and therefore dangerous, wizards. They likely don't care about a teacher. Maybe they're arrogant.

But we shouldn't make them too powerful without explanation. Usually magicians are given limitations in fiction to prevent them from being unstoppable. It can also humanize them. A common and believable limitation is that it takes energy to perform spells. Wizards save their strength for more worthy moments. Someone cocky might have no problem with wiping out defenseless people, but someone with pride might also see this as beneath them and let their henchmen do it.

There could be side effects to what they're doing, whether to themselves, others, or the world, with them largely ignorant of or indifferent to this. Do they learn of it the hard way? Do they resist such an inconvenient truth if others try to tell them? Do they know and don't care? Because they're evil or because their survival is more important? Do other species try to assassinate such wizards when one is known to exist?

A benevolent species is arguably more inclined toward civilization and therefore schooling, discipline, and access to at least more mundane supplies. Do they refuse to teach a nefarious species or do they do so anyway, knowing the problems this could cause and either not caring or doing it on purpose for some reason? Maybe one of our evil species is indeed well educated, etc., and teaches what they can do to less educated but no less evil species.

GODLY POWER

The gods, should they exist in our world, typically have powers they'll grant to a species. A classic scenario is a species laying hands on someone and channeling a god's power to heal the wounded. The power can be used in other ways, but whatever it is, this is different from magic as defined above because it's an issue of faith and not skill.

A species that lacks all that's required to become a wizard can achieve power through faith, leveling the playing field, though they're at the mercy of their god to answer their prayers. Might this not make them quite devoted, to augment their chances? This suggests a deeply religious species, or at least for some of its members. This can influence their relationships with others and their own kind, the priests reigning condemnation down on non-believers and trying to convert people, for example.

Whether evil or good, gods like attention and reward faith with their power. Imagine a god of cynicism who is also a god of poison and sickness, who grants his priest the ability to make someone wither and die from twenty paces. A god of innocence might be able to counter this by offering their priest the power of rejuvenation. Species can become part of a proxy war, caught in the middle but realizing it (or not) and taking what they can get. The role of priests can become quite strong but depends on a well-developed pantheon (see Chapter Two, "Creating Gods").

TECHNOLOGY

FANTASY

In a fantasy setting, technology means things like forging steel weapons, plate armor, or chainmail—the trade of blacksmiths, who are held in high regard. There are more rudimentary elements that our audience is unlikely to care about, including plumbing, irrigation, aqueducts, water wheels, and general tools for farming (a wood plow vs. an iron one). These are generally assumed to exist, but the question here is whether our new species is capable of such industry. Do they have architects smart enough to build structures that withstand storms and earthquakes? Can they build fortifications? Is the technological level enough to create more sanitary living conditions?

If not, they'll have to go without, live among those who do, or get these things by other means, whether stealing, buying, or conquering. They might have allies who'll agree to trade and train them in how to achieve something.

SCIENCE FICTION

In SF, we think of technology as being far in advance of our own on Earth, not the sort of rudiments mentioned under the fantasy section. Is our species able to design and build machines of any kind, not to mention something far beyond current human capacity? This requires intelligence, education and infrastructure for mining, refinement, chemistry, and more. Do we envision that they're chemists, engineers, and physicists? If not, they must steal everything, with it being more likely that they'll steal an entire ship, for example, rather than the parts to assemble one; this would be true of most if not all other techs.

Can we assume that some of these intellectual capacities and skills, like engineering, are needed to operate machines? That depends on our goal. Creators often grant spaceships advanced artificial intelligence (A.I.) that takes care of many functions. This gives a less than brilliant species far more opportunities, just as a gun allows a child to kill a samurai. Do the builders of these machines account for that and require more intelligence to operate something, or biometric security? A good approach would be a mix of these styles so that we can decide, based on our story needs, which option is in effect. For example, one species could make everything easy to operate while another does not. A third species that is contemplating stealing something would take this into consideration.

Decide what their life with technology is like. An ignorant and uneducated species can enjoy life in space even if they're not in command, because every space ship needs janitors, for example. This subservient position is something to keep in mind because it greatly broadens opportunities for them. While they might be in unenviable positions, they can still get around, and there's the mutiny idea of such a species taking over despite their limited technological skills. Maybe they bribe ship's officers into helping them. With some ingenuity, we can find a way to empower a weaker species.

Maybe our species steals or captures ships and is smart enough to operate but not maintain them; if something goes wrong, the crew might be stranded. Are they known for having to send out distress calls over this? It would likely get them captured and arrested, but they probably know all about this problem and travel in pairs, for example, the still-functional ship rescuing the other's crew before everyone flees. They might also set traps, taking over a ship that comes to help them, whether they really need that help or were just setting someone up.

More advanced species will be inventing technology and trying to safeguard it. They'll be the victims of ruses by those species who can't create these things. How has this changed or hardened/softened attitudes and laws about theft and tampering? With biometrics, devices could be set to only work with one species. We can invent all sorts of safeguards and ways of defeating them.

Not every species' society which lacks the ability to create technology will be "evil." Some might need the protection of another benevolent species. They might be taken advantage of by a nefarious one. There can be attempts to exterminate them or make them slaves. Fear about such outcomes could drive them to seek alliances, which may carry risks of their own.

If our species lack a society capable of producing technology (of whatever sophistication level), they may still be part of a mixed-species society that does indeed have the sophistication to create technological wonders. In this scenario, the smarter members of our species might be capable of gaining education, unless the society forbids them from doing so; a reason for that restriction is preferred, such as misuse of advanced information in the past. If our species can gain skills needed, they could introduce them to their own society with one degree of success or another.

COMBAT

Deciding on our species' morale, society, personality, and body (including dexterity, agility, strength, and constitution), will help us decide on their combat skills. A species that prides itself on "a good death" in battle is unlikely to run or retreat. The lack of this option might inspire more ferocity on the battlefield. But if there's no shame in running, and they run faster than everything else, perhaps our species has few battle skills, excelling at hiding and diversionary tactics.

Lack of dexterity and refinement reduce the likelihood of our species using bows except for the crossbow. Lack of finesse needed for the sword might have them preferring crushing weapons. A large species with big hands might be unable to wield many things designed for smaller species, but a club, mace, or staff could fit their hands better. A short species won't be using spears, long bows, or staves designed for anyone larger.

A flying species will likely use slings and other missile weapons so as to avoid bringing their wings into range of hand-to-hand weapons, but a bow might not be the easiest thing to carry unless it's small. Arrows in a quiver will need to be secured to prevent them from falling out, causing a delay each time they want to grab one. Rocks are often suggested as projectiles for slings, but rocks can become heavy unless their numbers are reduced, which in turn limits the number of attacks and might inspire our species to become quite accurate.

Does our species hunt others or get hunted? Does this occur for food, sport, or trophies? Decide how skilled they are at detecting threats or avoiding them. Do they stalk prey? Decide if they work in groups with their own kind or prefer going it alone. How do group tactics differ? Maybe they have special attacks or defenses. A species with a barbed tail might use it only for defense against a rear attack or whip it forward. Maybe it's poisoned, and if so, do they sting someone and wait for them to die or become immobile? Can they spit fire or something corrosive?

WHERE TO START

A top-down approach to inventing a species means viewing a species at a high level and working our way into details. We might decide on a sea-dwelling species and then face more detailed questions, like whether they have gills or can survive out of water. Can they walk on land? Are they seen often or rarely?

The bottom-up approach means creating details first and then slowly integrating them into a unified whole. Maybe we first decide on a species with sharp claws, a barbed tail, and which is rumored to carry people off at night while seldom being seen, and there's almost no trace of where it went. From this and other details, perhaps we decide this species is water-dwelling and the claws and tail are used for catching fish. The reason people disappear is that they're taken underwater and drowned, or perhaps held captive in underwater caves that have oxygen pockets, and since our species quickly enters the water from docks, there's no trail to follow. This big picture is suggested by details we created first.

CHAPTER FOUR

CREATING WORLD FIGURES

No book on world building would be complete without mention of those who live there, as they are arguably the whole point. That said, the creation of people will depend on our goals. If we're world building for gaming, then our world needs characters for the gamers to interact with. If we're a writer, then characters might be best suited to the stories we intend to tell.

Since this isn't a book on writing, I won't delve into the details of building memorable characters, because the goal of this chapter is to create well-known figures. Nonetheless, much of what follows can help us build characters. These are people we can reference at any time but which might not figure into a story. For example, on Earth we have Elvis, Oprah Winfrey, Tom Cruise, Tom Brady, Jesus Christ, Hitler, and the boy who cried wolf. In other words, a musician, television personality, actor, athlete, religious figure, dictator, and cautionary tale. In our world, we might replace them with wizard, knight, priest, and martyr. Or star fighter, bounty hunter, emperor, and Jedi knight.

Appendix 3 is a template for creating a world figure. It includes more comments and advice, and an editable Microsoft Word file can be downloaded for free by signing up for the newsletter:

http://www.artofworldbuilding.com/newsletter/

TYPES

Our world could benefit from heroes, villains, martyrs, and others who've become famous for whatever reason, such as physical traits, supernatural ones, or their role in world events. There isn't much difference between one type and another when it comes to inventing them, aside for the reason they're famous. Figure out what sorts of individuals are likely to be well remembered. This will give us a list of people to invent. Adding a touch of detail to the list will help inspire us. For example:

- A knight who turned the tide of war, maybe by sacrificing himself
- A knight who restored tarnished honor in the knighthood by doing something heroic
- A wizard who made people fear wizards
- An assassin who killed an emperor and triggered war (or stopped it)
- A passionate priest and good orator who inspired many to follow a god or way of life
- An influential leader who was assassinated/martyred, causing great social change
- A dictator who wanted to exterminate a race and caused large scale war
- A warrior known for incredible prowess but brought down by mundane health concerns
- A famous explorer whose ship vanished

If you're wondering where I got those, here are inspirations in no particular order: Martin Luther King, Bruce Lee, *The Princess Bride*, *Dragonlance*, and Hitler. By summing them up without their names, we start the process of making them our own and continue by creating details.

FAME

Our character is famous for something. This is the reason we're creating them. What are we hoping to achieve? Do we want someone whose name people fear to invoke? Someone to inspire others in times of trouble? Someone who is an example, good or bad, of what's possible? These motives (for us) needn't be dependent on stories we intend to tell. Our purpose is to have someone for our characters to admire, so what we need at the outset is a basic purpose for this person and how and why they are so revered or loathed. This can be a one liner in our notes: "He said a prayer to Lord Vallen, who at the Battle of Westin saved King Harin at the cost of his life and in so doing restored honor to the tarnished knighthood."

Whatever our character's fame, there are bound to be details about them, their life, story, and even what they did that people are wrong about. Maybe others have wishful thinking that someone was a certain way. People idolize heroes, ignoring ugly details, such as adultery or alcoholism. People demonize villains and ignore that they might've been truly devoted to their children. These exaggerations are part of humanity, at the least. When inventing your person, decide what people have right and wrong about them. Are there little known facts that might (or might not) change how they're viewed?

DEAD OR ALIVE

Decide if they're dead or still alive. If deceased, are they really dead or just presumed so? How did they die and was this satisfying in some way to the audience or characters? They could be incorrectly identified as dead and just be missing. If so, decide who the last person to see them was. Maybe they faked their death. We should have a reason and decide on the circumstances of that. What will cause them to return?

Are they imprisoned and is that known or not? If jailed or exiled, decide where, for how long, and why. The prison may have special properties or a unique location. How do they feel about being jailed (i.e., is it justified and do they agree?)? Maybe there's a release date everyone's worried about and preparing for. Have people become complacent about the threat this person poses so that they're easy prey when he returns without warning?

If the character is still alive, are they retired in old age, or out and about still doing things to add to that fame? Are they okay with that fame or hiding from it? Does anyone think they're past their prime? And how does our person feel about being viewed that way? Do they resent it or agree, perhaps sheepishly?

Our world has history and some if not most of these figures will be long gone (or at least thought to be—immortality, or the near equivalent, gives us options). Characters we'll never use except as a reference don't need much development, so when filling out the template in Appendix 3, don't spend much time on each section. It's living people that benefit from more thought.

We might decide someone is too much fun and we'll keep them around, changing their status to living, but this can cause a problem if we've tied the events of their life to the events of our world history and can't change it. But we can always write a story set in the past.

POSSESSIONS

A hero or villain with cool stuff excites the imagination. Who doesn't like Jedi Knights with light sabers (*Star Wars*)? Or albino weaklings with a sword that devours souls and transfers the victim's energy to the wielder (*Elric of*

Melnibone)? Or a warrior with a fierce bird that would devour lesser men but obeys him (Tarl Carbot of the *Gor* series)? Run of the mill items are nothing to get excited over and won't become famous and are probably not what we're looking for here. Jewelry, weapons, and animals can all be memorable possessions, but it's arguably better to choose one or two for each character. Otherwise the law of diminishing returns kicks in and the impact of each item becomes diluted by the existence of the others.

When deciding what our character has/had, consider giving them something suited to our purpose and their status. If they're a warrior, a weapon is an obvious choice. This can be one that achieved a famous result (such as it's the sword/gun that killed a certain bad guy) or one that was just generally used by them and had a special property that made it famous. Maybe the weapon was altered in some way, either a piece removed or something added to alter its functionality, power, or speed.

Armor is less exciting. Armor that saved our guy makes them a little weak, by comparison; we like people who save themselves. But it might allow them to enter something like a supernatural phenomenon no one else could enter, for example. But if the armor became cursed—or was all along—that's better, especially if it's still around on our world or believed destroyed (but isn't). What if the armor compelled them to do dangerous missions, as if it had a mind of its own? This is one way to meld a famous character with a famous item.

An item they are always seen with can also acquire a mythic reputation. A wizard's staff comes to mind, as does any outfit they typically wear or an item they use on their adventures. Something small like a ring is unlikely to capture much attention unless it has a giant diamond in it, for example. A necklace or belt are progressively more likely to get noticed, as is anything worn on the head.

Broken items are another area of interest. Can it be put back together? Some or all of the pieces might be lost. Decide who broke it, why and when, what led to this, and the aftermath. Was there a defeated hero/villain, a chaotic artifact, or explosion (one that created a monster)?

How did our character acquire this item? Maybe it was found, bestowed, or forged for them. It could be standard equipment that just has a fearsome reputation. Have they ever lost it and if so, with what consequences? Did they recover it? Perhaps it's no longer the same or has changed in some way, which might be significant. It could still be useable or dangerous in the wrong kind of way now. They may keep the altered item out of loyalty. Did anything happen to our character because they no longer had it?

If the item is still lost, is our character looking for it or have they given it up? Do you intend them to find it? Do you have any ideas who has it now? Are there any consequences if someone ill-equipped to handle it has it? This can apply to items that our gods have as well. In addition to weapons, armor, clothing, books, and devices to help with mundane or extraordinary tasks like food, shelter, and communication, we also have steeds and ships to consider (see the next section).

Did they get it by gambling? Maybe it was a trade deal, such as someone selling it without having any idea of its true value, which was then discovered by our character. The possession could have been the result of a quest our character went on specifically to find it.

Do others covet the item, causing our character to need to protect it? Either way, in a world with thousands of years of history, there are plenty of interesting items to be found and which no longer belong to their original owner; this goes up exponentially across multiple planets.

We might want to figure out who created the item. Did our character do it themselves? This is more likely if they're a wizard or engineer. We can also create a history for this item making its way through multiple hands, possibly causing problems along the way, most famously with our character?

STEEDS AND SHIPS

Steeds and ships (especially in SF) have a special place as a companion or a trusted way out of tricky situations. Audiences can become attached to them (like the Millennium Falcon of *Star Wars*), and that's what we want. Find a way to give it personality, which generally starts with a good name. If this is an animal, the way to make an audience care about it is to make the animal seem to care about our character, such as coming to the rescue, being loyal, and following orders, even showing initiative. Just like with dogs, we admire an animal loyal to a person, plus one who can be counted on. Sometimes having the animal injured, and the character to be upset about that, allows us to care, too. There is probably at least one famous dragon, horse, or enormous bird on your world, if they exist at all.

Ships have personality even if they're the non-AI man-o-war type of our Earth past. This has to do with characterization and other characters assigning traits to an inanimate object, so this might be harder in a video game. The more people consider it their home, the more personal a ship becomes. A great name is a huge benefit here and must not be overlooked.

With artificial intelligence, ships can be a step up from fantasy without talking AI. Sense of humor and banter go a long way with making an audience like the AI. If that AI is not perfect, making mistakes or being too invasive with unwanted body scans, for example, this humanizes them and can add humor. We can treat an AI as if it's a human (or other species) but with limitations on understanding emotions or physical impacts of a body on one's state of mind, disposition, and attitude; in other words, maybe they don't understand our character as well as they think. An AI can also become corrupted or be taken over by outsiders, and while obvious, it's still a good idea provided our version is done well. Talking ships are not the same as talking swords, too; we can get away with this one whereas an audience will skewer us for a talking sword.

The creation of AI is covered in *Cultures and Beyond (The Art of World Building, #3)*.

Relationships

When creating a world figure, their relationships may not be that important to us if we'll do little more than have a character name-drop their hero. This can be an area to skimp on until later, if ever, but should we decide to invent their relationships, this section may help. Some people are famous for who they kept company with, including who their enemies were.

Family

Parents, siblings, lovers, and children (and extended family) all provide benefit or add risk to heroes and villains alike, so decide who is in our character's life. Or what happened to those people if gone. Did family die first, breaking our character's spirit, or did family outlive him and mourn our dead character, possibly wanting revenge on a killer or responsible party? One of those mourners might be even more interesting than the person we started creating. A family of evildoers can be a lot of fun. A family of heroes can make us root for the lot of them. A family with both is even better.

If they have children, do they know about all of them? It's a cliché to have an unknown child turn up, so you might want to avoid that. Television shows, especially soap operas, desperate for a surprise twist, have ruined that. The unknown sibling is equally cheesy, so if we're going that route, make it good, interesting, and plausible. After all, it actually *does* happen, but we might want to only do that once in an entire writing career. If we need to introduce someone later, it's better to admit our character knew that the person existed and it just didn't come up in a story due to irrelevance (before now). Try to avoid playing the unknown relative card.

Has our villain been disavowed by relatives? This might be some or all of them. Some relatives might offer safe harbor at the risk of being cast out by the rest, or punished by society. What's in it for them to risk this? Perhaps they truly love our villain and feel they can save him one day. A mother who can't give up on her baby, now an adult, is overdone but understandable. Less common is a mother who has turned on their child. Potent emotions can be the reason our villain went bad in the first place.

Then there's our hero, who might wish to make family proud but whose actions have put family members in harm's way. Heroes have powerful enemies and there's no telling what some will do to family. Has our hero hidden children or a lover to protect them? Do the protected ones chafe at this? What kind of stress has arisen between hero and family due to this? Has anyone died despite our hero's attempt to protect them, and what effect did this have on them? Are they guilt ridden? Did they quit and let the evil they swore to stop go unchallenged, letting it win, and if so, what did it do to our hero? Destroy him? Is he a drunk now, unable to take all the guilt? Will he be redeemed one day? Are the children old enough to have a life of their own and cause trouble for their hero parent in other ways, as only teenagers can?

This raises a point that is often overlooked—there are descendants of this person. Maybe one of our story's characters is that descendant, whether one generation later or dozens. If other characters know that, it can be something they want to downplay. These relatives may have changed their name or done something to hide their association, and this may have worked for most people but not fooled everyone, possibly with consequences down the road. A common idea is of a deceased relative coming back from the grave to inhabit the body of a relative, so be clever if going that familiar route.

THE SPECIES

Since our character is famous, he's likely famous outside of his own species. With each species having a different world view, each might view this person differently. A hero to some will be a villain to others. Be sure to think about this to give your character added dimension. While elves and dwarves might view the character positively, each might have gripes about it. By contrast, ogres and goblins might view the individual as evil but again have slightly different issues with them.

While creating deeds, keep in mind that they may have run into conflict with one or more species while undertaking a mission. This can range from obvious encounters with ogres, for example, to enthusiastic help from elves and grudging aid from dwarves. Or the latter could've been openly hostile to what they wanted to do, not allowing our character to enter their lands, forcing him to take the long way around, for example. Make sure everything wasn't easy for them or there wouldn't be a reason they're famous.

HISTORY

ORIGINS, DEMISE, AND IN BETWEEN

While we don't need every last detail of where a character came from, it helps to know their original continent, at the least, and preferably a kingdom, too. The latter might wait until we've invented more and decided on the governments and quality of life there, as discussed in detail in *Creating Places (The Art of World Building, #2)*. Decide whether they still live there, have taken up residence elsewhere, or became a wanderer. Create a quick reason for their choice, which may have been influenced by familial concerns, such as keeping relatives safe by going far away and lying about origins. Or if the government made life horrible for people, they might have left. Or maybe life was wonderful and they left to help those less fortunate.

Our choices will impact much about their worldview, assuming we've created cultures as detailed in *Cultures and Beyond (The Art of World Building, #3)*. The society they came from will have beliefs and customs, and while the latter is not hugely important, the former is. There are basic ideas about how life should be lived, such as how different genders are treated. This is more important for characters that we intend to use as more than a reference, but if the Kingdom of Norn viewed woman as little more than sex objects and our male hero is from there, this would impact how well he gets along with people in other cultures that differ. Is this the reason he couldn't get along with peers and worked alone, for example?

Once we've decided where they came from, decide where they've lived or if they kept moving as if in search of something. Having multiple sovereign powers they've been influenced by helps create personality. This is another thing we needn't worry about too much at firs unless planning to use their residence in some way, such as a story where people end up there. Their home might have booby traps, whether mundane, technological, or magical. In SF, surveillance from a distance is likely, but we can still do this in fantasy with spells or magic devices. Decide how simple or majestic their home is. Personality will figure into this, but so will the fame heaped upon them and whether they've monetarily benefited from exploits or not.

If the character is dead, decide where the remains and any special items they possessed are. Is the body intact? Is it ashes? Is that grave actually empty but few if any know it? Maybe their grave is guarded, revered, or haunted. Their items can be buried with them or hidden. Maybe the items are lost, or just believed lost, and someone secretly has them, though it can be more interesting if more than one person has the various items, especially if they are needed together.

If they're still alive, where are they living now? What are they doing with their time? Are they hunted and living with lots of protection, or are they celebrated and afraid old enemies will destroy those they love? Are they imprisoned? Living world figures can be fun, though maybe nothing beats undead ones.

TRAINING AND SKILLS

While some individuals have innate skills, notable people like wizards, knights, gunfighters, and pilots often have training. We don't need a lot of details here, but decide if they went to an academy of some kind. Consider where it was, and whether they graduated, fit in or not, and if they're considered a great example of the academy's graduates or an embarrassment to the institution. Some of this will play into personality. They might've been apprenticed to a master, and if so, did they part ways peacefully? Does the master approve of him? Or did our character kill his master for his secrets or some slight, real or imagined? And is anyone after our person for justice or revenge? This could be the reason they're famous.

Another way to gain skills is by being captured and trained for something like gladiator fights. Or being conscripted into an army or as a sailor. Some of their skills can have less to do with fighting and magic, and more to do with navigation and tracking, wilderness survival, and the customs of various kingdoms. The latter brings up another point that some skills are gained in the field, whether military or social, instead of in a training regime. Unless our character was royalty, nobility, or aristocracy, they likely weren't trained in the finer points of etiquette, but they could still be a quick study, emulating what they see, though not without some gaffes.

Street smarts are either earned, innate, or both. Whether our character has this or not would help determine their effectiveness, whether it's actually being good on the streets or just the ability to read people and situations. Being bad at this might also cause them trouble that sours them on relationships and turns them into a villain.

DEEDS

The reason our character is known is presumably what they've done, though they can be famous for what they are, such as the last of a royal line or an exiled princess. Characters who never do anything aren't terribly interesting, however, so give some thought to actions this individual has taken. Actions that changed the world are ideal. For example, if we want magic badly restricted but don't have a reason, perhaps a villain wizard killed an emperor with this restriction as a consequence all must pay. Perhaps they've destroyed a kingdom, ruined a virgin princess by seducing her, or killed a terrifying warlord. Think about what you want them to have accomplished and make a list that can be as simple and short as below, and which can be expanded on further should the need ever arise:

1) Destroyed a given magic or technological item of great importance so that two or more groups would stop fighting to get it, earning a burn on one side of the face when it exploded
2) Invaded a given kingdom and turned the tide of power so that the kingdom fell
3) Recovered a lost weapon which they became known for wielding
4) As ship captain, destroyed a fleet and turned the tide of war

WHERE TO START

The first fundamental decision is what type of person are we inventing: good or evil? While it's true that some will consider a person one way while others consider them another, it's easier for us to decide on one to start with and decide later how enemies might view them. We should also decide their profession, such as knight, warrior, priest, or ruler. This will determine their capabilities and often how traveled they are, plus their influence. Next we should decide what we're hoping to achieve with this person. Remember that they aren't necessarily a character we'll use in a prominent way (we can do that later of course), but someone whose existence influenced the world and inhabitants. The deeds for which they became famous are often central to this, so focus on what they've done. Another major decision is how long ago they lived and died, or whether they're still alive. Other items can be saved for last, including possessions, steeds, ships, family, relationships, origins, and training.

CHAPTER FIVE

CREATING MONSTERS

A world with monsters is arguably more entertaining than one without. Appendix 4 is a template for creating one. It includes more comments and advice, and an editable Microsoft Word file can be downloaded for free by signing up for the newsletter:

http://www.artofworldbuilding.com/newsletter/

DEFINING MONSTER

We all know what a monster is, but since we might be creating species and animals, too, let's be clear. The term implies something harmful, unnatural, and morally objectionable, whether there's a physical deformity or psychological one. Monsters aren't real, of course, and are created by storytellers, usually to depict or highlight some of the above, sometimes as a warning. They are often a freak of nature and can result from birth defects, in which case it was something else, like a human, before being regarded as a monster by horrified onlookers. Their existence has often been thought to foreshadow something evil happening, which is one reason they are cast out.

In science fiction and fantasy, the word "sentient" is used to describe creatures that are human-like in their mental capabilities, even though that's not what the word means. Due to this convention, this usage will be retained herein anyway. The real definition of sentient only includes the ability to sense, feel, and experience, which means an animal is technically sentient.

As a side note, with space traveling characters visiting new planets, what they might term a monster at first might turn out to be an indigenous animal. Either that, or it's a member of a species that might've been stranded, for example, and terrifies those near through no fault of its own except appearance, and it's assumed to be a monster.

MONSTERS VS. SPECIES

The difference between a monster and an intelligent species is arguably their minds. A humanoid species is typically sophisticated in having what humans have: society, culture, philosophy, and other aspects that distinguish us from animals. This is a generalization, but monsters don't typically have these things, or at least, not in a way beyond that of animals. We can argue, rightly, that animals like dolphins and apes have a certain social structure, but these are communicated as much with body language as verbally. Any language is fairly limited compared to mankind. They don't read and write or pass down long histories. A generation today likely has no idea what was happening one hundred years ago, though this is admittedly conjecture.

None of this means we can't have an intelligent monster, but once we start giving a monster these things, it starts moving in the direction of humanity. We may find ourselves deciding that our monster is very cool and could be more useful, so we turn it into a species. No harm in that. Dracula is a good example of a smarter monster, but while he is a vampire now, he was once human. This is also true of zombies, who are typically portrayed as relatively stupid. We can use a similar approach (the monster was once human) to explain our monster's sophistication.

Does monster mean unsophisticated like an animal? In fantasy, SF, and gaming, yes. They're typically portrayed as things that can't be reasoned with when one corners us for dinner or we wander into its territory. In this sense, they're just like animals. We likely can't communicate verbally with it, either, but that's not a rule either. We can teach pets to understand what words mean, but that involves frequent time together, a reality that would make someone no longer think of the monster as such, most likely. This raises the idea of most people thinking it's a monster but one person having befriended it, which has been done with children's stories.

MONSTERS VS. ANIMALS

A major difference between monsters and animals is numbers. Just about every monster we've heard of was a "one off," meaning only one existed. The reason is the aforementioned purpose in a story—to teach a specific lesson that didn't require more of them—and because they are abnormal, which by definition means uncommon.

This is not to say we can't have more than one. Zombies and vampires are good examples, but in both cases, these originated from humans and we don't generally consider them monsters even if they're monstrous. In a film series like *Aliens*, we have what appears to be a monster but which is really an animal. Why? Numbers.

If we have more than one, can we still call it a monster? Sure, though "creature" might be a better term, but if we read the definition of that, it means animal. Does our audience care about definitions? Probably not. Either way, the existence of two or more identical monsters benefits from a good explanation, such as both of them being created at the same time as in a laboratory accident. Even then, there's no reason to say that the accident caused identical mutations. One accident could cause twenty different monsters, not twenty of one type, which are capable of reproducing and then being considered animals. Once we start multiplying them, we're going to start needing a name for them, at least, and unless they scatter, they might start developing more sentience (like society and language), sooner or later, and start becoming a species.

We needn't ever refer to our creation as a monster, but people use this term partly because there is only one. It has no name. It's an "it," as well, not a he or she, even if it appears to have a known gender. No one knows what to call it, unless it's been nearby a long time and someone gave it a nickname that stuck. In the book *Frankenstein*, the monster has no name, but because promo efforts for the movies use the monster prominently, people often think its name is Frankenstein when that's really the doctor's name.

ORIGINS

We needn't tell our audience where the monster came from originally, and in gaming it's arguably irrelevant, but the thought exercise can make the result more interesting. The first question should be whether it exists on purpose or by accident.

ACCIDENTAL MONSTERS

In worlds with magic, advanced technologies, or unexplained phenomena, the accidental route is especially viable. This is where many comic book characters originate. There are many possibilities that need little in the way of explaining how the monster came about. It encountered something and now it's a monster. No one is going to say our mutated human isn't possible.

This raises an important point—accidents happen to pre-existing entities, whether animal or a humanoid species. They don't generally cause a lifeform to spring from nonliving matter. We can do whatever we want, like having a broom become possessed of life as in *The Sorcerer's Apprentice*, but none of us regard that as a monster. It's an animate object.

This suggests that plants can become monsters even if we don't refer to them that way, but "monster" implies the ability to interact and to change location, not an inanimate object rooted to the ground. After all, a monster that can't change location typically isn't particularly terrifying. We could just stay out of reach or wall it up if desired. Maybe it can move but is tied to its lair, literally or figuratively, for some reason we'd want to reveal. Then again, maybe it has telekinetic powers and can influence people over a wide area, messing with their minds so that they have hallucinations, the most important of those being hiding its true whereabouts—or tricking people into coming near enough to become food, like the sirens of Greek mythology.

The accidental route means our monster having some intelligence is more feasible, if it was once human or another species. Years or even decades in the mutated state could have rendered that intelligence muted. Or the incident could've immediately rendered it dumber. Or vastly smarter.

Someone caught in an accident has one advantage—our sympathy. They're a monster now, but maybe once it was a good person with a family, one it wishes to see but is afraid to visit. It might either scare them or something worse, like feel a desire to eat them because that's what they do as a monster now, having poor impulse control. The monster may recall their past life and be hostile precisely because that old life is gone. This gives it motivation.

WHO CAUSED IT?

We'll need to decide who and/or what caused the accident. Readers want to know such things once one is mentioned. SF offers countless ways for this to happen, from alien weapons, physics gone awry, chemical experiments, or space phenomena. In fantasy, magic, otherworldly creatures, or other supernatural elements are likely sources.

Not all accidents just happen. Some are the result of a pursuit someone had, such as trying to manipulate matter or subdue forces. This is a good chance to dream up a scenario that led to the accident. We may have a story to tell as a result. Other characters crop up. Maybe our monster is the one behind the accident but blames someone else. Another option is for someone to have been purposely exposed to something that is intended to kill them but which results in a monster instead. Then there's the innocent bystander or even a hero who meant to stop an atrocity but is now a monster.

MONSTERS BY DESIGN

Some monsters might have been created on purpose, from something already alive or something inanimate. The latter suggests great power behind its creation, such as a wizard or god, both found in fantasy but often not in SF. This suggests that fantasy can get away with monsters that are farther removed from humans and animals than science fiction, where mutation of pre-existing life is more likely. But there's nothing that says technology, if it's advanced enough, can't create life from nothing.

Either way, our monster by design likely has a purpose. It's possible someone was experimenting with creating life, like Dr. Frankenstein. But that's been done, which is not to say that we can't do it, too, but we should strive for a fresh angle if we do. Maybe the monster's creation was successful and it's here for a reason, such as guarding something. Or terrorizing villages at a wizard's beckoning, which suggests story ideas. The creator should have some reason as to why they did it.

Maybe the monster is fulfilling its purpose. Is it proud of that, or does it wish it were free? Is it bound somehow? Perhaps its purpose is long gone and it doesn't know what to do. Perhaps its master has been destroyed and the monster is on its own now. Or the master was imprisoned and the faithful monster intends to free him. The monster may never really have a purpose at all. These monsters might experience an existential crisis like Frankenstein's monster, who is tormented by its existence and doesn't understand what it did wrong to be cast out by its creator.

This sort of monster can also elicit sympathy if desired. Slavery is still slavery. The monster can be tormented by its existence. Maybe it will even welcome death at the hands of those seeking to slay it, but maybe it fears that others want to capture it, and so it must fight back. There's always the monster that's content with being one, which is probably more likely with a monster created on purpose than with a monster created by accident (and which may remember the past or be disabled in some way that makes its existence especially hateful).

Humans have a moral and ethical code. Monsters are depicted as not having one. This helps us use them as they were often intended, as a warning about untoward behavior. But monsters may have a moral code, too, just one very different from ours, where the killing of sentient life is no big deal to them, for example. Their creator might've wanted to imbue them with certain traits, like protection of them or an item. That raises the question of how much control the creator had/has over the monster. Is the creator dissatisfied with his work? Are monster and master bound in mutual loathing but dependency? If the master is killed, will the monster die, and vice versa?

WHO CAUSED IT?

Who would create a monster on purpose? Wizards, gods, and "mad" scientists come to mind (like Dr. Frankenstein and Dr. Jekyll). So do bad people who've captured others and who want to see what happens when someone is exposed to something dangerous. It's possible that no one knows who created a given monster, meaning we don't have to mention it, but stories do well when there's some speculation about a monster's origin. Mystery is good, but not total mystery, which is why we all love clues.

Any character willingly creating monsters is likely up to no good. The creator's motivation should be understandable even if the logic behind what they've done is terrible and twisted. In fantasy, gods are a great choice because they might like creating beings for reasons never explained to the species. Or maybe they just want to keep life interesting for sentient inhabitants by creating monsters they have to deal with. SF offers many ways to expose someone to phenomenon, including viral infections from new worlds.

MONSTERS BY EVOLUTION

A monster can be a product of evolution, perhaps the first of its kind. In this scenario, our monster's habitat is likely to cause the resulting monster and its attributes. Evolution causes adaptation to solve a problem or take advantage of environmental factors that have usually been in place a long time. That's not to say that we can't have something happen shortly after a change in that habitat, but that's more suggestive of an accident causing the monster than evolution, which by definition takes a long time.

The *X-Men* took the route of evolution to explain the mutants, and though we may not consider them monsters, the non-evolved humans in the stories do. Superman has abilities bestowed by virtue of being an alien, even though those abilities are only explained as having something to do with the sun, and everyone accepts that. Our explanation can be as simple as naming the type of radiation that caused a mutation.

The changes in our monster by evolution might have no purpose other than to survive better than before. This can include adaptations that make it better at defeating our humanoid species. In this case, our monster will originate from an animal or species and therefore be seen as a perversion of that, much the same way a human with two heads was once considered a monster. Aside from the mutation, the monster will be similar to its original life form. Having been cast out, it might be upset with its own species.

Habitat

Where a monster lives is important to any story involving it, even if its home is never shown. What it takes with it from there, how far away it travels, and what it takes home will affect our uses of it. Showing its home gives us an opportunity to characterize the monster, while avoiding doing so, or just giving hints, helps create mystery about it.

Our monster may not have a lair, but the nature of monsters in literature has typically been cautionary, meaning those living near it are supposed to learn something about themselves from the existence of this monster. We don't have to follow that, but a monster that goes away for good may prevent a population from learning anything about themselves. On the other hand, traveling monsters provide new opportunities, even across other planets.

There's no reason our monster can't have access to easier means of getting around, such as a magical device or a portal near its home which it stumbled upon. For SF, a monster with access to an interstellar ship is very useful, and we can either have that ship be the monster's lair or function like a home away from home. Possible justifications are either that the monster was on a ship when it became a monster, or that a ship landed near it and it ended up onboard, likely killing the crew after launch.

A lair can include treasure, weapons, and the remains of victims, all of those being fairly standard furnishings reminiscent of Medusa's lair from Greek mythology. The bones are more likely from two occurrences—feeding on species or animals, and/or defending itself with the resulting victims left there. This is one reason to decide on our monster's tastes. And if our monster leaves dead bodies around, this says something about it, whether that it doesn't care about the smell, wants to send a message to visitors, or doesn't have a clue about disposing of bodies. It might also be unaffected by any disease this could spread.

The mystery of where one lives often occupies stories to the point of cliché, and yet it is such an obvious concern that it's nearly inevitable for characters to search for the lair. Rather than avoid this, make your search and discovery worthwhile. While a lair is often hard to find or reach (or escape from alive), making this impossible lessens the usefulness of our monster.

To aid this, decide what kind of evidence the monster leaves when it's away from home. Are there trails or footprints leading back? Does it cover its tracks? Are spores left behind? Does it kill and leave remains or take anything with it, particularly something (or someone) valuable and which compels action to thwart it? Is the trail it leaves a trap? Is magic (in fantasy) or special tracking equipment (in SF) needed? Can it thwart some measures?

Knowing whether our monster is nocturnal or not will figure into any stories. Things awake and prowling at night are more intimidating, but there's no reason it can't be active during the day. The effect on a population terrorized by it becomes all encompassing, for they'd still fear it more at night, just because humans, at least, fear the dark. Our monster's enemies will have some sense of its schedule and will plan their attacks for when it's sleeping, if they know its lair. If they don't, they'll be trying to trap or otherwise attack it when it's on the prowl.

MOTIVATION

What does your monster want?

TO BE LEFT ALONE?

Isolation isn't desired by most, but if everyone thinks you're hideous or evil, you probably don't want company unless it's other monsters, which raises the question of love between monsters (whether of different kinds or not). Is the monster being hunted simply because it's been seen and is feared, or has it done something to stir up other species? Do any of our species think the monster has a right to live unmolested or does pretty much everyone want to kill it? Such conflict is good for stories and a debate on the right to life.

To Hoard Treasure?

This idea is often used but doesn't make that much sense because treasure is no good when we can't barter it for other things. By definition, monsters aren't engaging in commerce with a larger society; it's not like the monster is going to waltz into town and buy something. One possible explanation is that it likes shiny things, which is indicative of low intelligence. A better explanation is that a given monster happens to have valuables from killing someone and taking all their stuff, possibly indiscriminately, and having little or no idea that some of it is valuable. After all, why would it know this unless the monster was formerly part of a society and remembers this? Treasure attracts thieves, but then maybe the monster considers it a good way to lure people there so it can eat them.

Food?

Everyone needs to eat. The bigger our monster, the more food it requires. Large, four-legged animals like horses, deer, and bison are probably staple foods. Making it a vegetarian significantly reduces the threat to species, so you might want to avoid that, unless a salad eating monster is desired for comedic effect. If the monster just wants to eat, then survival is all it's likely after, which causes an ironic problem if it feeds on the wrong thing...

For a storyteller, the biggest reason to have monsters eat intelligent species is for the horror it creates in others. For the monsters, they may have few other options. They also might not be sophisticated or moral enough to make a distinction. Feeding on the humanoid species, or livestock can rapidly cause conflict. Most monsters are remotely located, however, so wildlife is more likely to be a staple food. Humanoid species aren't that appetizing, in reality, due to the ratio of bones to muscle/meat on us. This is why sharks spit out most people they attack; we aren't a juicy seal, for example.

Security?

A monster that feels threatened is likely to attack others, especially those it believes to be encroaching on its territory. Monsters can be afraid, just like any apex predator. A monster could be smart enough to realize that attacking the species might bring greater numbers to destroy it, but it's entirely likely that a monster doesn't think that far ahead. Traditionally, monsters have a lair, which they presumably want to protect so they feel safe, but if our monster can fly or is otherwise quite mobile and a traveler, that greater freedom may give it less need of security. Then again, it might feel more vulnerable by not having a good place to hide. The idea of a monster who has recently taken up residence near a town is a good story premise.

REVENGE?

Whether our monster resulted from an accident or not, it might want revenge on its creator. Does our monster know who created it? A monster upset with life itself might just want to kill from jealousy or hatred, but it's often better in storytelling to have more interesting reasons than that. The "I'm a monster, therefore I kill" idea is stale. The monster might want revenge against the species that created it while leaving others alone. This can cause a perplexing mystery for characters. Imagine that elves caused the monster, who kills elves but leaves humans alone. The characters may not understand why at first until uncovering the backstory on this monster.

CHARACTERISTICS

PHYSICAL APPEARANCE

That monsters are hideous comes with the territory, usually, but there's no reason that has to be the case. Modern readers can consider someone or something a monster not for its appearance, but behavior. That said, a young adult audience is probably expecting a repulsive appearance. Sometimes it seems that everything ugly has already been done and that films, in particular, try to outdo each other, sometimes to the point of being unintentionally silly. The concept of beautiful monsters has also been done more recently, with anyone encountering that monster unsuspecting due to appearance, and this is sometimes an illusion. These are all valid options.

If we opt for the physically grotesque, inspiration can come from many of literature's existing beasts. Unfortunately, today's audiences have likely seen just about everything, so a monster will be made more memorable by having a rationale behind that appearance. Adding deformities or additional limbs or heads is easy and effective if not particularly imaginative, nor is merging different body parts from other animals together.

For this reason, it's suggested to figure out other aspects of our monster before working on appearance. When we get to this point, we'll already know this monster and give it physical attributes that help it achieve its motives or which derive from its origins. Justifications make the body choices more compelling, sensible, and our monster easier to standout. We face stiff competition on appearance so that we might have little chance of doing something that hasn't been done. The key to being memorable is backstory and justifications for the body.

Regardless of what we decide for appearance, having a clear idea of what our monster looks like, and the impression it creates, is important. If it looks just like humans, for example, few will think it's a monster. There must be some sort of mutation or transformation that has taken place; either that, or it is odd to begin with. Size is a simple way to make something fearful, but gigantism and dwarfism have been done before. If you go that route, I'd suggest additional reasons your monster is a monster.

A monster that results from an accident is more likely to be disproportionate in some way. One arm longer than the other, a misshapen hump, or an extra but useless limb (known as a vestigial limb) are examples. These are the reasons why humans have historically called someone with a birth defect a monster (nice of us, isn't it?). We judge by appearance, like it or not, and react with fear and revulsion to anything unusual.

SKILLS

A monster who can do unusual things is arguably more entertaining than one that's only creepy. These can be physical feats such as incredible strength, speed or endurance, the ability to regenerate severed limbs, or the power to influence minds to kill, submit, or lie to others about the monster. Whatever it is can be suggested by its appearance or we can make them a surprise. Supernatural skills offer more room for being unusual and memorable. Medusa could turn people to stone. Sirens could mesmerize victims into approaching. Try to think of something that's related to the purpose the monster will have in the story and you'll do better at inventing a monster.

WHERE TO START

We can start wherever we like, but if we have an idea for a monster, we should write down everything that has already occurred to us. The template in appendix 4 can help organize our thoughts and inspire us to think of areas we haven't yet considered. We often have an appearance and behavior in mind, possibly while imagining it scaring or attacking our characters. This suggests focusing on skills and its body. Its habitat should also be considered early on, and this may be part of our initial concept; but once decided, we can determine how this impacted its body. We can round out our creation by deciding on our monster's origins before its motivations, as one typically leads to the other.

CHAPTER SIX

CREATING PLANTS AND ANIMALS

It takes less time to invent an animal than a humanoid species, gods, or even monsters because animals aren't as complex. Plants are even simpler. First, we'll consider whether we should invent them. Then we'll look at specifics for each and then considerations that apply to both.

Appendices 5 and 6 are templates for creating a plant or animal respectively. They include more comments and advice, and editable Microsoft Word files that can be downloaded for free by signing up for the newsletter at http://www.artofworldbuilding.com/newsletter/

SHOULD WE CREATE PLANTS AND ANIMALS?

Creating plants or animals is one of the more optional world building tasks for fantasy, where no one expects it or will complain if we don't. We tend to assume a fantasy world is much like Earth, with the addition of elves, magic, and monsters, for example. We can create just a few plants or animals, tons of them, or none. Given that it's optional, we can benefit from thinking about why we're creating them, which is the focus of this section.

In SF that takes place exclusively on space craft, we can ignore the subject altogether unless the ship is from Earth or if we want to comment on what the crew are eating, for example. Or if they have an area like a greenhouse, zoo, or nature preserve for the same reasons we have parks in cities: respite from steel, plastic, and concrete.

In SF that takes place on non-Earth planets, or ships originating from them, we can't expect the same plants and animals. Even if the world is

Earth-like, the life could be very different. Something that looks like a bear at first glance might be an herbivore that makes a good pet. Details are what distinguish life forms from each other.

Vegetation doesn't need to be wildly different in basic form; there will still be trees, shrubs, and flowers, for example, but we have the option to imbue them with new properties, colors, and significance. This is fairly easy and maybe even necessary to be believable, but we don't need to invent an entire ecosystem.

Similarly, animals from another planet will still fall into broad categories like fish, amphibian, mammals, birds, and more. Since animals move and are prey and/or predator, behavior becomes an important aspect of inventing something different from an analogue. For example, a horse with two more legs will strike the audience as exactly that. The appearance, size, temperament, and behavior of such a non-Earth "horse" (we'll want to call it something else) should be different in meaningful ways so the audience does not have that reaction. Details are how we achieve this. How to do so is discussed more in the next section.

What is our purpose with inventing this life? Do we need an animal that's based on an Earth one but which has physical or behavioral attributes that Terrestrial ones don't? Our characters might use a horse-like animal or giant bird for travel. Maybe we need a lion that can be tamed and ridden like a horse. We might need a snake for its venom that an assassin will use. We might have a humanoid species that wears a bear pelt, except that in the absence of bears, we need a similar (but not too similar) animal. Perhaps we have a wizard who needs a rare plant for casting a deadly spell. And most common of all, we could have either a plant or animal that preys upon our humanoid species. Having a goal helps.

Creating Something Different

One reason to create plants and animals is that they can give our world a different look and feel. The more we create, the more pronounced this impression, especially when we link choices and behaviors of our characters to the life around them. This could be steeds that are ferocious and require great strength of will to control, but could be predators which cause travel plans to change. James Cameron did this to great effect in the movie *Avatar*.

Characters can learn hunting, attack, and defense skills based on those predators. Maybe they know what it means when a predator flees, such as when great white sharks suddenly swim away from a person in the water; it means an even bigger great white is moving in. This sort of thing is how we integrate everything. If done well, this can make our world stand out in a good way that makes audiences eager for more. The more life forms we create, the more different our world begins to feel.

How Often the Setting Will Be Used

If we'll only write one book in this setting, the extra work to create many plants and animals may not be worth it. Just do what you need for the project. Some of what we create for one world can be used in another instead, so inventing things we don't use right now is not an issue. In SF, we may have multiple worlds in a single work or across our career, so we can still just invent life forms for their own sake and figure out where to use them later. Integrating things is great, but that arguably matters more with humanoid species than plants and animals.

Time

It takes time we may not have to create unique plants and animals, though this time investment is less than with other things in this book. We can get around this by inventing during writing, but we must watch out for creating something without much depth or impact on our work. If inventing on the fly, always make a note to add this lifeform to your files and work it out in more detail, then touch up your depiction if necessary. Integrating it with other things is a continuous process anyway.

Do Our Creations Matter?

In the film and TV industries, having interesting plants and animals in the background is easy and fairly standard with today's special effects, and they need no more than an appearance. It's only when they affect character decisions or storylines that they achieve relevance, which is the point at which they should be mentioned in written stories. If we mention an irrelevant plant or animal in passing without some hint that it's a large cat, for example, it can be off-putting, especially if we name too many in a row.

As a case in point, in my story "The Epic of Ronyn," a character gets pelted with vegetables. I had originally named the different items he's struck with, but beta-readers commented that they had no idea what I was talking about and it took them out of the scene. I wasn't going to explain each item in the paragraph (and there was no room or reason to beforehand) because it wasn't worth it, so I replaced my list of vegetables with the word "vegetables." While not exactly descriptive, it helped the scene stay on focus.

On the other hand, "The Garden of Taria" story features a character who keeps invading someone's home and preparing a meal for himself and sometimes her, too. All of their conversations occur while food is being prepared, consumed, or cleaned up. This provided a good chance to name and very briefly describe various items, but it proved challenging to keep it to a minimum. A few choice words are recommend when writing.

For example, consider this line: "She saw a line of *yellow drops* leading from kitchen to couch, discarded *juna peels* tossed here and there along the way, the perpetrator licking the *running juices* from dirty fingers as he popped another *fruit* piece into his mouth." I added the *italics* to indicate the key words carefully strewn through this sentence to get across what the food is. Is this better than writing, "He ate a yellow citrus fruit called juna?" Both have their merits.

PLANTS

When creating plants, we must know their climate, which is covered in *Creating Places, (The Art of World Building, #2)*. But unless ours is an ice world, for example, it can be assumed that all climates exist somewhere, which means that we don't need to know which continents or regions our plant is found in just yet. It can be invented for a climate, and when we decide where on our world those climates exist, we'll know if it could be found there. We may want to name it after a place, or vice versa, but that's easy enough to accomplish later.

CLASSIFICATION

There are broad categories that plants fall into, but we're most likely interested in only a few.

The seedless plants include algae, liverworts, mosses, and ferns, with only mosses being something we're likely to use in our stories partly because no one thinks algae or ferns are interesting, and no one knows what a liverwort is (and it's not interesting or useful when you do). If we have sea dwelling species, algae can be more useful if there's a dangerous or useful kind that can develop.

The usefulness of moss is debatable, but it can be needed by wizards or have properties to make it deadly or otherwise cover a landscape with a color different than the green we expect on Earth. Mosses grow in damp areas and need plentiful water to reproduce. They can grow on rocks, trees, or discarded items. A special kind of moss, called sphagnum, can form floating islands found in bogs, where trees and other plants are growing in the shifting mat of clumped-together moss.

Among the plants with seeds are cycads, conifers, and flowering plants. An internet search on cycad will reveal plants that look like a palm tree, or an evergreen fern with very large leaves atop a branchless tree trunk (sometimes quite tall) and with cones in the middle of these leaves at the top. They grow slowly and live up to a thousand years, so they could be admired by a long living, humanoid species. They are in tropical and subtropical climates. These large cones can be imagined to contain useful material in them and to have predators who desire them.

A conifer also has cones but prefers colder climates and often forms enormous forests. Conifers include pines, cedars, Douglas-firs, junipers, redwoods, spruces, and more. Most are trees but some are shrubs. Their conical shape helps them shed snow and their wood is soft.

Then there are the flowering plants that dominate temperate climates; unless you live somewhere always cold or hot, this is what you see when you look out the window, and as such, these are the most common plants you'll be inventing. These include not only flowers, shrubs, and vines but trees like the oak, maple, elm, aspen, and birch.

Regarding trees, the deciduous variety lose their leaves in autumn while the evergreens lose them continuously all year in such a way as to appear, by contrast, that they never lose their leaves, hence the name.

What does this all mean to a world builder? Not much other than having a better understanding of what we probably want to invent: mosses, conifers, and flowering plants, with algae and cycads bringing up the rear.

LIFECYCLE

While trees live decades, plants like flowers don't. This matters because we can make a plant rare by shortening its lifecycle according to established (or invented) ones. And rare plants are considered more potent in spells.

Some plants are annuals. This means the plant's lifecycle is one season before it dies. If we want a petunia (an annual) in the same spot in our garden every year, be prepared to plant new ones annually. A biennial, less common on Earth, lives two years, producing foliage in one year and flowers the next; many are vegetables, producing food one year and leaving seeds the next. A plant that lives longer than two years is a perennial and usually drops all leaves by winter before returning in spring. Most vines are perennials, remaining in place year after year but flowering at certain times of the year.

A bulb is a short stem that has roots growing from one side and an undeveloped shoot from the other, from where the stem eventually grows. They go through stages, the interesting one for us being that if a bulb is dug up before the foliage stage is complete (the flowers aren't out), it won't bloom the following year but will in subsequent years; more importantly, if dug up after the foliage stage is complete, it can be stored for four months for planting elsewhere. Imagine a dangerous/useful plant that's a bulb and grows somewhere unique but can be harvested and transported and replanted.

ANIMALS

While there are many types of animals we could create, some are more likely candidates than others. To get started, knowing how they're classified might give us ideas.

CLASSIFICATION

Animals are either invertebrates or vertebrates; i.e., spineless or not. The distinction has no other significance.

Invertebrates, which make up 97% of animals, include worms, sea urchins, jellyfish, snails, arachnids (spiders, scorpions), crustaceans (lobster, crab), corals, and insects. On Earth, they tend to be smaller than vertebrates, but Jabba the Hutt from *Star Wars* was a huge worm, and the giant spider from *The Lord of the Rings* is infamous. Our characters are unlikely to use invertebrates for domestication, sport, guards, or transportation unless we make them enormous, so our use of them is limited, but they can be food, pets, and used for materials. These purposes will be discussed in the next section. Swarms of small animals, like insects, can pose a problem, and we can invent a swarm that takes place at given intervals (as with cicada) that people prepare for. Imagine that with giant insects.

Vertebrates include the animals you probably thought of when starting this chapter: amphibians, birds, fish, mammals, and reptiles.

AMPHIBIANS

Amphibians include frogs, toads, and salamanders, and require water to breed, laying larva that metamorphose into the adult form. They are capable of living on land or underwater but need moist habitats to keep their skin damp. They can acquire air through their skins to assist their lungs, with a few having no lungs at all; this allows them to remain submerged indefinitely. They are typically small but one extinct species on Earth was up to thirty feet. Being cold-blooded, they rely on environment to regulate body temperature and have slow metabolism, meaning they require less food and expend less energy. Their tongues are muscular and can often protrude surprisingly far, being coiled up when not in use.

Some species have glands that secrete poison, whereas some secretions just make them taste bad so they'll be spit out instead of consumed. Some are lethal to humanoids and this is a reason to invent some amphibians for our world, for use as poisons. The poisonous ones are often brightly colored as a warning and are more likely to actively search for prey, their appearance warning away predators. The camouflaging amphibians ambush prey.

Frogs can be venomous, too. The difference between venom and poison isn't well understood by lay people, but venom must be injected into the body. This typically means being stung, bitten, or stabbed. By contrast, poisonous animals can merely be touched and are relatively passive. Venom is typically for both offense and defense while poison is for defense.

Frogs and toads appear similar except the former has smooth skin and the latter warty; both have no tail, long folding legs, and big eyes. Salamanders look more like lizards, being low, flat, and possessing a tail. All have four legs, webbed toes, and no claws. Frogs and toads have excellent hearing. They periodically shed skin in one piece and sometimes eat it (yummy).

Virtually all amphibians are predators who hunt by sight and swallow prey whole, dining on small, slow moving insects and only chewing a little to subdue their meal. Holding still is how potential victims avoid being detected and eaten, but some amphibians hunt by smell and may be able to locate prey that doesn't have a scent, even in the dark or when it's not moving. Many amphibians are nocturnal and hide during the day.

While they are seldom seen (unless you invent large ones), amphibians are heard quite often during mating season, but their calls are fatiguing to themselves and could draw predators, in addition to attracting females. A deeper voice typically means a bigger amphibian. Frogs can actually scream when attacked and their vocalization can be aggressive to ward off competition. Some amphibians are territorial about sites for breeding, shelter, or food, and physically attack if necessary. Like reptiles, some salamanders can detach their tail if a predator has them by the tail, and regrow it.

BIRDS

There's a tendency to overlook birds during world building and storytelling, probably because they have limited use to us except as food or symbols (like associating a dove with peace). Birds consume food smaller than them, so unless we have giant birds, they'll be keeping clear of our species unless they've been domesticated and used like carrier pigeons, for example, or as pets, as in the parrot. Birds of prey like hawks can be used as hunters, possibly bringing our adventurers small game like rabbits or fish for dinner. Bird eggs are among the more useful aspects, but then what's different about our bird's eggs that we can't get from a run of the mill chicken, for example?

As with all animals, when deciding to invent a bird, consider our purpose and those of our characters. We may find there's little reason to invent one that isn't an analogue; we can just combine aspects of different birds, like plumage, behavior, trainability, and prevalence, and slap a different name on them and be good to go.

Migration is one of the characteristics of a world that might be more worthwhile to consider. Not all birds migrate, but land birds can migrate 1600 miles and shorebirds up to 2500 miles, with the longest distance for one species being 6300 miles. Some species don't necessarily return the next year, based on food availability (if that's the driving force behind migration, as breeding is the other big motive). It isn't just the carrier pigeon that can return to a specific place, as most birds can navigate incredible distances and return home.

Some species flock for safety in numbers, especially in forests where predators are harder to detect, and more eyes offer more chances to warn each other. Some birds also cooperate with other animals, such as sea-diving birds that take advantage of bait balls of fish; this happens when animals like dolphins herd small fish to the surface to eat, helping out the birds, too.

For general characteristics we might not be familiar with, most birds are diurnal but some operate at night, during twilight, or when tides are appropriate for feeding if they're a bird that wades in coastal waters. Some birds are more intelligent than most other animals, which could be interesting when combined with ferocity and large size. In contrast to reptiles and amphibians, birds rapidly digest food so they can fly again; they have no teeth and swallow most things whole. On isolated islands, birds may become flightless due to a lack of predators.

Not all birds create a nest for eggs but generally hide them from predators if so. Incubation is from ten to eighty days and in many species is only once a year, with from one to nearly a dozen eggs. This is useful to know if we're using enormous birds as in *The Lord of the Rings* because there would theoretically be a demand for such huge eggs.

FISH AND OTHER AQUATIC LIFE

Fish are aquatic animals that have fins and gills and are cold-blooded, their body temperatures affected by environment. This includes eels, actual fish, lampreys, rays, and sharks, but not some animals that have the word "fish" in their name, like jellyfish and starfish. Technically it excludes dolphin and whales, which are mammals. Some can breathe air just like us and can survive several days without suffocating. Fish may not hear well and instead depend on sensing motion, but they have excellent color vision, taste, and smell. A number of small fish have developed the ability to glide through the air for over a hundred feet, typically to evade predators.

Some fish form schools or shoals, which are slightly different. In a school, fish move at the same speed and direction, being tightly synchronized as if of one mind. By contrast, shoals are more loosely organized, the fish independent but staying close. Like birds, they are sometimes assigned religious symbolism, which we can leverage. For example, if there was once a drought on land and fish had allowed people to survive, they might be revered.

As world builders, our primary use for fish is as food during dining scenes unless we want one to threaten humanoid species that enter the water or sail upon it. People can be stung, paralyzed, poisoned, and outright killed by sea life, whether immediately or in time. We can have someone meet their end by drowning, by being swallowed whole, or most dramatically, by being bitten to death. Piranha, sharks, and other animals with significant teeth are good models for threatening sea life.

Only the largest marine life is likely to threaten or destroy a ship-of-the-line, but giant squid and octopus have been done. You'll want to invent something unique, either a single large creature or a coordinated group of smaller ones. If we invent some unusually smart sea life, maybe they'll have another agenda or just be attracted to pretty things, like those armored knights seen upon deck. This comes close to inventing a monster (see chapter five).

MAMMALS

Mammals are the largest and smartest animals, usually, though this can be different on a world. Most have four legs, though some have adaptations extreme enough that we may not realize they're a mammal (whales, dolphins).

Other sea mammals include otters, polar bears, and seals, and while some aquatic mammals can survive outside of water, others will die. If inventing one, this is something we must decide on. All of them depend on the sea for food and can submerge far longer than humans. Many must come on land to breed. Either blubber, large size, or waterproof fur can be used to retain heat. Large animals use their weight to stay down where their food is (on the bottom) while lighter animals have food that is more likely to be nearer the surface. Habitat is either open sea or coastal, with the latter including kelp beds, beaches, reefs, and even rocky cliffs. Sea mammals are hunted not only for food and fur but a substance like spermaceti, which is used to make wax. These give us product ideas.

Other mammals have developed aerial locomotion. Cats have a limited ability to essentially parachute themselves to slow their fall. Tree-dwelling animals can glide between tall trees that are spaced far apart. Bats can outright fly. These traits can be used in our work.

Living in trees poses challenges that cause adaptations, which include far better balance and ability to grip a vertical surface to prevent pitching backwards or slippage. Gaps between branches must be overcome by reaching between, jumping, or gliding. Longer limbs, claws, and a prehensile tail (i.e., one that can grab things) aid these.

Walking is a distinguishing trait that comes in three types. Primates (including humans) and apes are among those with plantigrade locomotion, meaning the toes and metatarsal bones (those between toe and arch) are on the ground, along with the heel. The disadvantage is speed, caused partly by shorter, thicker legs. The advantage is being more weight bearing. Digitigrade animals like cats and dogs walk on their toes and are faster and quieter as a result. Then there's ungulate locomotion, meaning walking on the tips of the toes, which sounds painful to us, but these animals have a hoof that is perpetually growing and wearing down like our nails; these animals are usually herbivores, are faster, and often have antlers (on males).

Most mammals give live birth and nurse with milk, but a few lay eggs. Communal raising of young is the norm with pack animals in particular, unlike with non-mammals. Mammals are warm-blooded, meaning the body regulates temperature instead of relying upon ambient air or water to do so; the ability has limits, which is why mammals can die from heat stroke or hypothermia. Being warm-blooded causes higher metabolism and therefore greater need for food. Mammals can replace a tooth once or never, but we could always decide that our mammal can replace teeth every time one is lost, like sharks.

Lastly, mammals are used for food, leather, wool, experiments, pets, transportation, and entertainment, discussed in a subsequent section.

REPTILES

Reptiles include turtles, crocodiles, snakes, and lizards. They either have four legs or none. Cold-blooded, they cannot control body heat without environmental help; while some have adapted to extreme temperatures, most stay in water or seek sun or shade as needed. A slow metabolism means less food is needed than for a mammal of the same size (as much as ninety percent less), and some can go a half year without food, though this means they aren't moving much; movement burns energy that must be replaced with a meal. Reptiles can dominate areas with little food, because there isn't enough to sustain birds and mammals. All of this also means reptiles don't do long chases and have a sit-and-wait strategy as predators, but this doesn't have to be true of ones we invent. Some small reptiles can glide through the air.

All Earth reptiles have lungs, but some have permeable skin, too, suggesting we can create a reptile without lungs if desired. Reptiles have watertight, horny skin/scales so they can live on land, unlike amphibians, but it isn't thick like mammals and can't be used for leather except in decorative fashion (as opposed to for protection or clothing). Most are carnivores or eat insects, but herbivores exist. Some reptiles consume rocks to help with digestion; such a stone is called a gastrolith. Reptiles are less intelligent than mammals and birds due to small brain size, but we can invent more intelligent and therefore more frightening ones. Most are diurnal (i.e., active during the day) but some that operate at night have a kind of thermal sight that we can make more extreme and useful, especially if we invent a humanoid species that's reptilian.

Reptiles usually produce sexually but some are asexual (where's the fun in that?). Genitals are stored within the body. Some do live birth while others lay hard or leathery eggs that almost immediately hatch.

Smaller reptiles rely on avoidance to not become a meal of birds or other reptiles. As such, they hide within underbrush and can often camouflage themselves, whether basic skin color does this or they can change it; the ability to lie still for long periods aids this. If unable to flee, they may hiss or make noise, like the rattlesnake; others make themselves appear bigger, like the cobra. Some are brightly colored to indicate they are venomous. Some actually play dead. Others can detach their tail and run away, the tail still wiggling for up to twenty minutes to distract their predator from their fleeing; some of these tails are brightly colored to encourage an attack there, but regardless, the tails grow back but not usually to the same length, and may be discolored compared to the original.

PURPOSE

Beyond our purpose in inventing a plant or animal, we can think about how they are used by our world's inhabitants. Food is an obvious way, and some food will have cultural or religious ideas associated with them; some items might be forbidden or ritually slaughtered first, though we'll want a rationale for such decisions, such as deciding an animal offended a god. Imagine a deity who was once on an important mission that became delayed by a herd of animals, or by a forest of a given tree type; now this is seen as the reason the god failed to achieve something. The resulting religion could forbid use of the item, either by the god's decree or not.

PLANTS

Plants are used in many ways that we can adopt when inventing one. The obvious example, besides creating oxygen, is for food, but there's also decoration, medicine, building materials, toys, clothing, tools, fuel, and everyday items like pencils and paper. Chemical processes often require or benefit from plants, such as fermenting beer or brewing coffee. Many of these aren't glamorous or of much interest to an audience, but when doing research on analogues, you'll learn what any given plant is typically used for and can leverage the information.

Often, not every part of a plant has the properties that make it special. The leaves can be deadly while the stem or seeds are not. When crafting a plant, decide which part makes it valuable and if anything must be done to that part for it to acquire its purpose. Leaves might need to be crushed. The pulp might need to be boiled.

DECORATION

Decoration is a useful subject if we decide that people in a given culture have assigned certain properties to a flower, for example, and assume that a female wearing one in her hair is revealing something about herself to others. Garlands of a given flower type can be used at ceremonies, such as burial or graduation. These uses require less invention of details because an audience will accept them as cultural and having little basis.

FOOD

Plants offer a good opportunity to have our characters and story affected by interesting foods. They can be poisonous, addictive, a bland staple for adventurers, freely found in the wild, or a cultural or religious expectation to serve or consume at certain moments. A culture clash can result for traveling characters. Even if we don't use plants in a significant way, they can still be briefly mentioned during any scene involving their consumption.

MEDICINAL

Invented plants are great for healing or poisoning our characters or for use in spells. We need no explanation for why a plant has these properties because audiences don't expect one, though in a more scientific world or story, one will help. Plants with supernatural properties are often said to grow near something like a special spring or dark place. The habitat can be the reason the plant acquires unique properties—or even loses them if away for too long, such as once plucked. Are the plants themselves supernatural?

ANIMALS

As with plants, humanoid species use animals in many ways, including as food, pets, transportation, entertainment/sport, guards, domestic work, and for materials such as hides, bones, and even fluids. Other humanoid species can also be used for these things, as distasteful as humans usually find the subject. We can use Earth animals or invent our own, which can be inspired by a desire to do something new or have an Earth animal do things one on Earth doesn't do. Maybe the only horses available for riding are similar but much harder to control or train. Or maybe they are carnivores and sometimes eat their riders. Maybe we can ride one but never with a saddle. Each of these might pose a problem for characters, adding dynamics to a story. We'd probably want to call this something other than a horse, changing physical attributes while we're at it.

DOMESTICATION

Domestic work like pulling wagons isn't thrilling, but such animals are likely to be more commonly experienced by characters in urban settings. They can be mentioned during scenes directly involving them or just in passing as they contribute to smells, filth, and other delights only animals can add to life. In SF, machines may have replaced such uses, at least for those wealthy enough to afford them. World-hopping characters may visit a world without such technology and have an inability to deal with animals like this, struggling to ride them, for example.

ENTERTAINMENT/SPORT

Humans often use animals for sport, whether hunting them, fighting them against each other, or racing them against each other. Some see animals as trophies and the hunt a sign of their virility. This can be used to characterize our characters. Inventing unique attributes for an animal can make this conquest worthwhile. While making it faster, more ferocious, or just rare is good, consider granting abilities like teleportation, hiding/disguising of its tracks, or greater intelligence and cunning than we expect of Earth animals. The name of such an animal can become a nickname for a ship or character.

FOOD

Animals used as food are either hunted or kept in a pasture. The former is a more entertaining use and requires preparation, skill, knowledge, and the right tools. This also exposes our characters to risk if the animal can fight back. Even if they can't, hunting typically means the wild, where other animals, species, monsters, and even supernatural phenomenon could impact the hunt. Dinner scenes can be spiced up with brief mention of the taste, feel, and desirability of what's being consumed. Animals can also produce eggs, milk or other fluids that others imbibe.

Animals kept in a pasture or pen are usually more docile, but not always; think of a bull. They can be docile until approached or threatened. They can also go wild if a predator comes near, howling with fear, which can aid a scene in which characters hear a bellowing animal and realize a threat to it—and them—is encroaching.

Ferocious animals are usually not considered food on Earth because the dangers they pose aren't worth the trouble, but maybe our characters have no choice or enjoy the challenge, even considering the eating of a docile animal a weakness, while the eating of something aggressive is strength; if that's the case, they probably want to hunt it, too. Such a scenario can suggest a cowardly character who dines on this beast to appear strong, but loses others' esteem when it is revealed he hasn't hunted them, but eats caged ones. This is one way we can use such animals.

GUARDS

Invented animals that can guard something are a staple of fantasy in particular. Ferocity, obedience, and difficulty killing are the usual requirements, but it can help to decide what this animal is like in the wild, too. What does it eat? It's almost certainly a carnivore that might pose a threat of eating interlopers; an herbivore is less frightening, and audiences are expecting us to out-do each other. Is this animal trained to perform its duty (more reliable) or is it chained up and ferocious enough to attack anything that comes close?

MATERIALS

Whether it is bone, hide, teeth and claws, or secretions, animals are harvested for what they can be turned into. This includes trophies, decorations like jewelry, and clothing. Horns and spines can become weapons. Some whales are harvested to make candles from wax in their heads. In a technological society, the processing for this can result in a larger number of products than the lower tech level found in fantasy. Consider what our animal gets turned into: soap, ink, paint, cosmetics, poison, oil, wax, wool, leather, and otherworldly things that fantasy and SF can allow, such as materials for spells and chemicals used for war or peace; the same is true of plants.

PETS

Pets are another common use for animals, especially in urban areas, but the subject is generally overlooked in both fantasy and SF. A scene inside anyone's home can include mention of a pet coming, going, or being passed. Films, TV shows, or video games can also show these in passing. Then there's the areas where it's fed, poops, sleeps, or is caged if dangerous. Some pets can travel well like dogs, while others stay at home like cats. Pets offer a chance to humanize and characterize people, though it's overly simplified to say that a vicious killer has a dangerous animal when he might just have a cuddly pet.

TRANSPORTATION

New steeds are an ideal animal to create. They can have advantages and disadvantages that Earth equivalents don't; modifying an analogue to achieve a specific purpose is a good way to start. Some will be lumbering, slow pack animals pulling wagons or just heavily loaded, while others can be faster and holding little more than a rider and his supplies. Flying steeds require creative license (something that big can't really get off the ground with riders, but no one really cares) and offer aerial threats if we've taken the time to invent them. They also pose a problem for our characters, who might be unable to take everything with them, causing a potentially painful choice for what to leave behind. They need to land sooner or later, too, and this exposes characters to risk, regardless of whether they've scouted first or not, for anything could've seen them in the sky and pursued on the ground, waiting for them to land; this would be a great reason to only land at night, after many miles of not being seen.

WHERE TO START

ANALOGUES

Inventing an animal or plant is easier if we base it on one or more Earth equivalents, of which tens of thousands exist. Analogues free us from becoming experts in botany, for example, because our lifeform has details that largely match an Earth life. By contrast, inventing from scratch means needing to understand more about what defines a lifeform type, though this chapter provided enough high level details for us to do so. Generally, we'll want to portray our inventions to an audience in simple, non-technical terms unless the details are required, as in the case of an actual botanist trying to create a serum from something to cure a disease, for example.

Remember the rule of three when using an analogue: make at least three changes. Some items to alter are coloring, the number of appendages, whether an animal is trainable or not, and how the life form can be used by our humans and species (if at all). We can borrow traits from other things, like inventing cats who obey like dogs.

Be aware that many Earth lifeforms are different than we might expect. For example, in America we're used to only seeing red tomatoes. We could create yellow ones, thinking we're being different, when yellow tomatoes already exist here. Cats can be highly trained. We may be accustomed to seeing something portrayed a certain way when that thing is more complex or varied than we realize.

Research will often surprise us and it's worth doing for our inventions and even personal enrichment, if you care about such things. Google any plant or animal that you want to start with and read about it, making a list of interesting attributes or things that could be mentioned when writing. The details can surprise us, and when we use those details, altered or not, to introduce our plant or animal, it's more engaging. Consider this example: "A large, four-legged, herbivore with huge tusks, they mostly graze or eat leaves and other plants. Their tusks are prized. They can be tamed and are often used as pack animals, either carrying the load or pulling it." That gets us thinking and picturing it far more than if we just said "elephant."

CREATING A LIST OF
ANIMALS AND PLANTS

There are so many things we could create that it's advantageous to have a categorized list of possibilities to decide on. Start with analogues in each class. Below is a small list of staples we might want to invent, using the rule of three to make each different from its source:

Mammals: boar, deer, bear, cow, goat
Sea Life: shark, whale, ray, plain fish, flying fish, dolphin
Lizards: snake, crocodile
Birds: vulture, pigeon, falcon
Flowers: rose, nightshade, lily
Trees: oak, weeping willow, pine, maple
Vegetables: corn, tomato, potato
Other Plants: wheat, rice

CREATING A PRODUCTS LIST

Another approach is to make a list of products our characters might need or use and then determine their plant or animal source. Goats are used for cheese, for example. Potatoes make chips and fries. Wheat makes beer and bread. Grapes make wine. Trees are turned into all sorts of products and have typical uses depending on the tree. Research an oak tree and how it's used (and why), and then give it some different properties and similar uses. We can write something like, "He dipped the bird-name quill into the sea-life-name ink and signed his name."

CHAPTER SEVEN

CREATING UNDEAD

In a book called *Creating Life*, a chapter on creating undead might seem out of place, but if it's still moving, we can consider it alive enough. A multitude of undead types already exist for our use, with most being public domain. These include vampires, zombies, ghosts, skeletons, and more. Most of them are excellent ideas that, just like elves, dwarves, and dragons, have stood the test of time. No one will roll their eyes if we use them.

SHOULD WE CREATE UNDEAD?

The first question we must ask ourselves is whether we should create our own undead. And the answer to that is—probably not. Not unless we have a good reason or an idea that is substantially different. Most basic versions of undead already exist, leaving little room for new ones that aren't rehashed old ideas with minor twists. If we create immortal bloodsuckers that burn to ash in direct sunlight and have superhuman strength and senses, and we call them something besides vampires, people will call us out.

Conversely, there's a limit on how much we can change something and still use the original name. This is a judgment call. The first consideration is, how quickly does the way we describe and use it invoke memories of the undead we used for inspiration? The sooner it happens, the more we just call it what it is. We want to avoid the "Oh, it's just a vampire with this and that added or removed" reaction.

The second factor is whether the changes we've made substantially alter the nature of the source. If our creation is a vampire but doesn't drink blood, we've changed something too fundamental to call it a vampire. Some will disagree and say authors can do whatever we want, and while this is sort of true, there are expectations that can be defied and ones that shouldn't be. If changing something fundamental, just change it more and invent a name.

THE MIND

This is an academic debate, but in death, does the mind go with the soul or remain with the body? Depending on our point of view, this can be used to determine the mental faculties of our undead. For example, we assume that if the soul goes to an afterlife, the mind goes with it and is fully intact. This would suggest that ghosts generally have their minds, whether those minds are impaired by their present state or not. Corporeal undead that have a soul would also have a mind, in theory.

But what about corporeal undead that have no soul in the body? Is that undead largely mindless? About as intelligent as an animal? It's something to consider if creating undead, or at least use as a rationalization point. It can help us determine what our undead is capable of.

Either way, we can introduce mental impairment of any kind so that our undead is "not right in the head." Such impairment includes denial of death. This might seem odd with a spirit. After all, a spirit doesn't have a body, so how can they not realize they're dead? Yet there are many ghost stories that include this idea. In such a case, the spirit is often behaving as if it's alive, going about its usual business, such as housework or even rocking a baby's crib. If confronted with the truth of their demise, these spirits can experience the usual wrath that even the living exhibit when an unpleasant truth is thrust upon them. The trouble with inventing this type of spirit is that we're not really inventing it—it's a standard ghost.

A generally accepted idea for undead is that they're tormented. We speak of "rest in peace" and other phrases about the dead, the connotation being that anyone not lying still must necessarily be upset about that fact. Even Dracula, for all his seeming enjoyment of his state, is shown as tormented when no one is looking. If life is an ideal state and death is the worst we expect, then being undead is an unexpected half-life with even less of a training manual on what to do. Torment can be emotional or mental in origin but affects both. The degree to which our undead is upset about its state may help determine its goals and traits, discussed in this chapter.

CLASSIFICATION

SENTIENT LIFE

The first choice to make with undead is whether they have a body or not. If so, the term undead is often used, as it implies a body that it is animated once again. If there's no body, it's a spirit, which is a slightly more generic term than ghost. That's not a rule, but I'm going with the following terms in this chapter:

1) Spirits—it has no body
2) Corporeal—it has a body, with or without a soul
3) Undead—a generic word meaning both or either of the above

SPIRITUAL UNDEAD

The existence of a soul is debatable and outside the scope of this book, but without one, we don't have spiritual undead. We may find it difficult to invent one that hasn't been done before partly because, without a body, our options are more limited than with corporeal undead, who can touch and affect the world.

One way around this is to decide that our spirit can interact with the physical world anyway, possibly with limitations. Perhaps they can only do so for short periods or under the right conditions. Maybe they become vulnerable while doing so, or afterwards for a time. Maybe the spirits that can pass through objects (an advantage) can't move them (a disadvantage), or the reverse, it can't pass through objects but can move them. Inventing such details is one way to create something unique.

Where is the spirit's body? This could be used for motivation or characterization. A popular idea is that destroying the body eliminates the spirit, which may know this and hide or protect its remains. The spirit might wish to reanimate the body. It might be unhappy with where the body lies, such as an improper burial, or if it's being used as a trophy. These speak to motivation, covered later, but the corpse may be irrelevant.

For more details, see the section under "traits."

CORPOREAL UNDEAD

Corporeal undead come in two varieties—those with a soul and those without. There may not be much difference at first glance. In the above section about the mind, if we accept the premise that the mind goes with the soul, then a soulless corpse might be mentally deficient. Perhaps this explains depictions of zombies, though I don't recall anyone explicitly stating they have no soul. The brain (not the same as the mind) is technically what allows for control of the body and it can be assumed to be impaired due to lack of blood supply, at the least, so this can be another explanation for traits. It's all make believe, but our willing suspension of disbelief is aided by something plausible.

The existence of the body gives us more options than a spirit. Our undead could have super senses instead of worse ones, leading to an altered personality or character. For example, an undead with super hearing might be able to learn things they otherwise couldn't by overhearing conversations not meant for their ears. The new knowledge might give them a feeling of power that might've been denied them in life. Consider how this might affect their minds, emotions, and motivations.

Being dead means a loss of body function, but this depends on our creation. In many recent works, vampires show heightened senses and don't appear dead, so much so that one can question whether these are really vampires or super human people who can't really be killed except by specific means like sunlight. We've even seen vampires having babies. The point is that we can decide on undead that are a vision of health, a rotting corpse, or just a skeleton. There are no limits, but each offers a very different experience for the undead and anyone encountering them.

In theory, a skeleton should be unable to move at all, having no muscles or anything else needed for locomotion, not to mention a brain to control limbs. This is largely true of a decaying corpse, as well, but at least the decay suggests movement is only hampered. Without the supernatural or technology to allow locomotion and more, corporeal undead are more nonsensical than spirits, so if we have a world without either, they may not make sense, not that anyone's stopping us from doing it anyway.

We might think that a skeleton implies that death occurred longer ago than with a partially decomposed or preserved body, but this is not true. The rate of decomposition depends on many factors, including exposure to air, water, or earth, and the level of aridity and even water in soil. A skeleton could be a decade old while a body preserved under the right conditions could be a thousand years old, whether this preservation was intentional or inadvertent. For some interesting if gross reading (not for the faint of heart), read this article:

http://www.memorialpages.co.uk/articles/decomposition.php

Non-Sentient Life

Plants

Undead plants? Sure, why not? We think of undead as having previously had a mind and soul (i.e., being sentient), neither of which apply here, but anything that's alive can die. And come back to life while not quite being the same. The subject is underutilized in fiction, maybe for good reasons.

Without a soul, spiritual undead plants are not an option, leaving only corporeal undead plants. Plants aren't mobile, typically, and are therefore easier to avoid than the slow moving zombies of yesteryear. This makes plants not particularly frightening. We also assume they can't grow, being dead, so they can't even extend their range.

If we want undead plants that terrify, a predatory and mobile one has better options once back to life. If there are walking and talking plants similar to the Ents of *The Lord of The Rings*, our options increase considerably. Wouldn't it be interesting for plants to not lose attributes as undead, but gain them instead? What if one became sentient?

Animals

We see undead animals less often than humanoids, making this a ripe area for originality. If undead humanoids have reduced capabilities, animals might, too, but authors have often given undead animals augmented ones instead. What if it's smarter now, even able to speak? The supernatural can grant this without explanation, as can technology. Great strength or speed are clichés but are done to make them more formidable, which could now be done with intelligence, too. An undead animal can continue with a behavior from life even if it's no longer needed, such as eating or hunting. The obvious thing here is for an appetite that's now sinister, such as preying on people. This can include swarms of insects who now do this and infect the living, who might in turn become undead.

Numbers

How many of this undead type exist? Is there only one? Is that because it just started existing yesterday and there hasn't been time for more yet, or because whatever caused it was a one-time phenomenon? Maybe someone created it on purpose and the creator's now dead, leaving no one who knows how the undead creature was created. We'll look more into origins next, but the issue of population count is tied to origins.

It might be possible for powerful wizards or those with certain technology to turn people into this kind of undead when desired. This is a good source of indefinite numbers when we need them for our work. The living can be instantly turned into one or killed and brought back. And the dead can be raised, requiring access to them first.

Can our undead replicate itself via a bite? This could mean a larger population, and a somewhat naturally occurring issue (compared to someone creating more on purpose), but in a limited geographic area, unless travel is unusually easy for the undead. Do these new undead have any allegiance to their creator? This has been taken to extremes in some vampire lore where killing the creators kills everyone they created.

Prerequisites and Prevention

Is there a prerequisite of some kind before something becomes a specific type of undead? Maybe any kind of person can be turned into this or only those people previously in hell or in heaven. We can decide they must have been buried in the earth, or not buried, or buried poorly, even cremated. Maybe they must've been sent floating down a river on a funeral barge, or jettisoned into space with not even a space suit on. Tying their origins to burial (or lack thereof) helps create something memorable.

Did the living or dead have to experience one thing or another to make them susceptible to this fate? This could be mundane, such as only sailors becoming those undead aboard a ghostly ship. Or a wizard in life becoming an undead capable of performing magic; one would assume that those without magic talent in life don't have it in death, but anything's fair game. What if someone had the talent but refused to use it until undead, when they're compelled to use it "for survival," by angst, or at the behest of the one who raised them?

Are there any people protected from such a fate by life or death practices? A priest comes to mind. If being turned into this undead is common, maybe people are buried in a way to prevent it, such as the head, feet, or hands being cut off. There's a custom to add to our species. It could be simpler and less gruesome than this, such as being buried with a religious item or something known to repel this fate; think of garlic and vampires.

TIME DEAD

How long was our undead not living before becoming undead? This affects appearance at the least, and possibly the mind. The latter is more affected if our world has an afterlife that this character has been wrenched back from. This sort of thing would be traumatizing, one would assume. Imagine the serenity they were enjoying. Or the horror they've escaped, for now. Having crafted an afterlife would help us here; see *Cultures and Beyond (The Art of World Building, #3)*.

In the case of vampires, the living die for a few seconds before becoming undead, which accounts for their lack of decay. They've essentially gone from alive straight to undead. Still, by definition, all undead must have been dead for at least a second, even if that renders the transition so nearly instantaneous as to be a moot point.

ORIGINS

Knowing the origins of undead is often a basic part of their identity and a good way to distinguish ours. A good story excites the imagination. In this case, we're talking about an undead who wasn't caused by the bite of another undead, for example, but an original undead of this type.

ACCIDENTAL UNDEAD

As with monsters, undead can be created by any number of accidents, whether natural, supernatural, or technological. This might be the most common cause because few people want undead to exist *and* have the ability to go around creating them. Undead created accidentally are likely to be few in number unless a large-scale event created many of them at once. How many accidents produce the same results? If we want many spirits that are the same, and in the same area, a large accident is one way to justify that; historically, our depictions of spirits have a tendency to show them as largely solitary. A type of spirit that works in groups could be a novel approach.

We might decide that there are certain types of phenomenon that are known to create specific types of undead. If those phenomena are rare but still somewhat widespread, the resulting undead can be as well. What if someone has harnessed that phenomenon and can unleash it on purpose? That could make this undead type more common; this works for monster creation as well.

UNDEAD BY DESIGN

It's safe to say that anyone who purposely creates undead is up to no good. Our perpetrator might be able to control the result. If so, we can decide who wants to do this and why, then figure out the resulting undead attributes, or do this in reverse. Once someone has created one, they don't necessarily need to continue doing so for them to propagate. Instead, the undead may have the ability to create more of themselves, making them widespread despite having a single, original source.

If our perpetrator can't control the resulting undead, he might be unhappy. Did he try to destroy it? Chase it away? Did it retaliate and kill or wound him? Or best of all, turn him into one, too, possibly under its control?

Does the creator have control over his undead? Do they obey? Chafe at this? Or do they seemingly like it? Are they crafty enough to pretend to obey only to look for an opportunity to attack him? How does he control them? A device? A spell that's still in effect and can be nullified by a zone where magic doesn't work anymore? Or did the means used to create them make his control a given?

GOALS

Even the undead want *something*.

Unfinished Business

It's traditionally said that spirits stick around to finish an important task or protect someone or something. This might be more of a character issue than one about an undead type, unless the latter always has the same goal that is apparent in behavior. Perhaps their appearance and behavior are often the same so that when taken together, the undead type is more identifiable. However, this is a basic idea about ghosts and is nothing new. We'll have to combine this with more unique issues to achieve something unique.

With unfinished business, two undead are unlikely to have the same tasks in mind unless they were created at the same moment and want retribution, for example. Two independently created undead might go about a similar goal in ways so different that this cannot be used to identify them. Revenge via murder will depend so much on their intended victim that the lack of patterns would make it harder to identify this undead as a given type.

Regaining Life

Being undead might offer someone a chance at returning to life. Logically, a spirit needs a new body to inhabit. Getting back the old one won't do much good if it's still dead and decayed, and yet you'll find no shortage of stories where that exact thing happens and the body is magically (literally) restored. Technology can also be used to that effect. People don't seem to question this, but maybe creators should. Decide whether body restoration is possible. If not, our spirit can forget about its own body. Either way we have some options, and so does our spirit. These can help us craft undead with certain capabilities that distinguish them from each other or standard ideas.

Body Restoration

First, decide what will heal a body and don't just gloss over this without commenting on it. Is it a potion? A priest? A device? How much healing can be done? If the body is nothing more than ashes because someone burned the body, can the spirit still get the body back? That would be extreme. Less extreme is a body that's been dead a couple days. It arguably takes less power to restore that one.

If the body can only be restored enough to support life but is wounded, the spirit will need to address that, and maybe know this in advance and have someone standing by to finish healing it. This would be a standard concern for this particular undead type. Imagine people sighting this undead and realizing that it must be lining up a doctor and how this might affect their decisions to stop it.

What kind of person would be willing to help? Family? Someone in it for money? Or being coerced by that spirit? A spirit terrorizing someone into helping carries an interesting side effect—if the undead is brought back to life, it loses its newfound powers (if it had any), and can become vulnerable to the one who has just been terrorized into restoring it. Is the undead character smart enough to foresee such an outcome and take precautions against revenge, keeping leverage that continues into its new life?

BODY POSSESSION

Whether our spirit's own body is available or not, it can try to take someone else's. There are several options to consider. First, will the new body need to be missing its soul? In this scenario, a smart spirit that is capable of jumping into a body should hover around places where young, healthy people die, like an army in battle. But there's still the problem of inhabiting a body that's now dead, unless this spirit is powerful enough to force locomotion and then get someone to heal it, too. This seems impractical.

Second, if the spirit can take over a body with a soul, what happens to the existing soul? It is ousted or still there but suppressed? The former case causes another spirit to be on the loose. The latter offers an internal struggle; will our spirit be powerful or forceful enough in personality to win or end up the one suppressed but now trapped within someone else? Or can they jump out whenever they want?

IF SUCCESSFUL

An undead who gets itself restored to life faces an interesting prospect. Now what?

If they've got their own body (healed or not), how will people react to this? Will old acquaintances and family have some sense of what's happened? Is this person known to have been dead and then resurrected or is he assumed to have been in an afterlife? The latter suggest a peaceful return and time prior to that. The former suggests sinister, unsettling issues. And what of all their worldly possessions, especially if they've been legally declared dead? Do they have options for restitution? Is our world a place where people return from the dead all the time and have certain rights they can expect? A Bill of Undead Rights is just what the world needs.

If they have a different body, what are they going to do? Embark on a new life as that person or try to reintegrate themselves into their old life as their old self? In the latter case, will anyone believe they're who they say they are? How would people react? Has our undead done anything to prepare for such an issue? Wouldn't it be better if a spirit attempting to do this has made plans for this while still disembodied, and that there's a type of spirit that typically does these things? That makes this less an issue of that character and more a behavior of this undead type.

If they start a new life in the new body, might they run into someone who knew the previous owner of that body? Such a concern could have them moving far away, so have they planned for this? Would our undead be intending to start up a new life and therefore engaging in certain behaviors that are typical of this undead type? Imagine a spirit who can steal gold for their new life, and haunt a place they want to live once they have a body again, driving out the living so no one will take the home until they arrive in their new skin later, buying it with that stolen money. This can be a character, but it can also be a type of undead.

FINDING PEACE

Undead are considered damned to wander for eternity and likely want to be at peace instead. The longer they're undead, the more this could be true, and the more upset they could be. It may not know how to reach this goal. Does our undead seek priests or family members for help? It may not realize the fear it will cause or naively think help will come when an attempt at destroying it might be the result instead, though this could achieve peace of a different sort anyway.

An undead may simply want to be left alone, lying in a grave until compelled to emerge, such as vampires that need to feed. Spirits might want to exist in a perpetual state of denial that they have indeed died, haunting their homes in a dream-like state where the passage of time doesn't register on them, as if they died this morning when decades could've passed. Some might want to simply retrace steps from a happier time and be content with this existence, only to have frightened people interfere with them. Such an undead would be harmless but assumed to be dangerous by those unfamiliar with this type's traits. These are standard ideas.

CAUSING TORMENT

In theory, everyone wants peace, but some enjoy riling up others in life. If they become undead, especially spirits that can appear and disappear at will, tormenting others is easy. This can be innocent fun or an attempt to mentally and emotionally destroy their victim. This can be for revenge against one person or all humanity (or a species).

APPEARANCE

If our undead can only originate one way, they might have a look common to all. We judge and classify by appearance, like it or not. For example, decide that our undead is a skeleton or rotting corpse, not that it's both. The caveat is that if corporeal undead are created by raising bodies from a cemetery en masse, the result will indeed be a mix of these two, unless a spell or technology used to create them is targeting one type of remains versus another.

Can people tell our undead is undead? With spirits, this is usually obvious, but there are stories of ghosts looking alive. The truth presumably becomes more apparent if contact is made or it does something to give itself away. Or someone gets close enough. If a spirit has the ability to open doors or otherwise interact with the physical world, then it could be virtually impossible to tell what it is. Usually in stories, we want a clue, meaning at least something is a bit off, such as it casting no shadow or being translucent.

For corporeal undead, the presumed answer is that people can immediately tell it's undead. We like the horror a corpse produces, but then vampires are most often shown appearing alive. The degree of decay can be everything down to a skeleton. Many corpses will show evidence of what killed them, including missing limbs or gaping wounds.

A skeleton presumably doesn't carry disease. It wouldn't wield a metal weapon with any skill, for the weapon would slide around in their hand more than a wooden one like a club; this is assuming we care about being realistic. Maybe these undead are really keen on finding gloves to solve such problems and this is an indication of their intelligence and an identifying trait (i.e., a glove-wearing skeleton is type so-and-so); they might also want footwear. Thinking like this is one way to make something more believable.

Skeletons with no clothes imply either being buried that way or being dead long enough for whatever they were wearing to completely rot or fall away once they rose, so consider having a certain amount of clothing, even armor, on the undead. They can acquire more once moving around, so it makes sense that some of it will have deteriorated (giving a clue what they were buried in) and some will be newer.

TRAITS

The distinction between spirits and corporeal undead notwithstanding, when creating undead, the difference between one and another will largely come down to what they can and cannot do—or even what they tend to be doing regardless of capabilities.

SPEECH AND OTHER SOUNDS

In theory, a corporeal undead would have difficulty talking due to a tongue and more drying out. If a skeleton has nothing to talk with, spirits are even worse off. We may opt to ignore all of this so that they communicate effectively, or give them telepathy. Try to be consistent; if the undead walks funny, it should have trouble speaking clearly. It doesn't make sense for one part of the body to be impaired but another to be unaffected by decay. If we want an undead to speak fluently but have trouble walking, we can fix this by having a leg wound cause the latter.

Completely silent undead or those making tormented attempts at communicating can be more frightening. An undead might be able to say only a few words, and if so, those are probably the ones associated with a goal. This could be the name of their child they want to save (or failed to save), for example. Another option is for it to emit a sound meant to draw others to it or affect them, such as causing a trance-like state in victims. Such a sound would make this undead type identifiable.

TOUCH

Corporeal undead have no trouble touching the world they're still a part of, but does their touch corrupt in any way? It can be poisonous, infecting a limb that must be removed. It can just cause unbearable cold that lasts. We can decide it causes the person touched to have visions of what the undead sees, like who its master is, or what it wants, or what horror it faces now. These results and others of our invention can be part of our undead type.

Since disembodied spirits don't inhabit a body, by definition, it's logical that their ability to interact with the physical world is compromised, and yet we've all seen movies where they can move objects or directly touch the living. Sometimes this touch is something they must learn or which takes a toll on them to perform; otherwise it's too easy and they don't have limits on their powers.

Decide how much our spirit can manipulate the physical world, how often, for how long, and to what end. Are they only able to pass through some kinds of objects and not others? Does the material something is made of affect their ability to touch it? Are they only hurt by something like silver? Can they touch people and if so, what affect does that have on the living *or* spirit?

The ultimate version of touch is possession of a body. An appealing idea involves the victim gaining the inhabiting spirit's skills—becoming an expert musician or gymnast, for example. A caveat here is that the body won't have the training. The body simply wouldn't be capable of it, but this again depends on how realistic we want to be.

MOVEMENT

The slow-moving undead of yesteryear seemingly paid more attention to realism but has given way to faster-than-humanly-possible corporeal undead. Assuming we want to justify anything, the latter can have either a supernatural, technological, or possibly genetic cause (in the form of mutation). Slow moving ones don't seem frightening anymore unless sheer numbers have blocked escape routes. Today's audiences expect better than victims who just stare in horror until undead surround them.

If we're giving our undead superhuman abilities, a good rationale sells this better. Knowing their origins will help; if a spell designed to grant speed to someone killed them instead, then making them fast in death makes sense. An animated corpse is presumably powered by unholy forces that also allow it to experience little or no fatigue.

Spirits are often shown gliding around or just appearing as if teleporting; the latter suggests knowing they're dead while the former suggests ignorance of this fact. Can spirits pass through objects? If so, this can be because they don't recognize a change has taken place, such as a bookcase being placed in front of a door long after they're dead; doing so might not indicate awareness of their death but being stuck in time, seeing the past instead of the present.

CONSUMPTION

If our corporeal undead needs to consume something to remain animated, is it really dead? Logically the answer would be no, but we accept the idea that vampires need to consume blood, as if a dead body has any ability to process liquids, not to mention oxygen in blood. What else might our undead need to consume? Souls is a good answer, as is energy of some kind. Maybe there's a supernatural substance they need. In SF, this could exist only in space, causing the undead to be a traveler.

If we've invented plants or animals with special properties, perhaps our undead is compelled to feed upon them for an advantage thus gained. Decide if our undead can't survive without it or just gains something like abilities. Or maybe it uses narcotics to dull the misery it feels. Imagine a drunk undead. Finding that narcotic would give it a goal.

Our undead might be consuming out of habit, as in the case of a primitive, mindless undead. In this case, it may not be aware that it can't digest food, or that drink leaks out of its innards. This can give our undead a typical, identifiable appearance—freshly stained with food and drink.

Spiritual undead have no body to consume with, but physical items aren't the only sustenance. Maybe the spirit wants or needs to feed on emotional turmoil it causes. Or it could drain the life energy from the living. Or devour their soul. It can feed on magic or energy from technology. Are there supernatural phenomenon that attract them? Can our species harness those and use them as a lure?

RESIDENCE

Corporeal undead have to be somewhere when not terrorizing people, so decide where it resides. We're looking for a dwelling type more than a specific place, unless we're creating something that's only found in one region of the world. Do they return to a grave or spend time in caves or abandoned ruins? The latter is arguably the most interesting. Undead are sometimes depicted as being only a creature of the night, but they still exist during the day. There's no particular reason they must be in hiding, with one obvious exception—if they're hoping to do bad things without getting caught, fewer people are out at night and they could meet the goal more easily.

Spiritual undead have less need of a residence but are often thought to be tied to a place by sentiment. This is usually a home or the place of a big event, including their death. If they died long ago, other things could've been built there since. In space faring stories, an individual spirit could end up on a ship that takes it away from home but the desire to return home is a character issue, not an undead type.

Aside from the mortal world, is there somewhere they go when not haunting someplace? This is something few creators address. Are they in an afterlife? Do they have any sense of time passing? Are they just dormant like a hibernating bear? While this doesn't need addressing, it could help us imagine something unique.

DEATH

Nothing lasts forever, including undead. Our characters will be highly interested in the question of whether this thing can be eliminated or not, and how to do so, so we'll need an answer.

SPIRITS

The final outcome for a spirit is typically banishment to an afterlife like heaven or hell, unless we have somewhere else to send them, such as a prison for ghosts. That would seem to be a temporary measure, which is fine but suggests unfinished business might come up later. Another option is for a soul to be destroyed, which is very final and not terribly nice. If that spirit was irredeemably evil then this might be fair, but innocent spirits exist.

Achieving the desired outcome is another matter. Does our spirit need to be confronted with a truth to let go of this world? Does it need to be trapped by spells or technology, such as the infamous pentagram drawn on the floor with blood, holy water, or some kind of salt or other material they cannot pass over? Does a priest need to channel the power and word of a god through prayer and blessed objects? None of that is original but if we invent objects required for this, then we turn these into something more unique.

If a spirit has possessed a body and is driven out, decide what happens to the now-vacated victim. Are they insane? Do they return to normal albeit traumatized? Do they have any knowledge of what was going on while they were possessed? Did the spirit communicate with them? Was the spirit able to guard its knowledge and plans from discovery or was the victim privy to knowledge that could be sinister or horrifying? Perhaps the victim knows things they shouldn't. They could now be under the control of the spirit (even though the spirit is gone) via manipulation, threats, or an ongoing compulsion to obey in a Stockholm syndrome sort of way.

CORPOREAL

When destroying corporeal undead, the focus tends to be on the body, with little concern given for what happens to a soul, if one is present. Soul and body are seen as bound so that truly rendering the body unusable is seen as resolving the matter entirely. This needn't be the case, for such a loosed spirit could then become a spiritual undead instead; it may have even started that way.

Entrapping the corporeal undead is theoretically easier, given that there's a body to ensnare and ordinary mortals could do so (or at least think they can). The difficulty may lie in the qualities of the undead we've created: super strength or something so like a wild animal in ferocity or being a disease-carrier. To craft an idea truly our own, we can imbue an ordinary object, such as rope, with a special property that counteracts our undead's unique qualities. Bless it. Irradiate it. Soak it in a chemical or a substance that appears only in space. What danger do these things pose to the living?

Once destroyed, some undead types have a habit of returning to life unless other measures are taken, such as dismemberment, fire, or entombment in a special grave. Can ours come back? How can it be stopped for good?

Fire is the stereotypical way to destroy undead, the rationale seeming to be that a dead body is cold and therefore cold doesn't bother them. Conversely, heat must. Besides, encasing someone alive in ice will kill them. Doing that to undead will just immobilize them until thawed. Fire will destroy everything but the bones, and if the fire is hot enough, even those can turn to ash. This is something about the concept of undead that makes sense, which can possibly inspire you to invent things that do the same.

WHERE TO START

We should first decide if there's an existing type of undead that we can use or make minor alterations to. If there is, then we likely have some idea what we hope to accomplish. As with monsters, this can involve basic appearance or behavior and imagined scenes of this undead frightening or attacking our characters. Work out these impressions, deciding if this undead has a body or not, and if so, whether there's a soul inside. This will suggest other attributes. Then begin using the template in Appendix 7 to address subjects you haven't considered yet. This can be done in any order, but it's helpful to decide origins before figuring out what it wants, which in turn affects behavior and even abilities. Whether it can be killed, and how, can also greatly affect just how dangerous it really is.

CONCLUSION

I've often joked that I find it hard to believe that God created the world in only six days because it takes me forever. Hopefully this volume will speed you along in your own invention of life. It bears repeating that world building is optional and not everything in this series must be done. Try to avoid feeling overwhelmed. If this happens, take a break. You might be taking everything too seriously. As your world's ultimate god, what you say goes. This includes a decision to skip over the invention of something because you don't need it, don't care, don't have the time, or don't have an idea. This book and the templates should help you flesh out forgotten areas of invention, but it's okay to have blanks in your files where nothing is written about a subject; I have left things this way for over a decade. One day it will occur to you (or not) to write something for that subject, especially when you need it for your project.

Don't let this become a chore. World building is fun.

Appendix 1
God Template

Name

Nicknames/Titles

Gods usually have one or two titles or nicknames.

Overview

Famous For

Include the god's reputation and that of their followers.

Domain

What is the god's chief area of concern (love, war, death)? What other areas help readers or inhabitants of your world understand what this god is like? Are their secondary traits, like a god of love being the god of marriage?

General Description

What form does the god appear in? Human? Animal? Which gender? Are there famous objects in their possession? Are those feared or coveted by mortals and others?

ALIGNMENT

Is the god good or evil?

SYMBOL

Keep symbols easy to draw, not for your sake, but your characters. Artists can draw more elaborate ones, but your world's residents need something straightforward.

OTHER IDENTIFIERS

Is this a god of an element, season, color, or month?

PERSONALITY

Discuss the god's moods, outlook/vision, friendliness, etc. Mention the intelligence, wisdom, and charisma. If appropriate, discuss strength, constitution, agility, dexterity, and morale, but gods usually have these in abundance.

RESIDENCE

Where does the god live? What is it like? Are visitors allowed and under what rules? Who or what else dwells there? Are there guardians? Humanoids? Creatures?

HISTORY AND MYTHS

What has your god done in the past? Created or destroyed lives or items? Fought with other gods? What myths exist about them? Have the humanoid species tried to do things to this god, such as steal a possession, and did they succeed? At what cost?

MYTH 1

Explain your myth or story about this god here and state whether the story is true or not. Is there a moral to the story to instruct the species?

CREATIONS

SPECIES

Which did this god help create? The god's influence on them might be better described in that species' file, but you can say what effect they typically have.

PLACES

Has this god created a place? This could be an island, a forest, building, or sanctuary of some kind.

ITEMS/POSSESSIONS

Has this god created any items for others or themselves? What possessions do they have and what properties (supernatural or otherwise) do they have?

RELATIONSHIPS

FAMILIAL

Are they the parent/child, or sibling of other gods? Do they have half-god offspring? What form do those beings take? A monster? An animal? An intelligent, sentient life? If so, mention them here and use another file to describe those beings in detail.

How old is your god and how does this relate to others (younger, older)?

SPECIES

How do they view and get along with each species?

PATRONAGE

Who does this god support?

CONFLICTS

Has this god participated or abstained from any wars? At what cost, and to whom? How do they typically fight? Can this god be incapacitated or killed? What sort of weapon will do it?

APPENDIX 2
SPECIES TEMPLATE

NAME

NICKNAMES/TITLES

Do they have nicknames?

FAMOUS FOR

Are there attributes that this species is famous for?

GENERAL DESCRIPTION

OVERALL APPEARANCE

Include voice, posture, impression, sleep and eating habits.

THE HEAD

Eyes, brow, ears, chin, jaw, nose, lips, hair styles (and colors), tongue. Heart-shaped, round, square. Bearded?

THE BODY

Discuss height, stocky/thin, details on hands/feet, athleticism, stamina, strength, common ailments, clothing.

Special

Anything more unique about them, like appendages or supernatural skills.

Gods

Which gods created them, influence them, or are worshiped by them? How does this affect them?

Characteristics

Intelligence

Wisdom

Charisma

Strength

Constitution

Agility

Dexterity

Morale

Specific Accomplishments

WARS WON AND LOST

INVENTIONS AND DISCOVERIES

WORLD VIEW

CULTURE AND CUSTOMS

Do they work every day? Take lunch naps? Include marriage, death, birth.

SOCIETY

Do they build cities? Scavenge, farm, hunt? Live in tribes?

LANGUAGE

Do they have an oral or written language? Which languages do they typically know?

RELATIONS WITH OTHER SPECIES

HUMANS

SPECIES 1

SPECIES 2

THE SUPERNATURAL

MAGIC

Can they do it? What kind of magic, how powerful can they become? Are they afraid of it?

HABITAT

Where a species lives determines many characteristics.

TERRAIN

Where do they originate from? Land with rolling hills? Mountains? Plains? Forests? The sea? Which is their preference and why? Defense? Food? Overall environment?

CLIMATE

Where are they found? Where are they not found? Are they known for disliking a climate and grumbling about it?

SETTLEMENTS (TOWNS/CITIES)

Creating settlements is discussed in *Creating Places (The Art of World Building, #2)*, but here we can decide overall look, feel, layout, and considerations that distinguish this species' settlements from those of other species. Decide if they're willing to live in large numbers in joint settlements, abstain altogether, or just have quarters (like the French Quarter in New Orleans) in a joint settlement. Or do they live among everyone?

HOMES

Where are their homes? On land? In trees? Underground? Underwater? How are they laid out and protected? Are homes communal? Are their rooms with special functions, socially or supernatural? Ceremonial? Do they have weapons rooms? Are homes passed down generations? Are any living there?

STYLES & MATERIALS

What are homes made of? Wood? Brick? Straw roofs?

COMBAT

Do they fight at all or run? How do they fight? With what weapons and armor? Do they use cavalry, dragons? Any typical battle formations?

ECOLOGY

Mating, birth, rearing.

Appendix 3
World Figure Template

Use this for heroes, villains, martyrs, and any other famous characters in your world.

Name

Include proper name and nicknames.

Famous For

Summarize in a few sentences what people think of with this person. Details of events and traits are further down. Include legends.

The Facts

Are there things believed about him and which are false? Are some things true but doubted? Are some things unknown and would they change anyone's opinion of him?

Traits

Characteristics

Is this a knight? Star fighter? What profession or trait defines him? What injuries do they bear the scars from?

STATUS

Is he dead (presumed?) or alive? Missing?

POSSESSIONS

Does he have any -known possessions like a magic sword, dragon, horse or ship? Why and what is it?

FAMILY

Are parents around? Any children? Does he know he has kids? What are their relationships like? A hero might have earned enemies that go after family. A villain might have killed theirs or been disavowed by them. Are parents or children old enough to interfere with his plans or life?

RELATIONS WITH SPECIES

How does he get along with each of the species? More importantly, is he viewed differently by each species, or famous for different things?

HISTORY

ORIGINS, DEMISE, AND IN BETWEEN

Where is he from? What formative events made him who he is? Where did he live? Is he there now? If he's dead, where are the remains and his possessions? Is the grave protected? Dangerous?

TRAINING AND SKILLS

How did he get his skills? Innate? Training? Life experience? What are the rumored and real sources of personality traits or skills that led him to become famous?

THE DEEDS

This is it. Tell us what he did or achieved and how. Why did he become famous? Was there a reason no one else could do it or was this just the first one to do it?

Appendix 4
Monster Template

Monster Name

The monster might have a name it thinks of itself as, and another that others call it.

Nicknames/Titles

Do they have nicknames?

Famous For

If the monster is known to exist, is it famous? This suggests it's hard to kill because quite a few people probably would've tried, and failed, by now.

Description

What does it physically look like? Does anyone ever get a good look at it? Are stories about it exaggerated? How does it feel about its appearance and how people react to it? What sorts of stories do people tell about it?

Motives

What does your monster want? To be left alone? Hoard treasure? Food? Security? Revenge, and for what?

ORIGINS

Did someone create this monster on purpose or by accident, or is it a product of nature?

GODS

Does the monster recognize or worship any gods? Or work with them? Receive aid in return for something?

CHARACTERISTICS

INTELLIGENCE

How smart is it? Is its intelligence limited to things like hunting, and is that just instinct more than thought? Some monsters aren't much smarter than animals, but monsters who were once human, for example, can be very smart.

WISDOM

Monsters aren't known for wisdom, but is it wise enough not to step into obvious traps? Does it know better than to go into town and kill people because a bunch of people will come to kill it as a result?

CHARISMA

Monsters are usually called that for being hideous, but not always. Some are beautiful or have the ability to convince people they are with hallucinations or illusion.

STRENGTH

Monsters are often depicted as stronger than most other beings, so just how strong is this one?

CONSTITUTION

Does the monster have an unusual ability to withstand pain? Can it travel farther and faster than its pursuers without exhaustion so that tracking it is hard? Does it withstand wounds in combat, or heal faster?

AGILITY

How mobile is it? Fast or slow? Does its body hinder movement or help it? Can it chase down prey or flee those chasing it? Is it faster than a horse?

DEXTERITY

How much control does it have with weapons or tools?

MORALE

Monsters are usually the ones scaring everyone else, but is there anything the monster is afraid of? Does it flee from battles when too many are against it or is it fearless?

WORLD VIEW

What is the monster's viewpoint about itself, others, and its place in the world?

SOCIETY

Monsters are generally isolated and have no society of their own, but what about the monster's impact on a nearby society? How is it thought of?

Does it impact life there, such as people not traveling in its direction (or taking special precautions)?

LANGUAGE

Does the monster speak any known languages or is it reduced to grunts like an animal? Is it easy or impossible to understand? Can it read and write? If so, someone had to teach it, so who did that? That individual has befriended the monster and likely protects it, but possibly doesn't want that known.

CUSTOMS

Is there anything that the monster does that could be considered a custom or habit, such as stacking the bones of victims? Or displaying them? Does it attack at a certain time of the month, year, or decade?

RELATIONS WITH SPECIES

If the monster has a unique relationship with a given species, list it here. Also, how do the different species view the monster? Do some want it left alone while others want it killed? Captured? Enslaved?

HUMANS

ELVES

DWARVES

DRAGONS

OGRES

SKILLS

What can your monster do that is unusual? What is normal for a creature with its limbs and their physical features to do but this monster *cannot* do?

THE SUPERNATURAL

Is the monster supernatural in any way? Can it perform magic? Is it afraid of magic? Does it have a supernatural place nearby? Does it utilize it or avoid?

FOOD

What does the monster eat? How often? Are species on the menu? Why does it eat them (just for food or to induce horror)? Does it lure food to it or hunt it?

HABITAT

Does the monster have a lair? What is it like? Are there bones lying around—or even arranged neatly like trophies? Does the monster stay in its lair most of the time? Is it mobile within the lair? How far from its lair does it travel? Does it have more than one? Is it a wandering monster with no home? Is it looking for one now? Does it prefer a particular type of place (cave, abandoned city)? Is the monster nocturnal?

COMBAT

How does the monster fight (which body parts are used—arms, legs, tail, teeth)? Does it use brute force? Cunning? Stealth (stalking prey)? Does it lure victims into a trap? Does it have any special attacks or tricks it can use?

Ecology

Is the monster capable of reproduction? How often? How many offspring are produced at once? Are they born in an egg? Are they like sharks and immediately dangerous? How does it reproduce? Sex? By itself? Can it mate with species or animals and if so, is the result the same kind of monster or a hybrid? Has it ever reproduced? Is this monster the offspring of something?

Appendix 5
Plant Template

Use this for trees, vegetables, flowers, fruits, and more.

Plant #1 Name

Description

What is its climate, season, appearance, texture, toxicity, smell, feel, and taste? When is it planted, grown and harvested?

Uses

How is it used? What products are made with it?

Reputation

Are there any stories about it, whether harvesting difficulties or famous/infamous uses?

Analogues

What Earth equivalents exist? This isn't something to tell your audience but helps you easily remember what you were thinking.

Plant #2 Name

DESCRIPTION

USES

REPUTATION

ANALOGUES

APPENDIX 6
ANIMAL TEMPLATE

Use this for mammals, birds, fish, amphibians, and reptiles.

ANIMAL #1 NAME

What does it look like and how does it behave? How is it used?

TYPE

Mammal, bird, etc.

MATING/BIRTH

Do they lay eggs or have live birth? What's the litter size? How long does it take? Do the mothers raise the young and for how long?

LIFESPAN

HABITAT

Does it prefer mountains, forests, deserts?

CLIMATES

PLACES FOUND

What are some specific places it's found, such as a kingdom or forest?

SOLITARY OR PACK?

PREY

Herbivore, carnivore, or omnivore? If the latter two, does it eat animals or also species?

PREDATORS

Do species prey on this animal? For trophies, furs, teeth, poisonous spines? To capture and breed them? Do your species eat it?

ANALOGUES

What Earth animals is this similar to? This is something for your private notes more than to tell an audience, as you can't compare your world's animals (or anything else) to Earth unless the characters have been here.

ANIMAL #2 NAME

TYPE

MATING/BIRTH

LIFESPAN

HABITAT

CLIMATES

PLACES FOUND

SOLITARY OR PACK?

PREY

PREDATORS

ANALOGUES

Appendix 7
Undead Template

Undead Name

Nicknames/Titles

Description

What does it look like? Does it appear alive or obviously dead? If a spirit, does it retain a self-image of itself as healthy and alive as if its unaware of its death, or does it's self-image reveal it knows (such as a gaping wound)?

Type

Animal, plant, humanoid; spiritual or corporeal (with or without a soul?).

Life Cycle

Origins

What caused this type of undead to exist? An accident? If so, when did it happen, why, and who caused it? If someone invented the undead on purpose, why and how did they do so?

Replication

How many of them are there? Can it make more of itself? How long until someone/something else becomes one once exposed to the triggering incident? How long does something have to be dead before becoming this?

DEATH

Can this undead be destroyed for good? How? What happens to it? If not, what happens when attacked with enough force to seemingly kill it or render it immobile? Does it recover, and if so, after how long?

HABITAT

Does it prefer graveyards, the wilderness, or abandoned homes or those lived in?

PLACES FOUND

What are some specific places it's found, such as a kingdom, city, or forest?

SOLITARY OR PACK?

Is it found in groups, alone, or both? If a pack, can the pack communicate and move as if they're of a shared mind?

BEHAVIOR

CHARACTERISTICS AND SKILLS

What can it do and not do? What hurts it? How strong, fast, smart, and agile is it? Can it speak, read, write, and understand the living or dead? Can it perform magic? Do biological scanners and other devices work on it? Can it use them (like a fingerprint scanner)? Spirits can move through objects or touch them. Undead can withstand some forces or not.

MOTIVES

What does it want? If it gets this, does it stop?

PREY

Does it have anyone in particular it preys upon? The innocent? Those of a certain religion or with none? What does it do to victims? Turn them into one, use them like a parasite would (such as feeding on them but leaving them alive), or just kill them?

COMBAT

How does it fight? With weapons held in the hand, its body, or thrown objects? What hurts it? What cannot hurt it? Does it gain power from certain kinds of attacks, as if feeding off them?

VOLUME 2

CREATING PLACES

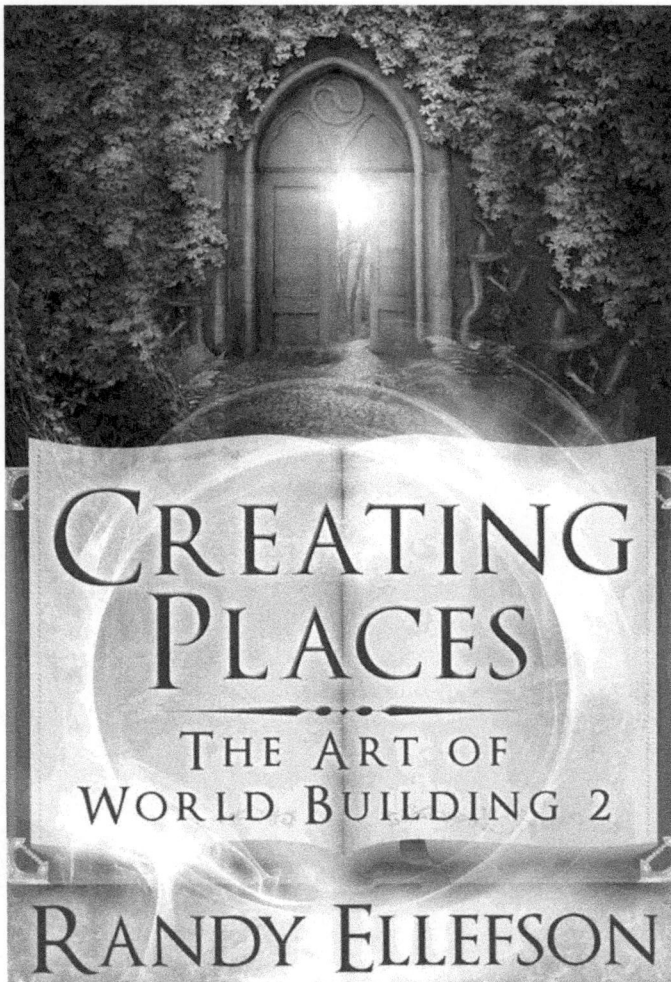

INTRODUCTION

If we've created gods, species, plants, animals, monsters, and more such as in *Creating Life (The Art of World Building, #1)*, we need somewhere for everyone to live. Creating the world itself can help us envision conflicts, alliances, and struggles our characters might endure while traveling across mountains, through forests, or over the sea.

In this volume, we'll discuss:

- Solar systems, planets, moons, stars, constellations, and more
- Continents, oceans, seas, and other water bodies
- Land features such as forests, mountains, and deserts
- Sovereign powers like kingdoms
- Settlements such as cities, towns, villages, and more
- Travel on land, sea, and in space by various means of locomotion (horse, wagon, dragons, ships) and how to consistently calculate travel times
- Places of interest
- History
- Drawing maps for continents, settlements, and more

The examples included in the text were created specifically for this guide and are not drawn from a setting of mine, except in rare instances and in Chapter One, "Case Studies" (drawing new maps is too time consuming).

WHERE TO START

The series and chapters within each volume can be read in any order but are arranged according to what might come first in a world's timeline. A planet precedes continents, which precede land features, et al. But our creations can be invented in any order. Only you can decide where to begin, but it's recommended to take any idea and run with it, writing down whatever occurs to you. If there are problems with it, they can be fixed later as you update and improve upon it. If you haven't read a chapter in this book and have an idea for something that's covered here, you can adjust your work later.

So where do you start? Where your heart lies.

IMAGES

Creating Places includes images, which are greyscale in the print copy and color in the eBook. Larger, full color copies can be viewed online at http://www.artofworldbuilding.com/creatingplaces/images. They are organized by chapter and provide more detail that make it easier to learn from.

THE CHAPTERS

CHAPTER 1 – CASE STUDIES

Three case studies show how the contents of this volume can aid in creating relationships we can use in our work. They discuss the effects of prevailing winds, climate, land features, rain shadows, and the impact of passages to travel through troubling areas. Each affects the sort of sovereign power suggested by a region and how alliances and enemies can be forged, some changing with time. Each power will have different ideologies and geographical features and needs, which can help us determine relationships between different powers.

CHAPTER 2 – CREATING A PLANET

This chapter focuses on creating an Earth-like planet. World builders should understand the role of the moon and its effects on tides, seasons, and more if we intend to have a moon different from our own or multiple moons. Mention of other planets, constellations, and comets can make our world seem like it's not an island. The equator, climate zones, prevailing winds, and rain shadows all affect how much precipitation falls in an area, which in turn affects all life there, including vegetation or the lack thereof. Understanding these basics will help us create believable landscapes.

CHAPTER 3 – CREATING A CONTINENT

Which hemisphere our continent lies in affects the seasons and might impact where we place constellations. Understanding plate tectonics can help us build believable mountain ranges and place volcanoes where they might occur. This can also determine where deep areas of the sea are, giving our sea monsters somewhere to call home. We have some liberty to name bodies of water what we want, but this chapter includes details on when to use which name, including seas, bays, inlets, and more.

CHAPTER 4 – CREATING LAND FEATURES

A continent will have mountains, volcanoes, lakes, rivers, forests, woodlands, savannahs, jungles, prairies, wetlands, and deserts, but world builders should understand each to place them in believable locations. While some aspects are obvious, minor details can change our decisions and augment our resulting stories. Why say characters have entered a run-of-the-mill forest when we can say it's a savannah instead, describing how it looks and what life is like for inhabitants and those traversing it? This chapter aids world builders in making a more varied landscape—one that is accurately depicted.

CHAPTER 5 – CREATING A SOVEREIGN POWER

Kingdoms, empires, dictatorships and more are types of sovereign powers that world builders can create. Before we do, a high-level understanding of the differences between them is crucial. Many variations to government types exist, which gives us freedom to tweak details for our needs, but we should know the rules before we break them. The role of sovereignty, including how it is gained and lost, is examined in this chapter along with the "divine right of kings." We also look at the head of state and head of government roles, the differences between them, and the conflicts that can arise. The nature of each branch of government is examined along with parliamentary systems. Democracies, federations, theocracies, monarchies, autocracies and more are examined for their key differences.

Inventing a sovereign power should include friends and enemies who shape policy, lifestyle, and culture. The form of government has significant impact on inhabitants and results from world view. History affects this as well, and while creating a history is optional, it enriches the dynamics of relationships and can create heroes, villains, and attitudes in the population. We should consider which species are present and in how great a percentage, and what languages are spoken or forbidden. Our power's location and climate will impact lifestyles and vegetation, which also influences what natural resources it has or lacks, and what the power does as a result. These can all lead to tensions both with other powers or the residents. Symbols, colors, flags, and slogans will be a source of pride and even fear for both foreigners and the population.

CHAPTER 6 – CREATING A SETTLEMENT

Location impacts a settlement more than many world builders realize, from climate to terrain and water supply, but our neighbors also determine how much fortification is needed and the number of armed forces, including their skill sets. Ancient and recent history can bring lasting change and cause attitudes that enrich our setting. Our population's diversity is also critical for determining what life is like for the majority and minorities alike, but first we need to decide who is who (and why), how much power they have, and whether they can subvert those who are supposedly in power. Whether outposts, castles, villages, towns, or cities, or even an orbiting station, a settlement will have secrets, a reputation, colors, symbols, and local lore that characterize it in the minds of inhabitants, friends and enemies.

CHAPTER 7 – TRAVEL OVER LAND

In settings without automobiles, we may struggle to determine how long it takes people to traverse a distance, whether that's between settlements or land features. Mountains, hills, desert, and vegetation all impact speed and endurance, whether one is walking, riding a steed (even flying on one), or hauling freight like a wagon. The presence and quality of roads alter this, as do life forms that might cause wariness and therefore slower travel. A methodology is presented to assist with organizing distance measurements and scale, determining the base miles per day (BMPD) for various mode of travel, and terrain modifiers to BMPD. Using both miles and kilometers, formulas are provided for making calculations, which can also be estimated for overall land area in sovereign powers. Newsletter subscribers receive an Excel spreadsheet that can be used to alter scale and modifiers so that all calculations are automatically updated, reducing the need for manual calculations.

CHAPTER 8 – TRAVEL BY WATER

Landlubbers have difficulty determining how long it takes for any ship, whether powered by oars or sails, to traverse a distance. This chapter explores the factors affecting sailing speeds and what vessels are most likely to be used during an Age of Sail period. Calculations are provided for realistic estimates. Both long and round ships are discussed, including the galley, brig, frigate, galleon, sloop-of-war, and ship-of-the-line. In fantasy, we have species and warrior types who might be part of our crew. We might also rule out gunpowder and cannon, which means having ships with no real fire power or which use alternative weapons, some of which are examined. Subscribers *to The Art of World Building* newsletter receive an Excel spreadsheet that performs calculations in kilometers, miles, and nautical miles.

CHAPTER 9 – TRAVEL IN SPACE

Science fiction features invented technologies for traveling the cosmos, but that doesn't free us from attempts to be realistic about life in space or how to maneuver. Modern engines operate on the principle of thrust, which requires rear-facing engines, and we'll need this for slower-than-light travel within a solar system. Imaginary propulsions, like warp, hyper, or jump drives can benefit from believable limitations. We should also remember that locations in space are ever changing positions so that how long it takes to travel between two points is seldom the same—or convenient for our characters. The need to enter a planet's atmosphere affects the structure of our ship, but world builders will be most interested in the internal organization and the effect we can make this have on people and story.

CHAPTER 10 – CREATING TIME AND HISTORY

History can enrich a world and provide us with cultural clashes, famous items, and world figures to which our stories and characters can refer or cite as inspiration. To save time, we can create a master history file with short entries that are invented in a few minutes and which do not need long explanations. Some could be turned into stand-alone stories if we stumble upon a great idea. Historic entries can be created at any time and can include events involving the gods, technology, supernatural, wars, the rise and fall of sovereign powers, artifacts, and famous missions by groups or individuals.

We also need a universal way to measure time because each sovereign power might have its own calendar, making the correlation of events across kingdoms harder. The merits of keeping timeframes similar to Earth's are discussed; this includes the reasons why minutes and hours benefit from little alteration, while the number of days, weeks, and months can experience greater variation without disrupting the audience's sense of time.

CHAPTER 11 – CREATING PLACES OF INTEREST

Even seemingly ordinary locations can acquire significance due to scale, features, or people associated with them. These include monuments, graves, catacombs and hidden passages, and unusual buildings, whether built in stone, flying in the air, or floating on water like Venice. Ruins offer places for treasure to be found or horrors unleashed, including magical or technological items. Event sites and shipwrecks also give inhabitants places to reference, seek, or avoid, and can be where items of our invention originated.

BONUS CHAPTER 12 – DRAWING MAPS

While drawing maps is optional in world building, they can help us visualize where everything's taking place, and if done well, can even be included in published works. Drawing skill isn't really needed, as modern map making programs allow us to place pre-existing shapes onto a map and move them around. Continent maps help us decide on the location and quality of land features like mountains, forests, and deserts so that we create a realistic ecosystem. The location of settlements, rivers, and bodies of water will also impact the stories and lives of characters we create. We can also draw settlement, dungeon, and ship maps to solidify our decisions and find new inspiration in our layouts.

CHAPTER ONE

CASE STUDIES

Whether we're new to world building or a pro, the following case studies can give insight into how the material in this volume can help our efforts. They demonstrate what can result from learning the contents of this book: how land features and map making can lead to decisions on allies and enemies, trade routes, and what types of sovereign powers could exist. Concepts are alluded to here but not explained; world builders can revisit these case studies as knowledge of this book's content is assimilated. The maps are also available online at http://www.llurien.com/continents/llorus/, where it might be easier to see what's being referred to.

Each case study will use my setting, Llurien, because I know what I was thinking while creating it, as opposed to someone else's world. It's a fantasy world with knights, magic, gods, and seven species of my invention instead of the staples—elves, dwarves, and dragons

CASE STUDY 1—TWO STRAITS AND A SEA OF ENEMIES

The first case is the effect two narrow straits have on access to a sea and how this affects the relationships of several sovereign powers. If following along with the maps online (instead of the one below), expand the following powers to see the maps: Erizon, Kysh, Marula, Niora, Pell, and Rone.

THE SEA OF FIRE AND STRAITS

On the western coast of this continent lies the Sea of Fire, which is accessible from the ocean to the west via two straits (two narrow channels) that flow north or south of the large island there (see the map below). The northern Strait of Erizon is not particularly treacherous due to its width. Technically, it's too broad to be considered a strait; even on Earth we sometimes use the wrong word, so world builders can, too. The southern Strait of Niora is narrow enough to fit the definition of "strait" better due to being narrow, so I decided it is treacherous to differentiate it from the northern strait (variety is good).

Figure 2 Sea of Fire

THE EQUATOR

The equator runs through the center of the sea, which means almost all the woods near the sea are rainforests. The equator's location also means the prevailing winds are from the east (i.e., blowing east-to-west). When drawing a map, we should know where land lies in relation to the equator, as this impacts forest types, skin color of inhabitants, wind direction, and where rainfall occurs, which in turn affects vegetation or the lack thereof.

ERIZON

Above the Strait of Erizon lies Erizon, a wizard-centric oligarchy, where personal liberties are fewer. It lies on the northwestern corner of the continent by the ocean, which suggests that Erizon is a seafaring power. Given its naval might and the proximity to the Strait of Erizon, it seems obvious that Erizon would want to control access to the Sea of Fire via the strait. This becomes the dominant factor in its relationships with every sovereign power to the east.

Figure 3 Erizon

KYSH

The Kingdom of Kysh is the heart of the Empire of Kysh. An empire re-quires stability, which suggested power not rest with a single person, so I decided the Kingdom of Kysh is a constitutional monarchy ruled by parlia-ment. The king/emperor is a ceremonial head-of-state, not head of govern-ment; this is not an absolute monarchy where the leader is all powerful.

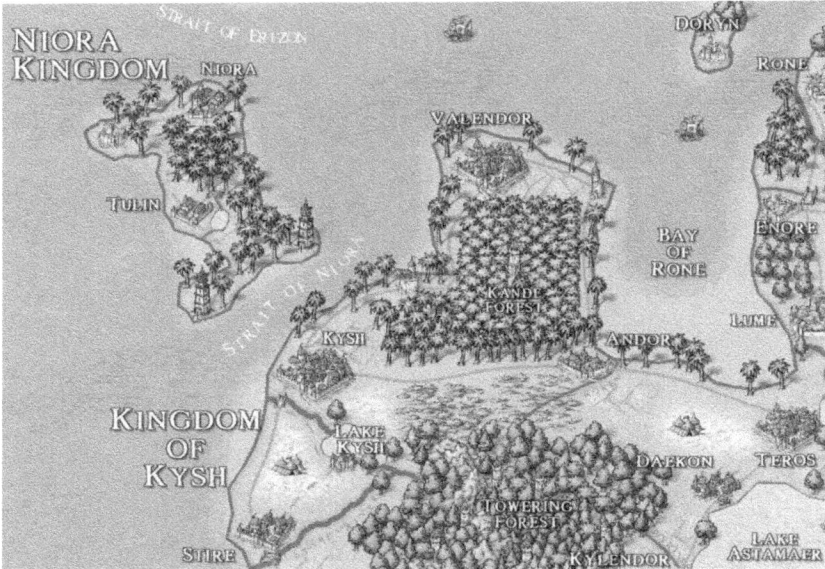

Figure 4 Kysh

Kysh and Erizon have philosophically different forms of government, setting them up as potential ideological enemies, so I made this true. Erizon has resisted annexation by the Empire of Kysh partly because powerful wiz-ards are in charge.

Kysh controls the difficult Strait of Niora just north of its capital. Since no one gets through there without Kysh's cooperation, powers adjacent to the Sea of Fire might want to be on friendly terms with Kysh. Otherwise, to reach the ocean, their only option is the Strait of Erizon and Erizon's ships. With Kysh respecting personal rights far more than Erizon, it is a potentially better ally. Both powers clash on the sea, whether in the Strait of Erizon or open ocean.

NIORA

The island Kingdom of Niora separates the straits and influences both. The larger Erizon and Kysh have each conquered Niora more than once over the centuries. Both have left a lasting impact on culture and architecture. Niora seldom had time to develop a constitutional monarchy (i.e., a bigger government) that lasted very long. I therefore decided it's an absolute monarchy, partly because it's small enough for one extended family to remain in power when independent. It is currently part of the Empire of Kysh, giving the latter more control over the Strait of Erizon. This is another reason that a sovereign power inside the Sea of Fire might prefer an alliance with Kysh over Erizon.

RONE

Figure 5 Rone

That brings us to Rone Kingdom, which lies on the right of the Sea of Fire, across the Bay of Rone from Kysh. For reasons explained in "Case Study

2—Stopping an Empire's Expansion," Rone prevented the Kingdom/Empire of Kysh from expanding farther north and is therefore Kysh's enemy. That leaves Erizon as Rone's only ally regarding these straits, but what's in it for Erizon? For one, enmity with Kysh implies friendship with Erizon, so Erizon will help Rone for a price, such as escort fees or high taxes on sold goods. Rone has also access to lands and resources to the east and south that Erizon doesn't, causing some mutual benefits to an alliance. This tense partnership has fallen apart more than once. Finally, I made Rone a constitutional monarchy to distinguish it from Marula, its neighbor.

MARULA

Figure 6 Marula

To the northeast of Rone is the = hot Marula Kingdom, located at the equator and with dark-skinned peoples. The Marula Mountains to the east block the westerly prevailing winds, causing a rainforest on the eastern side of them and a rain shadow and desert on the western side where Marula stands. A desert normally can't form near the equator due to heavy rains, but the tropical climate in Marula is really a temperate one due to high elevation, and this combination allows for a desert. Its people worship the sun and life-giving Alura River. Lacking many resources (like forests) and surrounded by enemies, it feels vulnerable, hence the ruling family's insistence on holding onto power, resulting in a brutal, absolute monarchy. Marula has a small stretch of coastline and can be easily cut off from the sea and everything beyond, so it became Rone's reluctant ally to gain aid on the sea and to prevent Kysh from conquering it next if Rone fell. The alliance is tense.

Marula and Erizon surround a common enemy (the Pell Republic) and are philosophically compatible, making them allies. This gives Marula two allies on the sea (Erizon and Rone) and two enemies (Pell and Kysh).

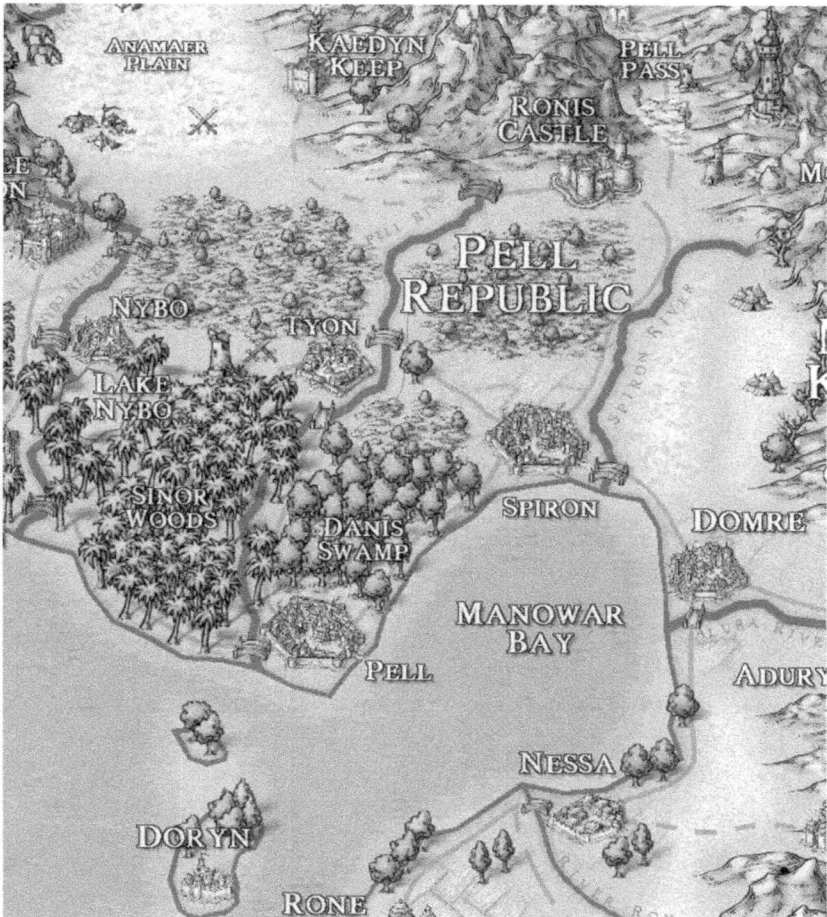

Figure 7 Pell

PELL

Between Marula and Erizon stands Pell, a federal republic with great freedom for its citizens, putting it at philosophical odds with those neighbors (see next map). Pell became an ally of Kysh for protection and access to the ocean. Pell has another ally to the north, a larger federal republic called Siara, who has encouraged Pell's transition from constitutional monarchy to republic. Siara and Erizon are enemies—they share a border—and Siara is another seafaring superpower with a small fleet stationed at Pell, its ally. Erizon tries to thwart Siara from sailing around it and entering the Sea of Fire, so Siara responds, in part, by just building ships *at* Pell. See "Case Study 3—Mountains and Murder," for more about this relationship and how geography suggested it.

NAMING CONSIDERATIONS

The sea's location at the equator and the often-heard command to "fire" during the frequent ship battles on its waters suggested a name: the Sea of Fire. Manowar Bay also received its name from the ships-of-the-line that sometimes blockade access to the sea.

CASE STUDY 2—
STOPPING AN EMPIRE'S EXPANSION

In this study, we see how one power's position earned it enemies and allies, and how a way could be found to stop an empire from consuming an entire continent. If following along with the maps online, expand the following sovereign powers sections: Erizon, Kysh, Marula, Pell and Rone.

In the lower right on the map, we see Rone Kingdom. The Empire of Kysh, to the southwest, must conquer Rone to expand northeast. When it tried, other powers came to Rone's aid for fear that if Rone fell, they'd be next. This included Marula farther to the northeast. Erizon joined forces with Rone because Kysh is their mutual enemy and Erizon doesn't want a stronger Empire of Kysh. Erizon believes it saved Rone, leading to some continued tension between these reluctant allies.

The Republic of Pell is an ally of Kysh but helped Rone instead, because if Kysh conquered Rone, then Marula, Pell assumed it would be absorbed next;

the country's enmity with Erizon meant that Erizon would not come to its aid. Since then, Pell and Kysh have had strained relations. To the north of Pell is Pell's ally, Siara, which aided the war against Kysh on principle; Siara, a federal republic, is opposed to sovereign powers conquering each other.

Figure 8 Controlling Territory

These relationships can impact stories and characters, such as someone from Erizon being haughty toward someone from Rone, a supposedly weak nation that needed so much help. A character from Rone might be bitter at the contemptuous way those of Erizon view him. This sort of dynamic is something world builders can create by drawing maps and creating different government types.

It can't be seen on the map above, but to the right are north-to-south running mountain ranges that cause rain shadows and deserts to their west. The rain forest in Rone Kingdom results from a large gap in those mountains, allowing moisture through. Other rain forests along the Sea of Fire result from the sea's moisture.

CASE STUDY 3—MOUNTAINS AND MURDER

In this case study, we look at the impact of mountain ranges on terrain and sovereign powers. If following along with the maps online, expand the following sovereign powers sections: Erizon, Marula, Pell, and Siara.

THE WINDS AND RAIN SHADOWS

In the next map, the equator lies just to the south (off the edge). This means the prevailing winds are westerly. On the map's right side is a large, north-to-south running mountain range, the Marula Mountains, which acts as a rain shadow that causes the desert to its left. The Nemon Mountains (also on the map's right side) have a similar effect, causing another desert on their west, called Pell Pass. The War Peaks to the west would once again drain water from the atmosphere, leaving none to fall on the wider Anamaer Plain, which is wetter due to some moisture from the Sea of Fire to the south, resulting in grasslands instead of desert.

Some of this is open to interpretation. For example, Anamaer Plain could be another desert but two already existed in this region and more variety is good. No one from this planet is going to show up on Earth and announce that, in fact, no moisture from the Sea of Fire is coming north to result in more rain. However, it's unlikely that a full forest would stand there. If you don't understand why, this book will change that.

Forests stand to the north of these mountain ranges, as there's no rain shadow; the Marula Mountains don't go that far north and therefore don't block moisture.

THE POWERS

On the left third of this map (and extending out of view) is Erizon, a sea-faring nation like the federal republic of Siara, on the northern coast. They are philosophically opposed and have competing navies with unrestricted access to the northern sea and a continent to the north. With the border between them short, most clashes are on water.

The remaining sovereign power in the image is the southern Pell Republic, which I decided has recently become a federal republic (in contrast with most other neighbors) like Siara. They became allies partly because Erizon threatens both from the west, launching wars on Anamaer Plain, a region filled with nomadic horse tribes. Caught in the middle, some of those tribes are allied to different powers, depending on who can benefit them. The landscape suggested these relationships, which is one reason to draw maps.

Pell Pass is how those of Pell and Siara meet and trade, but in the mountains to either side are unpleasant species and animals that attack any caravan or sign of life. Before Pell and Siara became allies, they contested Pell

Pass and guarded it with castles at either end, seen on the map. These are now where caravans prepare for the dangerous trip through. The War Peaks are named for the battles that have often raged on either side of them.

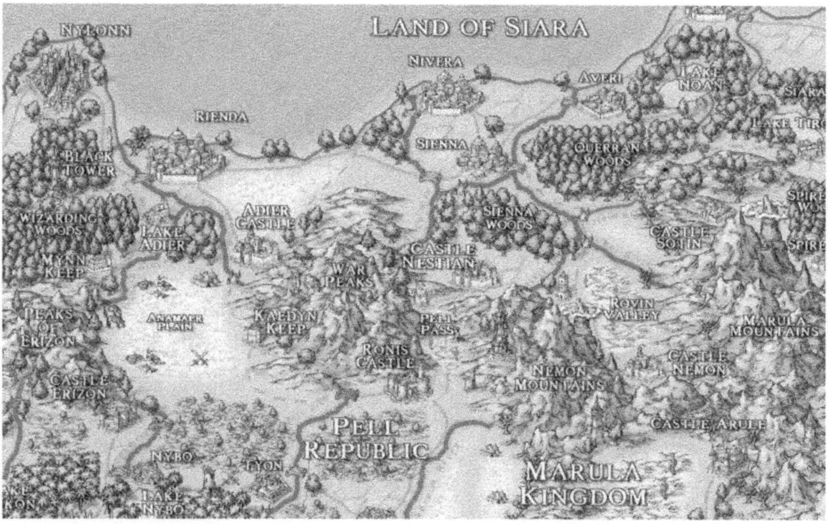

Figure 9 Impact of Mountains

The Pell Republic doesn't have the kinds of wood best for building ships and gets these materials from Siara, which has ships at Pell to access the Sea of Fire and lands beyond. This includes the Empire of Kysh, with whom Pell is on mostly good relations, partly because Kysh is also enemies with Erizon. Pell also has ships in Siara because it bought them from Siara.

The Kingdom of Marula to the southeast wants Pell's territory, including Pell Pass, partly to stop Pell and Siara from conspiring against it. Marula is at the heart of the slave trade and prefers those of Pell and Siara for slaves, increasing animosities.

CHAPTER TWO

CREATING A PLANET

There are global issues to consider in creating a planet, such as moons, climates, the sun, and the rest of the solar system. Unless we're planning something truly unique with these, like two suns or moons, we'll probably want to go with an Earth-like situation, which is the focus of this chapter.

However constant celestial bodies appear in our lifetimes, their relationships are always in flux. We can invent a scenario that isn't likely in a four-billion-year-old solar system, but which is possible in a two-billion-year-old one. The reason is that gravity slowly stabilizes relative positions. For example, gravity causes satellites to *eventually* orbit in the same plane. If we have them in two different planes, we're implying the solar system's youth. Either that, or one of those moons was recently captured by the planet and hasn't stabilized with it yet. By "recently," we're talking in billions of years, meaning this happened well before our species crawled out of the ocean.

This gives us leeway to invent a situation lasting long enough to tell our story, at the risk of eye-rolling by physicists. One goal of this chapter is to reduce such reactions and make reasonably informed decisions. Fortunately, physicists make up a relatively small percentage of Earth's inhabitants. Unfortunately, they make a higher percentage of science fiction readers!

Some ideas and terms apply to more than one section of this chapter. The alignment of three or more celestial bodies into a straight line is a called a syzygy. An eclipse is one type. Another type, called a conjunction, is when celestial bodies appear to be lined up from a low point in the sky to a higher one, as seen from another location (like Earth's surface). The term conjunction might be familiar to fantasy fans, as this has been used in stories, such as the films *The Dark Crystal* and *Pitch Black*, to indicate a rare aligning in the heavens, one that portends a great event. This is usually when some poor schlep is sacrificed, for example.

Appendix 1 is a template for creating a solar system and its planets, moons, and other satellites. It includes more comments and advice, and an editable Microsoft Word file can be downloaded for free by signing up for the newsletter at http://www.artofworldbuilding.com/newsletter.

ROTATION

Our planet is either rotating clockwise or counterclockwise. The Earth does the latter, which is why the sun rises in the east and sets in the west. We can reverse this for a quick way to thrust our audience into a different perspective. Of course, the stars, planets, and constellations will also travel across the sky in the opposite direction. Be aware that this affects ocean currents, covered later in this chapter. For world builders, this affect is largely that of which coast of a continent has warmer or colder waters. Prevailing winds will also be reversed in each hemisphere.

THE SUN'S IMPACT

Our lone sun is a yellow dwarf star of medium age. Most world builders, particularly in fantasy, will just want to go with the same and call their work done. More extreme situations might be better suited for worlds we'll only use for one story. In SF, with characters traveling across the cosmos to various planets, the viability of life in other suns' solar systems is debatable.

For example, a planet in the habitable zone of a red dwarf star would experience tidal locking (the planet's same side always faces the sun, just as one side of the Moon always faces Earth). This causes perpetual night on one side and perpetual day on the other. This sounds cool at first until we consider the huge temperature variations that would make Earth-like life difficult or impossible to form.

A moon orbiting such a red dwarf's planet could sustain life if it was also tidally locked to its planet, because that would cause the moon to not always have the same side face the sun. Even so, the lack of ultraviolet light also makes life unlikely, as does the variable energy output from the red dwarf (our sun is relatively stable). Maybe life can't originate there, but there's no reason we can't put a mining or research colony there. We can use such worlds but maybe not have much life originate there unless that life is extremely different from Earth's.

THE COMPLETE ART OF WORLD BUILDING | 199

THE MOON(S) IMPACT

Earth has a stable moon with no atmosphere, but other moons in both our solar system and beyond are volcanic, icy, or have toxic atmospheres. While our moon is relatively large in relation to the planet it orbits, and has a steady, close orbit, satellites orbiting other planets are often smaller, farther away, and have eccentric orbits. Most solar system objects orbit in the same direction, but some are backwards. This retrograde motion usually means a moon (or a planet) formed elsewhere and was captured by the planet (or sun). By contrast, a moon that formed when the planet did will orbit in the same direction. Large moons tend to match the direction while smaller ones can go either way.

TIDAL LOCKING

The term "tidal locking" will make many of us think of tides, but these are unrelated phenomenon. Our moon is tidally locked to the Earth. The same side is always facing us because the moon rotates on its axis in the same number of days it takes to orbit us. This might seem coincidental and unique, but most significant moons in our solar system are tidally locked to their planet; those nearest experience this first. Tidal locking is an eventual result caused by gravity. Early in a moon's orbiting, it might not be tidally locked, but ours may have become locked in as few as a hundred days (it's proximity and size having much to do with this). A moon that is not tidally locked may have recently formed or been captured by the planet. Either way, the stabilization process hasn't completed.

As world builders, we have some leeway to claim a satellite is locked or not. Most people are unfamiliar with the concept and we should only mention it if locking has occurred, as readers will assume the opposite without being told. Note that a close, large moon like ours will almost certainly be locked; during the brief period when ours was not, it and the Earth were molten and devoid of life.

Normally, only the satellite is locked to the planet, but they can become mutually tidally locked, as happened with Pluto and its moon, Charon. This means that each of them only sees one side of the other. If we stood on our moon, we'd see all sides of Earth as it rotates, but from Earth, we see only one side of the moon because they are not mutually tidally locked. If they were, the moon would stay in the exact same spot in the sky. About half the planet would see it, while the other half wouldn't even know it existed unless traveling to the far side of the world. This would eliminate most tides (see next section) except those caused by the sun.

We can create a planet that orbits the sun in the opposite direction from other planets, a fact which would likely be noticed. In a less technological setting, supernatural significance might be attributed to this. In SF, perhaps inhabitants of that planet realize it originated from another solar system and wonder what it's doing here. Where did they come from? We can also create a captured moon that orbits in a different direction than the planet or its other moons; these are typically farther away because gravity will eventually change that for nearer moons.

TIDES

Tides are variable. They are affected by coastline, currents, and other factors we can usually ignore as world builders and writers. But the moon is the greatest cause of tides, followed by the sun. If we want moons different from ours in number, proximity, or orbit, we should understand the moon's effect on tides. On Earth, tides can be so extreme that boats moored at high tide are sitting on the beach at low tide, which is one reason large vessels remain farther out and small boats are used to come ashore; such situations could be exaggerated with additional moons. Tidal forces are also causing our moon to get farther away, which would happen on any world we build (it if has oceans), but the rate is infinitesimal; still, a moon is unlikely to be getting nearer unless it's already very close. Gravity will pull it in and rip it apart. This can be a very real doomsday scenario for a world because the moon's debris will rain down on the planet's surface and cause destruction; the planet's tilt will also destabilize, affecting seasons and possibly causing dramatic and rapid-onset ice ages, for example (more on this in the next section).

Our moon causes high tide on the side of the Earth it faces because it is pulling the ocean away from the planet. The moon is also pulling the Earth that direction and away from the ocean on the opposite side, causing another high tide on the planet's far side. The Earth's other two sides experience low tide (see Figure 10).

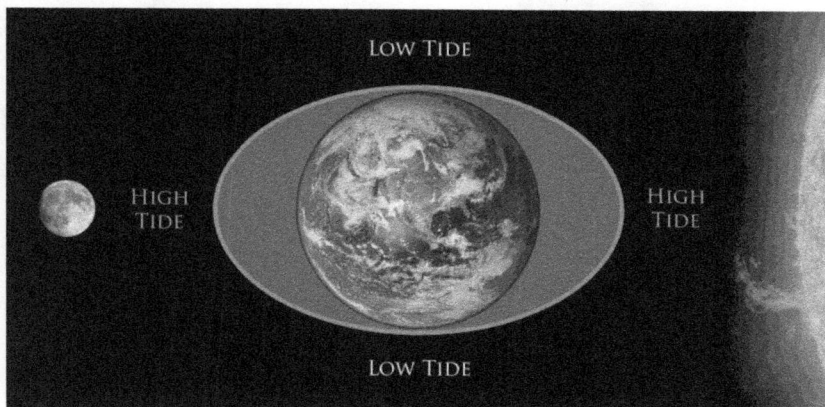

Figure 10 Tides

This causes two high tides and two low tides per day. Those two high tides aren't the same height, nor are the low. One reason is that the moon's orbit is not perfectly circular. If we invent a moon with a more elliptical orbit, the tide will be less pronounced when the moon is farther away. Imagine your characters being aware that such a moon is coming close in a week and they must get to higher ground or be flooded where they are, and that many settlements have taken this monthly flooding into consideration.

Among high tides, the highest tides are when the moon, sun, and Earth form a straight line, such as Moon-Earth-Sun. But the very highest tides are when moon and sun are on the same side, such as Earth-Moon-Sun (See Figure 11 below), because the gravity of both moon and sun are most strongly affecting the same side of the Earth. This is called a "spring tide" but has nothing to do with the season—it occurs twice a month, as does the corresponding lowest tides, called "neap tides." On a world of our invention, we might want to rename "spring tides" to avoid confusion.

A moon's diameter (apparent size) isn't particularly relevant for tides. Rather, mass and distance from the planet are the primary factors in tidal forces. Change either and we increase or decrease those forces and the resulting impact on a planet. More mass means more impact. More distance means less impact. Fortunately, our audience isn't expecting us to tell them the mass of a moon or how far away it is, especially as compared to Earth's, so we can usually ignore this, but we can at least know what we're ignoring.

We'll take a detailed look at how adding a second moon affects tides, as the observations can be expanded to additional moons and their impact. Using a clock face for orientation, with Earth at the center, what might the tides be like if the moons are:

• the same mass
• equidistant from the planet
• at 12 and 3 (to start) and never get materially closer or farther from each other while orbiting?

Picture Moon One's gravity pulling at the 12 and 6 positions (causing high tides there) while Moon Two's equal gravity does the same to 3 and 9 (causing high tides there, too). Would they balance each other's effect on the oceans, causing a constant water level (i.e., lack of tides)?

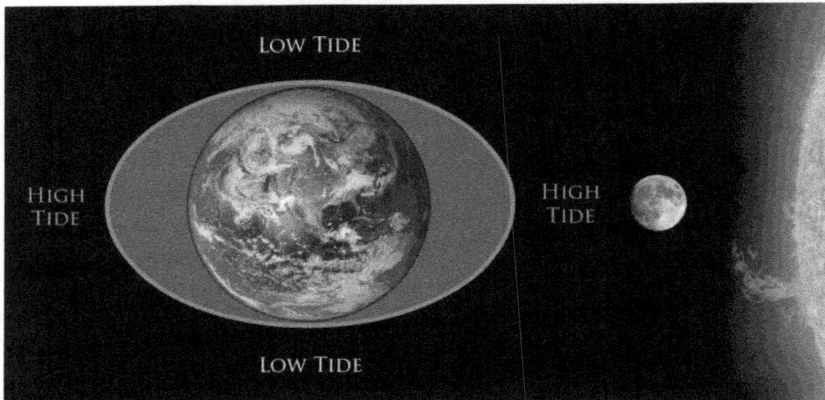

LOW TIDE

HIGH TIDE

HIGH TIDE

LOW TIDE

Figure 11 Highest Tides

Unless we're physicists, we can get ourselves into trouble with this kind of thinking, creating impossible situations. Is that's why it's called "science fiction?" Not really. SF is fiction which combines science that does not exist while hopefully getting right science that *does* exist. We have leeway to invent but should aim for believability.

Lack of tides isn't particularly useful, interesting, or likely (without mutual tidal locking; see previous section). The theoretical scenario above is a starting point for making observations that can help us make informed decisions. Altering that example, if two moons are at 12 and 6 and stay that way (always on a planet's opposite sides), we'd have more extreme tides. But if one moon had lower mass, it might have less impact on tides. This would also be true if one moon was farther away. Or had a more elliptical orbit.

Only distance, not mass, affects orbital speed. More distant satellites orbit slower, so two moons at different distances can't stay on the planet's opposite sides. Having two (or more) moons that are always in the night sky at fixed points to each other is unlikely. The nearer moon, moving faster, would appear to regularly catch and pass the farther moon. This will sometimes cause them to align in the sky. If they're orbiting in the same plane (and most moons of a planet do), this will cause at least a partial eclipse of the farther moon by the nearer. The degree of eclipse is determined by the relative size, not mass, of the moons. For a total eclipse, the nearer one must be large enough (as seen from the planet) to completely block the farther one as seen from the planet.

An elliptical orbit would also mean that a moon's effect on the world would ebb and flow depending on how far away it was; imagine it coming close once a month and causing a much stronger tide, and if this coincided with being on the same side as the other moon (and sun) every year, maybe we'd get a far stronger tide once a year.

If two moons are orbiting at different speeds (they do not stay at 12 and 6 in relation to each other), they can only do so at different distances from the planet. Otherwise they'd have crashed into each other, resulting in one merged moon and possibly a ring around the world from the impact's debris. The falling remnants would wreak havoc on life. If the moons are at different planes (but the same distance), they could theoretically survive, but gravity would eventually draw them into a collision because orbits stabilize to the same plane in time. This is a potential doomsday event for inhabitants.

When the two orbiting moons form a straight line with the planet, the tide would be more extreme. Otherwise, tides would be weaker.

In the most likely case of two moons orbiting in the same direction but at different speeds, at different distances, we could decide how long it takes for each of them to orbit the planet. We can just pick a number. Keep in mind that a number less than Earth's moon (which orbits in 27 days) means our invented moon is that much closer. A moon orbiting in 14 days is about half as close, when our moon is already very close. Anything that close will have a big effect on the planet, so unless we really want to emphasize the moon in some way, have the moon equidistant to or farther away than ours.

If our world has thirty days in a month, maybe we choose thirty days for one moon's orbit. Then decide how fast the other moon orbits. With this decided, we can then figure out how often they're on the same/opposite side of the planet. The formula is:

$$(P1 * P2) / (P2 - P1) = C$$

P1 is the period that the closer moon takes to orbit the planet. P2 is the farther moon's orbital period. C is the conjunction (when they're together), though this could be any two relative positions. Assigning P1 to 15 days and P2 to 30 days, we get this:

$$(15 * 30) / (30—15) = 30$$

Breaking it down, 15 times 30 is 450. This is divided by the result of 30 minus 15, which is 15. So 450 divided by 15 is 30. Every 30 days, the moons will be in conjunction (or any other configuration).

If you'd rather not do these calculations manually, the "Moon Orbit Calculator" Excel spreadsheet included with the free templates allows you to type in the number of days for two moons and get the answer. If we're after a certain result, we can keep changing the numbers until it produces an answer we like.

For example, on my world of Llurien, there are 28 days in every month (because there are 28 gods and each gets a day). I want the nearest moon to orbit in 28 days, heralding the start/end of each month. Three months is a season of 84 days. Each season, an arrangement of gods changes. I wanted a conjunction of moons to occur each time, adding increased significance to this seasonal event. That means a conjunction at 84-day intervals. So how long does it take for the second moon to orbit? I probably could've used math, but I just kept typing numbers into the spreadsheet until 42 for moon two's orbital period caused the conjunction field to say 84, my goal.

Knowing when two moons coincide can help us determine how often eclipses happen. It also tells us when the highest tides are. Sailors and port townsfolk will be aware of this. A water-dwelling humanoid species might be, as would animals, both on land and sea, possibly taking advantage of this during birthing, hatching, or forays ashore.

This exercise can be imagined with more than two moons, though you'll have figure out the formula for that. Effects on the planet start getting complicated unless we keep most of the moons farther away, give them less mass, and keep them in a mostly circular orbit. All of this reduces their impact so that we can include them, but concentrate on the influence of the one or two most influential moons have on tides.

What happens if there's no moon? Probably very little tide; the sun would cause some tides.

THE SEASONS

Our moon also causes the stability of the Earth's tilt. As the Earth orbits the sun, one pole tilts toward it and causes summer in that hemisphere, while the other faces away and experiences winter. Without a moon, Earth would wobble chaotically. Seasons would end, as would most life, especially plants that evolved in a specific climate and wouldn't survive rapidly changing ones that could last unpredictable lengths, from days to possibly centuries. Worse, this would destabilize the Earth's orbit around the sun and cause us to acquire an increasingly elliptical orbit, meaning Earth will alternatively roast and freeze in a year.

Earth tilts at 23.5 degrees and is a kind of Goldilocks tilt, just the right angle to allow life to flourish. More extreme tilts up to 90 degrees, or down to 0, would cause heat extremes at poles and the equator, making an Earth-like planet impossible. On a world that never had a stabilizing moon, life might still evolve but would be adapted to sudden, extreme, and potentially long-lasting weather changes.

HOURS IN THE DAY

Our moon also affects the rate at which both it and the Earth spin. Both are slowing due to tidal forces they exert on each other. They will eventually stop spinning altogether, except that the sun will become a red giant and vaporize both before then. The moon is also getting farther away. If the Earth spun faster, as it did billions of years ago, we'd have much shorter days. Therefore, if we want a plausible reason that our invented world has very short days, no moons is one solution. Either that, or any moons are too distant to influence the planet in this way. Both scenarios inhibit life, however, so it might be best to decide that the planet is relatively young and still has a stabilizing moon. We don't need to ever tell our audience this, but if we wanted a character to remark that the planet was 4 billion years old and only has 12-hour days, this doesn't make sense unless the moon was captured (not formed) recently, as in a few million years ago.

MOONLIGHT

Since our moon is barren, it reflects the sun's light down on the planet as moonlight. If we create a habitable moon covered in water, earth (much of it forested), and the moon's atmosphere, it would absorb rather than reflect sunlight. The result would be far less moonlight. We should consider this when deciding that our nearest moon is habitable or covered in thick, dark atmosphere or a non-reflective surface. A secondary, farther moon might cast some light, but the effect will be reduced.

OTHER PLANETS IN THE SOLAR SYSTEM

Our invented planet is unlikely to be the only one orbiting its sun. This section discusses others within a solar system.

In SF, interstellar travel is virtually a given, whether that's within a solar system or between systems and galaxies. In fantasy, other planets are seldom mentioned unless there's an event of some significance like a conjunction of moons, stars, the sun, and planets. This might be an oversight, for magic or other supernatural means could allow characters to move between worlds (and moons). If a magic portal can get people from one place to another, the difference between traversing two sides of a planet and between two planets might be negligible for all we know. It could take tremendous power from a wizard or we can decide the ability has become commonplace. Perhaps magical doorways have been created, the magic imbued within them so that ordinary people can use them, just like a technology. We could similarly have magic-powered spacecraft.

When inventing other planets in a system, we should have rocky planets like Mercury, Venus, Earth, and Mars closer to the sun, and gas giants farther away; temperatures are too high for gas planets to form close to the sun. Saturn isn't the only planet in our system that has rings; they are just more pronounced, so don't be afraid to do this.

There's a habitable zone that's not too far from or too close to the sun, where Earth-like life can develop. Only so many planets can fit within this zone, limiting the number of habitable planets. With a yellow star like ours, this is two to three planets. With a red dwarf sun, scientists concluded that a maximum of five could occur, and closer to the sun, because a red star is cooler. With trillions, not billions, of years for life to develop, life might flourish on more than one world. Life would likely be quite different from Earth, however. Decide if you need more than one habitable world.

Determine how many planets are in your solar system, their names, order, type (rock, gas, ice), and impact, if any, on your world. Some will be visible to the naked eye, though this depends partly on luminosity, a measure of reflectivity of the sun's light. These planets can be mentioned for added realism, making our main world seem less like an island. Planets are rarely visible; significance is often added to their appearance, particularly in less advanced worlds.

STARS ABOVE

While many stars are visible in the night sky, only the brightest are likely to receive enough attention to be named. Names could be given by sailors or anyone else who watches the heavens. These stars are given significance, often heralding an important event, mostly because they were in the sky when something happened. Stars and constellations are not visible all year, for as the planet orbits, the stars overhead change. The same stars will appear each spring, for example. This is also apparent with constellations.

CONSTELLATIONS

Constellations are an area of world building that can be avoided until we need it. A constellation is a group of stars that suggest an outline of a person or object. They are often attributed mythological significance. In a fantasy setting, people may still believe in such things. In a SF setting, the beliefs may no longer be held true but the constellations may still be recognized. The visible constellations change with the season due to a planet's orbit around its sun.

Creating constellations that matter to our characters can be done quickly. If we've invented gods or other world figures, like those discussed in *Creating Life (The Art of World Building, #1)*, we can use them here. Deities, or objects they possess, such as Thor's hammer, might be associated with a constellation. Mundane items might also be constellations, like our Big Dipper. People see familiarity and therefore comfort in the stars, and we have great freedom to do as we like.

We should decide which constellations are near each other. This can be done without explanation, as apparent groups of stars have no actual relationship. More important is whether each constellation is near the equator or not. If so, then people in either hemisphere can see it, though it will appear upside down to half the world. Any constellation closer to a pole is only visible to people in that hemisphere. For example, on Earth, most people in the northern hemisphere can't see the "southern cross" due to its location in the southern sky. This would be a poor location for a constellation we want everyone to see.

Figure 12 Constellations

If we want each of our gods to have a constellation, we might choose to place all the constellations at the equator so that the whole world can see them. Those living near the poles won't see all of each constellation, but they're a minority and we can resolve that concern for most inhabitants, if it matters to us to do so. We might choose to have a god's constellation only visible in the far north, however, if we want a stronghold of worshippers there and not in the south. What if all evil gods were north and all the good ones south?

If we have a winter god and their constellation is just north of the equator in winter, that makes sense for those inhabitants in the northern hemisphere, but those in the south will see that "winter" god's constellation in their summer. There is no solution for this unless we decide the god has no constellation or two, one near each pole, where each constellation would never be visible to those in the other hemisphere. The same formation of stars is unlikely, so one symbol might a trident while the other is a fish.

DARK CONSTELLATIONS

There are also dark constellations (such as the "Emu in the Sky"), which are mostly in the southern hemisphere on Earth and may be unfamiliar to some readers. Clouds of interstellar gas cause these apparent shapes, reminiscent of seeing familiar shapes in rain clouds. They appear dark because they're so dense as to block light from reaching us. This could be an interesting alternative for the constellations of evil gods. Good gods are light constellations. Evil gods are dark ones.

Figure 13 Dark Constellatio3ns

PASSING ASTEROIDS AND COMETS

Since the primary difference between asteroids and comets is composition, we can treat them similarly, with the caveat that the ice in comets causes their familiar tail. Our interest here is in those that come near our invented world and whether to invent ones that fly by at regular intervals.

Our world's inhabitants can see significance in them, inventing myths or imagining doomsday scenarios (which might be accurate). Combining a comet with a conjunction might foretell a particularly influential event.

UNDERSTANDING CLIMATES

While many factors affect life on our planet on the global level, climate is among the most important and has several world-wide aspects to it.

THE EQUATOR'S ROLE

The equator is an imaginary line equidistant from both poles. Days and nights there do not vary in length; this changes the farther from the equator we go. It's perpetually hot except at high altitudes. The four seasons of spring, summer, autumn, and winter hardly exist. Instead, residents think of a dry season and a wet one, which averages two hundred days a year on Earth; some places are uniformly wet all year.

If we're writing SF, the equator is a good place for space ports because the planet is spinning faster there and less fuel is needed to escape the atmosphere, though if we have imaginary propulsion systems, maybe fuel isn't an issue. On Earth, spacecraft must launch easterly to take advantage of this spin. Imagine a scenario where one nation has limited fuel and wants to launch easterly, but the spacecraft must then go over an enemy nation capable of shooting it down. This illustrates how research affects a story.

When drawing a continent, we should decide where it lies in relation to the equator. Position impacts climate and the direction of prevailing winds, which carry moisture that is either blocked by mountain ranges or not; see the section on "rain shadows." The location of deserts and forests (and what kind) are a direct result of this. The significance of position will be demonstrated by the rest of this chapter.

THE OCEAN'S ROLE

Ocean currents play a major role in climate. Oceans absorb more of the sun's radiation than the atmosphere, retaining and then distributing heat as the water flows around the planet. This effect is assisted by Earth's rotation, salinity, and tides (which are affected by the moon). If we have a world without significant oceans, this occurs less and the heat will be concentrated at the equator, leaving the poles more frigid. We can use this to create greater extremes between regions. For Earth-like worlds, we could ignore the ocean's role unless we'd like to leverage it, but the effect on our work will be subtle and might not be worth the effort to some world builders.

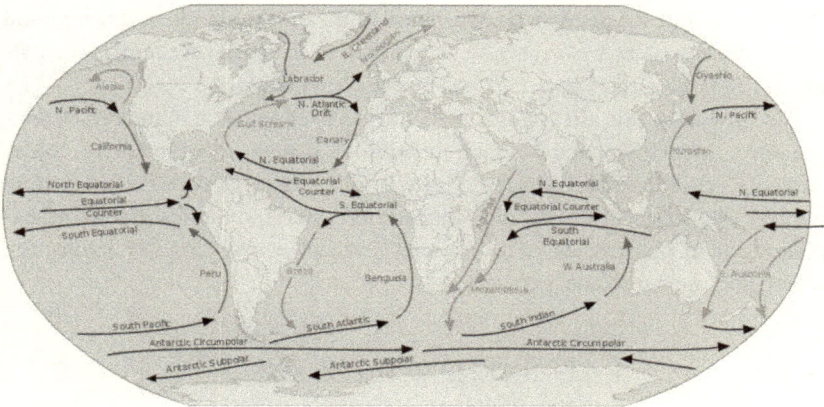

Figure 14 Ocean Currents on Earth

For example, we could invent animals, plants, or species that are found on one coast but not another. Why? Because it happens on Earth. The Gulf Stream that runs along the eastern United States pulls warm water up the coast. The opposite happens on the western coast, where polar water comes south, resulting in much colder waters there. Most seal types prefer colder water and are found west but not east. This is turn means predators like great white sharks are also concentrated where the food is.

If we do this on our invented world, we could have someone from the west coast express disbelief that those around him are about to enter the water on the east coast. Aren't they afraid to get eaten by a sea creature we've invented? They'd likely wonder what he's talking about, as they don't exist there. This depends on technological level, as the population of a more modern world like ours is more likely to be aware of differences even if not understanding the reason. In other words, this is arguably more likely in fantasy than in SF.

How do we determine where this might happen? According to NOAA (National Oceanic and Atmospheric Administration), "Major current systems typically flow clockwise in the northern hemisphere and counterclockwise in the southern hemisphere, in circular patterns that often trace the coastlines." This means that a current is either carrying cold water from the pole toward the equator, or warm water from the equator toward the pole. On Earth, the western coasts are typically colder than the eastern ones. The online, color version of the above picture makes the difference in coastal temperatures easier to see, as the blue arrows are for cold water and are red for warm.

The details of this will depend on how many continents we have and their shape, but we needn't go overboard and can just decide eastern coastal waters are warmer. A caveat here is that this all depends on the planet rotating in the same direction as Earth. If not, just reverse this.

So how does this affect climate? Warm coastal waters can moderate temperatures in one northern region relative to others, or conversely colder currents cause harsher winters. For example, parts of Norway have mild winters due to the Gulf Stream. We can note this in our files, but avoid explaining it in our stories, as explaining research we've done is among the worst, and most obvious, exposition errors.

UNDERSTANDING ZONES

The zones on a planet impact climate and will be discussed below. They are summarized in this chart:

Climate Zone	Latitude
Tropics	The equator (0)—23.5°
Subtropics	23.5°—40°
Temperate	40°—66°
Polar	66°—the poles

Figure 15 Earth's Climate Zones

The exact latitude where a climate changes is not constant, as it can vary from continent to continent, so these numbers are generalizations and world builders can avoid worrying about getting it right. Besides, we're inventing a planet. Who can argue with us?

THE TROPICS

Extending north and south from the equator to roughly 23.5° latitude is a region called the tropics. This area is not defined by latitude but by the point at which the sun appears to be directly overhead at its highest point in the day, which is affected by the planet's axial tilt. Since our imaginary planet can have a different axis than Earth's, and therefore a different tropical zone, we can invent the area that is our tropical zone. Most of us will want to assume 23.5°, never mention this, and be done.

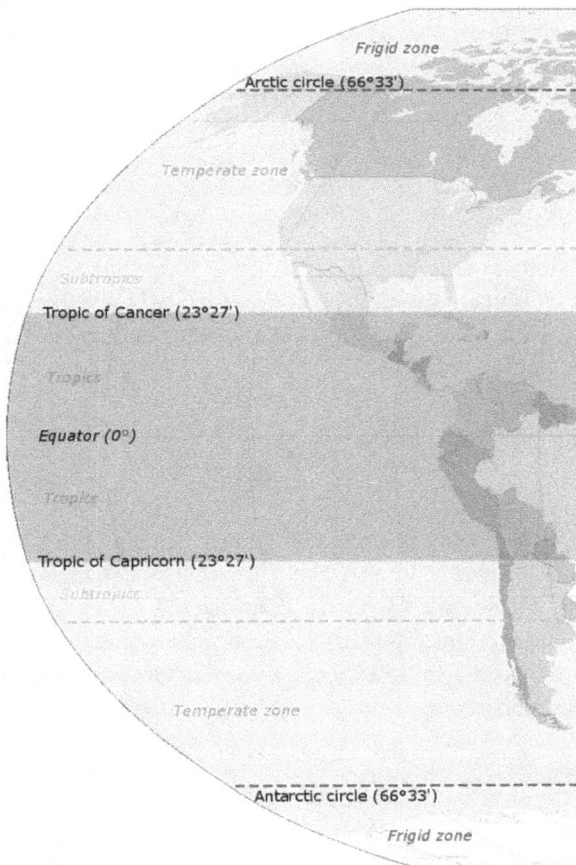

Figure 16 The Americas: Climate Zones

On Earth, the northern tropic is called the Tropic of Cancer while the southern is the Tropic of Capricorn. We'll want different names for ours. To make life easier on readers, it might be best to name a tropic after a prominent city located at 23.5°, though doing so requires having drawn latitude lines on a map. Or we can wing it. Stating that a map is not drawn to scale gives us some leeway to be inaccurate. Even on Earth, most people have no idea which tropic is which, where they end, or why they should care. Our readers won't remember either unless we name the tropics by something they're more likely to remember, like a prominent city or a kingdom in that tropical zone. The latter frees us from an exact location.

The tropics move heat from the equator toward the poles and are the primary influencer of climates on every continent. Ocean temperatures and mountain ranges further modify climate. A high-altitude area in a tropic zone might have a climate more like a temperate zone.

SUBTROPICS

The subtropics are the next farthest region from the equator, from 23.5° to 40°. On Earth, many deserts are in this zone, which seldom sees a hard frost or snow, but tropical storms and hurricanes can deliver as much as half of a country's rainfall.

TEMPERATE ZONES

In between the polar and subtropical zones, from 40° to 66° is the temperate zone, where most life on Earth exists. Coastal regions experience milder winters and summers than areas far inland, which experience a greater range in temperatures. Similarly, high altitude areas in this zone might have a climate more like a polar zone. The areas closest to the poles can be considered sub-temperate.

POLAR ZONES

The polar zones cover the north and south poles to 66° latitude and are largely covered in polar ice caps. There isn't much we need to worry about that isn't obvious. It's only mentioned to contrast it with the other zones.

PREVAILING WINDS

Wind direction varies at different latitudes (distances from the equator). These winds, along with geography like mountains, will determine where rain falls. This affects both climate and where vegetation and deserts are. Understanding this helps world builders create sensible topography.

If our planet is tidally locked to the sun, it won't rotate, one side burning and the other freezing. This extreme is not covered by this book, so we will assume our planet is rotating. On Earth, this rotation causes winds near the equator to travel east in the tropics, while winds in the temperate zones travel west. In the polar zones, winds are again eastward but are light. Technically, the westerly winds are not entirely westerly, as they move from near the equator toward the poles. Similarly, the easterly trade winds move toward the equator, not just easterly. Our invented planet can be rotating in the other direction, reversing these winds.

Figure 17 Prevailing Winds

A continent situated in the northern hemisphere like the United States or Europe will have westerly prevailing winds, which are called the westerlies for that reason. The easterly winds are called trade winds; sailors used them to cross the world's oceans, expanding trade. Ships benefit from sailing in the direction of the wind (prior to the invention of engines). We can call these winds what we want in our world, but it may only come up in the context of ship-oriented stories.

In areas with light winds, factors such as mountains, valley breezes, or the difference in air pressure between sea and land breezes affect wind patterns. These are local phenomenon and not something to consider when creating land features.

RAIN SHADOWS

Mountains cause moisture-carrying winds to rise. The clouds dump all the rain on one side of the mountain range, causing lush vegetation. On the mountain range's other side, there's no water left to fall. This causes a "rain shadow," an area that receives little to no rainfall. Deserts are the usual result. This process plays out across the Earth. A large list of examples can be found here: http://www.artofworldbuilding.com/rainshadow.

Rain shadows often occur near a coast and can cover half a continent, such as in the United States. Desert-like conditions occur closest to the mountains, though this is less severe farther from the mountains that are causing the rain shadow, partly because moisture doesn't come exclusively from the oceans and will be picked up in the atmosphere to fall as rain (albeit less of it). As we progress farther from the mountains, desert may give way to grasslands and finally forests.

THE CLIMATES

Climate impacts all life and is important for understanding how much rainfall occurs in various areas and the resulting vegetation, or lack thereof. It's an easy way to distinguish one location from another in stories. A humid region will impact the style of clothes and even customs of inhabitants. Maybe it's so hot and humid in midday that people work in the morning and late afternoon but take a long noon break. Those in northern climates might make the most of noon heat.

Climate is a long-term weather pattern, rather than day to day changes. Many factors influence climate and can be daunting to consider. Terrain, altitude, nearby bodies of water and their current, and latitude (distance from the equator) all impact climate. The ratio of land to water, how distant that water is, and the location of mountain ranges also have an impact. Another factor is the density and type of vegetation, which increase heat retention and rainfall. How far inland we are also changes things.

These variables cause the changes in rainfall amounts, temperature, and humidity. This might seem trivial, but areas can be well known for their climate. Examples include India's monsoon season, the humidity of the southeastern United States, and the dryness of the southwestern United States. As the latter two demonstrate, we can't rely on latitude to explain climate, as both areas are equidistant from the equator but one is hot and dry and the other is hot and wet. The prevailing winds and rain shadows from mountain ranges will be partly responsible for where forests and deserts lie.

There are different climate rating systems, but the Köppen climate classification is the one we're familiar with (even if we've never heard of it) because it has terms like subtropical and rainforest, so we'll use that one. In this system, climates are divided into five main groups, each with subtypes or subgroups. Much of the information in this section comes from Wikipedia's Köppen Classification Summary at:

http://www.artofworldbuilding.com/Koppen.

Africa map of Köppen climate classification

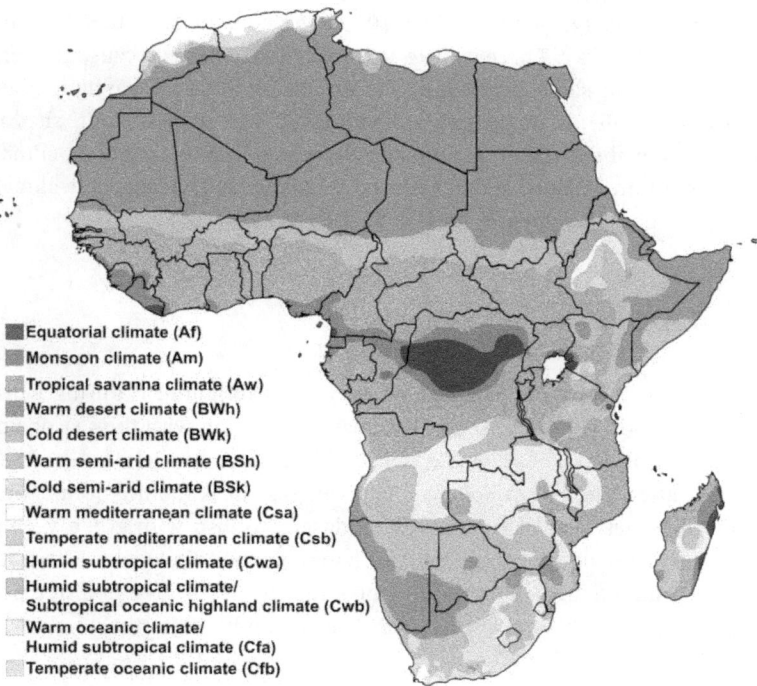

Figure 18 Köppen Classification Map, Africa

Some excellent color images online can give a quick peek into just how variable climate is on even one continent. One is below, but the rest of Earth can be viewed online at this link:

http://www.artofworldbuilding.com/KoppenMap

TROPICAL

Located in the tropics (nearest the equator), tropical climates have year-round high temperatures at low elevations, and average temperatures of 18° C (64° F) or higher. Of the three listed, we'll most often use the tropical rainforest climate, as the differences between the others are too subtle to matter to us; they amount to less uniform rainfall throughout the year.

TROPICAL RAINFOREST

In this climate, each month has average rainfall of 60 mm (2.4 in), and this climate is usually found within 5-10° of the equator but can sometimes extend up to 25° away. There is little seasonal change here, because the temperatures stay the same year-round, as do the number of daylight hours (changes are small). Many places are uniformly wet unless a rain shadow causes less rain there. Land at a higher altitude will have a milder climate and, due to a rain shadow, might even be relatively dry. Assign this climate to most areas near the equator, such as Brazil and Peru.

TROPICAL MONSOON

This climate is rare enough that we may want to ignore it during world building. Monsoon winds are those that change direction with the season and last several months. These winds cause this climate, which has a driest month just after the winter solstice. The wet season is months long. Some areas alternate between being arid, like a desert, to lush with green vegetation in the wet season, the stark contrast happening within weeks. The trade winds can bring enough moisture to cause rain in the winter months, preventing an area from having our next climate. Miami has this climate.

TROPICAL WET/DRY OR SAVANNAH

This climate has a more pronounced dry season of very little rain and is usually in the outer edges of the tropical region, farther from the equator. Some of the wettest places on Earth have this climate, with incredible rainfalls during the wet season, sometimes in a single day. Examples include areas of Africa, Brazil, and India.

DRY

Dry climates produce less than ten inches of rain a year. Some areas may receive more but lose it all due to evaporation. These desert climates can be hot, cold, or mild and are generally low in humidity.

The hot deserts have perpetually sunny, clear skies year-round and extremely high temperatures, though these can drop to freezing at night due to the same clear skies that permit heat dissipation. They are almost always in the tropics. Assign this climate to tropical deserts.

The cold deserts have similar hot summers, but the winter can be far below freezing. They occur at higher altitudes, are drier, and are in temperate zones (north of the tropics in the northern hemisphere, south of them in the southern). They are also usually in the rain shadow of a mountain range.

The mild desert climates are mild throughout the year and are usually found along the western edges of continents or at high altitudes (plateaus or steppe deserts). They are caused by cold ocean currents offshore. Deserts by the coast often have fog and low clouds.

TEMPERATE

Temperate climates are where most of Earth's population lives, though that's partly because much of our land is there. These climates have an average monthly temperature above 10° C (50° F) in their warmest months and an average monthly temperature above –3° C (27° F) in their coldest months. Some have dry winters, dry summers, or significant precipitation throughout the year.

There are several versions of temperate climates, discussed next.

DRY SUMMER

Dry summer climates, also known as a Mediterranean climate on Earth, usually occur on the western sides of continents between the latitudes of 30° and 50°. Summers are hot and dry except in coastal areas, where summers are milder due to nearby cold ocean currents that may bring fog but prevent rain. Winters are mild with rainy weather. Most rain is during winter, hence the name "dry summer." This climate is found around the Mediterranean and much of California.

WARM TEMPERATE

Warm temperate climates usually occur on the eastern coasts and sides of continents, from 25° to 45° latitude, such as the southeastern United States. Moisture from the tropics causes air to be warm and wet. More rainfall occurs in summer than in winter. The air flow out of the tropics brings warm, moist air to the southeast of continents. This flow is often what brings the frequent but short-lived summer thundershowers typical of subtropical east-coast climates.

MARITIME TEMPERATE/OCEANIC

These climates usually occur on the western sides of continents between the latitudes of 45° and 60° and immediately poleward of dry summer climates (such as north of them in the northern hemisphere). This includes the Pacific Northwest and New Zealand. They have changeable, often overcast weather. Summers are cool due to cool ocean currents, but winters are milder than other climates in similar latitudes, and very cloudy. This climate can also be found at higher elevations in latitudes that would otherwise be subtropical or temperate. These high-altitude climates are called oceanic even if they're not near an ocean.

TEMPERATE HIGHLAND TROPICAL WITH DRY WINTERS

This is characteristic of the highlands in the tropics. Winters are dry, unlike other tropical areas. Summers can be very rainy.

MARITIME SUBARCTIC OR SUBPOLAR OCEANIC

These climates occur poleward of the maritime temperate climates, such as Iceland. They happen on narrow coastal strips of land on the western poleward margins of the continents or to islands off such coasts. There is very little precipitation and temperature variations are extreme between winter, at -40° C (-40° F), and summer, up to 30° C (86° F). The ground is frozen in winter to depths of several feet.

DRY SUMMER MARITIME SUBALPINE

This climate is very rare and only exists at very high elevations where the ocean influence keeps the temperature from going below -3 C° (26° F). As a world builder, we can largely ignore this unless we need it.

HUMID CONTINENTAL

These climates have an average temperature above 10° C (50° F) in their warmest months, and a coldest month average below −3° C (−26° F). These usually occur in the interiors of continents and on their east coasts, normally poleward of 40°. Precipitation (with thunderstorms) is evenly distributed throughout the year, snow cover often being deep. Summers are warm to hot, and often humid. Winters are cold, sometimes severely. Forests thrive in this climate, including evergreen and conifers, as do grasslands. Oak, fir, spruce, and pine do well in wetter areas and the fall foliage is noteworthy.

From a world building standpoint, the subtypes offer little in the way of things we need to consider. That a summer is hot in one latitude vs warm in another is of little importance, but they are mentioned for reference.

HOT SUMMER CONTINENTAL

This usually occurs in the high 40° and low 50° latitudes, with an average temperature in the warmest month of greater than 22° C/72° F. This includes southeast Canada, some parts of the western United States (such as Utah, Montana, and Wyoming), and Serbia.

WARM SUMMER CONTINENTAL

This climate is immediately north of hot summer continental climates, generally between 45° and 58° latitude in North America and Asia, and in central and eastern Europe and Russia, between the maritime temperate and continental subarctic climates, where it extends up to 65° latitude.

CONTINENTAL SUBARCTIC

Climates occur poleward of the other continental climates, mostly in the 50° and low 60° latitude, although it might occur as far as 70°.

CONTINENTAL SUBARCTIC CLIMATES WITH EXTREMELY SEVERE WINTERS

Places with this climate have the temperature in their coldest month lower than −38° C (−36° F). These climates occur only in eastern Siberia. The names of some of the places with this climate have become veritable synonyms for extreme, severe winter.

POLAR

Polar and alpine climates are characterized by average temperatures below 10° C (50° F) in all months. The tundra climate has a warmest month of between 0 and 10° C. It occurs on the northern edges of Earth's land masses, in the north hemisphere. The ice cap climate is perpetually below 0° C and occurs at the poles and on extremely high mountains.

CLIMATE CHART

Highlights from the previous sections have been summarized in the chart below and are ordered the same, from the equator toward the poles:

Climate		Summary
Tropical	Rainforest	5-10° from equator, no seasons, steady temperatures, hours constant, uniformly wet
	Monsoon	Wet season of several months, otherwise dry, rare climate
	Wet/Dry or Savannah	Very little rain, outer edge of tropical region far from equator
Dry	Dry	**Hot deserts:** year-round sunny, clear, very hot (frigid nights), found in tropical region **Cold deserts:** similar summers but drier, brutal cold in winter, found in rain shadows/high altitudes and temperate zones **Mild deserts:** year-round mild, found in high plateaus and western edges of continents, prone to fog/low clouds if coastal
Temperate	Dry Summer	30-50°, western side of continents, hot/dry summer but milder on the coasts due to fog, mild winter with rain
	Warm	25-45°, eastern side of continents, warm/wet air, more rain in summer, frequent short summer thunderstorms
	Maritime/ Oceanic	45-60°, western side of continents, cool summers, mild cloudy winters
	Highland/ Dry Winter	Found in tropics at high altitude, dry winters, very rainy summers
	Maritime Subarctic	Found poleward of maritime/oceanic on narrow coastal strips/islands on western side of continents. Very little rain, ground frozen several feet in winter, temps from -40° F to 86° F
	Dry Summer Maritime	Rare, very high elevations
Humid Continental	All	40° latitude and above, found in continent interiors and east coasts, rain all year, warm to hot summers (often humid), cold winter

Climate		Summary
		(sometimes very). The four variants are all similar.
Polar	Polar	Average -10° C all year

Figure 19 Climate Chart

WHERE TO START

If we're using a sun unlike Earth's yellow star, we'll need to start there because this impacts much about our world, but otherwise little is dependent on another subject from a world building standpoint. Our biggest decision beside sun type is whether our world has a moon and how many. It's recommended to have at least one unless we're certain of what we're doing without one, because the absence of a moon will cause more changes than we might be aware of. The world's going to have an equator, prevailing winds, climates, constellations visible, and possibly other planets in the system, but none of these affect us until we start creating continents. Enjoy the rare privilege to embark on a world building subject in whichever order pleases you.

CHAPTER THREE

CREATING A CONTINENT

Despite the term "world building," we usually build far less than that in detail. Fantasy tends to utilize one continent. SF will typically use multiple planets, but on each, a single location (like a city) is used. Chapter Six, "Creating a Settlement," covers the invention of single cities, so this chapter discusses inventing a continent, even if we'll only use portions of it in detail. Multiples continents can be created following the advice herein. It's also possible to create a single, large supercontinent, like Pangaea or Gondwana.

We don't need to invent every region of our continent, but some basic thought should still be given to areas we won't utilize as much. It adds depth to our work to say that a product, like wine or furniture, came from a certain region. We can invent that on the fly instead of planning it, but there's more to life than products. Different sovereign powers will exist and have histories with each other. Allies and enemies flourish. Grievances are to be nurtured. Stereotypes, racism, and ethnic hatreds blossom. We can do all this and more by laying out a continent so we know where these people in conflict live. It's crucial for any story involving travel, like a quest, which typically involves a journey through hostile places; otherwise, any schlep could go get the quest token.

MULTIPLE CONTINENTS

We don't have to invent more than one continent, but to make our main one seem less like an island, we can name other continents and decide what they're famous for. We might never use them. But then maybe people on our main continent know of another where people are free, and those in an oppressed kingdom dream of going there. Travelers from faraway lands will eventually reach our shores. Why not have some ideas on where they originated?

Creating multiple continents doesn't necessarily mean laying out each in detail. Here's a simple process we can follow to get started for one:

1) Draw a rough shape on paper
2) Decide where the land mass lies in relation to the equator and where it is in relation to the others
3) Give the continent a name
4) Carve it up into sovereign powers
5) Add names to those powers
6) Decide what each power's like (Ch 5, "Creating a Sovereign Power.")

That can be it for now, or maybe we'll go one step further and decide on some reputations for the entire continent or various regions in it. Think about the Earth and what intrigues us about a place, then create such a one somewhere. We might want to save the best ideas for our main continent, but some things will be true of multiple places, like naval powers. There's usually at least one per continent. We can ask ourselves some questions for inspiration:

• Is there a kingdom known as a naval superpower, whose ships and raiders will reach our main continent's shores?
• Is there a slave trade somewhere?
• Huge rainforests?
• Impenetrable mountains?
• Vast deserts?
• Exotic animals?
• A spice trade? Or trade in something of our invention, like supernatural or technological elements?

WHICH HEMISPHERE?

The differences between a planet's northern and southern hemispheres is trivial but has consequences. What matters most is where our continent lies in relation to the equator. The reasons this is important are laid out in Chapter 2, "Creating a Planet," but amount to determining climate. We can draw mountain ranges without having decided this, but no desert, grassland, or forest should be placed without this decision. The combination of prevailing winds, which are solely determined by latitude, and mountains will influence the location of vegetation, as discussed Chapter 2 under "Rain Shadows."

Those who travel between hemispheres will note that any moons look upside down. So will constellations. Moon phases are also reversed, which can matter if we're planning to do something like supernatural spells that depend upon the moon's phase. An old game called *Ultima IV* had moon powered portals that only operated at certain moon phases, but the continent spanned only one hemisphere, presumably.

SEASONAL ISSUES

Those world builders who are used to living in one hemisphere might need to remind themselves, when creating a continent in the other hemisphere, that cold regions are not north/south but poleward. The seasons are also reversed; when it's winter in the north, it's summer in the south. This matters more during storytelling, but it also impacts constellations, as noted in the previous chapter. It can impact our calendar if we're not careful; this is discussed in Chapter 10, "Creating Time and History."

UNDERSTANDING PLATE TECTONICS

Understanding plate tectonics will help us add mountain ranges that make sense. A planet surface is composed of an outermost shell of slowly moving plates, which either converge on each other, diverge, or transform. The first two are the motions that create mountains ranges and volcanoes. Most volcanoes occur where two plate boundaries intersect, but some volcanoes exist in the middle of plates due to flaws in the plates; this means we can have a volcano anywhere on our map and no one can tell us otherwise.

There's a reason the western United States has major earthquakes and volcanoes and the eastern doesn't. The continental shelf is the area of land that's underwater just offshore. It is shallow compared to the deeper ocean. On the east coast, the shelf is wide, which means the plate boundary is also far away. By contrast, the west coast's shelf is narrow, ending just offshore. This means the deep ocean isn't far away. More importantly, the plate boundary is near the west coast, causing dramatic boundary activity that results in mountains and volcanoes.

Such a situation is true on other continents and is something to consider. If we say that deep water lies just off the coast of a continent, there are probably nearby mountains, some volcanic. We can also approach that in reverse: a coastal mountain range likely has deep water not far from shore. Ship wrecks there will be far under the waves. If we have a water-dwelling, humanoid species, or even sea monsters, they might be found here. Using the U.S. as an example, a giant sea monster is more likely to be encountered near the west coast than the east.

CONVERGENT BOUNDARIES

When two plates converge, one destroying the other's edge, the results can be varied.

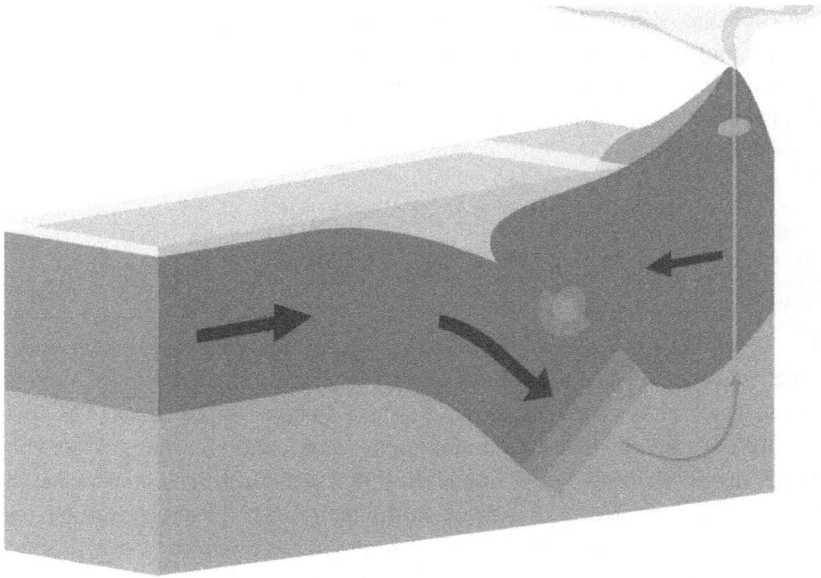

Figure 20 Ocean to Continent Boundary

If subduction, in which one plate is forced under another, happens at an ocean-to-continent boundary, the ocean plate plunges under the continent, causing a continental mountain range. This range will be parallel to the coast (plates), with volcanoes that are the most explosive.

If subduction happens with two ocean plates, one goes under and causes a chain of volcanoes, which will eventually breach the ocean surface and become land. These volcanic islands will form a subtle arc shape in relation to each other because a planet is a sphere. A deep ocean trench will also form. This can be over two miles below the rest of the ocean floor there. It can also be a hundred miles away. If we have a sea monster we'd like to give a home to, here is where it lives. In a world with sea monsters, a place like Hawaii would be prone to at least one creature; it almost doesn't make sense for one not to be there.

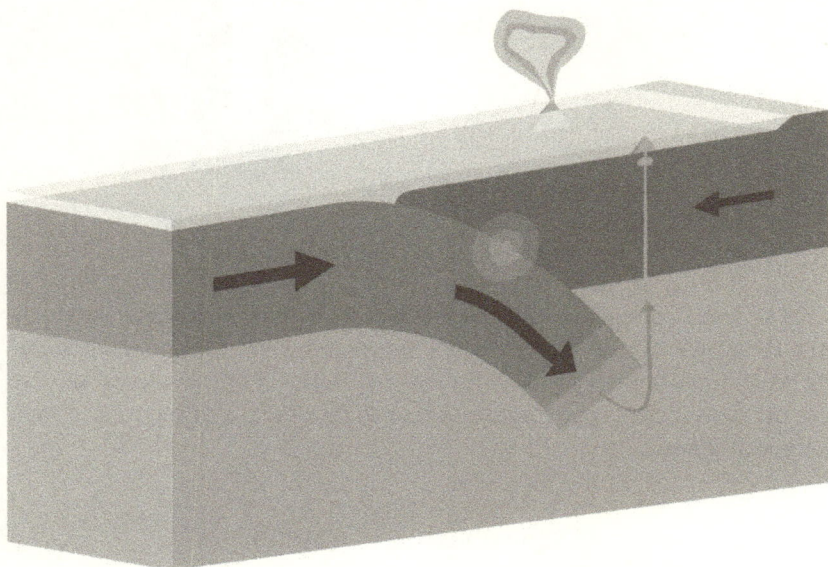

Figure 21 Ocean to Ocean Boundary

At a continent-to-continent boundary (shown next), the plates can converge, fold, and lift, forming very tall mountain ranges with no volcanoes. These will be the tallest ranges, located in the interior of continents.

DIVERGENT BOUNDARIES

When two plates move away from each other underwater, small volcanoes form, which can result in volcanic islands. When this happens on land, a low area of land can form and then fill with ocean water to create a sea.

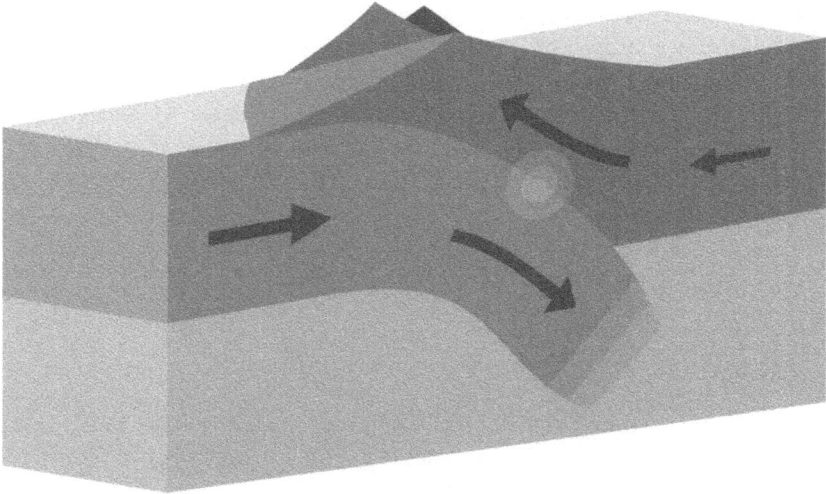

Figure 22 Continent to Continent Boundary

The Earth continents were once a super continent that broke apart. Divergent plates caused this. Evidence is apparent just from looking at the globe, as South America and Africa look like adjacent puzzle pieces. We can use the same idea for our continents, a small detail that may impress an audience if they notice.

TRANSFORM BOUNDARIES

Transform boundaries means two plates grind past each other without destroying either. These plates sometimes slip suddenly, causing strong earthquakes. Aside from this, evidence of their existence is less obvious. There are no mountains or volcanoes. If a paved road is broken, one stretch having moved ten feet away, this means the roads spanned the fault, an earthquake happened, and now the road will never connect unless repaved. We needn't consider this when drawing continents.

SEAS VS. OCEANS

Though there's no real difference between Earth's oceans, there are five that comprise the "world ocean:" the Pacific, Atlantic, Indian, Arctic, and Southern Oceans. The latter two are sometimes considered parts of the others.

Some oceans cover both hemispheres and are therefore said to have a North Pacific vs. South Pacific, for example. When creating our continent, we might want to give different areas different names, too. These names refer to huge areas of sea separating the continents but which are one continuous body of water.

If you've ever wondered what the difference between an ocean and a sea is, that's because there isn't one. They're the same thing. "Sea" is typically used to denote a smaller area than an ocean, an area that is surrounded by land on several sides.

By contrast, a lake is a body of water that is surrounded by land. Sometimes a very large lake is called a sea. This may happen because the lake is so large that it seems like a sea to those living on its shores. Or "Sea of So-and-So" might've had a better ring to it. Or someone unfamiliar with the differences named it and the name stuck. "Sea" can also suggest a wild expanse of water with nothing (or at least, no civilization) on the far side; this can represent a judgment by inhabitants that only barbarians, for example, are found on that far shore. World builders can do this, too, though some snarky know-it-all may tell us it's really a lake and we don't know what we're doing.

An ocean region may have a reputation not based on fact, such as our Bermuda Triangle, where ships are thought to mysteriously disappear with unusual regularity. We can invent such places, making them real or not. We can do this with aircraft, dragons, or anything else that flies. Maybe dragons refuse to fly somewhere because of such occurrences.

Some ocean areas are prone to hurricanes and tropical storms, which are affected by water surface temperature, air temperature, and prevailing winds. This sort of thing plays into culture and a region's viewpoints on the ocean and its consequences. There can be mythology about gods being angry with them and sending these powerful storms. By contrast, the Pacific Ocean is so named for its calmness, possibly owing to its enormous size (nearly a third of the Earth's surface).

BAYS AND MORE

The information here is mostly about naming water bodies.

 • Like a sea, a **bay** is a body of water surrounded on several sides by land. It can be part of the ocean or a lake
  • A **gulf** is a very large bay

• A **cove** is a smaller bay and is usually circular, with a narrow passage into or out of it.

• A **fjord** is a narrow bay with steep terrain around it

• An **inlet** is a narrow, long indentation of a shoreline and which often connects a bay to another body of water. A group of many inlets can be called a "sound."

• A **sound** is large enough to draw on our continent-sized maps; they can be as big, if not bigger, than bays. A sound can give ships places to hide.

• If two large water bodies are separated by a narrower area of water, that's called a strait, channel, pass, or passage.

Since bays lessen the effects of wind and waves, they are safer spots for fishing. Our world will have settlements along a bay. Some of our oldest cities will be there. It won't make sense to have a bay with no settlements on its shores, unless something is keeping everyone away, like a sea monster; in that case, the bay is likely named for that creature or its effect ("the Bay of Death"). Sometimes a monster is named for the water body instead, like the Loch Ness Monster.

ISLANDS

The difference between an island and continent is interesting reading but has no real bearing on world building. For most of us, it comes down to size. Use your judgement.

A continent often has large islands nearby, with those islands part of the same continental plate. This means shallow seas lie between the island and continent. This won't be the home of a sea monster that likes the depths.

These continental islands are distinguished from oceanic islands, where are almost exclusively volcanic in nature (whether that volcano is still active or not). Some oceanic islands result from plate tectonics, meaning we'll have a mountain range on it, possibly with the resulting rain shadow and desert.

Our world will have tens of thousands of islands, whether our species have discovered them or not. We needn't draw any but the largest near a continent. Most island nations consider their territory to extend far offshore in every direction. In addition to naming individual islands (or chains like Hawaii), we can name large regions that contains many islands. An Earth example would be Polynesia, which is a big swath of the Pacific Ocean and islands, all within an imaginary triangle. We also name land regions this way.

WHERE TO START

Though adding land features is part of the next chapter, making a list of the ones we'd like to include can help us determine how large a continent we need. Our story requirements can also help this. An early decision is hemisphere, as this determines whether hot or cold is north or south. We might also want to know other continents' direction and distance, as this influences population and more; try not to think of the continent as an island. We should also determine where bays and other water ways are when drawing our map, as this can influence the sovereign powers we place there. I recommend following the steps in the bonus chapter, "Drawing Maps." We can also start by imagining what powers we'd like in various areas of the land mass and rough ideas on their world view and impact, which can be fleshed out more by following Chapter 6, "Creating a Sovereign Power." There's no right or wrong way to start creating a continent because it's somewhat vague until we start filling it in, so use whatever inspires you to get going.

CHAPTER FOUR

CREATING LAND FEATURES

While laying out land features can be fun, it's even better when we've first reminded ourselves of the possibilities and what they can mean for our world's inhabitants, our audience, and ourselves. This chapter is a roundup of the salient details world builders should consider. We can start placing items without having outlined a continent or even a coastline, but it's often better to know where the sea is, to determine plate tectonics, covered in Chapter 3, "Creating a Continent."

MOUNTAIN RANGES

MOUNTAINS

Mountains are covered first because their effect on precipitation determines the locations of forests, deserts, and rivers. We all know what a mountain is, but scholars have not agreed on a definition. What this means is that our characters can refer to something as a mountain when it isn't that tall (less than a thousand feet), so remember this option. The land just needs to stand out from the surrounding area.

Roughly 24% of Earth's surface is mountainous. Glaciers can create various shapes, including cirques (an amphitheater-like circle) where lakes form. If two parallel glaciers recede and carve parallel valleys, they can leave a row of peaks between them. If three glaciers recede from the same central point, a pyramid-like, sharply pointed peak or glacial horn is formed, like the Matterhorn. While these are interesting, they seldom matter on the large scale for world builders and are instead ideas for characterizing individual peaks our characters have noticed.

The highest mountain discovered in the solar system is Olympus Mons on Mars. Its extreme height (69,459 feet vs. Mount Everest's 29,035) is due to the absence of tectonic plates on Mars. Land stays over a hot spot indefinitely, causing eruptions and lava flows in the same place, which increases local elevation. By contrast, on Earth, tectonic plates shift land (or ocean) across the hot spots, causing things like a chain of volcanic islands like Hawaii. If we want a truly enormous, standalone mountain on our world, we can decide tectonic plates don't exist, but this would cause various changes like a potential lack of earthquakes or mountain ranges (and a resulting lack of rain shadows). Such a world might have many very tall, volcanic mountains but few if any ranges.

Such enormous mountains may not be as interesting as they sound. Olympus Mons is so wide, as big as France, that our characters wouldn't realize they're on a mountain if walking on it. If we want something dramatic, than a single, solitary peak is better. Images of Mt. Shasta in California can give you inspiration. While it's only 14,000 feet, it's so large compared to its surroundings as to be majestic, and majesty is arguably what we're after. We don't need a giant Olympus Mons and its accompanying problems.

Mountain ranges can have peaks formed by different forces, meaning some are volcanic while others aren't. Several ranges can be back to back; this means one is north-to-south, and where it ends, another north-to-south range begins. To the layman, we sometimes don't realize this; neither will our audience, but we can give two different names to a range if they're separated by a pass or a little offset from each other. For example, the Appalachian Mountains include the Blue Ridge Mountains and White Mountains. These are regional names for the same range and are technically the smaller ranges that make up the larger one. If we have a truly long range, a thousand miles or more, it might not be realistic to say it's a single mountain range. It's probably several ranges.

VOLCANOES

We often speak of volcanoes as being active (they erupt regularly), dormant (it hasn't erupted in centuries), or extinct (it hasn't erupted in written history). These distinctions aren't scientific and a supposedly extinct volcano can erupt again many years after the last time. By human life spans, they're extinct, but active compared to the planet's life span. For our purposes, these classifications work, but we can surprise our species by having a supposedly extinct volcano erupt; maybe it's part of a prophecy.

Some volcanoes on Earth have been erupting continuously for hundreds of years, but these aren't explosive. We can have our characters believe an evil is ongoing in the world as long as Mount So-And-So is erupting. Or the reverse—a volcano's been erupting for as long as anyone remembers and then suddenly it stops as foretold, with consequences everyone's heard of.

A very large eruption of ash can cause a volcanic winter (when the sun is blocked out for a long time). This has caused some of the world's worst famines and even mass extinctions.

CHARACTERIZING MOUNTAINS

HEIGHT

Some mountain ranges are only 3-4000 (914 meters) feet tall while others tower above 10,000 (3000 meters). This is a critical difference. Lower mountains are less likely to cause a rain shadow, while taller ones absolutely will; the surrounding terrain is affected for as much as a thousand miles. Travel across a range differs according to how high one must climb to traverse them. Survival conditions deteriorate, too, as some mountains are so high that oxygen deprivation occurs (above 2400 meters or 8000 feet). The increased cold is another factor; it is possible to freeze to death. An underground species like dwarves may tunnel through, as could monsters, to solve this problem.

The ability of flying species, giant birds or dragons, to cross these peaks might also be impacted, particularly if they're carrying a load, such as our characters. We can narrate that our giant birds can take them as far as those peaks but no farther. The air becomes thinner at higher elevations and even birds struggle to fly over. The additional lift required by something the size of a dragon may preclude it from flying over the highest peaks, except that we like the idea that they're all powerful, but the point is worth making.

The higher the peaks, the less likely they are traveled, meaning a settlement there might be safer than one at lower altitudes. This will determine how many visitors the place is likely to get and even how receptive the residents are to that. This can work in different ways.

For example, a settlement in high mountains might be rarely visited and therefore suspicious and hostile toward outsiders. Then again, maybe it has no reason to be so hostile because no one poses a threat to it. Perhaps a settlement in smaller mountains is the one that's protective and suspicious, refusing admittance. We can create different scenarios for each range, making the settlements therein different. Higher altitudes also pose problems with oxygen deprivation and higher mother and infant mortality rates.

RESIDENTS

Which species live in each mountain range? It's likely that the same ones live in every one, but that may depend upon their attitude. I have a species that likes to prey upon other species but which is simultaneously at risk of being preyed upon by others. The result is that, if their prey isn't present, they tend to not be there either. Some of our species might have massive numbers in the peaks, which they use as a base to amass armies or from which to launch raids.

Another issue is whether we have a species, or more than one, known for tunneling into mountains, like dwarves. They can have underground civilizations that mine for gems and minerals like gold. This can make their lairs desirable for conquest. They may also unearth monstrosities buried deep in the earth and better left undisturbed. Maybe their place has been destroyed as a result, with all manner of ghosts haunting the ruin. Or perhaps they've controlled whatever they've unleashed and can send it after those who try to conquer them.

Dangerous animals and monsters can also be present and impact travel. Their presence can be known or not. Do our characters prepare for an encounter or try to evade them? Do they assume a certain number of them will be killed before they get through? If the mountains are low enough and our characters can afford aerial flight, maybe it becomes a moot point, unless these creatures can also fly or knock out of the sky anything that does. Then our people must escape alive.

EXAMPLE DESCRIPTIONS

Next are example descriptions similar to those you'll write for your files.

FORBIDDEN PEAKS

These intimidating mountains are shorter than most, being less than 5,000 feet tall, but the stories of evil wizard towers and all manner of monsters have kept most people from entering. Those who do often don't return or return insane, babbling nonsense about hundred-foot-tall cave trolls, talking trees, and rocks that come alive and chase people. The wizards of Nivera have investigated these rumors and found enough evidence to prove the claims, though they have admitted that only to the royal court in Nivera.

SOARING PEAKS

Volcanic in nature, these peaks still rumble with activity so that those nearby have long thought the gods must visit here. The tallest peaks are over 10,000 feet while the average is a couple of thousand less. Heavily forested, they are home to all manner of dragons and other flying creatures, many of them preyed upon by the dragons. The southern pass is inhabited by ogres and goblins, making travel hazardous and the city of Nivera hard to reach or escape. By contrast, the northern pass is well protected, courtesy of castles at either end and a legion of knights.

WATER

RIVERS

Rivers flow downhill to other rivers, lakes, or the ocean, but sometimes they dry up first. Other times they fall into a hole in the ground to become underground rivers. They seldom take the shortest route to their destination but simply go downhill, cutting through the softest material. Wide rivers can have a floodplain, which is where water goes when a river floods its banks. A floodplain can be many miles wide and have multiple settlements in it.

The age of a river can determine some of its characteristics because the erosion deepens over time. Young rivers like the Brazos River, Trinity River, and Ebro River tend to be steep and fast, with few tributaries but deep rather than broad erosion. Mature rivers like the Mississippi River, Ohio River, and Thames River are less steep, flow more slowly, and have more tributaries, with wider channels. Old rivers are slow, don't erode much, and have flood-plains; examples include the Tigris River, Euphrates River, and Indus River. When adding rivers, we should note their age in our files and consider how to draw them: a nearly straight line suggests a young river while a winding river suggests an old one.

The impact of rivers is mostly felt on settlements, but wide and long rivers have often been the boundary between nations. Keep this in mind when laying them out, for it's an easy way to decide where one kingdom ends and another begins. There will be many more rivers than the ones we put on the map, so when it comes to drawing, we're talking about the big ones, like the Mississippi River. Waterways can also impact travel, as we'll discuss later in the "Travel by Water" chapter.

LAKES

Lakes are found in natural depressions and along the courses of mature rivers, which are moving more slowly than young rivers. Most of them are also in higher latitudes. When deciding a lake exists somewhere, we need no explanation other than that a river flows into it. Sometimes two lakes that are near each other are connected by a strait. Most lakes on Earth are fresh-water, but some are not, such as the Dead Sea and Great Salt Lake.

Lakes have natural outflows in the form of rivers or streams, which serve to keep the lake level consistent (excess water drains off). But some lakes don't and maintain their level via evaporation or underground drainage; we can have a river end in a lake and not continue out the other side. Lakes sometimes vanish quickly, even in a few minutes, if something like an earth-quake opens up a hole through which the lake drains into ground water. This is another scenario we can use in our writing if our inhabitants attribute this to something supernatural. Incidentally, Baikal Lake in Russia is the deepest lake on Earth and is over 5,300 feet (1615 meters)—deep enough for a mon-ster, certainly.

There's no real difference between lakes and ponds and in fact there's ar-gument about what the difference is, the usual determining factor being size. That said, ponds far outnumber lakes. Geologically speaking, all lakes are temporary because they'll eventually fill with sediment, a fact which only becomes relevant if we have time-traveling characters who go far into the future and wonder why a lake is gone.

FORESTS

There are more than eight hundred definitions of "forest," and we're going to cover them all. I'm kidding, but if you're like many, you simply write "forest" in your stories and leave it at that. Here's a chance to be a little more specific and populate a world with different types of forests.

The tree types are covered in more detail in *Creating Life (The Art of World Building, #1)*, but it helps to know the basic types: evergreen (literally green all year), coniferous (needle-like leaves), and deciduous (seasonal loss of leaves, flowers, and fruit ripening). All trees actually lose their leaves but deciduous ones do so all at once in dry or winter seasons. The others lose and replace their leaves continually. Coniferous trees are the tallest in the world, including the redwood, so if we have elves that are living in enormous trees, they are conifers, which also means a single straight trunk.

FOREST

Most of the time, we will want to say a forest is just a forest. Only when choosing something more specific, as defined next, will we need to deviate.

Figure 23 Forest

A forest typically has a tree canopy covering 60-100% of the land within it. This allows for some underbrush but not something impenetrable. Half of the Earth's trees are in the northern temperate zone, though this is partly because there's so little land in the southern temperate zone. Temperate zones have both evergreen and deciduous forests; evergreens are the most common trees unless it's very cold temperate, where conifers dominate.

The latitudes between 53-67° (Polar Regions) have boreal forest, which are predominantly coniferous, with some deciduous trees.

Tropical rainforests are found within 10° of the equator and are *almost* the only kind of forest found there; the trees there are considered evergreens. Jungles are found there as well (see below). Smaller winged creatures can fly beneath the tall tree-canopy of rainforests but might find it difficult to reach the open sky unless a clearing is available. There is very little underbrush due to the canopy preventing sunlight from reaching the ground.

WOODLAND

A woodland has less tree density and therefore less canopy than a forest and is relatively sunny, with only a little shade. Otherwise the tree types are similar to forests. Most people probably think they're the same as forests and might call them "light forests." When naming forested areas, "Forest X" vs. "Woods X" can be used interchangeably, regardless of the tree density. In our notes about the area, we might want to specify it's a woodland.

Figure 24 Woodland

A woodland will be easier to ride horses or other animals through than a forest or jungle. The sparser underbrush limits ambush opportunities, so an animal or humanoid species we've invented and which relies on ambushing prey is less likely to be found here. While animal trails will still exist, the sparse underbrush means life doesn't need an existing path (created by other animals) quite as much.

SAVANNAH

A savannah has virtually no tree canopy despite the trees, which is one reason grass covers the land. This results in more grazing opportunities for animals than in forests. Some people wrongly believe that widely spaced trees indicate a savannah, but some savannahs have more trees per square mile than forests do. Savannahs cover a fifth of the world's land surface and typically lie in an area between forest and grasslands.

Figure 25 Savannah

There have been times in human history where we've set fire to a savannah on purpose. The goal is to prevent a forest from forming by killing the smaller trees and shrubs, maintaining the open canopy.

Animals that hide in tall grass will use a savannah to their advantage. Some of their prey will be skilled at climbing trees to escape. The lack of underbrush means riding animals or driving a caravan of wagons is easy.

JUNGLE

The term "jungle" is poorly defined in its vernacular usage. It's basically a very dense forest with enough underbrush to be difficult, if not impossible, to traverse unless we hack our way through. It's often implied to be in the tropics but needn't be. This contrasts with rainforests, which have very little underbrush due to the tree canopy that prevents light from reaching the ground. Jungles often border rain forests due to the light at the edge allowing underbrush to grow; we might have to cut our way through a jungle to reach the rain forest. The wildlife in jungles is dependent on where the jungle lies.

Figure 26 Jungle

If you're confused as to the difference between jungle and rainforest, that's partly because the latter term replaced the former. To quote Wikipedia, "Because European explorers initially travelled through tropical rainforests largely by river, the dense, tangled vegetation lining the stream banks gave a misleading impression that such jungle conditions existed throughout the entire forest. As a result, it was wrongly assumed that the entire forest was impenetrable jungle."

Due to underbrush, a jungle is largely impassable so that even people on foot will have trouble. Horses or other steeds cannot be ridden and might even be abandoned. Creatures who ambush will abound in such conditions.

CHARACTERIZING FORESTS

By now it should be clear how to characterize the forests we invent. The thickness of canopies and underbrush and the types of trees will determine what life is like for those who live here or pass through.

RESIDENTS

Which species and animals live in each forest? Benevolent species can make a forest safer to travel if they've been thinning out any nefarious species. Or obnoxious species, intolerant of others, may prevent travel. Or perhaps they've been driven into certain areas that are not safe to travel.

If we've invented any plant, especially ones that prey on species, are those plants here? Do people know that? What do they do to protect themselves? Avoid the place? Carry measures for protection, like an antidote to poison? Maybe those plants are only predatory at night so people feel safe in daylight but must stand guard at night.

If there are settlements near, people will use the forest for wood, hunting (for food and sport), and activities that possibly put them in harm's way. Their armed forces might have outposts or castles there and have cleared nearby areas to be safer. Or they might guard anyone going into the forest.

EXAMPLE DESCRIPTIONS

Below are some sample descriptions like those I use in my files. These might give you a sense of what we're after.

HORN WOOD

Named for adjacent Horn Bay, the Horn Forest lies near the southern coast, twenty degrees north of the equator, where the climate is temperate and often humid. It is a sparse forest with a mix of deciduous, coniferous, and evergreens and is known for its general lack of underbrush, sunlight streaming between the trees. Ogres and other obnoxious species are seen primarily near the eastern side close to the nearby Lima Mountains they call home. The woods are therefore considered safe and are used for casual riding by the residents of several cities nearby. However, in the event of a flying menace, there's nowhere to hide. A lookout tower stands toward the eastern edge as much for ogres as dragons that also call the mountains home.

Dark Wood

Dark Wood is so named for being seemingly impenetrable. Hacking through the underbrush is time-consuming, but using the few trails is dangerous due to the ogres and the like that wander those trails, but several monsters are believed to have made them. The trees are so thick it becomes difficult to see any threat coming. Poisonous plants abound here, as do criminals seeking to escape the law. For all these reasons, people generally avoid Dark Wood, skirting its perimeter by a wide margin. It is often not flown over either, for if a crash landing occurs, you'll never make it out alive.

The Adelia Forest

The beauty of the deciduous and evergreen Adelia Forest, which stands upon gently rolling hills on the eastern coast, has attracted visitors for years. Unfortunately, while the eyes draw people here, something foreboding makes them regret traveling far into the woods. Rumors swirl as to the cause—it may be haunted or protected by a wizard; both stories have attracted adventurers who have sometimes never been seen again—or haven't been right in the head since emerging.

Prairies/Grasslands

These lands are characterized by grass, whether tall, short, or mixed. The taller grass occurs where there's more rain, resulting in abundant grain crops.

The short grass can be less than a few inches tall. In tropical grasslands, sometimes all of the year's rain occurs within just weeks.

In North America, when the Rocky Mountains rose, they caused a rain shadow that killed the forests for hundreds of miles east of them, resulting in the prairies of the Midwest. For tens of thousands of years, Native Americans periodically burned these grasslands, preventing trees from growing there. This was done to extend the land for their livestock to graze.

Figure 27 Grasslands

Trees will steadily encroach on prairies without the interference of humans or grazing animals, so keep this in mind when placing them. They will exist due to rain shadows. Our species may cause them to remain intact; otherwise, the land will first turn into a savannah and then a forest. We'll want some nomadic peoples to dwell there, with herds of grazing animals, like the American Indians.

WETLANDS

A wetland develops its own water-oriented ecosystem from being saturated with water either seasonally or all year. The aquatic plant life is what distinguishes it. The water can be fresh, salt, or brackish (somewhere between). They are good places for monsters to hide, if they're fine with being wet all the time, because humanoid species are often uncomfortable with entering wetlands; we tend to like solid ground.

There are four basic types of wetlands; most are found in temperate climate zones or the tropics, but they can be in polar areas. Many fish species, including ones we create, use wetlands for nursery grounds, and many animals are typically found in them. This means food and products come from wetlands, including rice, honey, sugar, natural medicines, dyes and textiles.

There are far more lakes than we're going to draw during world building. Usually we depict the largest ones, which can have mires (discussed next) at various places along their shores. Take a moment to state in your files that there are wetlands in various places on these lakes and how far these are from various settlements. While this is good, it won't result in nearly as many wetlands as there would be, but the goal is not accuracy per se; it is including these potentially useful land features. I suggest that after building settlements, world builders take a moment to determine which settlements have a wetland nearby, what kind it is, and where it's located in relation to the community. This will necessitate deciding there's a smaller lake nearby, the kind not drawn on a continent-sized map.

MIRES

Bogs and fens are similar types of mires. Both get water from rainfall, but fens also have surface water (water that collects on the ground, contrasted with rain or a spring). The water quality is therefore different, but your readers will not care. Both form at the edges of a lake and can eventually cover the entire surface.

BOGS

A bog forms in land depressions or old lakes, typically in the mountains in colder temperate climates. They collect deposits of dead plant material (like mosses) and form peat. The water is acidic and sometimes comes entirely from rain partly because the bog is domed-shaped land that is higher than its surroundings. A bog can be many meters deep over a wide area. Evergreen plants can grow there, including trees in drier locations, in which case the bog can appear to blend in with an evergreen forest adjacent to it

Carnivorous plants can exist in bogs. They survive by eating invertebrates. Or we can have them eat bigger animals and our species. Some large animals like moose and caribou are found in bogs, as are otters and smaller animals. Peat is a product that can be used for fuel (heating and cooking).

Figure 28 Bog

In *Creating Life (The Art of World Building, #1)*, the possibility of undead plants was discussed. What if a bog contained undead plant material and the remains of either animal or humanoid undead? This could be where the undead emerge from and return to in between terrorizing the living.

FENS

Fens are similar to bogs but are covered in grasses and shrubs instead of peat, looking like meadows. They occur along lakes and rivers where seasonal changes in water level occur and are often in the mountains. Fens are located on slopes, depressions, or flat land. Water is supplied from the ground more than rain. A fen may eventually become a bog.

Figure 29 Fen

World builders can use fens for inventing plant life that is only found in one. Since fens are typically in the mountains, fetching an herb for a magic spell could place someone in danger from all those nasty ogres and the like that one must bypass to reach the fen. Some of the plants can be more dangerous if carnivorous and willing to consume humanoids. Since a fen looks like grassland, they can be deceptive so that characters enter them before realizing the potential dangers.

MARSHES

Marshes form along slow-moving rivers, at lake edges, or in depressions of land. They are often a transition between dry and wet ecosystems. Grasses and reeds dominate them (as opposed to trees) and they can be home to fish, birds, amphibians, aquatic mammals, and dangerous water-dwelling predators of our design. The water level is shallower than other wetlands. Saltwater marshes are found farther from the equator along coastlines where the tide floods them. They must be protected by lagoons or estuaries.

Figure 30 Marsh

SWAMPS

A wetland with a forest is called a swamp. They occur near large rivers and lakes. A hammock is a dry land area within one, albeit with aquatic vegetation that can survive occasional flooding. The difference between a swamp forest and a brush swamp is the amount of tree cover, as the shrub version has far fewer, and shorter, trees and is instead largely bushes. The shrub version is also drier and the shrubs are mostly on the hammocks.

While elves are known for their love of forests, they don't appear much interested in swamps, but maybe world builders can change this, creating a new variant on elves. How might these elves utilize the water and animals within it?

Figure 31 Swamp

DESERTS

Deserts take up a third of Earth's land surface but can be larger or smaller on the world we've created. They play a role in regulating Earth's temperature, so deviating from this could render our world less habitable, but our audience isn't likely to know that.

While lack of rain causes some deserts, others do receive rain, just not enough to compensate for high levels of evaporation. Our characters might express surprise about being rained on and not realize why the water doesn't remain. Ten inches or less of rain causes a desert, while semi-deserts receive ten to twenty inches. If there's grass, it's called a steppe. A given desert may be one of these, but have portions of another type, especially if the desert is large. Since rainfall causes the differences, we should use our understanding of prevailing winds and rain shadows to determine what type of desert exists where. Land near a mountain range might be a desert while the area of that desert that is farthest from the mountain might turn into a steppe (because it's getting more rainfall).

When it does rain in deserts, it's often a violent downpour. This can cause flash floods to occur miles away from where the storm is.

A desert normally can't form near the equator due to heavy rains in the tropics (from 0° to 30° latitude). However, high elevations (above 5,000 feet) cause a temperate climate to exist where we'd normally expect a tropical one. This can combine with a mountain range to form a rain shadow, resulting in a desert, such as those in Somalia.

Figure 32 Hard Desert

Only 20% of deserts worldwide are sand, and in some areas, like North America, sand only covers 2%. The rest is a virtual pavement of tightly packed small stones (like pebbles) left after the dust has blown away. Once this happens, the ground is stable. Therefore, it's not accurate to always state that humanoids or hooved animals are trudging slowly through sand.

Drifting sand accumulates as a series of sand dunes, or more rarely, a single dune. Extreme temperature changes from night to day cause rocks to break apart before further eroding occurs via wind, creating sand. Some deserts feature outcropping of rocks that help form an oasis when ground water remains. Established trade routes are often used to make crossing a desert less perilous. This is where we can add a settlement; most of these are likely to be small, not a megalopolis.

Hot deserts like the Sahara and Mojave have strong winds and low humidity. Cold deserts like the Gobi occur at higher latitudes and/or altitudes. Some deserts are farther inland because moist, warm air rises over the land closer to the sea and dumps rain there, leaving none for areas farther inland, causing a desert; this means we can have a forest between our desert and the sea. Some deserts are far from oceans or other large bodies of water, but others form to leeward of a mountain range, in its rain shadow, resulting in a long narrow desert near the coast. In other words, a north-to-south coast might have a north-to-south mountain range and then a north-to-south desert on the other side.

Sandstorms and dust storms aren't the same thing. The dramatic images of towering storms are dust storms. Sand is too heavy to be lifted that high and doesn't get much higher than a person when blown by the wind. It's inaccurate to state the sand is falling on people from such a storm; dust is falling. Sand will pelt people in the body and face sideways, not from above. People can die from repeated exposure to dust storms when dust causes an incurable respiratory illness that ultimately causes them to suffocate.

SETTLEMENTS

Chapter 6 includes details on creating individual settlements, but when creating our continent, it's wise to also decide where cities and towns are, drawing them on the map. Villages won't appear on a continent-sized drawing (there would be too many) but can be on maps of smaller regions. Laying out settlements helps start the process of imagining different sovereign powers and where those on our world live, travel, and what they must contend with to survive and get what they want from life.

Historically, people build near water to have a steady drinking supply, to dispose of waste in, and for transporting goods. The biggest cities tend to grow from a particularly useful spot on a river, lake, or by the ocean. We can't drink salt water, so such port settlements often have a river emptying into the ocean there, too. Always draw your settlements by water unless you've decided ground water, like a spring, is the settlement's supply.

CULTIVATION

We should consider how much impact our sentient species has had on the landscape. On Earth, we've done all of the following:

• Bulldozed entire forests out of existence, whether for wood, farmland, or to create living space
• Diverted rivers so that they've dried up
• Created dams that have caused new lakes to form

• Turned uninhabitable deserts into cities
• Tunneled through mountains and under lakes
• Altered our atmosphere with carbon monoxide and other emissions
• Caused global warming and sea levels to rise, altering coastlines
• Dumped toxic waste and garbage into landfills and the oceans
• Surrounded our planet with satellites and space junk
• Paved over seemingly everything
• Heavily fished the oceans
• Driven animals into extinction with many of the above

On our invented world, the current civilizations might be the most advanced ones. This can suggest they're the ones altering the environment in these ways, in which case the perpetrators might have protesters and supporters like Earth has. If an apocalypse has occurred (possibly resulting from these acts), then a previous generation might have been responsible; authors have done these cautionary tales before. Decide when the most advanced societies existed and what marks they might've left on the world and the psyche of those alive now. In the "Creating Places of Interest" chapter, we'll look at ruins they might've left behind.

WHERE TO START

Mountain ranges are the first item to place on a continent due to their impact on precipitation, which affects where forests, rain shadows, and deserts form, and which direction water is flowing. Mountains indicate where rivers start, while a coastline will determine the end, but we will be suggesting the altitude of the topography as we draw our rivers, so keep this in mind. Once we have determined winds and rain shadows, we can get a sense of vegetation as impacted by mountains. Use the knowledge gained in this chapter to determine which sort of forest, desert, and wetland is likely in each area; try not to bog down in doing this "right" because we have creative license. What we really want is to be plausible. If you have ideas on settlements and sovereign powers, indicate them and worry about the details later. Cultivation will also impact land features; we can determine how species have impacted this, though a decision might need to wait on placing settlements.

CHAPTER FIVE

CREATING A SOVEREIGN POWER

This chapter delves into the differences between kingdoms, nations, countries, empires, and more. In addition to allowing us to name sovereign powers appropriately, it helps us create different types with varied rights, outlook, and overall feel. Different governments are often ideologically opposed, and inventing such places, whether adjacent to each other or not, helps create friends and foes. The subject is an enormous one to which entire books have been written, so while this is not exhaustive, it's enough information for world builders to understand powers at a high level. Details on creating one are later in this chapter, but I highly recommend that world builders understand this material first; it may suggest possibilities that hadn't occurred to you.

Appendix 2 is a template for creating a sovereign power. It includes more comments and advice, and an editable Microsoft Word file can be downloaded for free by signing up for the newsletter.

http://www.artofworldbuilding.com/newsletter.

SOVEREIGNTY

A concept impacting all powers is sovereignty, which means the right to govern oneself without outside interference. It's a matter of recognition, both from other sovereign entities and from within. Generally, the power structure of sovereign powers is hierarchical, with the typical king or emperor at the apex and a dizzying array of nobles and aristocrats beneath. This book doesn't delve into this because the subject warrants a book by itself, and because this series is aimed at contrasting overall differences between power types—and what life is like for inhabitants. Those world builders who intend to write a *Game of Thrones* style narrative, one dealing with those nobles and aristocrats and their struggle for power within their hierarchy, can find details in any number of available resources to become informed.

The issue of whether sovereignty is recognized by others is crucial. Recognition broadly falls into two categories: external or internal. In other words, do other powers acknowledge the country's sovereignty? Do the residents recognize it? This impacts the attitude of others and can result in events like war, peace, or revolution.

EXTERNAL SOVEREIGNTY

A sovereign power may or may not be recognized as having sovereignty by other sovereign powers. When Napoleon declared himself emperor of France, most European nations refused to recognize his sovereignty and repeatedly attacked France (together) to prevent a French Empire. We can leverage such real-world events for our invented one. It's recommended but optional for world builders to read about the rise and fall of various sovereign powers through history to get a sense of how this works.

One factor influencing sovereignty is exclusivity. Is a sovereign power the only one claiming control over somewhere? This place can be the land itself or something on that land, like a weapon or source of power or wealth. If someone else is also claiming it, then one of them must be destroyed, engulfed by the other, or otherwise proven illegitimate, or neither of them is truly sovereign; they cannot both claim it and have this mutual claim last and be respected by the other. Sometimes a sovereign entity has a legal right to exercise control but doesn't have actual control due to lack of might, an uncooperative population, or other impediments.

It's possible to achieve sovereignty but not be independent due to needing help from other powers. This assistance can be military, technological, magical, or humanitarian, to name a few. To build ships, one might need access to materials located in someone else's territory. The territory could be landlocked and need an ally on the sea. Perhaps our power has no territory near the equator from which to launch spaceships, and must find an ally who does. Note that a desire for something doesn't necessarily cause dependence; it's only when a power cannot continue existing without support from another that it becomes dependent (but still sovereign). These situations can cause tension, assisting storytelling. Our monarch might need military aid for which he must bargain, possibly offering crops or natural resources. A power can be independent but not sovereign because sovereignty is claimed by more than one political group within it.

During a military occupation, a sovereign nation can retain its sovereignty because the occupying force does not contest it. Storytellers might be loath to waste such an opportunity for conflict, but this respect of a nation's sovereignty can show the benevolence of another power. The United States and its allies are a good example, such as after the Second Gulf War, when Iraq retained its sovereignty despite defeat. A republic may do this, but a dictator likely won't.

Sometimes one country can take over another's territory. The conquered sovereign entities (royalty) can continue to exist in exile and still be recognized by the international community, who see the occupying force as an invader and not someone with a true claim to that territory. This can lead to our deposed king claiming his rightful place has been stolen; perhaps he promises rewards to those nations who help him get it back. This is reminiscent of *Game of Thrones*.

INTERNAL SOVEREIGNTY

The relationship between a sovereign power and his subjects might also be strained. In extreme cases, the people overthrow him, and murder, imprison, or exile him. The latter two offer further chances for mischief by our deposed monarch, should he choose it or have those loyal to him who are willing to assist. Leaders are overthrown when they are weak. Weakness includes inability to:

1. Restore or create peace
2. Squash rebellion
3. Enforce laws when those laws are broken in particularly costly ways

Promises made to one's own police and military forces must be kept. Failure to do so can result in internal war and a coup, possibly resulting in a military junta or dictatorship. A strong leadership can bargain with opposition to keep peace.

Centuries ago, many believed a single person should rule because this provided a single voice of decisions. In time, this fell out of favor so that an elected body, such as a parliament, assumed authority.

GAINING SOVEREIGNTY

So how does a power acquire sovereignty? Conquest is the most entertaining for us. Other times, one power cedes land to another via a treaty, or grants the other the right to control a territory. If no state exists in that territory, a power can just take the territory, which explains the attitude of Europe on discovering North America. With the Native Americans not having a state recognized by the Europeans, British, French, and Spanish conquerors just took the land. Each declared sovereignty over different regions; overlaps between these areas led to wars. Then the soon-to-be United States declared its own sovereignty and threw everyone out. Other powers eventually recognized this sovereignty.

THE DIVINE RIGHT OF KINGS

You may have heard of the "divine right of kings," which on Earth means that someone is sovereign by the will of God and answers to no one but God. Tyrants tend to like this idea, which suggests any attempt to thwart them is treason. If our invented world is polytheistic (many gods), we can still do this by having someone claim a single god they worship has given this right. Someone from a different religion could make the same claim. Conflict is good. This also gives our protagonists someone to destroy.

This divine right can be expressed differently, both here on Earth and in ways we invent. For example, in some parts of Asia, such a sovereign is only considered legitimate if he is just; unjust behavior will have him stripped of sovereignty, which is then given to someone else—or taken by someone else claiming they've got it due to the tyrant's abuses. It's easy to imagine the tyrant seeking retribution on his replacement. This concept of the divine right justified rebellion against a tyrant.

Opposition to the divine right helped lead to modern ideas of democracy. Those questioning it can be philosophers or those who can write influential papers. We can have similar people in our invented world. We can have a monarch execute someone who has suggested that this divine right:

1) Is unjust,
2) Doesn't really exist, or
3) Should be abolished

Sometimes such rulers instigate mass executions like burning people at the stake as heretics. Such actions inevitably lead to more rebellion. Other monarchs are more benevolent toward individual freedom or have limits placed on their divine rights.

LOSING SOVEREIGNTY

The section on gaining sovereignty implies various ways to lose it. This includes being conquered, but a power can be overthrown from within, as evidenced by the French and American Revolutions. The concept of freedom and equality for all people led to rebellion that violently ended the rule of sovereign powers. A new government must take its place. If a weak one does or if the transfer of power doesn't happen fast enough, sometimes the military leaders seize control, resulting in a military junta or dictatorship.

OTHER FACTORS

It is possible for multiple powers to form a collective sovereignty, such as the European Union. This means they've reached an agreement that they will jointly make decisions on matters impacting a region or even the world. Those writing SF might find this particularly useful because technologically advanced worlds are often depicted as being so urban that there's hardly a blade of grass left. With nations competing for resources like water, cooperation must happen on some level to ensure survival. While mutual need can bring powers together for this, animosities can strain the relationship and eventually destroy it.

When space-traveling powers have an armada, they likely must leave some ships behind to protect their land and ventures. Other defenses might exist, but only something extreme is likely to cause all ships to depart for space. This will be true even if an alliance exists, regardless of how well allies get along. Importantly, if an alliance exists, isn't it possible, even likely, that ships will have crews drawn from more than one sovereign power?

Sovereignty affects a federal republic, which is a collection of individual states (like the U.S.). Each state has some sovereignty (to rule itself) but also falls under the federation's sovereignty. Members of a federal republic (the states) do not have the right to leave the federation. By contrast, in a confederation, they do. This is partly responsible for the American Civil War, when several states in the federation seceded to form a confederacy, but Congress declared the action unconstitutional. We can use similar scenarios.

CONCLUSION

Some sovereigns (kings and emperors) are absolute, meaning they can do whatever they want, being above the law. But others have restrictions by custom, laws (whether created by predecessors or not), a constitution, or even outside forces like other nations, with whom they have agreements. Due to the likelihood of the latter, absolute monarchs are rare. They also tend to abuse their power and get overthrown by their own people, which is one reason they're fun for fantasy and SF stories.

Not having enough military might to prevent this is one reason a monarch might not be absolute; they might be unable to enforce their own policies. An all-powerful wizard monarch, or one possessing a superior technology, might be more successful if he doesn't need to rely on troops.

If all of this sounds like too much to consider, think of it this way—does our monarch have the control to do what he wants or is something or someone in his way? Can he do something about it or not? Is his power recognized or disputed, and by whom: his own people or outside forces? Things change over time, too. Through history, no sovereignty remains the same. The British Monarchy of today isn't the same as 200 years ago.

ROLES

In any government, there are roles and titles. A few are most important for us as world builders.

HEAD OF STATE

The "head of state" is the visible representative of a sovereign power. He often has no actual power or authority, being ceremonial, such as the Queen of England. This leader sometimes appears to have power in making appointments to the government, but this is often a formality, as the real power to accept—or reject—these appointments lies in the legislature. Other functions are also ceremonial, including the signing of bills into law. The head of state is also the highest military leader, or commander-in-chief, but as with other matters, the responsibility can be ceded to others who have control (in this case of the military).

Examples of heads of state would be kings, emperors, and presidents. Presidents are sworn in. Monarchs are coroneted. In a hereditary monarchy, the head of state provides continuity with the past. Sometimes the image of the head of state (actual portraits, statues, or images on coins) replaces national symbols like the flag, resulting in a cult of personality. Ceremonial heads of state often attend events to add excitement to them.

One power they do have is to grant knighthood, nobility, and other honors. They can also declare martial law. As world builders, we can grant them whatever powers we wish. On Earth, governments and previous heads of state have granted the position a wide variety of rights, many of them reflecting the nation's culture. As a general rule, however, heads of state have few powers unless they're also the head of government, which is where their real powers originate.

Monarchs generally inherit their position as head of state. On Earth, the role is typically reserved for males unless none are available. If we'd like to be more modern, we can include females. These bloodlines and the order of succession are sometimes not clear, leading to wars when two people think they're the next king.

Head of Government

The "head of government" is the person leading it. He has a title like prime minister or chancellor. This person might also be head of state, in which case they'll have a title like king, emperor, or president. Be aware that the duties of a role, such as president, change from country to country. This means world builders have some leeway to give or take away rights from someone should our situation require it.

Writers tend to state someone's title without providing much idea on the person's powers. Some of this is natural to avoid some potentially boring exposition, but it might also be a lack of thought given to this subject. There are many potential acts various heads of government can do and it's worth researching them to gain some idea. For example:

• Can they veto laws or sign laws into existence by themselves?
• Can they be booted from office? By who? The congress or a popular vote?

• Are they protected from prosecution?
• Can they be executed?
• Can they raise and lower taxes?
• Do they need permission or cooperation from others in government to get things done?
• Can they get away with conflicts of interest?
• Can they declare war?
• Can they oppress/suppress media, communications, and the people?
• Are there exceptions to any of this?

Regardless of our decisions, I recommend a scene giving some idea of the person's limits. They could be in a bad mood because they're thinking about laws that constrain them. They can think about what consequences they might face. Rather than coming across as exposition, it sheds light on their turmoil, obligations, conflicts, and character, hopefully all of it relating to the present storyline and whatever is bothering them right now.

For example, "As the steward departed, leaving him alone, King Davos hurled his full goblet at the wall, red wine splattering like the blood he wanted to spill. It dripped down the painting of his grandfather, which seemed appropriate. What good was all this power if he couldn't quash a rebellion? He snorted in derision, powerless to crush anything more than the golden cup rolling around the polished floor. He was a useless head of state who knighted star fighters and blessed new warships. Prime Minister Kier had all the power, making his puppets in the parliament dance to his merry tune.

"The Davos line deserved better. That damn grandfather had signed away all their rights to parliament, the last act of the last absolute monarch. Maybe the time had come to wrest power back once more. He smiled coldly, knowing just the right people to stage a massacre. That new neutron bomb he'd secretly had developed would end this government once and for all. He could frame the rebels, too. And in the power vacuum to follow, who but dear old King Davos would the people turn to? He suddenly lamented the spilled wine. Revenge was thirsty work."

Such a passage not only gives us insight into a character, but their situation and how their role is impacted by history and their form of government. It's arguably better than just calling the guy King Davos and never commenting on any of it. Providing vividness to our readers requires having clarity ourselves. This chapter aims to provide this.

It can be assumed that if a sovereign power has a prime minister as head of government, there's also a ceremonial head of state who has less power. If you've ever wondered why the U.S. President (head of state and head of government) regularly meets with Britain's Prime Minister instead of the Queen of England, it's because those meetings are between heads of government. If the President and Queen meet, it is ceremonial, as heads of state.

Prime ministers can also have other titles and are sometimes temporarily a minister of something else (see next section), particularly in times of war (Minister of Defense). Some heads of government serve a set period of years while others can remain in power indefinitely; it depends on what the sovereign power (or the author) has decided on and passed into law. The head of government has an official residence like a head of state, though not nearly as grand. This home is well known, having a recognized name, similar to the White House in the United States. That's also the head of state residence, but you get the idea.

MINISTERS

There are sometimes multiple, other "ministers," each overseeing a different area like finance, defense, or foreign affairs. Or wizardry. Or interstellar travel. They usually have simple titles like Minister of Space. *The Harry Potter* series is full of ministers, like the Minister of Magic.

BRANCHES OF GOVERNMENT

It is important to understand the difference between executive, judicial, and legislative branches. The differences in how they interact with each other and heads of state/government are part of what distinguish one type of government from another. An executive branch administers the state and enforces the laws passed by the legislative branch, whereas the judicial branch interprets those laws.

This separation of powers exists to prevent tyranny and is an advancement over earlier forms of government like an absolute monarchy. To some extent, we are implying a level of government, political, and philosophical sophistication when we assign a form of government to our sovereign powers. The reason is that these improvements to governance arise out of dissatisfaction with earlier forms. That dissatisfaction stems from abuses of power that subsequent ideas on government are designed to prevent (with varying degrees of success). Sometimes a good improvement is made but has flaws.

Far more than two paragraphs can be written on branches of government, but when world builders are deciding what sovereign power type to create and where, we don't need much more than this. Such details are more useful when creating stories or doing a deep dive into political intrigue.

PARLIAMENTARY SYSTEMS

In a parliamentary system, the legislative branch, often called congress or parliament, has a prime minister as head of government. He answers to them and can be removed *by* them with a vote of no confidence. This means that the executive branch gets its power and legitimacy from the legislature, who can take it away. In some cases, the head of state (such as a king) can appoint and dismiss the prime minister. We can invent how this works for our sovereign power because variations exist on Earth.

In the example I wrote above, King Davos removing Prime Minister Kier from office isn't possible because I implied it isn't—that would've ruined my example. For this reason, it's suggested that world builders don't worry about such details in a sovereign power until setting a story there, because we might have to later change how that government works to make our story work.

As for how a prime minister is chosen, there are several versions:

1) Being selected by the head of state and then voted on by the legislative branch
2) Being outright appointed by the head of state
3) Election by popular vote (the people) or parliament

Despite the relative lack of power for the head of state, a king could usually still declare war. Similarly, a king could sometimes surrender without consent of parliament, which is an interesting scenario for causing the ire of the people, who then take action.

One advantage to a parliamentary system is faster passing of laws and avoidance of stalemates, which can happen when the executive and legislative branches are led by different political parties, as happens in the United States. If the parties can't cooperate, little progress is made.

Power is also more divided, which can benefit minorities, who might be better represented by factions within government. Only members of legislature can become prime minister, as opposed to anybody with the monetary and political backing to run for office, as in the United States, for example.

GOVERNMENT TYPES

Most of us don't find a discussion of government entertaining. We don't want to research it and explain what's it to our audience any more than they want us to explain it to them. But stories can be improved when told by someone with a high understanding of different power structures and their sources. These can cause conflict that affect our characters, whether our story heavily features government characters or just causes life to be hard.

The usefulness of Earth analogues abounds. Somalia's destabilized government has caused pirates to seek a better life through plunder, which can affect us if we sail near. The United States is admired for personal liberties, causing millions to desire fleeing to it; it is also despised by dictatorships. Some countries are known for their corrupt governments, police, and drug cartels, and the resulting problems citizens face. Our world's inhabitants should be aware of how desirable various kingdoms are or whether they should be avoided, and why.

This section provides details on sovereign power types. Entire books have been written on each, but we're not going that deep here. If you need more detail, this section can help you decide which government type you want to create before making such a deep dive via another resource.

Each name for a government type has implications, but sometimes a sovereign power has the wrong name. The Empire of Kysh might be a federation if one "looked under the hood" at how its government functions. A dictatorship is unlikely to call itself one. World builders should strive to get it right most of the time, but we might like "Empire of Kysh" better than "Federation of Kysh"—or our inhabitants might have some reason for the deception/inaccuracy. We have some leeway here.

Another issue is that a government type doesn't last forever in a given sovereign power. They rise and fall, replacing each other. For this reason, when writing in our world building files about our new sovereign power, include a note about what government type it has *right now*. We can also include other types from which it arose. Each will have left an impact on the present in some way, whether that's structures, statues, or military. The cultural impacts will be felt, too, including languages spoken and general feelings among the population, such as relief or dread about the most recent change. Working these out is optional but adds color and depth.

Government types can be organized, such as by power structure or power source. The latter is used here.

AUTHORITATIVE STATES

AUTOCRACY

A government where one person can do what they please without any inhibition, or fear of consequences from government or society, is an autocracy. These are great for fantasy and SF villains running a country. These are the sort of people our hero can destroy. However, when this individual is destroyed, the power vacuum can be devastating and lead to even worse. Absolute monarchies, like Brunei and Saudi Arabia, and dictatorships are the main forms of autocracy and will be discussed below.

TOTALITARIAN

In a totalitarian government, the state has total control of everything, including military, communications, and infrastructure. There's only one political party, which uses propaganda to remain in power and control minds. Citizens have no power at all and no laws to protect them or advance their wishes. Dissent can bring brutally harsh punishment, including death (and mass killings), long prison sentences, or hard labor. The military is used to enforce the will of a leader, who can often be part of a cult of personality designed to worship him. Many of Earth's most evil figures were leaders (usually dictators) of such regimes. They are typically very charismatic.

The ownership of weapons is highly restricted, as is free speech, assembly, art, science (magic?), morality, even thoughts. Even architecture symbolizes the hulking, brutish dominance. The state terrorizes its subjects into submission and has secret police.

This state will have an all-encompassing effect on any story we'd like to set there, as there's no such thing as living in this regime and not having it impact you deeply. Such states make for excellent enemies of our characters or threats to their way of life, particularly when the regime seeks to expand and conquer the place where our hero lives. Think Nazi Germany and the resulting world war.

This form of government can arise from the destruction of war, when a power vacuum is created and a political party seizes control, particularly when it controls mass weapons and then communications. Imagine a Kingdom of Illiandor defeating the Republic of Kysh, but Illiandor leaves because it lacks the resources to control Kysh, or its army is needed on another front, or some other reason. Now Kysh is on its own again but its government is destroyed. A military leader in Kysh takes power and it becomes a totalitarian government.

This government also forms after anarchy—a lack of government.

AUTHORITARIAN

An authoritarian government is a less extreme version of totalitarian ones. It has a single political power, whether an individual or group, and the leader is not particularly charismatic and may even be disliked. Separation between society and the state still exists, but the state constrains political and other groups, and the legislature, while also having so much red tape to regulate everything that it can stall out progress it disagrees with. Corruption is high and personal connections and favors are important to maintaining power. Elections, if held, are rigged. Unlike a totalitarian government, the state is only concerned with aspects of political life, not everything else. This allows the people to have some illusion of control. As long as society is not challenging it, the regime allows some liberty, such as a private business.

Examples include the United Arab Emirates, Laos, Egypt, and China, Sudan, Vietnam, and North Korea.

DICTATORSHIP

When one person or party rules a country, it's a dictatorship. It can also be seen more as a role in government than a type of one. This is partly because it's not possible for one person to truly do it alone; he must have others supporting him, such as with an oligarchy. Sometimes the apparent dictator is a figurehead, chosen by an inner circle that holds the power. The government is typically authoritarian or totalitarian. There are no elections and the people have no power, which rests exclusively with the dictator (and his inner circle) and is achieved by force.

Dictators sometimes arise after the collapse of a government, when they lead a military group that exerts force to take control. If the existing government is weak in any way, these soon-to-be dictators can seize power. Sometimes these military leaders appoint themselves political stature (like declaring yourself emperor). Elected presidents and prime ministers can seize power by crushing opposition and creating one-party rule, which is possible when the government is weak. These leaders typically live in opulence by stealing the nation's wealth.

Some dictatorships are temporary, to resolve a problem, with the dictator intending to return power to government after a crisis is over. Other dictators never intended doing so despite what they may have said. This gives us a few scenarios for creating such a character, though we'll need a motivation for their decision.

A stable dictatorship can last a long time. A dictator may avoid too much provocation. Why would the dictator risk their extravagant lifestyle by stirring things up? It helps if an established dictator refrains from aggressive tactics such as war against neighbors, because losing a war tends to undermine their stature. New dictators, however, may need war to establish their power, earn respect, and enrich themselves (from foreign wealth they promise to their people but keep for themselves). They have less to lose. If a dictator dies and is replaced by a son, for example, this individual might need to establish himself, destabilizing the dictatorship. When creating a dictatorship, decide how old and stable it is.

Examples of dictatorships include the Soviet Union under Joseph Stalin and Nazi Germany.

DEMOCRACIES

A democracy allows people to participate in government by having influence over what policies are made into laws. Direct democracy means that the public votes directly on initiatives that can become law as a result of that vote, but this becomes unwieldy as the population increases. In an indirect democracy, people use free elections to elect officials who vote on those initiatives on their behalf; the indirect approach is far more common on Earth, one example being the United States. Indirect is the one we'll typically want to use. Having representatives running government frees the rest of the population for other things. The ability to elect and remove government officials also eliminates the need for revolution to cause change.

While democracies have existed in some form for thousands of years, it wasn't until the last two hundred years that greater equality for citizens became the norm. Before that, there was often an elite class in control. Even in modern democracies, there are sometimes oligarchies or monarchs affecting affairs. This causes some ambiguity about the power structure, which is one reason world builders might want to avoid that.

Examples include the United States.

RIGHTS

In a democracy, laws are supposed to apply to all people, but this isn't always true. A democracy is a rule by the majority, which means minorities are sometimes overlooked, abused, and not offered equal protection. This is arguably truer in a newer democracy. In time, progress is typically made amid occasional setbacks so that an older democracy might offer more equal rights. Generally, greater freedom allows people to travel, learn skills and information, and have opportunities not available in something like a totalitarian regime.

Our characters can run into problems anyway. Someone with talent for magic might be prevented from training due to race, gender, or another issue. One character can be forbidden to carry a weapon while others can. If we don't want to focus on such things in a story, it's still a good way to give characters a sense of entitlement or bitterness about their life and opportunities. This can be the reason they've left home, to escape a lack of freedom. It can work in reverse, such as a female wizard allowed to be one in her home country only to arrive in another where it's not allowed and she is jailed.

Human rights abuses tend to be smaller or non-existent, compared with authoritarian powers. Citizens have laws on their side and courts through which to seek resolution of disputes. Freedom is central, including freedom of speech, political and religious views, and the press.

In theory, anyone can become a representative in congress, though money and influence often restrict this. In this way, a democracy can resemble an oligarchy, where a small group (the wealthy) are running government.

THE RISE AND FALL OF DEMOCRACY

A democracy can arise from revolution and wars that overthrow or otherwise destroy previous governments. Religion and economics can also cause a sudden change. The Great Depression in the United States caused hardship around the globe. It also sullied the idea of democracy, leading many to believe it was a failure. The result was a rise, in other countries, of dictatorships. A decade later, when those countries lost World War II, another swing back toward democracy took place; this was partly a rejection of such regimes.

Epic fantasy fiction often includes stories where someone must save the world, usually from an evil dictator or kingdom. Should our heroes be victorious, we can choose to have a similar rise in democracy in the aftermath, if we continue using the world.

A democracy can fail when it's not structured to prevent the balance of power from tipping too heavily. When a branch of government gains too much strength, it effectively stops being a democracy even if it doesn't re-brand itself. Some groups may be prevented from having power, which can also lead to trouble and an overthrow.

There's a tendency to take our current government for granted. In the United States, this complacency reveals itself in low voter turnout that some-times surprises those in foreign countries who wish they had that right to vote. In countries with less stable government and fewer rights, the average person is more likely to care quite a bit about the current government be-cause life under it isn't fair, kind, or likely to change. They may dream of escape. Give them somewhere to dream of.

TYPES

There are different types of democracy, but we'll only cover a few basics.

Direct democracy was discussed previously. So was indirect, which is commonly called "representative democracy," and when the head of state is also elected, indirect is called a democratic republic. A republic may or may not have the word itself in its name, like "Republic of Nivera." As with other government forms, the idea of a republic has changed over time, giving us some leeway to tweak details. Republics eventually replaced absolute mon-archies as the most common form of government on Earth.

Since a government representative is free to exercise his own judgment on how to "represent" the constituents who elected him, there's room for abuse and resulting dissatisfaction that may lead to being ousted from office in favor of a new representative.

In parliamentary democracy, the people elect members to parliament (the legislature), who in turn elect a prime minister as head of government from among their ranks. This prime minister is chosen from the majority ruling party. The people cannot remove a prime minister, but parliament can remove him via a vote of no confidence. The people can vote members of parliament out of office at the next election.

By contrast, in a presidential democracy, people elect the president, who is head of state *and* government and appoints his own cabinet. The election date is set, but the term of office (how many years they can be president) may or may not be. The president cannot be easily removed, nor can he easily remove legislative members. If the president is in a different party than the legislature, they can block each other, causing stagnation.

Even in a representative democracy, there can be aspects of direct democracy when the public votes directly on referendums or initiatives. This is how individual measures are voted on by the public, causing a kind of hybrid democracy. The United States allows this, particularly at the state and local level, as each has some sovereignty over its own affairs.

FEDERATIONS

FEDERATION

A federation is a union of self-governing states or regions that give up some of their freedom for a national government and the advantages it offers. A constitution outlines the status and division of power and cannot be altered by political powers, the federal government, or the regions in the union. One goal is greater stability, especially economic, but if the economy of one state experiences severe troubles, it can threaten the stability of them all. Territorial disputes are also resolved with the agreement, which also creates greater uniformity between disparate states.

The states have some sovereignty over themselves but nothing at the federal level or with other foreign powers. They have some rights to control local laws and administer their own affairs. Some states may have more autonomy than others, possibly because they joined a federation sooner, before the constitution changed. Federations can also provide a common military front to shared enemies. A federation is helpful in managing a very large area due to the ability of the small states (sometimes called provinces) to manage their more local affairs. Membership in the federation is not voluntary.

A challenge for all federations is that individual states sometimes have opposing ideas about what they can do and the central government must find a way to resolve this. Failure to do so can lead to civil war, states seceding, or even states being expelled. In extreme cases, the federation can collapse. One example is the United States Civil War, where southern states believed the constitution provided the right for slavery. Other states and the federal government disagreed. This caused the southern states to attempt seceding (to create a confederation, explained below). Seceding is not allowed in a federation and led to civil war as the federal government attempted to bring the southern states back in line. No foreign country recognized the south's Confederation of the United States as being sovereign.

Federations, like Canada, sometimes do not include "federation" in their name, but others will. Titles include federation, federal republic, confederation, dominion, kingdom, and union. In other words, we can't always tell what form of government a sovereign power has by its title.

UNITARY STATE

A unitary state is similar to a federation except that the federal government can eliminate the autonomy of the states. Their formation is also different, as a federation comes together from independent states joining forces. A unitary state originates from a pre-existing central government granting more autonomy to previously dependent states. What the government giveth, it can taketh away. These subdivisions can be created and abolished by the central government at will. Laws can also be forced on the states or taken away. Sometimes the states cannot create any of their own laws.

These details may be the sort of thing we and our audience don't care about, so we could ignore unitary states as an option for our sovereign powers and just have them be a federation instead, partly because we've all heard "federation." Fewer have heard of "unitary state," requiring explanation that is likely dry. If we use a unitary state, we may not want to call it one to avoid that reaction. This gives us the best of both worlds: a unitary state without reader confusion. If our story ever involves the government giving or removing rights to a state, then we can admit its form of government.

The United Kingdom is a unitary state.

CONFEDERATION

A confederation is a group of sovereign powers who form a permanent union so as to act together against other states. Membership is voluntary, unlike a federation. Any agreements made by the confederation are not binding until the member states enact laws in accordance with those agreements. The actual confederation has no real power and any changes to its constitution require a unanimous vote. The formation is usually by treaty, but a constitution will be created shortly thereafter. One confederation might be quite different from another, meaning we have some freedom to create the rules of one; some will be stricter, like a federation.

Switzerland, Canada, Belgium, and the European Union are examples.

EMPIRE

In an empire, multiple sovereign powers are ruled by a single power via coercion. The individual powers are still self-governing because the central government allows it, similar to a federation. An empire can include territories across the sea and other territories not adjacent to it, like the British Empire. Sometimes a ruler, such as a king, names himself emperor, making his territory automatically an empire, even when it doesn't fit the details outlined here (it's still a single sovereign power).

In addition to controlling by conquest, an empire can gain control by exerting pressure due to having an advantage of some kind. This can include superior economics that make another sovereign power subservient to it. Using force requires keeping soldiers in each country. This limits options for further conquest, so other forms of coercion are attractive.

A weak state may also seek to be annexed by an empire for protection and other advantages such as trade. Imagine being the ruler of a kingdom sandwiched between an empire and a wasteland of nomads known for violent conquest; we might want the empire's protection from the barbarian horde. This protection comes at the expense of current autonomy but is better than the alternative of being destroyed. In SF, a planet could be blockaded by space ships and prevented from interplanetary trade unless it joins the empire blockading it.

Due to this absorption of other countries, an empire includes multiethnic peoples and will typically force its culture on all its territories to consolidate its hold. When an empire fails, it often breaks into pieces based on these cultural and ethnic divisions, and the previously independent states (prior to the empire) don't necessarily return to what government they were before the empire. An empire's collapse is often catastrophic for its former territories, leading to enormous upheaval and uncertainty. If we want traveling characters to experience unexpected challenges wherever they go, an empire's recent collapse provides believable chaos across many areas.

An empire can become a federal republic or a more loosely bound commonwealth of nations all governed by the previously dominant nation. For example, Britain still governs states that were part of its empire. The impact of having been part of an empire is long lasting even when full independence is achieved. Economic and cultural changes take root more deeply the longer a state was part of an empire.

Examples include the Roman and British Empires.

MONARCHIES

A kingdom is technically a monarchy, which was the most common form of government on Earth until the republic took that honor. In fantasy, it's the most common, whereas federations seem dominant in SF. In a monarchy, one person (the monarch) is the sovereign until death or abdication, though there have been cases of a monarch serving for only a few years, with this planned in advance. This is done to achieve a goal, like quelling an insurrection. When the crisis is over, the monarch steps down.

Someone can simply announce they are a monarch after seizing power, as Napoleon did in France to create the First French Empire. Doing so resulted in other European countries repeatedly attacking France as a unified coalition because none of them wanted a French Empire. He rebuffed them but eventually succumbed.

Monarch titles are familiar: emperor, king, duke, prince, and so on.

SUCCESSION

Monarchies are typically hereditary, where only members of the family (usually male) can become monarch. Heirs are raised in a royal family and taught what is expected of them, and if the same family rules for generations, it's called a dynasty. The heir is most often known in advance to ensure smooth, uncontested transition. George R. R. Martin's *A Song of Fire and Ice* (aka *Game of Thrones*) is based on the failure of smooth succession. Competing ideas on who is the rightful heir can cause strain and outright war.

An heir can be chosen according to the proximity of their bloodline to the king. A son is in close proximity while a cousin is farther removed. Primogeniture is different and stipulates that the first born male is to inherit everything, followed by younger sons, then daughters, and finally siblings. We don't need to know too much about this for world building unless getting further into the details of a kingdom to tell a story there.

The rules for succession vary so that we can invent our own if desired. We could decide that the king's eldest son is next in line but only if he's been a knight or star fighter in the past. This becomes justification for forcing military service on a prince, but maybe such a prince fails and the next oldest male heir is now first in line to the throne. The quality of one's bloodline can be a determining factor, as can religion, age, and even mental capacity. The most famous disqualification is gender; our modern audiences might prefer the abolition of that one. Sexual orientation could also be used, one justification being that a homosexual is less likely to produce an heir.

Another option is for those within a group to elect the next monarch from those who are eligible. Maybe the next king must be a wizard, and this requirement trumps everything else so that even someone who is otherwise unqualified to rule becomes king. In SF, it could be a scientist chosen by other scientists. We can decide there's a reason for this, such as this specialized skill set enables the fulfillment of the king's duties. Or we can just decide it is part of the kingdom's constitution and never remark on why that is until we think of a rationale.

ABSOLUTE MONARCHY VS. CONSTITUTIONAL MONARCHY

In an absolute monarchy, the monarch has unrestricted power over the people, who have little or no say in government. He can enact laws by decree and impose punishments. He has full control over the military. In practice, he may be limited by a priesthood, the aristocracy, or middle and lower classes. The monarch also needs help from an inner circle that often acts like an oligarchy, since many are relatives. An absolute monarchy often gives way to a constitutional one.

If a constitution exists to place limits on the monarch, that's called a constitutional monarchy. The monarch is often the head of state but not head of government, making him largely ceremonial. Some constitutional monarchs are also head of government and have considerable power. Otherwise, power lies with the legislature and a prime minister who is head of government. Other powers can exist due to laws, precedent, or tradition. The monarch has an official residence and sovereign immunity (he cannot be sued and technically can do no wrong because the government is considered responsible). Succession is usually determined by law of the constitution.

OTHER LIMITS

A monarchy might not be absolute due to other limitations, such as military groups who retain authority over themselves and dominate the monarchy. In ancient times, there were several instances of the military electing a monarch or even killing one before replacing him; the Praetorian Guard of Rome exemplified this.

OLIGARCHIES

An oligarchy is any form of government where power is controlled by a small group of people. This can be beneficial in smaller populations, particularly if a group like village elders is in power, because wiser people tend to be less selfish. But in larger populations, oligarchies tend toward being tyrannical and make a good idea for evil sovereign powers on our world. Anything can be the basis for an oligarchy but is usually something like wealth, military power, status, family, higher education, or ability (like wizards). Owners of large corporations could qualify, especially in SF. There is sometimes a figurehead who appears to be the leader while the real power structure is unknown to the public. The military is used to maintain control and order.

Several types of oligarchies are discussed below.

ARISTOCRACIES

An aristocracy is a form of government where a privileged class, supposedly the most qualified, rule. They might be the most famous and will usually be wealthy or otherwise influential. Belonging to the aristocracy requires inheriting the right or having it conferred upon one by the monarch. The people have few if any rights while the aristocrats have many and might even be above the law.

Historical examples include medieval nobility in Europe and ruling classes in India, Athens Greece, and Rome.

PLUTOCRACIES

In a plutocracy, a small group of rich people are in control. The leaders may enrich themselves at the expense of the poor. And they do not make life better for everyone, just themselves, so we typically won't see them creating social programs to aid the general population. In such a sovereign power, opulence will dominate areas where the rulers dwell while poverty might spread everywhere else.

Historical examples include merchant republics in Venice, Florence, and Genoa, and the Holy Roman Empire.

MILITARY JUNTAS

A military junta results from a military conquest of a country, the power now being held by multiple military leaders as a political group. The state is fundamentally authoritative, as you'd guess, and there are no elections. There's also no constitution or laws adding legitimacy. Those in power typically emerge as leaders after combat, whether personal or military.

Past examples include Thailand, Burma/Myanmar, and Argentina.

STRATOCRACIES

Like a junta, a stratocracy is a military government, but this one has a constitution, laws and formal government, where every position is held by officers. If people can join the military, voluntarily or not, they become eligible to be part of this government. They therefore acquire the right to vote, for example, provided they are in good standing, such as having been honorably discharged. The rights of people are often limited, much the same way any military places limits on the conduct of its population. Since officers can be promoted on merit, this can be a meritocracy where only the most worthy advance.

Examples: Burma/Myanmar and the Cardassian Union of *Star Trek*.

TIMOCRACIES

In a timocracy, only property owners can participate in government. No one else can hold office or vote, for example, and their rights are limited. Acquiring property might be difficult. It's easy to imagine red tape and other barriers, or plots to rob an heir of property that would be inherited. Perhaps the government has recently eliminated the inheritance of property by individuals, which goes to itself instead of the heir.

MAGOCRACIES

We could also have a magocracy, where only people who have magical power can be in government, hold office, or vote, and no one else has much in the way of rights. There could other versions of this, replacing wizards with one thing or another—vampireocracy, undeadocracy, or elfinocracy. The latter could be more simply a "raceocracy," a term used regardless of the race in power, although it doesn't sound as good, but you get the idea.

OTHER IDEAS

Other ideas, which are sometimes theoretical or just rarely seen, have been suggested, going all the way back to Plato. Each of them amounts to rule by a select group, whether it's the strong, wise, technologically advanced, or whatever other criteria we invent. This is an opportunity to make things up. Another variant is rule by thieves, such as might be found in a corrupt city or pirate den. Rule by corporations or banks might be useful in futuristic SF. For more ideas, visit http://www.artofworldbuilding.com/government.

OTHER GOVERNMENT TYPES

THEOCRACIES

In a theocracy, a religious person or group rules and all laws are based on the religion's beliefs, which are based on the concepts of a god (real or imagined). The god is considered the ultimate authority, thus legitimizing the state; the god is head of state, which implies that someone (a mortal priest or "living god") is head of government. The latter is appointed by a group of high-ranking priests from their ranks, though in a fantasy or SF world, an actual god could make this selection personally.

Any laws stated by the leader are considered to have divine origin. These religious laws will be interpreted by religious courts. The leader may be responsible for appointing people to government positions, such as the military leader. Some theocracies allow people to elect officials while others don't. The level of control by the people can be negligent to substantial. This gives world builders leeway to invent what we desire.

Examples include Vatican City (Rome), Pakistan, and Saudi Arabia.

NATION

We've all heard "nation," but that isn't a form of government. The word refers to a people that have common characteristics (cultural, language, and especially ethnicity). The physical borders of a nation might not coincide with the physical territory of the state. For example, Russia recently invaded Crimea, on the grounds that Russians were living there and therefore the Russian state included that territory, which lay outside Russia's borders. Some Russians in Crimea agreed and welcomed this while others didn't.

We can leverage this scenario. Maybe some elves have left their forest kingdom Lorelai and taken up residence in another forest, which is inside a human-dominated Kingdom of Illiandor. The Lorelai elves could decide their nation extends into Illiandor and attack to acquire that other forest and the territory in between. This sort of thing can embroil our characters. We can include such incidents in the present or past of a region, causing lingering animosities and distrust.

The word "nation" is political. If we choose to call one of our sovereign powers either a nation or country, we'll still need a more definitive term (even if we never tell our audience what it is) for its form of government. Nonetheless, informally, nation can be considered the same as a state (which is a government) or country (an area).

Due to ambiguity about what constitutes a nation (there is no agreed upon definition), we may want to avoid calling our sovereign powers one. From *Creating Life (The Art of World Building, #1)*, you may remember that the concept of race (instead of species) is just a concept, one that may have no biological basis. Similarly, a nation is a concept more than a well-defined entity like a monarchy, which implies an actual border and a specific form of government. "Nation" implies neither, its vagueness making it less valuable to us. The concept of nations is relatively new on Earth; prior to (and even after) this, people sometimes felt allegiance to a ruler, religion, or their city.

COUNTRY

Like "nation," "country" is a vague term that is used as a synonym for a state, or former state. It is similarly not useful to us as world builders because it doesn't define a type of government. Why call Nivera a country and then point out that it's really a monarchy, when we could just call it a kingdom to begin with? The word "country" can be used informally to refer to a geographical region, one that has been associated with a sovereign state, and this is where this synonymous usage likely originates. Individual states of a sovereign power can be called countries, as in the case of the United Kingdom (the sovereign power), Wales, Northern Ireland and Scotland (countries).

Like nation, country is a word to use in storytelling but maybe not in our world building. There's no problem with having characters call a sovereign power a country, and if we've never determined its type of government and don't want to be specific, the vague "country" or "nation" nomenclature is a good way to dodge the issue. This is weaker than being specific, which should be much easier now that you've finished this section.

Next we learn to create sovereign powers.

CHOOSING A GOVERNMENT

The type of government is the first choice we should make because it affects so much of life in a sovereign power. A dictatorship, constitutional monarchy, and federal republic offer wildly different experiences for everything from personal freedom to opportunities for employment. Most of us take for granted the form of government in our own land because it likely hasn't changed in our lifetime unless we're in a war-torn country. But those who are suffering due to government failures for infrastructure, human rights, and other issues are keenly aware of their government and foster a desire for change or escape.

With the government type decided, we should decide who the head of state and head of government are; these may be the same person. Names are not important, just the roles. In a constitutional monarchy, just state the monarch is head of state and the prime minister is head of government. See the previous section for roles.

Decide the head of state's role. Does he have actual power, and how much? What can he make happen? If his role is ceremonial, what does he do, bestow knighthood and appear at big sporting events, like a joust? Does he bless new ships, space stations, or weapons?

No ruler rules alone. Decide who else has power (it may be a group) and whether they're helping or thwarting him. Is it the legislature in a constitutional monarchy? Is it an inner circle of trusted sycophants in a dictatorship? It might be the people in a federal republic, voting legislators out of office. Special interest groups can lobby for power and control events.

When deciding to use a parliamentary system, for example, we can write in our files something like this: "This sovereign power is a parliamentary system with a prime minister (head of government) chosen by the head of state (king) but who can be removed (by the legislative branch) with a vote of no confidence. The king's role as head of state is largely ceremonial."

To recap, follow these steps to get started:

1) Decide on government type
2) Decide on head of state and head of government
3) Decide head of state's role
4) Decide who else has power

HISTORY

The history of our sovereign power doesn't need to be created, but doing so often enriches our writing. A previous section provides ideas on how each type of power rises and falls, lending ideas for a changing political landscape and fortunes for our inhabitants. It's unlikely that our sovereign power has had the same government type through history. Changing it can provide opportunities for stories, such as abandoned places that might now be harboring something deadly.

In all likelihood, our characters won't know that a current aspect of their life originated in a previous form of government. But in certain cases they will. This includes shared coinage that a long-gone empire might've caused to spread. Grand buildings could be ancient and in disrepair like those of Egypt, the government that created them long gone. Common languages and customs arise from such things, too.

We don't need a complete history or many details. Just decide that some previous versions existed, choose a point in the past and work your way forward (dates can be added or altered later). For example, an absolute monarchy can give way to a constitutional one, which then collapsed during a war that left a power vacuum that a dictator filled. Maybe that guy was destroyed by a hero, who became an absolute monarch, then conquered other nations, becoming emperor.

States sometimes fail because they no longer provide something a state must provide. This could be economic stability, enough military might to control its territory, or basic services to the people.

Try to think of a legacy that each government left in its wake. Maybe it increased learning, language, and literacy (more likely in a democracy), voting rights, laws (which may not be honored later or can be), coinage, slogans, and improved the general disposition of a population. Maybe knights are far more widespread now, or plants and animals were imported from other regions. Perhaps a species was banned or allowed in after a ban and introduced cultural ideas. Maybe ships of a particular type weren't allowed but are now, or vice versa.

When creating history we can write something like this: "Up until a hundred years ago, this was an absolute monarchy. This changed as a result of the king burning heretics, a rebellion, war, or some other events. This led to the current system of government and a curtailing of the king's powers" (i.e., removal as head of government while keeping the role of head of state).

How Many Powers to Invent

Now that we have a high-level understanding of different power types, we can create one with better clarity. The process of inventing each is similar unless we go into details on roles and responsibility of individual government officials, which is not the focus here. We're taking a higher aim at overall subjects because those apply to the broadest issues in decision making and affect the most number of world builders. If you want the nitty gritty on any government type and its operations, numerous books by experts can provide the insight you need. I've created scores of sovereign powers over the years and have seldom needed more than what's discussed herein.

While this chapter focuses on inventing one sovereign power, we likely need more, particularly if we're going to reuse the world. The variety of government types outlined in a previous section should provide ideas for options. Strive to have differing governments.

Authoritative states and oligarchies will have abusive leaders and a suffering public. They are great for being overthrown by our hero, as the source of some evil that is threatening the world, or as a dangerous place that has valuable things our characters want to plunder at their peril. Monarchies can differ in severity. They can be benevolent but with few options for lowborn people to advance. Federations and democracies are more likely to be decent places to live, minimizing abuse from the state itself, but evil can lurk anywhere. Our characters from such a place might be better informed about the world and have far more opportunities to make their own way.

INVENT FOR TODAY

The invention of time and history is covered in more detail in Chapter 10, "Creating Time and History," but when creating a sovereign power (or settlement), we're usually deciding what it is like right now. "Now" is when we're planning to use it. We can just write in our files, "present day Nivera Kingdom is..." without deciding what year that is. Or we can omit the "present day" comment and assume that, unless we say otherwise in our files, we're always describing present day conditions. Eventually, we might decide present day means 5403 AE, but it isn't necessary now. Just make a note in your files or in your head about what you're doing.

POPULATION COUNT AND TYPE

When considering population, we should include land features in our thoughts. Dwarves are unlikely to be present in high numbers when there are no hills or mountains. The same is true of elves and forests. The form of government can also inhibit an entire species (or cultures within the species) from living somewhere if too much ideological separation exists between species and government. A territory may include land features that house undesirable species (and monsters), which in turn might cause repeated efforts to keep them at bay. The result will be armed forces who specialize in dealing with them, and possibly a famous hero for our world.

INCLUSION

Our sovereign power's population determines much of what life is like, partly because they'll decide the form of government. Or at least, the population around at the time will. We can look to the U.S. as an example, for with white men in power at the time of the country's creation, life has favored them ever since. The increasing introduction of other races has led to racial tension. While many believe other residents should be afforded the same rights, and these were intended by the founding fathers, this wasn't the case. New laws had to be enacted and other races and women are still trying to catch up hundreds of years later.

We can leverage such a situation. Decide who founded our invented power. This will be whoever we want to dominate it. Keep in mind that a power has a capital somewhere, and within the power's territory will be other settlements. As discussed in "Creating a Species: Habitat" from *Creating Life (The Art of World Building, #1)*, more than one species likely created our places. There's a tendency to decide humans built everything and all other species are bit players on that human stage. These locations can be dominated by another species instead.

We should decide what percentage of each species filled our sovereign power when it was formed, and what that proportion is today. And we should consider whether the percentage of any species rivaled or surpassed that of humanity. If the territory is half elven, that suggests they are present in many settlements (as at least a strong minority). In turn, they are prominent enough to insist on a form of government that takes into account their world view. By contrast, if they are only rarely seen outside their forests, they won't have a voice. Minorities are always excluded in some way, even in the most benevolent society.

Since government forms change in time, this means that a power could collapse and rebuild more than once. Earliest forms of government might not have considered the elves, for example, but a thousand years and several government types later, maybe now the elves are so numerous that they impact the current government type. There could be prejudice against this or not, but it gives us a realistic viewpoint into how a sovereign power can be more equal about who's in power.

EXCLUSION

Are there species that aren't allowed in our sovereign power or are suppressed, openly or not? We'll need a good reason, such as hostility, distrust, or other problems they might cause, like spreading disease. If a nefarious species is frowned upon, they might still be present. Sovereign powers cover much territory that cannot be completely policed, even with technology or magic designed to do so (nothing is perfect). Decide where in our land this unwelcome species tends to be, and how they reach that point. Do they land there (whether via ships or wings)? Maybe they can burrow to reach it. A spell or portal can put them there.

Why does an excluded species want to be here? They might be hunting animals or species for sport or food, whether there's a famine or not. They may covet a resource. They could be spying for later conquest. A benevolent species might come to spread its ideology or help people.

We might have sympathizers to the excluded species in our sovereign power. These can be people who want to overthrow the government. Perhaps they want to use these excluded species to help despite the risk. This might've happened in the past, too, and can be one way to create history and a fallen government long gone. The result of this can be an influx of the species and whatever good or ill they bring with them. It isn't just evil species that might be excluded, but the good ones during a benevolent power.

We might consider the price these species pay for being caught. Imprisonment, torture, forced servitude, and death are the more extreme options.

NUMBERS

Most of us have little idea how many people are within a geographic area. Rather than citing hard numbers, percentages can be more useful while also freeing us from unrealistic statements. Numbers might be needed when stating how large an army is, for example, but this can be bypassed with descriptions of how a sea of troops spread farther into the horizon than could be seen. This is more useful than a number, for it describes the impact or impression a force creates; a number tells the audience little.

WORLD VIEW

There is considerable overlap between a sovereign power's world view and government, but some ideas are bigger than the resulting government, which they can sometimes outlast. An idea can guide the formation of laws and the separation of power (or lack thereof).

We should decide what ideas drive our sovereign power. We can do this by deciding who the ruling class was/is at the time the current government formed. The group will promote its own self interests. This is true even in a democracy, where ideals of freedom for all are still seen as being in the best interests of not only all people, but those putting forth the idea.

If businesses are in power, they might craft laws that only they can own business, expand, or do advertising. Wizards in power might believe in the rule of might by magic and create laws and government supporting this. Those who fear wizards could undermine their power and might ban magic. This can be true of technological advances . Some people are selfish and want all the power and riches, being willing to force millions into poverty to gain it. A dynastic ruling class will try to preserve its way of life. Generally, any oppressive regime will undercut the people while also trying to prevent an uprising. By contrast, a more democratic one will empower the people.

The world view of those in charge can diverge from those they rule, regardless of the population's freedom. Those in a dictatorship might despise their government (quietly, to avoid being murdered by it) while democracies can have opposing parties that are starkly at odds with each other, despite sharing broader views that unite them. Inventing more than one political party can make our invented sovereign power more believable but isn't necessary unless we intend to write stories using them.

What we're looking for are a few broad ideas to characterize this place. They will be generalizations, as not everyone will hold the viewpoint. Take some ideas from here as a starting point:

• Wizards are evil and therefore magic is banned
• Aliens will only destroy us and therefore we must be prepared
• The ocean offers a chance to visit and conquer or explore other lands
• The world/cosmos is wonderful and must be explored for continued advancement
• Space must be explored because the planet is in jeopardy and another one is needed
• Territory or natural resources must be protected from aliens, immigrants, or barbarian hordes and therefore military might is cherished
• Freedom is a central right of all people and therefore democracy must be spread, prompting support of other countries and being "world police"
• The race/species in power is superior and deserves to rule the world
• Other races/species are inferior and deserve extermination or exclusion/expulsion from lands
• Gods have given a divine right to dominance that must be pursued

LANGUAGE

Decide if this power has its own language, which will often be named after it; sometimes the power's name changes, but the language's name doesn't, a minor detail that adds depth if we have occasion to mention it. Even if many cannot read and write it, a written language will almost certainly exist. Higher forms of governments arguably require it.

Secondary languages can also be widespread. These may originate from other species. The language of neighboring powers will be spoken by some but isn't something we need to consider unless these languages are widely spoken. The presence of other languages could bother those in power to the point of suppressing them, as an authoritative state might. Writings in other languages might also be banned. In extreme regimes, reading and writing might be withheld from the population to keep them ignorant. We should decide whether areas bordering other lands have secondary languages or not.

Humanoid species are often widespread enough that territory isn't the deciding factor in whether others know the language. Rather, personal experience with that species will cause people to pick up words. In such a case, understanding will be limited instead of deep and broad; this is known as a working knowledge of language—enough to get by on the streets but not hold deep conversations. In more educated worlds, a language could be taught in school much as it is on Earth. This might be truer in SF, where education is generally assumed to be far greater than in fantasy settings, but we can challenge that assumption.

Fantasy often includes the concept of a common tongue, one that most humanoid species can speak well. This concept is useful on film, reducing the need for subtitles at the least, but it also frees authors from inventing languages. Despite the nomenclature "common tongue," not everyone will truly be fluent, as barbaric species are often depicted as being barely coherent. Anatomy sometimes causes this. So can the common tongue diverging too strongly from their natural language so that they sound guttural in speaking it. This common tongue will be the language of somewhere. When choosing a name for it, we might first want to consider what empire of the past conquered so much of the world that its language became the common tongue.

In SF, language is rendered moot by universal translators. Characters are unlikely to learn other languages unless for curiosity's sake or because the equivalent of Starfleet Academy from *Star Trek* demanded it of officers. In the event of a universal translator failure, our characters may be unable to communicate with alien species at all without said training. It seems reasonable that on a large ship, at least one person would be fluent without the devices, not by chance, but due to protocol. A ship's A.I. would serve the purpose, but that can be comprised. The machine translators are typically not present onscreen but are portrayed as largely infallible when that's unlikely to be the case. Subtle nuances are lost on even people, let alone machines. Relying on just the words and not the tone or body language of the speaker is also problematic.

CUSTOMS

Customs will be affected by culture, a subject in volume three, *Cultures and Beyond*. In the context of sovereign powers, the kind of custom we care about is the kind that will cause misunderstanding between different powers. For example, a culture clash often results when a society has expectations that a visitor, ignorant of the custom, runs afoul of it. This can cause unintended offense, though that will depend on our characters; some people might recognize that the offense is accidental and attempt to educate the visitor. Others are more foolish and are eager to be offended, ignoring attempts to diffuse the situation. Maybe they behead someone for it, and depending on who that is, risk war.

Especially when deciding on greetings, we might wish to focus on these expectations. Do people in one power expect gifts of a certain value upon meeting? Or is that considered an insult? Is an amount of flattery expected? Do people expect a visitor to have researched the one being met, with well wishes given to the entire family by name? We can take cues from Earth societies. All we need is a set of expectations that might be unknown, or conversely, expertly followed by the more knowledgeable characters.

LOCATION

The adage that "location is everything" applies to an entire sovereign power. This determines climate, neighbors, and what natural resources are available (and which are not). The form of government will have little to do with location, however, as anything can exist anywhere.

Despite the latter, creators sometimes allow landscape to influence or characterize a power. If we desire this, then mountainous areas are good for an authoritative state and an impregnable fortress or city. An island nation lends itself to being a seafaring power that raids other lands, but it can be democratic or authoritarian. A desert's foreboding landscape can be good for authoritarian states, but then so can an area heavily forested enough that travelers must struggle through the vegetation.

If none of this seems definitive, that's because we can make a case for anything if we characterize it right. When we desire a desert dictatorship, claim the harsh landscape inspired it. Imagination gets us what we want and helps avoid oversimplified clichés. If we've already decided on our government type, we can consider this, or not, when choosing a region to place it in.

Having a map while inventing a sovereign power is advantageous (map-making is covered in Chapter 12). This allows us to place the capital somewhere and know where borders, other settlements, and land features are. If we don't have a map yet, then use a piece of paper to sketch regions as ovals marked with the land feature type, like "forest." We can also draw an arrow off the page and indicate an ocean or a dictatorship lies that way. Colored pencils can help; drawing a jagged coastline isn't much help if we can't remember which side the water is on. Use blue for water, green for forests, yellow for desert, and brown for mountains.

Having a sense of the sovereign power's overall disposition (benevolent vs. domineering) can lend ideas for the land features we might like there. This includes how those land features are characterized. A foreboding forest or mountain range might suit one need while a pleasant, coastal savannah with numerous islands offshore might suggest another use. If you have a map, look at it for possible areas to include within the borders and what features might be contested by neighbors. If you don't have a map, you can sketch it using the same mindset.

Decide on the overall territory and where current borders are. Leave room on a map for other sovereign powers, being aware that the more land this one takes, the less there is for everyone else. This is a greater issue if our map already exists and we don't want to alter it. Country boundaries on Earth make little sense to most of us, suggesting we can do as we please, although major rivers often form boundaries, as is the case in the United States with the Mississippi River.

CLIMATE

In "Creating a Planet," we discussed prevailing winds and rain shadows. With this knowledge, we should have a good idea of our sovereign power's climate. There could be more than one if the territory spans hundreds of miles north to south (changing its distance from the equator), or if it's east-to-west with a coastal mountain range on the windward side, or if the altitude changes significantly. The climates will determine the type of vegetation, or lack thereof. This will, in turn, impact what life is like.

For example, high mountains will inhibit travel, be a place for dragons or an underground species like dwarves to live, hide bandits, and be a source of wealth (precious gems and minerals mined from the earth). A forest provides wood for paper, furniture, and wooden ship building, but it can make

292 | RANDY ELLEFSON

travel difficult if nefarious creatures are within it. A rain forest provides unique plants and wildlife, some of them useable for medicines or spells.

Review the climates from chapter two and make a decision, which can be as simple as, "the west is hot, arid and dry while the east is very humid."

Climate will impact the inhabitants in other ways. People in a humid, wet, and warm area near the equator might be used to wearing little clothing and find nudity more acceptable. If not willing to go that far, they might still be more tolerant of showing skin, resulting in bared midriffs or legs for females. Tight fitting, long gowns might be unusual. The climate can inspire people to avoid working outdoors during midday in summer. Colder climates can have the opposite effect. *Cultures and Beyond*, will have more details on deciding cultural impacts.

RELATIONSHIPS

Whether a sovereign power is physically isolated (like an island) or borders other nations, it will have allies and enemies who shape the past and present. In the early stages of building a world, it's best to focus on the high-level aspects of these relationships, such as who is friend or foe. If we don't have a reason for our decisions now, we can add it later. There are some basic reasons we'll cover, however.

CAUSES OF TENSION

ETHNICITY

Ethnic hatred and other forms of racism are an unfortunate reality. We can pretend they don't exist in our world, but if so, that's best done by never commenting on it, not explicitly stating it doesn't happen, as this strains credibility. If we choose to invent this sort of tension, understanding the source helps. Generally, unfavorable attributes are assigned to a group of people who often share physical traits that make them more easily identified on sight; this is part of where the superficial aspect of this enters. Don't use only skin color for this, as facial features like eyes and noses can be used, too, such as how Asian and Jewish features have been on Earth.

The source of that unfavorable trait can be cultural, ideological, or based on government. For example, people living in an authoritative state might despise people in a relatively free democracy. This can be jealousy but is more likely to be propaganda put forth by that authoritative state condemning democracy and vilifying various aspects of it. Those in the democratic power might have similar negative views in return. Even if these governments change in time, the character assassination will linger (on both sides). These ideas are attached to the people.

In practice, borders change and people move, resulting in a mix of ethnicity that leads to conflict. This can cause one kingdom to attempt exterminating or expelling those of a different ethnicity. While we see this with humans, it can be done with other species, like elves against elves, or between species, like elves expelling humans from conquered territory.

This sort of expulsion can lead to perpetual war, particularly if cherished ground lies in contention. Jerusalem comes to mind. Retaliation can linger so long that each is convinced the other struck first or that they can never let an action go unanswered. The original reason for conflict can be lost to antiquity, which gives us some leeway to invent a conflict and a current claim by each side that justifies its stance, without worrying about having it "right."

We might feel that some of our species and powers are more enlightened than this, and they may be, but racism can run deep and be hard to eradicate.

RESOURCES

Natural resources can cause tension when powers can't share peacefully. This can happen when one power has the resource entirely within its territory or if the resource spans both powers. Newly discovered resources might cause a struggle to possess it. Weaker powers might also control a resource only to be threatened by a stronger one. While Earth-like resources are fine, materials of our invention can include items needed to power spaceships and weapons, cast spells, heal people, or anything we imagine. Rarer resources are more valuable and we can decide what's common on our invented world, but try to avoid making gold, for example, largely worthless, and something that's cheap on Earth be prized on your world; this tends to confuse and it might be better to just create a new resource than to do this.

TERRITORY

There are reasons territory can cause tension. This includes resources, ethnicity, religious significance, and the access the territory provides to other destinations. In the latter case, a landlocked power might wish to conquer another to gain access to the ocean. Territory sought is typically held upon acquisition unless something prevents this, such as the conquering army losing so many of its troops in victory that it cannot hold what it has gained. It might also become vulnerable to threats from elsewhere. Such fears can keep an invasion at bay unless something tips the balance. It might also succumb to local disease to which it doesn't have immunity.

WORLD VIEW

Ideological differences can cause one power to want another's destruction or to become allies against such threatening powers. These differences may be not only political, but cultural, religious, and moral. Some populations, or at least their government, want to impose their own way of life on others, and see differing ideologies as a threat. This is one reason the United States supports struggling countries and why Russia supports different ones. The resulting conflicts are proxy wars where two superpowers are fighting each other via smaller countries they seek to influence. This can make for strange allies.

INTERNAL CONFLICT

In extreme cases, internal conflicts can lead to rebellion, civil war, or government collapse. These dramatic events are useful in creating not only history, but a current situation that embroils our characters. A story taking place during such events is often about those events, however, so if doing this, we will need to work out the details of the conflict. If we don't want to focus on such extremes, then lesser tensions might be needed. These less dramatic issues can eventually reach the extremes we avoid until later, if at all. Don't be afraid to set these stories in motion out of a desire not to deal with the result now.

The conflict often involves freedom, abuses by government, or basic needs not being met, such as infrastructure or economic failures. It can be ideological; people have lost faith in a leader or what he stands for. These reasons often merge, such as when slavery led to the American Civil War. This was both ideological and economic, as the south's economy depended on slave labor that the north wanted to abolish for ideological reasons.

Ways to Identify the Power

A power is keenly interested in symbols, flags, and even slogans that are associated with it; this is also true in a feudal society. Although outsiders can stigmatize a place by associating it with something undesirable, this section focuses on inventing identifiers a power has chosen for itself. The goal of an identifier is to embody and portray a fundamental trait of a sovereign power. As such, the identifiers acquire power. They can inspire love, loathing, and indifference. They can be a rallying cry for resistance in war. They should not be overlooked. With travel such an elementary part of SF and fantasy, our characters will be looking for them when approaching space stations, ports, and fortifications. Failure to mention one is an oversight.

Despite this, world builders may need to invent them later in the process of creating a sovereign power when our idea of a place is more firmly established in our minds.

Symbols

A sovereign power often has a symbol, which its reputation may influence. Symbols may change when the government does to signify the change to outsiders and a country's own people. Inventing a symbol allows us to emblazon it on flags, ships, buildings and more.

To invent a symbol, we should decide how our sovereign power wants to be viewed by its citizens and by outsiders. An authoritative government will have a more intimidating and bold symbol (and colors) to imply oppression and dominance. A show of strength might be desired, either to intimidate potential attackers, or to bolster itself against a sense of weakness. A democracy might want to appear more inclusive and benevolent. Some symbols are negative like the skull and crossbones of pirates, while others show unity, like the United States flag and its stars representing each state. A symbol might not accurately reflect the power.

If we choose an animal to represent the power, this animal doesn't need to be specific to the landscape, or even be found there, particularly if it's considered wide-ranging. This is also true of plants. However, a distinctive landscape feature like a mountain with a peculiar peak should be located within the territory; for inspiration, consider Crater Lake, the Matterhorn, or the Devil's Tower. Other symbols can be based on the sovereign power's reputation (see the section in this chapter), regardless of which came first.

When deciding on a symbol, we should remark upon the impression it creates. If we're an artist, we can draw a hawk that looks vicious or that appears noble and proud. Simply saying it's a hawk doesn't convey this important distinction. While implying an impression can be fine, the ambiguity leaves room for uncertainty—and a sovereign power typically wants to be quite clear with its symbolism.

COLORS

While black or white colors can be used for identifiers, other colors can be used to increase the impression an identifier creates. Domineering governments often choose bold primary colors. The black, white, and red of Nazi Germany springs to mind. Benevolent countries might choose softer and lighter shades of colors like yellow and green. While this approach can yield results, it is unrealistically simplistic. Usage is everything. Don't be afraid to use colors for no reason. We needn't tell the audience what each color represents, assuming it represents anything. They'll care about the impression it creates. The meaning of colors will be lost upon us unless explained, and explanations are best avoided unless done quickly and artfully.

When choosing and creating sovereign powers, try to prevent too many of them from having the same color combination. Having a list of them will assist with this. Organize the list by continent, region, or alphabetically.

FLAGS

Flags often include the symbol in the power's colors, but not always. Many flags are quite simple, being strips of colored fabric. In a world with less technology, flags should be simpler to produce because they're likely hand made. This doesn't mean they need to be three strips of colored cloth sewn together, but simple geometric shapes are helpful. There are talented seamstresses who can embroider something extravagant, but this takes longer and there aren't as many of them to do the job. In SF, more elaborate flags (and symbols) might abound because machinery can crank them out.

On Earth, we often don't understand why a flag has its design unless it's from our country. In SF, with so many things to distract us, we might tend to care less about such things, but even in fantasy, fewer people will know, or care, about a flag's design. This gives us some leeway to invent without much justification. To make life easier, it's recommended that world builders decide on a symbol and place this on a flag, killing two birds with one stone.

SLOGANS

Our power might have a slogan. These are short, memorable phrases that epitomize a fundamental aspect of the sovereign power's outlook. They can inspire greater passion, loyalty or fear, such as "Resistance is futile" by the Borg of *Star Trek*, though the Borg aren't really a sovereign power as we think of it. Games of *Thrones* used this to good effect ("Winter is coming") and so can we. Inventing this calls on our skills as writers to sum up a truth in a catchphrase. Like the other subjects in this section, it requires knowing what our power is all about.

REPUTATION

Our sovereign power is likely associated with certain traits. These can include basic quality of life and freedoms (or the lack thereof), but we might want something more specific, such as an item from this list:

- A mad king
- Slavery (this includes being the source of exported slave s)
- A space craft design or type of man-o-war
- Raiders (like Vikings) or conquerors (maybe a specific individual like Genghis Khan)
- Wizards being banned
- Unique plants, animals, or products
- An unending war, either internal or with another country
- The first place something happened (a launch into space, a discovery, an invention)
- A horror, whether supernatural or technological
- Superior weapons, armor, technology, or devices
- Nomadic tribes with expert horsemen
- A seafaring or spacefaring superpower controlling territory
- Being near the elven homeland (or any other species, pleasant or not), and having good/bad relations with them

Make a list of options you'd like to cover and begin assigning them to the powers you create. Using Earth analogues makes this easier. Remember to change details and mix and match traits to obfuscate the source; see Chapter 1 from *Creating Life (The Art of World Building, #1)* for why. These issues don't have to dominate a nation, but they can be good starting points we expand on.

To get started, consider geography and government. For example, a naval or spacefaring superpower will need ship builders and may export ships. A seafaring one might be an island nation that excels at fishing and facing sea monsters, with legends, myths, and famous sailors. Animals or plants from the sea might be harvested. They probably also have a history of colonization attempts. Where am I getting some of this from? Great Britain.

WHERE TO START

We should first decide on a purpose for our sovereign power. Is it to be a force for good or evil? With that decided, choose a government that influences this disposition; more freedom for people is typically good in many ways while less is bad in many others. Next we should decide where on a continent it lies, as this will determine neighboring powers and what land features are near, which in turn affects who lives here; if our power covers a wide area, species' distribution will vary by location. With population so important, it's a good idea to decide on the general makeup of the residents. Are they 40% human, 20% elf, 15% dwarf, and the rest a mix of dragons, ogres, and whatever else? Now that we know who lives here, determine the power's relationships with its own people and other locations. This has a huge impact on our world building and could arguably come first when inventing a power. Remember that everything in this book is a recommendation but there's no right way to world build. Finally, we can attend to lesser issues like identifiers, language, and customs.

CHAPTER SIX

CREATING A SETTLEMENT

Without cities, towns, and villages, no world building project is complete. In this chapter, we cover how to create more vivid settlements for our characters. Appendix 3 is a template for creating one. It includes more comments and advice, and an editable Microsoft Word file can be downloaded for free by signing up for the newsletter.

http://www.artofworldbuilding.com/newsletter/

DETERMINE LOCATION

A settlement's location affects everything about the way it develops, from the reason it exists in that spot, to what it has to defend against, climate, species, culture, and more. Location is the first decision to make.

CLIMATE

Weather is much more than how the air feels outside. Consistent weather patterns, known as climate, affect rainfall, temperature, and air quality. These all affect life in the area, from native plants to animals and the humanoids who live there, including their culture and customs. Some life forms (including crops) will develop there while other life must be transplanted, which is more likely in worlds with good transportation, such as in SF. Chapters two through four touched upon what climates exist in which latitudes and elevations. If we've drawn a continent, it can be helpful to have also drawn rough ovals to indicate climates in each area. This largely solves the problem of determining a settlement's climate for us; we've already done the work. Just place the settlement in that zone. A high-level idea on climate is all that's needed at first, such as whether it's humid or dry, rainy or arid, hot or cold. Being more specific about when each of these variations occurs can be fleshed out later.

TERRAIN

In addition to altering a settlement's climate if the land is very high or low in altitude, terrain impacts how challenging it is to reach, not to mention live in, a settlement.

TRAVEL, FARMING, AND PRODUCTS

Mountains inhibit travel to and from a settlement over land, whether those mountains stand between this place and another, or if the settlement is among the peaks. The steepness is relevant as well, as this can largely eliminate farmland, requiring pastures be located farther away from the actual settlement. With airborne travel, these issues are reduced, as food can be shipped in, though this does make a settlement vulnerable to shipment tampering. Stones from the mountains can be used for construction, while mines can produce gems, precious metals, and fuels like coal.

Deserts offer few farming opportunities unless modern irrigation or magic is at play. However, the settlement needn't be surrounded by desert. An adjacent desert allows us to utilize it for our work while not causing too much hardship for characters. While travel over sand is difficult, many deserts are rocky; this hard-packed earth is unkind on the feet (or hooves).

A forest can also be adjacent to but not surround our settlement, but if it does encircle it, the trees can be cleared to make way for farmland. Woods provide rich biodiversity and therefore greater food and medicine choices. The trees can also be used for the construction of buildings, furniture, weapons and siege engines, tools, ships, and household products.

An adjacent river or lake not only provides drinking water and abundant food, but a trade route that can bring travelers to the settlement, in addition to providing fishing opportunities. Ocean water cannot be consumed, but the ocean provides wide-ranging exploration opportunities and more danger from enemy vessels. The livelihood gained from the sea outweighs its dangers, but a strong navy can be a significant aspect of the settlement's life. The sea provides for a multitude of products, from the fish themselves to items like the candle wax from whales. We can invent our own sea life and the resulting products gleaned from them.

IMPACT ON LAYOUT

Terrain can impact a settlement's layout, especially rocky areas that prevent anything from being built upon them. In stony terrain, consider placing the occasional boulder in random places. Some can be as high as a house and offer lookout opportunities, or even the chance for youths to climb it; such a rock might be named, and a town square might be arranged to include it because it's preventing anything from being built there. Rocky ground is harder to dig into for support beams for buildings, which may also result in open areas where only temporary, small structures are placed.

Higher areas are more easily defended, such as a castle location; they are also highly prized so that wealthier neighborhoods are typically there. A river or lake is also a highly sought area, but some industry will be located there, usually downriver from the settlement, due to pollution. Consider having the more luxurious homes farther upstream. Rivers, lakes, and ocean will cause progressively more room for docks, with the port dominating this region of town. This can bring out criminals, beggars, and other undesirable people, causing more touristy areas to be in a nicer section of port.

There are sometimes areas that offer natural protection, such as a rocky cliff or rock outcropping where a castle or other fortification can be built. A settlement will be planned around these and may be farther from a river precisely because a natural defense area is farther removed from it. A river can also serve as a one-sided moat.

Aside from these considerations, buildings need to be constructed on level ground or in such a way that uneven ground is taken into account. This can mean homes where the second floor is higher off the ground on one side, or leveling the ground prior to building.

Decide what terrain, if any, is impacting the layout and if it's resulting in anything typical of the settlement, such as boulders, homes built into hills, or the town being divided up based on zones for commercial, residential, or industrial needs.

WATER SUPPLY TYPE AND LOCATION

There must be water for our residents, which is one reason to place our settlements by water sources on maps. Our basic options are a river, lake, spring, or well; the size or number of these water sources will place limits on the size of community they can support. Remember that seawater doesn't count; it can't be consumed without making people sick. In an advanced society, desalinating large quantities of water (in treatment plants) is less of an issue than in medieval-like times; magic could change that.

The water supply is central to our settlement, whether it's physically in the middle like a well might be, or adjacent like a river; we always have the option of having a city with a river running through it, but this is more likely when the city expanded to both sides in time, not at the start. One justification for that expansion is to guard a bridge on both ends, first with a guard tower, then a garrison, then an inn and stables, and the next thing they know, the city straddles the water.

Decide where the water is early on because "Old Town," if it exists, will probably be closest to it.

OLD TOWN CONSIDERATIONS

Cities and larger towns often have an "old town," consisting of the settlement when it was just a town or village. This area often has a wall around it, one that's sometimes just a few feet tall. It might be badly in need of repairs, partly because its stones might have been raided for nearby buildings when the town expanded and the wall wasn't needed, thanks to a newer wall farther out. "Old towns" tend to be more crowded, with buildings in closer proximity to one another. This can become deadly in a fire that spreads between buildings.

Old town is the oldest and possibly most rundown area; in modern times, we've restored such places as tourist attractions, so this might not be the case in a more futuristic society. The streets will be narrow, the buildings in disrepair, and roads just spotty cobblestones or even mud. It might be poorer, with all manner of less desirable people here, from the innocently down-on-their-luck to scoundrels. It likely smells and will be the place where a plague takes hold. It might be a warren for thieves and worse. It's the perfect place for someone to lead visitors into an ambush.

Not all of this may be true, however, as this could be a good market district and the center of life. If a religious site is at the center, for example, maybe this has always been well kept and preserved. We have leeway to create differing old towns and have a character from one place be surprised by how old town is in another community.

WHO ARE THE NEIGHBORS?

SOVEREIGN POWERS

Our settlement is either deep within a power, near the edge of it (and therefore near another power's border, most likely), or in a land without a power ruling it. Each scenario will have some impact on that settlement.

A settlement deep into a sovereign power won't be reached by an invading army as quickly and therefore might enjoy more peace of mind. This depends partly on the relative strengths of the powers and invaders. A power may weaken due to famine, wars sapping its inhabitants and straining resources, or poor leadership. All of these invite conquests of our settlement, or inspire our settlement to conquer a neighboring power having those problems. This settlement might not always have been far from the current border, so it could still have substantial fortifications that may not be well manned or maintained anymore.

When a settlement has long been near a border, it has likely been attacked and even conquered more than once. It will have substantial and well-maintained defenses with an active garrison and some of the more elite fighters, some of whom may be legends. The military group might be famous too; an individual member might have esteem conferred just by association. This idea makes it easier to invent an intimidating character who has this in their background. This settlement is a likely first line of defense against invaders and may also be the source of attacks on others, even if the command came from another city within the sovereign power. This place may feel safe or perilous depending on the current state of hostilities.

While some cities are quite powerful, an independent settlement is more vulnerable even if it has a few allies. If it doesn't belong to a power, a nearby power may decide to annex it. Such a place may have good defenses, but without a sovereign power to lend it aid, it may not have the best fortifications or soldiers. Decide how long this settlement has been in its current state. Who last conquered and ruled it, and for how long? How did this end?

A rebellion? Or did someone manage to kill this ruler and oust his followers? What sort of abuses occurred? If he was benevolent, what sort of problems now abound?

If a settlement has been conquered, consider how long the occupation lasted. The longer this endured, the more a foreign culture will have imposed itself on life in the settlement or region to which it belongs. This is true even after occupation ends, though certain things will be eliminated while others last. Architecture typically remains, as do deeply ingrained cultural elements like widely accepted customs or even laws. It's the elements that people chafe against that disappear sooner. Some residents might be of mixed descent and will continue to live here, whether accepted by others or not; they might also be rejected by the ousted conquerors if they try to go there.

Weaponry will also determine how much a settlement has to fear. A country with long range missiles can strike deep into a territory. Magic portals that transport people—or bombs—can render location less relevant. So can aircraft or spacecraft that move at tremendous speeds or have cloaking devices. This is one reason we might want to decide the boundaries of sovereign powers before we start placing settlements there or deciding what life is like for the residents.

OTHER SETTLEMENTS

Virtually every settlement has friends and enemies.

Friends are easier to decide on if a sovereign power rules there, as cooperation between settlements under a sovereign power is part of the benefit of sovereignty. This sort of thing needs little explaining or working out for world builders partly because it's assumed and is also not entertaining for readers. Few are interested in how cooperation is working out for everyone or the details of it, such as favorable trade prices, crop exchanges, and shared military might or training of each other's soldiers. The latter is one of the few we could mention for a character, that they trained in so-and-so city known for its warriors. Decide which settlements have skilled warriors, healers, wizards, and more so you can leverage this when needed.

Despite all of this, some animosity can remain between settlements in one sovereign power even if that doesn't lead to open warfare. Think of different cities within your own country and how stereotypes persist and strain relations. Individual cities might have good or bad reputations. Decide how yours might be viewed and why, and if it's a fair criticism and observation or just inspired by jealousy, for example. What views have residents taken of other places, near or far? These will be generalizations, as not everyone will accept a stereotype, but one character being chastised for spouting slander helps characterize both the world and our cast.

Enemies offer richer conflict. Settlements of true enemies are unlikely to be part of the same nation. One exception is a settlement recently conquered by an enemy power, which is now expected to incorporate into its former enemy. This is a tough pill to swallow and can lead to openly acting like friends while secretly (or not so secretly) loathing new sister cities. For more open hostility, the easiest way is to not have them be part of the same power. Isolated settlements could also mean many friends and enemies.

Few settlements truly stand alone. Realistically, a city has towns nearby, and towns have villages, but we won't typically draw all these on a map or even name them unless needed. Some may be considered almost part of the larger settlement's domain and enjoy protection in exchange for something, like their agriculture or dairy, for example.

REGIONS & LAND FEATURES

We looked at how terrain can impact travel between settlements or even how they're laid out, but we should also consider the impact nearby land features and regions will have. With a forest or mountain range, dangers lurking within will influence the number and type of fortifications our settlement has. This can trigger decisions on where the castle stands, if one exists, or where the strongest weapons and troops are located. This will affect the city layout, as well. The armed forces might also venture into those land features to reduce the threat. Maybe warriors from other places come here for practical experience and training in dealing with a local danger.

Aerial threats are another consideration. Does our settlement have a wire mesh or something similar strung above it from towers as protection? Are there armed forces who fly on giant birds or dragons as defense and offense, undertaking missions into the peaks to cut down on the population of threats or report on their movements? Think about the impact of these dangers on settlement life.

A desert is less likely to be home to enough dangerous creatures that our settlement needs fortifications against them, unless we invent our own animals. Unless a body of water contains life equally at home on land or in water, it will not pose a threat. A large sea creature is unlikely to threaten the settlement itself unless it has huge tentacles or something similar, but even then, the water is too shallow in most places for such a creature to do this without getting beached.

POPULATION CONSIDERATIONS

Along with setting, our residents are the most important aspect of a settlement. This includes the species and their collective dispositions, leaders and others in power or exerting influence, and whether everyone is segregated into their own neighborhoods, or intermingled.

WHICH SPECIES ARE HERE?

We should decide which species are present in our settlement and in what percentages. Someone is a majority. There's a tendency in fantasy for that to almost always be the humans, unless another species originated the town. In modern times, a melting pot is increasingly common, and with travel easy in SF, a mix seems more plausible. In less advanced times, as is often the case in fantasy, with less travel, each settlement or region will be more homogenous. That's believable but a little restrictive. Perhaps we should have a few well-visited settlements that run counter to this assumption. If you choose one, select a politically neutral city along a trade route, rather than an out-of-the-way settlement that's also a hotbed of war, where strangers might not be welcome. This place is also more likely to be a city due to these factors. A port that lies on a continent edge, so that visitors from this land mass and others arrive here, is a good candidate, with visitors not necessarily moving on to other settlements.

Consider the nearby land features. In fantasy, elves go with forests and dwarves with mountains or hills, for example. A settlement near either feature with a native population is significantly more likely to have that species living in the settlement. However, with their homeland so near, they may not. If there's no such land feature near, then why would they be here long term? They likely wouldn't be if truly attached to their native habitats. We can invent species that aren't so caught up in their origins. Why can't a dwarf be sick of living underground? He can be, but would enough of them feel that way as to live here? What is it about this place that draws them? A good reason is encouraged. Perhaps there's work to be done cutting stone. Maybe tunnels are needed. Can they create a home away from home?

In SF, travelers get around a lot and might find habitats on other worlds which differ only somewhat from their home. This gives them enough of what they grew up with while providing something new. Consider that in artificial environments like ships or vacuum settlements, the climate control can be set to accommodate the species residing there—or purposely not set for them by those who are indifferent or cruel, like our villains.

With multiple species in a democracy, we might have an elf be president with a human for vice president, for example. In a hereditary monarchy, we may not have such variation, but who's to say that an elven ruler doesn't have some human in their ancestry? When this sort of thing is included, contempt for 'half-bloods' may surface, where that person is considered bad by both sides, but some societies might even insist the ruler be such a half-blood (to represent everyone). Strive for variety among settlements and powers.

The military might also have people of different species at different ranks. Restaurants can certainly be elven, dwarven, or whatever. Shops can cater to a niche or everyone, whether this is clothing or weaponry. Why can't the humans fancy elven clothes and buy some outright or just have human clothes influenced by other species? Integration has its advantages for making our world more believable.

As an example, let's take Jai, a human character. Maybe she fancies elven styles for aesthetic reasons and is considered to have high ambitions by her peers, who misunderstand her style choices because they like the idea she has a big ego. Maybe Jai spends a lot of time with dwarves and swears like one, or uses their expressions. Maybe she's considered a dwarven sympathizer when the dwarves have pressing political issues that are causing tension. Jai could love dragons and get herself an apprenticeship to one that can shape shift, so she's assumed to have access to all sorts of powerful items or information, which places her in danger.

To integrate species, we might have to rethink how they get along, and this can change from one locale to another, which also adds variety. We can have a traditionally segregated continent, and a more integrated one elsewhere. This can seem like a radical departure from expectations, but this is a good thing. It's also one reason to invent our own species—we're not beholden to anyone else's ideas. Despite this, there will probably still be settlements that are predominantly one species and which are preferred that way by the founders.

Decide how each of your world's species is welcomed and viewed.

WHO ARE THE LEADERS?

The smallest settlements, like villages, may have no formal leader but will still defer to someone who makes good decisions or who has some power, such as a wealthy farmer. This may change if that leader makes a few poor choices, or even one disastrous one is made. A large village, and certainly towns and bigger, will have a definitive leader, who might rise to power in the same way as a village leader, or through actual elections in a free society, or by appointment from someone within a sovereign power. This is largely a function of government, which is discussed in chapter five, so what we really care about within the settlement is who this person currently is, what sort of influence they wield, and what curbs their power.

On one extreme is someone who can enact laws or simply declare something a crime and someone guilty of it, and what punishment would happen. Such tyranny tells us much about a place and the quality of life. We may use this in authoritative states but not elsewhere. Conversely, a place with elections and laws that reflect the moral code of the population is likely to be fairer to all, though minorities can still suffer. Leaders of such settlements can be accountable for their actions, decisions, and even be the victim of poor situations, such as an economic downturn that isn't their fault but results in losing the next election. In between these extremes is a wide variety of possibilities that provides us leeway to create limits that impact our story.

DETERMINE POWER STRUCTURES

The larger the settlement, the more formal its structure, but unless our story features this, we can skip this stage and focus on our actual leader. If we need it, we can decide on a structure such as a city council made up of individuals who represent each ward, or neighborhood of town, each of whom are elected by their ward.

A mayor might be little more than another member of the city council, albeit one who presides over meetings and has ceremonial duties, but little power to act independently. He might have final say over financial matters or anything else we assign to him, such as decisions on magic or technology. Other mayors have more power, including veto rights, the ability to hire and fire staff within administrative bodies, and some legal authority. They are more definitively in charge but still need cooperation from the council on certain initiatives, which are at our discretion to decide upon. Great variety exists on Earth and gives us leeway to determine what we need.

When inventing a settlement, only decide on the details of power structure when you need to use it. Otherwise you might just contradict yourself later, or find yourself needing to change it for another story. That a council and a mayor exist can be assumed in any place larger than a town, so all we might need to do is decide who the person is and the influencers on them, then worry about council and mayor interactions when, and if, needed.

Our characters might need to understand relationships if they want cooperation from a settlement. This is when the mayor's power, or lack thereof, becomes an issue we can leverage. They might think they can appeal to him only to discover that he's powerless to help. An appeal must be made to the council, meaning several people must be swayed, not just one. This adds complexity and makes goals harder to achieve, even if an audience cares little for the details of government; the workaround is to make this about the council members' personalities, turning them into characters with agendas that interfere with our main characters.

WHO HAS INFLUENCE?

Before we decide on power and limits, we might also decide if there's someone other than the nominal leader who is in control. A clandestine group might have corrupted settlement officials and be getting their way. Lobbying groups can bribe and otherwise influence someone, or get their chosen people into government and then exert control behind the scenes. Some leaders become little more than figureheads. In these cases, the apparent authority they wield is sharply curbed. This creates a good conflict where the public might know the leader can do something but he refuses because someone is controlling him, and yet he can't admit this. Our characters might also run afoul of this influencer and find a more challenging situation than they had prepared for.

It doesn't have to be "evil" people who influence leaders. A benevolent wizard could insist things be a certain way. Those running a space port might need a degree of cooperation and assistance from town officials. A group of farmers may influence decisions that benefit the crops, which aid many in town. A resident hero might inspire not only the population, but the leaders into doing some things his way.

Decide what role this settlement plays in your story and whether a complication can help enliven it. If not, we can decide a leader is truly in charge and then change this later if needed. A new influencer can always arrive.

IMPORTANT PEOPLE

Aside from leaders, other significant figures could be associated with the settlement, whether they reside here, have been born here, or visit frequently. This includes world figures such as heroes. Monuments might exist for them, whether that person is alive or dead. Where do they reside in town? What made them a hero? Did those acts occur here so that they're adored for having saved citizens or the town, or did events happen elsewhere so as to make people proud they call this home? Decide if they were born here, or just moved in at some point, and whether that was before, during, or after the associated heroics. There might be some who resent him. This person might be one of our town's secrets or have powerful friends who come to visit openly. Is there any spectacle associated with the hero-in-residence?

Villains might also be here. They could be hiding after a horrible act or just use this as a clandestine base of operations. Is there something that tips off others to the villain's presence, such as a specific type of arrow? Clothing they're seen in, or even technological/digital trails could also lead some to realize their presence. Do they moor a distinctive vessel, whether a spaceship or a sailing ship, in the port? Do they have a feared stronghold nearby?

Our settlement might be home to similar people so that they fit right in; this could be the reason they're here. Just as heroes bring pride, villains bring shame unless they're expected, tolerated, or even welcomed. Remember that a villain to some people is a hero to others, so we might need to decide on their values and those of our settlement before we know how they're viewed. Their means might be despised while their end results are admired.

Wizards could have a tower here or a more modest home that doesn't call attention to them. A priest likely lives in or near their temple, if one exists, and makes their presence known for healing or guidance. We might have celebrities, depending on our world; actors, musicians, athletes, and other performers seem more likely in SF than in fantasy, where life is often too hard, and mass consumption is unlikely, for people to have elevated these people to celebrities.

We might also have monsters or creatures here, on the outskirts of town, in a tower, or beneath the ground in catacombs. We'll need a good reason why they haven't been destroyed, if known. Maybe someone has control of them. Perhaps there's a use for them, like the way Jabba the Hutt of *Star Wars* fed enemies to them. Decide on the creature's capabilities before figuring out how it can be used, where it is, and how it manages to survive if people know it's here.

POPULATION DISPOSITIONS

The quality of the population can be affected by settlement size. Small towns can be romanticized as wonderful places devoid of evil (no crimes are supposedly committed) but can also be prone to everyone knowing everyone else's business and gossiping. A large city offers the good and bad, from too many people and their problems and trash, to greater numbers of skilled laborers and higher quality of materials and goods. We might want a wholesome settlement in one place and an obnoxious one in another for variety, so don't be afraid to experiment with what's going on in a place. We should decide on the general feel, such as:

- Dangerous or safe
- Quirky
- Boring
- Sleepy or bustling
- Transient or stable
- Hard/easy to reach
- Welcoming (or not)
- Rich or poor
- Artful
- High-minded or down-to-earth
- Religious
- Militaristic
- Prevalence and use of either magic or technology.

Every settlement will have a reputation for one of these. How do we decide? We don't need a reason and can sometimes go with a feel we have, but if we want reasons, consider what surrounds it. A remote town will likely feel safe, sleepy, stable, poorer, down-to-earth, possibly religious, and have less technology, though magic may still abound if it's prevalent in the world; otherwise, skilled practitioners will be uncommon. A more urban settlement is likely more dangerous to live in, bustling, transient, welcoming (if more

312 | RANDY ELLEFSON

indifferent) to visitors and travelers, richer in some areas but poorer in others, high-minded, and has more technology and magic.

While these characterize an overall population, we'll need to consider which species are here and whether each has an attitude different from the overall feel than the dominant species. Is one species more high-minded, artistic, and welcoming than the norm? Is another one more dangerous, militaristic, and standoffish?

QUARTERS

You've probably heard of the French Quarter in New Orleans. The name originates from this being the original town, which we could call "old town," but it's called the French Quarter because the French founded it before Americans took over the city. We can do the same, having a settlement that was originally a town by elves, for example, before humans took over, resulting in an Elven Quarter.

Such a quarter might be full of trees like New York's Central Park. A city with dragons might have a similar huge park with plenty of livestock for them to devour. A water-dwelling species might have a quarter like Venice, Italy, with easy access to water, which can include underground rivers and lakes. A dwarven one would have buildings with smaller interior spaces, presumably, except for places catering to taller species, assuming they're welcome. A species' preferred architectural style will prevail, with customs being more honored here than elsewhere. If multiple species with differing environmental needs are traveling on the same space ship, they may have climate-controlled common areas in separate parts of the ship. This is especially true if that species' presence was expected, such as for crew members.

Consider where a quarter would exist based on each species and these questions:

- Why is it there?
- How easy is it to reach?
- Is it centrally located or off to one corner of town?
- Is the entrance guarded or open?
- Are visitors encouraged?
- Is the species' culture preserved within?
- What rules, if any, must other species follow while there?
- For what is the quarter known?

Decide which species have a quarter. There could be none or, in a very large city, one for each, but in many settlements, only those with a significant percentage of the population, and who are perpetually present, are likely to have one. A quarter doesn't necessarily have to be built for a species. They could just take over an area bit by bit, resulting in shops and other venues catering to their needs.

UNDERSTANDING ZONING

Young settlements will have no clear zoning, which is a designation of how the land can be used (residential, commercial, industrial, agriculture, mixed). The longer a place exists and the larger it becomes, the more zoning takes place to handle incompatible land use, such as dirty factories being beside homes. A place advanced enough to have sizeable industry is also advanced enough to have zoned that into separate areas. More mature towns may also have separate housing areas for the wealthy or upper class, but this is not always the case and we can have different classes mixed.

When laying out a settlement, consider whether these zones exist. Unless it's been rezoned, "old town" will have mixed use, possibly with buildings that are a store on the first floor and a home on the second; this might have been the original purpose, now changed. Upper-class areas might be by the river (upstream) or higher up a mountain, or near another natural resource like a glade or lakeshore, away from industry. Farmlands are obviously farther out from the settlement. Otherwise, we have residential and commercial zones, but they tend to be near each other, just like they are in your town; this sort of zoning is often on a block-by-block basis because no one wants to travel far. For that reason, the wealthiest might live in the center of town.

SETTLEMENT TYPES

The difference between settlement types is largely physical, determined by population size, defenses, and the availability of resources. Magnitude affects everything, including the amount of territory covered to how much of it can be farmed or protected and how often the settlement is visited. Those with a lot of traffic, something to offer residents, or both, are likely expanding. Conversely, those with less to offer may be shrinking. Most of this chapter will apply equally to all types, but we'll look at specific considerations.

OUTPOSTS

These are structures or groups of them where the population is too small (or not perpetually present) to qualify as a village. Whether we call them outposts or something else, the smallest permanent dwellings are anything from a single building that might not be perpetually manned, like a tower, up to a larger fort more like a castle. An outpost might only be needed during certain seasons or conditions, getting overgrown during the absence of people, or just minimally staffed. It could be a refueling station or scientific observation post, particularly in SF.

This has practical consequences. Farming is unlikely if no one is there year-round, requiring residents to either bring food with them, hunt for it, or be supplied from elsewhere, which is believable if the outpost is associated with a larger settlement that built or maintains it. We take for granted food and water supply or the presence of doctors/healers, repairmen (such as blacksmiths or mechanics), or police, but many of these may be missing from the outpost's staff. Decide which absences make sense or propel your story forward; wounded characters with no healers around adds tension, but a missing blacksmith is harder to make interesting or worth commenting on; in SF, those who can repair equipment are seemingly needed more often.

While it's typically known who built a larger settlement, an outpost might have been long abandoned and possibly used by someone else. This can offer mystery, such as hidden rooms or ones with disturbing contents and purposes. There's the possibility that whoever (or whatever) normally occupies it will return and catch our characters making themselves at home. It's important to decide who, if anyone, has been using this place lately, its condition, and what we intend to happen to our characters while here. Do they know about this place and think it's abandoned, or do they know something bad is here but they need it for shelter anyway and come prepared for battle? Unknown outposts that are stumbled upon are the most nerve-racking if something seems "off" about the place, as though danger lurks.

Our less civilized species are likely unable to create buildings. This suggests they're the ones to take over somewhere abandoned or often unoccupied. They may even do so seasonally so that the regular inhabitants know this and prepare, either by laying traps, making it otherwise less desirable when gone, or coming back heavily armed for the yearly reclaiming of their outpost. The unsavory inhabitants might also leave behind a mess, including carcasses of food, enemies, or both.

CASTLES

In this section, we'll look at castles that have no village around them.

Unless abandoned, castles are populated year-round and will be much like a village in which the residents live within the castle walls; there may be buildings scattered outside the walls, such as stabling for animals or guard houses, which are easily replaced if destroyed in a siege. The land around the castle offers farming and hunting opportunities, while the water source is typically protected (such as a well inside the walls). The castle is self-sufficient due to its defensive nature, and in times of peril, food may be stocked for a significant amount of time, but bear in mind that the ability to preserve foods is somewhat lacking in eras during which castles are widely used. Due to their self-sufficiency, castles typically have everyone they need, such as a healer or blacksmith.

Castles can be placed along important trade routes, at the opening to dangerous territory like a mountain pass, or near valuable resources. They might take advantage of a natural fortification that is easily defended and be a general defensive/offensive location within a sovereign power. They can also protect borders, though these borders can and likely have changed at times, often with the castle being conquered and finding itself part of another kingdom. Decide if each castle is currently in the hands of those who built it (or their descendants). Changing possession can mean that two opposing kingdoms have each occupied it at times, both knowing its secrets; this is seldom discussed or utilized in fictional work, as occupants are typically portrayed as knowing the castle's secrets while their enemy has no idea.

VILLAGES

While there are smaller permanent settlements, like a hamlet, world builders don't typically need anything less than a village. There should be a reason the village exists there, such as good farmland or natural resources, or even just being the halfway point between two other locations that can't be traversed in less than a day, requiring somewhere to stay. If there's a water source there, what starts as a known resting/camping place can become a village when inhabitants or passers-through begin adding buildings. If this is the case, an inn or two is quite likely and might be the focal point of town. Naturally, such a place is likely welcoming of strangers.

By contrast, a village that a group formed in an out-of-the-way location might be there to retreat from others, especially if the founders share a vision, such as a religious creed. We don't need to state why our village exists, but a detail like this can make it easier to characterize the place. It also creates reputation, which one of our visiting characters might know. Or they might find out the hard way. Villages tend to have a population with a limited number of religious and political views, which our characters can run afoul of if wearing a talisman of a despised god, for example.

A village is unlikely to have a dedicated, official protector like a sheriff, but the most skilled warrior living there will probably take it upon himself to protect others and resources as needed, with help from the able-bodied. These individuals may not be formally paid, as it's not a full-time job, but receive perks like a free meal or two for an act of bravery. They could also be trouble instead of a protector, intimidating others.

A village usually lacks a surrounding wall or has a wooden one at best, and less durable materials like wood are likely to be used for buildings. The quality of craftsmanship might be poorer due to fewer trained carpenters or blacksmiths, but if such individuals are present, they may be prominent. If our visiting characters have skills a village needs, they may be able to barter their work for food and lodging. For example, the town's blacksmith died recently—just don't make his death yesterday (that's too convenient). If this was months ago, not only is this more believable, but it means more work is needed as a village falls into disrepair. This sort of thing works with wizards or healers, too, or mechanics and scientists in SF.

For map making, we seldom draw villages unless doing a close-in view of where the story takes place. A continent or regional map would have so many villages as to become unwieldy. This means we can often invent a village on the fly for our needs. We're less likely to care about its symbol, colors, slogan, or anything else, and can skimp on much of this until needing it. Unless the village is famous for something, we're unlikely to ever mention its existence unless characters are arriving there or originated from it. Villages seldom have zoning and are more likely to have buildings that are a combination of a store on the ground floor and a home above it. And everyone knows everyone else, for better or worse.

TOWNS

Towns are the smallest settlement that we're likely to create files of information about and draw on maps. They differ from villages not only in size but competition and backup resources; to use the example from the previous section, multiple carpenters or blacksmiths if one dies. Our traveling characters are unlikely to get away with bartering their services for fare and lodging, unless the skill is something rare, like wizardry, healing, or specialized engineering skills. The variety of people and skills tends to raise the quality of everything, including town walls, gates, tools, buildings, food, clothing, and other merchandise.

The amount of crime will depend partly on population size and character, and which species are here. While some diversity of species can exist, one tends to be a majority and others less well represented. Smaller towns mean less anonymity, so if someone steals something and tries to sell it to someone else or wears/uses it, this is more likely to be noticed unless sold to visitors who leave before wearing it. Conversely, a business can cheat people more easily with the lack of oversight, regulation, and laws found in a city. Corrupt officials might also hold considerable power, intimidating residents and visitors alike; the towns in Hollywood westerns come to mind.

A town often has formal guards who report to someone. This is one reason that taxes are almost a certainty, as these professionals need to be paid. We can imagine a skilled swordsman from a village wanting to be paid for his services and moving to a town, maybe even to a city. In addition to guards (who act like police), specialized forces might be here and will depend on terrain; horsemen, knights, and archers are some skilled positions in fantasy, while sharpshooters and pilots are likely in SF, and we can invent others to go with technological weapons or defenses we create. The larger the town, the more likely a wall, and its height, materials, and the prevalence of archer towers, for example, also rises. Some buildings might lie outside the wall due to the town's continuing expansion after it went up. In a world where flight is common, newer walls might be rare, since they can be flown over.

A town will have considerable farming nearby and needs a larger source of drinking water, so these are often by rivers and lakes. They may employ irrigation. In our modern world, farmers don't get much respect, which is partly an effect of population size and industry making it easier to take our food for granted. In less civilized worlds, the importance of farmers and effects of floods or drought are harder to overlook. Especially in smaller settlements, any town council will likely focus in part on farming issues, and life will revolve around agricultural events like the planting or harvest. When inventing plants and animals for our setting, as covered in *Creating Life (The Art of World Building, #1)*, we may wish to decide if farmers can grow a crop and what the harvest cycle is.

A mayor and formal town council may exist, with individuals appointed by vote, reputation, or prominence, which could be influence, wealth, or land ownership. A family can hold sway over generations, too, for better or worse, and may be the ones whose name graces the town or areas of it. Larger towns are sometimes divided into wards, with each such neighborhood bearing a name and having a representative on a ruling council. Zoning also occurs, but this typically occurs as the settlement grows so that the oldest areas are more likely to be mixed use than later additions.

CITIES

Formality typically rules a large settlement. There are laws, regulations, police, a legal system, mayors, voting (in free societies), zoning, and even procedures like how to evacuate or handle certain emergencies. Everything is taken more seriously due to physical and population size and diversity. Otherwise, the chaos overwhelms, especially in times of conflict. This formality can become a problem, however, when groups are marginalized or taken advantage of, or when laws and regulations are unfairly and inconsistently applied, causing social strife that may boil over into protests, riots, and death. Congestion also makes the spreading of disease an issue. Cities offer the best and arguably worst of everything due to competition and quality.

The population is likely to be diverse even if some wish this were not so. Even hundreds of years after a settlement began, newer species can face racism from factions that want a return to the old ways, when their majority ruled and made no concessions to other species. A stark difference between poor and rich can be common, and stricter separation of crime-ridden slums and clean, wealthy districts is common. Marginalized groups will have less sway in town affairs and may be prevented from holding office.

Cities may have the best fortifications and military to staff them, with entire garrisons of trained warriors, many with elite skills; formal ranks are likely and a subculture for these people will exist, with inns, taverns, and equipment shops catering to them. All of this is more likely with somewhat isolated cities as found hundreds of years ago; such places weren't yet surrounded by suburbs, and police, not military, enforce daily order and the military is reserved for civil unrest and actual wars or excursions into other territories, for example.

Zoning will prevent industrial, commercial, or residential from mixing but will result in more traffic from commuting, even if that's mostly pedestrian in fantasy settings. Such a scenario lends itself to pickpockets and people hawking wares to passersby, making for noise. Main thoroughfares are more likely to be paved; otherwise, the mess after a rain storm is considerable. In SF, all roads are probably paved and parking is another concern, though public transportation may have reduced or eliminated this.

Pollution is a major concern and taxes help pay for better infrastructure to minimize the risk of illness spreading. Sanitization is generally better unless the city is run down. Increased anonymity in the largest cities means people only know a small percentage of the population and can fall back on stereotypes and prejudice to judge those nameless masses with whom they share a city.

Rivers and lakes provide the needed water for cities, so we'll want to place our largest settlements along them, though in SF we can use technology to create drinkable water from sea water, for example, and make better use of irrigation and the divergence of rivers from their natural course. Dams can also create lakes that didn't exist before. There are also likely man-made reservoirs, particularly if the area lacks water.

In SF, public transportation is common and might include a space port. We should decide where this is located, but the answer is that it's typically near industrial areas and somewhat out of the way due to pollution, traffic, and noise; think of airports and all they provide in food, other transportation, and nearby lodging.

The largest type of city, sometimes called a metropolis, is so large that it has often absorbed nearby villages and even entire towns. Individual towns may have retained their names and governments, but physically they've been absorbed into the metropolis, with no intervening gaps. These formerly independent settlements could have building styles unique to them and seem like neighborhoods of the larger settlement. If they had walls, those might still be there because in an attack, each walled area has its own fortifications.

IN SPACE

In SF that features space travel, additional considerations arise.

VACUUM SETTLEMENTS

Any settlement surrounded by a vacuum instead of breathable air has a multitude of issues. Everything which maintains life is artificial and can be arranged how we like for our story needs. This includes the presence or absence of greenhouses for potentially edible plants (and the oxygen they produce). Are food animals feasible in larger settlements? There seems to be no reason they can't be, given that we're inventing fictional technology, but one wonders how well animals would fare in such environments. Often characters are miraculously fed from things like replicator machines that can produce a sizzling steak to order, but this god-like ability is perhaps the most far-fetched in all of SF.

Aside from the fabrication of air and food (and possibly gravity), a vacuum settlement tends to be formal because it's not like just anyone can wander over and make themselves at home. Space and resources are limited and it takes considerable effort to get here from there. Under most circumstances, laws, regulations, and agreement are essential because violation can result in immediate destruction and death for everyone. In particularly large settlements, visitors causing problems may be less of an issue due to redundant fail safes and the strict enforcement of arrival and departure procedures that greatly reduce accidents.

ORBITING SETTLEMENTS

There are many opportunities for settlements on planets, moons, or asteroids, but settlements can exist in orbit around any celestial body with the gravitational force required; this is a function of the mass of two objects—so as long as our settlement is smaller than the thing it orbits, we're okay.

We should decide if our orbiting outpost is tidally locked or not (see chapter 2, "Creating a Planet"). This might have been done on purpose, with whoever placed the settlement in orbit causing this with some maneuvering (preventing rotation). Real estate values may be better on one side, such as the one facing a nebula, resulting in "The Nebula District," for example. What if something causes rotation to begin, such as sabotage by disgruntled residents who wanted the good life, too? What if the side facing that nebula also dealt with more radiation and had infrastructure to counteract that, and now the poorer areas are facing it without protection because they never thought of that?

DEFENSE AND OFFENSE

Earlier parts of this chapter touched on what threats might be near from wildlife, species, and neighbors, and how this can impact a settlement's defenses. Let's look more closely at the protection that might be needed.

FORTIFICATIONS

A settlement without defenses is unlikely to resist capture. Here we look at the types of fortifications a settlement may need.

CLEARED AREAS

While not an actual fortification, a cleared area devoid of trees often surrounds a settlement to prevent opposing forces from approaching unseen. Decide how far out this region extends from the city or whether it's been done at all. Trees might have been left there as a trap and the locals know better than to set foot inside.

ARCHERY TOWERS

Whether towers for archery or another missile defense, lookout towers provide the opportunity to rain missiles down on approaching forces. They could be located all around the settlement, but we should establish what's going to attack and from which direction. An army can typically approach from only one side; if they can do so from all sides, then this settlement isn't in a good location for defense. The direction from which the primary threat comes will have more towers, as will major entrances. A city wall might also provide an inner walkway that means archers can be anywhere and move easily; in this scenario, actual towers might be mostly for lookouts.

CASTLES

In fantasy settings, the castle is a major part of many settlements and the center of life. In addition to a strategic position for firing upon attackers and making itself harder to conquer, castles are used to shelter locals in case of emergency or invasion. In a village or small town, the entire population might fit in the castle. They'll be overflowing the rooms, sleeping in halls, maybe even in the courtyard, but it's better than being in the path of an opposing army. However, in larger settlements, not everyone's going to fit. No matter the size of the community so housed, there must be enough food and water to outlast a siege or surrender is inevitable. In cities, the castle's fortifications will be augmented by the city wall, which can protect a larger population and the city itself.

THE WALL

Small settlements sometimes have a wall, which controls entrance and exit in addition to providing protection from attack. Some are only waist high and made of stones, which may seem pointless to us for being so easily climbed over, but limited material might be the reason for this. A settlement near mountains is unlikely to have such small walls of stone. Similarly, a low wall of timber when a forest stands near seems less believable.

We should decide what this wall is designed to keep out. Anything with the ability to control fire will burn down wooden walls, though this is a time-consuming way to remove one, but a wooden wall can still slow an attacking force, especially if it's comprised of less-intelligent creatures, such as animals or monsters.

WHICH ARMED FORCES ARE HERE?

In fantasy, most settlements will have some archers, swordsmen, knights, and others capable of armed combat, but what we want to look at now is whether large groups of these will exist in a settlement, and why that might be. The use of technology in SF might reduce the skill and training required to operate weapons or defenses, allowing more generalized troops. Training is often required; still, this training is often more mental than physical. We'll spend less time looking at this because those technologies and the skillsets needed to operate them are imaginary, meaning we can invent restrictions as needed for our story. Reading about considerations for existing military may give you ideas.

LOCAL GUARDS

A larger settlement will have its local guards, or what we might call police on Earth. These individuals will have some skill, but nothing like those of more specialized warriors. This can be a sore point with them. Their reduced privilege or standing may cause jealousy, especially if they are mocked by more experienced warriors. This is a good way to add tension that occasionally erupts in a brawl, duel, or disciplinary action. These guards deal with more mundane issues among the population and less so with threats from outside. Minorities might feel unfairly targeted by them.

CAVALRY

In fantasy, a settlement with open lands around it is likely to have a cavalry, whether this is actual knights or less armored horsemen. Unless we invent different animals, this is the fastest way to travel on land without machinery. A horse charge is a devastating tactical move. A settlement surrounded for many miles with open land is virtually certain to have cavalry (and a large one at that). But if open land is only on one side, the size of cavalry is reduced in favor of other skillsets. Horsemen still navigate forests, depending on density, and there are often trails or roads, but higher density reduces the number of troops that may pass. The same is true of mountains. Few settlements will lack horses completely unless self-powered vehicles have replaced them, so what we're looking at here is the existence of a specialized force: cavalry.

KNIGHTS

While knights are often part of a cavalry, they may work independently of the cavalry, in circumstances where horsemanship is peripheral. Our settlement is likely to have knights if warriors with the greatest skill set and armament are needed. A settlement in the middle of a stable sovereign power without natural enemies (like an animal or monster in a nearby forest) is unlikely to have many, if any, knights in full-time residence. But if there's a horde of something dangerous in the nearby mountain range, or the settlement lies along a contested border, we'll have knights, and lots of them. Active war zones can change the need for such individuals, as well.

FLYING FORCES

In fantasy, giant birds or dragons are two options our settlement has for an airborne military. If we decide to include creatures which are tamable to this degree in the settlement's defenses, we need to work out their capabilities, including range. These airborne forces are more plausible in mountainous areas, due to flying creatures' greater ease of movement there. Forests prevent them from flying, and therefore seeing, below the tree cover, but they offer an advantage even when plains or deserts surround a settlement. We might have invented flying creatures that are too small to be ridden but which can fly beneath the canopy, but this is still perilous due to the ease with which they can be shot down from hidden archers, for example.

In SF, an air force is virtually a given, with machines replacing creatures, but not always; nothing says we can't have such exotic animals, too. This defense might have replaced cavalry and other land forces or augment them. Ships ranging in size from single-rider craft to troopships are options that give us great flexibility in what we decide is available and in what quantities, and what sort of training, if any, the riders need. It can be attractive to decide that little training is needed for one simple reason: our characters could arrive on a world which requires them to operate one of these and do so with a modicum of success, resulting in a hopefully thrilling chase on slightly unfamiliar machines through strange territory.

Consider the impact of machines on the ability to defeat or even bypass threats on land, such as creatures capable of interfering with them. A dragon that blasts fire or ice into an engine comes to mind, but any creature able to hurl a projectile a short distance into the air can bring down a low-flying, small craft if done right. There's a tendency to make machinery impervious to such threats; avoid this trap and your work might stand out in a good way.

NAVY

The navy is easy to overlook in fantasy, as so much is focused on land and even aerial threats. In SF, the battle is typically in space, making this ignored. Regardless of genre, consider using the details found in Chapter 8, "Travel by Water," to create a more robust presentation of naval issues. Lake-side settlements will have a decent number of ships, but their focus may be commercial rather than conquest.

The settlement's access to lumber, if that's the primary material for ships, will limit its building capacity. To be a seafaring power, the country requires both sufficient wood and access to the open ocean; by contrast, if they're located on a sea and must get past other navies to reach open water, they might be restricted to a smaller fleet. They might also become allies with a power that has a bigger navy. A settlement on the coast might be at risk for attack by ships that have cannon or a replacement for such firepower. This will mean fortifications like lighthouses, a castle, and a battery to repel an attack. Their own fleet is the best defense and keeps the fighting at sea.

DETERMINE HISTORY

To create a settlement's history, it can be beneficial to have already decided the history of the sovereign power to which it belongs. Is it part of one now or has it been part of different powers? Understanding where this settlement lies in relation to powers makes this easier to decide. Anywhere near a border has likely endured changes, but even places many days' travel from the nearest border could've experienced change. This is especially true if an empire has ever spread over it.

A city a thousand years old has likely changed hands, but one only a few hundred years old might never have. Decide how long ago this settlement was founded. If large scale wars are rare in that area, it might've only changed hands a few times, but more tumultuous places might have experienced this every generation, or more frequently. What matters is how much of a melting pot experience the community has had. This can cause a mix of building styles, materials, customs, and certainly population. And if a different species is the conqueror, we'll almost certainly have a more varied atmosphere than the mono-human one often shown in fantasy.

We don't need to identify or discuss these wars. All we need is the fact of the settlement having been embroiled in one, and the resulting damage or destruction. There can still be toppled buildings around. There might be monuments to individual soldiers or generic ones who represent a conflict. If a power conquered the settlement, erected such statues or buildings, and then disappeared, are these items still pristine, gone altogether, or defaced? Have some been repurposed, with their original meanings and inscriptions redone or removed so that the source is no longer apparent? Is a building abandoned? A tourist attraction? Such a building could be one native to the population, abused by conquerors, and still standing but unused, or taken over by vagrants. Sometimes these are an eyesore and sometimes they're a source of pride.

On a practical level, we don't need extensive details about which power it's been a part of, because in most cases we'll do little more than mention the fact in passing. We can just decide that it's changed hands to this one or that one a certain number of years ago, and various relics are around town as a result. But it isn't just structures but people who are affected, and their memories and attitudes about other places. Two places that were once enemies won't always be, nor will two that are friendly always be. Persistent strong sentiment is rare and is usually fueled by something like religion or ethnicity. Opinions and sentiment change over time, provided that situations have changed, and what remains is subtler lingering dislike or prejudice.

We can also have events that took place within a settlement, such as discoveries, inventions, accidents, and failures. Great fires, droughts, earthquakes, and other natural disasters sometimes leave a mark on not only the topography, but the living memory of a population. In a world with magic or technology, good and bad acts are likely, the number of them dependent partly on population size and settlement longevity. Is our settlement famous for anything having occurred here? Will it be?

LOCAL LORE

Settlements sometimes have local stories or legends. In a fantasy setting, this is arguably more common in villages and towns than in cities due to their lower education and worldliness, leading to myths. In fantasy, these may center on supernatural phenomena, such as magic or ghosts, even the appearance of gods. But in SF, these may be more technological in origin, such as first contact with alien species. Events are one way to create these, with a story surrounding those events. These stories often have missing details that could alter their interpretation, which also lends itself to there being misunderstandings about what really took place. Any unusual place or character, past or present, can cause lore. World figures who originated from here are good examples, and we can decide this person has unusual talents or skills that this settlement claims some responsibility for, though that's only likely in the event of a hero, not a villain.

HOW IT IS KNOWN?

Every settlement tends to be known for something, such as a product, event, or population skillset, like excellent archers. Do they make great wines? Weapons? Are their knights amazing? The wizards? Pilots? Or is the place just run down and a haven for bad people like pirates? The reputation can help us craft an overall viewpoint that adds character.

REPUTATION

The larger the community, the more likely we are to think of the settlement's reputation. This status is as much about the population's makeup, beliefs, or acts, as about what the settlement represents, though these are intertwined. We need a sense of what this place is like, and how we intend to use it, to form this reputation. Do we want it feared or a haven? Frequently or rarely visited? Humble and easily conquered or aggressive and out to dominate life around it? Are the warriors or rulers famous? For what? The amount of danger a settlement experiences can influence this.

COLORS

A settlement's colors will figure in our work in two major ways: characters might use them for personal or structural decoration, and flags, banners, or symbols are likely to incorporate them. During battle scenes, we're almost certain to mention the flags of the opponents. When characters arrive at our settlements, they may notice the pennants, and local colors may figure in awnings and other functional fabrics. Ships may use the colors on their sails or trim, while more technological vehicles could feature them on the designations painted on the vessel, and the interior.

The colors can be arbitrary, in which case it's recommended that world builders delay on a decision. By the time we need to be specific, maybe we'll have thought of a justification. If we'd like a reason, which is optional because we may never explain it, we can associate colors with something. Red makes sense for a settlement with a violent history, for red's association with blood. Blue might work for port towns, green for forest ones, and yellow for deserts or plains. Or we can use a suggestion of wealth, like gold and silver, whether the settlement has mountain mines for these minerals or just fancies

328 | RANDY ELLEFSON

itself wealthy (whether it is or not). A port city with a marauding navy that plunders other towns might also choose gold to show its wealth. Humility might figure in a settlement's sense of self, resulting in muted browns. A justification can be simple. And in a more primitive or isolated society, colors might be limited to what dyes can be created from local plants.

We might want a sovereign power to have a primary color that is incorporated in all symbols by settlements. For example, the Kingdom of Antaria's color may be blue, and the capital's colors are blue and gold, while a sister city is blue and silver. A nearby town is blue and brown, etc.

SYMBOLS

Many settlements have a symbol that's a source of pride, identity, and possibly fear among opponents. This symbol might represent the population's values and be humble for a peaceful place, or aggressive for a warlike or barbaric one. The settlement's colors might be part of it or even derived from it, so we can create this first. A wolf symbol suggests white. A raven suggests black. These can give us one of our two or three hues.

Symbols are often simple so they're easy to remember and therefore more powerful. Ones that don't require an explanation are better than those that do. Being easy to draw allows commoners to reproduce them, not just skilled artists. We can use animals associated with peace, war, or strength, or staple plants may suggest prosperity, though these won't exactly intimidate someone on the battlefield. Decide how often and what sort of hostilities a settlement faces before going with something warlike. A backwoods farming community probably favors tools of their trade. If a "first" happened somewhere, like the first launch of a ship into space, the silhouette of a vessel lifting off can become a new symbol. Crafting symbols isn't always easy, so consider saving this for when you really need one, and use the most obvious ones, which are often the best ones, first or on your most important settlements; there's a higher chance you'll be mentioning it.

SLOGANS

We seldom have reason or opportunity to mention a settlement's slogan, if it exists, but this may result from world builders not taking the time to invent them. Sometimes one doesn't exist until an event, like "Boston Strong" emerging after the Boston Marathon bombing. We can leverage this by tying our slogan to an event, recent or not. What is on the minds of the residents in the aftermath? Strength in the face of adversity led to the above example. Resistance might play on the minds of those in war-torn areas. We don't need a slogan for everywhere in our world and it could be difficult to conjure up so many, so focus on what you need for a given story. More can be added later; this is a prime subject to skip.

PRODUCTS

Every settlement has products it consumes or produces (or wants to). The population might be known for adoring particular wines, sweets, meats, or vegetables. Some will be delicacies due to rarity there. Others might be local and preferred for that, or coveted in various other locales far and wide. Locals might also have disdain for other products, particularly those with which they compete, or those from despised sovereign powers or regions. They might even enjoy such products while having contempt for those who produce them: "I hate elves but they sure do make good wine!" This sort of world building can be quickly mentioned in scenes to give an impression of a wider world than what we're seeing.

Forests provide plants for medicines and wood for furniture, tools, and building materials, including wooden ships, if the right kind of forest or trees are here. Mountains provide for gems and other minerals, even stone. The sea can be a product source for locals and an export to landlocked settlements. An import can be desired because it *isn't* found here. What if a port city doesn't have access to the trees needed to build ships? This sort of consideration can lead to trade with friends and enemies alike, helping inspire conflict. Inventing products doesn't seem glamorous, but much world building can be achieved by deciding what's available in a given region, and who they can sell to or get things from. Creating our own plants, animals, and resulting products gives us more options.

SECRETS

Inventing secrets for our settlement can be fun but is optional. Waiting until we have a need for a secret is recommended because a secret is unknown and we'll have no reason to mention it unless characters uncover it. Secrets can be incorporated into city layout, such as there being a building off limits to most people, for a reason that's a lie or which isn't admitted to at all. Maybe a building's location seems inappropriate, and the explanation lies underground, such as an entrance to secret catacombs, or a supernatural phenomenon, whether sinister or helpful. If we've created gods, world figures, and undead, the events of their existence can result in such places.

Secrets can be more mundane, such as benevolent or nefarious groups operating in the shadows; they might have influence over settlement leaders. Hidden doors or places are less exciting unless there's something truly interesting there, such as a portal. We can have landmarks like statues that have an unknown feature that is activated under the right circumstances. Maybe a statue is a being that can be reanimated, either as a stone golem, a living person, or undead. Religion is good for creating places with unknown (or largely unknown) features. See chapter 11, "Creating Places of Interest," for ideas.

HOW MANY PLACES TO CREATE

If we're creating a world, or part of it, to tell one story, our focus is clearly on those locales where events happen now or in the past, and which influence our work. Creating full details is advantageous for these places. Other settlements mentioned in passing can have little more than their sovereign power, location, climate, terrain, reputation (including defensiveness), population type and disposition, major products, and a few identifiers such as symbol and colors decided.

If we're creating a world we intend to use often, we can become overwhelmed with scores of settlements to invent. There's a way to manage this. Full details on a place are still only needed when we're going to use it in a tale, or if we happen to have ideas. For the rest, a master spreadsheet with high-level details on every settlement can make it easier to invent that information. We'll avoid creating the same symbol for two places, because we can see, in one file, all the ones we've already done. We can also more easily find this information when we need it.

A spreadsheet with columns like the following gets us started:

- Name
- Sovereign power
- Location
- Population size
- Species here (and percentage of overall population)
- Products
- Symbol

• Colors
• Military

Despite this information being in a spreadsheet, we'll probably want a file for each settlement, where this information is potentially duplicated, and get in the habit of updating both file and spreadsheet when we make changes.

Why would we want to create this high-level information for everywhere? We might want to remark that a character is drinking one of the fine wines from a place, or wearing clothes from there (or in their fashion). Maybe they're sitting on chairs from another place, evident in its design. Or they're sailing on a ship with a distinctive style. These little touches add realism and are easy to accomplish, but, as mentioned under the previous section about products, animosities and friendliness can result in added tension on regional levels.

WHERE TO START

It's wise to start with the settlement's location, as this affects everything about it, including layout, climate (and therefore dress), and neighbors, which can include not only other settlements and sovereign powers, but nearby species that live in adjacent terrain. The settlement size, and therefore population, is a second area to consider, as this affects the society and its world view. We might next consider the defense needed due to nearby threats. What it's known for can either be a starting point or a minor detail we add toward the end of our conception. Above all, start with whatever strikes you as a solid idea you won't change your mind on later, as this inspiration often colors much else about our invention.

CHAPTER SEVEN

TRAVEL OVER LAND

On Earth, motorized vehicles come with a speedometer to tell us how fast we're going. Using navigation systems, which are typically connected to GPS, we can even learn how long a trip will take and get continual updates on that. In a SF world with even more advanced technology, we can likely assume the same convenience, but in fantasy worlds, none of this exists. Few of us know how long it takes to get any significant distance by walking or riding various animals. This chapter focus mostly on a fantasy-like setting, where help determining speeds, capabilities, and the impact of terrain on non-magical travel is needed.

Most of the Earth uses the metric system. If releasing products, it's wise to state measurements for the culture where the product will be released. Despite this, miles were used instead of kilometers while writing explanations in this chapter because theories apply regardless of the measurement used and explanations are clearer with consistency. Conversions for kilometers are included for any formulas.

Writing "Not drawn to scale" on any maps we create is recommended. This provides some leeway in regards to stringent accuracy. A map is not needed for understanding this chapter, but the guidelines are written assuming that you have a map and now want to determine distances and corresponding travel times.

MODE OF TRAVEL

WALKING

Depending on the level of prosperity and technology in our world, most people will only have walking as an option. This is one reason people traveled less on Earth long ago. A trip can be arduous and fraught with peril from thieves and other bandits. Add to that the nefarious creatures in fantasy worlds and people will often stay put. Generally, in a world with poor medicine like in most fantasy settings, those walking are more likely to be between the ages of ten and forty. Those younger or older than this tend to suffer more from long walks. Their fitness level and our world's standards of health impact this. On Earth, few people lived past forty long ago, a problem that modern medicine has reduced. Now people are generally healthier, but if our invented society is based on a medieval one, our inhabitants might be somewhat frail by forty.

When traveling by foot, most people will walk the entire way—only trained warriors or messengers will run any meaningful distance. The ability to run for long distances requires conditioning and practice and is therefore not for the average person unless they happen to love doing it.

Armor, weapons, and supplies will encumber warriors, slowing them and reducing endurance so that they cannot travel as far in a day. A messenger might be less encumbered, but that depends on their location. If traveling in fairly safe lands, they need fewer protections and might carry less. A messenger for the royalty might receive free room and board, and need few supplies. Molesting one might be a capital offense so that they have little to fear. By contrast, in a dangerous wilderness or sovereign power, death from other species or animals (even plants) can happen at any time.

Most of our humanoid species will be close enough in height to humans for there to be no measurable difference. Those much smaller or taller have a shorter or longer gait. This can mean more or fewer steps to accomplish the same journey. This could, in turn, have them tired upon completion. They might also take more or fewer hours to complete the trip. We can alter them to compensate if desired. For example, perhaps our short species has better endurance and travels for more hours without fatigue, reaching a destination in more hours but still making it.

While carrying minimal supplies, the average human can reliably walk twelve miles a day, day after day, without needing to rest or be exhausted. A Roman legion could do fourteen to twenty miles per day. Someone could conceivably do over twenty miles in a day but be exhausted. A marathon of over twenty miles can be done in a few hours, but those people must train for it and must recover for days afterward. In other words, we can fudge travel times in our world based on story needs, but we should first understand a baseline.

Caravans are a special case wherein the entire group moves at the speed of the slowest traveler, unless that person can be placed in a wagon or on a steed. This often means that the slowest mover is an animal, so first we'll need to decide which ones are in the caravan and how encumbered they are, as this may reduce speed.

RIDING ON LAND

There are arguably three scenarios for ridden animals and their encumbrance—light, medium, and heavy. A horse outfitted for a casual ride and ridden by someone with minimal gear (spare clothes, a sword, some utensils and water) has the lightest load and will therefore be able to travel farther in a day, thirty or forty miles. By contrast, a fully armored knight (plate armor, with multiple swords and a lance) on a war horse that's also fully armored (plate armor) will have far less endurance and speed. This will reduce the distance that can be traveled in a day. A less armored warrior (chainmail, shield, one sword) and a lightly armored horse (just leather) will be able to travel father. This also relates to elephants, camels, and our custom animals.

Specialized horses can go over one hundred miles per day for several days in a row. The Pony Express riders could travel many miles, but they nearly rode a horse into the ground between stations, when they mounted another and kept going at the same breakneck speed. Horse-pulled wagons travel about fifteen to twenty-five miles per day without roads. Other animals like oxen, giant lizards, and elephants will have different speeds and endurance. We can use any of them as analogues for our invented animals.

FLYING

While flying can generally be assumed to be done in a straight line, factors change this, though this depends on the mode of travel, as what affects a dragon wouldn't affect a Boeing 747. Mountains can be tall enough that they must be circumnavigated. Real birds struggle to get over the Himalayas, for example, because the air is thinner. Dragons are often depicted as all-powerful, but describing their difficulty in climbing over mountains is one way to make them more realistic. This is one reason, along with rain shadows, for characterizing any land features we've created; in this case, we'll decide which mountain ranges are this tall (hint from Chapter 4: the tallest peaks are in the interior of a continent, not on its coast).

Hostile territories can also change flight patterns, whether that hostility derives from other animals or sentient beings like humans with missile weapons. A lone dragon might fear to fly through an area inhabited by other dragons, if the latter are territorial or of a hostile variety. If the dragon is unafraid, his rider might be more cautious.

Politics can also cause hostility. A dictatorship might have outlawed all dragons, for example, that aren't ridden by its own military so that borders are closely watched. Being caught could be a problem. While some might attempt passing over the territory using flight or subterfuge, some will simply go around. In such cases, we'll need to figure out the shortest path that is not a straight line.

ANIMALS

All flying animals that are depicted as being ridable are imaginary. The likelihood is that none of them would get off the ground with a rider, but there's no fun in that. We must take being realistic with a bigger grain of salt than normal, but the useful details and considerations that arise from trying to be realistic can make our work more believable.

Except for mountains, flying animals are unaffected by the terrain, whether that's roads, forests, rolling hills, or deserts. Flying low changes things a little, as foliage may hide threats, but we're focused on speed here, not dangers except as those that affect flight paths.

When deciding how far (and fast) invented animals can travel in a day, it can help to start with understanding what real Earth birds can do. A carrier pigeon can fly about fifty miles per hour and cover seven hundred miles in a day. Hawks reach twenty to forty miles per hour during migration. These guidelines can help us determine the speeds and distances of our invented fliers. If we have a species that is humanoid with wings, aerodynamics will ensure they fly more slowly than birds. Their maneuverability is also reduced so that a giant bird should have little trouble catching and killing our species, unless the latter is well armed with missile weapons. For these reasons, flying low and hugging treetops and mountains is wiser for our humanoid character than open air unless they have no reason to suspect such a foe. The sight of such a threat should prompt one to seek shelter.

AIRSHIPS

Whether we call them airships, blimps, or dirigibles, these aircraft use buoyancy to stay aloft. This chapter won't focus on the differences between them but rather how fast they can travel. The larger airships like the Hindenburg have higher speeds and other capabilities. The Hindenburg before its demise could reach 84 mph (135 k/mph), but smaller blimps are a bit slower—their maximum speed is 70 mph and with a typical cruising speed of 30-50 mph. The limitation is inherent in the shape and design; using a bigger or more powerful engine won't change this.

Figure 33 Zeppelin Airship

As opposed to a balloon, they are maneuverable. The large ones can ascend as high as 24000 feet (7300 meters), which means they can theoretically fly over any mountain range on Earth. However, their payload is reduced when that high and they mainly operate between 1500-8000 feet (460-2500 meters), though the Hindenburg typically did so under 650 feet to stay below clouds and monitor them for storms. The purpose of the flight will determine their altitude, as a passenger ship might sail lower to provide views while a surveillance blimp might be higher to avoid detection.

When planning a trip for our characters, we can assume a straight line unless we have some reason not to do so, such as the avoidance of a storm or hostile territory. Airships must refuel and this could restrict their uninterrupted flight to 24-50 hours, but the Hindenburg could fly over 100 hours, typically when crossing an ocean.

BALLOONS

Hot air balloons drift with the wind. They cannot be propelled through the air and their flight path cannot be controlled beyond a limited degree. Their speed is also rather slow, such as 3-6 mph for commercial flights, which range from 3-10 miles long and take roughly an hour. Longer trips are possible as the Earth has been circumnavigated in a single trip more than once; fuel, supplies, assistance, and navigator skill are the requirements for such a feat. For world builders, we mostly need to know the balloon's air speed and what sort of trouble our characters might get into if the flight doesn't go as planned, but this will depend on landscape.

AIRPLANES

There are many variations to planes and engine types that will determine how long it takes to travel between two locations by aircraft. This includes fuel capacity, wind, and the plane's purpose, as a passenger jet is far slower than an F-16, but also far faster than a crop duster. The variety is extreme enough that trying to summarize this may not serve a world builder well and has been omitted from the book.

What we need to first do is decide on the technological level of our society and what sort of plane we need (passenger, fighter). What's the purpose in our story, and do we want our characters to have a plane that suits that purpose or not? Perhaps only a two-seat propeller plane is available but they'd prefer a fighter jet. We'll also need a sense of how far they need to go. From here, we'd Google the plane type, learn its typical speed and fuel capacity, and get a sense of how long a trip might take if done in a straight line.

OBSTACLES

THE IMPACT OF TERRAIN

The terrain we travel over impacts our speed and reliability. Sand will impact a two-legged species less than a wagon, with wheels that are bogged down, but remember, from Chapter 4, that most deserts are rocky rather than sandy. A forest with thick underbrush slows everything. A light forest will have less impact. The density of underbrush in a forest is a moot point if there's a cleared road through it. Rolling hills, foothills, and mountains will slow everyone whether there's a road or not; it takes time to go up and down and this is worse on the legs of humanoids or animals, increasing fatigue.

Roads paved with cobblestones aren't smooth and can not only slow travel but fatigue feet and wagons, where the bumpy ride strains construction. Such roads are more common near a city, extending a short distance from the walls. Very dry, hard ground is tough on feet, which is why horses will prefer the grass. An unpaved roads means potholes and potentially mud.

Paving, when present, seldom extends far from a settlement due to expense. This is one way to indicate wealth, such as in an empire. We may want to decide that most roads are unpaved for most of their length.

Rivers can require traveling to a known crossing, which might be guarded by creatures or species who charge a toll or simply won't let others pass without a fight. Given fords' importance, such a crossing might be controlled by a city, sovereign power, or band of opportunistic thugs. But our main concern is to decide where a river crossing is between two settlements and measure the distance to it from both places, unless the bridge happens to be directly between them.

THE IMPACT OF LIFE

Wild animals and sinister species make traveling more perilous. On a wide open plain with low grass, one could see trouble coming from a long way off, but tall grass or a thick forest could slow our travelers even if there's a road through the terrain. Due to this, there's a difference between the theoretical travel time and the actual. This is another way to slow our characters.

CALCULATION PREPARATION

Multiple steps are needed to calculate distance and travel times. The existence of a map is assumed but not necessary. Just ignore those steps if you don't have one. If you're familiar with Microsoft Excel, some of this might easier to absorb.

GET ORGANIZED

If we're calculating distances for multiple journeys, we'll want to keep a list somewhere, like a spreadsheet. We'll need to write down the names of each place, of course, but this causes a minor problem with alphabetizing the list. If we write down Washington to Baltimore, then when scanning the list for Baltimore to Washington, we won't see it. We might think we forgot to write it down. It's recommended to alphabetize left to right, too, not just up and down in our list. It might be better to organize by geographic regions or kingdoms, too, if we have a large list of a hundred locations, for example.

What we're after is a listing like the below:

Start	Destination	Distance in Inches
Kingdom of Illiandor		
Arycndl	Illiandor	.5
Arycndl	Talendor	1
Illiandor	Talendor	.75
Kingdom of Kariah		
Cree	Kharlan	.25
Kariah	Kharlan	.25

Figure 34 Sample Distances

MEASURE

It's time to measure. We can print our map and do this in the physical world, or import a digital map into a drawing program that has rulers above and to one side. Or we can just eyeball everything. Adding a note to our map—"Not drawn to scale"—is also recommended to provide leeway.

We might decide to only include the distances between settlements, but we can also measure distances to nearby land features if those places are of interest to our characters or story. A forest or mountain range frequently traversed or skirted can impact character decisions and travel times.

If characters go through a terrain, we might want to measure how far that extends. For example, if Arcyndl to Illiandor is an inch overall, but a quarter inch is heavy forest and another quarter inch is rolling hills, we might want to indicate this. Each terrain will cause a different travel speed. This might be more detailed than we want, but it adds realism. It can be useful in stories as we remember to observe how much time will be lost on some parts of the journey.

This example shows what we're looking to do. The numbers are inches (modify for metrics if needed).

Start	Target	Road	Forest	Hills	Total
Arcyndl	Illiandor	.5	.25	.25	1
Illiandor	Talendor	.25		.25	.5

Figure 35 Sample Measurements

To those columns (road, forest, and hills), we should also add light forest, plains, mountains, deserts, and swamps.

SCALE

Determining our map's scale is easy. Just pick a number. Maybe .25 inches equals twenty miles. Based on this, we can calculate that one inch is eighty miles. Changing our minds about scale can become a problem unless we use a program like Microsoft Excel's spreadsheet feature. If we set it up correctly, we can change our scale at any time and have all our miles re-calculated for us. This book provides a free template that already does this, and a lot more, for you. See the "Template" section later in this chapter for more details.

Before choosing our scale, we should get an idea how far apart we imagine these places to be. One way is to reference familiar places on Earth. We might have the impression that two locations are as far as apart as our home and job are, or two cities we frequent. Use online mapping websites to learn how many miles separate them.

We might have a continent that we imagine to be as large as Australia, whether we've ever been there or not. Online maps can tell how far apart cities there are, giving us a sense of scale. Choose two cities and ask a mapping app for directions to learn the miles. If two similar locations on our map are that far apart, this gives us scale. For example, Melbourne to Sydney Australia is 867 kilometers. Then 867 divided by 4 is 216 kilometers per inch.

Sometimes such a number might surprise us and we might have to decide our continent/location is smaller or bigger than we'd thought.

With our scale chosen, we can calculate how far away all locations are and fill in a list of this information. In the example below, this has been done with two rows, using a scale of 1 inch equaling 20 miles:

Start	Target	Road (inches)	Road (miles)	Hills (in.)	Hills (mi.)	Total (in.)	Total (mi.)
Arcyndl	Illiandor	.25	5	.25	5	.5	10
Illiandor	Talendor	.5	10	.25	5	.75	15

Figure 36 Sample Terrains

There are better ways to organize this information, as found in the template, but this demonstrates the idea.

BASE MILES PER DAY (BMPD)

For simplicity, I'll use miles instead of kilometers for the acronym BMPD, but these guidelines may be easily converted to kilometers. We need to know or decide how far humans, wagons, dragons, and other species can travel in a day. We have leeway with invented species but should base them on something similar. Humans can reliably walk twelve miles a day without having to rest or recuperate. Faster or longer travel is possible with consequences, but we're first looking for a reliable base miles per day.

Horses do better on softer ground, making that their ideal terrain. This will be true of other hooved animals, too, regardless of what protections we put on their feet. In the next chart, we'll see that the ideal terrain is indicated by a zero in a column. The zero means that the terrain, such as a road for walking, has no negative impact and does not modify the base speed.

Research is the best way to determine the BMPD for our life forms. You can use the values I chose (in the next chart) or research humans, riding horse, wagon, and carrier pigeon BMPDs yourself.

TERRAIN MODIFIERS

As mentioned earlier, the difficulty of the terrain will modify the base miles per day (BMPD). You'll have to decide for yourself how much speed and distance is lost. Or you can take my current estimates as being plausible if not entirely scientific. My judgement calls are subject to change as I get smarter about all this. Either way, I don't worry over it too much for one simple reason—no one from the planet I've created is going to show up on Earth and announce to everyone that I was wrong about how long it really takes to travel between two places. Besides, my map is not drawn to scale!

Here is my chart of BMPD and the number of miles *lost* per day due to terrain.

Travel Mode	BMPD	Road	Plain	Forest	Hills	Mountain	Desert Swamp
Foot	12	0	0	1.8	3	6	4
Riding Horse	35	3.5	0	3.5	9	18	12
War horse (light)	28	2.8	0	2.8	7	14	9
War horse (heavy)	21	2.1	0	2.1	5	11	7
Wagon	25	0	2.5			17	
Dragon	500					160	
Carrier Pigeon	700					10	

Figure 37 Terrain Modifier Example

Looking at the first row, this means that humanoids travel 12 miles per day over level terrain. This speed isn't impacted by road or plains for the worse (as indicated by the zeroes). A light forest, without road or trail, slows humans 1.8 miles per day, travelling only 10.2 miles per day. In a heavy forest without road or trail, we lose 8 miles per day, due to thick underbrush we must hack through, moving only 4 miles. On rolling hills or foothills of mountains, we lose 3 miles per day, and mountains reduce speed by half, to 6 miles per day. A sandy desert or swamp reduces distance covered per day by 4 miles, to 8.

The greyed-out sections don't apply. A flying dragon is unaffected by roads, plains, forests, hills, deserts or swamps. Mountains' effect will depend on their height. Similarly, a wagon cannot typically pass through a forest, sandy desert, or roadless swamp. The presence of a road means that the existence of a swamp or other impediments can be largely ignored because the road bypasses the difficulties inherent in an untamed swamp, unless flooding has taken place.

You'll also note that the ideal terrain for horses is plains, indicated by the zero for plains. They lose distance on roads instead, because stones are hard on their feet, reducing endurance and therefore distance traveled per day.

Calculations were used to create the modified values. BMPD is reduced by a percentage. For example, mountains cut the BMPD in half. I used 25% for hills, 66% for heavy forests, 33% for desert, and only 15% and 10% for light forest and roads/plains. You can use my values or your own. Below are all my modifier calculations in the same chart as above, showing what I multiplied BMPD by. BMPD * Modifiers = Miles Lost.

Travel Mode	BMPD	Road	Plain	Forest	Hills	Mountain	Desert Swamp
Foot	12			.15	.25	.5	.33
Riding Horse	35	.1		.15	.25	.5	.33
War horse (light)	28	.1		.15	.25	.5	.33
War horse (heavy)	21	.1		.15	.25	.5	.33
Wagon	25		.1		.25	.66	
Dragon	500					.2	
Carrier Pigeon	700					.2	

Figure 38 Terrain Modifiers

OTHER MODIFIERS

What we're calculating is typical conditions. We can speed up a journey in ideal conditions or slow it down with poor ones. If desired, we can use additional modifiers, such how much people are slowed down in darkness, rain, or snow (of various depths). Danger along a route might also slow travel. I chose not to include these in my charts to avoid overkill but you can. For me, it's enough to know what's typical and modify an actual journey's time based on story needs or even whim.

CALCULATIONS

Now we need to calculate the number of days it takes to travel between two points on our map. The formula is distance divided by speed. First, we need to calculate speed by taking the BMPD and subtracting the amount of time lost by the terrain traveled over. The resulting formula is:

$$\text{Distance} / (\text{BMPD} - \text{Terrain Modifier})$$

For example, traveling by foot is 12 miles per day. According to my chart, if traveling through light forest without a road, we lose 1.8 miles per day, resulting in a speed of 10.2 miles per day. If our map's scale says that a quarter inch is 20 miles, and our journey is 1 inch, then 20 * 4 is 80 miles. Eighty (80) miles divided by 10.2 miles per day gets our answer: just under 8 days.

$$80 / (12 - 1.8)$$

Calculating speed for every mode of travel, through every type of terrain, for every two locations on our world, can be time consuming. Doing so has an advantage: once the calculations are done, we don't have to do them again. If we change our mind about scale and have used the provided spreadsheet to track our data, then our calculations will automatically update. This method might be more suited to those intending to use a world over many stories.

By contrast, there is a more manual method, discussed in the next section, that avoids using formulas to change things. Its chief disadvantage is that if we change our mind on scale, calculations we've logged before must be redone. Those using a world once or twice might find this is the most suitable approach.

PRE-SET CALCULATIONS

The easiest approach to calculating travel between two places is to be generic about it. Looking at the chart below will make the explanation clearer. This chart states in line 1 that everything on it is for traveling on a paved road. Column A shows inches on our map, while columns B and C shows the corresponding number of miles or kilometers; which we use is irrelevant for determining speed. Columns D through J are the number of days to travel each distance from the first three columns by foot, riding horse, etc.

This chart, and others for different terrains, is included in the free template given to newsletter subscribers. The file allows you to change the scale so that .25 inches could be 25 miles instead of 20, for example, and all the chart's data will change immediately.

Using these pre-set calculations, we never need to use formulas to determine travel time. Instead, we can take our measurement between two places, like Illiandor and Talendor, and see that it is 2 inches. Line 11 above shows us how far that is and how long each travel mode is. And we're done.

	A	B	C	D	E	F	G	H	I	J
1				Traveling on a Paved Road (or Flying Straight)						
2	Inches	Miles	Kilometers	Foot	Riding Horse	Warhorse (light)	Warhorse (heavy)	Wagon	Dragon	Carrier Pigeon
3		Distance				Days by Travel Mode				
4	0.25	20	32.2	1.7	0.6	0.8	1.1	0.8	0	0
5	0.5	40	64.4	3.4	1.2	1.6	2.2	1.6	0.1	0.1
6	0.75	60	96.6	5.1	1.8	2.4	3.3	2.4	0.1	0.1
7	1	80	128.7	6.8	2.4	3.2	4.4	3.2	0.1	0.1
8	1.25	100	160.9	8.5	3	4	5.5	4	0.2	0.1
9	1.5	120	193.1	10.2	3.6	4.8	6.6	4.8	0.2	0.2
10	1.75	140	225.3	11.9	4.2	5.6	7.7	5.6	0.2	0.2
11	2	160	257.5	13.6	4.8	6.4	8.8	6.4	0.3	0.2
12	2.25	180	289.7	15.3	5.4	7.2	9.9	7.2	0.3	0.3
13	2.5	200	321.9	17	6	8	11	8	0.3	0.3
14	2.75	220	354.1	18.7	6.6	8.8	12.1	8.8	0.4	0.3

Figure 39 Travel on Paved Roads

But what if the two inches between these locations are over different terrain? Maybe 1 inch is a road and another inch is rolling hills. We need to grab line 7 from both charts (the line for 1 inch). Now we have realistic data with thought behind it.

Inches By		Distance				Days By Travel Mode				
		Miles	Kilometers	Foot	Riding Horse	Warhorse	Hy Warhorse	Wagon	Dragon	Pigeon
Road	0.25	20	32.2		0.6					
Plain	0									
Light Forest	0									
Heavy Forest	0									
Hills	0.5	40	64.4		1.6					
Mountains	0									
Swamp/Desert	0									
Total	0.75	60	96.6	0	2.2	0	0	0	0	0

Figure 40 Travel Sample

In the included template, I've added an area for you to add up these values. It looks like this screen shot below. What I did here was take the inches by road and hills and typed them into the chart. Then I add the miles by looking at the other charts. I also added the values for a riding horse, in this case. It shows my final results for a particular journey.

The main problem with the above chart is that our data is not preserved. When we want to do a second journey, we'll have to replace that data, unless we save it somewhere. Also, if we change our mind about scale, that saved data must be redone. For this reason, some world builders might want to follow the steps in the next section.

CUSTOM CALCULATIONS

World builders who intend to use the world for many years to come might want to preserve travel times between many places in a single database. Doing this requires a time investment and familiarity with formulas that will scare away many people. This section is designed for the brave. I did this once for my main world, Llurien, and will likely never do it again, even for new continents, because it's too much work. There's also a significant risk of making a formula mistake. A major advantage of doing it is that, once done, it never needs repeating. A change of scale updates the entire spreadsheet.

The details of these custom calculations are discussed in the following template section. Explaining how to do it without the template as a visual guide is unnecessarily challenging. And setting up that template yourself is more pain than you likely want.

THE TEMPLATE

Most templates for this book are Microsoft Word documents that are downloadable but also printed in an appendix. For the travel calculations, there is a Microsoft Excel spreadsheet instead, which I discuss here. You can join the newsletter and download the "Travel Template" for free at http://www.artofworldbuilding.com/newsletter.

I'm not going to provide instruction on spreadsheet basics, just how to use my template, with caveats and tips. You will need to read this carefully and study the template. I suggest downloading it first, looking it over, and then reading along while keeping the template open to refer to. Those familiar with Excel and spreadsheet technology will find this much easier to follow and use.

The spreadsheet template has multiple sheets, which are discussed next. An additional sheet for calculating travel at sea is also included and discussed in the next chapter.

SCHEMA SHEET

The first sheet in the template we'll look at is called "Schema." The screen shot below shows two columns, "Inches on Map" and "# of Miles", or how many miles to the inch. This sets the map's scale.

	A	B
1	Inches on Map	# of Miles
2	0.25	20
3	0.5	40
4	0.75	60
5	1	80
6	1.25	100
7	1.5	120
8	1.75	140
9	2	160
10	2.25	180
11	2.5	200
12	2.75	220

Figure 41 Inches and Miles

The value in cell B2, highlighted in green, is the only one you need alter. Cells B3-B12 contain formulae to calculate distances based on the value in B2. In other words, B2 is the number of miles for a quarter inch. For example, half an inch is twice one quarter of an inch, so the number of miles is doubled. You can change the value in B2 right now and see how it changes this section of the "Schema" sheet. It also causes all the values on the "Travel" sheet to change. This is what we *want* because we don't need to ever re-calculate a value.

14		Base Miles Per Day and # Miles Lost Due to Terrain							
15	Travel Mode	BMPD	Road	Plain	Forest (light)	Forest (heavy)	Hills	Mountains	Desert
16	Foot	12	0	0	1.8	8	3	6	4
17	Riding Horse	35	3.5	0	5.25	23.1	9	18	12
18	War horse (light)	28	2.8	0	4.2	18.5	7	14	9
19	War Horse (heavy)	21	2.1	0	3.15	13.9	5	11	7
20	Wagon	25	0	2.5			6	17	8
21	Dragon	600	0					120	
22	Carrier Pigeon	700	0					140	

Figure 42 Base Miles Per Day

The second area of the "Schema" sheet, pictured below, is the BMPD and miles lost due to terrain. This should look familiar because I covered this earlier in this chapter. You don't need to change this unless you disagree with my formulas or the "Base" value I used. The green cells do not have formulas, so you can just type a new value. For the other cells, you'd need to modify the formulas if you don't agree with them. You'll notice that some cells have a little red triangle in the corner. This means I have a note, usually explaining my rationale for the formula, and you can see this comment by hovering your mouse over the red triangle. A right-click on the cell will open a menu allowing you to edit the comment.

TRAVEL SHEET

The travel sheet utilizes the schema sheet. I've provide sample data so you can see how this works. This sheet gets a little complicated so digest this in pieces and study what's happening closely. It is divided into sections. In general, the grey columns should never be altered as they are counting other areas of this spreadsheet for you, using formulas you'll never need to alter.

The first section, pictured above, is just two columns, A and B, which are the Start and Destination locations. This is the easiest part to fill out. Just add all your places here, organized by region or sovereign power.

The second section, "Inches over Terrain Type," is pictured below and is columns C through J. This is the measurement of how many map-inches separate two places. If the total distance is one inch but half is on roads and half is over rolling hills, you would enter .5 in column C (roads) and .5 in column G (hills). The grey-colored J column, "Total," totals the inches for you, and should not be altered. This section is also easy to fill out. Measure your map and type in your values.

	A	B
1	Start	Destination
2	Free Cities	
3	City 1	City 2
4	City 1	City 3
5	City 3	Town 1
6	City 3	Town 2
7	City 4	Wizard Tower
8		
9	Kingdom of Wherever	
10	City 1	City 2
11	City 2	City 3
12		
13	Kingdom of Nowhere	
14	Town 1	Town 2
15	City 1	Town 1

Figure 43 Start and End Locations

The third section, "Miles over Terrain Type," is pictured below and is columns K through S, with the last two columns adding up both total miles and total kilometers from the columns to the left (K through Q). For the other columns, we're getting the number of *miles* that corresponds to the number of *inches* from the second section. In the sample data, column C3 shows .25 miles over road. That means that column K3 should show "20" miles, because that's the scale we have set on the Schema sheet.

	A	B	C	D	E	F	G	H	I	J
1	Start	Destination	Road	Plain	Forest (light)	Forest (heavy)	Hills	Mountains	Desert - Swamp	Inches
2	Free Cities				Inches over Terrain Type					Total
3	City 1	City 2	0.25							0.25
4	City 1	City 3		1						1
5	City 3	Town 1	0.5	1.25						1.75
6	City 3	Town 2		0.25	1	0.75				2
7	City 4	Wizard Tower					0.50	0.5		1
8										
9	Kingdom of Wherever									
10	City 1	City 2	0.5	1.5						2
11	City 2	City 3	0.25						1.25	1.5
12										
13	Kingdom of Nowhere									
14	Town 1	Town 2	0.25	0.75						1
15	City 1	Town 1	1.5							1.5

Figure 44 Inches Over Terrain Type

Instead of manually looking at the Schema sheet, seeing that we want 20, and typing that into K3, we're using a formula to automatically grab that value from Schema for us. The reason for this is that, if we change our scale on the Schema sheet, the new value would appear in K3 without us having to alter K3. This takes more work to set up but will save you eons of time if you change your scale, as you probably will. Using formulas like this frees us from worrying about getting our scale "right" the first time and allows us to change our minds later without having to redo everything. If you click K3, you'll see the formula above that:

=ROUND(Schema!B2,0)

The text "Schema!B2,0" is grabbing the value out of B2 on the Schema sheet and inserting it here (in this case, the value is "20"). The value is also being rounded to a whole number, which is what the black text is doing. There's no automatic way to grab the red part. You copy and paste this formula into every cell that needs it, to complete this section of the Travel sheet. The same principle applies to .5 inches, except that you'd change the formula to use cell B3 instead of B2 from Schema sheet. And so on.

K Road	L Plain	M Forest (light)	N Forest (heavy)	O Hills	P Mountains	Q Desert - Swamp	R Miles	S Kilometers
Miles over Terrain Type							Total Distance	
20							20	32.2
	80						80	128.7
40	100						140	225.3
	20	80	60				160	257.5
				40	40		80	128.7
40	120						160	257.5
20						100	120	193.1
20	60						80	128.7
120							120	193.1

Figure 45 Miles Over Terrain Type

You can experiment with this right now. Go to the Schema sheet and type 10 into B2 and then come back to Travel and see the new numbers.

The fourth section, "Days by Travel Mode," is pictured below; columns T through Z are what we're after. This is the most difficult part. We want to take the number of miles from the previous section and divide it by the BMPD for that travel mode, minus the modifier for that terrain. In other words, if it's 20 miles, we divide that by our BMPD speed, such as a walking human (12), except that we first need to modify this BMPD by subtracting the number of miles lost due to the terrain. In the case of a road, a walking human loses no speed, according to our Schema sheet. We'd divide 20 by 12 to get 1.7 days. However, a riding horse moves at a BMPD of 35, and on a road, it loses 10% of its speed, or 3.5 miles, resulting in a speed of 30.5 miles per day. When we divide 20 miles by 30.5 per day, we get .6 days for a riding horse to go 20 miles. In other words, it will take just over a half day to go twenty miles under ideal conditions and without hurrying. You need to know this for storytelling.

T	U	V	W	X	Y	Z
Foot	Riding Horse	Warhorse (light)	Warhorse (heavy)	Wagon	Dragon	Carrier Pigeon
			Days by Travel Mode			
1.7	0.6	0.8	1.1	0.8	0	0
6.7	2.3	3.2	4.2	3.2	0.1	0.1
11.7	4.1	5.6	7.4	5.6	0.2	0.2
24.5	8.3	10.4	13.9	6.5	0.3	0.2
11.1	3.9	6.5	6.5	7.1	0.2	0.1
13.3	4.7	5.9	7.8	6.9	0.3	0.2
4.2	5	6.1	8.2	6.7	0.2	0.2
6.7	2.3	2.9	3.9	3.5	0.1	0.1
10	3.8	4.8	6.3	4.8	0.2	0.2

Figure 46 Days by Travel Mode

If this is confusing, just go through it slowly.

The formula is: =ROUND(SUM(K3/(Schema!B16-Schema!C16)),1). What this says is round (to the nearest tenth) the sum of a calculation, which is the number of miles to travel (K3) divided by the BMPD (Schema!B16) minus the modifier (Schema!C16).

For part of it, we could just write B16—C16, but those two cells are on the Schema sheet, which requires us to add "Schema!" in front of it, resulting in Schema!B16, for example.

It gets more complicated when our travel distance goes over more than one kind of terrain. In this case, we need to calculate each of them as explained above, and then add them together. In that sense, it's not that hard, but if you're not used to looking at Excel formulas, it becomes confusing. Study this one:

=ROUND(
SUM(L11/(Schema!B17-Schema!D17))+
SUM(M11/(Schema!B17-Schema!E17))+
SUM(N11/(Schema!B17-Schema!F17)),1)

This is for riding horse and basically says 1) divide the distance over plains (L11) by BMPD for riding horse—Modifier on plains, and add it to 2) divide the distance over light forest (M11) by BMPD for riding horse—Modifier on light forest, and add it to 3) divide the distance over heavy forest (N11) by BMPD for riding horse—Modifier on heavy forest.

I'm also using a rounding function so that we get results like 4.1 miles per day instead of 4.11341 or something equally annoying. The round function looks like this: ROUND(our calculation, 1), the 1 being how many places after the decimal we want.

You may find this spreadsheet to be a lot of work, and I agree. Consider doing this in small stages instead of all at once.

MANUAL TRAVEL

This sheet on the template is discussed in section, "Pre-Set Calculations." Each mode of travel has its own section. The numbers of miles, kilometers, and days needed to travel are based on the Schema sheet. No changes to this page are required.

AREA SIZING

On the template, there's another sheet called "Regions." This sheet allows us to figure out how many miles (or kilometers) long and wide our land features are, and the total square miles or kilometers. Though this has nothing to do with travel, this chapter's subject, it's on the same template to make use of the Schema sheet. Most of us likely won't care about the total square miles of land in a region or sovereign power, but for those who do, this sheet calculates it for you. The next image is a screen shot

Measure the length and height of each sovereign power or land feature on a continent. This will help you learn how big everything is. With the inches columns filled in, we can once again use the Schema sheet to determine how many miles and kilometers everything is by referring to the appropriate cells. In the image above, you can see "Continent Name" is fifteen inches long. Since I don't have fifteen inches on Schema (I stopped at 2.75), I used math to get my fifteen inches. In other words, the calculation is for two inches multiplied by seven (to get fourteen inches), then one inch being added to it. For example, =ROUND((Schema!B9*7)+(Schema!B5),1). The same was done for height. Doing it this way once again means that if I ever change the scale of my map, these numbers change for me.

	A	B	C	D	E	F	G	H	I
1	Area	Inches	Miles	Kilometers	Inches	Miles	Kilometers	Sq. Miles	Sq. Kilometers
2			Length			Height			Total
3									
4	Continent Name	15	1200	1931.2	12	960	1545	864,000	2,237,778
5									
6					Kingdoms				
7	Kingdom #1 Name	2.25	180	289.7	2.5	200	321.9	28,800	74,604
8	Kingdom #2 Name	1.5	120	193.1	2	160	257.5	17,280	44,751
9									
10					Features by Region				
11					Kingdom #1 Name				
12	Forest #1	1.5	120	193.1	1.25	100	160.9	12,000	31,070
13	Mountains #1	0.75	60	96.6	1	80	128.7	4,800	12,432
14									
15					Kingdom #2 Name				
16	Forest #1	1.25	100	160.9	1	80	128.7	7,200	18,637

Figure 47 Region Sizing

The calculation for square miles/kilometers is done by multiplying the values for length by height. However, this assumes your land feature is a square or rectangle when it probably isn't. The solution for this is another multiplication, this time by a percentage represented by a decimal value. For example, if we have a forest that is 100 miles by 80 miles, the square miles would be 8,000 (100 * 80). However, maybe it's not an actual rectangle, so we decide ten percent of that area is not included in the territory. We'd change the calculation from 100 * 80 to (100 * 80) * .9, resulting in 7,200 square miles. The same modification is done to square kilometers. This example is in the spreadsheet for "Forest #1 Name" under "Kingdom #2 Name."

Lastly

When experimenting with this spreadsheet, be careful of the way Excel works. We can accidentally change the formula in a cell if we click elsewhere. It's best to use the tab key to navigate out of a cell with a formula.

Where to Start

Determining the distance between locations for which we want to calculate times should be an early decision. Take terrain changes between each pair of locations into account. Then decide which travel methods will be used in books; there's no sense in calculating dragons' travel time if they don't exist in your world. Review the base miles per day that this book provides and alter them to suit your judgment. Do the same for terrain and other modifiers. Now you're ready to calculate the travel times. The easiest method is to use the pre-set ones provided. Otherwise, carefully study the equations in this chapter and the Excel spreadsheet and apply them as needed.

CHAPTER EIGHT

TRAVEL BY WATER

If you're a landlubber like me, you have little to no idea how long it takes a ship to sail from one place to another. That will change by the end of this chapter, but we have considerable leeway in deciding the length of any journey. Much of what follows here is about travel under sail, or by rowing, not by engines. In fantasy worlds, those engines are implausible. In SF, travel is typically through the air. The speed calculations in the section on ship speeds can apply to engine-powered ships as well, since a knot is a knot and it doesn't matter what's causing this speed, with the caveat that winds and oars cannot produce the constant speed of engines.

Several factors influence the difficulty of sailing between locations. The wind direction is chief among them. The ship building skills and seamanship of various countries also impacts this. All of it influences trade routes and which nations can conquer others. A ship would not be able to sail directly into a headwind. Taking an alternative route might force a ship closer to an enemy coastline.

There are several reasons we have leeway in determining the duration of a ship journey:

1) Our map, should one exist, is not drawn to scale
2) Oarsmen cannot row indefinitely and might have different levels of endurance and training from ship to ship
3) Wind speed is not constant even in the open ocean, affecting both the ship itself (if sail powered) and the height of waves that could further impact speed
4) Wind direction is also not constant, affecting the angle at which wind fills sails

5) Different types of ships sail at different speeds under the same conditions

6) Our ship is weighed down by people, cargo, food, and weapons/ammunition, any one of which can change in quantity during a voyage. A ship that just left dock is heavier than one at sea for six months, unless the latter is laden with treasure

7) Our ship might be damaged

8) Our ship is sailing on a fictitious planet, with possibly a different number of moons and whatever else might affect the seas

Maybe it comes as no surprise that we aren't sure how long a trip will take. What we're looking for is a reasonable approximation that a ship will take between X and Z number of hours to travel Y number of miles/kilometers, depending on conditions. But we don't have to do this. We can just invent numbers and not worry about it. Never stating the distance between two places helps this. Grounding our numbers in some real-world knowledge is an approach that more serious world builders might want to employ, especially if we intend to reuse the setting. Otherwise, we might be inconsistent. Regardless of our choice, the knowledge can help inspire believable details in our work.

For example, let's say that for our story, we need a trip to take 24 hours, but our calculations reveal that a ship usually takes 24-30 hours. We're in luck and can do it. When describing that journey, we could state that our sailors enjoyed nearly ideal conditions. This could allow for characters to undertake sword practice on deck or another activity requiring surer footing. A wizard could have time to mix materials needed for spells.

In another scenario, maybe we want our characters to feel confident they'll make that trip in time. But we want to surprise them and make them arrive late, in 34 hours. We can throw up a storm to slow them, making a character sea sick and preventing others from doing much of anything. Or maybe they battle a ship or sea monster and in so doing lose a mast despite their victory.

We don't have to do these things, but stories always need unexpected challenges, and if the sea isn't hard to predict, nothing in our world is.

SHIP TERMS

A few basic terms are helpful to know. This is not an exhaustive list of nomenclature, just what we need to know to understand the differences between vessels.

MASTS

A mast stands vertically from any ship that has sails. There can be more than one, depending on ship size and type. The center mast is the tallest and called the main mast. The mast at the bow (front of the ship) is the foremast and is shorter. The rear one, should it exist, is called the mizzen mast, and is the shortest. In a two-masted ship, the mizzen mast is the omitted one; however, the other two masts are farther back in the ship's body.

Figure 48 Ship with Three Masts

YARDS

Each mast will have at least one yard, to which the sails are attached. In many ships, the yard is horizontal. If perpendicular, or square, to the ship's length, the ship is "square-rigged". Most ships have from one to three yards of different lengths and thicknesses. By contrast, in lateen-rigged ships, the yard is sloped, running parallel to the ship's length, one end pointing at the sky, and there's only one per mast. The yards have names but these aren't needed to understand this chapter.

Figure 49 Yards

Some ships have a combination of square and lateen rigging. This usually means the main and foremast are square while the mizzen is lateen. This will be mentioned further when looking at actual ship types.

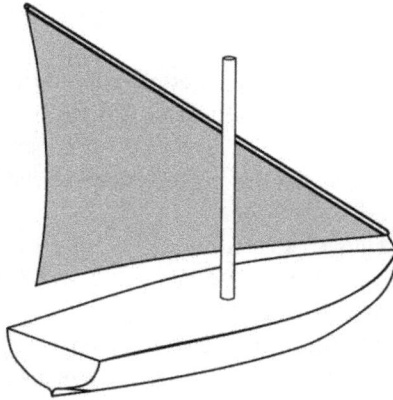

Figure 50 Lateen Sail

SAILS

In square-rigged ships, the sails are a trapezoid, being wider at the bottom than the top. On a lateen-rigged ship, a triangular sail is used. This is sometimes called fore-and-aft rigging because that's how the yard is aligned (forward and aft, or rear). This rigging allows for a closer point of sail on the wind, being more maneuverable. It takes advantage of rapidly changing winds such as in the Mediterranean, but in the open ocean, winds are more constant and a square-rigged ship does not suffer a disadvantage. Sails can be configured in many ways, most of which will confuse anyone not familiar with them, but this resource goes into more detail:

http://www.artofworldbuilding.com/sails.

SHIP RATES

In the British Navy, ships were rated based on the number of guns and personnel. This is something authors can mention but screenwriters might find hard to work into a conversation without being obvious about it. In either case, if we have a character say, "That's a first-rate ship," people will assume that means "it's a quality ship," not that it means the ship has over a hundred guns and more than eight hundred crew and is therefore in the biggest class of ships. The same applies to "second-rate" and so on, with many audiences assuming the ship is inferior when this isn't true. The ratings are not a judgement of quality, though in the "bigger is better" mentality, it is. Beware of this when writing about it.

Whether we emulate this or not, here is a basic rundown, according to *Men-of-War, Life in Nelson's Navy* by Patrick O'Brian:

"First rate: 100-112 guns, 841 men (including officers, seamen, boys, and servants)

Second rate: 90-98 guns, 743 men

Third rate: 64, 74 and 80 guns, 494, about 620, and 724 men

Fourth rate: 50 guns, 345 men

Fifth rate: 32, 36, 38, and 44 guns, 217-297 men

Sixth rate: 20, 24, and 28 guns, 128, 158, and 198 men."

Anything with fewer guns wasn't rated and all the above had three masts. Not including the forecastle and quarterdeck, the first and second-rate ships had three full decks for just the guns. Third and fourth rate had two gun decks and the rest had one. With multiple gun decks, the guns on the lower decks were the biggest and this was where crew slept and ate. High decks had increasingly smaller guns and cannonballs for the obvious reason of not making the ship top heavy. Weaponry is discussed later in this chapter.

This large image of a third-class man-o-war gives a great view of the rigging and interior of a vessel: http://www.artofworldbuilding.com/warship.

SHIP TYPES

While we could invent a new ship, there's little reason to, for several reasons. We aren't likely to engineer something that would stay afloat if constructed, but a large variety of ship types are available to us already. Within each type, even more variety is to be found. This means we once again have leeway to make alterations of our own if we need to, provided we get the basics right. Naval terminology regarding ships was somewhat flexible at times, but settled into more definitive terms. This works to our advantage because we can get things approximately correct and fudge details for our uses. In addition, audiences seldom know much about existing ships and probably don't thirst for something new. For these reasons, we'll look at the more prominent, existing ships, not learn how to build new ones.

Vessels comes in two groups: long and round ships. The latter aren't circular, of course, but are called this because they are wide when compared to the narrow and streamlined long ships like those used by Vikings.

LONG SHIPS

The earliest vessels are the long ships, which are largely powered by oars but also have sails for additional propulsion. The galley is the primary type, and there are variations on it. All were designed for war or swift transportation, as opposed to carrying cargo.

GALLEY

Synonymous with Vikings but used elsewhere, the galley is the basic vessel powered by strong, highly trained rowers. It often includes a single mast and a metal-shod prow for ramming, an act followed by boarding. It is highly maneuverable but has a wide turning arc and requires calm weather. It is also not for open seas (despite being occasionally used this way) and is consequently found along coastlines. The invention and addition of firearms to ships caused this to fall into disuse on Earth, but if our world doesn't have gunpowder or similarly powered gunnery, the galley might still be favored.

Figure 51 Galley

The later, 17th century galley on Earth had two masts and a captain's cabin at the rear, which adds usefulness to us as storytellers simply because a room exists in which conversations or acts not for others to witness may take place. If using this type of galley, we need another name for it, such as naming it after a sovereign power from which it's thought to have originated.

The galley type known as a galleass is quite large, having both a rear and forecastle for artillery and soldiers, and up to twenty-five oars per side, each oar rowed by five men. Above the rower's heads might be a deck for soldiers and operation of sails and gunnery. This ship wasn't as fast and often served in the vanguard of an armada as a commander's vessel.

Round Ships

Designed for carrying cargo and passengers, the round ships are also used for war and are what we've seen in every pirate movie. The round ships primarily use sails for power. When there's no wind, or an unfavorable one, oars can assist the smaller round ships (up to a frigate in size). Later ships are more maneuverable than long ships like the galley except in calm weather. The round ships mentioned in this chapter are square-rigged on all masts unless otherwise noted.

The man-o-war is not a specific ship type but a generic English name for a three-masted war ship outfitted with soldiers and cannons. This includes the frigate and ship-of-the-line, among others. On our invented world, we can apply the term to similar ships even if an Earth equivalent is not deemed a man-o-war.

While there are many specifications about round ships, the ones listed in this chapter offer a comparison regarding ship length, guns, crew, and maximum speeds. Finding definitive answers for each proves challenging due to conflicting specs cited in various sources. One source might say frigates are from 135-175 feet while another might say they range up to 200. Such details might be insignificant, especially given that, as world builders, we'd be discussing ships on our imagined world, where anything is possible and details could differ at our whim. Still, some effort should be made to know the guidelines before going so far outside of norms as to strain credibility.

To that end, the approach used to compile these specifications was to find reputable sources stating the range of widely accepted possibilities. Further, specific ships of each type with known stats were also considered. In the end, if two sources provided similar numbers, such as 24-40 and 24-44, the larger range is indicated on the chart. If one source provided a number far higher than others, such as 24-40 vs. 24-60, then the higher number was added in parenthesis with a question mark, such as the frigate gun count below, where it reads "24-40 (60?)."

Note that the maximum speed in knots is in ideal conditions with a strong wind on the optimum point of sailing (which direction the wind is blowing in relation to the ship's heading). No ship experiences such conditions throughout a journey, making the number somewhat useless for determining a trip's speed. These numbers are mostly for understanding a ship's capability.

Ship Type	Length in Feet	Guns	Crew	Max Speed (knots)
Brig	123	10-18	155	11
Frigate	135-212	24-40 (60?)	217-345 (815?)	14
Galleon	140-160	30-74	200-400	10
Gunboat	49-72	1-3	12	14
Ship-of-the-line	150-250	64-140	494-1280	11
Sloop	60	14	75	11
Sloop-of-war	60-110	8-24	112-125	11

Figure 52 Ship Chart

What follows are some of the more well-known ship types of Earth.

BRIG

The brig is a two-masted, square-rigged ship that has a single gun deck. It is fast, highly maneuverable, and can be used as a merchant ship, war ship, or scouting vessel. Pirates frequently employ them. A brig is arguably different from a brigantine but even sailing enthusiasts might disagree over any differences, and historically the names were interchanged; we can use either term. Early brigantines were often outfitted with oars, allowing for movement with poor winds or in and out of harbor more easily.

Figure 53 Brig

FRIGATE

The frigate is a fast and highly maneuverable, fourth-rate or fifth-rate ship with one gun deck. These are speedy attack ships and often used as scouting vessels for a fleet, escorting, patrolling or acting independently. They are the largest ships used independently because bigger ships are deemed too valuable to risk being captured or destroyed, which is more likely when sailing alone. Some frigates have two gun decks and are called heavy frigates. The term "frigate" is sometimes used generically to refer to quick ships.

Frigates are the same length as higher rated ships but have fewer decks. They carry supplies for six months. Any areas like a forecastle aren't as tall as ships-of-the-line. They avoid fights with ships-of-the-line due to being outgunned. During a line of battle, they do not join the firing ships but are instead in another row behind them, relaying signals up and down the battle line, as ships-of-the-line can see only the ship before and behind them, making communication difficult. They also aren't fired upon by the enemy unless they fire first, as it is considered bad etiquette; they are not only smaller but are present to relay messages, not fight.

Figure 54 Frigate

FIRE SHIP

Any ship can be turned into a fire ship, but as this means certain destruction to the ship in question, ships that have little to no value are used. The ship is rigged to burn from within the hold, where specially designed tubes vent the flames toward enemy ships and the rigging. The ship is sent floating into the general melee of a sea battle during engagements between fleets; it isn't something we'd see sailing around by itself. We might assume that something as valuable as a ship-of-the-line is an unlikely fire ship even if damaged beyond any other use; too many men would be required to sail it into position and then abandon it for other ships, but it could be done.

GALLEON

The galleon has two features that distinguish it from other round ships: masts and prow. Like other round ships, it has a mainmast and foremast, but the rear mizzenmast is lateen-rigged. It sometimes has a fourth, even smaller rear mast. This lateen style allows superior sailing that could save days or weeks over long voyages in the open ocean. An instantly recognizable feature is a long beak jutting forward from the prow.

For authors, these features require explanation that may gain our audience little in understanding. This is especially true of the beak, which has no functional benefit aside from helping sailors tend to sails, which few readers will care about even if we understand the details of such things and wish to convey them. The beakhead is where sailors crapped, the waste falling directly into the sea, but this is true of all round ships, not just the galleon; oddly, it is the rear of round ships that has an area called "the poop." This is also from where the expression "I gotta hit the head" originates, as the latrine is at the head of the ship and therefore downwind.

If we wish to explain what a galleon is and how it differs from other round ships like the frigate, the difference between square and lateen-rigging and the possible impact on maneuverability and speed is what to mention.

Figure 55 Galleon

GUNBOAT

Since our world might not have guns, a new name might be needed for this small vessel that carries one or more large cannons (or whatever missile weapon we invent). They are cheap and easy to build and therefore more expendable. Used in coastal waters, they are no match for large ships, but a score of them can do horrific damage to a lone ship, which can't sink them all fast enough. This boat is either powered by sails or oars.

SHIP-OF-THE-LINE

A ship with sixty or more guns, which includes all first, second, and third-rate ships, the ship-of-the-line acquires its name from being designed for the line of battle when two fleets fight each other in two parallel lines. This allows for firing broadsides at each other without fear of hitting their own ships. Smaller ships are not considered strong enough to withstand such a barrage from these vessels, the largest ships afloat, and therefore aren't part of the line, if present at all.

Figure 56 Ship of the line

For an interesting cross-section of the interior of such a vessel, view this diagram: http://www.artofworldbuilding.com/warship.

SLOOP

Figure 57 Sloop

To most of us, a sloop is basically a sail boat, having a single mast that is fore-and-aft rigged. If there are two masts, it's called a cutter instead (and is typically larger). There are other minor variations on this, each with a different name, but they are not ships of war and therefore might only figure in our work if our characters need a small, wind-powered vessel. Another option would be the galley (oar-powered long ship).

SLOOP-OF-WAR (CORVETTE)

This ship is not to be confused with a sloop. As its name implies, it's a warship, having a single gun deck with eighteen guns. It is considerably larger than a sloop and often has two masts. Eventually, three-masted versions were built and then resembled a small frigate. However, a frigate is square rigged; sloops-of-war have varying sail configurations, from all square-rigged to ketch riggings or snow riggings (googling this will reveal familiar images). The name corvette was later applied to them. The ships are not rated, having too few guns for the rating system of Britain, but we can rate them as we like on our world (i.e., seventh rate).

Figure 58 Corvette

PRIVATEER

A privateer is not a ship type but any ship operated by private individuals, or a group of them, for profit. They are given the right, via a letter of marque, to engage in acts of war on the seas by their sovereign power, which takes a percentage of any captured prize. Profits are otherwise split among crew and owners. The possession of the letter of marque, and the return and sale of prizes to the sovereign power, is what distinguishes a privateer from a pirate.

Not surprisingly, some pirates sought the letters (often illegally) to absolve their actions. Others acquired letters from opposing countries at war (not admitting to this, of course). They then attacked both sides as desired. For example, a privateer might have letters of marque from England and from France, using the former against French ships and the latter against English. Only he and his crew, and possible owners, might know this.

Privateers who didn't return captured prizes, or who otherwise violated their agreement, could be declared pirates. Some countries refused to recognize the letters of marque from their enemies and hanged captured privateers as pirates, or at least threatened to, leading to negotiations for an exchange of prisoners, for example.

As for the ships, they were heavily armed, fast, and highly maneuverable, as they were intended purely for assault. Since they captured ships and sailed them back (treasure inside), there was arguably less need for their own cargo space beyond provisions. Anything larger than a frigate was unsuitable (i.e., no ships-of-the-line).

SHIP SPEEDS

BY OARS

The top speed when using oars for propulsion doesn't matter much for travel because crews can't sustain it for long, despite one trip being done at 8 knots (which we can have our swaggering hero achieve because he's awesome). Ships would travel under sail for a trip of any length, with the oars being saved for a battle or a crisis. With favorable winds, a ship can do 2-3 knots while an unfavorable wind is half that (1-1.5 knots). For more details on calculating travel times, consult the next section.

BY SAILS

Now comes the challenging part—figuring out how fast our characters can get from one place to another on a wind-powered ship. This depends on where the ship is sailing. Not only are ocean winds more constant in direction and speed, but with sufficient crew to rotate duty through the day/night, ships sail around the clock. By contrast, sailing along a coastline or island means variable winds, requiring an adjustment to the rigging with each fluctuation. On such a trip, ships dock for the night at a port, if possible; the port has to exist and be friendly to them.

Note that explanations in this section are using miles. Calculations for miles and kilometers are included when we reach that point. Also, there's technically no such thing as nautical kilometers and any reference to this is only for those world builders more familiar with using kilometers than miles.

Speed is measured in knots. A knot is one nautical mile per hour (mph). A nautical mile is 1.151 land miles. Why the difference? The nautical mile accounts for the curvature of the Earth while the land mile does not. What this means for us is that if we've decided two ports on the same coast are 25 miles apart by land, divide this number by 1.151 to learn how many nautical miles this is (just under 22). If our ship has to go around a peninsula, for example, we'll need to measure that and take it into account.

Whether we measure in miles or kilometers has no effect on the time a trip takes. It only affects the numbers we use for our calculations.

Most ships have an overall speed of between 4-6 knots during a long voyage over open water, and 3-4 knots along coasts or along islands. This is not to say that ships cannot go slower or faster. Any ship can be becalmed or sail at its maximum speed under ideal circumstances, which is usually around 11 knots, depending on the ship (see the chart above). But it's rare for a ship to sail in ideal conditions for long.

Remember that some journeys might begin along a coast before using the open ocean, so we'll want the distance for the coastal leg, the oceanic leg, and then possibly another coastal leg. During coastal legs, a ship might put in to port overnight and therefore lose however many hours we decide they're docked or moored. If we assume a 24-hour day, for example, and one stop of 8 hours for the night, then a trip of 22 hours is extended by 8 hours and now takes 30 hours.

To calculate the hours needed to traverse two locations, follow the steps below. We'll use hours (instead of days) because our world might not have a 24-hour day. This also makes it easier to reduce travel time by the number of hours we decide that a ship is in port or is repairing damage while at sea.

1) Measure the sailing distance on the map. If using miles, skip to step three.
2) Optional: if using kilometers, convert the kilometers to miles by multiplying the distance by 0.62137
3) Divide the number of miles by 1.151 to learn nautical miles
4) Assuming average conditions (wind, cargo, personnel, etc.), find the range of hours your ship needs while traveling:
    a. At 6 knots: nautical miles divided by 6 knots = hours of continuous sailing needed
    b. At 4 knots: nautical miles divided by 4 knots = hours of continuous sailing needed
    c. At 2 knots (oar-powered): nautical miles divided by 2 knots = hours of continuous sailing needed

Here is an example, following the numbered steps above, starting with kilometers:

1) 125 kilometers from X to Y (along a coastline)
2) Optional: 125 x 0.62137 = 77. miles (rounded up)
3) 77. miles / 1.151 = 67 nautical miles
4) Speeds
   a. At 6 knots: 67 nautical miles divided by 6 knots = 11 hours (rounded up) of continuous sailing (no stops)
   b. At 4 knots: 67 nautical miles divided by 4 knots = 17 hours
   c. At 2 knots: 67 nautical miles divided by 2 knots = 33.5 hours

For the 33.5 hour trip, the ship could stop for the night. If we assume 8 hours each time, this results in 41.5 hours.

If you'd rather not make these calculations, join *The Art of World Building* newsletter to gain access to an Excel spreadsheet template that lays out the travel times for you.

ON RIVERS

Surface currents on rivers are arguably stronger than those on larger bodies of water due to the narrowness of the channel. The narrower the river, the faster the current, but depth can also make it faster. A river is not uniformly wide or deep and will become wider, and therefore slower, the longer it flows. This means river speeds farther inland are faster. A river's course also affects speed. Water flows faster in the center of a straight channel, but when it curves, the outer corner is fastest and the inner one slowest. Characters who are inexperienced sailors might be unable to utilize the currents well unless they happen to be keen observers and figure this out. How fast do rivers typically flow in knots? The extremes are almost 0 knots to 6 knots, but we'll typically want to aim for 1-4 knots for travel. Faster than 4 knots on a river might mean it is treacherous.

WEAPONS

On Earth, if a ship in the Age of Sail has weapons, it has cannon, which requires gunpowder, which in turn means our world almost certainly has guns. If we don't want guns on our fantasy world, then no cannons either. That means a ship with no fire power and hence a lack of drama. Where's the fun in that? We can either keep the cannons or replace them, the latter requiring some understanding of what we're replacing. We'll need some details on how fast cannons fire, how far, and how many people are needed to do this. Then we can consider alternatives. For example, wizards may provide an equivalent to gunpowder, but if that alternative exists in enough quantity for cannons to exist, then wouldn't guns, too?

THE CANNON

A 36-pounder, meaning a cannon that fires balls weighing thirty-six pounds, is among the largest cannon aboard ships and requires fourteen men. A powder boy brings gunpowder from below decks; gunpowder is wisely stored somewhere less prone to explosions. This role is eliminated in a world without gunpowder. If we invent an alternative to the cannon, and there are a hundred such weapons, we'd have a hundred fewer crew aboard, which in turn reduces supplies needed.

A chief gunner aims the gun and primes it for firing, but does not fire it; one of the other gunners does this. This role would still require an alternative, but the role would likely need a different name. The chief gunner is in charge of the crew, who practice together but seldom do so with live shot due to the cost. Not practicing with live shot affects the chief gunner's ability to practice aiming, but the rest of the crew can at least become efficient, affecting speed of firing, which is two to three shots in about five minutes.

The rest of the men are called gunners. Some gunners prepare the cannon for firing, as follows. One gunner shoves a wet cloth down the barrel between shots to put out any sparks before more gunpowder is loaded. One man inserts a cannonball while another rams it in. This is followed by another wet cloth wad to prevent the ball from rolling out if the cannon is aimed downward. These various details and personnel are specific to the firing of a cannon and might be replaced by a different number of personnel depending on what replacement weapon we devise.

Cannons require men whose primary job is moving the cannon back and forth. Prior to firing, it must be pulled away from the hull because it is loaded from the barrel, but must be fired with the barrel protruding from the hull. This means men pull the cannon back, several people perform various loading operations, and then the cannon is shoved against the hull before firing. Cannons have huge recoil, meaning they leap backwards when fired. This means several crew are needed to shove the thing back into place. We might not need these men with an alternative weapon that lacks recoil.

Smaller cannons still have the powder boy, chief gunner, and at least two other gunners for cleaning, loading, moving, and firing a cannon, so the number of men depends on cannon size due to how heavy it is to move around between shots.

ALTERNATIVES

When looking for an alternative to the cannon, we can look to siege engines used on land for inspiration. The trebuchet flings stones high into the air but can only be fired from the top deck of a ship due to the firing action. This would significantly reduce their numbers and interfere with sailing, crew movements, and melee. The catapult and similar weapons aren't much better.

Our best bet might be the ballista, which is like a giant crossbow mounted on a frame. Like the cannon, this fires in a straight line rather than hurling a projectile high into the air, meaning this could be located where cannons are instead of only on the top deck. It one were sized correctly for the space, it could function in much the same manner, though its firing action is quite different. Even so, it seems to be the only logical replacement. A ballista is highly accurate and can be aimed at a single person and hit them.

The main issue with a ballista is power and range. The Roman ballista fired over five hundred yards and was made of wood, but if we construct ours from iron for the frame and metal for the arms, this gives us greater power. Our world might have a fictional alloy of greater strength, like adamantine, providing even more thrust. Use of a fictional alloy gives us leeway to claim it fires much farther than the Roman ballista. A 12-pounder cannon could fire fifteen hundred yards, and while the practical range was far less, we can claim nearly similar distances for our ballista. Being plausible is the bar we need to get over. Creative license helps us.

Ballista are strong enough to fire straight through an armored knight and pin him to a living tree, the projectile embedding itself halfway into the trunk. Could one blow a hole in the side of a ship? Certainly. The missiles can be topped with our special alloy for superior strength and piercing ability.

Ballista can be easily modified to fire balls, which would be smaller than cannonballs. This further means that they could fire chain shot: two balls connected by a chain. This is used to destroy rigging. Grape shot (many small balls) to slaughter crew on deck is unlikely to work due to the firing mechanism being unable to contain it as a cannon barrel would. An alternative might be darts rather than a single large arrow/bolt.

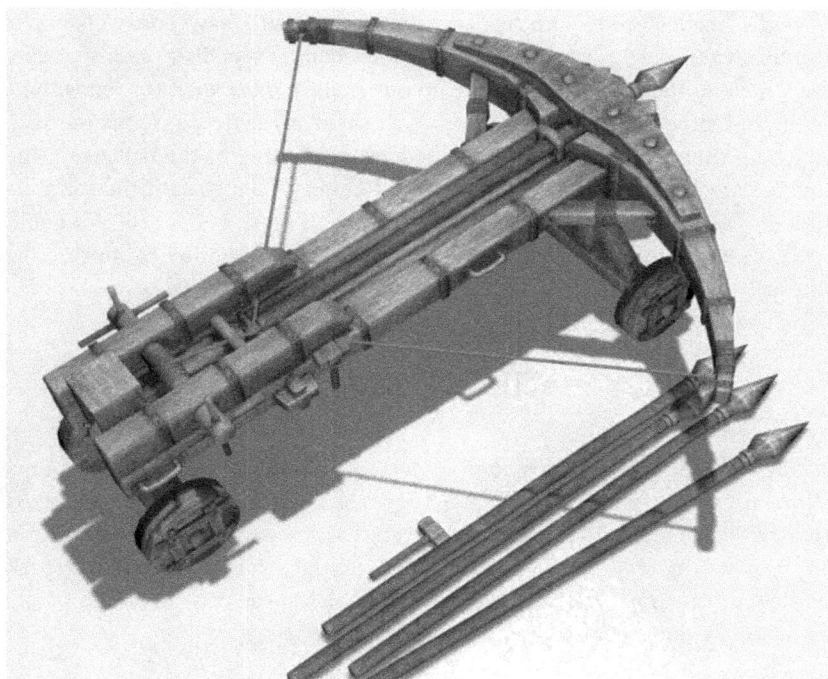

Figure 59 Ballista

Fewer crew are needed to operate a ballista. We'd need someone responsible for the team and who likely aims it and possibly fires it. Only one person is needed to place a projectile onto it, which can be their dedicated job. A powder boy isn't needed. Since there's no recoil, no men are needed to keep repositioning the weapon. That leaves operation of a winch to wind it. A team of two, one on each side, seems ideal for speed, though for larger ballista, maybe there's more than one team. From this, we can determine how large our crew might be. Do we need to get into this sort of detail? Not really, though in a visual medium, we'll want to show a reasonable number of people doing realistic tasks.

How fast can a ballista fire? As fast as the winchmen can wind it, plus a few seconds for loading and aiming. Much of time between shots for a cannon is repositioning it and the number of actions needed to prepare a shot. Most of this is gone with a ballista. Aiming is also faster because the frame mounting allows for easy pivoting up, down, or side-to-side. We can surmise at least two to three shots per minute, which is much faster than the two to three shots in five minutes for a cannon.

On a smaller vessel with smaller cannons, we could have crews of six per cannon. There might be a similar number of men for a ballista. As a ship gets bigger, so do the weapons. Bigger cannons require more men for repositioning it, but larger ballista don't. They don't scale the same way. This means a first-rate ship-of-the-line wouldn't need as many crew for the ballistae. During the Age of Sail, few ships could afford enough men to staff the cannons on both sides, requiring them to switch back and forth as needed. We could decide our ships have enough men for both sides, resulting in more crew after all.

SHIP PERSONNEL

It's beyond the scope of this book to describe all the personnel needed on a ship, but in a fantasy world, we have new humanoid species and occupations that can be added to the typical crew from Earth vessels. This can be true in SF, too, but the crafts there are usually spaceships. Ships often had livestock and even plants, mostly for consumption, which means our invented plants and animals can be aboard, too.

WARRIORS

Many fighting ships have military on board for the combat that might ensue when ships entangle (on purpose or not). Any sailor can engage in the fighting, but trained military are typically aboard during fleet actions. We can have such people onboard any vessel as standard crew, their numbers depending on overall ship and crew size. Larger numbers of such warriors will need quarters set aside for them (they may not be berthed with the sailors), but we needn't go into such details unless desired.

CLOSE RANGE

Knights are an obvious choice for hand-to-hand combat. They weren't on ships during the Age of Sail for the reason of gunpowder: bullets, and by extension cannons, had rendered armor useless. If we lack this issue on our world, then knights might figure heavily in the military aboard. A single knight could be present to represent knightly values or a kingdom on formal terms, or a group could be there in expectation of combat at sea. They can be available for missions ashore. However, even in a world without guns, knights still sink rather handily once overboard. They also make fine targets for archers.

Pirates wouldn't have knights on their ships and might think twice about attacking such a ship, if knights are assumed to be aboard. Why would they assume this? British ships-of-the-line were known to have marines aboard, so a ship belonging to a country of our invention can, too. Raising the country's flag might warn off pirates.

Ninjas or other forms of martial artists could be highly prized, due to their superior rope climbing skills and balance on those yard arms. Imagine how quickly they can board an enemy ship at close range.

Aboard a ship, unless there's a duel of some kind, the fighting is in close quarters, so space constraints would render weapons such as a staff less effective. Consider the weapons used by your warrior class which is routinely assigned to a ship, and whether they're appropriate under these conditions.

LONG RANGE

If guns don't exist on our world, archery is the obvious long-range weaponry fired by one person at a time (as opposed to a cannon). This can happen before and after ships entangle. These can be long/short bows or crossbows that fire flaming arrows into rigging or the hull (or people). Consider where such individuals might be stationed as ships battle.

WIZARDS

Is there a ship's wizard? A practitioner of some other supernatural power? They could stir a wind for a becalmed vessel, navigate, find enemy ships, and control sea life or the waves. Assistance in battle would be appreciated. They could create something that replaces gunpowder, allowing cannons to exist. They could teleport themselves or others from ship to ship or to shore, to save crew the task of rowing a small boat, exposing themselves to risks from sea creatures or those ashore.

On Earth, sailors are famously superstitious, but that needn't be true on our invented world. But if they are, sailors from one region could be afraid of allowing wizards aboard, while others allow it. A wizard might expect a welcome but discover that the crew is from another kingdom and fears him.

SPECIES

We might have invented species that could be part of a ship's crew. What special skills do they have and how might they be of use? One that climbs well would be suited to the rigging. What if we have a humanoid species that flies? Think how much easier it would be for them to fly high while looking for ships or land, compared to the humanoids who can only climb into the rigging with a telescope. If the flying creature of one crew were killed, the opposing crew would have a tactical advantage. There are numerous stories of ships sailing into a fog and being unable to find each other. Might not a flying species assist such an issue? They could get lost, too, but in theory they could use sounds from the ship to find it again.

Water-dwelling humanoids can repair underwater damage to the hull or rudder, chart a course through hazards, and catch fish. They can perform the equivalent of missions for which we'd use scuba divers and submarines, such as recovery of sunken ships and materials therein. Conversely, they could be antipathetic to the ships, and do damage below the waterline or silently sneak aboard. They might have traditional enemies beneath the waves, whether animals or another humanoid species. Maybe they even look like one of those enemies and one can go overboard, be killed underwater, and replaced by the enemy, who might at least initially fool the crew. They could even summon sea creatures to do their bidding. Do they claim an area as their territory and attack anything that sails through?

WHERE TO START

Where to start depends on our goal. If trying to determine the travel time between two places, follow the steps outlined in "Ship Speeds." You'll need to decide on the distance first, then whether the trip is along a coast, the open ocean, or both. Then consider what sort of issues you'd like characters to face on the journey. You may need to slow them or accelerate their travel based on story needs. If trying to decide what weaponry or personnel ships have on your world, the sections on this will assist a decision. The section on ship types will help you determine the style of vessel you want, but when it comes to rated ships, it's largely immaterial which you choose unless you intend two or more ships to go to war with each other.

CHAPTER NINE

TRAVEL IN SPACE

The previous two chapters focused on how to determine travel times using the sort of locomotion available on Earth-like worlds. Space travel falls under two categories: existing technology from Earth and invented technology. As I'm not a rocket scientist, the former is best left for those in the know to explain. World builders tend to be focused on imagined technologies anyway, and there's no telling what detail you might want to know and utilize about real technologies. More to the point, the limits of real tech eliminate interstellar travel and therefore whatever we're hoping to achieve.

THE REALITIES OF SPACE

Writing fiction doesn't free us from the realities of space, such as the intense cold or lack of oxygen. Some will think gravity doesn't exist either, but gravity is everywhere and causes all rotation (i.e. orbits). The conceit of artificial gravity has long been accepted so that we only need to address it if we want to, such as designing a rotating ship.

The question we must address is whether to pretend certain realities are overcome by technology (or magic) or not. It's recommended to be consistent in a single product. For example, in the *Star Trek* universe, food replicators that make lunch appear from thin air is as unrealistic as the teleportation devices that move matter (including people) between places. Being equally unrealistic (or realistic) is wise and helps the audience accept the reality we're presenting; otherwise, incongruities creep in. Having food replicators and teleporters but no artificial gravity would be an example, as the gravity, or a simulacrum, would be easier to achieve technologically.

When inventing technologies for space, creating a hierarchy of believability might be wise, if we'd like to have some things achieved while others are still imaginary, even to our advanced inhabitants. Maybe we want them to have achieved artificial gravity (so actors have a much easier time on screen) but still have the need to grow and cook food. At one time, the communication devices of *Star Trek* were considered fantastic but have been eclipsed by reality.

Generally, advanced communication is easier to achieve, as this often means little more than smaller devices with greater distance or computing power or capabilities, and sending of signals (not matter) long distances. Those signals can contain data just like here on Earth. This suggests that an advanced program, such as a hologram or A.I., could be sent vast distances, with the possibility of corruption in transit.

Any technology involving non-living matter is easier to create than something involving living creatures. This is especially true of transportation. Creating a new propulsion system using newly discovered elements from far flung solar systems is more believable than a technology that bends time and space and causes matter to just end up somewhere else in an instant. Such abilities are best seen as rare because making them commonplace implies the characters have other godlike abilities, too, and their lives become too easy, which reduces conflict, the heart of every story.

PROPULSION

Engines fall into two basic categories: those designed for space travel and those designed for atmospheric conditions. Both kinds already exist, but it is mostly engines intended for space travel which get mentioned in our work. There appears to be a correlation between how often an engine's functionality is explained and how fictional it is; the more fictional, the more explanations are given. Writers have as little interest in learning and explaining actual technology as the audience, who typically understands it to some degree. But fictional tech? We're all ears.

AIR BREATHING ENGINES

Engines for atmospheric conditions are the sorts of engines currently in use by planes on Earth. We don't need to invent anything or get into details of whether it's a rocket or turbine engine unless we desire to. We should just be aware that characters may need to remark that they're switching to "so-and-so power" as they enter a planet's atmosphere because the space engines they were using might not be suitable. This minor touch adds realism. Slower-than-light (STL) engines might also be used here and it's up to us to decide a given ship can use such engines both in space and in an atmosphere. This is one way to distinguish between ship types: some vessels might have engines that can be used anywhere and be considered more advantageous than ships that must change propulsion.

SPACE ENGINES

Space engines can be divided into two categories: those that allow faster-than-light (FTL) speeds and those that do not. For STL engines, propulsion is similar to atmospheric engines in that matter is ejected, usually from the rear, to propel the ship forward through normal space. This is one reason slower-than-light engines could be used in an atmosphere. STL drives propelling a ship at high velocities can cause time dilation, which is when two observers experience a difference in how much time has passed. Some stories discuss a captain not letting the ship go too fast using those engines, generally, to avoid this problem.

Some FTL engines are discussed next and are all public domain ideas anyone can use.

JUMP DRIVE

As the name implies, a ship with jump drive essentially teleports between two locations in an instant. This may be safely called a "jump drive" or something else. The main problem with such technology is that it eliminates all conflict involving travel and not having enough time to reach a destination by an important date. Consider using this sparingly or placing severe limits on how often such a drive can be used, such as it uses too much power, relies on a rare fuel source, is expensive to manufacture, or is too large for ordinary ships. Ships equipped with jump drive do not experience time dilation.

Hyper Drive

A hyper drive moves a ship into hyperspace, a fictional, separate dimension adjacent to normal space. As a result, ships in hyperspace are often depicted as being unable to communicate with those in normal space. Normal physics, such as the barrier to FTL travel, may not exist in hyperspace, allowing the ship to traverse great distances quickly. It takes time to travel in hyperspace but those traveling this way experience time normally and experience no time dilation upon returning to normal space.

Warp Drive

Warp drive is a conceptual FTL drive that is public domain despite being heavily associated with *Star Trek*. The idea includes multiple velocities of warp, such as warp one being far slower than warp ten. Instantaneous travel is not possible with warp drive. The ship suffers no time dilation and remains in normal space. Despite our use of the term "space", there are plenty of objects with which a ship could collide, which begs the question of how deadly such an impact would be. Without high-speed automated navigation systems and equally impressive shields, warp speed is unwise.

DISTANCE

To add realism to our space adventures, we should consider that all destinations are orbiting something. Moons orbit planets, planets orbit suns, and solar systems orbit their galaxy's center. If two objects are orbiting the same body, such as planets orbiting the same sun, the closer planet is orbiting faster. This means that the distance between two planets will change. They could be on the same side of the sun, opposite sides, or somewhere between.

This is different than fixed locations on a world's surface, and as a result, we have considerable leeway when announcing how far apart two places are at a particular moment, and therefore how long the trip will take. Due partly to the considerable time such travel takes, a destination is chosen not because that's where the target is now, but because that's where it will be when the ship also gets there.

This sort of thing can cause believable problems for characters. What if they realize a critical event is taking place on another planet in a week, but due to the worlds' current locations, it will take longer than that to get there? Or maybe they only have enough fuel to reach the destination if the trip is short, but they need to go now and don't have funds to get more fuel. Now maybe they hatch a plan to earn some money. Such details make stories better than ones where everyone just gets on a ship and goes whatever distance they need without much comment or impact on their situation.

Should we decide how far apart our locations are first and then invent propulsion systems according to our story needs, or invent propulsion systems and then alter how far away locations are based on story needs? The latter seems sensible because locations in space aren't fixed. If we need two locations closer or farther apart for a story, this needs no explanation. Conversely, it makes little sense to devise propulsion systems to go between certain distances when those will change anyway or you haven't decided how far the characters need to travel.

TRAVEL TIME

The amount of time to travel between different objects in space has so much leeway to it that we don't need the same sort of consistent precision that terrestrial travel may require. On land, we can fudge our numbers by writing, "Not drawn to scale" on a map. But in space, this isn't even needed. Nothing is in a fixed place except each planet's distance to the sun, and even that changes a bit depending on how circular its orbit is. And the technologies are imaginary, unlike the wooden ships from the previous chapter or the actual vehicles or animals from the chapter before that.

If you were hoping for a calculator like those in the previous chapters, there isn't one because most world builders will get along fine without worrying about this. It also involves a level of mathematics that is admittedly beyond me, and possibly you. And no one can come along and say that it would really take fifty-eight hours, not fifty, to travel between two invented planets in two imaginary solar systems, at a given time of the year (from the starting planet), at warp seven, especially since warp drives don't exist. This is one area where SF beats fantasy handily.

SHIP STRUCTURE

World builders in visual mediums will need to consider both internal and external ship structure, but authors may largely ignore this. Absent a schematic or picture, readers typically struggle to picture what we intend. This is true of other elements like the layout of a castle, for example. It's often better to not be overly specific about where each room lies in relation to another but rather focus on how long or difficult it is for characters to traverse locations within a certain time frame that matters to the scene we're writing. Still, even if we don't explain the structure, we should have an idea of it if for no other reason than consistency between scenes. We don't want characters to reach the engine room from the bridge in two minutes in one scene and in ten minutes during another.

EXTERNAL

There's a tendency to invent aerodynamic-looking ships used in space where air obviously doesn't exist. This is wise for two reasons: we expect such a design and are comfortable with it, and more importantly, it leaves open the option for the ship to enter a planet's atmosphere even if this is rare. Would ship builders make that nearly impossible with a non-aerodynamic exterior? Only if certain the vessel never leaves space. Since we've seen everything from aerodynamic ships to the Borg cube from *Star Trek*, we can get away with anything regarding aerodynamics.

Figure 60 Rotating Space Station

What other considerations are there for the exterior? One is the weaponry location, which determines which directions the vessel can fire in. Warships typically have this forward facing, with some ability to aim to the sides as well. Rear-facing weapons are for defense while fleeing. Some vessels have top or bottom mounted weaponry that can swivel and fire in all directions—except into itself, of course.

We might also consider where a ship can be boarded. Cargo is typically rear-loaded. People can be, too, or enter from the side, bottom, or even top hatches. Entering from the front is unusual. The decision can affect scenes where a ship has landed and a gunfight breaks out while characters are exiting or entering the vessel. The bottom-entrance seems problematic because if the ship crashes on its bottom, or the landing gear gives out, how does anyone get out? An emergency hatch elsewhere would be the answer. There's always a solution for these problems, so feel free to do as you please.

The other obvious subject for external structure is the engine location, but this is typically rear-facing, especially for any vessel intended for atmospheric conditions. The engine doesn't have to be in the actual rear, as propeller planes make clear. Even jet engines can be like this. With laser-guided weapons that can easily target an engine, it makes sense to avoid engine locations that are vulnerable in this way.

From the previous section on propulsion, remember there are fictional drives that don't operate on the principle of rear thrust; such engines could theoretically be located anywhere, preferably deep within a ship. What this means from a practical standpoint in war is that engines for STL travel might be rear-facing and vulnerable to attack, but FTL engines might be better protected and less vulnerable. Destroying those STL engines has a tactical advantage to inhibit maneuvering in the battle but won't stop the ship from going to warp to escape, for example. But if something volatile powers those FTL engines, then placing them deep in the ship might be unwise.

A ship that uses rotation to create artificial gravity will have this as the dominant feature of its exterior. The outside doesn't need to be round, however. It just needs to rotate. It's the inside that will be curved to some degree mostly because people and items will be pushed against those interior walls (that's the whole point), which act as the floor. Gravity increases the farther you are from the point of rotation. This is why we often see a configuration that looks like a spoke wheel; almost all of living areas are far from center.

INTERNAL

The internal structure of our ship is often important, unless it's so small as to have little more than a room or two. Characters need to move between locations such as the bridge, cargo, engine room, and quarters. We don't write about mundane scenes but active ones where the speed of transit is a factor in how the scene plays out. If it takes five minutes at a full run to reach the spot where aliens have breached the hull, and it will only take two minutes for the aliens to destroy the life support systems located there, we've got problems. Taking time to plan out our ship's structure (to some degree) is helpful for not only understanding such scenarios, but imagining them in the first place. No structure is foolproof, as organizing things to avoid one problem will likely cause another, so thinking about our story needs can help us build a vulnerability into our vessel.

Certain realities exist on ships, such as living quarters being near dining areas. Crew typically have smaller quarters in poorer locations than passengers, except for captains and officers, who may still not enjoy great privilege. Most vessels will need propulsion located primarily in the rear, an area often reserved for dirty or less desirable conditions such as cargo holds, loading areas for both supplies and sometimes passengers and crew, and machinery to power everything. The bridge or command center is typically forward.

Vessels which travel on water load from lower decks, especially for cargo, so the ship does not become top heavy; cargo acts as ballast and should be lower anyway. Also, loading from above just means having to create buildings and ramps to lift potentially heavy items unnecessarily. In space, this consideration is gone, but a ship designed to enter an atmosphere must still be balanced internally, whether that's front to back or side to side. In a weightless environment, heavy items could theoretically be anywhere, but artificial gravity is seemingly never lessened in areas with heavy cargo. Regardless, one could presumably float cargo to its location with relative ease.

Consider the purpose of our invented vessel before creating its structure. Passenger, cargo, and war ships will share areas like a bridge, engine room, and crew quarters, but entertainment, storage, and weaponry will all differ in size, quantity, and placement. Ships that are intended to permanently remain in space do not need aerodynamics.

DO WE NEED TO INVENT STRUCTURE?

In video gaming, a ship's internal structure is crucial because the gamer will guide a character room by room through the ship. It should make sense even if the layout or the purpose of rooms is not explained or apparent to someone who's busy killing NPCs onscreen. World builders are advised to plan a detailed internal structure so that the graphics team can implement it.

But in books or movies/TV shows, the structure often seems irrelevant. Seldom do we follow a character from a room, down a hallway, and to another room; doing so wastes precious screen time. I've seen entire series runs of *Star Trek* and still had little to no idea where one section of the ship is in relation to another. Even so, if we'd like to be consistent for a ship we'll use often, decide which deck each major department you'll mention is on. This avoids indicating that engineering is on deck six in one book and on deck seven in another. We don't need to be more specific than which deck and whether fore, aft, port, or starboard, if we really don't want to. Having a sense of difficulty and/or speed of access from various other places on the vessel is more important. If creating internal structure helps us do that, then yes, make decisions.

WHAT TO INCLUDE

The level of detail we invent should be specific to our use. The list below will provide ideas on areas that can be included.

The Bridge. Consider calling the command center something else for variety, but this is obviously where the ship is commanded and flown from. For visual reasons, it is typically forward as on Earth vessels, even if there's less practical reason in space. Sensors, cameras, and auto-pilot are often assumed to be responsible for something like docking, but those can malfunction or be destroyed, leaving a physical window as the backup. However, we can ditch this and have the crew using a TV, essentially, with the bridge located somewhere other than forward. Farther inside the ship seems wise, particularly for war ships. A command center with a wall of TVs to provide 360-degree views (inside and out) also seems more useful than a single, forward-facing window.

Living quarters (for officers and non-officers). Passenger areas are typically more spacious than those for crew, and both living quarters and dining areas for passengers are located in areas that prevent them from seeing the ship's guts. An easy way to resolve this is different decks, as on a cruise ship. On such ships, the exterior rooms will be for wealthier or more important people (for windows). Even ships that seldom have passengers may have one or two rooms set aside for a guest, even if that room is used for storage when not needed for passengers.

Entertainment. Passengers might be on a vessel mostly for pleasure, in which case we'd likely have what cruise ships have: musicians, dancers, live shows, lessons (like dancing), gambling, gaming, sports (like ping-pong, mini golf, rock climbing, surfing), exercise gyms, and individual practitioners (like ice sculptors). We'd likely want alternatives to these specifics in SF. A more military ship will have fewer diversions but will have something to let crew mentally and even physically escape their duties.

Shops. Even on a military ship, crew need to buy supplies for themselves beyond the basics the military provides (and which they might seek to augment or not use at all). On a passenger or cruise ship, many more shops will exist, generally in a concentrated area.

Dining. The main dining areas should be adjacent to living quarters while smaller eateries may be scattered about the ship, depending on size, and typically located near major work areas. Consider something special near the bridge, for example. A pleasure ship may also have bars and restaurants.

Cargo. Place this near the working area of the vessel, such as near engineering. It's an unglamorous thing that no one wants to see. If the ship specializes in cargo transport, or carries valuable cargo, then consider a separate area for items that might be under heavy guard, whether that's armed people or technology.

The brig (aka jail). This is not somewhere pleasant, meaning the bowels of the ship, such as near engines or cargo. Our characters may have other ways of confining someone, using imagined technology that eliminates the need for an actual jail.

Medical. A central location seems ideal on a warship, as casualties can come from all places, though perhaps it's closer to the most important people on the bridge.

The engines. Unless designed for only operating in space, all ships will have rearward facing propulsion, hence an engine room in the rear. There may be a second room for other forms of propulsion, with both controlled from another location. In *Star Trek*, this area is called Engineering, but a different word, such as Propulsion, is advised to distinguish our work from something so well known.

Main and auxiliary power. A ship that expects violence will probably have power sources separated from each other so that an explosion destroys only one and not all power sources. On some ships, this is located with the engines, a logical choice that requires less cabling throughout a ship.

Escape pods. These are located in convenient places. This means most are near crew quarters while a smaller quantity will be near all critical areas such as the bridge, engine rooms, and weaponry.

Weaponry. While weapons on star ships can typically be fired from the bridge, those weapons must be located somewhere, with possible manual intervention. Some are physical projectiles while others are energy, for example, but even the latter must be generated from somewhere. On the one hand, near the ship's exterior seems wise so that an inadvertent explosion doesn't blow the ship apart, as would happen with weapons stored farther inside. On the other hand, the risk of weapons being detonated in an attack also rises. Plan where your weapons are located and controlled from, including a decision on which fire physical projectiles and from where these are loaded (if not by machinery).

TIME AND DISTANCE

We may want to decide how long it takes people to move between locations in a ship, but this only matters if our story benefits from it. It's a moot point in small vessels. In an episodic show like *Star Trek*, where one ship will be repeatedly used, consistency is crucial. In many episodes, characters from the bridge are ordered to another part of the ship to deal with an emergency and arrive seconds later in TV time. We could conclude that the show just skipped ahead a few minutes, but often, whatever emergency was occurring, like two characters fighting, hasn't progressed more than a couple seconds. The presumed reason shows do this is so that main characters, i.e. actors, are featured all the time, but it's not realistic. We accept it, however.

If you'd like to be more realistic, approximate how long it takes to walk or run between all locations on a ship and whether something like an elevator is required. How long does it take to climb or crawl through maintenance corridors like the Jefferies Tubes of *Star Trek*? Are there stairs or only ladders? We seldom see a stairway except in places like engineering (and even then it's usually ladders). Why is that? Surely if they can invent warp drive they can still see the value of stairs over ladders if the turbo lifts (i.e. elevators) stop working. Are there no stairs (or underwear) in space?

WHERE TO START

The first choice to make in planning a vessel is to determine if it needs to operate in atmospheric conditions, or even if it might expect to do so. This will determine whether rear-facing engines are required, but STL engines will also require this. We should also decide what sort of ship it is (cargo, war, passenger), as this determines the amount and type of quarters, and dining or entertainment possibilities for crew. Next we should decide how passengers and crew typically board or exit the vessel, where they stay, and what they do onboard. We can also determine the purpose of our ship, such as travel within a solar system or between stars. This will help determine what sort of additional engines it has. Lastly, we should decide the events we're intending to take place on this vessel so that we can decide what sorts of vulnerabilities it might provide us with and how characters and story might benefit from these; but we can also start with this subject. The best choice is to go with the subject that gives you ideas first, then return to less inspiring areas later.

CHAPTER TEN

CREATING TIME AND HISTORY

WHY CREATE HISTORY?

While an elaborate history isn't needed, a sense of the past can add realism to our work. How much history we'll need depends on how much we'd like it to inform the present. A short story needs little, but an epic trilogy of adventurers traveling across many lands requires it. The sovereign powers they traverse have history with each other, and some of that will be recent, such as a war or a new ruler who is crushing freedoms for the people or reducing restrictions. Even if we don't want to comment on this sort of thing much, characters will be aware of these new ramifications of entering another land. Traveling through similar places results in a flat narrative.

Science fiction often focuses on the future, given the presence of technologies that don't yet exist, but that future is far enough away that there's still past that's ahead of our current timeframe. In other words, a story set on Earth in 2500 AD has 500 years of history that hasn't happened yet. In settings not connected to Earth, we can create future history without worrying about how we get there.

A common fantasy trope is that ancient, and long-vanished, civilizations have left relics that characters discover and use. These can include magic items, forgotten spell books, powerful creatures, and ancient, long overgrown cities that harbor horrors that will one day reawaken. The characters responsible for the demise of these civilizations can become legendary figures, which is covered in "Creating World Figures" from *Creating Places (The Art of World Building, #1)*. We should have a high-level idea of what culture created these items and how that culture disappeared, but details included in the narrative can be sketchy because in a world with limited technology, the average person knows less history. This is true even in an advanced society such as our own, where most people aren't worried too much about the past; that said, we pick up little details from the news and entertainment, so we have a general sense of events without depth of knowledge.

The architecture of ancient civilizations can provide a sense of being alien and therefore unsettling, allowing us to characterize a scene with description and our characters' reaction to a location. To do this, we should decide what form of government this decrepit place had. There's a tendency toward the brutish, hulking, and threatening styles associated with authoritarian regimes (and the foreboding they produce), but we can also have an elegant place designed by an enlightened species, whose city has been destroyed by war or plague (resulting in a sense of nostalgic loss for visitors). Deciding on the reaction we want can help inform our decision.

Post-apocalypse works need a cataclysm that has created the present scenario. The cause can be technological, biological, supernatural, or somewhat ordinary (such as an asteroid strike). A world with gods might want a moral reason for the destruction, such as gods abandoning a wicked species. In *Dragonlance*, human pride caused the gods to stop answering prayers for hundreds of years. Such a scenario allows commentary on humanity's failings.

We might have multiple continents and therefore a whole world for which we're creating history. In this case, we might want to organize the history we create into smaller sections, possibly in different documents. World events, such as gods inventing a worldwide species, or a plague that spreads between continents, would go into one file. But we otherwise might want to organize our events by a continent or region.

Sample Entries

Think of each entry in your history as a summary that only touches on the big issues. We don't need to know why a war was fought. Here are some examples of how to write logs.

Hessian 124—The Horn of Killian Lost

Legendary necromancer Killian of the Lorfrost suffers an ignoble defeat at the hands of Lord Sinias of Kingdom Norin, when Sinias kills a spectral knight who is in the act of blowing the Horn of Killian. The resulting vortex pulls all the souls into the horn, including that of Killian, who briefly disappears from the world. By the time he returns weeks later, destroying Sinias, the horn has fallen into unknown hands.

HESSIAN 227—THE ORB OF STARAN CREATED

In the Hills of Asawan, the Wizard Obin creates the Orb of Staran in a black pool of molten ore. Its existence and properties are unknown to all but a trusted acolyte, who kills Obin, steals the Orb, and flees from the Hounds of Asawan to Kingdom Illiandor. He will go on to suffer the same fate in five years when he is killed for the orb.

HESSIAN 248—THE WAR OF BEASTS BEGINS

Driven by famine and drought, an army of monsters and animals begins its assault from the far eastern reaches of the continent. In their immediate path lies the Kingdom of Norin, which mounts a defense and wins the first battle in the War of Beasts.

HESSIAN 250—KINGDOM NORIN FALLS

In the War of Beasts, Kingdom Norin falls to the creatures from the untamed lands to the west, including the Hills of Asawan, the Sea of Serpents, and the Crags of Forever. The capital, Dokken, becomes a haunted ruin where the damned king is rumored to still walk with a ghostly retinue that can only be controlled with the Horn of Killian, which has long been considered lost.

HESSIAN 251—THE WAR OF BEASTS ENDS

With the warnings provided by the fallen Kingdom of Norin, neighboring kingdom Seva is better prepared for the onslaught. The king is aided by the rediscovered Horn of Killian, found by a farm boy who becomes the unlikely hero of the war when he enters the city of Dokken in Norin and summons the fallen King of Norin. The beasts are no match for the undead and living warriors of Seva, who destroy them.

HESSIAN 252—EXPEDITION INTO HILLS OF ASAWAN DISAPPEARS

Following rumors that an unknown wizard instigated the advance of the beasts from the Hills of Asawan, Kingdom Norin sends an expeditionary force into the hills. It is never seen again, the last signs of it being near the Tower of Sorin, halfway into the hills. No bodies are ever found, nor are weapons, horses, or anything else. A follow-up expedition reveals the tower is gone altogether.

The above examples were invented in a few minutes for this volume. It doesn't take long and can produce world figures, creatures, legendary missions, and artifacts, all of which we could have already thought of or just be making up on the spot, to be fleshed out later. This begins the process of shaping a world; start small, then build on that. I now have two magic items, an undead army, two kingdoms, a famous necromancer and a wizard, and a land of beasts. Not bad for ten minutes of goofing around.

What I'd do next is open my supernatural items file and create an entry for the tower, orb and horn, then make up more details on how they work. I'd also open the files on kingdoms Norin and Seva and add entries about the War of Beasts. For whatever continent that is, I'd open the file on land features and write an entry for the Hills of Asawan and the hounds within, deciding where that is on my map. My file on animals would get an entry for the hounds.

CREATION MYTHS

In fantasy worlds, most cultures have a creation myth of some kind to explain where the gods and the culture originated. In more advanced societies, there's less myth, so this might not figure in SF as much. In volume 1, *Creating Life*, we discussed creation myths in more detail. These events are the earliest ones to fill out in that history.

TIME

MEASURING TIME

How is time measured in our invented world? This is a subject we can ignore if everything is Earth-like and we're fine with the audience assuming time is similar, as they probably will unless we remark on it. Markedly different time measurement is an area of unnecessary exposition that is best avoided unless it matters for our work. Readers don't want to remember how many minutes there are in an hour, hours in a day, how long the week is, how many weeks there are per month, and how many months the year includes. Each time we mention that two characters will meet in an hour, but that's really two Earth hours, is an annoyance.

Should we create different time measurements? That depends.

MINUTES AND HOURS

I recommend leaving minutes and hour lengths alone. Changing them offers an audience confusion with no payoff. There are better ways to make our world seem different. Even if we mention that an hour is ninety minutes, for example, but then we keep writing "hour" in our story, the reader will forget the different length. This is especially true if this alteration is arbitrary and has no rationale that makes it easier to remember. We can invent other words instead of "hour," but then those require explanations that must be remembered, too, doubling down on the encumbrance with which we've burdened the audience.

While it's true that time is likely measured differently on other planets, our audience is on Earth and needs to quickly understand time references in Earth terms. A workaround in SF that has characters from Earth is to have one mention "that's 1.5 Earth hours" to another person; the characters should likely go by Earth measurements for their comfort and that of the audience. In SF, a briefly visited planet is a good time to use different minute/hour measurements for a story impacted by this.

One reason to leave minutes and hours alone is that this unit of time measurement will be more frequently mentioned than days, weeks, or months. Story scenes take place in minutes, hours, and days. Having "minute" and "hour" be too different just messes with our audience's understanding of time. But scenes are less often separated by weeks or months, and once we're working in bigger units, does it really matter if "three months later" is one hundred days instead of ninety? Only a little.

As an example, on my world of Llurien, there are twelve months of twenty-eight days, resulting in 336 days. That's twenty-nine days, or a month, shorter than Earth. This means someone a year old on Llurien is eleven months old on Earth. But after ten years, a ten-year-old on Llurien would only be nine years old on Earth. While the gap has widened, the difference between a nine and ten year old isn't great. This is again true at 22 vs 20, and 33 vs 30. I don't need to ever point this out to my audience, but if I do, it doesn't matter unless characters from Llurien come to Earth (or vice versa).

On this note, it's important to figure out how long a year really is on an invented world. Once we've decided on all our measurements, do the math to figure out a scenario like the above.

We could name the hours of the day, but this can be another encumbrance that gains us little and requires exposition. Do so with a good reason that impacts your story or skip it. We can do these things and seldom mention them, however.

We can change the number of hours in a day, but it's recommended that day lengths be similar to Earth if we're building an Earth-like world. This means being off by a few hours at most, not having only twelve hour days unless we really mean for this to figure prominently. In SF, the life forms from a planet with different length days will have different sleep and eating cycles, but this will matter more when life forms from worlds with disparate cycles are brought together.

DAYS IN A WEEK

The number of days in a week is another area to change. There are seven days on Earth due to ancient civilizations naming them after seven celestial bodies that were visible (this included the sun and moon, which are Sunday and Monday). With planets named after gods like Thor (Thursday), we also acquired the names. We can do something similar on an invented world, using whatever rationalization we can make sensible. There could be eight moons that cause eight-day weeks. There could be six gods, each getting a day in a six-day week. We can depart from deities and decide the days are named after the six schools of magic in a world dominated by supernatural power. Or maybe there were six great heroes from long ago. Or six dragons. In SF, the days of the week are likely decided long before technological advances that could have days named after technology (or related scientists, explorers, etc.), but maybe a later empire forced change on everyone.

In the above examples from Earth, you'll note that Thor is spelled differently for Thursday. Most of the god names were altered in time from different cultures misspelling things, or just altering the spelling for their native language. We might want to do this, too, to make day names easier to say. For example, I could call a day Llurienday, but that's kind of a mouthful. Shortening it to Llurday or Rienday is a little better.

Regardless of our decision, we should take strides to minimize the use of day names in our writing because our audience will have no idea what we're talking about. This is true even if we explain it once. We can provide charts on a website, like a glossary, but skillfully handling this is the best approach. Our characters (as opposed to our narration) should be the ones most often using the day names, because they would. Take this example passage:

> Kier asked, "When will the sword be ready?"
> "Next Rienday," the blacksmith replied.
> Kier nodded. A week and a day. Plenty of time to run it through his beloved's heart.

If we change the number of days in a week, we might want to go with six or eight. The reason is that when we narrate "a week and a day" as above, this is still close to a week on Earth and the audience's sense of time passing is only slightly off. By contrast, if a week is twelve days, we throw the audience off quite a bit more and might have to keep reminding them of such a thing. In the above scenario, I would instead write, "Thirteen days. Plenty of time..."

WEEKS IN A MONTH

How many weeks do we want in a month? On Earth, this isn't set. Instead the number of days in a month is what determines how weeks are laid out. A month with thirty days could span four weeks one year and five the next, depending on what day of the week that month began. We might choose to standardize the weeks more, in which case the weeks might get names. On my Llurien world, every month has four weeks of seven days. Those weeks are associated with the four elements, resulting in Fireweek, for example. The fourteenth day is always the seventh day of the second week. No one needs a calendar to figure it out.

MONTHS IN A YEAR

How many months do we want in a year? Once again, and for the same reason, it's recommended to be off by one from Earth, meaning eleven or thirteen months in a year. Earth months are named and our invented world will need month names, too. Once again, our audience will have no idea what we're talking about, so they should be used sparingly and explained succinctly. Take this example passage:

> Kier asked, "When will the dragon give birth?"
> "In Dicerimon," the dragon keeper replied.
> Kier nodded. Three months, just in time for the winter sacrifice.

In this passage, note the use of the suffix "mon" on the month name. On Earth, we have "uary" and "ber" to denote half of the months. We might want to choose a similar approach to indicate to our audience that we're referencing a month. A common prefix or suffix can assist their understanding. As with Earth, perfect uniformity may not happen or be advisable and can even look like too much planning on our part. Feel free to make exceptions.

When revealing the number of months, we can also work this into narration instead of writing exposition about it. See Kier's fate for guidance:

> Kier asked, "When will I be executed for my crimes?"
> "Two years from today," the judge replied. "One for your beloved. Another for the dragon."
> Kier hung limp in the chains. Twenty-two months to agonize over his mistakes.

UNIVERSAL CALENDAR

In our modern world, we're used to the Gregorian calendar being accepted worldwide. This wasn't always true and in some places it's not official and is only used when trying to correlate dates between different countries. We could invent a datebook for every kingdom, but that's a lot of work for little gain. A universal calendar, meaning one that's acknowledged across a planet, has both advantages and disadvantages.

BENEFITS

In stories, we might have little reason to mention the year, but this depends on our needs and the world's technological level. A fantasy setting might be less concerned with information in general, not to mention date, but some SF frequently mentions this, such as the well-known "star date" for a captain's log entry in *Star Trek*. What's important is that, whether we mention dates or not, we need a universal calendar for our notes even if not used by our characters. Otherwise, we can't reconcile two differing calendars and understand when events occurred. There's no way to tell that year 734 D.C. in Kingdom X is thirty years later than year 343 O.E. in Kingdom Y.

Each sovereign power may have its own time measurement. Year one will be an important event, such as the kingdom's founding or the life and death of someone important. There could be a technology that shapes life, or a supernatural event or discovery. It should be something that resonates with society or which the power wants to champion, such as the first ruler in a dynasty. While we're free to invent these internal calendars, we need a universal one.

Whether our universal calendar is recognized on the planet is another matter. For this to happen, there must be a globally accepted event. On Earth, we use the birth of Christ, with years before that counting down like a timer and the years after counting up. However, this scheme wasn't recognized for hundreds of years and didn't become standard for hundreds more. Christianity slowly spread, and with it, the calendar. For an invented world, we might need something like the birth of magic or a new technology to occur and slowly spread, too. A swifter way is a cataclysm, which is especially viable in post-apocalyptic fiction and which will quickly dominate minds and ways of life. A mass exodus from a planet might be, too. We need to think of an event that most people in the world will think is a big deal.

If we want our story to be directly impacted by the event, by which I mean the characters and world are still recovering from it, the event should be recent, within the last few hundred years. Otherwise, place the event farther in the past. The invention of a technology might impact modern life, but the moment of that invention doesn't have to be recent.

Deciding no universal calendar exists is also fine, but be sure to choose one for your private notes if you're building a world intended to be used a long time, and which has multiple sovereign powers with differing calendars. If you can't decide, go with a believed creation date rather than the timespan required by evolution. It took millions of years for life to evolve on Earth, but according to some religions, God put us here less than ten thousand years ago. We can decide the first civilization is a marker, as that might've been much closer; years longer than five digits (10,000) can seem unwieldy.

When it comes to the initials like A.D. and B.C., whether for a universal calendar or not, we'll want a naming convention of some sense, such as B.M. and A.M., as in "Before Magic" and "After Magic." We don't need to use this style. Terms such as Heisei 12 in Japan means it's the twelfth year of the current emperor, named Heisei. People might want a positive spin on the years, but in a dystopian setting, a negative sounding term can be accepted.

CHALLENGES

If we're inventing a world for long term use or might use both hemispheres, there are some issues to consider for calendar names. On Earth, January is a winter month to some and a summer month to others, and since the word "January" has nothing to do with a season, we're okay. But what if it was called "Snowtime" instead? That would only make sense to areas which receive snow in January. Tropical climates may never get snow regardless of hemisphere, polar areas always have snow, and some areas have no seasons.

If we want to do it anyway, regional terms can add dimension. A character from such a place can express how different things are back home, now that they're away. On Earth, there's no shortage of people from the northern hemisphere saying how weird it is to celebrate Christmas in summer while south of the equator. Some holidays, like Christmas, have nothing to with a season but have become associated with it.

It's tempting to decide the year starts with spring, but this is once again only true for certain areas. For others, it would be the first day of winter or not associated with any specific season. How likely is it that everyone north of the equator likes that spring idea and everyone south of it likes the winter idea? Not very. The likely result is a different calendar, which might be local in focus.

So what do we start the year with? An event that has nothing to do with weather, climate, or seasons. In this chapter, the "Historical Event Categories" section may provide ideas.

CREATING AGES

Time periods are sometimes given names like the Stone Age or Bronze Age here on Earth. In fantasy, we can see an Age of Swords or maybe an Elven Age, for a time dominated by elves, possibly because their talents gave rise to their prominence. In SF, we might have a Terrestrial Age, meaning before space flight became possible, or an Interstellar Age. While the present age might not have a name, all past ages will get a name if we choose to do this at all; otherwise there's a gap with no name. At worst, we can all an age the "Pre" age, such as "Pre-Interstellar Age" when the following era is the Interstellar Age. A current age can lack a name because names are typically applied after the fact.

Ages are typically thousands of years but could be less. When creating events within that time period, be aware of the time frame's implications. If those of Earth begin space exploration more akin to *Star Trek*, that can be the start of an Interstellar Age. Events from our current time frame can either be fit into that age or the previous one. It's our decision how to group events as leading to a revolution and being in the previous age, or being part of the next age they trigger.

USES FOR HISTORY

Inventing history can have uses beyond world building. The main use is to make our present and future stories more believable and detailed. We might also invent world figures, artifacts, and mysteries we can utilize. These can offer twists and turns to our work. We could connect new ideas to previously created ones. Maybe we have a supernatural creature with an origin we haven't worked out yet, and we like the world finding this mysterious and creepy. Then we later invent an item that has some side effects. One day we bring them together and decide the item caused the creature. We can decide no one knows this until our characters discover it. With only two examples, this seems obvious, but in a world with dozens of inventions, an intricate layering becomes possible.

We can also write stories using the best incidents we conjure, so don't be afraid to let your imagination run wild, even if you create a bunch of stuff you don't think you can use at first. We can turn them into short stories that we send to loyal readers in our newsletter, as bonus materials. Or it can be on our website. We might even get such a tale published.

HISTORICAL EVENT CATEGORIES

There are different types of entries with which we can fill an imagined history. This list isn't exhaustive but can provide inspiration.

THE GODS

In some story worlds, the gods keep to themselves, but in others they interfere with life and cause events. This could be fathering children with members of mortal species, resulting in monsters or demi-gods. They might have sacred places that are built or destroyed. Perhaps most fun is that gods sometimes have very powerful magic items that fall into the wrong hands, causing events with long-term consequences. This can include the invention of new species or monsters that proliferate. A god can even be killed or otherwise inhibited (imprisoned) due to some event, whether they acted badly and were punished by the gods, or because a mortal somehow did something to them. Maybe some of these incidents are celebrated or otherwise noted, like an anniversary, by the species.

TECHNOLOGICAL EVENTS

Many technological events are possible, especially in SF. These include failed or successful missions, rocket/satellite/ship launches, explosions, discoveries, weapons tests, and first contact with other aliens/species. The latter is especially important; the longer the history between two species, the greater the odds of conflict and familiarity breeding contempt. Or those who've been hostile can learn the other isn't so bad, possibly due to help needed against a mutual threat. Disasters of technology, like America's space shuttle tragedies, often spur innovation and a memorial; a main character can be a descendant of someone lost. Classes of vessels might be invented, used, and retired. Another event is the discovery of special ore needed by ship engines or to forge metal in fantasy, or even the creation of famous items. Ships, fleets, and items can also disappear, be destroyed, or be captured.

SUPERNATURAL EVENTS

For fantasy worlds and some SF, no history is complete without the supernatural. Phenomena must start or be discovered, and possibly wreak havoc, and then be neutralized. We might have famous expeditions to deal with somewhere or something. Magic (in general or specific spells) can be discovered, expanded, and proliferate or be squashed in one region or sovereign power. Famous practitioners or victims will come and go. This is true of items, whether armor, weapons, scrolls, potions, or jewelry. Perhaps a useful material is discovered or exploited into nonexistence (or restricted by law). Monsters might result from events, too. Did something of the gods fall into mortal hands? Celestial events like a conjunction, eclipse, or comet can be assigned supernatural significance.

THE RISE AND FALL OF SOVEREIGN POWERS

No sovereign power lasts forever or retains the same government. The bigger events, such as the power signs an important treaty, or collapses can be noted here, but most internally relevant events can be kept in that power's file. How a kingdom came to be doesn't really require an explanation in our world history, and few will question this. However, its demise benefits from an explanation (see Chapter 5, "Creating a Sovereign Power"); these include being conquered, revolution, and a coup. Its fall will impact neighbors, but we might not need to comment on this unless an empire has fallen, as other powers that fell under its control will enter a period of instability.

WARS

A world without war isn't realistic. We can invent these while conjuring a history or while working in a sovereign power's file. Doing this requires an idea of the governments existing in those powers and their locations; otherwise it's hard to know why the war is being fought, not to mention where, or what impact it has on the powers or anyone else caught in the conflict. It helps to understand technological or supernatural level of the combatants.

Is there a goal we hope this war will achieve? Perhaps we want simmering resentments between characters of today. Maybe we want a disaster to result as the logical conclusion of animosities we've set in motion. Is a resource under contention? Is that place a danger that one power wants to secure but which another wants to utilize?

Remember that former enemies can become allies later, sometimes through government upheaval, defeat, or just the passing of time. We've seen this on Earth, where in as little as a few generations, animosities have given way to mutual aid and reconciliation. Don't be afraid to decide two friendly nations today weren't enemies as little as decades ago. The speed of change may depend on technology and information; worlds with less, as in fantasy, might harbor animosity for far longer.

"Ethnic cleansing", one group trying to eradicate another, has caused some of the worst wars; this sort of animosity won't quickly disappear. A power might try to unite ethnic groups that have become split across nations. For example, Russia recently invaded Ukraine with one justification being that the Ukraine has regions with mostly ethnic Russians, who want to be part of Russia. There were also natural resources at stake.

Pride is yet another reason for war, as a new dictator must make a show of power. Or the dictator feels pride in their nation and heritage and feel they and their people have been oppressed or wrongly scaled back in a previous war. Starting a new war to right wrongs from a previous war is a classic. Leaders may have a grand vision of superiority or desire a fate different from, and better than, their current reality, for themselves or their kingdom, and the stress of this simmers for many years before leading to open war.

Taking back territory, resources, or something else believed to rightly belong to a kingdom is another reason for war. Sometimes these are perpetual disputes—until an empire absorbs both opponents.

GROUPS FORMING

We might want to indicate when a special military group was formed. Use this for famous knight orders or naval/space forces, even dragon riders, spectral groups, elite guards, horsemen, archers, or whichever groups you've created. If there's a wizard or warrior order, like monks of a certain region, note their formation date, or when a powerful leader rose, influenced, disappeared, or fell. Did this group or someone from it accomplish something? Is there a force for good or evil, like the Justice League from comics? *Cultures and Beyond (The Art of World Building, #3)* goes into more details about groups we can create.

ARTIFACTS DISCOVERED/INVENTED

Creating magic items is one of the fun things about writing fantasy. For SF, legendary devices or ships are equally fun, particularly when they disappear, creating mystery, intrigue, and excitement when they show up in a story. These can fall under the protection of a sovereign power or individual and be contested. They can be feared or admired. They can come with a prophecy about the sort of person who might wield them one day, causing dreams and struggles. Each time you create an important item, add its invention date to the history, though lesser objects don't need an origin date.

MISSIONS UNDERTAKEN

Missions to explore, rescue, kill or kidnap someone/something, or investigate strange phenomena can be listed in our history. Be sure to indicate the outcome, whether this is known to the characters or not. This history is for your files, so it's okay to drop the truth in here and only reveal that to an audience in a story. Those who undertook a mission might be famous, giving us world figures. They might have also triggered an event, such as a war or new phenomenon, or discovered a new item or material.

WHERE TO START

History can be created at random, though at times we'll want to create multiple events regarding a subject at once. Entries needn't be related, making this ideal for piecemeal work. For any subject, such as a power or group, we can either start inventing the past in our history file or do it in the file for that power or group. The biggest items should go on the world history with minimal redundancy across files. The event categories above should provide ideas on what might need to be created before a history, but we want to work on history after inventing the thing for which we're creating that past. Otherwise, follow your heart and feel free to let creativity run free.

CHAPTER ELEVEN

CREATING PLACES OF INTEREST

Noteworthy locations provide our characters somewhere to stumble upon, avoid, or seek out on missions. They can cause interesting items or life forms to exist, possess, or flee from. World builders can place these in almost random locations, reducing the burden of logic needed to explain origins. Some phenomena simply exist where they do or are the result of natural geological forces (such as volcanoes or meteor strikes), while events such as explosions, battles, or experiments gone awry can cause others. Used in small doses, they can add complexity, interest, and variety to a setting.

ORDINARY PLACES

Not every location needs to be spectacular to be of interest. Anything unusual can do and should not be overlooked.

CATACOMBS AND HIDDEN PASSAGES

Catacombs, bomb shelters, sewer lines, tunnels, and subway lines, especially beneath a settlement, can provide somewhere to hide people, creatures, or possessions, and be used for stealthy maneuvering. We can decide they are known to all or a select few who are using them for nefarious purposes. Even if known, the extent of them seldom is; much of the fun lies in the mystery. When inventing these, decide why they exist. They might have been designed for covert work, such as in military locations. Royalty could have decided they wanted ways to move about without being noticed (or for their spies). Excessive heat in tropical locations might have led to these cooler places to dwell at times, or store things like wine or munitions. Perhaps there are secret training facilities.

In a world with dwarves, perhaps they just enjoy such locations as a reminder of home and have tunneled deep, with or without permissions. They might no longer live here, leaving abandoned tunnels that are partly in use by those with both good and bad intentions. Sometimes these locations aren't known because a civilization or population from a thousand years ago might have left it. The current settlement could even have been built atop such a place with no one realizing it.

STEP WELLS

For most of us, a water well might not sound interesting, but if you Google "step wells in India," the pictures will change your mind. These are elaborate pits in the ground with flights of stairs leading down to the water. The steps appear akin to an amphitheater, being wide and often on all four sides in a square or rectangular shape. Platforms can exist in these, and with some imagination, we might decorate them with carvings and statues. Some structures have cave-like openings into a cliff face and buildings that are carved from within. If we have a species which dwells in fresh water, they may swim up underground rivers to emerge from these wells.

Figure 61 Step Well

MONUMENTS

Monuments can be buildings, monoliths, or statues. Some could be more spectacular than others and qualify as famous locations. This can be due to size, complexity, or the individual or occasion being memorialized. Having world figures helps us decide on the latter. We should also determine the condition such monuments are in. Those in abandoned places might be in disrepair or have been vandalized, even destroyed utterly, whether this is known or discovered by characters in a story. Visiting such a place to acquire power or an item can therefore throw characters off their intended quest. Monuments located amid existing civilization might also be prone to thievery attempts and desecration.

On Earth, we have Egypt's great pyramids, the Great Wall of China, or Stonehenge. The ancient world included the Seven Wonders, which included a temple, two statues, the pyramids, a mausoleum, gardens, and a lighthouse. These seven were chosen because there were, at the time, seven bodies in the heavens: the sun, moon, and five discovered planets. An invented world might benefit from a similar explanation if monuments are being counted. The lists can be longer, and different lists have existed over time. The original seven don't sound impressive until one considers the unusual size, adornment, or subject (often a god) of most. Many of these wonders were destroyed by earthquakes or floods.

GRAVES

While most cemeteries won't be of much interest, other burial sites may be. One possibility is a system of catacombs, where skulls and bones have been stacked. Mausoleums can be enormous, uniquely decorated, or house famous people; these may contain items, such as treasure, which others plunder. These would require guards of ordinary or extraordinary kind, such as ferocious animals/monsters, or humanoids with demonic, technological, or magical powers. Graveyards could also have unique layouts where different classes of people are interred separately. Rituals might also be done at regular intervals. A day of the dead festival might exist, the macabre scene fitting for a story. Lone grave sites in the wilderness might also achieve significance for location or features.

Extraordinary Places

Underwater Settlements

While extraordinary to us, an underwater settlement might be commonplace on your world, if a water dwelling species exists to construct them. Are there dry areas or air pockets allowing land species to reside there safely? Or be imprisoned because there's no way to reach the surface? Perhaps magic or technological portals allow people to enter or leave such a city. Think about what sort of industry and skills a water dwelling species might acquire if they not only have water-filled areas but dry ones, assuming they can move on land. Might they craft a large enough space to practice with weapons they'd need skills for on land?

Floating Settlements

We've seen cities in *Star Wars*, and rock formations in *Avatar*, both suspended in the air. We can use magic, technology, or unexplained physics to do the same. Aside from this floating aspect, these settlements otherwise differ little from more ordinary communities. However, we should think about what opportunities are afforded. A flying species might be prone to inventing such places or find them very attractive. There might be few predators except the flying kind, making life safe. While no city walls will exist, what kind of aerial fortifications might be needed? Trade might be quite difficult without ships, large flying animals, or other means to transport resources. It may also be at extraordinary risk of crashing to the ground, which seems an obvious sabotage focus for enemies. How does this place protect itself from hurricanes, tornados, or strong storms? The obvious answer is that it's only built somewhere that doesn't experience these.

On Earth, we have Venice, which is built largely on stilts, but the impression is still of floating on water. This does not require magic or advanced technology, but we can invent a place that genuinely floats on the sea. A water dwelling species might find this accommodating and even be the ones to invent it. The setting can be a place where land and water species can interact more easily. This must occur where significant waves are rare if not unheard of, so look for a lagoon or otherwise protected inlet in waterways like bays or sounds. If there are large sea monsters that could easily wreck the place, then it won't exist, but if there's a new sea monster never considered before, we can have fun destroying the settlement in a story.

OTHER UNUSUAL HOMES

A species might build homes inside hills like the Hobbits of *The Lord of the Rings*. Elaborate mountain homes are a staple of dwarves. A flying species could build small homes inside enormous trees, but with no way to reach the ground so that predators, including other species, can't access them.

PHENOMENA

Strange phenomena are staples of fantasy and SF, especially when the latter involves explorations of the cosmos. Space offers nebulas, radiation, and alien planet environments. We can invent all manner of experiences that have no real explanation or at best, pseudoscience to impart believability or specific effects on characters and their environment, such as an interstellar ship. Space phenomena have a great advantage in that their location is flexible; we can place them wherever we feel like it and invent them on the fly.

By contrast, singularities on a planet or other body (moon, asteroid, etc.) are typically associated with a given location. They often benefit from at least speculation as to their causes. Technological or magical disasters, resulting from experiments or battle, offer easy rationalizations and even suggest world figures or famous items that might've been involved. Monsters or creatures can be a result, too. Does this phenomenon influence only things that come in contact with it or can it affect nearby objects? Maybe it can compel people to approach.

We can also create seemingly unrelated phenomena in different locations but which bear some similarities, but later associate them with each other. We might also have phenomena that begat other phenomena, with no one knowing this until characters stumble upon the truth. This sort of layering adds depth while fascinating audiences as oddities they've experienced before are revealed to have new significance.

There might be places where magic or technology doesn't work, is unpredictable, or is supercharged. Animals could go wild, which is a cliché, or become docile if we want a new impact. There can be locations allowing extraordinary travel, whether actual doorways, random spots, or the former built on the latter. These gateways can lead to other physical locations, supernatural ones, or an alternate reality or timeline. These methods may be predictable, controllable, or neither. Can only certain people or devices activate them? Or we can have a portal open constantly because no one knows how to close it. Beings could be summoned through them.

On Earth, we have places where strange behavior is believed to occur, like the Bermuda Triangle or crop circles. Then there's Area 51, a rumored place for storing unusual items. The origins of places like Stonehenge or Easter Island have been debated, but we can invent similar locations and attribute fantastic reasons for their existence.

RUINS

Abandoned places are ripe for death by misadventure. Monsters, treasure, and items can all lure people to investigate and figure out what's there or what went wrong. To that end, dropping clues is vital to intriguing an audience. Some of these places will be legendary while others are previously unknown. Both have their merits.

These can range from simple caves or tunnels, like a monster lair or dwarven home, to entire cities or even planets; if we want to be extreme, we can include solar systems or entire galaxies. The scale of abandonment suggests the scale of calamity that caused that abandonment, so choose accordingly. Danger is often assumed to lurk in such places, whether that danger is the new inhabitant, nature having taken over, or the remnants of the reason abandonment took place. Valuables are often assumed to have been left behind, attracting thieves and opportunists who might interfere with a band of characters going there.

Ruins are fun for audiences to watch people discover and explore. We can create mystery about what's happening there now and what led to its demise. Clues and rumors should evoke curiosity and maybe feelings of dread, foreboding, wonder, and excitement. The more suggestive these are, the better, but it pays to have a reveal that goes beyond audience expectations regarding how cool the truth is, surpassing it. The trick to this is being coy about the truth, and inventing plausible variants on that truth, each one compelling but not as cool as the actuality.

But not everywhere needs a big story. Disease, drought, climate change, natural disasters, and destruction in war are simple explanations that are likely culprits. Some places vanish for commercial reasons, such as over-exploitation of the resource (as in mining) or because a better commercial location usurped it, leaving a ghost town, which may have some residents.

Bear in mind how overgrown the location is. A rainforest or swamp quickly consumes a place so that it's nearly impossible to find and less likely to be known; roads to it will disappear, too. More exposed locations will endure wind erosion and may become buried by sediment. An underground place won't suffer much erosion but will instead lose structural cohesion from earthquakes, the toll of which we can tailor to our intended desire. Similarly, a mountain settlement might suffer rock falls. Sometimes people wonder why more dust doesn't accumulate in abandoned places, but dust is partly particles from people, so no people means no more dust accumulation or the tracking in of other contaminants.

The durability of buildings is greatly impacted by their material. In less advanced settings, the roof is often the first part of a structure to disintegrate, allowing more rain and animals inside and speeding interior erosion. Stone structures could last centuries despite deterioration, but remember that locals might steal these materials for their own uses. With the advanced technology in SF, a location could last far longer, unaffected by erosion except for becoming overgrown and buried. Then again, maybe automated machines are keeping it pristine long after life has departed.

Magical or technological items are among the best ones left behind, whether by accident or on purpose. They are begging to be found by heroes, villains, or a random fool. Depending on the item, this could empower someone who shouldn't have such power, raising them to king or overlord among their kind, such as goblins. Think of a weapon, armor, information found in books or scrolls, or a space ship or other tech, depending on your story. The object found might also be cursed. It doesn't have to be the item responsible for the ruin existing. We might want to create a group of people who see it as their job to find, neutralize, and store these items to prevent such events.

SHIPWRECKS

Wooden shipwrecks aren't always completely submerged, but if so, they become more useful if we have a water-dwelling species that can plunder them, whether that's items, coins, gems or something else worthwhile. The species can be benevolent or nefarious, and the items found can be dangerous or benign. We can empower sea-dwelling life in some way that makes them more formidable to landlubbers, possibly upsetting the balance of power. They can also become a threat to ships. Perhaps a good species rescues people or performs salvage missions in cooperation with land species. They might even raise a ship back to the surface, or use it as a home. They

416 | RANDY ELLEFSON

might claim that everything below the waves is in their domain and therefore theirs, causing conflict.

In SF, shipwrecks may be more accessible, whether in space or on the surface of a planet, moon, asteroid, or space station; they could also be underwater. The technology available on one could be a boon or threat to those who discover and salvage it. The most obvious reason for abandoned spacecraft are crashes, partial destruction, or literally abandoning ship. Wars in space can leave a huge field of debris in orbit, whether around a planet, moon, or a sun; such a ship graveyard must be navigated carefully and might even be named. When creating one, decide the reason for the battle, how many ships were involved, who won, and what kinds of craft were involved. Was it a fight between war craft? Or was this a peaceful convoy that someone attacked? This will likely be part of a larger conflict between sovereign powers across the same or different worlds.

We should decide what happened to the crew. The easy answer is that everyone's dead, but other options are more entertaining. Capture and being marooned offer chances for survivors to have new lives quite different than their previous ones.

Source of Fame

When creating a shipwreck of note, there must be a reason people remember it. It could be in a remote place that makes recovery hard. Or it could be in the mouth of a crucial river or outside a noteworthy settlement, or scene of battle. It could be on an asteroid or orbiting a unique body.

The ship could have been famous before crashing/sinking, whether for its attributes or missions it undertook, including the one causing its demise. Did it have a special engine, new A.I., or experimental weapons or defenses, some of which could be the reason it met its doom? Someone could have tried to destroy or capture it. Maybe it just had an appearance or configuration that struck fear into people's hearts. It could be famous for its captain or crew; the former allows us to create a world figure (see *Creating Life (The Art of World Building, #1)*).

The reason for a ship's demise can be famous. This can include a mutiny, striking a rock, reef, or iceberg, or a storm strong enough to overturn the ship. For spaceships, we often use technology to rupture hulls or propulsion systems, but they can also strike space debris, whether that's other manmade objects or leftovers from the solar system's formation (rock and ice). A disabled ship can become unable to maneuver away from an impending collision, but the disabling incident should be interesting. The event which damaged the ship may leave the wreck dangerous, such as with radiation or supernatural residue tainting it; maybe this causes monsters (see *Creating Life*).

A sea or space monster could have caused damage. We should decide who attacked whom; perhaps the way in which the crew brought demise upon itself rendered their fate famous. War is an easy way to destroy vessels, but since it's mundane, we might need to make the battle famous or assign another attribute to this ship to make its wreck renowned.

Cargo is an easy way to make a shipwreck famous. We can place anything we've invented for our world in the hold, provided that transporting it between two locations makes sense. If this form of transportation is rare, that makes the wreck rare, too. We end up with a "lost" item. The question then becomes whether this has been recovered or not. Stories to acquire lost treasure suggest themselves.

A creature inhabiting the ship now could be the source of infamy, especially if that creature can pilot the vessel. A ship that's fallen into the wrong hands provides opportunities for mayhem whether it remains disabled from travel or not. A stationary ship, if equipped with the right technology, could still be a great danger to anyone who comes near.

Combining two reasons for a ship's fame makes it more intriguing, but don't go overboard with justifications for fame; no more than two, generally.

EVENT SITES

Any interesting event can cause a location to acquire significance—a famous battle, if a high body count occurred, or if the tide of war turned there, or a species was massacred. Religious sites abound, whether a martyr died there, a prophet revealed something, or a sighting of a deity took place. A shrine, church, or other monument may mark a site. A first (or last) instance of anything can make a site known, such as the first execution of a king, the place where a species was invented, or if it's the first place a weapon was used. The location of natural phenomena can acquire significance, such as geysers, sinkholes, or the aurora borealis. Solitary mountains or volcanoes have inspired people, not just when they erupt, but as a place where deities may dwell. The trick to creating these is the associated story. Otherwise, they're only slightly more interesting than your average tree, for example.

METEORS

Meteor impacts leave craters that might leave less technologically advanced people wondering what's occurred. Myths might result. Meteors are sometimes believed to be carrying life forms that can now inhabit the world. These are often of a viral nature, but may be sentient, and capable of inhabiting and controlling people. Either way, the crash site can be a place of interest, one that might be worshipped. The sighting of meteors, comets, and eclipses can also herald important events in a fantasy world. In SF, a meteor still in space can be a destination if it possesses rare minerals.

WHERE TO START

Places of interest can crop up anywhere we need them to be. They can be created long after we're already using our world or right from the first story. But if we have wars or battles in mind, we can start with these as sources of phenomena. Any fight involving titanic forces, like great magical or technological power, can be the instigator. Decide where you'd like this place to be, such as in a remote location or a central one that impacts life all around it, probably via avoidance; the latter will be a major factor in stories taking place near the location—remote locations give us leeway to invent places of lesser impact. If we have a goal in mind, such as wanting a point of origin for a monster, inventing the creature first can give us ideas on where and what caused it. If we've already invented several places, we can invent a different type of place, in a different location.

DRAWING MAPS

Whether we're an artist or not, creating maps has advantages. They help us visualize a location and think about what lies where. This can be anything from land features on continent or region maps, to buildings and public areas in settlement maps, cells and escape routes in dungeon maps, stations or ships (whether those vessels are wooden or space-faring), and even planets, moons, asteroids and suns on star maps. Seeing empty spaces to fill on our map can inspire invention that leads to more creativity, realism, and realization about what's feasible or even likely, given our design. Impossible scenarios can be avoided. A map also helps us remember what we visualized, should we be absent from our story world for an extended time.

Some of us are good enough artists to include our map in published works, but even if we can't draw, there are programs that can greatly assist us. They don't require drawing skill; rather, the ability to place pre-existing objects, like a city or mountain icon, is all that's needed. Then we just repeat this as often as needed or desired until we're done. And maps can be created piecemeal. Even if we don't use such a program, we might want to hire someone to depict a location for us, and even squiggles on a page are helpful in telling an artist what to create.

CONTINENTAL MAPS

Whether it's a continent map or just a region of one, we should consider the merits of creating a map and how to do so. We can create one ourselves or hire artists for a few hundred dollars, which is comparable to the cost of book covers but which can be used repeatedly.

SHOULD YOU DRAW ONE?

For a world that an author will only use for a short story or one book, a map may not be needed or worth the time, but worlds we'll use often (across a series or not) will benefit from maps. The more the characters travel through the wilderness, the more likely this need is. Even stories that take place primarily in cities might need a regional map if the audience must follow two or more storylines that are concurrently happening in different locations that the audience struggles to understand; *Games of Thrones* comes to mind. A city-centric tale has little use for continent maps unless referencing nearby locations, whereupon a regional map is helpful. Game designers may need one for the same reasons, even outside of digital gaming, where it is often mandatory.

If we want to calculate travel times, a map can help us measure with accuracy, even if we decide our map isn't drawn to scale. We can discover problems with intended time frames in our story and find adjustments that might be creative. If a journey will happen too fast, we can cause calamity to slow our travelers. We might use magic, steeds, or technology to increase travel rates. Or we can change our story. If we'd like to cite specific distances, like "it is one hundred kilometers to Illiandor by horse and it will take two days riding hard," we can make such statements with greater confidence.

Drawing maps can be fun and may provide ideas for both stories and setting. Chapter 1 on "Case Studies" provides examples. But if we don't want to draw one, there's a good way around this: base locations on Earth ones. We might use England, France, and Spain as our respective countries, calling them something else. In our notes, we can just write that "Illiandor is England," for example, and even use its geography. Readers will never know unless we provide a map with a familiar shape. We can do this on a smaller scale as well, such as using the provinces of Canada as different countries, even while changing the latitude to something balmier near the equator.

HOW TO CREATE ONE

We should decide on our initial goal: are we intending to draw a continent or the region around where our story takes places?

CONTINENT FIRST

For a continent, we can base the overall size on an existing Earth one or just a region, like a country (or several). A smaller area, like a U.S. state or province like those in Canada can also be used but might be designated an island. In all cases, we'll just surround it with water instead of other land masses. This analogue can help our sense of scale, distance, and travel times.

With this decided, we can begin drawing a shape for our coastline. Nature doesn't create straight lines, typically, so the inability to draw one is not a disadvantage. We can once again base part of this on Earth analogues. Just don't use an entire coastline for even one side of a continent. We can take the west edge of Spain, the south edge of Britain, the region between North Carolina and Florida for the east, and the northern coastline of South America. We can also draw all of these on the "wrong" coastline. Stealing continent edges this way takes the difficulty out of this, and if you miss draw it, so much the better. We could also trace these.

We should have a general sense of what climates we want. This will determine how far from the equator the continent is. A broad, inclusive climate range means a land mass that runs thousands of miles north to south, if the planet is at all Earth-like in size. Make this decision early because it determines which direction the prevailing winds are. And as we learned in Chapter 2, "Creating a Planet," this predicts where rain shadows from mountain ranges develop. This affects the amount of vegetation, causing everything from dense forest to arid deserts.

First, we'll want to decide where those mountain ranges are, using what we learned from "Creating a Continent." Nature often places one range along the edge of a continent, with deep water (and possibly sea monsters) offshore. Find a place you'd like this, the best culprits being on the eastern or western shores; a northern or southern range means a single climate (cold or hot) takes place in that mountain range, which provides less variety.

For a second range that's somewhat parallel, choose a different length and starting point rather than starting at the same latitude or longitude and traversing the same distance. With a range that's more perpendicular to existing ones, try not to form right angles like an upper case "L." Placing empty space between two such ranges helps prevent this. Remember that there are different kinds of mountain ranges and that we can place solitary peaks, or a few in a row, virtually anywhere. We don't have to create every mountain range at once, being able to work on one region of our map at a time, but it can be helpful to do so if we have ideas.

With this decided, and with our knowing which way prevailing winds blow at the latitude where this mountain range stands, we can determine where rain shadows and therefore deserts exist. If there's a significant gap between two ranges that are north and south of each other, for example, moisture may get through there and cause a forest near that gap. Also, remember that smaller mountain ranges cause less of a rain shadow. Knowing these things allows us some flexibility to justify having a forest where a desert might actually lie if the peaks were taller. Using Google maps, we can look at satellite images of continents and figure out what typically happens; these show ranges, vegetation, and deserts.

We'll want to draw some rivers that flow toward the sea, possibly stopping at a large lake first. And this fresh water is where our settlements will be, as humans cannot consume salt water without becoming sick (but we can invent a species that can). When creating a continent map, we don't need to draw every lake; in fact, doing so would be impractical, just as every river would be. This is one justification for putting a settlement somewhere that water doesn't appear on the map, but do this on purpose, not by accident.

Vegetation will grow around rivers and lakes, but it will also grow on the opposite side of a mountain range from the desert that a rain shadow causes. Generally, we'll want a forest on one side, a desert on the other. However, if the prevailing winds are east to west (or vice versa), and the mountains are also running that way, then the winds aren't being blocked by the peaks; the winds are parallel. This makes forest on each side likely, but desert on either side unlikely.

LOCAL REGION FIRST

If we're creating a map for a specific story, we might only need a regional drawing that focuses on the area where our story occurs. This requires knowing our story's requirements regarding land features that impact storytelling and whether weather plays a role. First make a decision about what you need for each. Weather determines latitude, as does the need for a rain forest or frozen tundra. If only one is needed, we could move our continent north or south (depending on which hemisphere it's in). If both cold and hot are needed, a more temperate zone or longer continent (north to south) might be needed. With this decision made, we can choose latitude, basing this on an Earth continent or country if needed for better understanding.

With latitude and hemisphere decided, we can understand which direction the prevailing winds blow. We might not be drawing the whole continent, but if we decide to place mountains along a north-south trajectory, then wind direction will determine rain shadows and vegetation locations. For example, if the winds blow east and we place a north-south range on the eastern edge, then a forest will be between the ocean and range, and a desert will be to the range's west. If we don't want a desert, then put the mountain range somewhere else, such as on the western edge or more east-to-west.

With such information, we can decide what land features surrounded the settlement or region where the story takes place. While our focus might be on that area, approaching development from the continental mindset helps us be realistic. We don't need to ever draw the rest of the land mass. It does help to have some idea how much land is in either direction, however. A region at the coast has an ocean or sea available to it, and therefore shipping and trade options unavailable to a landlocked area. The number of potential allies and enemies in every direction also matters to overall mindset, but these are less mapping issues than world building ones.

MY PROCESS

I use Campaign Cartographer 3 (CC3) to draw my continent maps, which I also use for region maps by zooming in. There's an add-on called Fractal Terrains, which can be used to generate continent shapes with the click of a button. It actually creates entire planets but I've typically looked for a continent that I like the look of. Mountains, hills, vegetation, and even lakes or bays, etc., are also depicted. If I don't like what I see, another click and I get another planet. There are changeable parameters to generate more or fewer land masses, for example.

I take a screen shot of one I like, crop it to size in an image program like Windows Paint, and save it. In some cases, I take two different continents and overlay them atop each other to create a composite shape that I like. I then import the image into CC3 using their instructions for doing so. Then I use CC3's tools to trace the continent outline. I sometimes change little features I don't want to include, or add them.

I'll have already decided the continent's latitude, hemisphere, and which direction it lies from any existing continents I have. For the latter, the reason is that on Earth, tectonic activity sometimes separates one large continent into two smaller ones that appear to fit together like a jigsaw puzzle; see the western edge of Africa and the eastern edge of South America for an example. I might want to imply such a relationship between two continents.

In CC3, I use the hill and mountain tools to drop these icons over the Fractal Terrains image, though I'm free to ignore or add features that weren't present. For a mountain range, it's best to drop the foothill icons first because these will be farther out from the range's center. Then I drop the mountain icons on top of the foothills, starting at the top of the range and going down. The reasons for this would be apparent if you did it in reverse yourself. Basically anything you add will cover what's already on there, so the southernmost mountain should be fully visible but partly covering the mountain icon to its north. To achieve this, just start at the top and move down. Top to bottom is generally the way to work.

Once I have outlined the continent and mountains/hills that were depicted on the Fractal Terrains image, I no longer need the latter and can hide it in CC3. I add some major rivers and lakes. There are tools to draw rain forests, shrub land, deciduous and coniferous trees, and more. I start at the top of my continent and work my way down, adding items as I deem appropriate, with an eye for the information in this volume and with what little artistic sense I have. I add cities and towns at fresh water locations and by the ocean. I tend to use the rivers as country boundaries.

For each settlement, I give it some farmland, maybe a bridge over the rivers, and roads/trails to the neighboring settlements. Then I start filling in clear areas predominantly with trees, unless I have reason to believe rainfall is limited, in which case I give it grasslands or shrub lands. On the windward side of mountains, I put thick forest due to the rainfall. Desert goes on the leeward side, then maybe grasslands farther from the mountains as moisture is picked up in the atmosphere again. I just repeat this process as I work my way around the map, dropping icons for whatever I need.

CC3 comes with different color icons for settlements, with some blue, gold, red, etc. To help readers (and myself) understand the country boundaries, I tend to stick with one style of icon for a given country, such as the gold ones for one country and the blue ones for a neighbor. If you're zoomed in enough, you can tell just by looking at the map what areas are in a territory. The results are good and publishable with my manuscripts, and yet I can't draw to save my life. You can see the resulting maps at http://www.llurien.com/Antaria and http://www.llurien.com/Llorus.

DRAWING THE WORLD

Creating a map of the entire world we've invented can be a challenge. As mentioned in the section above, the Fractal Terrains add-on to CC3 can create an entire planet with the click of a button. However, while it will have continents, oceans, bodies of water, mountains, and vegetation, that's all it will have. If you happen to like the entire planet and need one, you can follow my process above to incorporate the result into CC3 and then re-draw each land mass with the missing features, like settlements. This can give us the best of both worlds: a globe that looks like a Google map photo without data, and smaller, more detailed areas.

Another option is to create continents, and then manually place an image of each continent on a blue background which simulates the ocean. This can give us a world map. If we have a program like Photoshop, we can paste high quality, full size images of our continents to make a giant, detailed map.

SETTLEMENT MAPS

SHOULD YOU DRAW ONE?

For game designers who'll have characters roaming within a settlement, the map is essential for knowing where everyone, and the dangers they'll face, are located, but few if any books include maps of cities or towns, so one isn't expected with stories. A map may even interfere with a reader's ability to form their own mental picture as the story progresses. There comes a point where an audience doesn't care where we said something is; what matters is their impression. Referring back to a map included at the beginning of the book is optional but might jar them. Placing the map toward the book's rear is less advisable because they'll have their own ideas by then. Including it within the text, when the layout is described, is the best option.

If our settlement's layout is distinctive enough to impact story events, then a map is more important, whether we share this with an audience or not. One reason to create it is that we may forget this layout in time if we need it again. However, these issues can be solved without a map, just by notating locations in a file.

The existence of a map does not free us from the responsibility to succinctly describe our location, in ways which are easy to visualize. It can be best to say that a church stands at one end of the town and a mayor's hall is at the opposite, rather than that one is east and the other west unless the compass points matter in some way. For example, if the sun sets on the mayor's house and we like foreshadowing his demise, we could try that. Including specific details which are irrelevant to the story implies those specifics matter when they don't, overwhelming our readers. Unsure what to remember, they may remember nothing.

A settlement map can make us think about locations we haven't considered, such as segregation of the wealthy and poor, or crime-ridden areas. The wealthy will likely live near rivers or a treasured location like a shrine or park, the latter being more important in very urban areas because so much of the land might be paved or occupied by buildings. In larger settlements, the poor will inhabit the areas that are heavily trafficked or polluted, and the wealthy will be upstream of this, if on a river, or in a separate area of a lake.

Urban planning is a subject few of us know about, but zones are often created to improve the quality of life. Factories are not typically near homes. Commercial locations can be almost anywhere. Homes are often grouped into neighborhoods. Infrastructure like roads, sewage, and power are carefully planned. It's a massive subject deserving of its own book, and yet few of us will ever need to know where these locations are unless trying to draw a map, because our audience will assume these things are somewhere logical without us being specific. The depth of this subject is one reason not to draw a map, but that depends on how many details we intend to include. Sometimes being vague has advantages.

One way to avoid drawing is to use Google Maps and find a place of similar size to the one you imagine. For fantasy writers, we might want to choose an older location like those in Europe. Then we can zoom in on a town and make a screen capture or print out. From this, we can write names of places on it (and just use this for our personal files, not publishing it). Either that, or we can still draw it ourselves using this as inspiration.

How to Create One

Decide what the settlement's water supplies are (lake, river, wells?) and draw this on a map, whether with pencil and paper or a program like City Designer 3 from Pro Fantasy. Then choose an area as "old town," which is where the settlement began before spreading out. There's probably an original set of buildings, possibly surrounded by a small, dilapidated wall. Here lie crowded streets and possibly thieves and the poor. An original mayor's hall could be here. Sometimes these old towns are preserved but other times they might be demolished due to the space being needed for something better. There's likely to be some industry near the river, too, including anything that produces waste.

Upriver from here, if applicable, create the wealthy area, which can be one of several. We might have another location that qualifies, too, such as higher land or a castle or other fortification. There's likely to be a port, and related commercial industry near the river but not fully occupying the territory. We don't need to be specific about the latter, just that factories and the like are there.

Figure 62 Village Map

Remember that while a small village might be on level ground, larger places seldom are due to expansion and variable surfaces. Higher areas are often used for the wealthy, fortifications, or important buildings like a shrine or mayor's residence. Lower areas might flood, especially along the river, lake, or ocean. If this happens or the tide causes extreme fluctuations in water level, consider how this might affect structures along the shore (such as being built on stilts).

If you have multiple species living here, decide if they have their own sections of town and where those areas are. A water dwelling species is by the water source, most likely, unless they're salt water creatures, and their ability to come upon land will impact their influence. Elves might be near a forested area, but if there isn't one, then is there a town gate with a road that leads toward the nearest forest, and which provides a better view of it? The same holds true of other species like dwarves wanting a view of hills or mountains, but there's no reason they can't live all the way across town, too. The question is where is a concentrated group of them dwelling?

Now that we've chosen a few locations for "old town," the wealthy, species quarters, and important buildings, we can begin filling in housing, commercial, and industrial locations. We can include spaces for parks, a stadium, cemeteries, and public gatherings. An array of other specifics could be included, such as the prison, but these are only worth noting if we intend to use them.

Before depicting any of them, decide which kind of neighborhood each is. The reason is that if we want a crime-ridden, poor area, we probably want more industry there, too, and fewer parks; parks may exist, but they will be poorly maintained (a detail we can ignore). What we're after is the knowledge of what reputation each section of town has. We then want to create our neighborhoods with that in mind. Think about where you live; somewhere is considered nice while another is run down, while a third might be downright dangerous. Naming neighborhoods can be as simple as compass points: southeast is unsafe while northwest is wealthy. I'd probably say that northwest is therefore up on a big hill, has more parks, and a great shrine to a cherished god. Southeast might be near the river, industry, and a place of frequent muggings, unrest, and dissent, with close, crowded streets and smaller, old homes.

We'll need to leave space for roads. Consider leaving a wide avenue in wealthier areas or from the castle to a major gate. We should also determine where a garrison is, if it exists, and what the likeliest point of attack is, as that's where the castle goes (on a hill). We should also form an idea of where the main city wall is; does it surround the entire community or has further development taken place since its construction so that some buildings are now outside the wall?

This should be enough to get world builders started on map creation. Once you're working, you'll have ideas on how to proceed.

Dungeon & Ship Maps

Should You Draw One?

If relative locations matter to your work, creating a map is a good idea, even if it's just for your reference and never published. We seldom see a map of ships, lairs, or dungeons in stories, suggesting authors might avoid this without complaint from an audience. Gamers and game designers might benefit from such maps, as the audience's characters will need to navigate through locations. For readers, a map could be beneficial. My experience in reading about someone's journey through a dungeon, castle, or similar labyrinth is that I have little to no understanding of where they are. Maybe the characters don't either, being lost, but these scenes often lack orientation.

Even if we don't show a map to the audience, it's crucial to accurately convey the layout we've envisioned. Otherwise we can describe a series of twists and turns that doesn't make sense to readers with a strong sense of direction. This can be one reason to be slightly vague. Rather than writing that a hallway turned left twice and then right once, we can say it turned to one side twice and then the other, but to some people, that's worse.

One reason for a map is to determine what rooms exist and what's in them. This can be problematic; few of us understand how a dungeon is laid out, assuming there's a standard way, and we might have trouble assigning a purpose to rooms. Some room examples are cells, guard stations, weapons rooms, torture chambers, latrines, pantries, mess halls, and visiting areas. Depending on the setting, some might have a library, laundry area, kitchen, a mini-hospital, anti-magic zones or cells for wizards, bullet-proof rooms, or areas where prisoners are forced to do hard labor (of various kinds). Think of modern prisons for ideas on room types and potential layouts, including security zones for different levels of dangerous prisoners. All of this matters because of the tradition of adventurers exploring such a place and finding monsters and valuables in various rooms, with some sketchy justification for these things existing where they do. Some thought can raise our dungeon above the competition, and having a map can give us ideas.

In SF, maps of a ship could be invaluable as a reader because explanations can be difficult to visualize, though it may not matter for your story. When I watch TV, I seldom understand where parts of a ship are in relation to each other, but characters typically solve this for me with explanations like, "We have to crawl through this tube and up two decks to reach engineering." To write things like this, we'll need to remember our layout, but that may not require a map. We could just jot down what deck everything is on and whether it's fore, aft, port, or starboard. For example, engineering might be aft, port side, deck 5 of 20.

HOW TO CREATE ONE

For dungeon maps, we can use lined graph paper to draw hallways, doors, and rooms, each with a width determined by the scale we've chosen, such as a square on the grid being five feet. We need to decide where the entrance is but may freely arrange areas such as those named in the previous section. A dungeon is typically below another structure like a castle, meaning foundation walls, pillars, and other supports will be incorporated into the design.

For space ships, we should determine a list of areas we need. This can be based partly on something like a cruise or cargo ship or actual military vessels on which people live. In addition to places like the bridge, engineering, and propulsion, living areas are needed, including dining, recreation, sleeping quarters, general stores, and more. An interstellar ship could keep travelers on it for a very long time and need to satisfy their needs. See the next section for software that can help create a spaceship map.

For wooden vessels, we'll want to find a resource (possibly online) that shows us typical configurations, such as this one: http://www.artofworldbuilding.com/warship. We can model our design on this, removing decks in smaller vessels. This might take some drawing skill, but the point is that we don't need to invent internal layouts so much as understand how these ships are already structured. We can print such an image and trace it, or hire an artist to do it, or suggest readers refer to a link included in an author's note at the start of a tale.

For wooden ship layouts, most people don't understand existing ones and aren't bored with them, so we should research what's commonplace on Earth and use something similar. Creating a layout might be beneficial for readers, in order to clarify little-understood nautical terms like port, starboard, orlop, bow, stern. We may point readers of an eBook to an online resource, but print books lack this capability. Including an existing image requires gaining the copyright, but we can hire an artist to create one similar or attempt to draw it ourselves, using a program like Cosmographer 3.

MAP GENERATION SOFTWARE

There are programs available which require no drawing experience to create maps. I recommend checking out ProFantasy. Campaign Cartographer, which is excellent for creating continent and region overland maps, has optional add-on programs. One is City Designer, which allows us to create villages, towns, and cities using everything from fantasy-looking buildings to futuristic ones. Dungeon Designer can do the same for dungeons. Cosmographer can create star maps and space ships. With some ingenuity, we might be able to create deck plans for wooden ships, too.

These products produce professional-looking results that can be included on our websites or within the pages of our books. Game designers can use them for campaigns. Hobbyists can have endless fun inventing places.

A quick internet search will turn up other options for drawing maps, or you can follow this link http://www.artofworldbuilding.com/mapprograms to a list of programs.

CONCLUSION

While this volume focuses on creating places, world building doesn't need to start with the planet itself, or anywhere on it. We could start with inventing species, plants, animals, gods and other beings as described in *Creating Life (The Art of World Building, #1)*. More often than not, we'll crisscross between subjects as we refine our ideas. Everything is optional, but if you're stuck on deciding what to do first, follow your heart. Start with what matters most to you so that you don't burn out on creating things you care about less. It's also vital to remember your goals; create what you need for your story or career but don't invent anything you can't or won't use. The templates will help you stay organized and might even inspire more invention. And if you ever get frustrated or overwhelmed, take a break.

Remember, world building is fun!

SOLAR SYSTEM TEMPLATE

SOLAR SYSTEM NAME

STAR

What type of star is it (yellow, red dwarf) and does it have a name? Are there two stars?

PLANETS COUNT

How many planets are in the system?

GALAXY

In what galaxy is this solar system found?

NAME

TYPE

Is this a spiral galaxy?

PLANET 1 NAME

PLANET TYPE

Rocky, ice, or gas? Does it have an atmosphere and breathable by humans or another species? How far from the star is it? Is it in the habitable zone? What is the temperature range? What species live here?

ENVIRONMENT

What is the axial tilt (23.5 degrees like Earth)? Does it orbit counterclockwise or clockwise? Is it tidally locked to the sun? How long does it take, in days, to orbit the sun?

SATELLITES

Does it have a ring system and if so, what is it made of? Ice, gas, stone? is it visible from other planets with the naked eye?

MOONS

How many moons does it have?

MOON 1 NAME

Is it tidally locked? Is it the nearest moon or not? Is the orbit circular, elliptical, retrograde? Is it habitable?

SOVEREIGN POWER TEMPLATE

POWER NAME

GOVERNMENT TYPE

Your sovereign power's government is an important factor to decide because it will impact most other items in this template. That said, government can change in the course of history. Decide what type it is in your "current" time period. You can create a different historical version later if you want.

Example text: Since 510 AE, Nivera has been a federal republic of fifteen provinces governed by a constitution, congress and elected president who is both head of state and government. The president's official residence is in the capitol and called the "The Spired Dome" for its iconic dome, which is also the national symbol.

WHO RULES

Your government type will determine who is head of state and head of government. Now name someone who is currently in those roles, such as: "King Huma is a ceremonial head of state with limited powers. Prime Minister Olina is head of government. The two are often at odds with each other privately but publicly pretend they aren't—a poorly kept secret."

WHO REALLY RULES

Sometimes other groups have power or affect things considerably. For example, in the United States, powerful lobbyists and special interest groups are often thought to be buying influence. Who in your realm is doing such things? It can be the wealthy, land holders, or even clandestine groups or an evil wizard who has the head of government (or legislature) in their power. The public can also be in power by voting people out of office, or applying pressure to get their way.

HISTORY

If you want to, create previous versions of your power. Examples suggested below. I wrote these in chronological order (oldest first) because it's easier.

ABSOLUTE MONARCHY (1-150 AE)

Nivera was an absolute monarchy for many years, with the king claiming the divine right of kings gave him authority to do as he pleased. His abuses, and those of his descendants, slowly eroded confidence in the monarchy and led to demands for more freedom. These rebellions were crushed brutally, heretics being burned at the stake, earning Nivera a bad reputation for harshness. During this time, many castles of the realm were built.

CONSTITUTIONAL MONARCHY (150-340 AE)

After the War of Whatever with Kingdom Nemon, the King of Nivera was forced by the people to sign the Treaty of Whatcamacallit, ceding much power to a newly forming parliament. The king became an increasingly ceremonial head of state while the prime minister ran the government. Prosperity for the common people increased due to their voting power to elect members to parliament, which enacted laws to grant more personal liberty.

DICTATORSHIP (341-388 AE)

When Kingdom Sumor conquered Nivera in the Ten Years War, a power vacuum remained because the conquering kingdom didn't have the men to hold Nivera, whose remaining forces regrouped and expelled their conquerors. The military general seized control and ruled Nivera as a dictator.

Federal Republic of the Empire of Fain
(388-510 AE)

Nivera became a state of the Empire of Fain, which defeated the dictatorship that had previously existed, annexing Nivera in the process and installing a republican government so Nivera could manage its own affairs. With the collapse of the empire, it remained a federal republic.

Identifiers

Famous For

Think of any country on Earth—what comes to mind? Add something for your power. Products, wars, rulers, heroes, villains, and influence are good choices.

Symbol or Banner

Before deciding on one, it helps to know what sort of government exists. Make it simple and memorable.

Slogan

Does your power have a slogan?

Colors

Most powers have two to three colors associated with them. The colors don't need to symbolize anything but it's often better if they do.

Location

What continent is it on, and in what general region (north, west)? Use land features to specify its borders where possible, and use the names of other powers for this later when you've established them.

SETTING

Name the land and sea features found here and how the population feels about them. Are some foreboding? Just dangerous? A source of pride and wonder? Are some coveted by other sovereign powers? Has the land feature changed hands at times?

CLIMATES

Is your power large enough to have territory in more than one climate, or differing elevations, which may themselves have different climates?

SETTLEMENTS

List the major settlements found in your sovereign power and how they relate to the power. Details on each will be in their own file, but a few comments here can help shape your power. For example, "Valendria is the wealthiest city in Nivera and home to many spectacles that bring visitors from all over the kingdom and other lands. Most in Nivera aspire to visit Valendria one day."

UNIQUE PLACES

Are there any places which have acquired significance due to supernatural phenomena, or a field of famous battles? How well known are they?

RELATIONSHIPS

ORGANIZATIONS

Discuss groups that live in your power and whether they're supported or the power tries to curtail their activities.

SOVEREIGN POWERS

Explain relationships with other powers.

POWER 1

Example: "Nivera has long been allies with Kingdom Fain due to their mutually threatening neighbor, the authoritative state Iruna."

POWER 2

Example: "A long history of aggression from Iruna has made Nivera a traditional enemy, with multiple major battles going back centuries. The strife is largely ideological in nature, but Nivera also controls access to the valuable ore found in the Nivera Mountains."

SPECIFIC ACCOMPLISHMENTS

INVENTIONS AND DISCOVERIES

Has anyone from the power invented or discovered something special? It could be weapons no one else has, such as those made here but nowhere else. Maybe there's an important plant only found within its borders. Or a supernatural phenomenon.

PLACES BUILT

Has the power built any place like specific buildings, infrastructure (like damns or aquafers), or even entire settlements that were formed on purpose (for a reason you'll want to cite) after the power came to be?

World View

Languages

Is there an official language and if so, what's it called? Naming it after the sovereign power is easiest. What other languages are widely spoken here? It might be dependent upon region. If you have species, which of their languages are spoken here? Read and written? Is a language forbidden? You'll need a reason for that one, such as elven being forbidden because war with elven lands nearby has occurred frequently and those speaking it are thought to be elven sympathizers who can't be trusted.

Society

Your society will be greatly affected by the current government, and to some extent, previous governments. What's the work week like here (number of days and hours)? How much freedom do people have in personal lives? Are they mostly content and complaining about trivial things, or do basic needs of food, shelter, and health occupy their times? Are public places well kept?

Customs

The Inhabitants

Population

You don't need to know how many people there are, as figuring this out can be rather difficult. It may be more helpful, and less restrictive to you, to decide on population percentages. How many are human or elven, for example? Moreover, how do they get along? Are some concentrated in certain areas more? What about ethnicity?

Sample text: "The overall population is considered to include all of the good species, humans, and elves within its borders. Any evil species like ogres are not considered part of the population despite numbers in the hundreds of thousands."

HUMANS

Humans make up the majority of the population, at 45%. They dominate the legislature and are usually chosen as prime minister.

ELVES

The elves are 30% of the population, including half-elves, which are estimated at 1% of the elven total.

DWARVES

Dwarves are believed to be 25% of the population, most living in the mountain strongholds so that less than 5% are regularly seen elsewhere. The result is that they appear to be less of the population than they actually are.

ARMED FORCES

You might have knights, elven archers, or more in your sovereign power's army, or as part of the royal court, or just in the land as independent warriors. Decide who's around and what they're used for. How much prestige do they have? Are they feared or respected or both? Are some of these guys the sort who could become dictator should your power become weak?

IMPORTANT CHARACTERS

Who is important in this country aside from the obvious government people? Any wizards? Knights? Heroes? Villains? You can invent some individuals without worrying too much about them as characters—that's a storytelling issue for another time.

PUBLIC PLACES AND OCCASIONS

NOTABLE FESTIVALS AND HOLIDAYS

On the anniversary of your power's formation, there's probably a public holiday. Just pick a date. It doesn't have to mean anything prior to that. While you're at it, decide on other important ones, such as when a dictator fell from power, or a hero was born or saved "the world." You can just make up some stuff, spreading these out in the year. Hopefully you'll have a chance to use or mention that in your work. A new year's celebration is almost universal.

NOTABLE BUILDINGS, ESTABLISHMENTS, AND GUILDS

Settlement Template

Settlement Name

General

Alliances

Is this an independent city or part of a kingdom? Who are its allies? Note how many smaller settlements are nearby and in which directions; if this is a city, then is there one town ten miles to the north and a dozen villages on the other sides, or is one area devoid of settlements for some reason?

Identification

Symbol and Banner:
City Colors:
Slogans:

Famous For

What comes to mind when people think of this place?

Location

What continent, and where on it (northeastern, south)? Nearby land features? How accessible?

Setting

What is the terrain (forests, mountainous, desert, plain, sea/river port?) Climate?

Relations with Other Settlements and Places

Town 1

Elven Forest 1

Important Features in Town

Is there a distinctive land feature? City layout?

Notable Religious or Magic/ Technological Sites

Other Special Sites

Fortifications

Walls/Gates

Is there a wall around it? How many gates? Well-guarded? Has it ever been breached?

Castle

Where is it and what condition is it in? Ruined or intact? What's it made of? How many towers? Ever been destroyed?

LOCAL LORE

Any legends or mysteries about the place?

PRODUCTS

This depends on geography. State why this is a product, such as having wood or fish from nearby land features.

HISTORY

What events are important in the formation of this settlement?

YEAR FOUNDED

WARS

BATTLES

Outcome? Who attacked them? Or did they attack?

THE INHABITANTS

What is their attitude toward magic, technology, gods, the supernatural, the species, and strangers?

LEADERS

What sort of government is here and who is currently running it? What type of mayor is here and what is his relationship with the council?

INFLUENCERS

Is some organization or individual really in control of the city?

POPULATION

What is the overall population count and which species live here? How do they get along? Are they segregated? What are they afraid/proud of?

HUMANS

RACE 1

RELIGION

What religions are taught/tolerated/shunned here?

ARMED FORCES

Is there an army? Garrison? Just local guards? Militia? Knights? Star fighters?

THE LOCAL GUARDS

How many? Well trained? Well equipped? Who's in charge?

KNIGHTS

IMPORTANT PEOPLE

PRIESTS

WIZARDS

Are they in town or nearby in a tower? Is magic tolerated? Feared? Can wizards cast spells in public or only in secret? Are they a rare/common sight?

HEROES

VILLAINS

NEARBY MONSTERS/CREATURES

Which ones are near and how many? What is the effect on the inhabitants and fortifications?

PUBLIC PLACES AND OCCASIONS

RELIGIOUS TEMPLES AND SITES

FESTIVALS AND HOLIDAYS

TAVERNS AND INNS

Are there any? Are they in a designated area or just anywhere? How friendly or suspicious of strangers are they? Are they safe or might you wake up dead?

GUILDS

EQUIPMENT SHOPS

What kinds of items are available for purchase or trade here? Is this place famous for making anything? Two-handed swords? Full plate armor? Silk tunics? Strong ropes? Devices?

WEAPONS

ARMOR

CLOTHING

GENERAL GEAR

SPECIAL CONSIDERATIONS

SUPERNATURAL PHENOMENON

UNKNOWN

Are there are any secrets about this place, whether known to a few or not?

VOLUME 3

CULTURES AND BEYOND

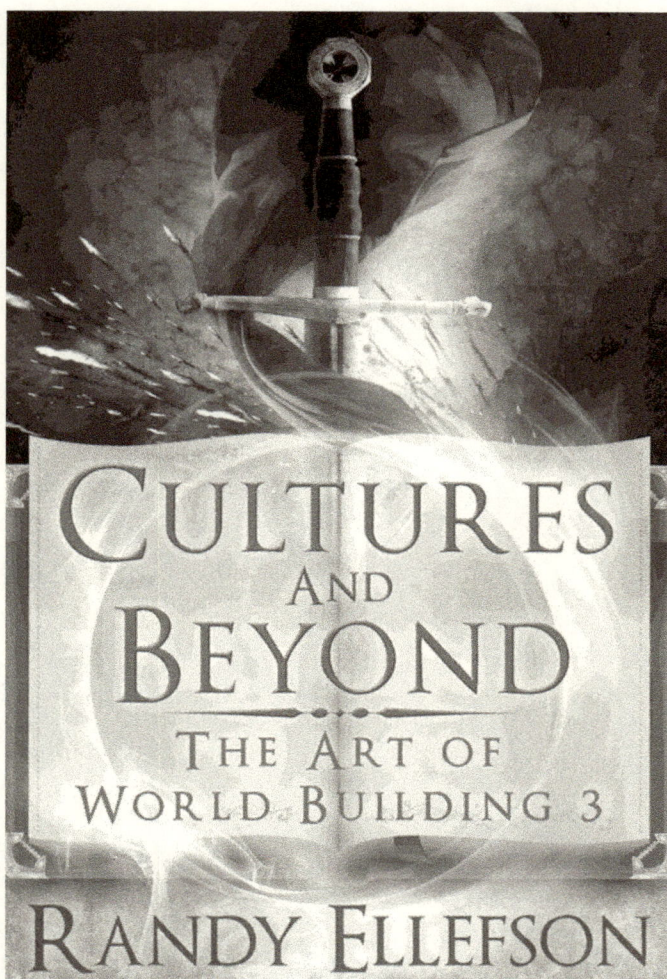

INTRODUCTION

With creating life and places covered in volumes one and two, we turn our attention to everything else about setting that characterizes our world, inhabitants, and storylines.

In this volume, we'll discuss:

- Cultural vision, scope, origins, and manifestations
- Organizations like organized crime or secret sects
- Armed forces (the army, navy, and air force)
- Religions and how to leverage deities we've invented
- The supernatural and its impact
- Items, whether supernatural, technological, or neither
- Languages and the impact they have on setting
- Names and techniques to invent them
- Educational, legal, commerce, health, and IT systems
- Approaches to managing world building development

Examples included in the text were created specifically for this guide and are not drawn from any setting I've created, or stories I've written or published.

Chapter 1 from *Creating Life (The Art of World Building, #1)* includes discussion of some principles referred to here, the main one being the use of analogues. This means inventing something that is based on an Earth equivalent but making enough changes to it that people are less likely to recognize the influence. This is known as the Rule of Three.

The book has a website where you can find additional resources, information on other volumes in this series, and other items as they are added.

Visit http://www.artofworldbuilding.com

WHERE TO START

The series and chapters within each volume can be read in any order but are arranged according to what might come first in a world's timeline. This volume is an exception; one chapter has little to do with the next. If you have an idea for something covered herein, write down everything you're thinking of before reading about other things you might consider. This will keep you from forgetting your idea or becoming overwhelmed with feelings of needing to get it "right;" there's really no such thing. Then you can read on for new ideas to enrich your setting.

So where do you start? Where your heart lies.

THE CHAPTERS

What follows is a brief summary of what's included in each chapter in Volume Three, *Cultures and Beyond*.

CHAPTER 1 – CULTURES

This chapter discusses the differences between a culture and a custom, and that morals, values, and beliefs underlie everything. World builders can determine the scope of an invented culture, as some are regional or extend throughout a sovereign power. Cultural depictions can have visible, audible, and behavior aspects that can be defined. These include issues such as body language, hair styles, gestures, clothing, and more. Greetings and farewells should be defined because characters will use them. Similarly, swear words, slang, verbal expressions, and colloquialisms can be created to characterize interactions. The daily life of a culture is depicted in dining, bathing, sleeping, employment, and transportation rituals and behaviors; pastimes, holidays and more create a respite for the everyday activities. Even architecture can be influenced by culture.

CHAPTER 2 – ORGANIZATIONS

Organizations for good or evil are a staple of both fantasy and SF. This chapter discusses both group types and their world views, plus common traits like goals, enemies, friends, and their source of (and quest for) power. How members join and leave such groups is an important element; some organizations might prevent or inhibit departure. Prerequisites can also bind a member to the group. The history and actions of a group are an important part of its reputation.

CHAPTER 3 – ARMED FORCES

Military groups such as the army, navy, air/space force, and knights are a staple of fantasy and SF. We can leverage existing ideas or craft our own. Doing so means deciding how someone joins and leaves, including requirements, tests, and training. Some species and races might be forbidden or assigned special roles. Throughout history, famous members can inspire pride or loathing. When devising military units and ranks, it helps to understand Earth analogues, so some basics are included in this chapter. The world view, locations, place in society, and symbols are all important elements of memorable armed forces and this chapters covers them all.

CHAPTER 4 – RELIGIONS

While some aspects of the societies we create have history as a minor element, history is crucial with religions, so first we look at where and how the religion formed, including a prophetic figure and the role of a god, should one exist. Creation and end of world myths, and the afterlife, are important elements that potential followers consider, along with the requirements for worship and the penalty for failing to follow the rules. How someone joins and leaves a religion can be trivial or significant and includes the possibility of expulsion. We'll need holy sites, too, and a decision on holidays, customs, sects, relationships with everyone from species to other religions, and what members of the clergy are like and their role in society. Most importantly, we need the symbols and beliefs of this religion.

CHAPTER 5 – THE SUPERNATURAL

Supernatural elements exist in both fantasy and SF and can be used to add surprises. The audience may expect magic, for example, but not our version of it, so there's room for originality here. We can create energies that give rise to phenomena, beings, or places like magic pathways or alternate worlds and realities that impact our setting and stories. How much impact and prevalence these supernatural elements have, and how to determine this, are an important focus of this chapter.

CHAPTER 6 – A SYSTEM OF MAGIC

Magic systems can be simple or complex, but they should always be consistent. This chapter discusses the methods and principles of good systems and how to create them. This includes the importance of names, deciding if spells are needed and what those are for, whether spells can go wrong and how, and different types of magic we might want to include in our settings. We'll also look at how much training someone might need, what forms that training takes, and learn how to decide what's right for our setting. And no discussion of magic is complete without a look at how to invent spells.

CHAPTER 7 – ITEMS

Whether magical, technological, or more ordinary, memorable items exist in our setting even if we don't mention them. SF likely expects them, and fantasy often has at least one magic item someone has or covets in a story, but even ordinary items can be given significance through association with important people, places, or events. This chapter discusses how to invent their properties, origins, and form, and how to determine who is likely to use or want them. The creation of an A.I. is included.

CHAPTER 8 – LANGUAGES

Creating a language is one of the most challenging aspects of world building, but it's also one of the few that we can outsource; how and where to do so is discussed. Even so, some basic terms must be understood so we know what we're buying and receiving from our expert. If we choose to do it our-selves, we should consider whether it benefits our audience and how, or even whether it's a burden that we can save both them and ourselves. This chapter will not teach world builders how to invent a language because there are entire books on the subject, and those are referenced here, but it will discuss the pros and cons of constructing a language and what we lose by not having one (or more).

Chapter 9 – Names

Many techniques exist for creating names of people, places, and things, and all of them leverage our creativity to make the results and process more satisfying than using name generators, which are also discussed. Caveats and pitfalls abound, for while a great name elevates our story, bad ones turn off audiences, or keep them from talking about a character with an unpro-nounceable or unspellable name. We look at the differences between given names, surnames, compound names, and different ways to use parts of our invented world for all of them. The tips in this chapter will make this re-quired activity fun and rewarding.

Chapter 10 – Other Systems

Other systems exist in our setting and warrant development. We'll exam-ine educational systems and their impact on employment, plus where and how people are getting educated or being disqualified from it. Health sys-tems include medical and mental, and they range from great to terrible, each having significant impacts on lives. Information systems aren't just for SF, because fantasy settings need to disseminate information, too, and have their own ways of doing so. Understanding monetary systems and how to keep them simple is another focus of this chapter and includes how to determine the value of time, labor, and materials. And no world is complete without laws, crimes, and punishments, so developing a legal system is a critical world building task we breakdown into a manageable one.

CHAPTER 11 – CONCLUSION

In the series conclusion, we look at how to organize our files of world building notes so that the info glut doesn't become overwhelming; this includes some tools others have created, whether free or not, and the pros and cons of using them. We'll also look at different approaches to world building and how each affects our working methodology and results. Final thoughts include the merits of following our own rules per world and whether partnering with another world builder is a good idea or not.

CHAPTER ONE

CULTURES

There are so many customs and culture-related items that we could disappear down a research rabbit hole, so we'll focus on things likely to be useful as storytellers and gamers. In addition to working out details in advance, world builders can refer to this chapter when creating scenes.

While much of culture can be invented when we need it, the disadvantage is inconsistency if we're not careful and take notes. We can invent something earlier in a story or series, then forget and contradict it later. Generally, people (like our characters) don't care about customs until encountering ones different from theirs or when expectations are not met. In the latter case, judgment about the offender results. This is one value to us as storytellers.

If we need a reason for characters to not be accepted warmly, failure to follow customs is a solution. This can be individual characters or whole groups rejecting someone. It can be wise or fun to include a character who is more well-traveled than other characters and understands how to navigate other lands without offense. This requires at least two cultures: the one our characters are from and the one in which the story takes place.

WHAT IS CULTURE?

Culture is an abstract, complex concept. Most of us have a vague understanding of what it means, but when we're building cultures, we need clarity to know what elements to invent, why, and how. Culture is a social group's lifestyle. It is symbolic communication and often taken for granted, which is one reason we have troubling grasping the concept. It is a set of expectations. It evolves over time, though slowly, sometimes with bursts of social change. It not only differs across sovereign powers, but within regions and settlements. The culture of football players is different from that of rock musicians. Nonetheless, if they exist in the same society, they'll share other elements of culture; to coin a term, we might call this "cultural scope," which will be discussed further in this chapter.

The case can be made that values, beliefs, and morals are the origins of culture. These are ideas. And they manifest as rituals, habits, customs, art, music, and the use of language. When broken down this way, it becomes easier to determine what work must be done, and in what order: the ideas, then the manifestations. This is how we'll approach inventing culture, rounding out our concepts before deciding what they've resulted in.

Even if inventing the ideas first is helpful, we may have a few of the resulting manifestations in mind because we thought of them first, but this is fine. We can work backwards from them and try to determine what ideas they imply. For example, if rigid formality exists in greetings, we can infer that people feel oppressed or suppressed, or that open expression of feelings is frowned upon. This can help us create more manifestations, but it can also suggest some values: that emotion is considered weak, that dignity is prized, or that appearance is important. We'll look more closely at this.

CULTURAL SCOPE

Every culture exists somewhere: in a sovereign power (or several), a region, a settlement, a social group, or a race or species, to name a few. Every sovereign power has a form of government, which will greatly impact the cultures within it. We must therefore know what this is. Residents of a democracy have leeway to create culture whereas a totalitarian government may be forcing culture upon people; the culture will be very different.

Creating Places (The Art of World Building, #2) detailed our primary government options and, at a high level, what life is typically like for inhabitants of each. We want to consider how much freedom and control people have over their lives. The less freedom, the less variation in culture at the lower levels of region, settlement, and social group. And the more oppressive and rigid a government, the more likely residents live in fear and avoid any violation of expectations, which could result in imprisonment, torture, forced labor, or death. Before embarking on the invention of a culture, decide what the sovereign power's government is, even if you're creating culture at the social group level. It's wise to create culture in the following order:

- Sovereign power
- Regional
- Settlement
- Social group

The reason is that ideas and manifestations at the sovereign power level influence the regional level, and so on down to the smallest social group. If this seems like a lot of work, most of what we need to invent is at the top level and, being inherited by lower levels, only needs modification as appropriate if our tale or characters need it. Each person will belong to every level above their social one.

For example, Kier could be in the knight social group while Antar is in the archer one, but both are in the warrior one, the settlement culture, the regional one, all the way up to the sovereign power level. Some elements can be true in multiple cultures, such as nerds acting roughly the same way in Japan as in the United States; in reality, each will have its own nerd culture, but we'd still recognize some similar elements, in theory.

We may want to invent the most universal items early, then more localized variations. But we should always make a note about scope in our files. For example, "Throughout the Empire of Antaria (including sovereign powers and settlements that once belonged to it), wedding bands are worn on so-and-so finger."

Every species and race is likely to have variations. The elves and humans in Kingdom Illiandor will not have the same dining etiquette, but some similarities will exist, just as the elves of Illiandor will share some dining etiquette with elves in another kingdom. This means that we could scope certain aspects as being typically elven and others as being of Illiandor. For example, let's say that all elves drink only from the right hand, place a napkin in their lap, and never talk with food in their mouth, regardless of the elf's origin (never mind that individuals can defy these customs). But all species of Kingdom Illiandor swear an allegiance to the king prior to dining. While more involved, this is believable depth.

THE IDEAS

There are arguably three types of cultural sources: beliefs, values, and morals, with some overlap. Deciding which of each matters to a group depends on what impression feels right to the world builder=. Think about the group's role in society and its goals and motivations. We needn't feel locked into our decision. If we don't think of a manifestation of a specific value, that's okay. These are guiding ideas that we're unlikely to explain to an audience anyway, unless a character is monologuing their thoughts, which is a great way to reveal these ideas.

MORALS AND VALUES

An individual's values come from within, can change over time, and are personal principles. By contrast, morals are taught by society, are usually deep seated and slow to change, if at all, and guide us on how to live rightly. Morals sometimes result from a fictional or true story; the fictional ones are often designed to demonstrate a moral. While these differences between morals and values exist, we can treat them the same when using them to invent culture. Here are some traits we can leverage:

Acceptance	Integrity
Compassion	Kindness
Cooperation	Justice
Courage	Perseverance
Dignity	Politeness
Equality	Respect
Fairness	Responsibility
Generosity	Self-control
Gratitude	Tolerance
Honesty	Trustworthiness

A more high-minded society will value different traits (like dignity, equality, politeness, and tolerance) than a barbaric one, which might value self-reliance, courage, respect, and integrity. A society with more freedom might value most items on that list while individuals in an oppressive one might value courage, responsibility, politeness, and perseverance, while longing for things denied them, like kindness, dignity, and quality. The oppressive society itself might prize obedience, humility, and sacrifice, expecting citizens to adhere to these. The society's government may prize values that are different from its inhabitants.

BELIEFS

Many beliefs in culture originate from religions; those beliefs and how to invent them are discussed in chapter four in this volume, on creating religions. As we invent our world, we can take any religious idea and make it more cultural. An example would be Christmas; most would agree that the religious nature of this holiday has been taken over by the cultural aspects of it. There are other concepts from Christianity that permeate life in the U.S., including heaven, hell, the devil, and common swears. Religion's influence on culture runs from holidays to working schedules and beyond. Leverage the beliefs of a dominant religion to create parts of a culture.

For example, if one day a week is for religious observance, or a few hours of every day are for prayer, then many will have work schedules structured around this. Even those who don't practice the religion will be aware of these times if widespread. We tend to expect fewer people at stores or on the roads on a Sunday due to church goers, just as stores are often closed on Christmas. Our world's inhabitants will be aware of these times and may plan for them, which is one way to sneak cultural elements into a scene.

As for non-religious beliefs, some are based in superstition. For example, walking under a ladder is considered bad luck, as is breaking a mirror, stepping on a crack, or a black cat crossing our path. If we've invented an animal for our world, we can use it in the same way, choosing a physical trait that makes it ominous, such as one type being poisonous when the rest aren't (such an animal should be uncommon but not too rare or it never comes up).

Understanding the origins of such ideas can help us invent our own. Some are practical, like passing under a ladder being unsafe. Some may originate from a nursery rhyme. Then there's the talisman that can keep evil away, whether it's garlic and crosses for vampires or a rabbit's foot. Associate an animal with something good like a benevolent deity and a piece of one's body can become a talisman. Perhaps a plant has a root shaped like a humanoid and therefore any part of the plant, like garlic, is seen in either a good or bad light.

The black cat idea likely came from being associated with witches, so if we have a world with magic and a type of animal is often seen with wizards, who are also considered dangerous, a similar belief can arise; we can make this true in one culture and the belief may spread across others even if wizards elsewhere don't often have such animals with them.

The idea that bad luck comes in threes is an example of confirmation bias, where we believe something and then look for the pattern, such as two bad things happening, prompting us to look for the third item. There's debate as to the origin of this one, but the trinity is important in Christianity and we can do the same thing with a different number in our world. If we go with three, we earthlings will associate it with Earth.

Touching wood for good luck also has debatable sources. Some say it dates from when relics that were believed to be pieces of the cross Jesus was crucified on were sold. Some religions also worship nature and believe trees had spirits in them. Churches of wood were once used as sanctuary and knocking on them in a specific pattern was a signal for entrance. Perhaps pirates (who are notoriously superstitious) knocked on their ships before a bad storm. We leverage rationales but it's important to note that not only do most of us have no idea where these superstitions originated, we don't care, simply accepting them. Our characters will be the same, but our audience may wonder at the new ideas we invent, but explaining is best done in a single sentence, like this:

As she'd done since childhood, Tianna clapped her hands twice for luck, like the famous knight Kier had done to summon the horse he rode to glory at the famed Battle of Evermore.

The breaking of a mirror is another superstition, which arose after we stopped gazing in water to see our reflections. Technology provides ever greater possibilities for image capturing, and at my local Renaissance Festival, there's a running joke that photographers are stealing the souls of those whose picture they take. Such literal interpretations are less common in a more educated world like ours, but they can be fun and useful to remember for fantasy settings. Disturbing that which holds the image, such as breaking glass or causing ripples in the water, is seen as sinister portent. Leverage such a belief as desired, forecasting how many years of misfortunes are thus foretold.

Friday the 13th is considered bad for reasons that aren't agreed upon, but again, examples can give us ideas. Perhaps it's due to Christ having supposedly died on a Friday, or one of his twelve disciples betraying him (13 were around the table, including him). Some speculate that 13 full moons in a year caused calendar problems and was considered unlucky; if we have any similar pattern in our time keeping system, this is one way to attach meaning to it. Another way to make a number and day unlucky is to have a prominent group of good people treated badly (i.e., executed) on that day in the past. Confirmation bias can make people start seeing bad events on such a day, thereby "proving" the superstition.

As we continue, we'll see how beliefs like these can lead to culture's invention. They are a point of origin, just like morals and values.

CULTURE VS. CUSTOM

Confusion can arise about the difference between culture and customs. Customs are *part* of culture, are a way that culture is represented, and are expected behaviors in given situations. When we invent customs, we're also inventing culture. Since culture is a somewhat esoteric term, we'll be talking more about creating customs, with culture revealed *through* them.

The words "custom" and "tradition" are sometimes used interchangeably because the only real difference is the length of time that they're practiced. A custom becomes a tradition when it is passed down generation after generation. Customs are therefore newer. There's no rule on this, but if we're inclined, we can decide a tradition is over a hundred years old and a custom is more recent. Use "tradition" to refer to truly enshrined behaviors, the violation of which would cause a stronger reaction. Custom implies less formality, weight, or expectation – and less offense if violated.

CULTURAL VISION

World builders could invent various manifestations, like greetings, dining, and attire expectations, that contradict each other instead of springing from a common element. Imagine a culture where very formal greetings occur, with multiple bows, gestures, and elaborate phrases. At dinner, we might expect fine manners. Instead, we're shown people pushing unwashed hands into food bowls, eating off their hands and licking their fingers, and finally shoving the hand into the food again. While this is extreme, these greetings and dining etiquette examples clash and don't spring from a unified vision.

Before we get too far into inventing cultural elements, we should determine a vision that seems appropriate. These are related to values, beliefs, and morals. Some example visions are:

1. Formal: Refined, cordial, dignified, high-minded, controlled emotions
2. Exuberant: Hearty, boisterous, unrestrained, familiar, informal, crude, open emotions

3. Timid: Overly apologetic, not being a bother, polite to a fault, restrained in affections

4. Brash: Entitled, demanding, bold, proud, self-righteous, self-absorbed

5. Modest: Sincere, polite, down-to-earth, informal, compassionate, humble, folksy

6. Calculating: Friendly but distant, cliquey, rumor mongering, disloyal, fickle

If we wanted to be stereotypical, we might assume that royalty exhibit the formal one, while barbarians typify the exuberant. The timid one is based on a few 1980s comedies set in England, while the brash one is how some people describe Americans abroad. Those in small towns sometimes get the modest reputation, and teens sometimes experience the last.

In addition to those previously listed, a seemingly infinite number of cultures exist on Earth that we can leverage. As with every analogue, we should follow the Rule of Three – make at least three significant changes to it to prevent audiences from recognizing it. Otherwise they might recognize Japan, for example, when they see it by another name. There are so many aspects to culture that more than three major changes might be needed. How do we keep everything coherent? By following a cultural vision.

Regardless of our culture's source, whether an analogue, entirely invented, or somewhere between, we should choose a guiding principle or vision. Taking the first example, of formality, we need only imagine how people act based on these. If Kier is from this culture, he won't be chugging ale, slapping people's backs in congratulation, eating with his hands, being unkempt in public, or revealing his affection for a woman in anything but the most subtle of ways. But if Kier has a visitor named Torrin, who hails from the second culture (hearty, boisterous, unrestrained, familiar), we can imagine Torrin doing all of those things. If this is happening in Kier's homeland, Torrin may be judged as uncouth. If visiting Torrin's homeland, Kier would likely be seen as boring, stuck up, and arrogant. This is the sort of conflict we can leverage, whether we keep the impact subtle (as in a comedy of manners) or deadly (so much offense is given that execution or a duel is demanded).

RACE AS CULTURE

World builders are sometimes criticized for a mistake – making a race or species synonymous with a culture. This means each settlement of dwarves, for example, has the exact same culture as every other dwarven settlement. This is as unbelievable as humans having a mono-culture across a world. Avoiding this is easy; just create different cultures. That's time consuming and may explain why race as culture dominates the work of world builders, but all we need are variations.

We can leverage the cultural scope inheritance, where beards are prevalent on all males in a sovereign power, but those in one region or settlement braid theirs while others grow it to their waist, and yet another keeps it close cropped. This way, people can tell on sight where a dwarf is likely from. We don't need to justify differences because few people understand where cultural elements originate. But we could always decide that long beards are the norm and the short ones resulted from a deadly case of lice generations ago. Maybe the braided style came by emulating a war hero who did that. Just make these up. It's fun.

CULTURE DEPICTIONS

Culture could be divided into three types of depictions that storytellers and gamers employ, singly or in combination: what's only seen, what's heard, and what's performed. This organization is for clarity as we investigate what to invent and what to bypass, which may depend on medium. We'll look at depictions that are subtle but which can permeate society. More pronounced depictions of culture, like greetings, clothing, and etiquette will be discussed later in this chapter, as most deserve their own section.

VISIBLE

The visible aspects of culture are seen but seldom commented upon by storytellers. This includes architecture, clothing, hair styles, and body language. Much of this can be quickly taken in by a viewer in a visual medium like film, TV, or gaming, where the set and costume designers will be charged with inventing most of it. This is not to say that storytellers can or should ignore it, but in the written medium, we devote most time to actions, dialogue, and thoughts. Some readers even dislike much descriptive writing as the story stalls while we describe something, unless we've learned the art of description as action or revealing of a character's state of mind.

With many visual depictions in the written word, it's often good to focus on the impression someone or something creates rather than going into details about how this is achieved. One reason is that most of us don't recognize terms for various clothing, hairstyles, or architecture, to name a few, and conveying these to an equally ignorant audience accomplishes little, while also making it seem like we researched this stuff so we could tell them. Don't name a hairstyle unless quickly able to describe it and what it's thought to suggest about anyone using it; that opinion will vary by other cultures.

AUDIBLE

The words our characters speak are most of what we need for audible depictions of culture, which often dictates what we say and how, or whether we say anything at all. There are times when we think it's not our place to comment on something because of how that's viewed. For example, if you say something rude about your absent spouse, am I expected to change the subject or wait until you do? Am I allowed to comment on it? Can I agree with or disapprove of your behavior? These cultural non-responses are due to perceptions about what a behavior means and the underlying value, such as minding my business or warding off a further venture into a personal subject. When inventing culture, we should consider what is expected to be said *and* what is allowed to pass without comment. It reminds me of the adage that sometimes it's not what we say and do but what we *don't* that is revealing of ourselves.

For example, humility is (at least theoretically) prized in the United States. If someone gives us a compliment, it's customary to politely acknowledge it before changing the subject, rather than gushing about how true their remarks are and encouraging more of the same. When determining what (or if a) response is expected, think about what moral value is exemplified by doing so, and what offense is avoided. Also think about the belief that is attributed to the action or inaction. If ignoring a compliment is *believed* to be rude, then it effectively is so, possibly because a *value* of modesty is violated. The quietness of a library or church is also respectful, but does it need to be in every culture? It's customary to mute a mobile phone when attending a meeting. Loud music in bars makes it customary to yell in someone's ear to be heard, causing a violation of someone's personal space that is accepted in that environment due to necessity.

Our voices, and the way we speak, can also be part of culture. Some languages are considered, by non-speakers, to be eloquent and flowing while others are harsh. But it can also be culture to speak softly/loudly, to speak at length or say very little, or speak with a prompting inflection so that even statements sound like a question; this is deferential and may reflect values of humility and respect. The "ums" and "ahs" of speech might be rampant or non-existent; these can be unnoticed or frowned upon, maybe because they're believed to result from an unsound mind. Perhaps interrupting people is unusual because it's considered disrespectful, or commonplace as a sign of enthusiasm and sociability while remaining quiet is believed to show unfriendliness. We can spin interpretations.

Songs may be prevalent so that we write lyrics to print in a book. There are other sounds like the tone of alarms, phone rings, and even when applause occurs (in some cultures, there's no clapping between songs at a rock concert). We should consider the impression and quality of these sounds; for authors, that's most of what we can give the audience, whereas other media allow the audience to hear it. Other instances of audible depictions of culture will be covered later in this chapter in the form of greetings, curses, colloquialisms, and more.

PERFORMED

No culture is complete without actions people perform. We'll once again look at more subtle ones here. One of those is eye contact, whether this is maintained, averted, or avoided altogether, and for how long. This is influenced by attitudes about respect, deference, and domination. Use this as a guide to decide what people do. Some view maintained eye contact as challenging, while looking away is meekness. If a culture values personal strength, they likely approve of sustained contact and frown on looking away, while a culture that values knowing your place might feel the reverse. If an action is considered respectful, we don't need to explain why, but dialogue is a good way to do so if required. Consider this scene:

Kier burst into the throne room, bloodied sword in hand. "My lord," he began, addressing the king, "the ogres are minutes from breaching the defenses. We must leave at once."

The captain of the king's guard intercepted him. "You dare to carry an unsheathed sword before the king? Show some respect!"

Kier frowned. "You had better, too, or will you fight them with your pretty face?"

Amid the muted laughter from those assembled, the king caught the captain's eye and nodded. As one, the king's guardsmen ripped swords from sheaths and took up defensive positions.

The expectation to not bare a sword before the king, and the reason for Kier's doing so, is summed up in two short sentences that are relevant to the action. It also causes brief tension. This is why we need culture.

What side of streets, paths, and halls do people walk or drive on? The left side is preferred in countries where people are predominantly right-handed and physical combat (i.e., swordsmanship) was/is common. A swordsman wants his sword arm facing the potential opponent approaching him. The scabbard is also worn on the left hip and less likely to become entangled in anyone (people are walking on the other side of you). It's also easier for right-handed people to mount a horse from the left, which would be while standing in traffic if they're riding on the right of the road, so this is avoided.

But once wagons are in the picture, things may change. Picture a wagon pulled by two horses side-by-side. There was nowhere in early wagons for someone to sit, so someone is riding the left horse because it was easier to mount. As traffic comes toward him, he wants to keep his wagon wheel away from approaching traffic, which is easier to achieve if that traffic is on his left. The result is driving on the right side. If you want to prevent this, decide that even the earliest wagons had somewhere for him to sit. While this is interesting, we're unlikely to mention the reason for our choice.

Most of the actions we'll depict are incorporated into hybrid subjects (where what's done, heard, and seen are combined) like greetings, so we'll cover those after a word about social classes.

SOCIAL CLASSES

A social class can mean different things depending on the society, but it is a way of defining not only income levels but lifestyle generalizations and expectations. People of each class will think, dress, and act differently than those of other classes in the same society. They will also have different needs and therefore values. Everything from spoken expressions and body language to rituals will depend upon one's class, and it is typically quite difficult, even impossible, for one to switch between classes, which people are sometimes born into. We can do this with our invented classes.

In the United States and similar countries, there are five, each largely focusing on income. This economic indicator doesn't need development as we can leverage real world examples. These classes, with examples, are:

1. Upper Class (Elite): landowners, heads of companies and universities, "old money."
2. Upper Middle: professors, engineers, managers and directors, accountants, lawyers.
3. Lower Middle: clerical and support staff for the classes above.
4. Working: craft and factory workers, food and health service staff, repair shop staff.
5. Poor: the homeless or those on public assistance (welfare, food stamps, etc.), or earning just enough to rise above this, with full-time wages but still below the poverty line

Some suggest a sixth class, that of "new money"—when someone from a lower class becomes wealthy due to an invention, a lottery, or otherwise vastly improving their financial situation. If class is based on wealth, they have technically changed class, and yet they may act quite differently from those who've been in that class far longer. They may even be rejected as equals because their behavior doesn't morph overnight as their finances did.

In feudal Japan, people were born into one of three classes, each with internal divisions. The highest was the royal class, which included the emperor and royal family only; the emperor was head of state, with little real power. Next came the noble (military) class, those who ran the country, which included shoguns (political and military leaders), daimyos (feudal warlords), samurais, and ronin (samurai with no daimyo). Roughly 90% of Japan was the lowest class: peasants (farmers and fishermen), merchants, artisans (entertainers, artists), and criminals. In a society dominated by a single group, such as the military or wizards, we might leverage Japan's model.

When inventing our own class system, we define a hierarchy and who belongs to each. We can see that in the U.S. model, the highest class includes those who are in charge, but in the Japan model, the highest class is partly figureheads while those in charge are at the top of the second class. As is often the case, there may be no getting it "right" in world building but getting it plausible; we're the one inventing the society.

Generally, the elite class members are rich, powerful, or of royal blood (or an equivalent), or some combination of these. They have the most prestige and power, unless someone like the feudal Japanese emperor is merely a ceremonial head of state, rather than the head of government; as covered in *Creating Places (The Art of World Building, #2)*, the latter is the one with the real power. The elite class is very influential, often holding the purse strings within a society. They may only be symbolically in charge but could be those who are running the country, or the industries and institutions that drive it.

These are the leaders who define policy, laws, and how life functions for themselves and the lower classes. In a constitutional monarchy, these would be members of parliament. In a military junta, they'll be warriors at the upper ranks, like generals. If corporations dominate as is often true in SF, then CEOs and other leaders of industry will be here. If wizards are widely accepted instead of feared, this could include the most powerful.

The second highest class will be the most important professions in the society. Those who produce food, such as farmers and fishermen, can be in this class in a fantasy setting, if they are revered instead of taken for granted; in SF, machines have likely taken over, and in some instances on Earth, these professionals are only peasants, the lowest class. In SF, scientists, engineers, and higher officers would be here, including many who build or command ships (regardless of what we call the rank). In fantasy with wooden ships from the Age of Sail, commanders might be here. In a fantasy setting, knights and other important warriors could be included, like the Jedi of *Star Wars*.

These first two classes will likely exist because the most elite will want to distinguish themselves from those just below them and upon whom they rely to run the country, even though those people are subservient to them. We can assume that roughly 10% of the population falls into the top two classes, which leaves us to decide on how to divide the remaining population. We can decide that it's multiple classes like the U.S. model, which is arguably more likely when industrialization causes additional groups of skilled laborers, who may need support staff (another class). Or we can leave it as one large class containing most of the population, which may be more likely in less technologically developed settings. The next table breaks down social classes in both fantasy and SF. What we see in fantasy is the three lower classes being merged into a single one.

Class	Roles	SF	Fantasy
Elite	Figureheads who direct next class	CEOs, presidents	Royalty
Upper Middle	Highly skilled, valuable, powerful professionals, those running country	Captains, engineers, doctors, lawyers	Nobility
Lower Middle	Supporting upper middle class	Admin staff	Serfs
Working	Entertainers, service industry, factory staff	See roles	
Low	Unskilled labor, poor,	See roles	

Class	Roles	SF	Fantasy
	homeless		

Figure 63 Social Class Roles

It might seem like more work to define subclasses within these, but sub-dividing the groups can make sense. For example, an admiral or general has more prestige than a lieutenant, so while they're in the same overall class, each might have different expectations thrust upon them. On my Llurien setting, there are at least four distinct, named warrior types, and while they'd all be in the second class, there would be a hierarchy/subclasses among them due to their rank and what roles they serve. Before I decided on a class system, I already knew who was considered more valuable and the resentments this caused in others, and by understanding classes, I knew how to define and use this more effectively.

Once we define our classes and who is in each, we can invent culture for them (this is our cultural scope). We would decide on the morals, values, and beliefs of each group, and a cultural vision based on the hierarchy. It's safe to say that the elite class expects deference, though even in our modern society, they are often mocked (out of sight) by lower classes. The most rigid and elegant depictions of culture will be here. A trickle-down effect is in play, where lower classes are increasingly flexible and less formal, with their casual lifestyles an object of scorn from those above, who can be seen as elitist snobs. We should decide on these classes before inventing culture for any because the culture of each is partly in response to the culture of the others. Each class wants to distinguish itself, its members believing their way superior for one reason or another (because it supports their values, morals, and beliefs better than another class culture).

To determine a class cultural vision, look at the roles each fills in society and how important its members are, what problems plague them, and what traits allow them to overcome this. While the working class supports many people, individuals may be considered easily replaced as compared to an upper middle class admiral; there are only so many of the latter and yet anyone could probably become the former, like a waiter (no offense to waiters). A working class person is more likely to suffer certain kinds of abuse on the job than an engineer, but even the latter has problems, just of a different nature. A waiter must deal with poor tips, unexpected shift changes, and difficult customers. An engineer must deal with sloppy work by peers, shifting priorities, and clueless or obnoxious clients and managers. The waiter may value generosity, consistency, and kindness. The engineer may value diligence, planning, and patience. We don't need to work out every scenario, but if we have one that needs clarification, this is one way to achieve it among social classes. Try not to go too far down the rabbit hole on this.

CREATING CULTURE

Now that we've considered our guiding principles behind culture, it is time to invent the manifestations that reveal it. Our focus will be on elements we're likely to use, though some of us will need items others don't. This chapter can't be comprehensive because there's simply too much. However, the techniques behind the cultural manifestations presented here, and their rationales and considerations, can be applied to any item not included. Music and art are two areas we won't cover because they don't apply to the written word except as we describe them, and other mediums are likely to have dedicated composers or artists defining them.

Be aware that borrowing anything from Earth might result in accusations of cultural appropriation, a recent term implying that cultural elements can be devalued and insulted by use as something shallow when someone from outside that culture uses them in ways not considered respectful. Do world builders need to worry about this? Maybe. Whether they've thought about it or not, audiences likely don't expect storytellers to invent entire cultures because the work is vast and therefore, borrowing ideas from Earth can often feel like an homage. They can even feel pleased for it to be included. It helps to tie this manifestation back to our cultural vision so that it seems part of it, which we want to do anyway.

Remember the Rule of Three from *Creating Life (The Art of World Building, #1)* – make at least three *significant* changes to an Earth analogue. If we don't, people may recognize it; I always think James Cameron swiped Native American culture wholesale in the *Avatar* movie; it's pronounced distracting, and regrettable. Other works often steal Asian cultures with little conscience. Moderation is often best.

HOW MUCH CULTURE TO INVENT

As with many items, we could spend the rest of our lives building culture, so we need to limit our work. Asking why we are inventing culture can help. The answer is threefold. We are inventing aspects that will:

1. Portray a more engaging, realistic world
2. Make our story appear to take place somewhere other than familiar (i.e., Earth).
3. Cause culture clashes, in the form of tension due to expectation and misunderstanding. There is a further question of degree. How much tension do we need?
   a. Minor, offended feelings to make characters dislike each other
   b. Serious breaches that lead to ruined agreements (like treaties), imprisonments, death, or alteration of story or character trajectory

This will help us decide how much culture to invent in any given location, and how much we need cultures to differ, and on what subjects. If bowing while greeting is considered a minor offense, we don't have a character thrown in jail for not doing it. But if it's considered major, perhaps we do. It will also depend on how touchy our characters are or if they're looking for an ulterior motive to imprison someone.

Rather than inventing specific cultural items before outlining a story, we may want to only note that we want a culture clash to happen in a given scene we're planning and the consequences of it. One advantage is that we can first plan our tale, then create cultural elements of great impact where we need them, then less impactful elements. We should also know how many locations we'll need. In a *Lord of the Rings* style narrative, characters travel across many kingdoms, each needing a culture. We might have characters from differing places that might also need cultural tweaks. Add up all the people and places and that's the number of cultures we might need. If we have three sovereign powers with very different governments and resulting lifestyles, such as a democracy, an absolute monarchy, and an authoritarian one, readily distinguishable cultures are easier to imagine than if we have three absolute monarchies. This can be a reason to vary the government types in our tale.

We can sometimes give the appearance of a culture being synonymous with an entire sovereign power, for example, even when differences exist within it. This may happen if we're only using one of several regions or cities, for example, and not showing the others. Some might say we've created a mono-culture, so just be aware that we can create this impression. If we care to prove we haven't, then we'll benefit from a character thinking a rude (or kind) thought about a style of clothing or hair they see someone wearing when that style originates elsewhere. A few ideas like this sprinkled throughout our narrative can at least suggest we know culture varies. Using this approach, we can minimize the amount of culture inventing we'll do.

THE BODY

The body may not seem cultural, but it is. Long ago, larger women were considered desirable due to a belief that they were more likely to survive pregnancy and childbirth. Today, many women face great cultural pressure to be thin. The rising obesity in the United States is seen by some countries as a decadent sign of wealth while other countries suffer malnutrition. Judgement is heaped upon the overweight and such nitpicking exists that healthy young women are shown doctored photos that make similar women appear even thinner, as a false standard of beauty that many consider harmful; this is cultural pressure and a *value* judgement.

Ageism is real and felt at all ages, while often targeting the old. A society which values youthful productivity might consider the elderly a problem that should be locked away in retirement communities and denied rights, like a driver's license and human dignity, because that society values youth and productivity. Another society might teach great respect and reverence for their elders because they value wisdom and experience. There's more to ageism than the body, of course, as mental capacity and maturity are related.

Someone's general appearance is also cultural. Social norms change with our location and even time of day. In business, we make ourselves more presentable while being more casual at home and on the weekends. But perhaps we have a culture where formality reigns so that even a trip to the drug store means not having a proverbial hair out of place. Or perhaps a culture acknowledges that people can be very productive at work despite casual attire. There's also the question of a bare minimum of make-up for women (or men), groomed hair/beards, and clothes that aren't wrinkled, for example.

BODY LANGUAGE

Facial expressions are considered universal across cultures, so that's one element world builders don't have to worry about, at least among humans. To make our lives easier, we can take the same approach to other humanoid species. We might decide that an ogre is smiling for a different reason, like the pleasure of imagining bashing your head in, but it's still pleasure. Changing a smile to mean what a frown does, for example, will not only confuse characters but our audience. There are other ways to have characters misunderstand something, such as seeing the smile as benevolent when it's not.

Posture, walking, standing, sitting, and even how we hold our head or carry ourselves can be specific to an individual but also part of culture. A dignified culture might espouse standing tall, with chin up. An oppressive culture might see that as arrogant and have dominated people so much that being hunched, with head hanging low, has become a cultural expectation. Sitting with back straight is a sign of a strict culture, whereas slouching might be accepted in a lackadaisical one. Walking might be brisk in a fast paced one, but slow shuffling or casual meandering might reflect oppression or peaceful relaxations. As with most cultural issues, we want to determine what's common so that we know when someone is deviating from it and how that deviation is perceived.

The concept of personal space is one that can vary among cultures and across fictional species. Being close can express dominance, aggression, or signal intimacy. It can make people uncomfortable for all three reasons. Too much distance can seem impersonal, standoffish, and dismissive. To decide how close is considered normal or unoffensive, think of the cultural vision. A more reserved society will want greater distance while a boisterous one might find that distancing an affront, as if we're better than them.

Eye contact can range from too constant to too fleeting. Some cultures see looking down or away as appropriate deference, particularly when facing someone of higher station, whereas others see this as contemptible weakness. It can also suggest aggressiveness, whether that's simple meeting of gazes, a glare, or even refusing to look at someone at all. I've had some people stare at me so relentlessly that, aside from reminding me of a cat, they gave me the creeps. In a culture where status is highly valued and strictly enforced, deference is likely, but in a society where status is gained through conduct (whether social skill or achievement), a show of visual strength through maintained eye contact might dominate. We can tweak the length of expected gazing, but audiences don't want to be told that four seconds is fine, and anything less is not; instead, just state that a character looked away sooner than expected.

HAIR STYLES

The way in which hair is worn often symbolizes the social group to which one belongs. As fashions change, these associations can come and go; therefore, it is best to determine the fashion of a time rather than the past thousand years. Hair styles change more rapidly than that, generally, over the course of decades or a few hundred years. However, a more insular society might retain them longer. We often mock both current and previous styles as embarrassing as a way of distancing ourselves from the period or the perceived values of that group.

An association may be all that's needed to establish a hairstyle. In the 16th through 19th centuries, many men wore white, powdered periwigs. This spread from France to other parts of Europe because Louis XIII covered his baldness this way; the wigs became associated with power and eventually became quite elaborate until a taxation on the powder set in motion their demise. Women didn't typically use them unless they, too, had lost their hair, but men had their heads shaved so they could wear these wigs, which were considered cleaner than their own hair due to sanitary conditions at the time. In our invented world, we can ditch the powder, use something besides white, or make them shorter and more functional. We can also make wigs less or more ridiculous, but remember that we need to describe it to a reader unless we're in another medium.

In the U.S., long hair on men was once considered feminine and counter-culture. In *Game of Thrones*, a Dothraki warrior with a long ponytail signified how long it had been since he'd known defeat. Samurai wore the chonmage style to help keep their helmets on during battle. This functional origin remained while also becoming a status issue. What country (and culture) do you associate dreadlocks with?

As this is not a treatise on hair styles, it's recommended to perform an internet search and make a note of what's been done or invent something yourself. Decide which group uses each style. In our world, we don't need to define the source of one and can assign them without a rationale, though if one occurs to us, we can note it. People generally accept that a style belongs to a group without questioning it; so will our audience, simply because we said so. If we want a species to have a style, choose one that has variations, such as most elves wearing periwigs but one culture going short, another long, and both use white while a different one uses green, for example. This gets us unity but avoids a species monoculture.

While hair color is not typically cultural, it can be. East Asians so often have black or dark brown hair that we can be surprised when someone's is different. Denmark, Norway, and Sweden have long been associated with blonde hair and blue eyes. Punk musicians have often dyed their hair colors that don't naturally occur.

Facial hair can also be cultural. A long beard may symbolize virility, strength, manliness, or health. A shaggy one can suggest someone is wild and crazy, while a neatly groomed one suggests refinement and civilization. We once again want to decide what's expected based on cultural vision: do we foresee people being meticulous or not?

BODY MODIFICATION

Regardless of type, all body modifications might take place before, during, or after an important ceremony or event, such as a wedding, childbirth, or age milestone. They therefore signify a rite of passage having taken place, and the absence of the expected modification indicates it hasn't happened. These can both come with judgments, positive or negative, about the *value* associated with the change. If the body is believed to belong to your god, then modification might be prohibited without permission from said deity; or the god might demand it.

Tattoos can be part of culture, whether that's the placement or style. We're talking less about individual expression here and groups denoting membership for their individuals. We can choose black or other colors, use symmetry or not. Women might have more feminine styles while men have bolder ones. A religious group can require them, as can social groups wanting a specific tattoo to show membership that must be condoned. In some cultures, it might only be criminals and gangs who wear them. Some tattoos, like henna, are not permanent. As for what's shown, these are typically symbolic, even if only being lines of some kind.

Piercings are another body modification that can be more than an individual's taste, but part of a culture. Many body parts are available, and invented species might have more, but ear and noses are the most widespread and ancient on Earth. Stretched ear lobes and lips are another form. The number, size, material, and style of piercings can all be expected and represent a value. They can be signs of nobility or wealth. Gay men used to wear only one earring to indicate their orientation. Beliefs and superstitions can result in them, too, such as an idea from the Middle Ages that a specific piercing improved long-distance sight, resulting in explorers having them. There can be practical ideas, such as sailors thinking a gold earring can pay for their burial if they wash up somewhere.

Branding isn't typically accepted on Earth in modern times due partly to associations with slavery; it not only marks property but can humiliate if the brand is always visible. It can be done as punishment, such as slaves who've run away, or military people who committed an offense like desertion. Any crime that we feel others should be alerted to can result in one. We can choose that those with inclinations deemed offensive by the state can receive one. We have leeway to decide where it is done (very visible or under clothing), how large, and its design.

Implants take on special significance in SF, where technology can become part of the body. These can enhance abilities and senses or simply replace lost or damaged areas. There may be backlash against this or full acceptance by all of a culture or only parts of it. Tension is always desired in storytelling, so it may be best for some groups to oppose while others adopt. Questions of authenticity may arise, in the sense that someone is no longer who they were born as, if enough changes have been made. Are they still human? Do people feel augmented or like they're losing themselves? What is the psychological and philosophical impact of too much change, and where they draw the line at "too much?" What value is being offended or championed by the changes? This will decide how culture views it.

GESTURES

A sampling of gestures from Earth can give us ideas on what to leverage or invent; as long as we have a rationale, we can make up new ones or repurpose existing ones. Gestures that are a part of a greeting, for example, will be discussed later in this chapter because they include other elements, but some gestures stand alone. This includes one designed to show displeasure and give offense to the source of that displeasure. In much of the world, this involves raising the middle finger, a gesture that goes back to at least Roman times, with the finger representing a penis and the remaining finger knuckles representing testicles, though modern folks seldom know this.

Some cultures have alternate versions of this, such as two fingers (two penises) raised with the hand facing one way or another, or extending the arm before slapping the opposite hand into the elbow and bending the struck arm upward. Making a fist, with your thumb sticking out between your index and middle fingers, is called the fig and, to some, resembles a woman's privates. Putting your thumb behind your upper teeth, facing outward, and flicking the thumb is another variant called cutis. The "talk to the hand" gesture, arm extended, palm outward, all fingers spread, is called the moutza.

The "OK" symbol in the U.S., where the index finger and thumb form a circle and the other fingers are straight, means "asshole" in some countries. The thumbs up gesture can mean putting that up your rear instead of everything being okay. The devil horns can represent any animal with two horns but reminds some of a bull and suggests the target person's wife is having an affair (with the bull, i.e., a more virile man); we can do this with an animal of our invention. Another rude gesture is pointing to your other hand, where all five fingers are spread, indicating that the person you're doing this to had five potential fathers (a promiscuous mother). Crossing your fingers for luck can be seen as representing a woman's privates and is the same as calling someone a "c*nt."

Shaking your head for "no" and nodding for "yes" is not universal and is reversed in some countries. Crossing the arms is standoffish in some countries and arrogant in others; I personally just find it comfortable and wish people would stop reading into it! Punching your fist into the other palm is a threat of violence to some, but our fictional world's warriors might see it as wishing another warrior a good battle, whether literally or figuratively. Shaking two fists means good luck in Austria but could easily be seen as a threat in others. The foot can be considered very unclean and therefore, showing the bottom to others is highly offensive in some cultures; similarly, not taking shoes off inside is considered rude in others.

Sometimes our location while doing a gesture is an issue. Doing one over a threshold might be good or bad, or while sitting verses standing. A doorway is a transition, so a gesture that normally means peace could be seen as rude, meaning we hope the person's life changes for the worse. The opposite could be true if their life is unpleasant, in which case we're wishing them well? Think about what a location means and how we can spin the gesture's normal meaning. A church is a holy place to convene with gods, so being outside one, or in the doorway, and gesturing for someone inside to come to us could be interpreted as seducing them away from a god.

CLOTHING

Concentrating on specific clothing styles is time consuming; we're after a general sense of style. For example, the existence of buttons as a fastener, rather than as decoration. We take those for granted, but they didn't exist until the 1300s. What do people do without them? They wear looser, baggier clothing that may be tightened with a string of some kind; the clothes may just be wrapped around them (like a toga). This can impact culture; when buttons were introduced, so was tighter clothing, which could leave less to the imagination; resistance to the button could therefore happen because it causes a shift in culture, one that challenges ideas on modesty. Decide if buttons exist in this region or sovereign power and whether tight clothing is possible, and whether the existence of buttons is new or taken for granted (just like tighter clothing may be).

This is just one of countless examples, but it illustrates how the technological elements of our world impact and change culture. If we're thinking that only a fairly simple society may not have buttons as fasteners (decorative buttons are much older, to 5000 BC), such as a nomadic one, the Roman Empire didn't have them either, and yet they had aqueducts, dams, and ballistae. This surprising incongruity is real but if we do such things ourselves in a story, the audience might think we're making a mistake, so it may behoove us to meet expectations. Maybe we shouldn't have our star fighters not knowing what a button is.

Clothing can be used to indicate status, gender, rank, and social class. Plainer clothes suggest something lower while more adornment is for finer folk. Tunics in ancient Rome were adorned with colored bands, where the width, number, and color of these indicated standing. We can make up our own interpretations, such as wide and golden meaning better, and narrow, fewer, and more mundane colors meaning lesser. Decorations can be around the hem, neck, or wrists, but the front or back design was less common long ago on Earth, unlike today. Finer fabrics also suggest wealth while coarser is for the poor. Richer colors, or even clean and bright ones, can also indicate higher status. Consider how important status is to the culture and invent such expectations for cultures where status matters the most.

But even in cultures where visual indications of status are less important (possibly due to being a melting pot), situations will still call for traditionally finer or more mundane clothes (church, a job interview, being on vacation). Those with the highest status might still indicate it with designer clothes, even if just wearing a skimpy bathing suit.

This means that we can still decide what constitutes higher fashion and a reason for this. Tailored clothing makes one look better, so this is an easy one. On Earth, even those of us who can't afford Louis Vuitton or Prada have heard of them, so we just invent a few names on our fictitious world, and we're done. We need only reveal its value in a quick line:

She strode in with a diaphanous Olliana gown flowing about her, the price of which would've fed a city block for a year.

Clothing can reflect what is important to the society, groups, or individuals. If hard work is admirable, then sturdy, dependable, simple, rustic, coarse, and unadorned clothing may dominate. Or is clothing ostentatious with embroidery, jewels, and richer fabric like silks? This might appeal to high society that want to wear the latest fashion, sacrificing comfort and durability for appearance.

Modesty is a major cultural element that manifests in clothing, not only in adornment, but how much of the body is visible. Are women allowed to show cleavage (but not "side boob")? How far up their legs can hemlines rest? Above the ankles, above the knees, mid-thigh, or can they wear a thong in public? Do bras exist and are they expected to hide any appearance of a nipple, or do they push breasts up, as we often see in medieval period films? Can the belly be shown? The shoulders? We should consider how sexually open or repressed the culture is; religions can and will impact this.

One option is to decide that culture is static, regarding clothes or anything else, and therefore newer, more revealing styles (possibly originating from another culture) can cause one culture to harshly judge another as promiscuous and not caring about family values. We can see how values lead to cultural ideas that manifest in clothing, in this case, and an observation of another culture's clothing leads to a (contemptuous) judgment about what they value. This is what culture is for with world building.

Do men wear pants? What about women? In the United States, a woman wearing pants was once considered to be acting like a man, and this was frowned upon. It brought accusations of not acting like a lady, not knowing one's place, and being an unacceptable companion. We can do the same thing in our setting, regardless of what men's fashion a woman has chosen to adopt. Imagine the contempt heaped upon a man if he chose to wear dresses. In our designed culture, we can decide on norms for gender and then have characters violate it for reasons that are often practical; pants are more utilitarian compared to dresses, for example. A rebel will oppose norms just to do so, but such a character typically has attitudes that cause this.

Our cultural vision should influence these decisions.

The economy can also impact clothing due to choices or lack thereof. Those who cannot make more sophisticated clothing must do without or barter/buy them. An isolated culture may have this problem, but so can poorer individuals in societies with significant trade. This can result in limited options and predictable styles for lower classes, ones that become part of culture so that someone who comes into significant money and upgrades their wardrobe might be seen as putting on airs. Note the value judgment.

Footwear can also be cultural. In warm climates, sandals or even bare feet might predominate, while fur-lined, leather boots may in cold locations. A traditional style can exist for either so that those who go against this are judged. While climate affects the choice of how much covering is typical (a universal consideration), the exact styles are not important to our audience and we have leeway to decide what's expected and what's a deviation and what the value judgment is.

ACCESSORIES

Accessories can also be cultural for having expectations associated with them. This includes what can be worn and when. Consider this partial list of items:

Arm bands	Jewelry
Bags	Neck wear
Eyewear	Shawls and wraps
Footwear	Watches
Gloves	Weapon holders
Head gear	Wearable devices

Types of hats can be customary based upon the event so that a baseball cap is incorrect at a polo match, for example. Some cultures insist that a hat not be worn indoors because it's considered rude, particularly in front of a woman. A woman's hat is often considered part of her ensemble and therefore does not need to be removed. In recent years, it's become customary for golfers to briefly remove their hat when shaking hands of the other players at the end of a round. These expectations fluctuate and we have leeway to invent justifications, which are often unknown to people from the culture. Just assign a value to a behavior's meaning. Other head coverings, like a scarf, can be treated the same.

Wedding bands being worn on the left ring finger is customary in many Earth cultures because the Romans believed that the vein in that finger led directly to the heart, but at least a dozen wear it on the right hand. We could decide a culture recognizes the importance of the thumb and therefore a ring signifying family (if not marriage) is worn on one thumb. Which hand? Just make something up. Maybe people are predominantly right-handed, and the left does less practical work, or one hand is reserved for ceremony and rare occasions, and therefore it is more sacred. Therefore, a man who resents his family, or if cast out by them, might wear the ring on the opposite hand in protest. Other types of rings or accessories are much the same. As with everything cultural, we don't need an explanation but can just make it up if we want one.

Some accessories result from function. A winged humanoid species working as messengers, rather than carrying scrolls in the hand, might attach them to a scroll case worn on the hip or a sash. Meaning can be attached to how it is worn—when carrying a message, it's worn on one hip, if not, on the other. Or perhaps it's not worn at all when off work, or it's simply left at home at certain times. Continuing to wear it at social occasions could be considered rude, as if saying, "I'm only here in official capacity, not because I care." Another species might be known for strong drink and always have a flask with them. While being drunk might be customary at rowdy moments, being sober at important events can be seen as respectful; perhaps still wearing the flask offends.

There are seemingly endless variations to accessories, so we won't cover more. Hopefully these ideas help you decide. As with all cultural issues, assign a value and its associated behavior and choose how that can go awry and what bad meanings can be associated with failing to meet the expectation.

GREETINGS AND FAREWELLS

One way to distinguish a culture is their greetings and farewells, but what all cultures have in common is the willingness to do them because it's a hallmark of goodwill, respect and civility. We can surmise that in a truly barbaric society (one that also has little culture), these greetings don't exist or are not much more than eye contact and/or a grunt, but most societies that world builders need to invent have more than this.

Greetings are typically more involved than farewells because they set the tone for the coming interaction, but when there's to be no real interaction (such as passing someone on the street), they're short. An acknowledgement is among the most basic of expectations, and yet some situations do not call for them and not everyone will comply even when they do (just as some will do them when not required). In a big city, people walk past each other on the street with no acknowledgement and it might even be considered weird for us to say hello to anyone.

As world builders, we should aim for brevity because the audience doesn't really care about these moments unless something goes wrong during them. Why waste a paragraph or five minutes of screen time? It's similar to an issue in *Game of Thrones*, where Daenarys had so many titles by the end that it took thirty seconds to rattle them off, and the show repeated this in every introduction instead of bypassing them. Never make the audience want to skip ahead.

Many potential failures exist in both greetings and farewells; storytellers can leverage all of them for tension. Some people will not respond to one at all; we don't need to first establish that a response is expected because our audience will assume so (it's implied), especially when other characters react to this. The unresponsive person likely knows they're failing in this, unless they didn't hear/see it or are distracted. Reasons for this are a storytelling issue, as culture doesn't explain a total lack of response or acknowledgment when doing so is universal across cultures.

By contrast, culture can explain responses that are considered inadequate, a fact that may surprise the one giving the inadequate response. It's almost a given that, without previous experience in another culture or someone telling us what to do, we will make mistakes. The degree of these will depend in part on how different the two cultures are (the one we're in and the one we're from). Ignorance is not the only reason for giving offense. Shyness can cause it, as can previous bad experiences that leave some fearing more of the same and performing poorly. Some people use too much or too little strength in gestures, such as a meek or crushing handshake. People are always interpreting the actions of others and some cultures might be more prone to finding offense.

We may want both formal and informal greetings in our setting. In English, "hello" is more formal than "hi," which is not as casual as "hey," which still stands above "yo." Then there's "What's up?" or its shortened "'sup?" We don't need so many as this, and there are plenty more in America, but it's realistic that our traveling characters will greet comrades one way, strangers another, and those of a different station a third. Consider creating these variations.

Greetings sometimes have a practical origin, such as the handshake being designed to show that neither person has a weapon, or even to dislodge a dagger hidden up one's sleeve. A variation on this is to grab the upper arm. With alternate weapons in SF, we might think of a different greeting that has a similar purpose. Think of how a sneaky person would conceal an item and what gesture might reveal it and become commonplace.

In addition to greetings, some of what follows can also be done to congratulate others, thank them, say farewell, or confirm an agreement.

THE WORDS

Analogues are useful when inventing greetings and farewells, but first, a few observations.

• There's often a word that means "hello" and a more casual version like "hi."

• We can wish pleasant times on them, such "Good morning" and "Live long and prosper."

• We often inquire about their well-being, such as "How are you?" This can be rhetorical.

• We can state how happy we are to see or meet them, such as "Pleased to meet you."

• We can use a title, like "sir," "Lord Kier," "Mr. Smith," or "Grand Master of the Seven Realms."

• We can introduce ourselves first, last, or in between (when additional people are there)

• Using a given name is less formal than the surname

All we need do is combine these ideas while inventing variations that make sense for the context, which can be social, about station/rank, or both. Our cultural vision may have less impact on our decision because most greetings have certain values in common, those being respect, well-wishing, and a show of good and peaceful intentions. If an individual doesn't want to show those things, they don't make the greeting or include every part of it.

Some ideas are a bit religious, like "many blessings" or "may the Lord bless you." Then there are military ideas like, "May your sword never break," "May your bowstring never snap," and "May your arrows fly true." Just think of a peril that might befall a profession and we can invent an expression. Or we can avoid these slightly negative sounding ones for something more upbeat: "may your staff always shine," or "may your blade always gleam." A scout might be simply told, "many sightings."

PHYSICAL GESTURES

In addition to (or in place of) words, both greetings and farewells can include gestures that may be optional, required, or at least expected. We should decide on this along with the gesture itself. That way, if something is required but our character doesn't do it, this is a larger offense. If it's only expected, it's a smaller offense. If it's optional, we pay little attention, and if it's highly unusual, we notice it being done and perhaps wonder why, though being offended isn't common.

There are different analogues we can leverage from both real Earth cultures and ones that other storytellers have imagined, but first, remember that touching others can spread germs. In a less technological society, like those in fantasy, people may be (and likely are) unaware of this. A prevalence for gestures that spread germs might exist unbeknownst to them, so we maybe shouldn't have them avoid it as if they know something they don't. In other words, don't project our knowledge of this onto them and have them prefer other greetings because of it.

Beings from different planets have different germs and immunities, which naturally arises more in SF. It's reality, but storytellers often overlook this because acknowledging it could place a substantial restriction on character behaviors and plot developments. This is a personal call each creator must make. Just as European diseases infected Native Americans, killing many, planet-hopping characters would do the same. Those big SF movies where aliens need incredible weapons to wipe us out may miss the mark in that they may only need to drop even a mild pathogen (or several) here and come back later when most of us are dead; the exception would be when they can't wait for that.

THE HANDSHAKE

The handshake done on Earth in modern times is so common that we often want something else on our fictional setting, with good reason. This gesture is too much like here. Variations already exist and we can invent our own or leverage these, which is recommended for speed of world building. For all of them, we want ease of depiction; no one wants even two sentences describing it.

Some easy variants are:

• Forearm, bicep, or shoulder clasp
• Interlacing fingers
• Fist bump
• Two hands

The details of handshakes vary by country on Earth. They are typically done barehanded, meaning failure to remove a glove could be seen as disrespect. In some countries, only the same gender shake hands, or sometimes one gender is expected to be greeted first this way. A religion like Islam discourages gender-mixing. Children can be included or excluded. Some prefer a weak grip, others a strong. While some use right hands, they simultaneously use the left to grasp the other's right hand by the elbow. Sometimes a senior person is expected to initiate the gesture. One country considers it rude to have the left hand in a pocket during a greeting. While most handshakes are brief, some cultures expect people to hold hands for several seconds after the initial shake. In another country, that might be considered odd. There's a lot of opportunity for misunderstanding for foreigners. There are also combination motions that must be known in advance to perform. They're usually done by those belonging to a specialized group, such as athletes, musicians, wizards, or organizations, such as a secret society.

Speculation about the origins of handshakes is that soldiers did this to show they didn't hold a weapon, which could also have been a dagger hidden up one's sleeve. Refusal to shake hands could be a bad sign. We may find this useful in a scene.

The Kiss

As a greeting or farewell, a kiss on the lips would be too intimate for most cultures except among lovers or family, but it's an option, one that shows great comfort with physicality. It's easy to imagine other cultures viewing this as a sign of promiscuity or lasciviousness. It's also far more likely to spread germs. A kiss on the cheek is tamer and can either involve lips touching the skin or a cheek-to-cheek gesture with a kissing motion (or sound) from the lips, as if imitating. Sometimes a single kiss is done, but we've all seen each cheek getting the treatment. A kiss on the forehead is another option but can suggest patronization because adults sometimes do this to children, but maybe they don't in our world. We have leeway to invent the interpretations, too. Finally, there is the kissing of the hand, which has been presented for the purpose. This has often been done to women or those of higher station.

The Bow

The bow seems more formal and may be appropriate in a culture where shows of respect are valued. It isn't just the important people who may need this deference, but the whole population. The degree of bow is commensurate with the level of respect shown; while it might be customary to kneel before one's king, if one is truly humble, prostration might feel appropriate.

That might seem excessive to others. Even when one remains upright, there's still a degree of bow, such as a slight bend or much more. What is appropriate might depend not just upon the relative social standing of those present, but upon the occasion, as something more serious and formal requires a deeper bow. In some cultures, people are exact about it and bowing too much is just as bad as bowing too little. We can decide for ourselves how touchy our peoples are.

A mere head nod would be the smallest gesture, followed by kneeling (one knee is less formal than both) and finally prostration (lying full upon the ground). These are levels of submission, which is why the more severe versions appear in religions. One version of bowing on Earth is Namaste, where we would place our palms together before our chest, bow slightly from the head, and say "Namaste."

THE SALUTE

A salute is typically reserved for the military and can be any number of fingers, though it's typically all or the index and middle finger in a two-finger salute, with the other fingers bent and the thumb touching them. This can cause problems and has done so on Earth, as the Polish do the two-finger variety, like the Cub Scouts (children), and this led U.S. troops to assume the Polish were being disrespectful, as if implying they were kids. The result was Polish troops being arrested until the misunderstanding was cleared up.

In some places, a salute is only when a hat is worn. Others only allow it indoors when formally reporting to a superior officer. If enemy snipers are known to be nearby, no saluting happens (to avoid identifying an officer, who becomes a target). The palm can face downward as in the U.S. or toward the one being saluted. The downward version resulted from lower level troops working on tasks that dirtied their hands, and presenting the dirty palm to a superior during a salute wasn't considered polite. A closed fist can also be used, and the arm can be extended forward (instead of bent to bring the hand to the forehead).

The origins of saluting are suggested to be from knights raising their visor to identify themselves, which was partly a show that they weren't afraid of their foe, either. This can easily be used in the context of a knight who refuses to raise a visor and is taunted as a coward. In SF, salutes can be done with rifles. A salute can also be done with the sword, with enough variations in gesture that we can invent what we like. Pointing the tip at the ground is a sign of submission.

Others

Sometimes we only nod at another person in passing, raise eyebrows, or just smile. We might say the briefest version of a greeting, such as "Hi." We may give a small hand gesture, like a wave, but without raising our arm. What all of these have in common is not so much a greeting as an acknowledgement that we saw the other person and we aren't pretending we didn't. This is more important when we know them.

The military salute manifested in the tipping of one's hat, by civilians, toward others as a greeting and gesture of respect. Sometimes the hat is merely touched, while other times it is removed, particularly indoors. Even today, some still consider it wrong to leave a hat on inside. After some gestures, like a handshake, the hand is placed on our own heart, though secondary motions are less common on Earth.

We can borrow ideas from animals, as this might feel more appropriate for beast-like species, such as trolls, ogres, and dragons, all of whom might use sniffing like dogs. A winged humanoid species might stretch and/or shake wings. Maybe subtle ways of fanning those feathers mean something, like annoyance, impatience, or happiness. Folding them in might be a blow-off. Wrapping them in front of oneself might be seen as evasive or a sign of being uncomfortable; maybe they're just cold and this can be misinterpreted.

A species with a tail might raise it in a lazy swing, or crack it like a whip, making an actual sound. Some of this can be considered friendly or hostile. An Earth cat raises the tail in greeting, or slaps it on the floor when annoyed, and casually wags it when relaxed. Then there's the fluffy appearance when startled, though that requires fur. Cats can extend their claws at will, so maybe we have a species that does the same, even giving a friendly scratch or bite. A dragon might puff some smoke out, but a little fire is an offense.

A society where everyone has a bladed-weapon at all times might gesture with it, whether sheathed or not. Maybe the gesture is just to unsheathe it by an inch and put it back, and doing more so is considered a sign of aggression. "He bared his blade!" an outraged character might shout, drawing his.

In worlds with magic or technologies we don't have, wizards might make their staff give a pulse of light in greeting. A gun that has lights, whether a laser sight or just a flashlight, could be used for the same, especially if something like Morse Code signals are used on the field and have become a way to recognize allies. Maybe people position the staff or rifle a certain way almost like how a hat is tipped or a head is bowed. Since the powerful end of a staff is the top (usually), maybe it's considered rude for a wizard to tip the top toward someone they're greeting, but sliding the bottom forward can be seen as submission just as kneeling might be. Use your imagination.

LANGUAGE

Our use of language, which is covered in detail in chapter eight, is also cultural. Phrases enter the vernacular from common usage in a variety of ways, often from music and art, but world builders don't need to explain origins. What we do need and should invent are expressions, styles of speaking, and general tone, such as casual or formal, harsh or pleasant, etc. As always, culture is about expectations.

TONE

The way we speak carries as much meaning, if not more so, than the words we use, but those in auditory media can convey tone with greater ease than authors. Despite this, world builders should decide how people from a culture sound even when the words are not considered. Hollywood films are a good way to get a sense of how different cultures and their language come across from the tone of speakers. The French are depicted as haughty and pretentious in tone. Germans and Russians are gruff, hard, and cold. The British are overly polite, to a fault. The Japanese are elaborate, formal, and distant. Use these analogues as a guide.

COLLOQUIALISMS, SLANG, AND EXPRESSIONS

We can invent words and phrases that are often spoken in a culture, whether these are part of curses, greetings, or other elements we'll discuss further in this chapter. A colloquialism is usually understood regardless of any socioeconomic factors while slang is for smaller subgroups (like teenagers) so that those outside that group may not understand it. This can help scope expressions we invent, noting in our files if everyone "gets it" or just a subgroup. A colloquialism might contain slang.

A well-known example is the different ways people in the United States order carbonated drinks. This varies by the region. Some variants are "pop," "soda pop," "soft drink," "soda," and "coke." The latter doesn't mean "Coke." The phrase "chop your breakfast on a mirror" refers to cocaine use and may only be known by fans of Metallica, as the line is in their song, "Master of Puppets." The contraction "y'all" is associated with those in the southern U.S. For inspiration, Google is our friend and yields tons of ideas.

There are some basics we might want to focus on because they come up in conversation. For example, what do people say when they agree? In the U.S., we have "okay," "sounds good," "alright," "yeah," and "right" as some examples (there are more). Pirates say "Aye." When disagreeing, we tend to be less direct so as not to offend, saying "I'm not sure about that" or something similar. We don't typically say, "you're wrong." How do people tell someone they're a liar? You're "full of shit" is common in the U.S. Just think about things you say to people and invent alternates.

SF is infamous for technical jargon. To this, we mostly need to invent the technology and then refer to it. In both SF and fantasy, we can turn a noun into a verb to create jargon. Casting a spell on someone can result in them being "magicked," for example. If there's a common spell to cause changes to a person, this can be used the same way, such as a charm spell resulting in someone having been "charmed." If a common device gets the jitters, we can invent an insult that someone has been "jittered" one too many times, as if they're personally developed that trait. Names of devices can be used this way, too.

In our modern world and a SF one, the source is often media (TV, film, books, songs) and needs no explanation when a world builder invents them. Audiences come to realize it's such an expression when more than one character uses it over the course of a work.

SWEAR WORDS

Not all swear words are created equal. Some types are used far more often than others. Words for excrement are bound to exist in all languages and be in frequent use. We can just use Earth versions, because they're so common as to not cause a reaction, but it's better if they stand alone. By contrast, "I don't give a shit" is a colloquial expression and shouldn't be used.

The word "fuck" is unique and powerful. Some writers avoid having characters say it unless they're from Earth because it's too much like here. This is also true of "shag" from Britain. An infamous world building version is "frak" from *Battlestar Galactica*. That might bother people more, and if *Game of Thrones* used the f-bomb, so can we. A benign word in one language can be a swear in another, such as "bloody" in England; to create these, just use a slightly graphic word (like bloody) in a context where it otherwise doesn't fit (and is not simply an adjective) and do it several times in a row to get the point across that we're not being literal. An example would be, "I'm not bloody doing it. No way do I bloody pick that thing up." On the other hand, if we write, "I'm not picking up that bloody thing," it just seems like an adjective.

Invoking a god is often part of swearing. Sometimes it's literally just their name said harshly, or this can be combined, as in "Goddamn" and "Goddamnit." We can also merge words to create hybrids, like, "motherfucker," "dumbass," and "shithead." Animals can be leveraged, and if we've invented our own, this helps with uniqueness; examples include "sheepfucker," "bullshit," "horse piss," and "dragon spittle." All we need to do is find something objectionable, which is why bodily waste is popular, as are the body parts from which they originate, or other "private" parts. Other kinds of waste, such as something industrial in SF, can substitute. Perhaps magic leaves a residue we've named and can leverage.

DAILY LIFE

DINING

There's an etiquette to dining, which means there are values that lead to expectations. Does this culture value savagery and baseness (like lust and gluttony) or rising above animalistic instincts to one degree or another? This leads to a general level of hearty gusto, decorum and refinement, or something in between. It impacts everything from how people are called to a meal, how it's presented and consumed, and what happens when it's over. To keep things simple, we can decide that there are three defaults: hearty, refined, or moderate. Subtle variations on them become what we tweak for each culture we invent.

To be stereotypical, the hearty choice might best suit barbarians, nomadic peoples, and those whose civilization is in its early stages. Meals might be had at any time, while standing around or right after an animal is killed. No one washes up beforehand and they show up smelling however they smell, wearing whatever's already on them, likely dirty. Perhaps there's no table or silverware, and if people gather at all, they stand or sit on the ground or maybe a pelt. To call others to a meal, they might simply holler once and leave it at that; if you don't show up, that's your problem. Or they expect you to notice and come over. Food is eaten with hands. Dirty fingers and mouths are wiped on sleeves, if anything. Belching might be common, and loud songs, stories, and ale flow. Anyone who needs to step away just goes, possibly losing their spot if they've even got one. To relieve themselves, maybe people don't go far, doing it in sight. Those who want more of something just take it. Perhaps they eat too much, don't share, and there's no such thing as leaving some for someone else. When it's all done, no one cleans up other than to lick something clean or throw a bone elsewhere, like to dogs, who might be allowed to help themselves during the meal. This is a social event but mostly about eating.

Contrast all of this with the refined approach, again going for an extreme. Meals are likely had at a specific time that, if subtly changing from day to day, is still told to people in advance, usually politely; a guest might be asked to spread the word to others, and the meal doesn't start until everyone is seated and perhaps a prayer is spoken; there's no nibbling allowed before this. Hosts might also provide choices, such as stating that steak is the main dish and asking if corn or peas is preferred by the guest. The food is presented well, like a piece of art, with sauce dribbled over it and a sprig of parsley to one side. Everyone washes their hands beforehand and wears relatively clean clothes and is washed enough to prevent poor scents and appearance. Ornate silverware, china, and crystal goblets may adorn a beautiful table with napkins and possibly an elegant tablecloth, candles or soft lights bathing everyone. Food is not only eaten with utensils, but multiple forks, for example, are designed for use on specific dishes. Whether servants are present or not, food and drink are politely passed and/or served for dedicated bowls/trays and utensils no one's eating with. Even an unheard belch results in someone saying "excuse me," and permission is asked to leave a table for any reason, including the bathroom. Those who want more ask for it or go without if eating too much is considered gluttony, or perhaps they wait to be offered (and must accept?). No one ever takes the last of anything. When it's done, everyone concludes at the same time and departs together, helping (or letting servants) clean up and restoring order, pushing chairs back in, wiping mouths a final time and cleaning the hands, too. This is a social event where eating is almost secondary.

In between these extremes are what we'd typically see and experience today in modern cultures. This means a roughly expected mealtime, casually announced. People are expected to wash up but often don't, and only blatantly dirty clothes get a reaction. There's one fork and knife per person; you get anything else you want/need yourself and come back. People serve themselves from plain dishes with either a serving spoon or something of theirs that hasn't been in their mouth (think knife, shoving stuff out of a tilted bowl or plate). Someone eats the last of something without much regard for anyone else wanting it. People leave when they need, without permission, and often only the adults who live there clean up anything. It's informal, satisfies a bodily need, and may not be particularly social.

These three basic scenarios can be altered, with more or fewer acts of refinement added/subtracted. In theory, a younger society might be rowdier while an older one could be more refined. Standards of cleanliness (which education influences) will impact the move away from the first example. There's more judgment in the refined scenario, where minor offense can be given for something as trivial as using the wrong spoon for soup.

Here are some additional questions to consider:

1. Can people invite themselves or others to dine? Are impromptu guests accepted?
2. Is there expected attire and what might it be?
3. Seating
   a. Who sits first?
   b. Are seats assigned an order or not, and how if so (rank)?
4. Are some tables reserved?
5. Does anyone enter or do something after everyone else is present or seated?
6. Serving
   a. Who gets served first and last? Is that based on gender, seniority, or do guests or the hosts receive the privilege?
   b. Are extra portions viewed well or poorly? Is it considered rude or wasteful to not finish what you've taken? Is it bad to not eat much as if disapproving of the fare?
7. Is it permissible or forbidden to brings weapons to the table?

We must still consider how many meals are common in a day, when they're consumed, and perhaps what types of foods are associated with each. There are often traditional items. What comes to mind for breakfast, lunch, and dinner? Few world builders have the time to invent an array of meals or even occasion to show them in our work, so we likely want to be generic. For example, in looking at the food groups, are certain ones associated with one of these meals? Fruits might be consumed primarily for breakfast, snacks, or as a side dish, as often happens in the United States. But perhaps a fruit or veggie salad is a common lunch item instead. Fish might be eaten later in the day after it's been caught, but then fisherman are often out early and maybe it's ready by breakfast, though that means fishing closer to shore.

In fantasy worlds, there's no refrigeration and we can use this to decide what is often in a meal.

In the United States, the early bird special means eating a few hours before most people, at restaurants. This originates from the expression that "the early bird gets the worm" because rain causes worms to be on the surface and the first bird gets plenty of options. We can do this or reverse it, meaning most people eat early and restaurants are eager to lure people in later, after the rush. Here we might use the expression 'second mouse special', referring to an idiom "the second mouse gets the cheese" meaning a mousetrap kills the first mouse and, having been sprung, poses no danger to the second, who eats their fill.

A big family dinner (or other meal) where everyone sits down at the same table is a part of certain cultures, but in others, people might eat while on the go or standing in the kitchen after making the meal. The latter is often caused by necessity. If family togetherness is a value, however, eating together is likely as well. Dinner is usually the most important meal for this, with the day's events complete, but in our fictional world, it could be lunch followed by a siesta. Or breakfast with well-wishing for the day's events. Find a rationale to justify which meal is for family gatherings, while another, like lunch, may be with coworkers or friends. A character from a culture without this may place no value on the experience and not understand it; this can help create a culture clash.

There are cultural aspects to guests. If someone happens to be present near a mealtime, it's often courtesy to invite them, but perhaps our culture suggests politely showing them the door because this is a family occasion. We can spin these things. The guest might be expecting to leave and be embarrassed that they haven't already. Perhaps when they smell the food cooking, they become uncomfortable and begin to excuse themselves. But it could be reversed, where the smell has them assuming they'll be invited as in their culture, but it's not what happens, leading to offense. Perhaps a guest is expected to invite themselves or even help themselves to any food and drink in our house. Or a host is supposed to offer, the guest declines once, the host offers again, and only then does the guest accept. Doing so sooner might be considered hasty or greedy. Remember that culture has a lot to do with expectations, whether those are met or not.

FOOD

Cultures always have their own foods. For inspiration, we can easily leverage Earth analogues. What do we think of with Chinese, Indian, and Italian foods to name a few? Even a city like New Orleans has associated dishes. There's New York style pizza and Philadelphia cheesesteaks. France and Champagne, Germans and beer, the U.S. south and moonshine. We only need to decide that something is particularly delicious somewhere or that they invented it. A drink or food can be known for its effect, taste, or smell.

But individual foods do not a culture make. Rather, there's a taste, aroma, and consistency often associated with a culture. This could be red or white sauce. It can be pasta or rice (Italy vs. Asia) with seemingly everything. What is often unique is the sauce and spice combination. Are foods bland, spicy (mild to hot), rich, creamy, tart, tangy, etc.? We could go on, but food is one area where the values we decided on earlier are of limited use in deciding what a culture's food tastes like. We can instead simply assign a style, though authors sometimes like to say something like, "Their food was as spicy as their lovemaking." This can help us decide.

Its presentation, however, is another matter, as culture influences this. Japanese culture is often refined in appearance, manners – and how food looks on a plate. There's a design aesthetic. Another culture might heap everything onto a plate, or pile meats and veggies atop a bed of rice. Granted, every approach can exist in the same culture, but we have the option of creating expectations. The dining style likely accompanies the presentation. How stately do chopsticks look, and the white bowls of rice, soup, or tea?

When inventing foods, it's often the impression we want, as the audience will never get to eat them. We want to comment on the reaction to be served, not to mention consuming, anything. Why reaction? In the United States, fish is served without a head, but in other countries it will still be attached, a fact that bothers many American diners, to cite one example. There are also body parts some cultures eat and others won't, like pigs' feet. The existence of rice, noodles, various meat types, and vegetables will not change much on even imagined worlds, even if the details do or we create analogues, so we should spend more time on impressions and reactions.

Specific foods are often consumed at traditional times, such as turkey at Thanksgiving in the United States, or ham for Christmas and eggs for Easter. Believe it or not, KFC is a traditional Christmas food in Japan since the 1970s. We likely need a few of these items if a holiday is occurring amidst our story; we can take common foods and simply decide they're had that day, possibly prepared or served a certain way.

Crops are harvested at different times of the year. This can result in seasonal foods that are also part of culture. Absent refrigeration or being stored somewhere cool, most fruits and vegetables only last a day or two without quality loss, but they can still be eaten days later, though there is risk of bacteria having grown on them, depending on the item. There's a lot of variation to this, but some plants can still be associated with a whole season because not every apple tree, for example, needs to be harvested at the same time, and in our fictional world, with invented variations on plants, we have leeway for our decisions. In *Creating Life (The Art of World Building, #1)*, we covered creating plants like Earth ones, with minor changes. We can learn when a food is harvested and mimic this with ours.

BATHING

In a modest society, bathing is in private, but some cultures have people bathing together, whether coed or not. We typically mean using soap, but a Korean Bathhouse has people soaking in a variety of pools of varying water temperate, even saunas. These can also be coed or not. A culture clash on modesty is easily done for this, with value judgments being made.

How often do people bathe on average? This often reflects a society's understanding of hygiene, with SF worlds tending toward better education. Our fantasy characters may get one bath a week, taking any reasonable chance to swim in the interim. And a bath it likely is, not a shower, due to technology. Rarity may promote the use of perfumes as deodorants, with higher society possibly overdoing it, though they likely have more frequent bathing, a fact that easily distinguishes them from commoners; better kept clothing does the same.

Parents bathe children, but when does this stop and kids go it alone? If self-reliance is important, this may be earlier. If a child is rare (due to something like overpopulation that means a couple only gets to have one), then perhaps the parents fawn over a child until he's older. Does one parent or both assume responsibility for this? A child may also join either parent in a bath, meaning the parent is bathing, too. We might also see a family bathe together, all genders. If hot bath water is a luxury, decide who enjoys it first and last. We can use this when a character who got it last as a child, for example, gets the rare chance to go first as an adult and thinks about this during the scene, thinking back to childhood. Even without the luxury of warm water, who gets to go first when bath water in a tub must be shared?

At what time of day do people bathe, morning or night? It's seldom mid-day but could be, particularly in a culture with a midday siesta due to heat. Those who are apt to get dirty during the day will likely pick night to avoid getting their bed dirtier than necessary, so this may apply to blue collar workers more than princes, for example.

SLEEPING

A culture can be known for varying degrees of sleep, which the species/race makeup of that society can impact. A race that needs little sleep might have an active nightlife. One that needs a lot might have afternoon naps as commonplace. If that race dominates the culture, the impact will be felt. If it does not, then other races may judge them for how much or little rest they need.

In many Earth cultures, it's standard for a couple (especially if married) to sleep in the same bed, but that's a custom. It isn't necessary. Consider keeping this in a society with low temperatures much of the year; in *Game of Thrones*, some women are referred to as "bed warmers." This is unlikely in a hot climate and people may prefer their own beds, which don't need to be in the same room, either. Imagine a race where the males always snore; the females may be used to it, or they may insist on different rooms.

Some other questions to ask are:

1. Do children sleep with their parents, either in the same bed or room?
2. What age is this frowned upon, if ever?
3. Is the culture aware of Sudden Infant Death Syndrome and preventing it?
4. Do babies have traditional items slept with, like a teddy bear? We can mock an adult character who retains such an item or simply has one around for some reason, such as intending to give it to a niece.
5. Do people sleep with a light on or total darkness? Perhaps a scented candle is traditionally lit on some occasion. If the environment is typically bright or daytime naps occur, maybe masks are worn just then or all the time.
6. Do window coverings exist because of this and allow for easy manipulation?
7. Do people sleep nude, in undergarments, or specific bed clothes? Naturally, regional air temperatures influence this.

The shape of beds is assumed to be rectangular due to our bodies being longer than wide while lying down, so no one will question this. But we can imagine that a bed for two does not anticipate them lying side-by-side. How about feet-to-feet, or head-to-head, in a very long bed? Circular beds are an option, as are those inspired by a culturally significant symbol, such as a heart for a honeymoon suite. There are also bunk beds, water beds, air beds, pods, ones that can be retracted into a wall, those on the floor (without legs), or even suspended ones, like a hammock. Something is likely to dominate. Decide what it is, what's traditional, and what's the latest craze. Don't forget to mention those useless, decorative pillows, should they exist.

EMPLOYMENT

Unless independently wealthy or living with their family, most people need a job. On a cultural level, what we're looking for is a typical number of hours worked in a day and how many days per week. A related question is whether positions pay enough or whether people need additional employ-ment, or to combine income with a spouse, extended family, or friends who share living expenses. Working out this detail for every position would be very time-consuming without much payoff for us or audiences, so focus on what's most common. Do most people at a given class level need to work two jobs or is that uncommon? If it's very common, it can become part of a cul-ture and is therefore expected.

The 40-hour work week is a decent average for humans, who work more in some industries. But consistently going beyond an 8-hour day, 5 days a week leads to worker burn out (and to make our world different, we should alter this). If we need many characters with lives that are miserable in our setting, exceeding this is one way to achieve it. Laws sometimes forbid such a thing, which can lead to secondary jobs, though perhaps there are laws against that as well. But the state often mandates minimum pay rates, though such a thing is more likely in SF than fantasy due to increased government. Some companies allow variations, such as 4 10-hour workdays a week, so perhaps this is common in our fictional world. Maybe people must work al-most every day but only 4-6 hours. Do they have long days mixed with short ones, with a name for each type?

Another employment issue is how early or late people tend to work in a day. Perhaps early rising is standard, or working into nightfall (or both). Tak-ing a break during the afternoon, such as for an extended lunch break of hours, might be common in the culture. This is called a siesta and results from a combination of a big, heavy meal at lunchtime and excessive heat, both of which can lead to drowsiness. Consider adding this to any culture near the equator or other hot areas; that culture can spread to other regions that don't have the heat. Many businesses will close for 1-2 hours during this period, a fact that characters will take into account when they need supplies. A siesta also lets people stay up later, extending social life. Is a siesta so common that sleeping chambers are part of the office environment? Imagine the privacy and security concerns subsequently raised and steps to mitigate them. These sleeping rooms might be coed or not; imagine the combination of coed and nudity.

Are children allowed to be brought to work? Can a woman breastfeed at work at all, and is this openly or is a room set aside? Are daycare facilities available in this society and do they provide adequate care? Maybe it's so expensive that some mothers or fathers don't work and stay home to raise children while the other spouse works.

On that note, are women in the workforce? Are men? What about children, and at what age? Is any gender or age group discriminated against, given better pay and benefits, or denied certain types of employment? Is there cultural shift underway or is the status quo rigidly maintained? When rights are restricted in a supposedly free society, there's often a "two steps forward, one step back" shift toward more freedom, due to resistance. Decide if such a movement is needed in the setting and how it might impact the story. We don't need incredible details on this unless it's a major story element, but a decision about employment opportunities will certainly impact the outlook of all genders. For example, a woman who can't get a decent job might take to adventuring (or piracy) if she's got the skills and personality for it.

We can consider many aspects of employment, such as whether people get vacations or holidays at all, health and other insurance benefits, pay raises, and what type of abuses must be endured from management, coworkers, or the public. We can model a SF world similar to but more advanced than an Earth society, but fantasy might require reimaging employment; on the plus side, with less formal organization (i.e., companies), there are fewer policies, for example, to decide upon. That someone has a great or crap job, in their opinion, can sometimes be enough, and all we may need is their comparison to a better or worse life that someone else has, with a few details that amount to discrepancies between what is and what could be.

TRANSPORTATION

Transportation may not seem like a cultural element, but it is. Some cities, like Los Angeles, are known for their cars, while another might be known for motorcycles. Venice is known for gondola boats. Cities are known for pedestrians, bicyclists, and traffic jams, not to mention extremely limited parking. Residents and visitors take this into account; sometimes, they plan their lives around it. A science-fiction setting might similarly be known for certain types of craft.

There are subcultures that trick out of their cars with all sorts of aftermarket accessories. The same can be done for motorcycles or spaceships if those are personally owned. With a little imagination, perhaps we can do the same with wagons, horses, or even dragons and the gear we use to ride them.

The existence and state of public transportation can also have cultural impacts such as whether a settlement is known for people having to walk everywhere because public transportation doesn't exist. Or maybe it's free, or really expensive, either extreme impacting the willingness to travel. Crime with public and even private transportation (think of unlicensed taxis or services like Uber) is also on everyone's mind. What kind of security is typical in the culture we're inventing? It depends partly on the wealth available for police and infrastructure to deal with criminals.

Long distance travel is another concern. In SF, this is almost a given, but in fantasy settings, many people can't do long-distance travel. Here, the horse or wagon are the typical methods of getting around, but they're not the fastest or most comfortable way of doing so and necessitate either camping or staying in an inn. Both offer dangers depending on how safe the landscape is. In our modern world, we tend to assume that we can go on a hike without being mauled by an animal or killed (depending on where we live), but this isn't true in a fantasy setting. Traveling over land poses risks, which come from other humans, species, monsters, animals, and possibly even plants, whether those are predatory or just poisonous.

If only a few people do have personal experience with distant cities or lands, those people might be admired. This can also cause people to lie about it. Significant ignorance or simply false information about faraway places could be prevalent in society. This can mean that word-of-mouth and rumor predominate. It can also mean that those who officially travel in some capacity, whether sanctioned by the government or knights errant, are looked to for news of the outside world. This, in turn, could lead to "street criers" hanging out near the city gates, collecting information from incoming travelers, and then going to the town square to disseminate that at specific times, like morning or evening, when people are drawing water from a central well.

In volume two, we covered calculating travel distances and times, but here we're looking at the impact on culture. In a fantasy setting, many roads and paths are dirt—mud when it rains—more so in a village, less so in a town or city. The likelihood of muddy feet can impact footwear, dress hems, and pants cuffs in an entire region if rain is common; details of where steady rain is likely is part of *Creating Places (The Art of World Building, #2)*. This, in turn, can impact culture, such as people staying indoors during the rainy season. Perhaps going barefoot becomes common and it is part of culture to wash one's feet on arrival inside somewhere, and locations are expected to provide the opportunity. The same could be done in dry climates, but now it's the removal of dust that is a concern.

Is it customary to have somewhere to stable a horse for visitors? What about a parking space for vehicles? Do people double park and is that expected or an irritation? Imagine what sorts of issues might arise with SF vehicles that can hover or outright fly. Then decide what is considered customary and courteous; the ways people react to violations are likely similar to road rage here on Earth.

PASTIMES

How people spend their free time is a cultural element we can develop. If they are out adventuring and saving the world, they may lament not enjoying their usual pastimes, or find ways to inject them into their adventuring life. Using the United States as an example, men stereotypically watch a lot of sports on TV and may attend sporting events in person. Women shop, talk about their feelings, and gossip (or so men believe). Those with dogs must walk them or take them to the park. Both might take fitness classes or enjoy exercise like swimming, jogging, or biking, to name a few. Some people enjoy cooking while others enjoy eating out and can't cook a thing. There are countless activities like fishing, off-roading, or travel.

We don't necessarily need to invent pastimes for our world. Many of those just listed are universal, as are countless others. However, we can put a new spin on them. If we have a pet dragon, that presumably comes with different responsibilities than a dog. Decide what they are; this can be used on multiple worlds, with some minor variations. If hunting is a pastime and we've invented new animals, we can decide how challenging each animal is and what trophy typically results. New plants and animals may impact cooking (such as very long times at a low simmer to make something edible), but this is the sort of thing we can invent on the fly. Any plants, animals, magic, or technology that are involved in a pastime gives us leeway to decide how it influences that hobby.

It's recommended to create a handful of activities for a novel-length work, less for something shorter, more for a longer work. With a novel, one or two can be shown during a scene, such as characters hunting or playing a game of cards or dice during an important conversation. The others can be mentioned in passing; a character can lament not doing one or mock another for their hobby. Two people can look forward to doing something upon arrival at a destination known for that pastime (or not). A character can be made to feel like they don't measure up because they spend too much time on a hobby. These briefly mentioned ideas don't need long explanations about rules or anything else. Consider this example:

Kier remarked, "I can hardly wait to reach Illiandor and play valends with someone who doesn't lose within minutes." He smirked at those around him.

His companions rolled their eyes and one replied, "If you spent half as much time on swordplay as on card games, we wouldn't have to save you every other encounter."

"Right." Antar flashed a grin. "Maybe next time we'll just let you be killed and take back your winnings that way."

The captain strode in. "No time for gambling ashore boys. We've a hanging to stop!"

What may take longer is the invention of games or sports, if the details are to be shown. Smart world builders will take existing games and modify or combine them. This is easier when the existing Earth game features an animal and we're substituting one we've invented. It's differing abilities might mean new rules, especially if it has abilities that create unique advantages; we only need to decide what those are and place restrictions on whether they can be used at all, under what conditions, or how frequently. Most Earth sports involving animals feature horses, elephants, or camels, as these are the few ridable options. Some games involve animals fighting each other, but there are likely few rules in such a case because animals, by their nature, are not going to understand or obey them, unless our invented ones are smarter.

Our invented species may also have attributes that are forbidden or restricted in use. Perhaps a team can only have one elf, for example, due to their skills. Maybe dwarves aren't allowed at all because they can't compete due to height. We can just decide how the game is played (by humans) and consider the pros and cons of others and what problems their attributes cause; these problems will result in rules to deal with them. All of this applies more to sports than something like card games, as physical attributes greatly impact the former but mental ones the latter.

RITUALS, FESTIVALS, AND CEREMONIES

BIRTHDAY OBSERVANCES

Many celebrate a birthday on the day they were born, but all birthdays in a month could be officially the same day in an authoritarian regime that restricts and standardizes such events. An important religious day could affect this, especially if the god is believed to have come into existence that day; everyone is sharing a birthday with a god. We can make up other scenarios.

If we do this, people could have two birthdays: the actual day and the universal one. The former might be privately and quietly celebrated by family and friends; if the universal birthday is state sponsored, other celebrations may frowned upon. We can even use this to get our characters in trouble for celebrating their actual birthday.

There are other religious holidays that might be observed across multiple cultures, but only if that religion is prominent in all of them (think of major religions on Earth for inspiration). In a later chapter, we will look at creating religions and these events, but for each, we should decide how these impact culture. The simplest variant is that people take the day off from work to observe the holiday; a formal government, likely in SF, might sanction this so that people are paid that day. In a fantasy setting, this is less likely, as the concept of paid holidays might not exist.

HOLIDAYS

Most of us look forward to holidays because we're paid and get a day off, especially a three-day weekend. This is something that'll be on the mind of characters in similar situations. Others may know that a day is coming up and expectations need to be met for prayer or family gatherings. Even characters who are off adventuring will be aware that they're missing a holiday and loved ones might be wondering what happened to them. An exception would be when they're so busy running for their lives that they not only forget about holidays but what day of the week it is. Still, can you remember the last time a character thought about a holiday in a story? Authors tend to ignore this altogether.

Some holidays are reserved for civil rights leaders who impacted culture, a political figure like a first president, the military (especially in a military junta), or even wizards if wizardry is commonly accepted. Major wars, disasters, or first contact with an alien species (that become allies) are potential holidays. More events were discussed in *Creating Places (The Art of World Building, #2)*.

There may be several holidays, or even a season of them, that strongly impact the culture, like Thanksgiving in November through New Year's Day in the United States. Retail has turned this into a major shopping opportunity, but themed movies and decorations abound, too. Such a scenario is arguably more likely in a modern or futuristic world than in fantasy, but we can still have sales of smaller magnitude at festivals. Some cities might be known for better festivals, causing widespread travel to reach them.

Some countries may refuse to acknowledge a holiday or ceremony for ideological reasons. An authoritarian regime is unlikely to appreciate people celebrating a holiday from a democratic country even on their own time, particularly if that holiday celebrates a political figure who pushed for greater rights. Conversely, those in a democracy are unlikely to appreciate a holiday from a regime that promotes civil rights violations, even if the celebration is tolerated due to something like freedom of speech laws.

CEREMONIES

Ceremonies are often religious in nature and we can leverage a religion we've created to invent them. Some ceremonies dominate a culture for weeks, such as Ramadan in Islam, but only if that faith is widespread or even state sponsored. People may plan in advance if a pilgrimage is needed, meaning this impacts them before and even after the ceremonial period.

If people have left this culture for another land where the ceremony isn't acknowledged, they may return home for it, possibly meeting resistance to the idea. Their parents might have originated there and instilled the faith in them, though they've never returned; it's still on their minds even if their current homeland ignores the ceremony/holiday. Imagine needing to take a day of vacation for Christmas day because your country doesn't acknowledge it. Adding a small detail like this to a character's thoughts can make our world look more believable.

When inventing ceremonies, decide how widespread they are and if everyone is aware of one due to unusual prevalence. Some of us might've heard of one but know nothing about it if it's less practiced. The details of a ceremony only matter if we're going to show it, and in this case, we don't have to explain each moment. If we say anything, it's often best revealed quickly as a character's thoughts. Have them think about what each step means, such as consuming a liquid that represents a god's blood, or food that equates to their benevolence, or kneeling to show deference and humility.

FESTIVALS

Festivals can be based on holidays, ceremonies, or the reasons *those* exist, but they can also be seasonal, such as a harvest festival, a spring one, or a solstice. These need fewer explanation. Festivals are easier to create in the sense of justification, but if we have little reason for inventing one, the details of what take place can be harder to imagine. Fortunately, we can leverage Earth festivals for ideas.

Sporting contests are common, whether these are light-hearted (such as bobbing for apples) or potentially deadly, like a joust. Races are particularly rousing if our characters gain something important by winning. Food and entertainment, whether plays, singing, or other contests are bound to occur. If we're out of ideas, we can also visit a Renaissance Festival for inspiration. For those writing SF, just replace everything with modern equivalents. A race would be in space craft. Fighting against holograms might replace jousting. Games may employ technology.

FOLKLORE

Folklore can include jokes, stories, songs, and proverbs that establish and maintain collective identity with a culture; types of toys might be included, particularly if they represent a character from a legend. These are elements not taught in school, but which are picked up via word of mouth by living in the community. They aren't created by individuals with copyrights, which means we don't have to worry about the origins other than understanding what value system gave rise to one, to make it feel appropriate. The folklore must always be relevant to the group or it wouldn't exist, unless it has achieved a significance beyond its original meaning. An example would be Halloween, which shows us that holidays or events can result from folklore.

Given this, story characters who exemplify a value, and those who don't and paid the price, are good ones to create in folklore. Hansel and Gretel, Cinderella, and more teach a lesson, and in a fantasy world, they are likely to still be relevant ways of instructing the young in community values. These tales often include a simple premise and setting, one or two characters with one goal, and a villain in the way. We don't get things like backstory, and even character motivations might be missing. A character wants something, and the more universal that desire is, the less it needs explaining.

Folklore can be divided into verbal, material, and customary (i.e., behavioral) elements. And each may be present in a single manifestation of folklore, such as birthday parties where a song is sung, a material item is presented, and guests, hosts, or a person being honored perform actions like blowing out candles. We don't have to explain them, though a quick line about it is often better; meanings may be lost in more developed societies like ours or in SF, but simpler societies may remember.

Folklore must be performed because without it, an item like a birthday cake is just a cake. This is known as "framing," which is a cue to the audience that we are entering a moment of fairytale. Both performers and audiences understand that it's not intended to be real, but symbolic. This is one way that folklore is separated from witchcraft, for example, though one could be mistaken for the other. These performances are partly to remove us from daily life for a brief time and may involve going to a specific place, such as a shrine in the woods, or be done at a given time, like midnight. Verbal folklore may begin with a phrase that reveals it is folklore, like, "Once upon a time..." We can invent our own, but the audience will not recognize it and we'll need more improbable moments in the story to indicate this. For example, "In the land of mist and spice" can be a common opening, followed by, "a man with two heads" because we know that's not normal and this story isn't real.

ARCHITECTURE

If we haven't traveled to other regions or countries much, we might not think architecture is part of culture, but it can be. We take the architectural style of where we live for granted but notice it in places that look very different. In some rural regions, a wrap-around porch is very common. In towns, bright pastel colors may dominate exterior walls, or everything is bright white stucco. In still others, murals or graffiti abound. Each of these influence the impression architecture creates, and this impression may be what we're most after.

Saying construction is brooding and menacing, or quaint and homey, is more useful than using technical terms for building styles because many of us (including audiences) don't understand those terms; authors should use them sparingly if at all. Materials can be commented on, such as clay, wood, stone, and metal, because these imply sophistication, sturdiness, and overall impression, and are easy visualize. The vibe that materials impart can influence how we feel about a place.

A log cabin with a thatched roof, or one made of bamboo, gives a very different impression than a steel and glass building. In between are buildings made of stone, tiles, and synthetic materials. The hue of these contributes to the impression of a location as drab or colorful, but this becomes cultural when such a style is not just in architecture but clothing and more.

Regardless of material, we can leverage the reality that villages often have narrow streets from when people only walked or rode a horse. Many roads aren't wide enough for a wagon. Anyone who's traveled to Europe has likely seen an "old town" where everything about the architecture is smaller, including the space between buildings.

One way to decide on styles is by government type. An authoritarian regime may be reflected in menacing, dark architecture that intrudes upon the psyche. A democratic one may favor bright colors and greenspaces. One that prizes order is likely to have well-designed spaces, possibly with geometrical layouts that include how gardens are structured. A poorly run or chaotic government might have housing that has sprung up wherever it could, where little planning has taken place; this could be true if war has taken a heavy toll, causing governments to rise and fall in quick succession over the past hundred years, leaving people on their own to "make do." Even when a more successful government takes over, it may leave such slums as they are, even if crime and disease run rampart there. Such places intrude on culture because people consider the safety (or lack thereof) of them. It isn't just homes that are affected, of course, but public buildings that are likely financed with taxes. Private businesses built and paid for by a company are impacted less in a fantasy setting where these companies don't exist.

Necessity often dictates culture. Those in a medieval town may dump a chamber pot out a window into the street. Is this considered standard in a culture or are they breaking a local law? The stench of many doing this could lead to people wearing a perfumed scarf over their lower faces; this becomes cultural and can outlast the original cause when society advances and people stop dumping poop in the street. Urban, suburban, and rural areas often have different styles, sometimes due to necessity or industry.

Culture affects the interior of buildings, too. In the United States, for what's called a single-family home, we expect certain rooms. On the first floor, it's the kitchen, dining area, formal dining room, formal living room, casual family room, an optional garage, and the laundry room (which might be on the second floor instead). On the second floor, we mostly expect multiple bedrooms and associated bathrooms. There may be a basement, and this could either be finished or unfinished with multiple rooms. Two stories with the optional basement is common in many areas, while single story, rambling houses appear in other areas and times. We can add expected rooms, such as ones dedicated to magic, religion, target practice, or weapons play. Rooms can also be designed with certain activities in mind but converted to another, such as a spare bedroom being used for a nursery. If our culture has a siesta, there is likely to be a room for this, or part of one, if people don't always do this in their bedroom. This room might be closer to the front of the house for not only themselves but a guest to use.

Consider whether there are species and races of different heights in the setting and whether this is considered. For example, do dwarven homes have a front door tall enough for humans, and social room, too, but father inside, where guests are rare, the doors and rooms cater only to dwarves? If this is true in a society, people will expect and reach a conclusion about a dwarf whose home is exclusively dwarven-sized. Is he anti-human, for example? Or was this the only one available, prompting him to apologize to human guests all the time? Do people talk about him being anti-human behind his back?

Something we can leverage from history is the existence of utilities such as running water, power, and appliances. These impact the cleanliness of our inhabitants and their general fitness and longevity. Technology and medicine are the primary reasons that those of us alive today live much longer than in the past. In SF, we may just assume these (and better versions) exist, but certain things may or may not in fantasy. For example, running water actually can because it doesn't depend on electricity.

WHERE TO START

The order in which we create culture isn't hugely important, with one major exception: decide on ideas and beliefs, and then a unified cultural vision early on. This doesn't have to be first, as having a few ideas of culture can inspire the vision, but try not to go too far until an idea is achieved. If we still can't decide on one, we're risking incongruity.

It's also important to create the social classes so that we know where the group for whom we're creating culture falls, since this impacts many aspects, including their formality. The rest can be done in random order, but we'll arguably get the most mileage from greetings, farewells, cloth-ing/accessories, dining, past times, and daily life. It can be wise to keep ideas we don't use for one culture but associate them with another instead. This helps set them off against each other. Or we'll use that other one in another world altogether.

CHAPTER TWO

ORGANIZATIONS

O rganizations for evil or good, like the mob, Avengers, X-men, Arthur's
Knights of the Round Table, or Robin Hood and his merry men, help us
create a dynamic setting. These groups are less formal than military ones
discussed in the next chapter, like knights, and are less structured, being
more loosely held together by common beliefs.

GROUP TYPES

FORCES FOR EVIL

Most groups arguably don't think they're evil, even if the majority of outsiders think otherwise. Even terrorist organizations seemingly believe that
they're doing good things when blowing up civilians, killing children, and
worse. Their worldview is at the heart of their machinations and is therefore
among the elements to focus on first. If we don't know what our group
wants, how can we decide what they'll do to get it?

Whether religious, social, or philosophical, evil organizations often justify their actions, and it is their behaviors that make them evil, not their beliefs. Such groups often disagree with that, however, and frequently murder
others for having different ideas, which are a threat to them and their goals.
This is one justification for killing "innocents," people who don't deserve
death. Evil groups can declare others are evil and try to destroy them. Some
such groups seemingly attract members with little conscience.

Either way, decide what the group's guiding principles are. Do they want
to spread a religion? To topple a kingdom whose way of life offends them?

To get revenge in the name of a fallen idol or cause they appreciated? How far are they willing to go to get it? Did the group start off less "evil" but due to circumstances we'll name, they've lost their way and become something more abhorrent? Are they justifying a means to an end, such as killing civilians because they're in the way?

Forces for Good

An informal group as a force for good is unusual on Earth because we have police and organizations like the United Nations to oppose wrongdoers. This is different in fantasy because police forces aren't as formidable as they are on modern Earth. Evil organizations may also engage in activities outside of a jurisdiction, which is far worse in SF, where it can extend planet-wide and beyond. A formal group that is bound to a sovereign power may lose the right to counter the evil group's actions outside the power's jurisdiction. But a force for good can be devoted to doing that very thing.

A good group can have a mix of high-minded and realistic reasons for existing, such as upholding certain virtues and stopping the spread of nefarious regimes that will impact them or loved ones. The ideas can be inspired by religion, philosophical justifications, and a sense of fairness. These people are virtuous but grounded in humility, compassion, and other positive traits that inhibit a slide into being an evil organization dominated by idealism, lack of reality, and selfishness.

We'll need to decide what guides this group and if it's written down or just an understanding. The latter gives way to misunderstanding and assumptions, which might result in bylaws being written. Perhaps there's an oath people repeat at meetings, to remind of what they stand for. These groups will also try to forge a positive relationship with not only those who can help them, like city leaders, but with the public whom they help and protect. Reputation is important and can be aided by charitable actions. Fantasize about what sort of group you'd like to form yourself if you were a powerful wizard or knight with equally strong friends who agreed with your world view. Tired of certain kinds of atrocities in life? What would you do about it?

Common Traits

Whether evil or good, group members have certain things in common. Invent a symbol or traditional colors, and whether anything is given upon joining, such as a tattoo or medallion. These can cause quick reactions among characters and are a fast way to reveal who someone is.

GOALS

Every group wants something. Knowing their objective is crucial. We must also define the current state of their goals, so we know how far or close they are and how they feel about this.

OBJECT CONTROL

Sometimes a group's goal is an object they can hold in their hand, like treasure or a device, but only a few may be able to literally do so. If the object has religious or supernatural significance, then obtaining, recovering, or protecting it can be a goal, but additional motives may apply.

What will the group do once the coveted item is obtained? Use it for something or just possess it? The latter isn't particularly interesting. Money is typically used to buy other things, but members could have different plans for their share of the loot, assuming it's not seen as belonging to the group. If it's divvied up, the group may disband unless a desire for more keeps them together. If it's an item to only possess and not use, why will the group stay together after getting it? They might need other reasons, such as undertaking missions. This is true of a good group that wants to confiscate dangerous items and prevent usage by evil groups.

LAND POSSESSION

Land can be great appeal for security, strategy, or to control assets like a mine. A religion's followers may seek to control and preserve a holy site or use it to interact with a god; a real-life example is the Middle East conflict over Jerusalem. Using territory as a group's goals is problematic because disputes over land are typically between sovereign powers or settlements, not groups that, by their nature, might be more mobile. The solution is to have them working to benefit a power through that acquisition. They can be officially sanctioned (or not) by that power, able to perform acts the power can't do. A group can also deliberately destroy diplomacy to cause war.

POWER

While power can be a group's goal, it's usually a means to an end. It's a cliché of poor storytelling for a villain (or his henchmen) to want nothing more. It makes them cartoonish. Make sure there's a more complex goal than this, as power only works in the short-term, such as ensuring the survival of the group or individuals within it.

UPHOLDING IDEAS

Many groups have philosophical or religious reasons for existing. They want to uphold the virtues they've learned. This can mean either promoting those ideas or destroying those who defy them. Intolerance is a staple of humanity; an invented species can be different, which can allow us to comment on this aspect of humans. Whether good or evil, such groups and their members are often willing to risk their lives for the cause.

We may need gods and religions for this, but general-outlook philosophies can work. Examples of the latter can include believing in equal rights (for all genders, races, and more), abolishing slavery, spreading democracy, and ending the abuse by aristocracies. We may have philosophers like Plato or Socrates who have imagined ideal states that inspire groups. The advantage of using gods as inspiration is that each will have a vision their followers support and which can become the basis of multiple groups, which is easy with a pantheon where the gods are divided by their chief areas of concern. But consider how many religions arose on Earth, with a single god.

ENEMIES AND FRIENDS

Whether individuals, species, kingdoms, or other groups, the one we're inventing will have friends and enemies. We might need to draft several groups before deciding their relationships, but whenever we're deciding what they support, think of who that might upset into forming an opposition group. Sometimes one group will indeed inspire another's formation and, if the second destroys the first, it may no longer have a reason for being unless it has found more purpose elsewhere. Creating multiple reasons for a group's continued existence is wise as organizations have more usefulness to us and seem more well-rounded than focusing on the destruction of another group.

An organization with more than one purpose can result in multiple friends and enemies. At times, a hostile group might even become an ally, which makes for dynamic settings. Doing this requires having a clear understanding of the group's goals, passions, and beliefs. A list of gripes about the misdeed of others, and actions to right those wrongs, or uphold positive ideas, will suggest people who oppose or support them. Do they thwart or respect authority of nations and other groups? What does the average person in their region think of them? Other regions? Are they a symbol of something? Are they feared or respected? Much of this is about their history.

POWER STRUCTURE

Knowing how the group operates has much to do with the power structure. World builders and audiences gain much from having clarity about this. While some groups have a leader, others are run by an inner circle and others might have member votes. Nevertheless, a single leader, even a figurehead, can be useful, speak for the group, and do things like break a tie. Power struggles within an inner circle can be useful for tension; they may arise from the lack of formal structure we'd see in the military.

Power comes in many forms, such as physical or supernatural might. This may be more prized in evil organizations, a leader possibly chosen by killing a previous one. That might cause fear that keeps people in line in an evil group, but likely causing dissention in a good group, where intellect might be more favored.

Wealth can be power when properties are acquired, such as a group's headquarters. For the rich, this can confer power over the group unless it can choose another HQ. Money can also purchase supplies, whether weapons, armor, transportation, or basic necessities. It can buy spies and corrupt officials. But others might covet it, putting the individual at risk. Some groups won't respect it. And wealth can be lost.

Connections and influence are impossible to steal and difficult to acquire. Influencing those outside the group, such as political leaders, tends to be for older people, who've had time to forge relationships over decades. Within the group, anyone could forge influential connections, making others see them as a leader, despite not being an official one.

Mental acuity can be prized in leaders, especially in good organizations, where leaders rely on input, showing respect for those they disagree with and giving kudos when ideas help, which increases loyalty. They can become the leader even if someone else has more money, connections, or physical strength. This power cannot easily be taken from them. They conceive great plans that further the group's goals and foresee flaws in others' plans.

Aside from leadership roles, the rest of the group may have no defined structure beyond an inner circle, who earn that place through the influences just discussed. New recruits may be treated differently, but once accepted beyond a probationary period, the new individuals may be on their own to form allies within the organization. Unless we have a specific reason for being detailed with group structure, such as writing a story about someone's time joining a group, participating, and eventually departing, a non-structured group is a good choice.

HISTORY

While the group can be new, one with a history creates depth. This should include the formation story of how, why and where the group originated, and what actions they've attempted to do, why, and the result, both for themselves and those impacted by their existence and efforts.

ORIGINS

A group's location will influence their origins. We can use any regional conflicts to inspire their rise. If two sovereign powers are at war, for example, we should know what each wants, why, and the tactics used to pursue it. Do they force people to serve in the military? Do they commit war crimes? Are they harming people and livelihoods? Is injustice being forced on the population? Are riches (like access to a mine) being withheld by one power to the detriment of the other? Any of these and others can inspire opposition that leads multiple individuals to ban together and form an organization.

Another option is a weak king who lets forces overrun his kingdom, or an evil warlord threatening destruction, or a supernatural phenomenon that must be contained. These are events that thrust people into action, and when they realize others want to take the same actions, the group arises. War might trigger groups' creation in other ways; for example, if it ends, leaving something the group considers unfinished business. For example, maybe the "evil" army is defeated, but many groups that comprised it are still extant. This group will go on a search and destroy mission, the first of many. Others might admire this and join the group.

The group may arise from a shared philosophy about what is right and wrong in the world, whether that's inspired by specific events or not. Each individual will largely agree with the group's outlook. Such a group may form in peaceful times, where social injustice is in their sights to correct. The group may exist informally before an event triggers them into becoming a more serious organization.

ACTIONS

No history is complete without attempts, successful or not, to achieve the group's goals. Create a half dozen attempts with a mixture of failure and success. Have they fought in battles with others? Just on their own? What famous incidents are attributed to them or foiled by them? Both failure and success should result in the death of members, only a few of whom might be noteworthy. Others outside the group will also have died, including members and leaders of opposing groups, warriors, wizards, and civilians. The latter may be inspired to join this group's enemies. All will have left a mark on someone, somewhere. Lives might also be saved and cause similar recruitment or supporters.

Some actions may only partially get their goal, which allows us to grant some success without eliminating the need for their continued existence (if that goal makes them disband). For example, an organization dedicated to keeping powerful magic items out of the wrong hands might perpetually be recovering and storing them. If there's a wizard cabal that keeps causing trouble, this can cause multiple events. If we want the group gone, killing them is one way, but a more peaceful end means their goal might've been realized, but sometimes a new group arises from the ashes of the old.

IN AND OUT

Once the group exists, we should decide the circumstances under which it accepts or rejects members. The larger the role this group plays in our story, the more we benefit from this. A character from one will be aware of possibly being ejected for a failure while another may be determined to prove he's worthy to have been accepted. A more established character may be involved in the inner circle or aspire to be. All of this helps us create depth.

JOINING

Accomplishing deeds in line with the group's goals may prompt an invitation to join, with possibly repeated recruitment attempts. The organization will need a sales pitch, so decide what benefits they're offering someone. Is it safety (in numbers), intel, prestige, allies, or better rates of success? Some are material concerns, but there might also be philosophical benefits of a world view strengthened by joining with others of like mind. Is there a problem someone seeks to alleviate by joining? This can be lack of supplies, high failure rate of their own missions, great danger, or anything that being alone in a pursuit exposes oneself to. We'll have people joining an organization for different reasons, which can also create internal conflict when some are more interested in one aspect than another. We can imagine someone stating that they're here only for the money while another character scorns them for not supporting the group's grand vision more.

Existing members can recommend new members, though this may require having their own membership settled; a new member's recommendation may not carry much weight. This provides an opportunity for conflict if the suggested person behaves poorly and casts a bad light on the guy who vouched for him.

What causes someone to be accepted or rejected? Informal groups often don't have formal tests, so someone may join on probation of a certain length or number of missions. They may be assigned to work with one or more people who have responsibility for them, any of them able to give a recommendation to the group's leaders about membership. During that time, it's likely that the organization's secrets will remain unknown to this person, and even upon acceptance, only the inner circle may know certain things.

What happens if candidacy is rejected? This may depend on how quickly this happens and whether the group is benevolent or nefarious. We can see an evil organization killing a failed recruit or sending them on a suicide mission; in the latter case, what if they survive? They may be forced to commit serious crimes and failure results in expulsion or death. A good organization is more likely to let someone walk away peacefully and have tests that amount to matters of character, judgment, and ability to support the group, including following orders. A group intending to physically fight might require skills tests. A supernatural group might need a display of talents.

LEAVING

People will leave an organization for many reasons that we don't need to invent here. We only need to decide how the group handles departures.

For evil ones, we can make this simple in that exiting means death. This might be a well-kept secret or one visibly demonstrated. This is an easy way to characterize them early in a story, such as showing a minor character earning this fate. It can shed light on why a more important character intends to disappear instead, possibly faking their death. Or maybe the important character tries to kill everyone else in the group, knowing they'll be hunted forever if they don't. We can also have their mind erased or a similar act that safeguards the group's secrets.

With good organizations, such tactics are highly unlikely. Members are free to depart at any time, though they may incur a debt that needs repayment or which the group could waive. If they're truly valuable, they may be talked into a temporary departure, but informal groups likely aren't insisting that someone's decision is irreversible.

Regardless of group type, a member may not have been important enough to warrant much concern about their exit. An inner circle member is more likely to face scrutiny. This could include inquiries into their motivation. Loss of life or limbs is a risk to many groups. A member can become disillusioned with the group's stated goals, or exhibit behavior that goes against it. A change in leadership can result in unwanted changes, especially if it's a coup. During these, factions might appear, leading to infighting and death. These are some issues to consider when creating a history.

WHERE TO START

The first decision with organizations is to determine whether most people view them as basically good or evil. We should decide how we intend to use them, such as being allies or foes of our main characters. Are they on the same side of a conflict but with different value systems, or in genuine opposition? Decide their goals and the tactics used to achieve them, as this determines reputation. We can then envision past actions and start creating the history, including an inception point. The power structure and how members join and exit can come later, as can a decision about who else is their friend or enemy. Be sure to decide on a symbol and use other considerations found in appendix two.

CHAPTER THREE

ARMED FORCES

M ilitary groups like knights, cavalry, and star fighters will exist in our setting whether we invent and mention them or not. However, not creating these is a significant oversight. Some will become an army, navy, or air force (or space force), each possibly comprised of multiple specialty groups. We might also need to create them for other species who have very different ideas. World builders often resort to generic groups that are not well-defined, even if characters from those groups are major characters.

Well-crafted groups can add believable tension and detail to a setting and achieving this is the goal of this chapter. As with many subjects, it's possible to invent far more than we can realistically use, but as with character back story, inventing some items helps us portray the world. This chapter includes a set of items to develop, but world builders are encouraged to decide on which aspects to invent, based on story needs or preference.

We must decide what type of group we're defining. Is this the navy, air force, or army, for example? We can ask what purpose they serve, but the military is typically for both protection and conquest, as needed. Once we know which type we're creating, this will help make other decisions discussed in this chapter.

Virtually all armed forces work for a sovereign power. This means that, in a story with two different kingdoms, for example, we might need two armies; this is needed if we'll use characters from either and those details inform our plot or characterizations. This could become overwhelming to invent, so we must be realistic and only create what we need.

The type of government will impact much about this group. An oppressive one will provide a strict environment, including mandatory service, while another might have far more freedom, at least when people are off duty. It's a mistake to create a military group without understanding the government that controls them. *Creating Places (The Art of World Building, #2)*, went into details on many government types and it's recommended to become familiar with them and their likely impact on all aspects of life.

LOCATION

Specific relations with settlements and sovereign powers, or even regions of land, can be determined in the world building files devoted to those. Large forces like an army are comprised of people throughout a power, but they'll have military bases in specific communities. This will be strategic locations and often large population centers, so if we've created a map or otherwise decided where major settlements are, this decision can be made for us.

Smaller forces like a knighthood may exist anywhere there's a need, including in or near smaller settlements. It is these that we may be able to decide on a case-by-case basis for which communities have them in quantities beyond the lone person. Assess the threats posed by animals, monsters, and species found in each land feature (such as mountains and forests) near a settlement; armed forces are designed to protect against such threats.

TERRAIN

Creating Places (The Art of World Building, #2) taught about the different varieties of terrain: open land, forests, hills, mountains, deserts, and swamps/jungles. Few military groups operate equally well over these terrains, and not at all in some. This helps us decide how commonly encountered they are. Terrain also impacts their transportation choices. For your files, state what types of terrain they're found in or what sort of encumbrance they experience if traveling there, such as being slowed down or having to go around.

For example, horsemen would be stopped by a jungle, but a savannah would be more like open land; the difference is underbrush. We don't need to note how they fare in every forest type. Instead, state that underbrush and low branches slow them and that the latter can also impede the use of certain weapons like the sword, leading them to use shorter blades. We may need to remind ourselves of their reduced effectiveness in certain conditions so we can more realistically portray and use them. They may become known for one, which may have led to their development. Horsemen excel at open land, whereas a force that rides dragons or large birds might specialize in mountains because they can fly over the terrain that hampers others.

Multiple species help us because each may be helped or hindered by different terrain. Imagine our armed forces reaching a jungle and stopping because the humans on their horses can't continue, which prompts a recruitment effort seeking out members of a species which can. This is unlikely to be a secret, leading to open acknowledgement of the need and role these species fill. Maybe every squadron of these horseman is expected or required to have them.

These terrain decisions help us determine where the armed forces are found. A city surrounded by jungle won't have a cavalry at all, but one with open plains in every direction certainly will. A mixed-terrain settlement will utilize the most appropriate group based on circumstance. This can also lead the population to think more highly of one group than another, namely the one seen as more responsible for protecting them. That can cause tensions and resentment among rival military groups. All of this adds believability and layering to our setting. It's easy to create a character who belongs to one group and has an attitude about anyone from the other group. The amount of each territory within their jurisdiction aids the decision.

SPECIAL SITES

Our military group may have special sites, such as training facilities with unique instruction in weapons or even withstanding types of pain. Members may be sent to areas where a foe they're expected to specialize in are found in high numbers to gain practical skill fighting. Giving these places names, like "The Citadel" or "The Dark Abyss" adds mystique. Characters can remark on their time spent there, inspiring audience curiosity. More mundane training centers will exist, typically at major settlements. The best teachers can impact the most people there.

If they are religious or highly ceremonial, sacred places that come under threat can upset the military group or cause periodic pilgrimages. Destroyed or damaged places help us create history even if we don't comment much or at all on what happened. Who doesn't love a ruined or abandoned site? Traditions can impact reverence and trigger long-standing animosity toward whatever creatures or sovereign power was responsible. Sites of great battles can also achieve relevance. We're looking to invent some lore for our group.

Are there places where they store weapons, defenses, ships, or other equipment? Some of this could be ordinary, some unique or magical and rare, and others acquired in battles, as gifts, or from deceased members. All may be guarded, physically, magically, or technologically. The more valuable, the less likely they openly admit to the locations or types of defenses.

We may need to solve practical problems for our group with special sites. For example, a group which specializes in riding flying animals embarks on a journey too long for a single flight, requiring an overnight stay. Maybe they've planned ahead and built a series of towers in the wilderness, each inaccessible from the ground. This aids with keeping the riders (and animals) safe while asleep. Try to think of realistic problems and their solutions.

TRANSPORTATION

In this section, we look at what the military group provides or is expected of members. They may not provide steeds, machines, or training in anything, though that doesn't mean our members cannot acquire and use them. How members of this military group get around might not seem important, but it can generate decisions. This is especially true in fantasy, where riding animals on the ground or in the air can impact where this military group can operate and how they're used for scouting or in battle. In SF, this aspect of transportation might matter less if everyone is getting around on flying craft. Everyone must disembark eventually, but in such cases, we typically see people on foot or in another vehicle. When was the last time you saw someone exit a spaceship on a horse, for example? This could be plausible, however, if they know the terrain they'll find and think this is superior; perhaps machines scare local people or wildlife, or cause harm they wish to avoid.

WALKING

Walking, running, or even rolling along the ground (for our ball-shaped humanoids, should they exist) requires little invention. However, the number of legs impacts both speed and endurance. For anything humanoid, we can decide they're not much different from us unless we're altering a characteristic by at least 10%. Maybe they can reach somewhere in 9 or 11 hours instead of our 10, or travel 9 or 11 miles or kilometers in a given time frame instead of 10. For anything with four or more legs, we should base its capabilities partly on a similar animal, so if the species is essentially a large feline, base its speed and endurance on lions, tigers, and similar cats. Quick research will turn up numbers, which we can modify. The goal is believability. Reasons they use their own locomotion include terrain that inhibits other options, they only operate within a settlement, or a lack of alternatives. The latter may mean not enough horses or equipment (like saddles) to equip them, for example.

RIDING ANIMALS

Especially in fantasy, riding animals is an option that facilitates speed of scouting, spreading information, and maneuvers, the latter being especially advantageous in combat against unmounted forces. This is so decisive that wars have been won this way. Riding animals may be expected if the military group operates outside a settlement's walls; it speeds travel, scouting, and other acts in emergencies. However, terrain may inhibit this, from trees to steep, rocky inclines; specialized groups might be needed and operate primarily by foot.

Think about why we're inventing this group. If their role is to protect a settlement, they'll bear resemblance to cavalry or knights and we can leverage these. If they're messengers or patrollers who must be able to fight their way out of trouble, then they'll act alone or in small groups and require self-sufficiency and light encumbrance; they'll have a known response to encountered trouble, such as calling for reinforcements that will take the form of more serious military might. If creating knights or cavalry, they fight from horseback (or a similar animal) in an organized manner. The existence of both groups is horse-centric, but other military groups may mostly use the same animals for transportation or hauling supplies. In these cases, decide how prevalent the riding skill is and what degree of mastery is expected.

A flying animal poses a similar problem as a ground-based one: encumbrance. Loading them down with supplies, plus our rider, limits speed, endurance, and maneuverability, all placing the rider at increased risk of defeat by opposing forces. If problems with that are avoided, the great advantages are speed, perspective from above, escape from all land-based threats (unless flying low), and the ability to bypass difficult terrain.

Any military group typically furnishes animals that are required, but if not required, members may still be expected to have a fundamental skill. Consider a town guard that operates primarily on foot, but which occasionally needs to guide riders through town, or escort them to somewhere out of town. Would their leaders want the limitation of knowing some of their guards can't ride a horse? Probably not. Decide which animals they're expected to master and to what level; basic proficiency is the bare minimum. Perhaps they can ride but not fight particularly well from atop this animal.

RIDING MACHINERY

Whether cars, motorcycles, tanks, planes, space craft and more, SF worlds are more prone to ridden machinery than fantasy, where it is mostly wagons that might be used to haul supplies. We can invent machines, including their pros and cons. The limits we create for a machine can give us ideas for other machines that were developed to compensate for that weakness. Variety makes settings more believable and creates chances for the characters to settle for less than ideal equipment, with consequences we control. As with other transportation that can be used for making war, decide what vehicles are typically available to members of this armed forces, what they're trained in and to what degree, and what they are given and expected to have.

THEIR WEAPONS

Military groups and their members are often known for their weapons, skill using them, or both. A distinctive choice makes them more memorable and entertaining. Think of the light sabers Jedi wield in *Star Wars*, or the phasers from *Star Trek*. There are special weapons in fantasy, too, though seldom by an entire military, presumably due to manufacturing limitations, but we don't have to abide by that. And weapons don't have to be spectacular to be associated with the military.

Do they all have a two-handed sword because they specialize in fighting something like giants? If they're archers, we can decide whether bows are always made the same way, using wood from one type of tree or another. It sounds better when we've invented the tree and can write something like, "Kier lowered his solanaen bow as the loosed arrow slammed into his nemesis." With repetition, naming the type of material helps associate it with a mythic quality. Audiences begin to wonder why we mention it and how such an item is special, even if it's really nothing.

At a minimum, we should decide what weapons are required and bestowed by the military (and replaced by it if broken or lost in the line of duty). On Earth, members were sometimes required to supply their own weapons and armor; not having them would prevent inclusion.

We can also determine their preferred weapons, such as a long bow instead of crossbow despite having proficiency in both. Do they prefer a short sword to a long sword? What weapons do they rarely use? Are there any for which they have contempt? Snobbery exists in all things and a master swordsman might find a bashing weapon crude. A sense of their outlook and missions help us determine these. If we can't decide now, return to it later when we understand this military group better.

THEIR DEFENSES

Defending against threats is a basic reason for military groups. While a settlement may have fortifications manned by this military group, what we're looking at here are their ways to protect themselves.

ARMOR

Regardless of genre, a military group typically mandates a minimum requirement for armor. When was the last time we saw a knight wearing only leather? It could happen if he's on light guard duty deep inside a well-fortified city that hasn't been attacked in a decade. Even then, his superiors would have approved this before it happens unless he's headed for disciplinary action. This sort of detail brings our world to life.

IN FANTASY

We don't have to invent armor types in fantasy. Unless adding magical properties to it, everything we need probably already exists: leather (studded or not), chain mail, plate mail, plate armor, and variations on these. Understanding the differences helps us decide what they wear, including cost, how cumbersome they are to don, fight in, or wear for extended periods.

For example, chainmail is heavy but can be donned by one person, so a character prone to solo travel might prefer this. By contrast, full plate armor generally requires help, which is one reason knights have squires. Plate mail, which can be light and easier to put on, is a compromise. Since we're talking military groups, it can be surmised that they often work with others, but perhaps not. Form an opinion about their likelihood of working alone as part of deciding that they use plate armor. Similarly, if they go many successive hours on duty, perhaps chainmail isn't their usual garb due to the fatigue.

We may want to decide that those of a given rank have superior armor; after all, commanders are more valuable. Consider the chart as an example, using army ranks to demonstrate.

Rank	Typical Armor
Private	Leather
Warrant officer	Studded leather
Lieutenant	Chain mail
Captain	Plate armor
Colonel-Generals	Plate mail

Figure 64 Armor and Rank

If you're wondering why a captain would wear the heavier plate armor and the more senior generals would only wear plate mail (arguably less protection), captains are the highest rank that's in the field and expected to fight. Plate armor is unwieldly and impractical, so there's little reason to believe a general would wear it; plate mail is easier to deal with while also conveying supremacy due to an appearance like that of plate armor. Throw in an elegant cloak or sash and the generals can look more regal.

In SF

In SF, ranged weapons like guns (regardless of what sort of projectile they fire) reduce the need for the sorts of armor we expect in fantasy. Even so, body armor does exist. The mundane Kevlar and similar materials found in real life can be used, but we can invent armor that deflects or lessens the damage of our invented SF weapons. World builders should think about protective clothing so that everyone isn't only wearing their uniform. Some range weapons will work on the principle of a projectile, meaning the force of it striking causes damage. Other weapons like a laser can cause burning wounds, so heat resistant armor is more effective. Another beamlike weapon may emit radiation, whether a known kind or something of our invention. Either way, just like real world clothing offers limited protection against radiation, we can decide that some protection is incorporated into body armor but that it has limits.

SKILLS

Our military members might be trained in hand-to-hand combat with and without weapons. Is boxing part of training or do they only brawl? Our sense of their refinement and dignity can help us decide. The kinds of missions they go on can, too. Covert work often leads to close fighting – so close that swords (and longer) aren't feasible. If such work is reserved for special forces like Marines, then perhaps the special skills are, too, with only basic fist fighting practiced elsewhere. Never being disarmed is unlikely.

There are various forms of martial arts on Earth and we can invent hybrids or our own. We'll want a new name regardless of how much we borrow from one either in philosophy or form. It's okay to describe one in such a way that people recognize what it is but realize we've changed the name, because most people won't identify it anyway and the names of many are specific to Asian countries that don't exist in our fictional world.

THE ROAD TO ENLISTING

PREREQUISITES

While most if not all military organizations will train recruits, some skill and/or aptitude is typically required before training so that less time and resources are wasted on training someone who won't be up for the job's rigors. If we've already decided the expected skillset of accepted members (or ones that have completed training), this can help us decide on the prerequisites. For example, if advanced horsemanship will be acquired during training, basic horsemanship is a prerequisite.

Some level of proficiency with various weapons is likely required, and these can be divided into broad categories: long and short bladed weapons (swords and knives), blunt force weapons, and range weapons (bows, guns). Elite groups may require more skill across a wider array of weapons. We can decide that if there are six requirements and someone only has four but shows great promise in those, that they are provisionally accepted. There are no rules except for those we invent. Some organizations will churn out elite fighters while others may only produce average warriors who are half-expected to die within two years of enlisting.

Not all prerequisites involve something physical. Knights may require noble birth. Perhaps they must show strength of character, which may either be tested or vouched for by reputable sources. There might be educational requirements or the ability to read and write certain languages. This can make characters more believable, especially if they aspire to belong to this group and must prepare for an initiation test. If they've failed once too often, maybe they cannot be considered anymore and have feelings about this, ones we can exploit. Remember that some underprivileged people might try to join the military precisely to gain access to things they can't otherwise acquire, such as food, lodging, clothing, and pay.

CHARACTERISTICS

In *Creating Life (The Art of World Building, #1)*, we looked at intelligence, wisdom, charisma, strength, constitution, agility, dexterity, and morale as traits to define for species like humans and others. While writing a description of each and how it manifests in a species is preferred, we can also assign a number from one to ten as a quick indicator of what is typical. We can do the same with the characteristics that a member of this military needs in order to be accepted or successful.

Officers will require higher mental traits, while enlisted troops, expected to do most of the fighting, need better physical ones. While deciding the latter, think about what weapons they prefer. It takes greater dexterity to use a sword or bow than a cudgel. Superior dexterity is a needed trait for skilled swordsmen, but a crushing weapon depends on strength. Knights aren't known for their agility due to wearing heavy armor, at the least, but if we're creating a group that wears less, perhaps agility is expected. Wearing heavier armor might require greater endurance, too.

For wisdom, are they skilled at battle plans, or do they make foolish mistakes? Can they learn from history, keeping and reading old plans? Do they have military and advanced training for officers in matters of running a large military? Officers must pass tests, which are designed partly for measuring intelligence, not just education.

Morale is highly prized but is not the same thing as courage. Rather, morale is partly the ability to maintain formation in the face of peril, instead of everyone running away. Militaries require this and do things like court-martial those who run, but a specialized group that doesn't operate in formations might have less regard for it (and value courage instead). Morale is a hard trait to determine beforehand, however. We can still jot down a note about their reputation for it.

While working out the details, we may be unable to decide on everything. Returning to rework items is part of the process, so do what you can and move on for now.

INITIATION TESTS

A candidate may face initiation tests to verify if those prerequisites are met. The exam also allows someone to demonstrate how good they really are at a skill. If they're already advanced, maybe they can skip some training, have a superior trainer, or be singled out for honing into a finer warrior; we can also use this to make peers resent that person. We should decide what weapons are tested and what level of skill is required for each, with some preferred over others.

Tests can also focus on how a candidate reacts to failure or challenges. Someone who whines about unfairness is likely frowned upon. Does a combatant get back up or otherwise shrug off a blow? Some of this is to be expected, but consider if a trait like unusual perseverance is required. Must members of this military stand for a day without fatigue? If so, this might be tested, but development of it might be expected during training rather than being there from the start. Imagine ways we'd use this military and its members and then concoct tests to demonstrate potential.

An example of what to write for a knighthood might be: "The minimum requirements are: demonstrated skill with the sword, average proficiency with a horse, average skill with at least one missile weapon, a willing desire to learn weapons skills, and honorable conduct at all times."

TRAINING

A military group without formal training makes for one that is easily defeated due to inconsistent skill levels among personnel. Knowing what weapons, steeds, machines, and knowledge they require helps determine what training they receive. Some basic ability to make minor repairs might be needed, especially in SF. Are they expected to know certain languages, and does that include reading and writing them? What about understanding some neighboring settlements or sovereign powers, whether allies or enemies? The latter points are almost a given for officers, but the lowest ranks can be captured and find themselves trying to escape enemy territory. We might also decide that they're expected to know or utilize whatever is handy and be generally resourceful.

Officers receive advanced training, typically, being college or something similar. We don't need to specify details but can assume it includes superior knowledge of language, societies, customs, tactics, politics, and anything else that helps them run an organization better.

We should keep all training simple unless showing a character going through the details of becoming a member. But we may want to decide how long training lasts in months or years. Base this on their expected skill level but don't get too specific unless you've researched what's likely. We might say someone can become an expert swordsman in six months when an educated audience member knows better.

Decide where training takes place. There may be cities or universities that do much of it before people are deployed. This will impact the culture of a settlement due to the number of recruits there.

FINAL TESTS

If we've done the previous work in this section, determining final testing is largely done, but we can add drama by claiming two candidates must fight to the death, for example. Maybe they must defeat a monster. Tests can be spread out over days and be an ordeal designed to test their mettle. Are these tests feared or are relatively benign? Are people tempted to cheat and can they get away with this? How strict is the governing body? In a lawful place, good oversight might exist, but a barbarian horde may allow cheating under the premise that you'd accomplish a mission no matter what must be done. Officers will have written and oral tests of knowledge.

IDENTIFIERS

The identifying marks of the military are on clothing, items, skin, buildings, and vessels. Consider the impression the group wants to make. Some example options are listed and grouped to create a brand:
- Noble, proud, strong
- Bold, intimidating, forceful
- Elite, precise, elegant
- Covert, deadly, efficient

COLORS

Choosing colors for our military group can be challenging. It is therefore best to go with no explanation or with something obvious, like silver for steel if favoring blades. Black suggests stealth and nighttime operations, or those in space. Red is obviously for blood. Gold, silver, and bronze can suggest wealth and elegance. A good source of ideas is to research flags of Earth countries and find the explanation for the colors, then leverage these. Rationalizations only matter if someone's really going to care about the color choice; few in our audience will. However, military members will be taught the significance and can think about this during a scene.

SYMBOLS

Armed forces both protect and conquer. A symbol can inspire ferocity from its members or a willingness to sacrifice themselves for an ideal. They can intimidate opponents and impact their morale. Sometimes it takes a reputation to go with these symbols. Consider their sophistication. Expert swordsmen have more refinement than those who bash people; their symbol can reflect a fighting style. Education matters, too; if ordinary people can join and find a calling, perhaps a symbol reflects a universal appeal, whereas a highly trained group might want to appear elite.

Animals and weapons of war (especially one that the group is known to use) are frequent symbols. If we've invented animals, we can leverage their reputation. Using Earth examples, what comes to mind for a lion, snake, eagle, or horse? Symbols that require explanation are less powerful, so if we're using an animal the audience hasn't seen, show it and establish its reputation before revealing it's part of a symbol.

SYMBOLS OF ACCEPTANCE

Medals, pins, clothing, armor, weapons, and transportation can also show that someone is a member of this military group. However, the purpose of medals and pins are often to denote rank, whereas clothing signifies membership. A uniform is often head-to-toe, but in fantasy, it may be less comprehensive. We sometimes show them wearing their own attire but with an item like a cloak to denote service, as if uniforms don't exist, possibly due to limited manufacturing.

Militaries have requirements for armor and weapons, the style of which can reveal service, though this assumes mass production more likely to be found in SF but not fantasy. Either genre can cause symbols to be added. In fantasy, just as clothing might not be supplied, weapons or armor might not be provided for some soldiers so that they're using their own. In addition, a soldier might own something unique that they might not be allowed to use, whether it's weapons, armor, or their own steed, because uniformity is encouraged. Getting special exception can be problematic if others resent it.

For transportation, if they require something to do their job, like a highly trained animal, they may be given this. It still belongs to the military, who is responsible for its stabling and care when not in use. Do they form bonds with an animal so that it's considered theirs despite this, or are they expected to use whichever one is available? People are sometimes sentimental about ships, which have their quirks, but these almost always belong to a military, sovereign power, settlement, or wealthy privateers due to sheer cost.

THOSE WHO SERVE

MEMBERS

We should decide which species can join. Humans may comprise the majority, with others in specialized roles or in locations where their skills assist, such as elves stationed near a forest military base. But a military group for another species might work very differently, with humans a minority or not allowed. Use the world view of both the species and this military to decide if it's a good fit among them. As mentioned in *Creating Places*, joint settlements and sovereign powers can exist, implying a species melting pot and leadership is shared, which can lead to joint military groups, too. If elves revere life but a group doesn't take prisoners, preferring to kill them, we can assume elves don't join. The prerequisites may be designed to eliminate them, either for world view or physical reasons. A knighthood might require using a lance, eliminating a dwarf.

This raises an important point: not all members of the military are fighters. Those in a modern Navy on Earth are unlikely to engage in hand-to-hand combat, but in the Age of Sail, they were expected to if boarding or boarded (or on land excursions). In the case of our life-revering elves, perhaps they are the equivalent of doctors. Such details add believability to a military, where good uses can be found for species with specific traits and concerns. Isn't it good to show that the elves are there but in a typical role, and perhaps the dwarves are, too, operating artillery like catapults? They can be officers, too, as they seldom fight. There are plenty of support personnel who don't.

Consider whether members are part of the military, in what capacity and what rank they have. They might be fighters, healers, counselors, or all three. Today we're all aware that soldiers become traumatized and need psychological support, but even if our world is too barbaric for that sophisticated level of support, soldiers die, and many will desire last rites.

IMPORTANT MEMBERS

Whether they're still active, alive, or long dead (and revered or despised), notable members are figures that our characters can aspire to be like, or dread being compared to. All we need is a name, a reputation, and the deed that caused their fame, plus maybe a sense of how long ago and well-known this is. We benefit from at least one good and one bad member, one to cause pride, another to cause shame for members. It's realistic. People can simply fail to do a job, or they can do something deliberate, such as betray their fellows and run from battle. If we have a specific set of job functions this group performs, have someone fail in that, as this makes the character more memorable.

RELATIONSHIPS

Our military group has a relationship with the rest of our world and it's smart to at least quickly decide what those are like.

WITH OTHER MILITARY GROUPS

A world without rivalries is less entertaining and realistic. In any region, sovereign power, or settlement, it's possible for two or more military groups to exist and be called upon for different reasons. This can lead to resentment and more. If the knights are always given the toughest jobs of fighting the most feared creatures, it's reasonable that another group might wish for an opportunity to prove themselves capable of this task. The knights could also be condescending towards others. Our multiple groups don't have to suffer discord, of course. Perhaps they complement each other well and look forward to working together.

Bear in mind that two groups who don't get along in one location might be great comrades in another. This may mean deciding on a city-by-city basis, but as that's time consuming, we can decide on several typical relationships that happen and then just assign one of these to each settlement as needed when we're using that setting. The usual reasons for this discord or cooperation will be found in our file about the military group. In our settlement files, we'll only say which version is happening and possibly a specific incident that triggered the current (or usual) status of relations. This keeps us from repeating explanations in one settlement file after another, beyond, "They resent and bicker with each other here."

Below is not an exhaustive list of options for how they could get along, but it can give you some ideas, all of which might be true on your world in different locations, between the same two groups. These might not be mutual, or one group could be more at fault than another.

1. Mutual admiration and respect, cooperation and appreciation on joint missions, seeing themselves as collectively part of a large picture
2. They work fine together but disrespect each other privately (usually)
3. On joint missions, they contest the other's authority and are difficult to work with
4. They avoid joint missions and are known to openly sneer at each other
5. Brawls between them are common in bars
6. They sabotage each other's missions
7. They are in open conflict (for control?)

WITH SPECIES

Not every species will view our military group the same way. Clearly, knights who destroy an evil species won't get admired by their victims, but even a species that receives protection from said knights might take it for granted. Even so, we should decide what every species' typical attitudes are toward this military group as a whole and its individual members (these can be different).

We should also decide what this group officially thinks about each species, as attitudes are often shared. Sometimes an organization promotes a viewpoint that its members are indoctrinated with, whether this is good or bad. This will depend on the dominant species. Some members might disagree with that attitude but learn to keep their mouths shut, while others speak up and get themselves into trouble. To decide attitudes about each species, we can leverage the relationship they have.

Using the knights as an example, if they're always saving the dwarves in a region, they might have either contempt for dwarves or amused condescension. This might be true even if they admire and like the dwarves for other reasons. They might enjoy saving them, but they might also resent it, particularly if their friends sometimes die in the process. It's easy to imagine the less noble among them thinking that their friend would be alive if the dwarves could defend themselves. While we associate knights with good deeds and bravery, etc., that doesn't mean some of them aren't asses. But we wanted to decide what the entire military thinks, so why does this matter? Because this sort of experience can cause many to share this attitude.

A supposedly evil species that our military group is routinely defending against, or driving away from a settlement, is sure to cause a uniform attitude among the group. They likely think disparaging things, perhaps rightly so. Maybe they want to exterminate them altogether.

Another possibility is someone holding attitudes from his home organization, getting involved with soldiers from somewhere else, those who don't share this stance. Maybe a knighthood in a different region needn't rescue the nearby dwarves, who can fend off the threats facing them. When these knights air opposing views, an argument can ensue.

WITH SETTLEMENTS

Most groups will be based in a settlement they are charged with defending. Unless they're poorly performing their duties, they probably have a good relationship with the town's inhabitants. There are shops, bars/taverns, and more that cater to them, offering discounts, supplies, or social activities. We need only point out especially friendly or hostile establishments in our files. The military may get too rowdy, starting brawls, resulting in confiscated weapons upon entry. If two military groups don't get along, an establishment may cater to one and ban the other, or make them sit in designated areas. Strict militaries will have better behaved warriors, generally, at least at home, but some forces are less so. Decide what makes sense for them.

How well behaved they are in other settlements will depend on several factors, including their leadership, how they're viewed and treated, and whether that settlement is considered an ally and has its own military. If the settlements are in the same sovereign power, they may have a rivalry that falls short of physical altercations leading to death. Consider whether they've saved the other settlement in the past or failed to and earned some discontent or worse.

WITH SOVEREIGN POWERS

If our settlement exists inside a sovereign power, the military groups are associated with the power more than the city in which they're based. This is especially true if they have more than one location. Each power could have a different relationship with their knights, as well. They could be nonexistent in other places, known only by reputation. We could think that an authoritarian power is unlikely to have knights because the latter is noble and the former can be brutal, but it's not always the case. A republic could, but we most often associate them with monarchies. All of this may be true with other military groups.

WITH ANYONE ELSE

We may have created organizations as per another chapter in this book. If so, we can decide how that organization gets along with this military group. The military may be an obstacle to avoid or overcome, or allies who protect and help the organization's members. Such interweaving of our inventions makes our world stronger.

There can also be types of people who are collectively viewed a given way. In a world with magic, are there any generalizations we want to make about how wizards and this military group view each other? Are wizards included as special ranks, like the Marines? Are they forbidden? Does this military feel like wizards are often causing problems that lead them into battle, such as raising an army of the dead (or living) to conquer lands this military is charged with protecting?

These are generalizations, but take the time to mature the outlook of this military and then compare and contrast it with everything else in the setting to determine relationships. This task is one to return to often for a few minutes at a time, tweaking our decisions. Always be thinking of how to cause tension, even among allies, who might fight on the same side but bicker over minor differences in form or substance.

MILITARY UNITS

Large armed forces are organized into military units, each led by a commander. When combined, these units form larger groupings that can amount to an army, navy, or air force (or space force). The armed forces we're inventing now may not exist in such large numbers; maybe they're more of a specialty group, like the U. S. Marines, who have special training and may accompany members of larger military units. Decide which type you're creating as this determines whether you need to organize them into military units or if they accompany the units of other forces.

The following chart shows typical army units, numbers of individuals comprising each, and the rank of the usual commander. Each unit is comprised of multiple small units. For example, a platoon is composed of multiple squads. This means that a lieutenant (in charge of a platoon) has several subordinate sergeants (commanding those squads at his direction). We can alter these numbers. This can be a guide or used wholesale.

Units	Number of Soldiers	Commander
Fireteam	2-4	Corporal
Squad	5-14	Sergeant
Platoon	15-45	Lieutenant
Company	80-150	Captain/Major
Battalion	300-800	Lieutenant Colonel
Brigade	1000-5000	Colonel/Brigadier General
Division	10000-25000	Major General
Corps	30000-50000	Lieutenant General
Field Army	100000-3000000	General
Army Group	2+ field army	Field Marshal
Region	4+ army groups	Commander-in-chief

Figure 65 Army Units

The following chart shows several air force units and how many aircraft are in each and the usual commander. Regarding groups and wings, significant variations occur across countries, making it harder to generalize, but these names can be used interchangeably.

Units	Numbers	Commander
Flight	3-6 aircraft and support crew	Squadron leader
Squadron	3-4 flights	Squadron leader
Group/Wing	3-4 squadrons	Wing Commander/ Group Captain

Figure 66 Air Force Units

TROOP NUMBERS

Those wishing to write war stories can struggle to determine how many troops are in a settlement, power, or in an army facing another army. This will depend partly on things like forced military training, expectations, the level of threat in recent decades and today, and even the sort of government that exists. This allows some leeway, but a military junta is likely to have a high per-capita number of available soldiers compared to a monarchy, which might count farmers in its ranks, as opposed to trained warriors.

For perspective, the United States has almost 7 soldiers (combined military branches) per 1,000 people, or nearly 7 per 1000 capita. A city of one million can therefore produce 7,000 soldiers. It's not quite that simple, of course. Army, Navy, and Air Force bases create concentrations of personnel where those bases are located. But the soldiers may have joined the military from a broad area. Some cities or regions will contribute more or less than others, partly for cultural reasons.

We don't need to get this detailed, and we can fudge the per capita higher or lower based on our needs. This number varies considerably across Earth nations, from about 2 per 1000 capita to over 100, with many below 10. We can choose a typical per capita and assume this as a default. Then state in each settlement or sovereign power file whether these armed forces produced from here are at, below, or above the typical per capita. If we ever need a war and want troop numbers, we can add the total population of cities and towns in a power and arrive at a likely army size.

Formula: Population * Per capita = Troops
Example: 1,000,000 * .007 = 7,000

This becomes useful when determining who has the bigger army. We can change the numbers if we want Kingdom 1 or Kingdom 2 to have the larger number of troops. There are more towns and settlements on our map than we've likely drawn, so we can also raise the number upward by 10-20% for all of those unaccounted for settlements. Recent battles or famine are just two of many scenarios that could've reduced one power's available forces. Such details add believability and are arguably better than just deciding one army is bigger than the other because we said so.

RANKS

Using ranks makes our armed forces more realistic. The simplest approach is to use a standard naming convention from Earth. It's familiar and already understood (especially by those in a similar military branch here) while creating the necessary and believable structure that would likely exist. But we can also strike out on our own, carving out specific roles and their associated ranks. Renaming existing roles creates the sense of another world, but the audience won't know what we mean without some minor exposition. If we choose to rename them, it might be wise to keep track of what they're normally called for our internal world building files. Preserving the rank name lets us research more about them should we need to later.

The following chart lists ranks in order of highest to lowest and compares the titles of similar ranks across the army, navy, and air force.

Army	Navy	Air Force
Commissioned Officers		
Field marshal, or General of the army	Fleet Admiral	Marshal
General	Admiral	Air chief marshal
Lieutenant general	Vice Admiral	Air marshal
Major general	Rear Admiral	Air vice-marshal
Brigadier general	Commodore	Air commodore
Colonel	Captain	Group captain
Lieutenant colonel	Commander	Wing commander
Major	Lieutenant Commander	Squadron leader
Captain	Lieutenant	Flight lieutenant
Lieutenant (first)	Lieutenant junior grade	Flying officer
Second Lieutenant	Ensign or midshipman	Pilot officer
Officer cadet	Officer cadet	Flight cadet
Enlisted Grades		

Army	Navy	Air Force
Warrant officer or sergeant major	Warrant officer or chief petty officer	Warrant officer
Sergeant	Petty officer	Sergeant
Corporal	Leading seaman	Corporal
Private or gunner or trooper	Seaman	Airman

Figure 67 Military Comparison Ranks

Aside from those in the military (or their loved ones), most people have a limited understanding of or interest in relative ranks. Authors need to navigate this ignorance during storytelling. What the audience most needs to understand is who is higher and lower in the chain of command during a scene, not what their day-to-day responsibilities are; the audience can infer major duties from a scene involving the character carrying out some duties, such as during a battle scene. Ranks don't accomplish this because most of us don't know what someone with a given rank does. So why do we care about rank? Because soldiers refer to each other by rank in dialogue.

If we're writing a story that is heavy on the inner workings of a fictional military group we've invented, then we'll need to invest more time in working out duties. This can also be easier than researching all of these ranks and trying to determine what they do. When I've investigated this, I've often come up empty, which is why there's no chart listing every rank and its responsibilities. This also changes from country to country, meaning we have leeway to invent. Plausibility is the bar to get over; we are inventing a fictional group, not correlating it exactly to Earth military. Obviously, we don't want to call an army private a general, and we should form a sense of hierarchy, but beyond that, little is needed by most world builders.

COMMISSIONED OFFICERS VS. ENLISTED GRADES

In the previous table, ranks are divided into commissioned officers (CO) and enlisted grades. The former is appointed by a formal document issued by the head of state (the individual running government; *Creating Places (The Art of World Building, #2)* discussed heads of state in detail). The generic word "officer" typically means "commissioned officers" even though it could refer to non-commissioned officers. COs are trained in management and leadership and often have college degrees, which are required at higher levels. If such education doesn't exist in our world, we can decide that experience matters more. If they have little to no experience or practical knowledge of being in the field, they'll have trouble understanding the life of the enlisted grades they command.

By contrast, enlisted grades means any rank that is not a commissioned officer (who also outrank them). These are the bulk of any military—the fighting men and women and those who support them, such as pilots, engineers, technicians, and more. They can be promoted to higher enlisted grades and sometimes become a non-commissioned officer (NCO).

An NCO hasn't earned the commission yet, and is promoted from the enlisted grades due to experience and seniority (as opposed to being an officer from the start). They aren't paid as well, are less educated and trained, and have fewer legal responsibilities. Despite this, they are considered crucial to the military for several reasons: they're the most visible leaders (higher officers are seldom seen by most soldiers); and the senior NCOs are the main link between enlisted grades and COs. Because they rise through the ranks, they have practical experience as soldiers, as opposed to COs, who may have none. They outrank lower enlisted grades. An army sergeant is an example.

COMMANDING AND EXECUTIVE OFFICERS

Commanding and executive officers have different positions that are quickly summarized here.

A commanding officer (CO) is responsible for planning strategy and tactical moves, finances, equipment, duties, discipline, punishment (within military law), and more. Available positions are limited, with seniority determining who is promoted into an empty spot. Any unit that's expected to operate independently can have a CO but the term is generally reserved for major units like an army, regiment, and battalion; smaller units have a commander, who is an officer, but is not a "commanding officer" with the rank, pay, or responsibilities/duties of one; they are often referred to as a leader, not a commander, as in "platoon leader." As an example, a platoon leader cannot administer judicial punishment, but a CO can.

An executive officer (XO) is responsible for running a military organization and reports to the CO. By running the day-to-day activities, the XO frees the CO to concentrate on his own tasks. The XO is typically second-in-command in navies, but in other branches, they may not be in command, only overseeing administrative functions. We can change this, of course. Companies, battalions, regiments, and brigades each usually have an XO.

RANK AND ROLE

While the details of what roles a rank has can change from country to country, and in our imagined world, there are some high-level leadership positions we benefit from understanding. In other words, who leads a battalion? What's a rear admiral do? What about a wing commander?

For each military branch, the ranks and roles are listed next. By necessity, these are generalizations due to variations on Earth. Use these wholesale or as a starting point for customization. In some cases, you'll see the role repeated for two adjacent ranks, which suggests either rank could perform that role, or both individuals at once, with one subordinate to the other. Use your imagination.

Rank	Role
Commissioned Officers	
Field marshal or General of the army	5-star rank, commands a sovereign power's army, sometimes honorary or only used during wars
General	4-star rank, commands an army, highest peacetime rank
Lieutenant general	3-star rank, second-in-command (of an army corps)
Major general	2-star rank, commands a division
Brigadier general	1-star rank, commands a brigade
Colonel	Commands a brigade
Lieutenant colonel	Commands a battalion or regiment
Major	Commands a battalion
Captain	Commands a company, sometimes second-in-command of battalion, can be entry-level rank for those with advanced college degrees (doctor, lawyer, wizard?), highest rank that's still in the field (as a fighter)
Lieutenant (aka, First)	Commands a platoon, often second-in-command / deputy to a captain
Second Lieutenant	Entry-level rank for officers. College graduates can skip this rank, and even others are often in it less than a year
Officer cadet	Trainee rank
Enlisted Grades	
Warrant officer or sergeant major	Warrant officers are typically technical experts, pilots, military police, etc. Sergeant major is highest

Rank	Role
	enlisted rank
Sergeant	Commands a squad or fireteam
Corporal	Commands a squad
Private or gunner or trooper	Entry rank of 4-6 months duration (rank can be skipped if given awards). Troopers are cavalry, while gunners operate artillery

Figure 68 Army Ranks

Rank	Roles
Commissioned Officers	
Fleet Admiral	5-star rank, reserved for wartime, commands multiple fleets
Admiral	4-star rank, often the highest rank in peacetime. Commands a fleet
Vice Admiral	3-star rank, commands the vanguard of a fleet
Rear Admiral	2-star rank, the least experienced of three admirals (at the rear of a fleet)
Commodore	1-star rank, commands more than one ship at a time (flotilla or squadron of ships that is part of a fleet), temporary rank (usually a captain)
Captain	Commands the largest ships, highest rank to command a ship
Commander	Commands smaller ships like a frigate
Lieutenant Commander	May be the CO of smaller stations/ships, or XO of larger ones
Lieutenant	Senior-most junior officer rank, formally second-in-command of a ship (behind captain), multiple lieutenants on a ship used to be numbered by seniority as "first," "second," etc.
Lieutenant junior grade	May require two years of service
Ensign	Commands squadron or team. Entry-level rank for officers. Named for carrying the flag.
Officer cadet	Trainee rank
Enlisted Grades	
Warrant officer or chief petty officer	Requires passing special exams and with high scores, plus enlistment time

Rank	Roles
Petty officer	Often specialists
Leading seaman	The senior-most seaman
Seaman	Entry rank

Figure 69 Navy Ranks

Rank	Roles
Commissioned Officers	
Marshal of the air force	5-star rank, typically ceremonial (like those from the royal family) if at all (it's rare)
Air chief marshal	4-star, commander of the air force, highest rank
Air marshal	3-star rank, commander of a large formation/vanguard of fleet
Air vice-marshal	2-star rank, commands large formation/rear of fleet
Air commodore	1-star rank, commands multiple groups
Group captain	Commands a group (aka wing)
Wing commander	Commands a wing or squadron
Squadron leader	Commands a squadron or flight, most junior of senior ranks
Flight lieutenant	Manages team of airmen/specialists/NCOs, can be second-in-command of squadron
Flying officer	Applies to ground crew too
Pilot officer	Entry-level rank for officers, can be skipped for those with training
Flight cadet	Trainee rank
Enlisted Grades	
Warrant officer	Warrant officers are typically technical experts, pilots
Sergeant	Commands a squad
Corporal	Commands a squad
Airman	Entry rank

Figure 70 Air Force Ranks

HISTORY

While we don't need an extensive history on our armed forces group, some details make them realistic. We don't have to say what caused them to exist; people will assume that a need led to it. If the military group and need is quite specific, such as dealing with a type of creature with unique abilities, then we might want to decide when and how it formed. What were these creatures doing en masse, and repeatedly, that made people realize a standing force of trained warriors to deal with them would be needed? The obvious answer is threatening a settlement/power or critical resources; there's no reason to get fancy.

Decide how long ago they formed. We have three options: very recently (the last ten years), a long time ago (five hundred or more), and somewhere between. The latter is our default option when a formation period doesn't matter to us. Truly old organizations are likely widespread, with strong history, meaning they've been influential in multiple major battles and wars. They have proven their value and are held in high esteem, with numerous legendary characters along their long history. By contrast, a very new group might not have been tested even once. They may be less trusted or relied upon. No heroes exist, or maybe one, who might be considered an anomaly. If going this route, our story likely features the formation of this group, so do this when the details of a group forming are of interest to you and you can make it a good story.

We may also want to decide where they formed. This is useful when trying to decide where they've spread to since inception, how long ago, and how ingrained in society they are in different places. This allows us to create variety without much work. They will have spread out from this origin point in one or more directions. Using general population and the United States as an example, Europeans settled first on the east coast; as a result, despite hundreds of years passing, population is still denser than farther west, north in Canada, and even south – the directions people spread. A similar phenomenon can happen with a type of armed forces becoming popularized.

In worlds with flying or water-based ships, this gradual spread over the land may be supplemented with the relatively sudden appearance of these armed forces in locations far removed from locations already having them. The idea of them will have been brought with the travelers. Designate somewhere as "The birthplace of the knighthood," for example, and then decide to where they spread. If we have a file for every sovereign power or kingdom, and have used the templates provided with these books, we'll see an entry for "Armed Forces" for us to jot this down.

With the number of world building tasks before us, creating a history for a military group is one to keep brief. If we already have wars invented for the past, add a mention of their role. Some examples:

• "They entered the Battle of Evermore late due to the distance to traverse, but they turned the tide and helped ensure victory, leading to their celebration as an elite force."

• "At the Battle of Evermore, they led the vanguard and were destroyed to a man in the first assault."

• "In a position of leadership throughout, their forces controlled the pace and tactics of battle, leading to yet another victory and an increase in their reputation as masters of warfare, without whom many evil regimes would dominate the land."

We may also want to invent specific missions they undertook and whether they were successful. We need their objective, which can be stopping someone, recovering or destroying an important item, or rescuing someone. We'll also state what they overcame, such as enemy, supernatural, or science fiction forces, and the ultimate outcome. If the mission augmented or damaged their reputation, say so. Remember to focus on what you can use in your work, what makes the group more believable, or both.

FAMOUS DEEDS

Unless our military group is less than a decade old, there's a likelihood that some of its members, while on official missions or not, have been part of famous exploits. This can be admirable or not, depending on our goals. Even if we have a group, like knights, that are esteemed, we can still have them be part of an ignoble event, possibly because they made mistakes or failed, not because of nefarious intent that we don't associate with a knighthood. Such discrepancies can humanize them. Conversely, a group known for bad deeds may have helped stave off a disaster because it might've affected them, too, adding dimension.

It bears mentioning that a group considered heroic by some will be despised by others, sometimes even by the people they help. For example, jealousy of knights could lead some to think they're arrogant, causing disrespect by the people they protect. Esteem is never universal; nor is loathing. When we decide and describe their relationships with others, we can comment on these aspects of them. Create a story with thought given to how both sides view the deed. We can invent a nickname that different participants assign a character, such as "Kier the Valiant" and "Kier the Butcher of Illiandor."

LORE AND MYTHS

New groups are unlikely to have much myth behind them unless they formed as the result of a momentous occasion or achieved prominence during one. They might have been the elite force that finally killed someone who promoted great evil, for example, possibly during a prolonged war or battle. Such a deed, heard around the world or across the cosmos, can give quick mythology to a group or its members.

Older groups are more likely to have multiple instances of heroism or impact in their past. This is where having invented historical events aids us because we can decide someone from this military unit did something important in one battle or another.

Some military groups also like to create a mythology around them. It typically includes an historical person who does something that embodies a trait the group admires, such as sacrifice or courage. This is an opportunity to create a mythical figure and a deed that our present story's characters may reference as a hero or role model. We can create a 2-3 sentence blurb on what they did like this:

"At the Battle of Evermore, Kier led a band of knights to rescue the elven high priestess, but found himself surrounded by a dozen ogres. Knowing it was certain death, he ordered his men to carry the elf to safety while he remained behind, fighting to his end while his men escaped unharmed. A statue in his honor stands among others at their compound in Illiandor, and the elves improved their relations with humans in the aftermath, a tradition that continues to this day." I wrote this in about the time it took you to read it. These are easy and fun to do, while adding depth and history. These stories can be a bit off from the truth, as often happens, but unless we have reason to mention that the narrative is off, it may not warrant inventing it.

WORLD VIEW

LANGUAGES

We may have little need to specify which languages this military group can speak. Instead, we can take a predictable but believable route and decide they know enough about the language of any nearby species that they must communicate with regularly in the performance of their job. This will change from sovereign power to sovereign power, even city to city. It's a fast decision that makes sense and gets the job done. It provides flexibility to decide on a more case-by-case basis that they don't live up to this somewhere, or are particularly fluent in a language somewhere else. We can leave a note about this in our files and be done with this.

We may also want to specify that they're expected to know, and be trained in, the languages of species with whom they have frequent interaction. We'll need to decide if this is only speaking it or also reading and writing. In SF, a universal translator may negate the necessity of this learning, while a language considered universal, like "common" in fantasy, can also make this requirement unnecessary.

PLACE IN SOCIETY

How does society view this group and its members? With reverence? Fear? Suspicion? Or are they taken for granted, their protection and sacrifices hardly noticed? This will impact their place in society. Respect can result in being present at ceremonies, gifts bestowed on some occasions, and people gathering to see them leave or return. Contempt will not. Fear will cause avoidance; perhaps they can only dine in back rooms so people don't feel uncomfortable, or maybe they refuse this restriction and end up chasing away other occupants of a tavern with their presence alone. Are there shops that cater to their needs and inclinations, even if it just means having their favorite items ready? Or are such things absent altogether to avoid tempting them to enter? In many cases, unless we have a need for one extreme or another, moderation will be best, meaning there's nothing special about how they're treated or welcomed. Remember that their place in society might be slightly or even dramatically different in one settlement or sovereign power from another.

Customs Among Them

As with all customs, we want to focus on the ones we're most likely to use: greetings, farewells, and in the case of military groups, toasts, burial rituals, and pre-battle customs. Think of an expression and gesture they use upon meeting, and what physical and verbal response is expected. Farewells are typically less formal or ostentatious and an expected one is arguably more likely to be absent altogether. Such actions of familiarity, shared among only their group, strengthen the bond between them; this is useful in battle, where people die or are scarred for life, physically, mentally, and emotionally. These bonds help with morale, which we touched upon in *Creating Life*: the willingness to stand firm, together, in the face of mortal peril.

Toasts are likely to focus on body counts, performance in battle, and things like weaponry or armor withstanding the forces at work, the idea a kind of well-wishing visited upon those being toasted. Below are examples:

- May your arrows fly true
- Break heads but not blades
- A blow for Kier! (a hero)
- May Sinistria (a goddess) favor your hand
- To hell with our enemies (use an afterlife of your invention, not hell)
- May heaven bring you peace – many years from now!

Where to Start

Our first choice with creating armed forces is to decide whether it's a smaller, specialized group like the U.S. Marines or a larger force, and what kind it is: army, navy, or air/space force. This will determine where they typically operate, which will impact every subsequent decision. We should then envision what role we see them playing, particularly in a large conflict such as the world wars that are so common in speculative fiction. If our story only needs a high-level depiction of them in action, we can skimp on many details of invention, but if our characters (even minor ones) are current/former/ future members of this force and are impacted by this, we'll need more. Decide on the scope you need. Most other aspects of their invention can be done in any order.

At a minimum, we must invent their symbols, colors, and any slogans. If they wear or utilize specific armor or weapons, we'll be showing this and must decide on it. Envision their place in society as this will inform what and how they do things and how those actions are viewed by other characters; this includes working out relationships with others, at least at a high-level. We can skip a complete history if we don't need it, but an historical figure or two is recommended. Another area we can skip is how such individuals become one or creating ranks that differ in any meaningful way from the standard ones listed in this chapter.

CHAPTER FOUR

RELIGIONS

To create organized religions, we'll need our god(s) worked out in some detail (refer to Chapter 1 of *Creating Life, The Art of World Building, #1)*). Many religions focus on a single god, even if others exist, but some will worship several gods together. The techniques and considerations in this chapter apply to both. It also helps to have our species created so we can decide which ones tend to be part of which religions and even if those religions exclude one or more species, for example.

HISTORY

Major religions on Earth are thousands of years old, but minor ones are sometimes new. In either case, we don't need a detailed history, but some significant events are worth inventing. Many aspects of a religion originate from its inception. It's therefore recommended that we begin creating one at its source.

CREATION

The story of a religion's founding is crucial to how it is viewed and often what is expected of converts. A prophetic figure is an expected source. This person speaks in (or receives) the words of a god and brings those messages to people. To create this, some basic ideas are helpful:

1. Their name (previous and potentially new)

2. Their occupation before becoming a prophet – they are typically transformed by the experience
3. When it happened – a calendar may use this as a starting point
4. Where it happened – this can result in a holy site
5. How it happened – this can generate relics, symbols, and rituals

We can keep this brief, like this example: "In the year 12 A. K., the horseman Vicen rode into the Dark Peaks in what is the modern day Empire of Amarysh, emerging as the prophet Kier, Chosen Voice of the God of War, Arian, whose golden sword he pulled from a petrified Lluvien tree, whereupon he heard Arian's voice commanding him to return and form the Blades of Arian, an elite force of mounted, religious warriors." In a sentence, we have two potential symbols (the sword and a specific tree type), plus a generally holy area (the mountains) and possibly a specific location, assuming anyone can find the petrified tree.

This can result in pilgrimages at an interval of our choosing. While that can be a literal returning to a site, it can also be figurative when being literal is too challenging for many (due to distance, cost, etc.) or even impossible (the site is lost or destroyed). Religions make use of symbolic gestures. Instead of traveling 5,000 miles to Kier's petrified tree, perhaps someone would travel to and pray at a replica that is only 100 miles away, and which is said to have grown from seeds of the same tree or grove as the original. We've all heard of "guilt by association." Religions practice a kind of holiness by association.

That tree type is probably planted at other holy sites like churches or even the front yards of converts; sighting it while on missions might be seen as a sign from the deity. Maybe furniture is made from it, or a wooden practice sword. Priests might wear a wooden talisman of a sword around their neck. While on his journey into the Dark Peaks, perhaps our prophet survived on a kind of fruit found there. Eating this then becomes part of rituals. The juice from it can be a drink consumed only at holy times. The spilling of that juice can be seen as an offense.

What these ideas have in common is the finding of ordinary details and assigning them significance because they're part of our prophet's experience and story, either at the moment he became a prophet or in a subsequent moment from his life. Or death.

Decide how long this prophet lived and when he died. To create these, invent these details:

1. Did he die naturally?

2. If killed, who did it, why, how, and when?
3. How did the religion react to this?
4. What did the god do?

New religions are seldom met with affection by rulers, who want the hearts and minds of the population to be theirs rather than with a religion, which is often seen as competition. It is easy, natural, and believable that a prophet meets an untimely demise. Martyrdom also raises the prophets' importance, as dying for your beliefs is considered by many to be the ultimate sacrifice and proof that those beliefs are valid. A wise world builder kills their prophets. This can also result in holy sites (where they died), artifacts (based on what killed them), and rituals to commemorate the occasion. It can also create enemies, at the time or in the future, where the people who killed the prophet are long considered enemies of the religion and its followers, leading to tensions.

DESTRUCTION

A religion can cease to exist without the end of the world happening, too. In a world without real gods that interact, all we really need is people to stop believing. This is arguably one of the reasons that religions insist people believe in the god and the religion's practices. Why would they stop believing? A foretold event not happening is one reason; smart religions avoid specific dates for future events for a reason. According to Church Times (UK), individuals can lose faith at any time for a number of reasons, such as when several of the following traits are found in the person:

• If other practitioners are hard to live with
• If the religion is too hard to practice
• If the teachings are too hard to understand
• If they resist submitting to authority
• If they're above average intelligence
• If they crave experience

These can happen to someone even if the gods are real, though it begs the question of whether one gets smitten for leaving the religion.

For a religion to die, we may need nothing more than a sufficient number of people abandoning it. This can happen en masse if major life events cause inner turmoil in enough people, and the religion cannot offer comfort. Rather than having an epiphany of belief, a revelation of perceived false promises occurs instead. If the religion was a state religion, meaning a sovereign power made it official, and the state collapses, the religion can vanish, too. This might be easy for world builders to implement because destroying a sovereign power is simple; see *Creating Places (The Art of World Building, #2)*. One religion can also supplant another.

In "Creating Gods" from *Creating Life (The Art of World Building, #1)*, we discussed creating end-of-world myths. Every religion will have one. That demise may not be inevitable, which could mean that worshippers can prevent this with their conduct. Or the righteous can be saved while everyone else is damned. If we've already created that myth, what we want to decide now is how this end of world scenario makes practitioners act because this can motivate devotion to religious practices, some of which might exist to bring about a positive end for adherents. If the myth comes true, that's the end of the religion, but if a specific date was given and nothing happens, that can also end the religion due to lost credibility.

Are people expected to pray at intervals for this myth? Do they avoid certain foods or behaviors thought to bring an untimely end to themselves or the world? Religions focus on daily life and its morality much more than the end of the world, so this tends to be a background idea or connotation that is only occasionally mentioned. Or the avoidance or destruction can be part of prayers and, when recited every day or week, become familiar enough that people don't worry about it much as a practical matter.

Since destruction hasn't happened yet, we don't have the advantages that creating a religion offers. There are no artifacts, for example, or holy sites. It is therefore wise to keep the behaviors inspired by the potential end of the world simple. Incorporate them into prayers and expressions. "May Armageddon never be," characters could say, to use a name from Earth.

BELIEFS

Without beliefs, religions don't exist. There's a difference between facts and beliefs. A fact is provable and accepted by those who lack a bias for ignoring it. But a belief exists in the absence of proof. If we had proof, it would be a fact, not a belief. Some might debate this, but it's relevant with religions and gods because, on Earth, most of us accept that no gods are real, with the possible exception of the one God. No one believes in Zeus. But people once did, and when they stopped, Zeus vanished. We had invented him.

This is relevant because we should answer the question as to whether the religion we're inventing is centered around a real god or an imagined one. If real, that god likely has directions he has given to the species. Or the religion is acting on its own and may have concerns about doing its deity justice, given the lack of direction. Or it may be a combination of the two. If the god is not real, none of this arises.

Using the history we've created, and the traits of the god (real or imagined), we can invent beliefs within the religion. They are typically centered on spiritual, mythological, and supernatural elements of either the deity or the religion. Here are some fundamental subjects about which to create beliefs (some may be facts if the god is real):

- Where the god originated
- What the god represents
- What the god wants of the world, his followers, and possibly his/their enemies
- How the god wants to be worshipped
- What followers must do to be accepted and remain in his good graces
- How the god rewards or punishes, and for what
- How and under what circumstances the god's power manifests in the world, including interaction with mortals and other beings

These basic ideas can result in several behaviors that come to define this religion. Religions are known for their beliefs and how its followers behave (in service of those beliefs), so this cannot be skipped while inventing one. Invent an answer for each, and much of the principal work to create a religion is done.

NAMES

A religion's name can be based on someone from its origins or a major lesson or attitude. Islam means submission. Christianity is obviously named after Jesus Christ, but the word Christ means chosen one. Buddha from Buddhism means enlightened one. We don't need to deviate from such things and can invent a word that means one of these or anything else; we may never explain it anyway. Create a word we admire and like the ring of, but ensure that a suffix can be added to create additional forms of it, like Buddhism from Buddha. Nicknames might also exist but are optional. A god of fire's religion might also be called "the burning faith." To create these, we'll need this religion well-defined. Chapter nine has many techniques for inventing names.

FOLLOWERS

BECOMING A FOLLOWER

Many religions have no requirement for becoming a follower. This is the easiest route for world builders as our work is mostly done. People can believe in a god or religion without attending church, praying, or giving outward sign of faith. Others will do some or all of these things and become part of a community that bolsters itself through shared belief, regularly seeing each other at places of worship. None of this requires much development. But we might want a religion that requires specific acts that are witnessed before someone is allowed to officially join the church. This could include:

• Donations of money, food, or possessions
• Visible adherence to requirements for dress, prayer, food/alcohol, and more
• Missionary work to spread the word
• Sacrifice (of lifestyle or killing of something, or someone)

That list is in rough order of severity, and the farther down it we go, the more this religion impacts the life of the follower, since killing people can lead to the killer's imprisonment or death. Going so far can cause the individual to feel more heavily invested in their beliefs, and this degree of devotion is one reason a religion might ask such things; not only does the believer demonstrate the strength of their faith, but the extreme act, once committed, makes the belief that much stronger. The god we're creating a religion for can suggest sensible alternatives that make these decisions easier. Consider their attributes, what you'd like to achieve with this religion, and how you will use it.

LEAVING

In religions without formal admission, departure is a choice and nothing more. But in others, one might need permission to leave the church. Members might be questioned (even tortured?) to find out why they want to go. They might be banned from entry into that religion's holy sites thereafter. If a tattoo or other permanent mark was affixed upon joining, this might be altered to make them a pariah. A more benevolent religion is more lenient, naturally, and may allow for return one day, whereas a nefarious one might condemn someone to death for merely being suspected of wanting to leave.

EXPULSION

Only religions that formally accept members are likely to expel them. The obvious reasons are failure to adhere to the teachings and behaviors mandated in that religion. Being seen with those of opposing religions, or conversing with them, or having friends, lovers, or children with them, could be considered a sin. We can invent whatever heresy makes sense for our deity, based on their attributes. The stricter the religion, the easier for this to befall someone. In the more extreme cases, the person could be put to death simply to sow fear in others, or to hide that this has occurred from outsiders (who might perceive the religion as losing its hold on people – dead men tell no tales), or simply because the deity, like a god of death, demands it.

WORSHIP

We can decide the details on how and when people worship (whether characters follow this or not). If our story doesn't need much, keep this simple. It helps to know when a priest or religious character is unavailable because they must worship somewhere at a given time, with other characters aware of this.

For location, they could use a church/mosque or shrine to worship. The former will have priests who can lead prayers. A small shrine is likely to have fewer priests, if any, and the level of formality may be lower, but shrines can be churches by another name, and their size will reflect this. A god of war might want a large, formidable structure, as a god of greed could want something ornate. We can spin this in different ways so just choose something that seems sensible for the deity.

Followers might also use their home or something in the wilderness, like a sacred grove. The latter is more likely for a nature goddess, for example, while it's a practical matter to worship from home. This can also suggest a time of day, such as morning or night. A more domineering god may be strict while a more benevolent one might not care, but this is also about the religion, and species create these, which means they might be the strict ones. We can decide that people must attend a formal worship at a given interval, such as once a week, with less formal worship expected other times.

When people pray, do they kneel or stand? If on the floor or ground, do they use a mat and what is it made of? Maybe there's a sacred kind of reed or cloth it's spun from, or it must be decorated with a symbol or color. Do people use a talisman in their prayers, like the cross or rosary beads? Things used during worship allow an easy way for enemies to defame the god, by defacing what the worshipers use, which can be as simple as stepping on it, if the bottom of the foot is considered unclean?

Some religions require fasting, which can be an interval of our choosing, such as one day a week or a period of sunrise-to-sunset for several weeks, once a year. The timing will coincide with the most holy of periods in the religion. There are advantages to the body, such as increased metabolism and improved concentration, but the reasons for religions to desire fasting is for purification of the body and, by extension, the mind and soul. The goal is often akin to seeking a god's forgiveness or a similar, humble virtue. Gods that might desire this could be those where purity or devotion seem desirable, and this can extend from food and drink to sex. Specific foods can be forbidden due to a negative association, such as that animal playing a role in a story; if the prophet was searching for his lost flock of some animal when he became a prophet (or when he died), then this can result in not only food from that animal, but fur and other products, being desired or shunned. It's possible that a god or religion could also insist on certain foods and drinks being consumed in great quantities, such as a week-long feast once a year, and smaller feasts being once a week. Sacrifice can include animal life – and that means the humanoid species, too.

Many religions have a holy text, regardless of form (book, scroll, stone tablets, iPad), but some may be oral. Illiteracy can lead many to depend on priests, which gives them more power. Religious songs like hymns will exist and if we'd like a character to sing a few lines, we'll need to compose a portion. Some songs might be in a language some characters don't understand.

HOLIDAYS

Religions can declare days or entire weeks as holy periods. Whether these are recognized by a settlement or sovereign power is another matter to be indicated in our world building files. These times will correspond to significant historical events, such as the day the prophet became one, died, or was born (or reborn). This is one reason we need history. If sacred texts or artifacts were revealed, created, developed, destroyed, or used memorably, each can be associated with a holiday. We may be developing multiple religions and can end up with a holiday every week if we're not careful. Two opposing religions can clash over a shared holiday.

Religious events can involve specific prayers on a given day(s) and at a holy site that is mobbed by crowds, which can cause problems, from lack of adequate food and shelter to stampedes and accidental death. A largescale pilgrimage is likely only once a year. A commemorative event like this is based on a historical one. Leverage the history we've invented.

LOCATIONS

Not much is needed to determine the location preferences of religions, as most want to be a central point of life and be present if not dominant in settlements everywhere. We can assume they prefer having a church in each. What we'll need to work out is where they are accepted, adored, despised, banned, and just tolerated. This is not a single decision for our religion template, found in the appendix, but in each settlement and sovereign power file for our world. The reason is that this will change from location to location.

What we *can* decide here is whether they have special sites. These are places where a significant act occurred. Many will have the equivalent of a small shrine or at least statue to note the location, which might be remote and unguarded; they might have supernatural or technological elements to protect these sites from vandalism. Churches can acquire mythic status due to age, rarity, uniqueness, or treasured artifacts or remains there (such as bodies of saints). Such places are easy to invent because we can state, with little justification or explanation, that it's the oldest place, or the only one with something, or lots of saints are buried there.

IDENTIFIERS

COLORS

Color can be used to indicate mood and state of mind, both of which religions hope to influence. Some Earth religions believe that achieving an enlightened state is expressed using a color for wardrobe, buildings, and decorations. This could mean that someone is expected to wear those colors at ceremonies or significant events like marriage or a milestone. Priests of a lower rank might be denied white, which is the most enlightened state because it represents all colors; a rainbow can carry the same significance.

We can put any plausible spin on a color, making it seem good or bad. For example, red is often associated with passion, sensuality, and blood. Another association would be purity (Hinduism). Most of these are good, but while blood keeps us alive, we tend to ignore this unless it's spilled, which is bad. Yellow can be associated with fire, which is good unless it's out of control, but others associate it with happiness. Blue is considered cool and soothing, but some religions find it brave and manly instead. Make it believable and our decision is taken as truth for our inhabitants.

SYMBOLS

All religions have at least one revered symbol. To create this, use an attribute of the god, a prophet, or a story involving them, their behavior, or the actions of the most prominent followers from the religion's earliest days. The average person, not a skilled artist, should be capable of drawing this symbol, which needs to be simple.

Obvious examples of attributes include a depiction of the sun for the sun goddess, a lightning bolt for a storm god, or a skull for the deity of death. We can be more creative, but expected icons are powerful and easy to remember. Practitioners want strength, clarity, and confidence, not confusion, wondering, and trying to decipher meaning. As world builders, we have other opportunities to be creative. If the god uses an item, like Thor's hammer or Poseidon's trident, these are easy choices, but a god might lead multiple religions, so if one is already using a symbol like Thor's hammer, another is less likely to do so, or at least with a twist on it.

CLERGY

Some religions accept anyone as potential priests while others might have strict requirements. Prerequisites could include being beautiful, a virgin, or having taken a life. Some professions might be desired, like warriors, while others are forbidden. The ability to read and write is likely mandatory if the religion uses holy texts, but not if they don't exist. Some religions might require an experience like an out-of-body one, or a demonstration of the ability to communicate with the divine. Perhaps a priest must reach out to a god and receive reciprocal contact, implying that the deity has chosen them to serve. Someone might need to heal with their touch. Consider what role you'd like priests to play in the story and don't give them more demanding requirements than is necessary; if they don't need to heal, for example, then don't make that required.

A religion must typically accept a priest into it. Imagine a Catholic person declaring themselves a priest without the blessing of the church. Such a person won't be allowed to do sermons or other behaviors in a holy location and might be shunned or even imprisoned, but very informal religions can exist, with someone declaring themselves a priest. In remote areas, this can happen, and if a sovereign power's people arrive, their formal religion might declare that person a fraud. We don't need to work out how a priest gets accepted unless the detail matters, but a governing body will interview and investigate the person. A candidate may be accepted on probation.

Once accepted, most will undergo training that we don't need to develop unless featuring this in our tale. Much of it will involve administrative functions or theological interpretations that this religion teaches about a holy text, to ensure a consistent message from priests. Most religions are a bureaucracy and people start at the bottom and work their way up, meeting new requirements and gaining approval to advance. Keep it simple:

• Someone died or was transferred, and a position opened up, and they're promoted
• They reached a service requirement, such as two years in a previous role
• They performed a deed (on purpose or not) that warrants recognition/promotion

Are all genders and species treated equally as either clergy or practitioners? Are some not accepted at all, or with a reduced role? A female goddess might turn the tables and insist that males cannot attain higher positions in the priesthood. Adding this detail can cause a reputation among that religion, its followers, and those who dislike it. If a religion condemns us as bad for gender, sexuality, race, or anything else that we feel is not a choice, we're likely to disrespect the faith. Decide if your characters can benefit from the tension this adds.

Important Members

A religion may have saints, prophets, and other religious leaders who impacted the faith, sometimes negatively with a betrayal of an oath or the god and teachings. Perhaps they went too far in pushing an agenda and either gods or species turned on them. They could also have inspired brutal administration of policies that result in harsh treatments. On the more positive side are those who inspire people. Create a few names, decide when they lived and died, and what they did to earn their esteem; just have them embody what the religion stands for, or part of it, with a significant deed or years of adherence to the ideals. They are a symbol. Focus on ones our characters reference or who will appear in our work.

Sects

A religion can have sects that disagree about interpretations of texts. Go easy on this if creating a pantheon due to the volume of work that could result. If we have two or more thoughts on how something could be done, use both, assigning ideas to sects. Each will oppose the other(s) and likely want them eradicated or drawn "into the fold," making this a good source of tension. This is especially helpful if our world has only one god, because one religion causes little tension, whereas multiple interpretations and doctrines cause conflict. Create a few incidents in the past, ones that solidify dislike of the other(s) and exemplify and justify the animosity.

Relationships

This religion, its followers, and its clergy have relationships with settlements, sovereign powers, species, and other groups, whether that's another religion or the military. This can be a lot to work out, and most of that can be decided on a case-by-case basis when we need it, not in advance. Species are different and should be fleshed out in our overview of this religion. One, like humans, might be drawn to this faith while another tends to be repulsed by it. To decide this, we'll need to have a solid understanding of the species and its outlook, which includes areas of turmoil that a religion can calm. This might be one of the last things we decide for this faith because a comprehensive sense is needed to form this association.

Does the religion feel that members of a species are in particular need of their teachings? Are they known for targeting elves, for example? Elves would likely know this and possibly feel irritation or outright hostility if this is considered condescending. Exasperation with a religion is a common feeling, while bonding with those of a different one is another. Decide what's typical of a species, using their outlook, the religion's, and the story needs.

WORLD VIEW

LANGUAGES

To decide on the religion's official language, we should choose which species the prophet(s) belonged to. The other option would be the god's language, should one exist. It could also be the language of those the god most wishes to reach, which could be a species other than the prophet's. For older religions, the language could be one no longer spoken, such as Latin, which can make it unique, prized, and mysterious. Holy texts are likely written in the official language unless translated.

Choosing where this prophet became one can help determine a likely species, but arguably most religions will want to convert other species, too. If they're not considered worthy, by mortals or a god, this inclusion or exclusion will determine the availability of translations to other languages. Even if the clergy don't create them, others may. The willingness to reach others will also decide which, if any, species languages clergy are expected to know and to what degree.

PLACE IN SOCIETY

It can be difficult to generalize a religion's place in society because this will depend on the society. It might be a state religion in one place and banned in another. What we want to decide is, for places where it is accepted, what role can it play in society and the lives of individuals?

For example, it could be prominent at sporting events if the religion promotes athletics or prowess in battle. Priests could be blessing the games or acting as fair judges. If the religion helps alcoholics and others similarly afflicted, it can provide hostels or treatment for free, perhaps with backing from the settlement or sovereign power (which is paying their bills). Which religion's priests perform marriages, burial rituals, or life's milestone ceremonies? All of this will be based on the god(s) we've created and what they care about.

One reason these matter is that members of a society will think of a religion's reputation when it is mentioned, their buildings are passed, or their priests are encountered. Even the followers, if wearing the religion's symbols, can elicit a reaction, whether subtle (a frown or smile) or excessive (taunting). Arguably, every character we invent should have a religion (and might have switched in their past) or none, but there's typically a reason for the latter, such as trauma or upbringing causing loss of faith. This will cause their reaction to their own or other religions; such details are realistic.

CUSTOMS

Invent religious customs based on a deity. A god of war might want a show of strength that results in a firm handshake. The words might be bold and decisive, such as, "Fierce is the heart!" A god of peace might wish blessings and be gentler in touch. A goddess of pain might slap a hand painfully. We can invent these beforehand or while writing. They often don't need explanation because the depiction tells the audience what they need to know. Refer to chapter 1 on creating cultures for what to invent, using the deity as inspiration.

OUTREACH

Some religions may send clergy out as missionaries early in their career; older priests are more established in the community and will be missed if sent far away. They can be inspired to do this or commanded to by clergy or deity. Are they aggressive or passive about proselyting? The same religion might be aggressive in one area and less so elsewhere due to local leadership or situations among those to be "saved" by conversion. Determine if there's a set number of years this work must be done.

COMBAT

Some religious orders forbid the use of force or carrying weapons while others have armed and trained warriors. A decision is easy for a god of war or peace, though the latter could acknowledge that people must defend themselves and that peace can be achieved through might, so we can once again put a spin on our invention. If we go with a less obvious rationale like this, we can state why with exposition or a scene like this one:

Kier disdainfully glared at the priest, hefting his sword. "Stand aside or be cut down."

The priest patted the blade slung at his waist. "My goddess may treasure peace, but she's not foolish enough to simply turn the other cheek. I know how to use this."

"You had better, or you will meet her soon enough." Kier advanced only to find the priest swiftly raising a blade that clanged against his twice before his fell to the floor.

For each religion we invent, a sense of the god's impact (through clergy) on the world and our story can guide our decisions. Do we want priests to be passive and easily bossed around or do we want more strength of behavior like the one depicted just now? Decide what feels right.

When weapons are forbidden, there's often a rationale, which can be a deep part of a religion's views. With Christianity, Jesus taught about turning the other cheek, and this humility is an inherent part of every religion that is based on his teachings. With our invented religion, do we have a rationale we can use to justify a lack of violence? A god of greed might want followers to fight to gain or keep what they have, or at least see it as a practical necessity. But does a goddess of the forest feel this way? Maybe not for a long time, but if species begins decimating woodland like we've done on Earth, and all manner of non-violence has not inhibited the destruction, perhaps a change of approach is in order. Either way, don't be afraid to challenge perceptions and expectations, which can lead us to assume priests are defenseless wimps.

We should also decide if priests are to accompany warriors, whether this is for war or smaller outings. This may be sanctioned, or the clergy may find themselves in this position against their will, such as trying to save a wounded soldier only to find himself and allies fighting for their own lives. Are priests members of the armed forces and what rank do they have? It is presumably not every religion, so which ones gets this role? They sometimes must also administer last rites to the dead and dying.

If we've decided they use weapons or wear armor, we should specify what they are expected to have...

WEAPONS

We should consider the effect weapons have when deciding what priests are likely to use. A religion might forbid the spilling of blood and therefore suggest blunt weapons like the staff or mace. These still cause bleeding, of course, but it tends toward being internal. Blood is not only a symbol of life but also carries diseases, so whether it's symbolic or a practical matter, this viewpoint can arise. Gods of war or death might prefer its spilling and allow especially destructive weapons like hollow-point bullets. Technology allows for weapons that kill in other ways, such as radiation. Light sabers or similar laser-like weapons cauterize wounds and prevent bleeding.

Consider whether suffering is something they want to minimize or maximize in victims. A faith might promote a swift death if it's to happen at all and prefer bladed weapons (blood loss kills in minutes verses hours or even days). Others might prefer subduing someone and train people in martial arts. Such a tactic might leave the practitioner relatively defenseless against better armed and armored opponents.

ARMOR

Priests are only likely to wear armor when sent into combat on purpose, just like everyone else. For everyday living, local hostility levels will determine the feasibility of wearing light protection. What we want to decide is, *if* they're armored, what is it? If there's a lightweight chainmail, this can be worn under robes. Leather is another option, but even knights only rarely employ plate armor, so this is less likely. In SF, we might have technological armor akin to Kevlar, and we can invent these to be light and slim. These can also absorb or resist magical, godly, or technological power (like radiation).

Decide what sorts of forces they're likely to encounter because this will determine the armor choice. Is there an aspect of this religion that informs the choice? For example, if leather is made from an animal that they consider unclean or sacred, then this is ruled out. If metal somehow interferes with communing with a god, so much for chain mail and the like. Armor might even be considered a barrier to being reunited with their god (through death) and therefore be frowned upon. Being creative with a choice makes this more entertaining for us and audiences. Otherwise, keep it simple.

THE AFTERLIFE

Our first decision on the afterlife is whether it's real. If it's real, then likely a god created it and the rules are incontrovertible. In this case, our religion is probably right about anything going on there or how to arrive, though having them be wrong is one way to make someone lose faith. Being right can add considerable weight to pronouncements about what one's behavior may cause. That, in turn, could inspire devotion. The question is how people learn that the priests are right and then tell people, given that they're dead?

But if the afterlife isn't real, this means that a species invented it, if the concept exists. This means they're wrong, and if they're wrong about this, they probably are about many other things. One aspect to consider is that, if wrong, the followers have likely tailored the concept to fit the religion and its teachings. But whether they're wrong or not, we'll craft those lessons and world view to create an afterlife that fits. If the good are rewarded and the evil punished, we only need to invent those environments to our muse.

There may be more than one afterlife, depending on how we count it. Heaven and hell can be considered two, each distinct but both arrived at by the same means: your conduct and/or faith. If each religion has more than one and we're creating a number of religions, this could become overwhelming. It might be better to have a few afterlives that are universal (because the gods created them and they're real) and which are less tied to a religion. Either that, or a religion has a special area in an afterlife, such as Catholics and Protestants both going to heaven but having their own version or area, whether they ever meet or not.

Can people visit the afterlife while still alive? Fantasy tales are full of this trope. This is one way for the truth of it to be confirmed or compromised. Communing with the dead is another way. If an afterlife can be reached by the living, we must decide how, such as a physical or spiritual journey, one often fraught with peril. The challenges faced can have no meaning or be based upon gods or just the story we're telling and its needs for character development or plot coupons. Some of the perils can be real while the species might have invented others that either don't exist or are quite different than imagined. This can cause problems for those journeying there if they've mis-prepared based on a lie. Besides, there's less tension in a journey that goes as expected.

In Earth's history, there have been various overarching ideas on the afterlife over the centuries, the details tweaked for the times, and we can leverage any or all of them. The first three here are considered good while the others are bad:

• Paradise (heaven) – a wonderful place without needs or wants
• Ascension – becoming a higher being, such as a demi-god of a trait you exemplified
• Rebirth – another life with or without memory of the previous one(s)
• Oblivion – the soul simply ends upon bodily death and that's it
• Torture (hell) – perpetual horror and pain
• Boredom – monotony unending

Finally, remember to name the afterlife(s) with a word that suggests whether they're menacing or hopeful. A great name can elevate these to being memorable, though what we decide exists in them helps, too.

WHERE TO START

After determining the god this religion follows, world builders should start with history because we can incorporate this in the invention of a religion. Almost every religion pays great attention to its beginnings. This will include historical figures that performed influential deeds, and the symbols that are crucial to it. The world view and place in society is another early subject to flesh out, as are relationships with species and which ones are typically members and/or clergy. How people worship can come next. The details of becoming a priest are an area to save for later unless we need it. Combat is perhaps the last subject to work on unless fighting is a major aspect of the religion, as with a god of war.

CHAPTER FIVE

THE SUPERNATURAL

Some could argue that a fantasy world without the supernatural isn't really fantasy, though we can still consider it that if it has all the other trappings, such as fictional species and races. But in SF, we can skip the supernatural altogether and not ruffle any feathers; unexplained phenomena are considered science we don't understand. In either case, the supernatural can significantly impact the world(s) we invent, so we should look at what we can invent. Chapter Six covers magic systems and there is some overlap of subjects covered, so readers may want to peruse both.

SUPERNATURAL ENERGY

The most obvious type of supernatural energy is magic, but divine power also exists. While radiation, dark matter, and similar items that we might find in SF aren't necessarily supernatural, they can be considered this way by both us and inhabitants; this means we can invent fictional types or decide what happens when characters are exposed to those or real ones. Humans have seldom if ever been exposed to many real energies in large doses, or at least, most of us don't think we have. This allows us to do things like invent The Incredible Hulk, Spiderman, or the Fantastic Four due to exposure and audiences will believe it. As usual, plausibility is the bar to get over.

Regardless of the source or what we call it (magic, radiation, etc.), we are inventing details about:

1. Its origins
2. Its properties
3. Where it occurs

4. Whether it can be controlled and how
5. What protection against it exists
6. Past incidents involving it

Origin is an area we can skip if desired because scientists often don't know the source of an energy in the real world; it can take decades to discover this and omitting the source adds mystery. But gods are typically considered the source of their own power, while magic is thought to derive from them if they exist in our setting.

We may want to name the types of energy because inhabitants will, and it eases all references to them. SF authors can invent them or use existing radiation, like gamma rays, while inventing new effects, and fantasy authors may have even greater leeway to start fresh. Try to find a name that sounds cool or intimidating; a nickname can help and can be based on something that once happened when someone was exposed to the energy.

Decide where this energy can be found, such as only in space, in a lab, in areas prone to supernatural phenomenon, or in seemingly random places. Are there conditions that must be met before this energy is detected or surges to life? With this decided, we'll know how often it's encountered and by who. If such a location is near an elven settlement, for example, they'll probably be local experts. This can help when the energy (or something like it) is found elsewhere in our world, with that expert elf present for our story, to explain facts and suspicions to audiences and companions alike.

Inventing the properties of our energy is useful and fun to do. This includes its appearance, with invisibility being one option. Does it remind people of anything? If it looks like blue fire, there's a nickname we can use. Does it give off heat or cold? Maybe it does neither until we touch it. Can people detect it before making contact, and if so, what does it feel like? Electricity, heat, and cold are some options. How close do people need to be before they are affected, or is there a range of effects based on proximity? How intense is it at each distance? If the phenomenon is temporary, we can also decide on duration, such as it happening in a given location but each flare up is only a few minutes and maybe predictable (like the "Old Faithful" geyser).

Deciding if and how this energy can be controlled is another subject for the imagination. The ability to control it may come and go. Perhaps long ago no one could, now they can, but in a nearby future, technology needed for that control will be destroyed. What if it's been brought into civilized areas and now it's out of control? Or unforeseen circumstances, such as interaction with a nearby and different energy, causing changes to its behaviors or properties? For SF, we'll invent technological devices that include weapons, defenses, and containment fields. In fantasy, this energy may be assumed to be magic unless we offer some explanation that it's different. If people can control magic with spells but not this energy, that helps distinguish the two. We may want some supernatural energy to still exist naturally so that people encounter it either by accident or on purpose.

We can add interest to this energy by inventing past incidents involving it. This can result in monsters, tall tales, myths, legends, and famous characters that may provide a cautionary tale. These can be as short as a few sentences tossed into our narrative, like this:

> Nasha blanched at the idea of passing through the Nifling Hills on the way to Illiandor. "Isn't that where Olian the Fool had half his face burned off?"
> Kier nodded at the legend. "They say the flames got him, if you believe that story."
> "You don't?"
> "Blue Fire coming out of the ground without warning? Seems far-fetched."

A template in the appendix can assist with the invention of supernatural energies.

MAGIC PATHS

In some fantasy settings, there's an alternate way of traveling that amounts to magical paths, which may have a corresponding magical doorway for access. Using these paths typically offers an advantage accompanied by great risk. A common advantage is much faster travel, which can help story issues when we need them to get somewhere faster than possible. The usual dangers are nasty and dangerous things one might encounter, whether living, dead, or inanimate (and possibly supernatural). This adds adventure, as well.

Other people could be walking these paths, posing another risk. Maybe they (or our characters) are lost and have been so long that this place has changed them, whether actual mutation or desperation leading to mindsets they've never had or acts they wouldn't normally commit. Do they prey on travelers for survival? The normal rules of physics sometimes don't exist in these places, such as time moving differently.

In the real world, a path leads through and around other locations. We can invent these within this supernatural landscape, from buildings like castles, homes, and magical towers, to land features like forests, rivers, and mountains, all with supernatural properties or life within them. If we create enough sufficiently interesting places, they can become another reason people enter this land, to acquire something found within, rather than to travel through it. Perhaps wizards can find rare items to use in their spells, or send someone else to fetch them; this is the basis for my free novella, *The Ever Fiend (Talon Stormbringer, #1)*.

The doorways into this other world can be wholly supernatural or physical with supernatural properties. They may be located in places that are inherently dangerous or which have become that way due to being guarded by something, or that territory being controlled by something nefarious. Consider naming not only this supernatural land but the doorways. Inventing an origin is optional but helps with realism and our invention of additional details. An obvious source for a supernatural land is the gods. Omitting an origin adds to the place's mystery, though we might want to decide in our files and withhold the revelation from an audience.

A template in the appendix can assist with inventing supernatural lands.

ALTERNATE REALITIES

Most of us have probably seen an alternate reality depicted, especially in SF. There used to be a TV show called *Sliders* where, in every episode, the characters were forced into an alternate reality from Earth. These variations can be easy to create. All we need to do is make some changes that have a significant impact, even if the average person doesn't realize the influence it would have (until reading our story). For example, on Earth, what if the Nazis had won WWII? What if we'd never invented GPS? What if global warming has raised the sea level by ten feet?

These examples are extreme, but we can do variations that impact far fewer people, such as just our main characters. One who is married in one reality is not in another, or is a parent, or lost a sibling in a way that affected their outlook. When we've developed backstory for a character (to shape who they are), and then we want an alternate reality for them, we can change that backstory. We're trying to change who they are by presenting them with an alternate view of themselves or their life, one that causes them to question their life choices or even their personality in their own reality.

SUPERNATURAL BEINGS

DEMI-GODS

A chapter from *Creating Life (The Art of World Building, #1)* covered the creation of gods and pantheons in detail, but here we'll cover lesser beings: the demi-gods.

The term can mean many things, so for our purposes, we're discussing any supernatural being that has less power than gods but is related to them, and works with them in some capacity. They are often the offspring of gods or a human who has been given divine powers or rank. Some, like Hercules, are the result of a human (or another species, even an animal) mating with a god. The term would include angels and demons on Earth.

In mythology, demi-gods often serve a specific purpose, such as being a messenger of the gods. As world builders, this means we can invent someone when we need them for our story, though we may want a few of them in advance. Such a universally used character, as the messenger, might get more frequent use and mention by us and our world's inhabitants. On the other hand, a figure like Cupid only comes up in love scenarios. For these beings, we need little more than a name and function until we show them in a tale. This means they're easy to create and flesh out later. Decide if any are needed. Here are a few roles they can play:

1. Harbinger of doom
2. Harbinger of love
3. Harbinger of good
4. Messenger

Other figures can be invented when we need them, though it helps to hint at their existence beforehand so that it doesn't seem too convenient that just the right one has popped up when our story needed it.

If we invent half-gods, meaning they have a mortal (i.e., human or other species) parent, too, we need to decide on their abilities, which don't need to come directly from the divine parent. Deriving talent from the divine parent makes it easier to decide who their divine parent was, but there's an idea that talent skips a generation, for example. I have musical talent and so does at least one of my kids, but neither of my parents do, though a grandparent had some. When we invent these half-gods, we are implying that deities have sexual relations with mortals. Does that conform to the view we've developed of their relations?

CREATURES

In *Creating Life*, we discussed both animals and monsters, so these won't be covered here, but we can take any of them and add supernatural elements.

We don't always need to decide where a creature originated, but it helps us determine everything else we need to invent for it. Under circumstances we invent, predetermined sources of energy can give rise to this creature. Having decided where such energy is available helps us establish a physical point of origin. How and even if our creature relocates can also add believability. Does it need a new habitat due to the way its body now functions? Perhaps it can't abide certain temperatures or other environmental issues, or just craves a specific environment now and adapts its habitat accordingly.

The creature's physical properties and capabilities are often linked, though they needn't be. What changes can we make to its appearance based on its supernatural abilities? Perhaps there are marks on the skin that react to external stimuli. That said, it can be advantageous to have this creation externally indistinguishable from the source; that allows for surprises when they prove to be other than they appeared. Decide on whether this subterfuge is helpful. If not, pair the skill to the body, such as ears that can move in odd ways because their hearing is superior, or eyes that look different (color, pupil shape, etc.) because their vision is altered.

FIGURES OF NOTE

Earth mythologies are full of interesting characters that are not gods or humans. This includes Charon, who ferries souls across the rivers Styx and Acheron. There's Cerberus, the three-headed dog in Greek mythology, who prevents the dead from leaving Hades. For ideas, all we need to do is look at other mythologies. We may want to start with a role or job function, which will also give us a location this individual occupies, and its characteristics. If the River Styx has properties we've already invented, and effects on people, then our version of Charon might be able to control or counteract these for at least himself.

The gods are often the source of such figures, who arguably need their approval to perform the function they serve. But these figures can come from any source, such as supernatural accidents before they are put to the use they now serve. A god may be the only one who can control it, possibly using a device that can fall into the wrong hands. Other times, an individual from a species or race might have been transformed into this figure, possibly due to their devotion to an idea that the god agrees with. For example, Charon could believe that everyone must be judged upon death and was so fervent about this in life that Hades assigned him to transporting souls. This gives such a character an attitude that can be revealed while interacting with our characters.

SUPERHEROES

We may not think cartoon characters like Spiderman or the X-men as supernatural, but they're close. Most would agree that they have supernatural abilities though not intrinsically supernatural. There are few limits on using these elements to transform them if it's credible. What happened to them, when, why, and how did it affect them physically? Decide how much control they have over their skills at the point of the story that they'll be used. Like any character, they need backstory, just one with extra information.

FAMILIARS

Another supernatural being is the "familiar" of wizardry. They originate in medieval folklore and were though to assist witches, or perhaps in our case, wizards, including protecting them, whether that means physically or scouting and warning. They may also possess specialized knowledge, particularly of a different plane of existence. They are usually in the form of a small animal and appear corporeal rather than ghostly, though we're free to do either. We can make them invisible to others. Whether they're considered good or evil depends on who they serve; they might be considered fairies or demons. Familiars are sometimes given as a gift, or appear when someone is alone or in trouble, after which they are bonded from weeks to decades.

PREVALENCE

Throughout this chapter, we've touched on the idea that supernatural elements may only sometimes be available for our characters to encounter. This is true for beings and energies that might exist all the time but only periodically flare up in a given location. However, we also need to decide how prevalent the supernatural is generally in our setting. Do we want a world that is mostly like Earth in the medieval ages with a little bit of magic? This is a default depiction found in fantasy.

Or do we want a setting where the supernatural is as common as electricity is in Earth's modern times? This will have a significantly greater impact on the world and our story. If we want this, we can benefit from reading fantasy works where others have already thought through this impact and given us ideas. Otherwise, we'll have to do a mental deep dive into questioning everything about everyday life. This can be an exhausting exercise due to the sheer number of modifications we'll envision, but it can be well worth it; we'll look more at this in the next section.

The prevalence includes attitudes about the supernatural. People fear the unusual, but even the deadliest phenomena can elicit indifference if it's commonplace. If we are used to harnessing and controlling the supernatural, this can also lead to complacency about its dangers. This correlation is built-in; we just need to be aware of it and make a note in our files about it. If the supernatural is everywhere, only someone traumatized by it is likely to react strongly to its use.

THE IMPACT

The influence that the supernatural has on a setting can be enormous unless the supernatural is rare. In fantasy, places are often presented as if they're medieval-like with a smattering of wizardry thrown in. Theoretically, this only makes sense if magic can only be performed by a small group of people. By contrast, if everyone is capable of performing a degree of magic, this would impact society, depending on the nature of this magic and what people can do with it.

Let's imagine a world where most people can perform simple spells. First, we should define what is meant by "simple." There are many options, but what if we can move small objects? Wouldn't we use this ability to clean our homes? Who wouldn't like the ability to cast a spell or two and have everything put back in its place and wiped down? This could eliminate the entire housekeeping industry, plus the tips we leave after a hotel stay (unless we're too lazy to cast the spells and hire people to do it for us). What if we can cast a spell to prepare food? This might eliminate the restaurant business and the concept of dining out. But maybe some recipes are too complicated and only people with more power can pull them off; restaurants and "chefs" still exist. If I can cast a spell to style and color my hair, then I never need to visit a barber, eliminating another industry, unless, once again, some choices are too advanced for me. If we can cast a spell to dress ourselves, perhaps we have no wardrobe, or closets in our house, and there's no such thing as department stores. In a world where all of this is possible, does anyone even have a job? Doing what?

If we can make food for ourselves, do we have it have it appear on a plate or right into our mouth? Why not go one step further and have it in our stomach? Imagine how easy it would be to lose weight if we could transport the food into our stomach and bypass the tyranny of the tongue that tempts us to each too much due to loving the taste. We could use magic to brush or repair/replace our teeth, eliminating the dentistry profession.

A more advanced spell might be teleporting between locations, which would eliminate the need for vehicles and parking, not to mention fuel. But it might cause other problems, such as someone appearing in our bathroom when we're not wearing anything. Perhaps there's a law against such a thing, or spells to prevent that by protecting a certain room. We would have no need of roads either. This would suggest that the path between one home and another is grass or whatever naturally grows there, if anything. This also makes it possible to have a house in unusual locations, assuming one can be built there, because getting to it isn't an issue. Magic can be used to construct one and there's no issue with builders needing to reach our chosen spot. Maybe magic can be used to alter the shape of a home at any time, or simply move the entire house from one location to another. That might make finding someone difficult unless there is something in the house that acts like a location beacon, which can be turned on and off for privacy so that no one can find us if we don't want them to.

This thought exercise can get us thinking about how just magic, not to mention other supernatural issues, can influence life. What if supernatural creatures can appear at any time? How would this change us and our environments? If the gods can appear and smite us, then would anyone swear with a god's name? If there are magic paths available and a doorway near us, do we purposely live farther away so that nothing nasty comes out and wreaks havoc on us? How do people compensate for the existence of each supernatural element, and are these issues positive, negative, or a little of both? We must decide the prevalence of each element and where it occurs.

We should also consider the limits on each, including the toll that performing magic takes on people. Are there restrictions, and are they natural or imposed by laws or preventive measures that others have taken? For example, if I can teleport myself, then, in theory, I can send you somewhere as well. Presumably, this is frowned upon when done without your permission. But if there were no witnesses, how can someone prove that I sent you somewhere? Is there a class of police investigators who can determine what happened? If not, then what's to stop me from teleporting myself somewhere and claiming that you did it, getting you arrested (if that's a crime)?

Unless we want to invent an entire system of laws and methods to investigate crimes of magic, we may decide that teleporting another person is not possible, for example, or go one step further and decide that magic has limitations to prevent this from happening. This seems to be the default approach for many world builders, and it works when those limits exist. The problem is when everyone can do some magic and we haven't considered how this would realistically change a setting.

We can't cover every scenario here, but these examples should get us thinking about how much impact the supernatural has on our world and what elements can be eliminated, altered, or replaced by it.

WHERE TO START

When we start inventing the supernatural, we should determine how large an impact we'd like this to have on the setting and stories. This determines the prevalence and character reactions or ability to manipulate. Elements can be developed independently of one another, so that there's no particular order to follow. Don't be afraid to revisit ideas to see how they hold up, and try connecting them to other elements we've invented in the meantime.

CHAPTER SIX

MAGIC SYSTEMS

Some may assume that only fantasy settings involve magic, but SF can have it, too. There's a tendency to assume worlds have one or the other, which begs the question of what happens when planet-hopping SF characters land on one without technology, but magic instead? Regardless, world builders will know if they need or want magic for a world. If so, read on. But before we invent spells or systems of magic, we should understand our options and some theories.

PRINCIPLES OF GOOD MAGIC SYSTEMS

Before creating a magic system, we should consider some guiding principles.

SANDERSON'S THREE LAWS

Author Brandon Sanderson once proposed three laws of magic that we'll examine for perspective. Any quotes in this section are from his website, brandonsanderson.com, unless otherwise stated, with the rest paraphrased.

Sanderson's first law is "an author's ability to solve conflict with magic is *directly proportional* to how well the reader understands said magic." Try not to give characters abilities unless we've already shown they possess them. Determine how problems can be solved without magic or within the existing magic system, before altering it. And if we do change it, don't give them abilities that perfectly solve their problem. Breaking this law can make magic too convenient.

Sanderson's second law is: "limitations are greater than powers." What characters can't do forces them to stretch and forces our story in other directions. This adds dimension, depth, and tension, so we gain more with limits than we do by granting powers that just resolve everything.

Sanderson's third law is: "expand what you already have before you add something new." We can make our system too complicated if we're adding new elements rather than refining what we have. We also run the risk of contradiction when the goal for our characters might be achievable with an expansion of our current system.

SOFT MAGIC VS HARD MAGIC

Sanderson also discussed what he calls soft vs. hard magic. In his view, soft magic is not rigidly defined (if defined at all), allowing for authors to "preserve the sense of wonder in their books." By not explaining how magic works, we feel a sense of amazement because we don't understand how it works or what is possible. It is mysterious and exciting, but also dangerous and unpredictable. It adds tension. Authors who use such systems don't let magic solve problems for their characters, who seem like a small part of a vast world that can overwhelm them with its power.

By contrast, in hard magic, "the author explicitly describes the rules of magic." We identify what it can do and what it can't. Therefore, when a character needs to do something, we aren't surprised by their ability (or lack thereof). Though it's a comic book character, his example of Spiderman is a good one: we already know his abilities and simply accept it when he uses one of them, but he doesn't acquire new abilities on the spur of the moment. He has to use the tools we've already defined.

Sanderson also talks about a middle ground, where some things are defined but others aren't, allowing for flexibility and that feeling of mystery that soft magic allows, while also providing the structure and understanding that hard magic gives.

WHAT'S A LAW?

Sanderson's use of the word "law" led me on an interesting thought exercise that adds clarity to creating magic systems. According to Merriam-Webster's The Third New International Dictionary, "Law is a binding custom or practice of a community; a rule or mode of conduct or action that is prescribed or formally recognized as binding by a supreme controlling authority or is made obligatory by a sanction (as an edict, decree, rescript, order, ordinance, statute, resolution, rule, judicial decision, or usage) made, recognized, or enforced by the controlling authority." Laws are authoritative, definitive, to the point, and arguably avoid explanation to minimize public arguments when accused of breaking one.

By calling his principles "laws" and asserting that there are three of them, Sanderson invokes comparison to Isaac Asimov's famous Three Laws of Robotics. However, Asimov's laws were invented for specific stories and societies described in those stories, meaning they are actual laws there. By contrast, Sanderson has proposed three laws for building magic systems. But no world builder is beholden to another's ideas on this (and he admits he does not intend that). His laws do not apply to any society, invented physics/limitations, world builders, or even stories. He cannot enforce them except on himself, which applies to us: we can choose what to enforce on ourselves.

Sanderson's laws are restated here as a single sentence for comparison. None are declarative and each leaves room for interpretation:

1. "An author's ability to solve conflict with magic is *directly proportional* to how well the reader understands said magic."
2. Limitations are greater than powers.
3. "Expand what you already have before you add something new."

LOCAL LAWS

Compare those to the following laws I invented for this section. These are laws that might exist in a city or sovereign power, both of which have authority to impose and enforce laws. They are designed to instruct people on what's permitted and when. We might craft something similar for localities.

1. Magic shall not be performed within the city limits except within designated areas or by those holding a valid permit.
2. Magic shall not be used to inflict physical harm or death on a living being except in defense of one's own life or that of another.
3. Magic shall not be performed on the Holy Day.

LAWS OF MAGIC

What about laws of magic? These would delineate what is possible and what isn't, due to the equivalent of physics for magic, like nature's "laws," such as the law of gravity. These would be *discovered* and defined by the species/races through experience and observation of what [usually] works and what doesn't. Here are some examples:

1. Black Magic and White Magic cannot be performed by the same wizard.
2. Magic cannot be performed by virgins.
3. Magic can only be performed by spells, or by items imbued with spells.
4. Wizards of the Moon must be exposed to two hours of moonlight each night to perform Moon Magic between then and the next moonrise.

WORLD BUILDING LAWS

What about laws that world builders should follow when creating a system? This is what Sanderson intended. These are ones that will impact the storytelling and what local laws and laws of magic we design; as such, they should come first in our work. The next section has my thoughts on this.

ELLEFSON'S SEVEN LAWS

World builders can choose to enforce any, all, or none of my laws for creating magic systems for themselves. These laws are not about how to use a magic system once created, but how to create those systems. Most are self-explanatory with a single sentence, but a few words follow each. Some include examples, which are not meant to build upon each, but rather offer possibilities and world building prompts. Use these ideas as guidance for what we should do to craft a magic system.

FIRST LAW

World builders shall decide what the laws of magic are.

The universe (or another authority such as gods) has determined what works and what doesn't, and under what conditions. This should be defined for all magic types. Examples:

1. Spells are required.
2. Magic can be performed at-will like a god.
3. There is a finite amount of magic energy and once consumed, it is gone.
4. Naturally occurring places exist where magic doesn't work.
5. With rare exceptions, a wizard can only perform one type of magic and they do not get to choose.
6. Elves cannot perform elemental magic.

SECOND LAW

World builders shall define what makes someone capable of performing each magic type, and how common practitioners are.

Examples:

1. Anyone born with the talent can perform magic. These people are rare.
2. The gods decide who can do magic and can grant or revoke ability at will.
3. Anyone who consumes a specific item with a specific frequency acquires the ability as long as said item continues to be consumed.
4. Witchcraft requires a deal with Satan. Witches are common.
5. A near-death experience is required to become a shaman. Shamans are rare.
6. Consumption of alcohol eliminates the ability to perform magic for several days.

THIRD LAW

If multiple types of magic exist, world builders shall define what is possible in each, the differences between them, and whether practitioners can perform more than one type (and under what circumstances).

Short examples (yours should be much more in depth):

1. There are two types of magic, with most practitioners relegated to one type:
    a. Low magic: only simple spells to assist daily living (like cantrips)
    b. High magic: all higher level, more powerful spells
2. There are several magic types:
    a. Alchemists: can only work with materials to affect personal change
    b. High wizardry: can draw on magic energy in the environment
    c. : must work with spirits or demons for power

FOURTH LAW

World builders shall determine what happens when an attempt to use magic fails.

Examples:

1. A spell either works within its parameters or fails. There are no accidental results.
2. A failed spell will visibly/invisibly release gathered energy chaotically/safely.
3. A failed spell traps gathered energy within the caster's body until released
4. A failed spell produces an unexpected result of a different nature but not extremely so.
5. Magic (done without spells) energy is safely released back to its source when the casting fails.

FIFTH LAW

World builders shall decide what local laws exist in each location where a story takes place.

Examples:

1. Alchemists must register with the local guild.
2. Wizards must surrender their staves upon entering the city limits.
3. Only valend wizards may create magic items.
4. Only those with a valid permit may use magic items within city limits.
5. Wizards will be killed on sight.
6. Necromancy is forbidden except within 48 hours of the deceased's burial.
7. Wizards are not allowed on the city council.
8. Those accused of witchcraft must identify another witch to avoid execution.
9. Unlicensed mindreading, without written permission from the subject, is illegal.
10. Public sources (such as the water well, torches, etc.) are not to be used for elemental magic.
11. Elemental wizards who do not participate in resolving a public crises (like a flood or fire) are to be sentenced to one year's hard labor.

SIXTH LAW

World builders shall follow the rules they set forth.

This rule applies to all world building, not just magic systems. Fantasy and SF audiences are adept at noticing our mistakes, so keep a list of all rules and abide by them. It can be best to narrate a rule with some flexibility. For example, "*most* wizards cannot do so-and-so." One trick is to narrate the law this way: "people said wizards couldn't do so-and-so." That makes it popular opinion, not a statement of fact. Another trick is to have a character, not the narrator, state a law. Characters don't always get things right, so when our story proves them wrong, it's not the author breaking our rule. However, do this on purpose. Why would we want to? Because we might want to suggest something to the reader, and then surprise them later, but it must be a good surprise. It is effective when a character finding out the truth protests that another character told them so; this also channels the audience's potential upset into acceptance.

SEVENTH LAW

For each location, world builders shall decide if magical training is available, what form it takes, what is involved, limitations imposed before graduation, testing criteria, and what restrictions if any exist on those who graduate.

This one is more of a suggestion; not doing so is unlikely to cause problems, while doing it will almost certainly benefit us. Examples:

1. Training is only available via an apprenticeship where sanctioned by the sovereign power
2. Wizards must pass the Kierdyn Test by the third attempt or have magic ability suppressed for life
3. Prior to graduation, only low magic spells can be performed outside the guild
4. Wizards are tested for the ability to release magic energy safely

DO WE NEED A MAGIC SYSTEM?

Creating a magic system is about organization; without it, we don't have a "system." The problems with an on-the-fly approach are numerous, one of the biggest being inconsistency. Readers are astute. If rules prohibit a character from doing something at one point, and we have them do it (or something similar) later, in defiance of that rule, readers will notice. This can happen due to forgetfulness and not writing down any spontaneously invented rules. We also sometimes imply a rule without realizing we've done so, only to break it later. And breaking our own rules makes it apparent we don't know what we're doing.

Another problem is giving people the ability to solve something with magic right when they need it. Deus ex machina is considered poor storytelling. If we want to do this, we shouldn't make the magical solution perfect. If they need to go fifty miles, make the spell only transport them forty miles, depositing them somewhere that presents new issues. Perfect solutions eliminate conflict, which is the heart of any story. Having a system helps us create limits. Without a system, it's harder to contrast multiple styles or types of magic. Each should have its rules, limits, benefits, and problems. The point of a system is to decide who can do what and under which circumstances, bringing order to the potential chaos of magic being everywhere and there being no limits.

But we don't always need a system. If we're writing a short story, we're less likely to break rules, for example, because our tale will end before we can. The longer a work is, or the more times we'll use the setting, the more we need a system. And if magic is very prevalent, we'll need a system to impose limits and be realistic; without one, we're at greater risk of inconsistency and mistakes. But if magic is rare or a minor part of a story, we may do well enough without one.

TYPES OF MAGIC

When most of us think of magic, we mean wizardry unless indicating a subtype as described in this section. Wizardry is broadly defined as the harnessing of magical energy, using any combination of words, gestures, and components (aka ingredients), with practitioners in a robe, wielding a staff, and being of advanced age; all of these clichés are best avoided.

Once we define types of magic, we begin breaking them into groups that people can perform or not. What follows is a high-level discussion of several types, but more can be found with an internet search. There are specialized forms of magic that other world builders have imagined, which are public domain, and which we might want to include in a setting in addition to anything we devise.

When deciding on our needs, we should consider how many people can perform each type of magic and why that is. Rarity means more valuable and feared. The specialists in this section are just that and can be treated as generally less available unless our setting and story requires a lot of them. The next chart lists reasons for magic being rare or common.

Reasons for Rarity	Reasons for Commonplace
It's dangerous	It's safe
It's feared	It's accepted
Practitioners are feared	Practitioners are admired
Training is unavailable, limited, hard, or costly	Training is available, easy, and inexpensive
Materials needed to perform it are hard to acquire	Materials are plentiful

Reasons for Rarity	Reasons for Commonplace
Spell books are rare or poor	Spell books are common and good
Talent is rare	Talent is common
There's no money in it	It's lucrative
Family and friends shun you	Family and friends are not impacted

Figure 71 Magic Rarity Chart

For each magic type in our setting, we can mix and match commonplace and rarity, such as making the talent or spell books common, the magic dangerous, and the materials rare. Such variations make our worlds more believable and help distinguish types from each other.

WHITE AND BLACK MAGIC

Magic can either be beneficial or harmful to others and the environment. These are referred to as white and black magic, respectively. We can also think of them as good and evil, possibly associating them with good and evil beings (gods, demons, etc.) as the provider of each. This can mean that a wizard aligns himself with a deity, who might have requirements for behavior and their mental or spiritual state. A white wizard might need to be noble, benevolent, and kind, for example, and perform mostly for the benefit of others (rather than the self) or access to the power fails.

Black magic may include voodoo with its hexes, curses, poisons, and association with zombies. What must a black magic wizard be like or do regularly? Sacrifice animals or people? Sow discord? Black magic is considered bad due to being used for selfish or evil purposes. In popular culture, practitioners are feared and shunned not only for their practices, but what those practices say about them as people. This is a way to characterize someone.

Those with a poor understanding of either may confuse someone doing white magic with one doing black magic; this trope has been used with witches, where all are branded evil due to ignorance and fear of their practices, reputation, or appearance. Other types of magic in this section can be considered black, such as necromancy or shamanism, but this often results from ignorance about the practices. People fear what they don't understand, and we can cause conflict by including magic practitioners that act, dress, or talk strangely or secretively (even if for good reasons). For all magic types, consider dividing them along this good vs. evil axis. Another option is "grey magic" that lies between these extremes.

ALCHEMY

Alchemy is the practice of turning one material into another, usually an ordinary item to a valuable one, such as lead into gold. While this is not possible on Earth, it might be in a world we invent. The practice held other goals of interest, such as creating healing potions, an elixir of immortality, or a universal solvent that can dissolve anything (called an alkahest). If you've ever wondered why the British edition of the first Harry Potter book is titled *Harry Potter and the Philosopher's Stone*, this refers to a legendary item that combines these powers and which was the ultimate goal of an alchemist.

The morphing of material is thought to be an analogy for personal transformation into a better, purer state, meaning alchemy is considered a spiritual matter, not just physical. We could see alchemists as a cross between the wizards and priests of our world. The transmutation of specific materials can be thought to cause specific changes within a person, and we have leeway to invent these. For example, if I turn a piece of lead in your hand to gold, perhaps I've made your spirit more noble and high-minded, too. Maybe this can reform a criminal, and the opposite can be done to someone pompous, like an absolute dictator. Or maybe the impact is to make you more knowledgeable, or change your desire or aptitude for learning rather than outright granting knowledge.

Due to the power inherent in these changes, alchemists guarded their knowledge so that any written information was done in a language only they understood or which had a cypher to obscure understanding. Their books and scrolls could be quite cryptic. Most were trying to create the aforementioned stone, a project known as the "magnum opus," which in ancient times had four stages, each associated with a color, the final state being the goal of personal development via alchemy. In later times, these were expanded, but the original four stages, each with a spiritual or psychological aspect achieved through the listed physical transformation, were:

1. Nigreo (blackening): facing one's internal demons, through a cleansing and decomposition/putrefaction of the base material.
2. Aledo (whitening): achieving an awakened, receptive soul, caused by purification.

3. Citrinitas (yellowing): achieving wisdom (in one's soul), by the transmutation of moonlight to sunlight (silver to gold).
4. Rubedo (reddening): discovering and attaining one's true nature in body, mind, and soul.

Alchemy has an advantage over magic for writers; magic is often thought to be nothing more than physical manipulation to achieve a physical result. By contrast, alchemy achieves change within the self or others by transmutation of physical objects that represent something. As authors and audiences enjoy symbolism, this makes alchemy useful in adding meaning to an alchemist's behaviors. It's a missed opportunity to portray one as solely wanting to become rich by changing lead to gold, for example.

Adopt symbols to represent these stages. On Earth, birds have often been used to represent the progression. This includes the phoenix, already known for its transformation. The colors are sometimes emblazoned on the clothing of those interested in achieving a higher state. We can add both symbols and colors to anything, including government buildings, homes, or institutions that consider themselves to be in pursuit of enlightenment.

WITCHCRAFT

While we all know what's typically meant by witchcraft, also known as witchery, the term is a broad one. Both white and black magic interpretations exist on Earth. It can mean using the supernatural to cause harm or be more beneficial such as divination. Using spirits for these practices is assumed to be dangerous and possibly evil; there is an assumption that spirits who have not gone to the afterlife, or are willing to be contacted by the living, must be nefarious. This rises from fear, ignorance, and lack of comfort with all of it, with people assuming the worst about what these spirits and those contacting them are capable of.

Pagans have often been considered witches, which has led to many associations, such as full or partial nudity, being barefoot, wearing loose and flowing clothing, chanting, singing, and dancing in the woods to conjure spirits, typically at night and during specific moon phases. The celebration of basic natural elements can be seen as championing base human needs and instincts like sex. This combination, along with fear, leads to the assumption of copulation with the devil or similar figures as a means of gaining supernatural powers.

One practice common to witchcraft is the use of archaic runes or symbols inscribed on a target, such a person, building, or item that is the focus of the spell. Another is a poppet, a figure made of wax or clay to represent another person, with the spell cast on this. Incantations differ slightly from speech in other magic types in that they are often chanted or sung rather than simply spoken, sometimes specific actions being taken at moments within the incantation, rather than there being no coordination. Witchcraft that involves scrying often makes use of reflective materials such as a mirror, blade, or scrying ball. This reliance on a material, the existing properties of which offer some aid, helps distinguish witchery from other magic types.

As with necromancy, we should understand the afterlife in our world if any interaction with the dead is to take place. And if beings like demons are to be communed with, we'll benefit from having worked out places like Hell, where they dwell. The rules we've devised for such places can impact the rules we craft for witches and others to interact with the beings there.

NECROMANCY

Magic that involves the dead is called necromancy, which can be its own type of magic in our world. Communication with the dead means understanding how the afterlife works. After all, if spirits are simply obliterated, bringing one back or interacting with it is impossible. The nature of an afterlife might also aid or inhibit the recruitment with or contacting of the dead. Would a Satan-like figure make that contact easier so that more hell is loosed upon the Earth? Would a God-like figure inhibit it? Or would God allow interaction because it might be benevolent? Having a justification and multiple barriers can make scenarios more plausible.

Communication can mean the equivalent of a long-distance phone call, meaning the spirit never leaves where it resides. This seems easier than summoning the spirit to cross boundaries; this is where inventing afterlife barriers figures more heavily. A third option is raising a body from the dead and restoring the soul into it, a more intense experience for both necromancer and victim. This is especially true if the target does not become undead but a living person once again. By dividing these concerns this way, we can begin creating a system of magic for necromancy.

We should also understand what death has been like, as this impacts the mind or emotions of anyone thus contacted. That, in turn, will affect behavior, including how cooperative they are, though perhaps our necromancer can force obedience – at least until he's incapacitated and the undead either get free and go their own way, return to the land of the undead, or take revenge upon the necromancer who awoke them into servitude.

We can decide that the undead have acquired unlimited knowledge, increasing their value, or only have firsthand knowledge just as in life. The Roman poet Ovid speculated that an underworld marketplace exists where undead exchange news and gossip, which not only expands what undead know, but creates a place where the living can travel. Perhaps knowledge isn't the only item traded here.

THEIR PRACTICES

Necromancer rituals can last for hours, days, or even weeks, and sometimes use moon phases or the placement/configuration of other heavenly bodies. These often take place in or near graveyards, tombs, and mausoleums, though the churches of evil deities are an option. While words, gestures, or materials might be involved, these rituals often involve a circle drawn in blood, holy water or an equivalent, salt, or writing. These serve to protect the practitioner from possession, assault, death, kidnapping, and more, from the very forces they seek to control, which are a threat to their lives and soul. These circles can also concentrate magic power where the target dead will be imprisoned after summoning; bringing a potentially malignant being to this realm is inherently dangerous and unpredictable, making this precaution wise.

Sacred talismans, relics of the dead, and body parts such as bones may be involved, whether worn, laid on circles or altars, or used during gestures. They could be mutilated, incinerated, or otherwise destroyed, which naturally means they can't be reused, which places emphasis on success the first time. Placing a limit adds urgency that benefits stories. The practitioner may be wearing the deceased's clothes or an item that held importance to them.

Foods that symbolize death, and fluids like blood, are often present. These are consumed by either the necromancer or enthralled spirits. We can invent a reason for this, such as giving a spirit more substance and therefore power over a world of which they are no longer a part. Perhaps consuming it binds them to the world, to the necromancer, or to do the deed for which they're now recalled. Can the necromancer force them to consume it?

A more extreme practice involves sacrifice, which could be an item, animal or human (or an invented species). This might mean a life or the soul, too. The victim could be the infamous virgin, but an excuse for this might help alleviate this cliché to something more palatable. If we state that innocence, more than virginity, can counter the evil forces involved in necromancy, or fool a guardian of the underworld into letting our necromancer access a spirit by suggesting we have pure intentions, this concept makes more sense. Youth also seems plausible for younger people's strength, but a baby has little, so a teenager might be ideal.

Shamanism

In shamanism, the shaman communicates with spirits or other beings believed to be in another plane of existence, one that intersects with ours. It often involves an altered state of consciousness achieved through meditation, trace, or hallucinogenic drugs. In SF, we might choose to inject something or more advanced technology such as direct brain stimulation or implants, but in less technological settings, we're likely using liquids (drinks), solids (food), gas (to be inhaled), meditation and ritual, or a combination. Shamans experience dreams or visions that have messages, but they can also physically, or more commonly, spiritually enter a spiritual realm. A shaman may also try to bring energies from the spirit world into his own. That there can be benevolent and malevolent spirits adds danger and unpredictability to shamanism.

Within a culture or village, different shamans can exist, specializing in functions. We can divide these as we wish. Some functions include healing, communicating, fortune-telling, leading souls to their rightful afterlife place, or keeping traditions alive by knowing and relating stories that teach, instruct, and bring the community together. Reasons for such divisions can include the difficulty or danger inherent in certain tasks. Perhaps a younger and physically stronger shaman should do certain things, or if a shaman dies performing a function, only some of their knowledge dies with them because other shamans perform other duties. Another shaman can always contact them in the afterlife for that information, assuming another can do it.

To become a shaman, someone is expected to become so sick as to risk death, and possibly die, before returning to life. This will assist their later ability to access the afterlife/underworld. The thought is that, to understand sickness and heal others from all ailments, they must have experienced something as severe first. It should come as no surprise that some would-be shamans don't survive this. Others might be scarred physically or another way from the ordeal, though being of sound-mind and not having "a demon" would be required; if they haven't healed their mind/soul from the ordeal, how can they do so for others?

A spirit guide may help a shaman, who can acquire more than one. These acts as guides, messengers, or protectors. As world builders, we can choose the form and power a guide may take, including animals of our invention. These spirit guides can lend strength to the shaman on his journey and even provide the power needed to enter the spirit realm. The guide's form, such as a duck, is sometimes chosen as one that is comfortable both below and above water (including flying), which symbolizes the ability to navigate both the normal world and underworld.

GOALS

The goals of shamanism vary but include:

- Communication
- Divination
- Bringing otherworldly forces into ours
- Healing

Communication with the undead allows access to what ancestors knew when alive or knowledge that they gained in the afterlife. This trope gives our characters another way to learn something about the world or current situations (in other places or the earthly one). Whether that intel, or the person providing it, can be trusted is another matter, and this creates another storytelling dynamic.

Divination, the practice of gaining knowledge of the future, can come through visions or direct interaction with spirits who may know, or claim to know, what is to come. When ancestors are contacted, a presumption of truth telling and well-wishing toward the living may give confidence in the answer. This will still depend on the ancestor contacted, for as we all know, not everyone gets along.

Bringing forces from another realm into ours requires more power, experience, possibly training, and maybe a stronger connection to the ancestors, possibly through increased interaction as a shaman; this is unlikely to be a task for a novice. A willing force is much different from an unwilling one. Either may require compensation.

Healing via shamanism is an alternative to supernatural healing by priests. Perhaps the latter invokes the [consistent] power of gods while shamans invoke the unpredictable, potentially evil power of spirits, who might exact a price from healer or healed. Moreover, if an ailment is considered to arise from one's soul, that's the kind of illness that shamanism is thought to heal, as opposed to a physical matter. In a world where wandering spirits (or something like a weapon) can cause supernatural damage, perhaps such a wound is on one's spirit in a literal sense, not just the figurative.

The latter means someone has "a demon" that causes bad behavior. For example, a trauma in childhood could create a demon that leads to alcoholism. The demon is a metaphor, not something literal, though in SF and fantasy, we often make it so. Similarly, we may say their spirit is wounded. Thus, on Earth, a shaman attempts to heal this figurative wound. Or in our invented world, it's a literal wound, maybe one that doesn't respond to other means of healing.

This conjures a philosophical debate for figurative wounds of the spirit. Is it better for an external source, like a shaman, to fix us, or should we self-heal, possibly by forming a better understanding of ourselves and our psychology, growing as a person and overcoming our demon without such outside assistance? The former offers a quick and easy fix for the wounded. Where would modern psychology be today if shamans could wave their metaphorical magic wand and my demons, and yours, could be vanquished so that I'm just a happy, productive member of society instead of argumentative, boozing, and generally screwing up my life because a demon haunts me? Am I stronger because I grew as a person, the hard way? Yes. Am I stronger because a shaman "fixed" me the easy way? Not really. I only lost a problem that made me weaker.

Psionics

Psionics is the ability to communicate or perceive beyond the five physical senses. This fits our definition of magic. While fictional, these are considered innate talents people are either born with or develop. They're usually depicted as natural, meaning they don't require spells, but we've also seen them portrayed as needing an external element. The crystal ball is the most famous of these. We can add anything we desire to make these unique in our setting, while also making them easier or harder to accomplish. Multiple subtypes exist and are briefly summarized next. Any combination of these can exist in the setting. We can treat all of them like magic, meaning we decide their prevalence, training needed, the distance restrictions, and other elements discussed in this chapter.

Ability	Description
Clairvoyance	This is the ability to see events or people beyond the range of normal sight. This can be broken down into precognition (the future), retrocognition (the past), and remote viewing (the present). It can also imply clairaudience (hearing) or be mutually exclusive, meaning some people only have one talent. A theme of this chapter is imposing limits, so don't be afraid to restrict them.
Empathy	An "empath" can read or sense another person's emotions and may even be able to control or influence them.
Mind control	One person impacts another's mind, including removing, suppressing, or replacing memories, or causing the victim to sense phantom pain.
Psychometry	The talent for gaining foresight by touching objects.
Telekinesis	Telekinesis is the ability to move objects with the mind.
Telepathy	Reading another person's thoughts or communicating directly with their mind.

Figure 72 Psionics Chart

ELEMENTAL MAGIC

Using the elements is one way to organize our magic. In addition to the four elements of water, air, earth, and fire, people sometimes decide that spirit is a fifth. We can also invent other elements, especially on non-Earth like worlds. Whatever we decide, this is a convenient way to divide spells because many spells will only use a given element. If we want our wizard to be able to do something with fire but he is a water wizard, this restriction is built in. We can also have rare individuals who are able to do one or all of them. But we don't need to decide that people can only do one element. Perhaps everyone can do all four but there's a "high" and "low" magic that distinguishes them. Or some are just better suited to one and, while they can do all, struggle with some.

We can decide that practitioners need the element to manipulate and cannot conjure it from "thin air." For example, in a desert, a water wizard would have nothing to work with. Or we can decide they're able to sense and draw it from wherever it is within a given range; while there may appear to be no water in a desert, it's still there. Water and fire are the only two that might be unavailable, generally, but even water is usually around. It's fire that's less naturally occurring, putting such wizards at a disadvantage.

Element	Possible Uses
Air	The ability to fly, manipulate weather, suffocate others, breathe underwater, cause fog
Fire	Starting/extinguishing fires, fireball spells, wall of flames
Earth	Causing earthquakes/sinkholes, softening or hardening of earth (to create mud or stone), creating or commanding stone golems
Water	Dehydrating someone, hydrating them, creating drinking water, parting the sea, walking on water, causing rain, and possibly controlling sea life
Spirit	Control, communicate, or summon/banish ghosts

Figure 73 Elemental Magic

MAGIC PREVALENCE

Just like with technology, we need to determine how common magic and the ability to control it is. Rarity makes it more special, valuable, and feared, while it being common tends to get it taken for granted. We don't need to explain the prevalence unless it has changed in the setting, such as hardly anyone having the ability and suddenly almost everyone does. We can just state it's one way or another, but how do we decide what we want? By understanding the impact on setting and stories.

The more common magic is, the more it affects life (and stories), just like Earth technologies today. Do we want it everywhere? Magic will dominate. If we skip thinking this through, we risk a mistake: magic can resolve plot problems when we didn't want it to. Let's say we plot a story where the characters need to get somewhere in two days by horse, and along the way, someone joins their group, and they acquire both important information and an item. Then we decide magic is pervasive and there are magic gates they can use to traverse this distance in ten seconds. Now it doesn't make sense that they'll go by horse. They won't learn the information and don't have the item or companion. Now we must fix our plot. Avoid this by working out the magic prevalence first.

If magic is rare, we get the usual fantasy setting of a few people being able to do it. Most life happens without magic, which is used by individuals mostly for their own benefit. If magic is common, it's likely been commercialized so that society benefits from it. Just as we have engineers who work for a settlement/government, we might have wizards whose jobs involve using magic for the benefit of all. We must decide the degree of this. An easy way is to think about modern technology and its advantages, and then determine a magical equivalent. It helps to divide life into categories, such as farming, manufacturing, government, communications, and daily life. What can they do with it?

Magic items are a primary result of this. Think of appliances in your life and whether something comparable exists, but don't do a one-for-one switch where the only difference is whether there's a plug for electricity or not. A magic toaster likely works and looks differently than an electric one. We're not just replacing the energy source, but reimagining how the end result can be achieved via an item with the same purpose. Combining purposes is one way to achieve this. We may have a toaster, microwave, stove top, bread maker, panini press, and oven in our house, plus a grill out back. Do they just have one thing and the spells are the difference?

Instead of items, we can have wizards who use their skills "in real time." An example would be that there are no magic gateways to travel between locations, but there are wizards who excel at transporting others and they work for the government doing this, stationed at specific locations, just like a train depot, for example. They'd likely have insurance via their employer for accidents. Do they have an 8-hour workday? Imagine the fatigue. They may work in teams for that reason. We could have different spell types for this, each named, with some being preferred and more expensive. We can do this exercise with any aspect of modern Earth life.

WHERE DOES MAGIC COME FROM?

Even a physicist might say that magic must come from somewhere. There's a fine distinction between the origins of magic and its sources.

ORIGINS

The origins of magic in our world is the answer to the question, "Where does magic come from?" And the answer can be the universe (nature) or the gods (or a being with god-like abilities). There aren't many more options, though we can get more specific than the "nature" option, such as saying it's radiation, or a lifeforce, or some other energy. We don't need to explain it to an audience. Magic is accepted. Its origins are a philosophical question and therefore ignored if we choose to, whereas the source of a wizard's power is a practical matter to which we should pay some attention.

SOURCES

To perform magic, a wizard must draw power from a source regardless of the origins of that source's existence. Inventing sources is an easy way to create multiple types of magic, one per source, if desired. What follows an inexhaustive list of possible sources:

- The planet
    - Elements
    - Gravity
    - Magnetics
- The solar system
    - The sun
    - The moon(s)
    - Ring system (like Saturn)
    - Comets
- Other realities
    - Other planes (like the Astral plane)
    - Parallel dimensions
- Beings
    - God(s)
    - Demons/angels, etc.
    - Aliens
    - Plants, animals, humanoids, etc.
    - Souls (possibly from the living) or "lifeforce"
- The "force" from *Star Wars*

The latter option is an implied one in many stories, though only *Star Wars* calls it that. The energy just exists all around us and those with the talent can sense and manipulate it. A large source, such as the universe, has an advantage. When a wizard draws energy from a source, it seems reasonable that the source is temporarily drained. An analogy would be blood drawn

604 | RANDY ELLEFSON

from us. It replenishes in time, but of course someone can take it all, killing us. A truly powerful source like the sun or the universe is unlikely to be noticeably drained.

But if magic draws energy from living beings, it seems clear we could kill them by taking too much at once, or too often. Wizards could draw from multiple sources to mitigate this. We should determine the source of our magic and within what radius from the wizard that source must be. This is irrelevant with some sources that permeate everything or are seemingly always the same distance; while a planet gets farther or nearer to the sun, this is imperceptible to the naked eye, but what if wizards are always weaker in winter because their source, the sun, is dimmer? But then perhaps it doesn't matter that the radiation and other elements the sun expels in our direction change distance. It's up to us to decide. But we're always looking for ways to limit what sorcerers can do and this is one way.

If a wizard draws from the living, it's an obvious way to kill people, intentionally or not. But perhaps only some species can be so drained. Either way, imagine this person leaving a trail of corpses or people who've suddenly got a type of "sickness" with symptoms indicating a wizard used them as a source, likely in violation of the law. Consequences make for conflict, which makes for story. If we don't have a need of this source being impacted, then we can decide the source is everywhere, in which case, we can also avoid mentioning it at all.

THE COST OF MAGIC

Everything requires energy, and magic is expending it, or at least redirecting it elsewhere. We can say the same amount of energy exists before as after, and we've repurposed it, but this is a philosophical subject. We care more about the cost to the practitioner here. Those who suffer few or no effects of performing magic are almost gods, but mortals aren't so lucky. Adding a cost to wizardry is an easy way to limit their powers.

The obvious and default answer, which no one will feel is a cliché, is that it's physically draining to perform wizardry. Everything else is, so why wouldn't it be? We also can decide that using it is like alcohol, which is a depressant but, in the short term, acts as a stimulant instead; people can feel energized during a magical battle but "crash" when it's over, needing a deep sleep if they expended a lot of energy; use an analogy of your choice with different side effects to invent something original. We can decide that magic ages the practitioner prematurely, or reduces their ability to have children due to exposure to the energy, as does radiation. An old idea is that a spell needs to be memorized and, once cast, the wizard forgets it and must relearn it; what if casting it affects the mind in other ways? Maybe the spell isn't the only thing they forget. Or perhaps magic makes them have nightmares or slowly go crazy. Just be sure to invent a price.

SOCIAL ASPECTS

Whether magic is rare or not, there may be laws that vary by location about its usage. We can create an entire area of law, crime, and punishments. These often originate from problems that have already occurred, so think about wizards doing bad things, especially in public, and how society has tried to deter this. We can invent some history and infamous incidents and characters (including victims), after whom a law may be named.

How can they inhibit wizards? The purposeful use of anti-magic zones is one way, or a device that can be placed on someone to cut them off from magic. Maybe they've figured out how to permanently remove the ability. Perhaps they can only limit access, such as making someone weaker so that only minor spells can be done. If they don't have a supernatural way to inhibit, they could just drug someone so that they're too weak to do it and regularly administer this. We can invent plants that have this effect once properly prepared. Where there's a will, there's a way.

The more common magic usage is, the more social customs will arise from it. Casting a spell on our date without their permission is probably frowned on! But is casting a spell on ourselves prior to it okay? That likely depends on the result. If it's considered dishonest, like making us appear 100 lbs. lighter, this is probably bad, but if we only changed our hair color, maybe not. It depends on whether we're up front about these things. To create these, think about how life would be and what you'd want to do if you had magic and how others would react to you doing it.

There's always a power disparity between wizards and muggles, to use a Harry Potter term. Do people consider it rude for a wizard to use magic with non-magical people? How concerned are people about this? Imagine being one of the few who can't do magic and how intimidating that might be, and how we might try to hide it or compensate. What if we're the lone person who's unaffected by magic? What sort of bullying is done due to magic or via it? Be prepared to think about these elements if magic is prevalent.

Some communities might reject magic while others take advantage of it. Religious beliefs or conservative values (that resist change) can affect this.

So can fear and significant historical acts. It's an oversight to not have such places, or even zealots who denounce wizards or are on a crusade to capture, kill, or render them magicless. By contrast, some will worship the powerful or seek to be an apprentice, resulting in fierce competition. Sorcerers might be viewed like athletes are here. Give serious thought to what social elements are impacted.

WHAT'S IN A NAME?

The words for magic users can be generic or imply meanings. The phrase "magic user" is a catchall that includes everything: wizards, mages, sorcerers, magicians, necromancers, witches/warlocks, and more. Many of these are virtual synonyms that carry no specific meaning unless we decide to differentiate them.

"Magician" sometimes implies a trickster or a charlatan. If we have true magic users and charlatans, "magician" might be for the latter and seen as an insult. On Earth, a magician is an "illusionist," who appears to be doing magic. Such people can exist on a world with actual magic, so it's likely there's a word for them, and real wizards hate being considered one. This adds a dynamic. If we use "magician" for real magic users, we need another term, such as "trickster," or "illusionist," for these other guys.

"Mage" is familiar to fantasy audiences as a synonym for magician, but some haven't heard this term. A simple reference will educate them, like this example: "Kier was a mage, or magician, of great renown." This is slightly better than, "Kier was a mage, or wizard," because the first ties "mage" and "magician" together better than "mage" and "wizard." The word itself is archaic and fell out of usage until fantasy games like as *Dungeons & Dragons* revived it.

If we've invented types of magic for our setting, each needs a name. The inhabitants will have named them even if we try to skirt this issue. We can append other words to it, such as "high magic" and "low magic," or create new words altogether, like my "valendry" from Llurien. We can also use the words in this section to refer to different practitioners.

ARE SPELLS NEEDED?

It may seem obvious that spells are needed to perform magic, but that depends on our definition of "spell" and "magic." Magic is considered powers that don't exist on Earth. But in our fictional world, magic is real, so does this definition fail? On that world, yes, but our audience is on Earth, so it still holds. But any physical changes that can be done without manually manipulating something, or using tech, can be considered magic. As for spells, this typically means words, gestures, physical materials, or some combination of these, to perform said magic. If all of this seems obvious, there's a reason the distinction is being made.

Gods are considered real in fantasy worlds especially. And gods make things happen that don't occur in the real world of Earth. Does that mean they're doing magic? Unless we have a pressing reason for using a different word, yes. Perhaps gods and mortals are tapping into the same well of supernatural power, but one difference is that people are weakened by this and gods either aren't, or to a lesser degree, but we can safely say gods (usually all of them) are capable of magic.

But are gods using spells? Or are they doing magic by force of will? I'm inclined to say it's will power for several reasons. One is that we should distinguish between gods and mortals. It seems clear that gods can innately do magic (will power), but mortals must struggle to learn and master it, even if they have the talent from birth. Gods may have imposed limits, via spells, on what mortals can do. We can find other ways to impose limits, but it still raises the point: either beings can do it by force of will or they need spells.

We've seen depictions of gods making gestures or speaking words to achieve their result, which suggests they're using a spell, but perhaps they're just controlling the force better this way. In visual media, people are typically shown doing these as visual/audible cues as to who is causing something to happen. This is sometimes omitted when it's already been established who in the scene has the ability, such as Darth Vader in *Star Wars*, or when ambiguity is desired (either by characters or storytellers). Since will power is innate, gods may not need spells. Non-gods are typically portrayed as needing to learn how magic works; they study various things like the language of magic (an innate skill for gods), and then read spell books to learn how each spell is done. Then they practice. What little power they start with grows with that practice. We assume gods aren't doing any of this because we show them as strong. Whether gods are using spells or not is semantics, except that if we have a choice between gods and mortals using willpower, the least sensible option is gods needing spells and mortals using willpower; the latter suggests fewer restrictions and more power, both of which apply to gods.

What about mortals? Can they do magic via will power or are spells the only way? We may want to have both in our setting and use a name for each, like wizard vs. sorcerer.

SPELLS ARE NEEDED

Let's say spells are needed to perform magic. The spells would harness magical energy, but if the spell is performed wrong, we have two options: nothing happens, or magic still happens but in unintended ways. Both are plausible. Failure can mean that the energy wasn't harnessed at all, which seems the safest poor result. Failure can also mean the energy was harnessed but discharged improperly, resulting in an alternate outcome, whether that's a deadly explosion or a minor variation in the intended result. It's up to us to decide which we want.

Comic results are sometimes desired, particularly in children's books like Harry Potter. But we can also show the dangers of magic with perilous failure. Imagine how few people would want to do this if it's so dangerous. By contrast, if nothing happens, an attempt is less fraught with worry. We might badly need the spell to succeed and feel pressure for that reason, but if we can't do it right, we and others aren't dead or worse. Decide how dangerous magic should be in the setting. It's easy to imagine wizards who are a nervous wreck when doing something powerful if disaster could result. This can also cause strong restrictions by governments and others. It also ramps up the apprehension people feel when someone tries a spell. If you're a wizard and about to do something, I might run for my life even if you're my friend and I trust you. All of this can be significant reason for training facilities. But if nothing happens when failure occurs, everyone would be far more casual about it. What do they have to lose?

We can also invent solutions per situation or spell type (or even magic type). What if I'm a spell author and I know how to make my spell recipes safely dissipate energy when done wrong? But another guy had no idea and his spells are therefore more dangerous? My spell recipes are more desired. Why would anyone use the other guy's spells? Because those are the only ones they've found.

Breaking a spell down into parts helps with this. Maybe the energy must be harnessed first, then manipulated before being expended. Can a wizard sense the harnessing? If so and it's not working, he might stop right there.

This failure will not expel energy and therefore nothing will happen. But if the energy is harnessed, and then the expulsion part of the spell is where failure occurs, an accidental result seems more plausible. For this reason, maybe some wizards craft their spells in reverse: the part to control the energy comes first, followed by the gathering of energy. This way, if failure happens during the first part, the harnessing also fails and nothing happens. Regardless of the order, some spell authors might've put in a failsafe that causes energy to be quietly released back to where it came from or safely dispersed elsewhere.

It seems plausible that all of these options would exist in the same world. We can have individual spell creators with a reputation for one thing or another. There can be entire schools of magic that only teach one kind of spell, whereas rogue wizards are willing to do the more dangerous spells. Perhaps the latter are only created by rogue authors trying to achieve an end result that sanctioned places, like a school of wizardry, forbid. Or maybe truly powerful spells require so much of the wizard's energy to perform that some spell authors dispensed with the safeguards because it made the spell that much more taxing or complicated. Short cuts happen in all parts of life, even when unwise.

SPELLS ARE NOT NEEDED

Now let's decide spells are not needed. Mortals can do magic without them. All those safeguards we just discussed will be absent. There's no recipe, path, or guideline to follow. There's no "if I do this, I will get this result." We may will something to be and have unconscious thoughts intrude and also be willed into reality. Or maybe we weren't thinking of one aspect of our intention and it's omitted as a result. We may be able to fix these mistakes at once, but it might also be too late, such as willing an arrow fired at us to veer to one side, causing it to strike our best friend and killing him instantly. If we're not powerful enough to bring someone back or reverse time and opt for a redo, we're out of luck.

This willpower business is inherently more dangerous and uncontrolled – and one reason to reserve it for gods. The odds of a mortal wizard doing something wrong but still achieving an accidental result are probably far higher. And this might be why *optional* spells still exist, to achieve and control a specific result (within a defined range of possibilities). Spells would therefore place limits on magic, not make magic possible.

Given this, does it make sense to cast a spell and have it go wrong but still do something? If we wanted that to happen, we wouldn't be using the spell. It should be a pass/fail scenario – either we do it right and it works (within parameters) or we do it wrong and nothing happens. This is a viable option to consider for our world.

But there can be more to this. Willpower wizards can clearly draw energy without help from a spell. This suggests that the point of spells is to control the energy's release, which they can also do, but that this will aid them in doing so. There might also be issues with controlling the drawing of energy (such as taking too much or from poor sources), and therefore spells *do* include this. And authors of spells can include or omit safety features or be better or worse at inventing them, as we discussed in the previous section.

So where does that leave us? Whether using spells or not, we can have magic go wrong and still produce a result, even when the whole point of spells is to do it right. But we should generally opt for a pass/fail scenario if spells aren't required. If spells are likely to be of little help, then many people wouldn't bother with them. Perhaps they're viewed like training wheels on bikes and few people use them after a certain experience level.

THE LIFE OF MAGIC-USERS

We won't look at how a wizard, shaman, or other type of practitioner spends his day so much as the phases of his career, from how the ability is gained and lost, their training, what life is like at the height of power and then if they begin to lose strength with age.

HOW THE ABILITY IS GAINED AND LOST

Even if everyone in a setting can perform magic, we must decide how the ability is gained (or lost). Our default is that it's like talent; you've either got it or you don't. However, even among those who do, they sometimes don't know it, feel it, or have it until they reach a given milestone. This can be an age or event, such as losing virginity, a first period for a female, or the first time we draw blood or kill someone. Maybe we even need to die and be reborn. Perhaps the ability can be given like a gift under certain conditions. We might have to consume something once or regularly, like a potion, pill, plant, or animal.

What about losing the ability? This seldom gets a mention but is worth focusing on. If magic is a talent, then it theoretically never goes away. But maybe it depends on how the magic works. Songwriters always have the talent to write music, but as we all know, some are better than others and there are times when a band seems unable to write great music anymore. If performing magic requires some originality or inspiration, then maybe some wizards have fallen from grace, their "heyday" behind them. They can still do it, but they're out of ideas for new actions. They're the equivalent of a "has been" band still touring and playing their greatest hits.

If an event causes magic ability, can another make it stop? Maybe a potion, pill, plant, or animal takes it away. Perhaps someone must be celibate like a priest; this raises the unfortunate prospect of rape being used to render a wizard non-magical. What if killing someone, drawing blood, or another act causes the ability to weaken or fade? The gods can make this a reality to punish people, particularly if magic was used to perform the act. A benevolent god might do this, but perhaps a nefarious one grants the talent for causing mayhem.

If the ability is gained or lost, decide if this is permanent or not. Maybe having it was never forever anyway. Maybe the sun gives the ability, but the sun is too far away in winter and wizards cease to be one for part of the year. Do magic items stop working at that time, too? What if an item was holding up a building?

TRAINING

Even wizards who can do magic with will power, not spells, can benefit from training. One element that distinguishes mankind (at least on Earth) is the ability to learn from predecessors. And wizards are likely the elite, having more specialized knowledge that can be passed down. While some of that can be done via books or scrolls, personal interaction tends to be superior to written material. To determine how much training is available and what form it likely takes, we should determine the prevalence of magic as previously discussed.

At its rarest, magic will only be taught by individual wizards in a master/apprentice scenario. At its most common, there are wizardry schools, possibly many of them held in differing esteem, and with practices. Aside from prevalence, the other major factor determining this is public and government attitudes toward magic. Naturally, where it's forbidden, the secret apprenticeship is more likely, but where it is openly accepted and plenty of wizards are around, a school may exist.

We can use this to develop character backstory. If they have little to no training, that will explain some mishaps and inconsistency. They may even be able to do some spells without all of the words, gestures, or ingredients, somehow compensating for it. Someone who goes to a prestigious wizardry school will be known for that. Those who had a secret internship, possibly with someone disreputable, may keep quiet about it and refuse to admit to their master's whereabouts. Every wizard is likely to have an accident of some kind in their past, and training certainly influences the number and severity of these, plus the emotional and even physical scars that result. A wizard without fear is a fool.

To create a school of magic and its curriculum or books, we can leverage subjects from our own schooling. What typically exists? Potions, summoning, communication, creating and using items, material usage (plants, animals, etc.), history, school of magic, types of magic, general spell casting 101, and more. Unless we're planning to have a character in a Harry Potter-like setting, we don't need too many details, but it's worth inventing this once and having it in mind for most of our fantasy worlds because much of it would exist on all of them, even if the class or book titles change. Inventing a magic curriculum can be fun.

Determine how long school lasts in hours per day, months, and years and if there are ranks that people achieve at various stages. This can help break "wizards" from one organized mass into smaller groups distinguished from each other. An obvious decision is for multiple years, and with this chosen, we can choose ranks. For example, if it's seven years, we can use the seven colors in the spectrum to denote those at each stage of completion, and maybe they wear robes of a given color to show it. If it's four, maybe we use seasons or elements.

Are there tests that must be passed to advance? It seems obvious. We don't have to decide what they are, but it can add interest, particularly if each year has one test that is more feared than the predecessors. It's a chance to invent stories about what happened to one person or another when failing. We shouldn't go too far with this sort of thing unless our story is to heavily feature it.

At what point do graduates become eligible to teach others, whether at school or in an apprenticeship? Why would someone want my teaching instead of yours? Expertise and prestige are two reasons. We can gain the latter due to pedigree, training, accomplishments, and fame. Or even having past students of a given instructor go on to achieve greatness. Invent a famous instructor in the setting and determine why this is so.

We should also determine what happens if someone fails training or is expelled. Are they literally marked, like a thief with a notch in their ear? Or perhaps their abilities have been removed. These people will be around and it makes our setting more believable that one should be encountered, particularly in longer tales. Their fate should be a warning to those in training.

HEIGHT OF POWER

When wizards are in their prime, we should determine their options in society. Deciding on magic prevalence once against helps us decide their prospects. For example, if magic is common and accepted, they might begin to instruct others, possibly at schools. They can live openly, make people feel safe, be honored (with statues or presiding at ceremonies), and enjoy good relations with leaders, military, and anyone else. When magic is rare and wizards are feared, they may teach in secret, maybe far from others, hide their location or nature, be shunned, and have an attitude about all of it. All of this would be on someone's mind when entering into wizardry just as we envision our prospects in any career. Don't overlook this. Use the techniques in chapter one to invent a culture for them, and be sure to vary it by sovereign power and, to a lesser extent, within regions and settlements.

Wizards are often thought to amass powerful items and wealth, whether it's true or not. When magic is common, there may be special vaults and banks like what we see in Harry Potter, but without this, keeping their hoard close (such as at home) is more likely. This can lead them to become a target, one who has various kinds of protection (magical or otherwise) to conceal and protect their homes, whether there's anything valuable there or not. We need to think about where they might choose to live, based on how magic and its practitioners are viewed. They'll want to feel safe, whether that means living openly or in secret, and with physical or supernatural protection or not, and even though they might be very powerful and inspire fear, the terrified often attack in the name of preemptively defending themselves.

All of this affects a wizard's family life, too. They're so often shown to be loners that we can easily overlook this. Don't they have friends, lovers, children? Are some of them magical? Or strong in other ways, like knights? Many will be just as respectable or disrespectable. It's tempting to see a wizard as all-powerful, but even they get sick, injured, or tired. Fantasy is prone to sorting people as good or evil, but many supposedly "evil" people just have a different viewpoint, one shared by many others, around whom they'd feel safer in weak moments.

THE WANING YEARS

Powerful wizards have powerful enemies, but sooner or later they are going to start aging and become increasingly vulnerable. Who is going to protect them? Maybe this is a scenario where the wizard's apprentices protect their former master, or do they prey upon him? This is part of the magical culture. This could also be one reason that there are magic guilds, with one of the benefits of joining being this protection as we age and become weaker and vulnerable to our enemies. Might not a wayward wizard in youth curb his worse tendencies as he ages so that he'll be accepted – and protected?

Just as we imagine our prospects for a career, we might think of our retirement. How is a feared wizard going to live peacefully? Move away so people don't realize? Who wants to end their life in hiding, away from anyone they care about? It seems reasonable to find another way. Might not a wizard cultivate good relations for just this issue? Even an evil wizard, if smart, would find a kingdom where they're see as good and retire *there*.

ATTIRE

The default attire many audiences have in mind is the robe, with the color or something else denoting the type of magic or skill level the practitioner has attained. There's no reason for the robe other than cliché, but they do offer the chance to have an unknown quantity of pockets within, each holding ingredients. However, other clothing can achieve the same; cargo pants come to mind, though the pockets are visible. Do we really need a wizard to hide how much stuff they're carrying? Quick access to pockets during fights is wise, but a belt or bandoleer (used for bullets) can do the same.

Question how practitioners are dressed and why. A robe could be considered formal and mostly worn while at official functions. Perhaps a shorter version is for travel, worn with trousers to cover the lower legs when it's cold. A robe might be tradition or enforced on wizards in societies that insist on immediate identification (in this case, via clothing) of practitioners. Some wizards might wish to hide their abilities for any number of reasons.

Another old cliché is that wizards can't wear armor. This may have been conceived to make such powerful characters more vulnerable, but we have other ways to do this. Armor interfering with gestures doesn't make sense as a justification, given that sword fighting, for example, requires far more mobility. But another explanation is that metal somehow interferes with the wizardry; we can make such a factor true of one magic but not another to create distinctions, but it also seems that an enterprising person would fashion armor that doesn't cause this, with such armor being hard to acquire.

Consider that the audience only benefits from a visual cue in visual mediums, so print authors have greater leeway to completely abandon all stereotypical garb. In other mediums, we may want an immediately recognizable style in our story world. Then we just need to establish it, which takes no more than a line of dialogue when someone comments on the outfit. In *Star Wars*, we know who's a Jedi knight at once due to inference.

CREATING LIMITS

A system is all about limits. Whether we're doing hard or soft magic, we must still decide on limits unless we genuinely want an all-powerful being. There are arguably two kinds of limits: those imposed by the universe/gods and those caused by mortals. For the latter, this means that someone has devised a system of magic on our world.

For example, the arch wizard Kier discovered and developed a series of spells now known as Kierzadry. Another wizard called Taria invented Tariandry. Both had their talents, knowledge, inventiveness, research ability, and access to materials with which to experiment. They also ran into problems, solving some and not others, and deciding they'd found a limit (whether true or not) to one thing or another. And they built on their work over possibly decades, crafting spells that considered their learning. The result is two different schools of magic (or types), each with their own rules.

Let's say Kier lived with varied landscapes nearby, with unique wildlife and plants, like the Amazon on Earth. It's likely his spells use exotic materials, and maybe gestures or magic words are lesser parts of his spells. But Taria lived in a desert city when none of that was available, so her spells rely much more on words and gestures. Maybe she even contacted spirits, demons, or the like, and these supernatural forces are part of what she developed. Do we need to explain any of this to the audience? No, but imagining the origin of a magic type helps us develop it and use the natural limits of the physical world to define it.

Maybe those who practice Kierzardy are very good at the manipulation of materials but struggle to perform Tariandry due to the complex gestures and words, and lack skill in contacting spirits, who might be unfamiliar with them and therefore reluctant to answer. A Kierzardist might subsequently imagine this is another limit and wrongly tell others Tariandry can't be done by them. A Tariandist might decide that it's difficult to get the materials needed to perform Kierzardry, even at stores, and that even once acquired, processing them in the correct way is too much like cooking with rare materials that they don't understand. It's also possible that these are rival schools of magic and practitioners generally refuse to teach each other. The last thing they want is someone who's adept at both.

GET ORGANIZED

Creating limits has much to do with organization. An obvious example is elemental magic. Given that there are four elements, this is already structured for us. We can also create high and low magic, black and white (and grey), moon and sun, light and dark, good and evil, and color magic. We can also decide a specific requirement is a type, such as blood or sex magic requiring an item (blood) or act (intercourse).

Explanations are optional. They can significantly impede our ability to create and define magic types because we're trying to justify many fictional things. It's time to act like the world building gods that we are; things are this or that way because we said so. End of story. If we think of an explanation for any decision, that's great, but avoid getting bogged down in this. Besides, we can say Tariandry and Kierzardy are incompatible without saying why because our world's inhabitants may not know either (some mystery is good). A simple explanation could be that Kier and Taria are not mortals, but gods who hate each other and don't want their wizards crossing over like that, so they included limits.

PROS AND CONS

Even magic systems have pros and cons, which is one way to further define our system(s). Some pros have little to do with the type but rather the society. For example, if training or materials are widely available or cheap, that's a plus and may result in easier refinement of the talent. On the other hand, this could also result in numerous practitioners so that it's harder to gain employment as one or distinguish oneself, for example. There may be pros and cons that are specific to the type, rather than general benefits of wizardry. For example, many practitioners can help their community, or make a difference in life, finding meaning and purpose in their powers, but this is true across magic types. We're looking to define what's beneficial about a type.

CREATE BENEFITS

Why does anyone want to perform this type of magic? If they don't get to choose between types, this matters less, as they only have one option: develop their talent/ability or not. Reasons to forge ahead can include the obvious ones, like power, prestige, wealth, personal safety, and gaining advantage for ourselves or others, but even if none of these appeal to someone, there's a default reason: they have an innate ability and may sometimes cause things to happen by accident, so they need to learn control.

Regardless, we should craft some benefits of each magic type. A built-in benefit might be that a necromancer can communicate with the dead and possibility comfort the living by fostering interaction. If the dead have advance knowledge of the future, this can also be advantageous. Alchemy is thought to cause noble changes within a person, whether the practitioner or the target, and doing so may align with a person's outlook to make the world a better place; it's the similar set of reasons for why people become priests. For an elemental wizard, bringing rain to a barren land is an example. Psionics can help us understand each other or avoid problems. To craft these, consider what uses practitioners have for this magic. What are their goals? What can be done with it?

Our intended story, if we have one, can also assist. What problems will the characters face and how might this magic type assist them? If a trap lies in their future, perhaps they can see it in advance. If they can't find an item physically, maybe this wizardry can locate it. Reading minds helps overcome an enemy, or creates allies. How can they resolve conflict? Be careful not to perfectly solve the plot or character issues with magic!

While pros don't help us craft limits to define a magic type, they can help us envision cons that do by way of contrast. And these benefits are only possibilities, not guarantees. The cons can prevent realization of these benefits.

618 | RANDY ELLEFSON

CREATE PROBLEMS

What problems does this magic type pose? All types can be dangerous, so we're once again trying to decide on specifics for a type. Reasons to not develop the talent can be economic, lack of education, lack of materials, social problems caused by being a practitioner, personality traits (lack of desire, follow through, and more), or other problems inherent to the type.

Necromancy can revive the dead, who may have ideas about obeying commands or what to do now that they're animated. They may now have supernatural traits that can harm the necromancer or expose the practitioner to knowledge that haunts them. Some types like witchcraft may require a bargain with an evil entity like a demon, who eventually comes to collect. Either of these could result in prolonged contact with other conscious forces (demons, ghosts) that increase the risk of being compromised by them. We could become enthralled by them, enslaved. We might die and our spirit enter their world. To avoid such fates, a spell may have a time-limit on it.

Practitioners aren't the only ones for whom problems can be caused. Do I want a clairvoyant in my head? Is society okay with necromancy? A government or high-minded individuals can place limits, not simply by creating laws, but by incorporating limits in the spell. Imagine that our wizard Kier, who invented Kierzardy, tried to protect himself, devotees, or people in general by adding the limits. Or maybe he didn't and decades later, a government hires a disciple to alter the spells and does so, with older versions being confiscated. This thinking allows us to imagine catastrophes and then what people did to imbue spells with limits.

Our intended story can help us determine problems. What sort of issue might the character face because they have this talent or ability? Breaking laws is not what we're after, but magic going wrong and causing problems, which might have resulted in limits being imposed on the magic system by practitioners, or the spells' creators, or those who control the source of the energy (such as gods).

HOW TO INVENT SPELLS

As we all know, spells are a combination of words, gestures, and ingredients. One way to invent spells is to decide that each of these serves a different role in each magic system. If we can't make up our mind, we can have one type of magic use gestures, for example, in one way, and another type use them for another. It's the divide and conquer approach to not only inventing spells but magic systems. One choice to make is whether gestures, words, or ingredients are the difference between two spells; we might have a single spell to make a pie, with ingredients determining whether it's apple or blueberry. Or maybe ingredients don't include the fruit at all and there are indeed two spells, one for each type of pie.

GESTURES

While gestures could mean anything, it seems sensible that they're used for assisting with the width of spell for the area affected and the distance from the caster. If I only want people before me to fall asleep via my spell, I would control my gesture to indicate them but omit people to their left and right. If I want to affect people who stand within 20 feet of me, perhaps my arm is a given distance from my body but not too far, so that those more than 20 feet away are unaffected. If I want them to fall asleep instantly, perhaps my gesture is quick, whereas a slower motion might cause a less sudden effect and a gentler fall into sleep (and to the floor).

A spell that targets individuals more precisely can be imagined in a similar way. If three magic missiles will depart my fingers, perhaps I point them at the chosen targets. This could be done in succession with three pointing motions or all at once with one or two hands; we can imagine some inaccuracy with this, plus people being tipped off as to what's coming. Some variants on spells might require contact with the target, such as wanting to make a single person be the victim. Generally, the more people or wider impact area, the more difficult and tasking we can imagine the spell to be for the caster.

Gestures might also indicate the power level due to the force with which they're made. Imagine that we're casting a wind spell and merely flick our finger, versus a strong sweeping motion with one or both arms. The first might blow out a candle's flame leaving the candlestick standing while the other might knock over everything in its path. This is not a rule, but it's another way to decide what is required of the wizard. Viewed this way, a gesture might indicate passion and determination, which might please the source of that power if a god is the origin and they approve of the result; this could, in turn, convince that source to grant greater power to the wizard.

We can also decide that the wizard has harnessed energy and that, to disperse it away from themselves, these gestures are necessary, or the spell goes off in their face. With that in mind, if others know this, they might try to inhibit such a gesture, so the wizard hurts themselves. A bound wizard might be unable or unwilling to cast various spells. Imposing this limit lets us understand when they can and can't do something.

INGREDIENTS

Whether creating spells, potions, or items, viewing ingredients like those for a recipe is a useful analogy. Everything has a purpose, or it isn't there. The combination of water and flour make dough, needed for anything requiring bread or a crust. Yeast is to make dough rise. Spices are optional flavoring. Fruits, meats, and vegetables are for flavor and nutrition. For cooking, the heat can melt items together, bake some ingredients, or convert separate items into a whole. The type of pot matters. Some things can be fudged ("add spices to taste") while others will botch the result if not exact.

We can use all these cooking techniques to determine spell ingredients. Just as yeast is used to make dough rise, we can decide a common plant is used to bind elements together. A spell that has words, gestures, and only one ingredient doesn't need this plant, but one with two or more ingredients does. Similarly, maybe there's a spell type that results in a glass object and we therefore need a bit of sand, warm water (for its heat), or actual glass to achieve this. Whether someone is creating a crystal ball or an orb for light, these same ingredients would be needed even though the spells differ in other respects. Quantity would depend on the object's size.

The point of a spell is to achieve a specific result, just like cooking recipes. If we're following the recipe for apple pie, but don't get the preparation or quantities and/or ingredients right, we don't end up with a blueberry pie. Or an apple. Or a plant. We also don't melt the countertop, destroy the baking dish, or grant life to the apple slices. That said, it is possible to substitute ingredients, which is a good way to allow a wizard not fully prepared to cast a spell produce something similar with the ingredients available in the moment. Decide how flexible the spells are. If they need two oz of white sand but only have two ounces of black sand, what happens? If they have the white sand but only 1.5 oz, does the spell still work but results are smaller than it would have been? Less range? Less powerful? To answer these questions, know what each element of a spell is causing. We can start with our cooking analogy, the purpose of various items, and then imagine substitutes.

Element and Purpose	Substitute
Warm water and flour (wheat, bread, whole, etc.) to create dough	A liquid and a grounded plant. The liquid could be ordinary or unusu-

Element and Purpose	Substitute
	al/magical
Dough to form a container, base, or new whole, and which can be shaped many ways (pie, pretzel, muffin)	"Dough" to act as containers, projectiles
Yeast (makes dough rise)	Grounded plant to alter/accentuate ingredients
Water to cook (noodles, rice), sanitize, break down or congeal ingredients	Any liquid to boil, purify, breakdown or congeal ingredients
Spices for variations in taste	Small materials for variation in power/other details
Meats, fruits, and vegetables for nutrition	Meats (for strength), plants, and other elements for shaping results
Pots, pans, containers of metal, glass	Same, possibly of unique materials
Tongs, spatula, etc., to handle hot items	Same

Figure 74 Spell Ingredients

WORDS

The mystery of magic is often the viewers' inability to understand what a wizard is doing, or how, and finding out that the words mean something unimpressive ruins this. So we may not want to decide them for every (or any) spell. But we should still decide what they're for.

The words might be the "ties that bind" bringing everything together. Without the words, do we just have gestures and materials? Words can be what makes magic work, from the gathering of energies, to the merging of this with any gestures and ingredients, to the channeling of those elements. Seen this way, words serve as the control, with gestures assisting in any stage of this. They're a kind of "on" and "off" function for spell casting, words at least beginning if not ending the casting. Some spells could still be manipulated with gestures once the speaker goes silent, though there's likely a time limit on that. Does a wizard have five seconds or thirty to manipulate the energies he's collected?

If we invent a magic language, this implies that those words grant access to magic so that the same words spoken in another tongue have no effect.

Whether we show this magic language or not, working out what must be said can distinguish one spell from another. A generic pie spell might only have a single word different (rhubarb vs. blueberry) in a placeholder sort of way, or the entire spoken lines could be different. If we have an invented language, it will be less effort (and cheaper if someone must do it for us) to just replace a word than the entire contents.

Let's say these are the words:

"Oh god of plenty, hear my prayer,
Make this joy of many layers,
A scrumptious treat of apple pie,
Without which I shall surely die."

This generic spell is specific only once, the word "apple," and can be swapped with blueberry, cherry, pumpkin, or whatever. This is not only easier for us, but for the wizards in our world. If we have two types of magic, we can decide that one type uses this simple word substitution, allowing for wizards to quickly learn a range of only fractionally different spells. Contrast that with another magic type where the spells are so different that it is more difficult to learn. What if this is what was required just to switch to a blueberry pie?

"In the land of Kingshire grows,
A fruit that cures all hunger woes,
Blue and berry it rightly be,
Till baked as pie and had with tea."

The length of the lines should be kept short for simple spells and lengthened for more complex. We want to avoid similar phrasing, unlike those examples. We can use names of places and individuals as appropriate, making some almost like prayers. We can decide the lines are a bit like recipe instructions, where we tell the magic what to do with the ingredients, how, in what order, and what the result should be. This can take the place of gestures, and if we'd like spells that don't feature a motion, then perhaps the spell's words are what impact this. For example, a spoken "strike down those behind me" would take the place of needing to turn around and wave an arm.

WHERE TO START

Early decisions to make in creating a magic system include what types of magic we want to include in the setting, how prevalent each is, what the source is, and whether mortals need spells to do it. These choices will guide everything that follows. Then we can consider the cost of magic to a practitioner and other limits. We should also decide if we're inventing more than one type of magic for the setting and the limits of each, adding a name. With this in mind, we can then decide on training. We can invent specific spells, being careful not to craft many, if any, that solve a plot problem in a story we're planning. Finally, we can invent local laws.

CHAPTER SEVEN

ITEMS

There are three main categories of items we can create: magical, technological, and ones that are neither. In this chapter, "technology" means
SF items that don't exist on Earth, as we don't need to invent things that *do*
exist. Such items are in their own section, "Regular Items."

OWNERSHIP

Regardless of type, the question of ownership matters for world builders.
We need to know who's got the object now and whether they're considered
the real owner or not. Lost items add intrigue, especially if someone's got it
and doesn't know what it really is or who owns it – and how much peril this
may place them in. Even an item created for someone may never have found
its way to that person. Decide if the current possessor is the rightful owner;
if not, invent another character and a story about how it transferred. It's likely that the owner, if still alive, wants it back and may appear in our tale. Or
the item might be famous, and others covet it.

Games like *Dungeons and Dragons* are full of items our characters acquire
and little is done with origins, but storytellers should pay attention to where
they found it. If characters are in a ruin, long abandoned, this suggests any
claimants are long gone. But if they find something lying in the middle of an
alley in a thriving town, that means someone (who is still around) owns it.
An ancient item covered in rust is likely the discoverer's to keep, but a freshly oiled blade may provide conflict.

REGULAR ITEMS

Our world can benefit from important items that are neither supernatural nor technological. In the former case, people can attribute supernatural properties to objects that don't necessarily have them, as is the case on Earth. Religious ones come to mind. Something associated with a prophet can be considered holy. These include the Shroud of Turin, the Holy Grail, and even John the Baptist's head. But we also have items that were present at an important moment or which were memorably used, such as a weapon that killed a famous villain, or a possession of that villain or a hero.

Our regular items won't have unique properties quite like those of magical or technological ones, so we don't need much more than its description. A unique appearance makes it more identifiable in visual mediums, even if that was achieved not by design, but by usage. An example would be a sword that had no special properties but was used to kill a powerful villain and is now revered.

The origins are likely as mundane as the item itself, but needn't be. Sometimes people like the idea that a seemingly ordinary item was special all along, but it only revealed itself to be when someone did something with it. This is mythological thinking. People may later decide that a sword which slew a victim had a property incorporated by the forging blacksmith. We can even have such characters build a reputation on this. Maybe our current hero wants a sword forged by that blacksmith, thinking it has an advantage that it doesn't. This adds realism.

When creating a regular item, the form may matter if our characters will use it. A coveted decorative wall hanging may be anything, but if we need them to wield it as a weapon, then it needs to be a blade. If our characters won't use it, consider making the item a less expected form, like a tea pot. If poison was in that, or it was the last one from which a ruler was served before death, this can make some think it's special.

MAGIC ITEMS

Any item can be turned into a magic one by assigning it supernatural properties. We have some standards to choose from, such as rings, bracelets, and other jewelry, and the stereotypical wizard's staff. By contrast, a wand is something no one has unless they're a wizard (or a classical music conductor). Every item we see around us can be given magical properties, but we shouldn't make everything magical unless it dominates our setting (even then, moderation is best). How do we decide on a limit?

PROPERTIES

One way to create limits is to invent problematic items. For example, a cloak that always makes us invisible is an issue because we must securely store it somewhere when not in use. Make an item difficult to control and people will avoid using it. Study how real-world tools you use malfunction, then imagine how the invented item does this. Is the item defective? We can have fun with this, such as that cloak making our body disappear but not our shadow and the character not realizing the cloak doesn't take care of both. Does it sometimes go on by itself? Is it expected to deteriorate in time? Does it have the coveted "on/off" property?

Not all items are created equal and we can have different versions of anything. Poorer characters might get by without features while wealthier ones expect them. The existence of some features might not be apparent to some users, or they could assume one exists and be disappointed that it doesn't. Maybe they even counted on it and found out at the worst time that their assumption was wrong. We can use such things to aid story, as tales where everything goes as planned offer less tension.

Limit an item's unique powers through quantity and quality or our characters have too much power. Most magic items have one or two related uses, which is sensible, but a wand or wizard's staff are exceptions because it's seemingly their nature to provide assistance on a wide array of matters; they're also controlled by those with talent, skill, training and more, which may be untrue with other items. For everyone else, dividing up abilities helps us focus and not create the equivalent of a Swiss army knife.

Some items are sentient, but the infamous talking sword has become a symbol of unimaginative writing; some magazines immediately reject a story with one. Getting away with such things has much to do with originality and whether it's downplayed or in the audience's face. We may have better luck with SF where an AI can be the source of that speech.

ORIGINS

The more commonplace an item is, the less we need to decide its origins, but the more unique it is, the more audiences will wonder. Are there people who specialize in creating magic items? If so, these are presumably for sale. Their items are likely higher quality as they are more experienced. They and their store likely have good protection, physical and supernatural. How common is this? Depends on the prevalence of magic; if magic's rare, these would be correspondingly unusual, probably located in the populous and wealthiest cities. The profession for these people can be named for ease of reference, possibly by the type of magic. By doing this, we can create more highly prized items that characters are thrilled to find or possess.

Some items may originate with the gods, whether for their use, for use by demi-gods (like Cupid's bow), or for mortals. If it's for the gods or demi-gods but a mortal possesses it, it's likely been misplaced or stolen. Why would deities create items for mortals? The mischievous or villainous ones might want to give their followers an edge. Benevolent gods might try to counter that by granting special items to their own, but they may just wish to reward someone. Or perhaps use of the item benefits the god in some way, such as attracting followers eager for it to be used on them. The recipient is likely a member of their religious order, but needn't be. Consider the god's aims.

FORM

The item's physical form has implications that render inventing them easier, but form often has little to do with function. A magic broom may be used as transportation, which has nothing to do with its form and function (to sweep). Rings and wands have little to no impact on how they're used, but a weapon or tool does. Consider our use for the item and if it makes sense to marry function to form.

Wearable items have the advantage of seldom being left behind by accident. They're also with us when we suddenly need them. This is why jewelry is so commonly used it's become a cliché. Jewelry often serves no real purpose, making it ideal for magic properties that have little to do with form. A ring that makes the wearer invisible is more plausible than one which bakes cookies, as the spell applies directly to the wearer. Worn items typically affect a person for as long as activated. Whether magic or not, some weapons can be worn but might not be allowed in certain places, which can pose a problem if characters must leave behind a crucial item. They might just skip going in.

Some items are not expected to travel much if at all, like a tea pot or genie's "lamp" unless an existing one elsewhere won't do. Smaller magic items lend themselves to being carried in hand, bags, or pockets; transporting others might not be feasible. This is truer with freestanding items, such as furniture, transportation, or magical doorways. Such items tend to be guarded. What sort of protection does it have?

USERS

We should decide who can use each magic item. Knowing the item's purpose and our story's need for it guides this decision. If the item accentuates a wizard's power, like a staff or wand, then it may not work at all for others or only provide simple functions, like casting a light. Generally, a wizard wouldn't want a non-wizard gaining much ability from their items.

Can someone without magic talent use it? Without a "magic word" to control some, even they might fail. Some items could be activated or deactivated only by wizards but be functional for others. If there are different types of magic in our world, are people able to use all of them, or only the types for which they have affinity, talent, training, or skill? When inventing a magic system, we will decide on such rules and can apply them to items. Worn items can be lost and used by someone else, while anyone can come across a freestanding item, depending on where it's located. Consider the likelihood of someone else using it and whether the inventor would've inhibited this.

TECHNOLOGICAL ITEMS

Unlike with magic items, technological ones are unique, rather than repurposing an everyday item, like a ring, to have technological significance. Both can be done. A smart watch is more than just a watch but was created to have those extra features, rather than being repurposed. With all tech objects, we'll want to balance the good with the bad so that few items are without their issues. How to do this is covered throughout this section but amounts to altering properties, forms, and origins to produce pros and cons. Characters complaining or praising these details adds believability, as does their avoidance of some things and pursuit of others.

TECHNOLOGICAL PREVALENCE

How common is technology in the setting? This will have an impact on how it's perceived and the likelihood of our characters having technological problems. Many objects will be taken for granted, but how often does technology fail or get in the way? We notice a failure more than expected results. The frequency of technology ruining plans may be on par with how often they help. This can be a story issue, but the more technology that exists, the more likely things are to fail and affect lives.

PROPERTIES

Aside from what purpose this item serves, we should determine considerations such as battery life (and if its rechargeable), reliability, durability, usability, its interface, and data connectivity abilities. Technological items almost always have an "on/off" switch, and possibly a battery that will eventually die. Decide that most can be switched on and then we only need to decide which ones miss this feature – or have a flaky one.

Reliability doesn't need an explanation because we all understand that some items are great and others aren't. Just decide some manufacturers produce items at one extreme or another, based on what we know about the species/race, sovereign power, or company involved. Battery life may be an issue at the item, product line, manufacturer, or species level. It's less common that everything by a race, for example, has poor battery life.

For durability, higher priced items are typically better, but manufacturers know that if an item lasts forever, we'll never buy another from them, so the conspiracy theory that some are designed to break down after a given time— right after the warranty expires, say—is quite believable.

Usability and the interface are major areas for us to characterize. Who hasn't complained about how something is designed? Give every manufacturer a reputation and our characters will have an attitude about their other products. The interface can mean how intuitive or cumbersome it is and is a way to give a good item a flaw. Maybe it's powerful but hard to use.

For connectivity, our default should be that a technology does not play well with tech from other planets unless someone has purposely built that in, which requires previous interaction with species from that world, or at least acquisition of and familiarity with their technology and language. This is a believable limitation. Even on Earth today, if we travel from Europe to the

U.S. or vice versa, we need an adapter for something as simple as electricity. The tech for advanced systems is interdependent and simply hooking up to something shouldn't be as easy as it's often shown in SF.

ORIGINS

In SF, the origins of an item are often overlooked, which is fine if it's commonplace, or assumed to be from the military if the character is a soldier. Many items are likely for sale. Characters care who made their items just as we do about our smartphone, vehicle, computer, and appliances. This will be truer if species/races on other planets created them. Everything should have distinct traits, such as the difficulty of use or reliability. Even the look and feel or its reputation will affect response to one. Someone might wish for the power of a Nissen plasma gun with the reliability of an Muirdo one and the accuracy of a Raita one, these being races or corporations. One character might be pleased to find one of the Nissen guns only to have another say it's unreliable.

To improve the impact of origins, we can decide different species or races are capable of different qualities (and even quantities) of production. Both cause value. Maybe only the Nissen can create that plasma rifle, or they're the only rifles that are worth having. Spend a little time dividing up item types and deciding which race (or even sovereign power of that race) is good, bad, or mediocre at creating each. As with magic items, we can have individuals who excel at creating them, rather than companies or kingdoms. As long as we juxtapose origins with properties or values, we're creating believability – and finding ways to give characters something they need but which doesn't perfectly do the job. If they really need a plasma rifle but it's not the Muirdo kind, then maybe it's going to fail in a crisis. This is how we use origins.

It's worthwhile to create several manufacturers for any SF setting, their names emblazoned on products and ads. Each will elicit a response from people, that opinion differing according to the individual and company. We can characterize both and make the world and people more relatable. And when their items show up in faraway places, people can be surprised, even comforted by something from home. They may be amused if another species thinks it's great.

FORM

Form and function may go together with technological items, but not always. Some devices like a smart phone offer far more functions than a person unfamiliar with one might guess, such as GPS or motion sensing tech. Since we're inventing tech, we can decide whether form and function have anything to do with each other. Items that scan or transmit signals can be in any physical shape; the days of needing an antenna are long over on Earth, but maybe not on our invented world. Anything computer related can be divorced from its form. This is also true of wearable items, though not those designed to augment the form, such as a cloak that makes any covered part of us invisible.

Weapons would appear to be those where shape matters, but this depends on the type. If we're swinging it like a sword, for example, and the technology in it has something to do with this, such as increasing the force or accuracy, then the form still matters. Weapons that fire physical projectiles also need a barrel, so a gun that shoots a smart bullet likely still looks like a gun. But what about weapons that fire lasers or the beams of light we see in *Star Wars*, for example? They're always shaped like a gun, but is that necessary? If the laser requires manual targeting, then it is possible characters are used to using guns with physical projectiles, and the accuracy is improved this way. By contrast, it might be hard to aim a weapon that's a round disk held in the palm, with the beam emitting from the center. And of course, audiences are used to the gun shape and won't question it. Should we?

If the laser is not manually targeted by the hand, then yes. We can manually target a large gun like the cannons seen on space craft, but in those cases, the gun itself isn't held. It's attached to the ship. The character might be using a computer to fire. Think of any game controller, ones with multiple buttons for each hand and little levers controlled with thumbs, that you've used while watching the action on a TV via the gaming console. Even though we're manually controlling the aiming, the actual weapon needn't have a barrel. These are virtual guns. When this is the case, consider changing the form to something with fewer limitations, like an orb that can fire in any direction without requiring turning.

When manual targeting isn't involved at all, and no physical projectile is fired, why would we have a gun barrel shape? Think of a good reason or opt for something more unique. The missile fired may begin dispersing once shot and a barrel delays how soon this happens. Or perhaps the energy needs to be collected before it can be fired in a given direction and the barrel aids this. Maybe the weapon's engineers just aren't smart (or original) enough to go without this. Any weapon designed to affect a wide area is also a candidate for avoiding a gun shape.

USERS

Technology tends to be user-agnostic, but a species might want to put biological controls into their items so that only they can use them. This is especially true of weapons and informational items, depending on what sort of data the latter typically holds. Many items require specific knowledge for how to control them, so we must decide if the device is intuitive or not. In TV and film, we often see people facing no obstacles at all with this and it's not realistic. Plan for them to need an item that they can control and make them work to find it, instead of just being able to use whatever is on hand. If a species uses biological controls, a human won't bother trying to steal their ship, for example. Instead, they may opt for stowing away, or an alternative, to flee their present situation.

Which functions are necessary to an item we're inventing determines how technical it must be. The complexity will affect the degree to which users unfamiliar with it can figure it out. Consider having simple functions more obvious but more elaborate features less intuitive and beyond the characters. Even experts in that field may have difficulty figuring out something designed by another culture. We need things to go wrong and not understanding how to use an item is a believable way to achieve this. We can also have them achieve the opposite result they wanted or even cause problems with this unfamiliar device.

The gun is infamous for being a way to "level the playing field." Before that, physical prowess mattered more during conflicts, but now even a toddler can kill an adult. This is why the "safety" exists, so does the item we're inventing include such a thing? SF often features particularly deadly items, so the obvious answer seems affirmative, but include known hacks to get around that equivalent (known to a select few, like our wiliest character, of course). Weapons aren't the only leveler. Think of disadvantages the protagonists have compared to their nemesis and figure out what possession of the latter can fall into the hands of the former and even the fight. Then avoid making it too easy for our heroes to use it.

CREATING AN A.I.

An Artificial Intelligence (A.I.) has become a staple of SF, particularly in the form of a ship that can be controlled via the A.I., which typically gets a name for ease of reference. Let's call ours Surance, which sounds female, and that is a decision to make. Is the gender fixed or can users change it? This arguably matters more in TV/film because every change of voice or appearance means another actor, plus a brief explanation, which can be as short as someone answering raised eyebrows from crewmates with a shrug and saying, "I changed her." This change matters less in books because the reader won't notice, which begs the question of why we'd do it.

And the answer is that Surance may have the ability to impersonate others, both visually and vocally, because it can be useful for the crew (and us). We live in a world where genders are not viewed and treated equally despite attempts to change this. What if our crew welcomes aboard a race, hostile to females, which takes offense at Surance? It's both a storytelling decision and a character one for whether the crew changes the A.I. gender to be sensitive, takes a "too bad for you" attitude and leaves it as is, or splits the difference (leaving gender unchanged and explaining to and "educating" the visitors on their own cultural views). We can think of other scenarios for gender changing, with the caveat being that gender is theoretically irrelevant with a non-living being, but we all know that most of us look male or female. We can choose a neutral one to bypass the whole question.

We must also decide where the A.I. "lives." These are often shown as part of a vessel or structure like a house, but there's no reason Surance can't be portable and as small as a pendant. Think of how we use Siri or Alexa devices and the possibility of having it everywhere if desired. Surance can manifest as a full body projection standing near a character (decide on the range of this), or maybe she's a floating head, or just a voice, one that maybe only the wearer can hear (via a matching earpiece). If Surance appears, is it apparent that she's an A.I. or can she seem real? Can she appear as more than one person at once? Imagine needing to give the impression you have more fighters by your side so that someone pursuing you backs off.

We should decide if there's the equivalent of an internet or if all of the A.I.'s data store is local to them. How much info can they take with them? With the advances in memory storage on Earth, we can give them everything but the latest changes. But this may not be true in a universe unconnected to us. Then again, a society capable of producing some A.I.s must surely be able to create portable memory storage? They can likely connect to other systems unless we decide to restrict them.

PERSONALITY

Personality is another major area to invent, but we'll do so much like with any other character. While we can make them human-like, we can also assign the A.I. another race and culture, which makes sense if an alien species designed the ship. This can make them less cooperative unless hacked and altered (with one degree of success or another). Unless Surance has been programmed to respect something like modesty or secrets, this can result in awkward situations, including being watched or listened to without permission. Decide how much of a conscience has been included.

An A.I.'s personality can be used as a counterpoint to those on the crew. Being more serious is likely, even a default. Think about it from a manufacturer's point of view. You might like a sarcastic A.I., but plenty of people don't. If I'm in the market for a ship and you're a spaceship dealer, you could lose a sale over an obnoxious A.I. This certainly suggests that Surance is modifiable, possibly with aftermarket parts or programming. Consider this and the age of an item (a ship for example), not to mention its origin, to determine the status of the A.I.

LIMITS

An all-powerful A.I. is as problematic as anything else, maybe even more so. They're designed to control an entire ship, house, or wherever they reside, deeply impacting living beings, even sustaining or killing them via environmental controls. It's important to determine a way they can be turned off while leaving the item (let's say a ship) still controllable, albeit with minimal systems? This has been done before but it's an obvious plot device to have someone hack the A.I. or for it to suffer other problems. This is as realistic as a computer bug or car maintenance problems, so don't avoid it. Just use it when it permits a new spin on the story. In our modern world, virus attacks are constant; they will be in a world with A.I.s, too.

Decide what tasks the A.I. is designed to do and to what degree. What can't it do? What does it need living beings (or at least physical machines) to do for it? How many backups are there and how robust? A spaceship would likely have more than one, given its importance, but of course doing so is less fun for storytellers because restoration can happen quickly enough to ruin the tension introduced. An A.I. with less important functions is more likely to have one or even no backup.

Can Surance's abilities be augmented? It's a program. Maybe there's a crew member tasked with maintenance and enhancements. As a professional software developer, I see tons of poor work and processes resulting in bugs. Cocky coders make mistakes, and the geniuses often shown in SF are likely worse. Prudent design requires teams of people, with a project manager and others in oversight roles, involved in any such effort. This would likely be true on a large vessel, so keep this in mind. Imagine living in a ship where everything about our life is on the line if someone codes a mistake into the A.I. The idea of a single coder is not believable in many situations.

WHERE TO START

We can start in one of several places with inventing items, including how we intend them to be used and how we want characters to think of them. Is it a plot coupon they need to acquire to accomplish goals? If so, decide why they can't reach those goals without it and how they'll use it to be successful; it helps to think of what can go wrong, too, because tasks that go as planned offer less drama. Its function determines properties, which can then help with form. Origin is optional but adds a good detail that can also determine where this item is now and why, a little history adding depth. A final decision can then be which one of our characters has the skills or attributes to use it. But all of these can be done in whatever order works, and starting with an idea is always best, wherever it leads.

CHAPTER EIGHT

LANGUAGES

Constructed languages, known as conlangs, are a staple of fantasy and science fiction stories and gaming. Creating a language is one of the most optional subjects in world building. It has a limited positive return, given the difficulty of the task, the learning curve, and the time-consuming nature. And no one will be able to understand it; we need to translate everything anyway. For authors, this relegates the words to a visual display, one that's generally incomprehensible. For those in film, TV, and gaming, a constructed language can at least be spoken and go a long way to characterizing the speakers, but in those situations, it's likely that the studio has hired an expert to do it.

If an author has an audiobook made, they will have to speak the language well enough to narrate personally or teach a narrator. Some narrators may be unwilling to do this or charge extra for it.

This chapter will not teach you how to create a language. There are books on the subject, written by experts, and it is recommended that interested readers consider them. What this chapter *will* do is look at what is involved at a high level, what we might be getting ourselves into, and the cost to world builders of skipping it.

As of 2020, the following books about the art of inventing languages are available and are recommended resources to start your journey. I have read the first two – and they convinced me not to do this.

1. *The Art of Language Invention*, by David J. Petersen, inventor for *Game of Thrones, Star Trek*, and more.
2. *The Language Construction Kit*, by Mark Rosenfelder
3. *Advanced Language Construction*, by Mark Rosenfelder

SHOULD WE CREATE ONE?

We often benefit from questioning what goal we hope to achieve with our world building. This is true of inventing languages. Clarifying our motivation will help determine the degree to which we do this, if at all.

One reason to invent a language is vanity—we have a language all our own. This is arguably a poor excuse. Having a successful writing career or writing a bestseller will impress more people, if we care about such things. Time spent on our writing/gaming craft (or how to promote our work) is probably wiser.

Creating a naming language, discussed later in this chapter, is among the better reasons to craft a language as, at a minimum, it prevents every location or character in our world from having similar names. That said, if we look at a map of Earth, many names are similar across countries. One reason is the influence of Greek and Latin, which influenced not only English, but French and Spanish. We can therefore use a similar naming style in different sovereign powers.

A good reason to invent languages is that we may have different species in our setting and they sometimes greet others in their own language before switching to a common tongue. They might mutter under their breath in their language, or talk openly to members of their own species, thinking bystanders won't understand. It can be good, and natural, to *show* these words. The other option is to *tell*, such as narrating, "They exchanged words in their own tongue right in front of the humans, not realizing that some of them knew enough to understand." However, storytellers tend to not show greetings, etc., after initially showing some because they don't advance a story; people who are often together may not bother greeting each other at all anyway; when was the last time you really greeted your friends or family in more than the most cursory fashion?

Creating the feel of another world is another reason to create a language, which lends credibility to the idea that this place is real. After all, it's even got its own language (or several). This also makes us seem serious about our work. However, there are many other ways to do both, with a better return on our time investment.

We may feel that a language is expected, but that depends on medium. Book audiences don't necessarily expect one whereas gaming, TV, and film probably do; a studio is likely to hire an expert for this. People may understand that this is a significant time investment for an author, but a studio has tons of people working on a project and money, too. Many authors just throw in phrases invented on the fly and which do not originate from a working language. This can give the impression that we've made a language when we haven't. For some of us, this is enough.

But if our work is ever turned into a film, etc., much more language will be needed. Are we prepared to supply all of the phrases and train actors? Can we even do so? Because if we invented the language, no one can do it for us. And if we just made up junk phrases that don't work, it can cost us respect among real conlangers. Most of us don't have the luxury of worrying about this (our stories are unlikely to be optioned for film, etc.), but it's something to consider. If a conlanger is hired to take over what we've done, they may have a hard time creating a complete language because our work is unusable.

We should also think about how often we'll use the world. If it's for one book, we could spend more time inventing the language than writing the book. By contrast, if this is the only or most in-depth world we're going to create, one that we intend to use for decades, then the time or money investment is much more worth it.

THE MEDIUM

Conlangs are arguably best suited to being spoken because we can hear inflection and tone despite not understanding it. Gestures and expressions help us infer meaning. Sometimes a character translates for other characters and us. Subtitles render these a moot point but can be tedious for the audience if it goes on for too long; this is one why some scenes start with actors speaking a conlang before switching to English, as if a universal translator has been switched on via the camera. That device helps characters *and* audiences bypass the impractical nature of invented languages. And of course, if we're working in TV or film, someone else may be tasked with this project, another reason we don't have to worry about it as much.

Readers have none of these to help them. Authors must repeat the sentences, doubling the word count of the sample, though it's doubtful we'd do this enough to significantly impact manuscript length. Sometimes we'll have a character sum up what's been said. If the audience is like me, they just skip over the conlang rather than trying to sound it out or understand any of it, since they're unlikely to succeed. This makes our effort a waste of time. Something else to consider is that pausing to examine the conlang will pull readers out of our story. We should avoid this. The main takeaway a reader will get is a general sense of the tone, such as guttural versus elegant. A conlang allows us to show this rather than tell. This can be an important way to characterize a race/species or society, more than just the speaker.

OUR OPTIONS

We have several options for inventing a language.

First, we can ignore the subject altogether. This means that a book written in English has every last word in English. At best, we allude to other languages by narrating something like, "He said hello in his language before switching to Common." For authors, a minority of readers will object, but many won't even notice. For other industries, especially in SF, the universal translator idea spares us complaints.

A second option is to not invent a language but just make up words and phrases as we go along. This is what many world builders do. The only real downside is that any linguist or conlanger can tell we're doing this, but this minority understands how complicated inventing languages is and, while disappointed, likely understands our avoidance. How important is their opinion to you? Will you feel ashamed when they call you out, assuming they do (they won't)?

A third option is to create a language to one degree or another, such as a naming language. If we do this, it's recommended that we read more than one book on the art and invest ourselves in it. If we don't do it well, we're only pretending to do better than options one and two. This is only for those who:

- Are not intimidated by the books noted at this chapter's start
- Really want to do this
- Have the time, and
- Possibly intend to use the setting and therefore the language for a long time

The fourth option is to hire someone. Those with money to spare, or who are already profiting from their career, should seriously consider this, especially as a first foray into constructed languages. After all, we will have one of our own that we can learn how to use, and this may help us if we later invent one ourselves.

How to Hire Someone

We can hire a conlanger via the Language Creation Society's (LCS) site at https://conlang.org/. Simply fill out an application that includes details of what is needed and by when, and potential conlangers will contact us about fulfilling the job; LCS recommends providing 2-3 months lead time. As they note, clients (that's us) always want to know how quickly we can receive a translation for our needs; patience and planning are helpful.

Even when hiring someone, they're likely to use terms we don't understand if we haven't read any of the books mentioned in this chapter. For example, do we know what phonology is? Our conlanger may use terms like this and it behooves us to know what they're talking about and what we're buying, not to mention how to use it.

LCS suggests four order options, based on how much material we receive from the conlanger, who retains the right to suggest their own pricing. What follows are quotes, as of 2020, from their website: https://jobs.conlang.org/pricing

Option 1

- "Naming Language"
- Phonology (the sounds of the language)
- No grammar at all
- 2 dozen names
- $100 United States dollars (USD)

Option 2

- "Conlang Sketch"
- Phonology (the sounds of the language)
- A few basic forms of grammar
- 50 lexical items (vocabulary words, including names)
- $200 USD

Option 3

- Phonology (the sounds of the language)
- Basic grammar
- 150 lexical items (vocabulary words, including names)
- 5 sample sentences
- $400 USD

Option 4

- Phonology (the sounds of the language)
- Detailed grammar
- 500 lexical items (vocabulary words, including names)
- 20 sample sentences
- $800 USD

Where to Start

The first decision is whether we want to *use* an invented language, for what, and how often. This will determine whether the time or money invested is worth it. We should also decide if we're comfortable with inventing phrases as we go along without worrying whether they make sense to linguists, a small portion of the audience. If we think we will frequently use extensive passages, or the world is one we intend to use for decades, inventing (or hiring) may be worth it. Time spent on this world building task is time away from another task; do we have the time? For those who are already making money with their work or can afford it, this is one of the few world building tasks we can hire someone else to do for us. It's worth considering. The next recommended step is to buy one of the listed resource books, because even hiring someone requires knowledge – unless we've decided to ignore the subject altogether.

CHAPTER NINE

NAMES

Creating names for people, places, and things can be a challenging but necessary part of world building. This chapter will discuss techniques for inventing names, how language invention can inform our choices, and options regarding the different parts of names.

PEOPLE NAMES

In order to explore naming, we should first understand which parts of one we're discussing. Differing terms are used for the parts, such as given name, surname, first name, last name, and more.

HOW MANY NAMES?

Up until about the 12th century on Earth, not everyone had a first and last name, known as "given name" and "surname," which means having both is optional for our invented world. People in some countries have two or more surnames (and which can come before the given name). Hereditary last names are also not universal. Knowing the reasons for these variations will help us decide where on our world we could do similar things. We have flexibility.

The order of these names can vary, but in Western countries, the given name is typically the first name and the surname is the last. In Eastern countries, this order is often reversed. In Spanish-speaking countries, the given name is followed by the father's surname and then the mother's. This mostly matters to us if we're presenting both names to our audience. It's a simple way to distinguish one culture from another.

On Earth, some religions have saints, and those names have sometimes been adopted by others. One result is many people with the first name John, for example, resulting in a need for surnames to distinguish between them. One point here is that if we have famous knights or wizards in our world, their name can be highly sought.

GIVEN NAMES

The "given name" is bestowed (hence the term) upon the person, usually by their parents, but it can be decided by other relatives, particularly if the parents are absent or incapacitated. Or the cultural choice can be different, like grandparents doing it. Or an older sibling. We might decide that the state does it, especially in an authoritarian regime or a futuristic one where people are given a number instead. Consider the government type that this person was born into for whether people have freedom to name a child or not.

The name is typically given at birth but could be changed later if an important event or religious ceremony occurs. This could be as simple as the child's first, eighteenth, or twenty-first birthday. We can decide a boy becomes a man on losing his virginity and then he gets another given name; the same can be done with a girl, or when she bears a first child. They'll be known by something else in the meantime, or perhaps their initial name is replaced by another in a coming-of-age milestone of our choosing. If a character obtains magical power at puberty, for example, perhaps they get a wizarding name then, whether they or their instructor choose it. Names are sometimes changed when immigrating, possibly to fit in. Ethnicity might be downplayed this way if the character has reason to fear hostility.

How might world builders use such information? Explaining via narration is the least attractive option. Dialogue might be better, such as one character noticing another's ethnicity but that their name doesn't quite match and then remarking on this, possibly snidely: "Your name won't hide what you are!"

On Earth, the given name distinguishes one person from another in a family or clan (because they'll all have the same surname/last name). Sometimes there is more than one given name, which means that one of them, referred to as the forename, is spoken first if both are used. Either one could have more prominence and be the main name for this person, but it's often the first one.

As for why a name is chosen, the reasons vary and are often combined. The simplest reason is that parents like the name. This may not apply to world builders, but wanting a name that's clear of negative associations can also rule out some choices; a relative of mine gave his daughter the name of a despised woman I once knew and for years, I thought of this every time I heard the girl's name. Names can be chosen in hopes that the child will have the character trait, such as Hope or Faith. On our invented world, we could decide a word like Kier means "heroic" in an old language and give this name to a character. We're only likely to mention such things on occasion.

Occupations can be another source of names, which is especially true of surnames, such as Smith. Objects can be chosen, as can places, the time of birth, or physical characteristics. Sometimes a surname becomes a given name, like Harrison.

Many names have a meaning that we may be unaware of because the name is based on old disused words. One issue is that names based on something can come across as literal unless we explain them, and it seems less like a name. For example, few of us know that David means beloved, so we'd have to explain that or call the character "Beloved," which might seem odd. As a result, this information is interesting but potentially not useful. If you're like most people, you may not know your own name's meaning. Your parents might not have either. Or they looked it up out of curiosity and then forgot what it means a month later.

It is possible to voluntarily choose a new name, in which case the phrase "given name" makes less sense unless we think of this as giving ourselves a new name.

SURNAMES

In contrast to the given name, the surname is inherited from either the family or a clan, but not all surnames are inherited. They are often chosen or changed, either by the individual or someone else, such as a servant's lord, or even government officials. Many who immigrated to the United States were simply given new surnames upon arrival. Sometimes those new names had something to do with their original name, such as a misspelling or Americanization of it, while other previous surnames were simply ditched by officials.

The original meaning of a surname is often lost in time. This is especially true if the spelling has been altered. In our work, we're more interested in giving characters names that mean something to not only them and other characters, but to the audience.

Any of our characters might have earned a name or simply inherited it.

USING PLACES

Surnames are often used to distinguish between two people in the same settlement who have the same given name. This means that in a small town or village, surnames might not be used. Galen is simply Galen. If he travels, he might be asked where he's from, resulting in others calling him Galen of Norin, which in time might become Galen Norin. This could become his surname if he's moved into a culture where others have one and there might be more than one Galen. One's place of birth need not be the surname, as later residences can apply instead.

If there's a prominent land feature, this can be used, as can names of castles or prominent buildings. The name of an actual hill can be used, so that Galen, who lives near Ardo Hill, becomes Galen Ardo, or the generic word for the feature can be used, resulting in Galen Hill. Regions such as counties, states, kingdoms (including long forgotten ones) and more can be used.

A knight might wish to suggest he comes from a respectable city instead of the less-favored one from where he actually originated. Said knight need have never even visited, much less lived, in that city. Few if any are likely to contest such a claim unless advanced technology, the kind found in SF, allows them to easily verify his origin. That said, a character doing this might have an accent that betrays him, for example, and be unaware his ruse is known or suspected.

In some countries or regions, an article is placed before the surname, such as "de" in France, resulting in Galen de Borun, and this is sometimes later altered to d'Borun or Deborun. When using an apostrophe in names, remember that the punctuation is replacing something. We can make a list of articles used in a given country; remember that not every name should have them as that looks too consistent and planned.

USING OCCUPATIONS

Surnames were often derived from an occupation, such as a blacksmith or ironsmith. This latter point raises an issue for fantasy authors. There are almost certainly blacksmiths in your world. If you call someone Galen Smith, that surname looks too much like a name from our world, which interferes with our attempts to create a world that appears different from Earth. The way to avoid this is, well, to avoid this. Choose occupational surnames that are likely for your world but don't exist in ours. Another option is to leave that example as Galen Blacksmith, because that's less familiar. This also allows us to introduce a character and state their profession simultaneously (unless it's different, in which case this can be a problem).

In some countries, servants took the first or last name of their employer as a surname, adding an "s" to the end. Galen's maid, Sori, becomes Sori Galens, or maybe Sori Isa-Boruns. An actor who always plays the role of a king in plays becomes Galen King.

USING FIRST NAME

A surname is sometimes created from a first name. Using Galen again, his son could be Rogin Galenson or Rogin Galen. This first makes sense but also looks a too little Earth-like. His daughter might be Galendaughter, a common naming convention in some European countries. A shorter suffix might be simpler. In Russia, girls inherit their father's last name just like boys do, with one distinction: the letter "a" is added to a girl's last name. For example, Galen's son would be Rogin Ori Isa-Borun and his daughter would be Suri Pia Isa-Boruna. Simply adding "a" works for some names but not for others, so we'd need more than one version.

USING NICKNAMES

While we sometimes associate nicknames with being unflattering, not all of them are, and in either case, these can become a surname. Those who've refused to choose a surname are sometimes given an unflattering one. In our world, Trollman could be someone who has specialized in dealing with trolls or who resembled a troll. Any physical or even personal/mental characteristic can be used. If someone acts haughty like a hated nobleman, they could end up with that nobleman's surname, which is the reason some people on Earth have Caesar for a last name. To be more precise, a relative may have been given that surname derisively and then passed it down. In some cases, families remove unflattering names in later generations.

Another variant is using something unrelated to the individual, sometimes as an affectation. Someone can be named after the morning sun, a beautiful (or even deadly) flower, or an animal known for its strength.

COMPOUND SURNAMES

Where an individual has two last names, this is called a compound surname. Several varieties exist on Earth and can be leveraged for our world. Each of the two names is typically derived from one parent. Let's take the name Galen Sori Isa Borun and break it down:

First Given Name	Second Given Name	Paternal Last Name	Maternal Last Name
Galen	Sori	Isa	Borun

Figure 75 Compound Names

Galen Sori is his first and second given name. Isa is his paternal last name (i.e., his father's surname was Isa), and Borun is his maternal last name (his mother's surname was Borun).

If Galen has children, they can either inherit just Isa or both Isa Borun, but in Hispanic cultures, seldom if ever is only the maternal name (Borun) inherited alone. There's no reason we have to follow that, of course, but it shows some variations are available even here.

If Galen has children who inherit Isa Borun, and then they have children, it can become more complicated. For example, let's say Galen's son Rogin Ori Isa Borun marries a woman whose last name is also a compound name, Sine Tiona. They have a son, whose name could be Uron Dain Isa Borun Sine Tiona. Those wanting to shorten his name can call leave off his middle name "Dain," but they can also use only his father's surname, calling him Uron Isa Borun. Since it's not okay to use only the mother's surname, Sine Tiona, we can't call him Uron Sine Tiona. Variants on all of this exist.

Similarly, his father's surname being Isa Borun means it would be wrong to call Uron by just one of those: Uron Isa or Uron Borun are both wrong. This is again assuming we're following the Hispanic convention. We can invent our own rules.

To help avoid confusion, we can use punctuation: Galen Sori Isa-Borun has a son Rogin Ori Isa-Borun, who marries a woman with the last name Sine-Tiona. Their son is called Uron Dain Isa-Borun Sine-Tiona. In our work, we're seldom going to want to use all of these names, as audiences expect to be on a "first-name basis" as the expression goes in the United States, with our characters. This is considered more personal, and audiences want personal connections with characters.

PLACE NAMES

Naming places has a few unique considerations.

In our modern world, at least in the United States, few of us have any idea why any location bears its name. This may be true in our invented setting as well, and likely depends on how old places are. Since many places are named for someone, the person for whom they are named also has an impact if that association is remembered. Being named for someone that a culture has forgotten relegates the connection between person and place to the unknown. This is also affected by how long ago that person lived.

For example, we assume anywhere named Washington is named after the first president, but Dallas is just Dallas. In reality, the latter is named after George M. Dallas, but few know that, care, or have any idea why they should. In a world where travel is easy, such ignorance is more likely due to the sheer number of distant places (over a hundred miles) we can visit. But in a fantasy-like setting with restricted travel and far less information about the wider world, it's more likely that people know why each location within a certain distance bears its name. This is partly due to a lack of information overload that comes with technology. Consider this before spending too much time inventing justifications for names; your characters may be unlikely to know or discover this and we therefore have little reason to worry about it ourselves.

In a single work, we should avoid explaining the reason every place bears its name. It can start to sound like we're educating the audience or doing exposition housekeeping. Strategically pick the one or two places that are worth this, and briefly sneak in any such exposition. We decide based on whether the place's name and its origin can characterize the setting or not.

We can have our characters see a statue, painting, or carving, at city gates, on flags, on awnings, or on prominent buildings, possibly with a plaque that commemorates the namesake. Something that depicts the person is a little better because their appearance can give an idea who they were without explanation.

For example, "As he entered the gates of Kierdon, Antar smirked at the statue of Kier overhead, sword aloft, plate armor emblazoned with the knighthood's symbol, cloak swirling around him, for if Kier had still lived, he would've been mortified at the squalor and seediness that scurried around the town." We would then go on to paint more details about what Antar experiences as he goes about his business, hopefully making this relevant, too, such as someone stealing from him along the way. We could alternatively have him being chased through town by ruffians before finding himself cornered beneath that statue, which adds commentary to what's occurring.

We can invent place names using several rationales and techniques discussed next.

USING EVENTS

Names of places sometimes change, which can happen for several reasons. We don't have to worry about what the place was called before unless desired.

One of these is an event that creates the current name. If a shipwreck happened there, the ship's name might have renamed the place. A named weapon fired from that location could be the source. A nearby land feature can be the source of a disease name; Ebola was named after the Ebola River near one of the initial breakout sites.

Being conquered often results in a new name connected to the conquerors. An obvious example from Earth is the litany of cities named Alexandria after Alexander the Great conquered them. He could've named them after a god or hero, too. This is one way to create a name in a region, where that name is unlike those already there; sometimes these new names stay long after the conquerors are gone, though this seems more likely if occupation lasted a number of years; otherwise the conquered might just switch back to the old name.

The opposite is also true – the name of a place is given to an event, like a battle named after it. In SF, we might have an item being built here, like a well-known ship, weapon, or device named for the town of origin or mass production.

Another type of event is weather or other natural phenomena. A well-known example would be Winterfell from *Game of Thrones* . On Earth, places have been named Hurricane, Rainbow Springs, Frostproof, Waterproof, Cyclone, Snow, Tornado, Summer Lake, and Winter. The more literal names are less artful than something like Rainbow Springs and can suggest we didn't put much effort into them.

USING PEOPLE

One option is to name a place after a character or a surname. We see this on Earth all the time with names like Jacksonville or Harrisonburg. Other examples include the Cook Islands (named after Captain James Cook), Dominican Republic (Saint Dominic), and Seychelles (Jean Moreau de Seychelles). This can be done from villages all the way up to countries. We can add requirements, such as the person needing to be royalty before a place can be named after them. For more ideas, look at this very long list at Wikipedia: http://bit.ly/PlaceNamesPeople

The main issue with naming places after people is that it means inventing another character; we probably aren't naming a location after someone who's in the story we're telling. They'd have to be pretty old, for one, but it also makes things a little odd. However, if we've invented gods or other legendary figures (as discussed in *Creating Life, The Art of World Building, #1*), we can leverage those names here. This is one area where building a world used for our entire career, rather than only the story currently on our minds, has an advantage, because we're more likely to have invented people we can repurpose. We might want to do an alternate version of their name to avoid confusion between the place and the person; using prefixes and suffixes (see the next section) makes this easy.

If we've already invented place names, we can retroactively decide these were people. We don't need to spend much time developing them as characters, as a line or two in our notes can suffice. For example, "Kierdon is named after the knight Kier Moonbright of Illiandor, who exemplified honor and valor at the time of the town's founding, for his heroic sacrifice at the Battle of Hestia, where he saved the crown prince at the cost of his own life."

For what reasons do we name places after people? In addition to heroes, legendary figures, and important discoverers and political figures, we often use religious saints. If people embody a positive character trait, such a person may be chosen in a show of optimism about the quality and character of the location's citizens. This trait needs no basis in fact. Those with both good and bad characteristics will exist in every location, so this is a technique we can use to quickly invent past priests or wizards in our world.

ADDING SUFFIXES AND PREFIXES

Some names are based on a surname, which can be more obvious when we're familiar with that surname, such as Washington or Jackson. This familiarity doesn't exist on invented worlds. While we can certainly use such names without alteration, we can also alter them with either a familiar suffix or prefix from Earth or one of our invention.

The examples below can spark imagination:

- Ville (Jacksonville)
- Burg (Harrisonburg)
- Sted (Christiansted)
- Caster (Lancaster)
- Chester (Manchester)
- Avon (Avonmouth)
- Burn (Blackburn)

- Don (Abingdon)
- Den (Willesden)
- Ford (Stafford)
- Gate (Helmsgate)
- Ing (Reading)
- Mere (Windemere)
- Ton (Hamilton)

Doing this in fantasy or SF might result in places names like the following:

- Flamecaster
- Magedon
- Fluxton
- Stafford
- Spellburn
- Orbdon
- Laserton
- Droidsted
- Spellcaster

- Beamdon
- Blasterville
- Cryoton
- Cyberburg
- Rayburn
- Hivemere
- Moonford
- Aeongate
- Unimere

COMPOUND NAMES

We can also combine words, whether we leave a space between them or not. For example, East Haven and Easthaven both work well. This lets us take two somewhat ordinary words and fashion something unique from them. More examples include Black Hollow, Broken Shield, Hero's March, Goldleaf, Ironforge, Oakheart, Raven's Nest, and Silverhelm. A partial list of source words is here (and don't forget to use colors, directions, and plants and animals, either of our invention or not):

- End
- Keep
- Break
- Dale
- Spring
- Streams
- Horn

- Vale
- Ridge
- Falls
- Pass
- Den
- Heart
- Crest

• Field   • Moor

Uniqueness

Inventing a name that no one else is using appeals to both world builders and our audience. But it's possible to invent a name that's already in use without realizing it, and we can always claim this excuse, partly because it's unrealistic for us to know every name ever used by every creative person in history. The odds of any author coming up with a name no one has ever done before, or ever will again, are slim. Even so, we should try, because uniqueness prevents confusion and a reader associating the name with something that's already familiar. We often hope that a character, place, or thing we've invented becomes famous; a distinctive and cool name helps this. It's worth noting that combining familiar words helps audiences absorb them quickly. The examples in the previous "Compound Names" section demonstrate this.

Sometimes people who have multiple names become known by just one, like Cher, Bono, and Sting. They are said to be mononymous. But it's far easier to create a unique name by combining words (for places) or given and surnames (for people). There are far more Lukes than there are Luke Skywalkers. There's only one Han Solo. Only one Princess Leia, who could almost be considered mononymous in that she's got a title and one name; it's not clear in the films whether Leia is her given or surname (it's her given; her surname is Organa even though her family name could also be Skywalker were it not for adoption).

When inventing a name, don't worry if you invent a word that, as it turns out, already exists, even if you're naming a plant, animal, or species instead of a character. It's not ideal but also not a big deal. There are countless words in English that have two meanings and there's no reason yours can't become meaning number two. On the other hand, if you find that the word exists and is objectionable in some way, or easily confused with what you're doing, you might change it in one of the ways mentioned in this chapter.

As a case in point, I used "drek" long ago only to later learn that it means "shit" in German. Go ahead and laugh. I did. And then I stopped using that. It pays to Google any word you invent. Ignorance can be bliss until someone in the know sends you an email and you cringe. As "drek" illustrates, a word that doesn't exist in English may exist in another language.

It can become an exercise in futility trying to avoid every last word, so don't worry too much. I once invented "kryll" for one of my Llurien species only to discover many years later that "krill" are a type of marine life. I de-

654 | RANDY ELLEFSON

cided I don't care partly because I spell it differently and few people are going to know that word. And if they do, they know krill are a small crustacean whereas my kryll live on land, meaning there's little reason to confuse one with the other. Nonetheless, a beta-reader once pointed it out with "LOL! Why are you naming this after tiny fish!?!"

A more recent incident brings up another problem: someone far more prominent than you can invent a similar name long after you did. In this case, Seth MacFarlane's show, *The Orville*, also has humanoids called krill. I still frown every time I hear it, but I'm not changing a name I've been using since 1991 because Seth used a similar one starting in 2017. I know some people will ask why I stole Seth's name instead of using one of my own, criticizing my lack of originality and even claiming I'm a Seth fanboy. On the plus side, I published *The Ever Fiend* in 2016 featuring a kryll, so I have proof I used it first. Still, I wonder why Seth named his humanoids after tiny fish!

LEVERAGING EXISTING NAMES

If there's a name we really like, we can sometimes use it without consequence, but this depends on the name and how much of it we use without alteration. A famous name like Luke Skywalker is one to avoid. Even the surname can't be used due to its heavy association with him. A variation like Airwalker might work, but the similarity in subject matter between air and sky is also more problematic/reminiscent of him. On the other hand, Nightwalker doesn't immediately call him to mind, unless his full name is Luke Nightwalker. Even Lucas Nightwalker might tip off people as to what we're doing. As usual with an analogue, follow my Rule of Three: at least three significant changes. In the case of a name, just two changes may suffice, such as Kier Nightwalker.

There are other names that might not be household ones, but which are still too well known in the genres to use, even in an altered state, without raising some eyebrows. This includes Legolas from *The Lord of the Rings*, Raistlin Majere from *Dragonlance*, or Voldemort (*Harry Potter*). Be careful leveraging such names. It's arguably better to borrow a minor character's name or use one from a lesser known work or author.

GENERAL TIPS

Making any aspect of our work challenging for the audience can kill enthusiasm and conversation about it, and this includes names. This issue can manifest in several ways, each with its own solution.

KEEP IT SHORT

Long names tend to be harder to read, remember, spell, and pronounce than shorter ones. This includes too many names, or syllables within a name.

More than three names may be excessive. In English speaking countries, we typically use just the first name, the surname only when being formal, or both when introducing someone. The middle name is almost never used unless it is part of a stage name or someone goes by that *instead of* the first name. We can invent something different, and other cultures have already done so, but the point is that we seldom use more than this. We can invent a long name like Liminera Solto Ariso Nubien Arta Astol Munir, but few people want to see that more than once.

Names with too many syllables are hard, too. Four syllables is considered long but not unwieldy. Exceed this infrequently (once a story). Strive for between one and three syllables much of the time.

With long names, such as Limineraslyvarisnia, people tend to skip much of it rather than working it out as we did when inventing it. In actual usage, such names get shortened anyway, such as to Limi or maybe Nera. It can still be advantageous to invent such a lengthy one to create a sense of cultural differences, but we'll want to use the long version once or twice, such as when introducing the character in narration, or at a formal ceremony.

In addition, sometimes parents or other authority figures will use the long version when expressing disapproval or affection. By contrast, the short version can be a show of familiarity, whether that's appropriate or not. If we want to use this device in a story, maybe we should still use the short version in narration (implying this is how the character thinks of themselves) and only put the full name in another character's mouth.

When writing content such as a summary or book blurb, use the version that's easiest to absorb. The long version could give the impression we'll be doing that all the time and possibly turn off a potential reader. However, using first and last name can be good if the combination sounds very cool and gives a hint about their character or type, such as Talon Stormbringer, the name of my all-purpose fantasy action hero.

KEEP IT SIMPLE (APOSTROPHES AND HYPHENS)

People are drawn to simpler things, and that includes names. World builders can easily create a sense of somewhere different from Earth (or another culture in our invented world) with unusual naming conventions, but some approaches can be overused or otherwise annoy readers. This includes too many consonants, hyphens, or apostrophes. One of these per name is better than several, even if spread across a character's given and surnames.

One problem with too many consonants together, like Ghlnalenkm, is the difficulty in pronouncing it. Some readers may find this easier than others due to similar occurrences in their language, but others won't and something as simple as a name shouldn't be a point of consternation for our audience. In the case of Ghlnalenkm, the "h" adds no value. We could also surmise that there's a vowel somewhere in the start, such as "Gal" or "Glen," producing Ghalnalenkm or Ghlenalenkm. Why not just write them that way ? Or get rid of the "h" and get Galnalenkm or Glenalenkm.

Hyphens are used to connect words, like Smith-Davies when a married woman wants to keep her surname when taking her husband's surname, too. While the culture might use hyphens, that doesn't mean we need to show it to our reader all the time. In the above case, maybe mention Smith-Davies and then reduce it to Smith for the rest of the work. We can write something like, "She went by Smith instead of her legal name, Smith-Davies, out of laziness, but never in the presence of her husband, who'd been known to arch an eyebrow when she didn't add his Davies." This smoothly gets in some characterization and tension while doing some housekeeping exposition.

Why is an apostrophe used? It takes the place of an omitted letter, or potentially several of them. This justification reveals how truly optional this is – and therefore how easy it is to avoid. Do we really need to replace a letter? What's wrong with it?

Before doing this, decide what letter is being omitted and whether it seems better that way. Fantasy writers have been using (abusing?) apostrophes for a long time, and this is precisely why many people loathe it. A quick Google search will reveal a heaping of scornful posts about this. Do we want our audience rolling their eyes? That's contempt for us, so probably not.

To avoid that reaction, we should have a justification for it, though the obvious problem with this is the need to explain it. However, a single sentence can do. What justification do we need? Making a long name shorter by replacing letters with an apostrophe is a good one. We can replace Smith-Davies with S'Davies; that's an awkward example because it sounds bad, but you get the idea. We can explain, "Recruits were called Marmillionor partly to haze them with the unwieldly mouthful that had produced widespread derision for eons, and which shortened to M'ionor upon graduation."

An apostrophe is also used for a contraction, such as "can't" instead of "cannot." The main issue is that people won't understand what we're contracting unless we explain it, so it looks random. We can get around this with characterization: "He'd been a wizard of the Marmili Order before becoming one of the famed knights of Ionor, and while the combination was rare, the title of M'Ionor struck awe into everyone but the surly guard barring his way." Note how in this case the "I" is capitalized due this resulting from two titles being combined, unlike the previous example, where letters within a single word were omitted. This could be written Mionor, but the significance of two merged titles is then lost, though many won't realize this detail.

We may want to use the apostrophe to suggest pronunciation. This often happens when several adjacent vowels should be sounded apart rather than as one. For example, the word "Tourten" is likely read as two syllables ("TOR-ten"), but writing it as "To'Urten" makes it three ("tow-UR-ten"). We could further decide that the first two letters are short for "Torni," for example; this means "To'Urten" is short for "Torni Urten."

The one thing we don't want to do with apostrophes is have no reason for using one (or giving the appearance of this). Making a name sound like a fantasy one by including a senseless apostrophe is not a reason. It is the most loathed justification and considered shallow. Even when we have a good reason, we should use them sparingly. "All things in moderation."

THE ISSUE OF SIMILARITIES

There's an idea that an author should avoid having two characters whose names start with the same letter, such as Adam and Aiden, in the same story. The reason is that people often don't read very carefully and mostly notice the first letter, especially if the names are also roughly the same length. In misreading it, they can think a different character is saying or doing something, causing confusion.

The same principle can be extended to naming places or things in a given work. Don't name one place Newall and another one Norall; in this case I've also made the ending the same to illustrate this point. A variety is easier to accomplish if we're world building to tell a specific story, because we can invent the names just for that story, but if creating a world for general and repeated use, we do run the risk of inventing two places that appear in the same tale sooner or later. While not a guideline to obsess over, the trick here is to not name adjacent places too similarly, as they're the one most likely to be visited within a single story.

SOUND

A name's sound matters more in mediums where people will say it, but authors should still think about the impression it creates and how easy it is to say. Be sure to say your invented words aloud. This tells us much about how feasible it is and whether other characters are likely to use the full term or shorten it. If we're struggling to pronounce it, that's a bad sign. Don't worry if your audience doesn't say it right, as it's bound to happen for even mono-syllable words. If accuracy really matters to you, we have the option of providing a pronunciation guide on the book's website. This can take the form of a short audio file of ourselves saying the name. Modern technology makes it very easy to produce such recordings.

APPEARANCE

Books aren't really considered a visual medium, but the look of a word matters for style. While we can't read elvish, Tolkien's flowing script creates a smooth impression, while many hard consonants can suggest brutality and coarseness. Adding silent letters can change appearance while not interfering with pronunciation. We may want to use certain letters within one culture, such as always using a k instead of a c, or replacing i with y. For example, Lonnieri vs. Lonnyery. Letter combinations can also be frequently repeated, such as "ier" as in the names Kier, Lonnieri, and Raediera.

Techniques for Inventing Names

We can use techniques while inventing names, which can be more fun than using a name generator. It's more creative and gives a feeling of ownership and pride. These techniques are presented in no order and can be combined.

Silent or Repeated Letters

Taking a simple or known word and adding silent or repeated letters is simple. H is great for this. Galen becomes Ghalen. Add an extra l to create Gallen. An extra n makes it Galenn. This can change the pronunciation but that's fine as long as we like it. Other good choices for silent letters are s and m, while many letters can be repeated depending on their position in the word.

Vowel Substitution, Addition, or Subtraction

Vowels can be changed, added, or subtracted to and from existing and invented words. An extra vowel gets us Gaalen or Galeen (with a possible pronunciation change). Maybe Gaelen is better. Or Galan. Swapping y for an i or e gets us Galyn or Galin.

Capitalize Another Letter

We can capitalize additional letters, but only two is likely best. This works better in longer words, like GaLendria, but this might work better with an apostrophe, such as Ga'Lendria. We typically capitalize the first letter, but there's no reason a culture can't choose another, resulting in gaLendria or ga'Lendria. We might want an explanation for this, such as humility being prized so that less importance is placed on the self; therefore, the initial letter isn't so tall. That viewpoint could result in the entire name not being capitalized, like some modern performers such as k.d. lang, but it may cause audience confusion and should be used wisely. It might also look like a regular word, not a title. Capitalizing a different letter might also benefit from an explanation, such as galenDria, where galen is the given name and

Dria is the surname; the surname takes prominence so that family members have a "family first" attitude.

SWITCHING FIRST LETTERS

We can switch the first letters of known words. Woman becomes Soman, Doman, Roman (maybe not that one), or Loman; I could go on. The computer manufacturer Dell becomes Kell or Xell. Look at your keyboard's letters while doing this. It helps.

ADD SUFFIXES OR PREFIXES

Adding a one syllable suffix to the end of a word helps add style if we use it with some consistency. It can help characterize a region or culture, too. Galen now becomes Galenor or Galendor, though the latter sounds like a place. Instead, maybe Galenda. A prefix could create Dagalen, though that no longer looks like a prefix, partly because it's so short. We could change the capitalization to daGalen. If we used a hyphen or apostrophe, we get Da-Galen, Da'Galen, or da'Galen.

BREAKING KNOWN WORDS UP

A challenging but fun approach is to look at products around us and steal a syllable or two, and maybe change some letter. This often produces very good names. As I wrote this, "Galen" was on a nearby product, which is how that got chosen. So is "solutions," which I can turn into "Lucion" by dropping the first syllable and replacing a letter. More examples: "Plantronics" becomes Ronik, "Contigo" becomes Tigo, and "moisturizer" becomes Irizor and Sturin. If you don't like the result, play with it until you do. Maybe Kirizor and Asturin are better?

FOREIGN LANGUAGES

We can take names from languages foreign to our own, either wholesale or as a basis for modification. This is particularly useful if we want to create a sense of shared names in a culture; if we need many words, inventing them from scratch can be difficult. This is known as an analogue, and while my Rule of Three doesn't apply as much, it's still good to make at least one change, instead of three, to prevent people from recognizing the name. From Asia we can take the names Amida, Bae, and Kaede and convert them to something of ours using techniques in this section, resulting in Amidar, Baedin, or Kaedi, for example.

BE CONSISTENT, JUST NOT TOO MUCH

When inventing names of people or places within a region, some consistency helps create the impression of unification. To adopt a naming style, use certain elements repeatedly. Which elements will depend on our preference. Any aspect of a name can do. For example, the suffix "or" can be added for Galenor and Ravenor, or the "ae" combo to cause Laeryn and Novinae. Then create a place with both: Daelinor. It's also okay to have names that don't meet these conventions because too much consistency looks too planned.

NAME GENERATORS

Free name generators exist on the internet. Most focus on character names, but we can leverage the results for places or things, too. Some of them allow us to choose what sort of name we'd like, such as Elvish or Klingon. We can also choose the gender. The resulting names will fit the style we've chosen, though this feature won't help us much if we've invented our own species.

The generators can make naming much faster and easier. With a button click, we get dozens of potential names. If we don't like them, another click generates another batch. A side-effect of so many shown to us is that we can become picky and quickly dismissive. This may be why I personally have found most of the results to be poor and unusable, but your luck or standards may differ. We can also use such a name as a starting point, altering it using the techniques in this chapter.

One negative to this is that it lacks creativity. A program is doing the work for us. This reduces or eliminates a personal connection to the result; having less investment in the world we've invented can make us care less about it, which might show in our work and impact the audience's connection for the worse, too. Our personality is also missing. If there's an impression we're hoping to create with names, the name generators are less likely than our minds to produce what we seek.

A few name generators are listed here, the first having over a thousand styles from which to choose and includes places, objects, and more:

- http://fantasynamegenerators.com/
- https://www.name-generator.org.uk/
- http://www.seventhsanctum.com/index-name.php
- http://www.fantasynamegen.com/
- http://www.rinkworks.com/namegen/
- https://www.behindthename.com/

WHERE TO START

We should start inventing names of people before places because we can name those locations after some of our characters. Objects should come later because these are sometimes named after places where they originated or were used dramatically. For people, choose a sovereign power where you wish to create names and think about the culture you've envisioned for them. Do they place importance on family names? Do they wish to honor both mother and father so that both surnames are taken by a child? If so, considering hyphenating that for clarity. This may also suggest names tend to be longer. Choose a rationale for the number and order of names. Decide if an initial given name is replaced by another at an important milestone in life. While inventing names using the techniques in this chapter, choose a few letter combinations, such as prefixes and suffixes, that are common, to begin creating a style of names within that sovereign power.

We'll likely be creating names for multiple powers in our career, so we can just practice with this and improve as we go. I'm much better at this now than twenty years ago and you soon will be, too. Our story or world might also have multiple sovereign powers for which we intend to invent names, so try to vary the style of one place from another, but don't worry over this too much. Countries that speak the same language will have some similarities.

For naming places and objects, the techniques in this chapter can get us started, and we can leverage some of those people names. Using a little ingenuity and some techniques, name generation can be fun. Sometimes we might have momentum doing this and it can be wise to just invent many names at once and save them for later. Lastly, we might also get started with those name generators and modify the results if they're close to our desire.

CHAPTER TEN

OTHER SYSTEMS

This chapter covers other systems that will exist in our world, including educational, health, legal, commerce, and information systems.

EDUCATION SYSTEMS

Educational systems aren't the most glamorous subject but should be given a thought because every character has either gone through one (to one degree of success or another), skipped it, or one didn't exist during their coming of age. Unless every character had the same experience, the differences between them will impact interactions, opportunities, and more. Developing character backstory is incomplete without this.

A system can be easier to devise if we omit explaining it. Few of us know why the system that raised us exists as is, which is one reason we'll accept a different one if presented authoritatively. This is also a subject few are curious about, including audiences. Unless we intend to set a story in a school, we can skimp on inventing details.

Systems are often public, meaning that the government pays for them, likely through taxes, but a church can be the provider as well (paid for with donations?). This means students do not have to pay to attend, but they may need to purchase supplies, including textbooks, and we can change such a detail. The schools that require students to pay are known as private schools that, in theory, provide a superior experience. It is likely that if public education exists, some private instruction might, too. We can decide when we want a character to have attended one, at which point we need a name, specialties, and reputation for the school and students.

Systems can be broken down into basic and special.

BASIC EDUCATION

Basics are the subjects that most of us take for granted: reading, writing, and arithmetic. History, sports, music, art, culture, and more are typically included in earlier years and more specialized extensions are taught to teenagers. That would also mean biology, chemistry, different versions of math (algebra, geometry, trigonometry, etc.), and increasingly advanced uses of language, including foreign ones. The latter is especially important in fantasy and SF that includes multiple species, each with their own verbal and possibly written language. In a world like ours or a more advanced one (SF), we and our audience can assume these subjects exist and characters can learn them. This allows us to largely skip inventing details if desired.

But in a less developed world, less of this will be taught formally if at all. This impacts fantasy authors with a setting like a medieval one. Education may not have gone beyond the equivalent of fifth or sixth grade if it was required at all. One reason is that children must often work in the family business because earning money or performing labor is more important than book learning. The invention of machines to automate or improve the speed of tasks, or increase the yield of something like farming, helps create more resources and "free time" that becomes available for education. Consider whether basic needs are being met in the society without great physical labor. If they're not, it's likely that education is a lower priority.

When this is the case, only a few people will achieve more advanced education, meaning what we might learn in our teenage years (in middle, junior, or high school, or whatever we call them). We can consider this a kind of second tier of basic education, rather than specialized education, which we'll examine next. There will be a criterion for those who are chosen for this extra instruction, such as being wealthy or unusually smart, and special permission may be required. Certainly, nobles are not assigned mundane tasks and therefore have the time for this. It's one way they can easily distinguish themselves from peasants.

Decide how education works based on the story needs for characters who know more than others. Given that basic education may not be forced, this creates ample room for ignorant characters, who only know what they hear and may get by with streets smarts and people skills far more than learning. This seems likely in fantasy settings. Larger settlements provide for people with more specialized skills and this also suggests training for them and better education. It is believable to decide bigger settlements means better (or simply more) education opportunities and therefore that our most educated characters come from cities rather than rural areas.

Our setting might include magic or advanced technology, and if their prevalence is high, basic instruction in them may also be provided. This won't turn someone into a wizard or engineer, but just as grade school teaches students high-level concepts about music or art, the population might know basics about magic or warp drive, for example. Those who become engineers need subsequent advanced education (i.e., college or technical school). Here's what we might write in a file for basic education:

For SF: "At age 6, students are legally required to enroll at a public Kierdyn School (named for the famous scientist, Kier), which they attend until age 16. After this, each student must enroll in a technical school for 2 years, learning space sciences. Advanced education beyond this is available in three-year stints, each resulting in a degree."

For fantasy: "At age 6, students may enroll in a private Kierdyn School (named for the god of knowledge, Kier) if their parents can spare the child's work hours and afford the modest price; students may work at the school in lieu of paying in gold. Enrollment is not required. School ends at age 12, though students can leave prior to this. Advanced schooling beyond this is only for nobility or those considered unique or special, and who must pay with not less than ten years of service in their profession after graduation (refusal results in lifelong servitude)."

Special Education

Any education that takes a deep dive into a subject can be considered specialized training that not everyone receives. For example, musicians might take specialized lessons as teens or earn one or more college degrees later, becoming an expert. Without basic education, advanced education is unlikely to exist, though we can decide by subject; focus on skills characters need. Someone can become an expert without this education, but there are typically gaps in their understanding or knowledge.

If schooling ends before the teens, this type of education is unlikely except for nobility and rare individuals. In fantasy settings, we typically see less formal schooling. This suggests special education is rare and therefore private, via an apprenticeship or guild. With its advanced technology, SF suggests that specialized education is widespread, but it depends on the setting. A dystopia may feature a destroyed or depleted infrastructure. Many tools are so easy to use that people need only training in how to design and repair them; we don't need to work out the education system to determine this.

So what do we need to decide? Mostly how common different kinds of educated learning is, per subject, if they matter to our story. We can make anything rare by limiting the number of resources available to teach it, whether instructors, actual schools, or textbooks. For anything common, colleges or technical schools will teach it. If we need details, determine prerequisites, training duration, subjects taught, the awarded degree, and professions. Unless it's art, like music, few people get an advanced degree for personal enrichment, but for employment opportunities thus raised. Characters can bond with each other by discussing how much they both hated a subject you decided was disliked.

THE APPRENTICESHIP

With both knights and wizards, we see squires and apprentices respectively; other versions of this can exist in both fantasy and SF. But this is sometimes not part of a system if it's private instruction. Being a knight's squire might have defined expectations and a wizard's apprentice may not, unless that wizard belongs to a guild that sets forth rules; we have leeway here. These understudies typically live with their master for years, doing menial work and otherwise attending to their master's professional and even household needs, in addition to receiving instruction. Decide if this makes sense in the setting for any profession. It is more likely when public education is lacking or when someone is an especially sought-after master. It can also be true when the master or subject is evil, for lack of a better word, because it's unlikely that public education teaches their methods.

Since this is less formal, we may not need to decide at what age apprenticeship can begin, and what duties are expected, what life is like for both master and understudy, and how it ends unless these are standardized. It could be a privileged life of fine dining with powerful people or a miserable one of squalor, suffering, and fear. If the profession is dangerous, this apprenticeship likely is as well. What sort of protection does the master provide, whether physically present or not? What are the benefits beyond the chance to acquire knowledge and skills? Forging personal connections could be a significant attraction, but then it depends on how much respect the apprentice is given. Someone may have had more than one apprenticeship in their past, with wildly different experiences. This is as much a character building as world building issue, other than deciding whether it's available and for what professions, typically, and whether something like a guild or knighthood establishes guidelines.

OTHER CONCERNS

For all systems, we should decide how many years of school are typical and at what age it begins and ends. Some governments mandate this so that it's against the law to skip it; the parents are typically the ones responsible for ensuring it happens and the ones punished for refusing, not the child, but we don't have to do that. The child could be punished instead. The problem with doing so is that children understand consequences less than adults, but if you had to complete your homework to get any food, you'd learn the lesson pretty quickly. We can be inventive with this. While that seems cruel, maybe an invented species of ours values self-reliance and isn't above teaching hard lessons.

Are students expected to be separated from parents at any point in their education, living at a school or with a teacher (a boarding school)? This may be only on school days, through a semester or school year, or until graduation. Does segregation exist, such as by gender, species, race, ethnicity, social class, blood line, delinquency, or other elements? Does the school have facilities, such as dorms, gyms, libraries, labs, and other specialty rooms mingled with classrooms, in a separate building, or away from school altogether? These details mostly matter if we're setting a story at school or a character has been impacted, such as not seeing their family for years. But we can also drop little details into stories, such as a wizard's lab being crowded with students after school hours because it's off campus, and now our wizard character must contend with people being in the way.

HEALTH SYSTEMS

MEDICAL

Medical care varies widely between fantasy and SF worlds, though sometimes the latter has systems just as poor. Regardless of genre, it's too convenient for wounded or sick characters to be instantly healed, without needing convalescence. It's like when death loses meaning because dead people are easily revived without consequence; why fear for a character who can return? A recent vampire show featured them snapping each other's necks during disputes. This would kill a mortal, but all it did to them was render them unconscious for an hour or two. Despite this, even other vampire characters would react as if someone they loved had just been murdered and they'd never see them again. Wouldn't they be blasé about it? The neck snapping thing was little more than an inconvenience, so why react with horror? Similarly, if an audience knows characters can return from the dead or be instantly healed without issues, there's no drama in health problems. For this reason, fights in superhero movies have no tension because everyone's going to be fine! Removing tension is the opposite of a smart storytelling device.

It can be hard to generalize about average life expectancy before 1900 on Earth, due to it rising and falling, but it was seldom above thirty. However, if someone made it to age twenty, they could often expect to live another thirty years, especially among the wealthy, who had better access to health care. Children are more susceptible to sickness; the percentage of those reaching adulthood could be as low as 60%. In our fantasy settings, few characters will have living grandparents, or may not have both parents still alive. Most in their twenties are probably long married (even widowed, sometimes more than once) and with a few kids, and yet we seldom see this, perhaps because it gets in the way of adventuring and our escapism. When lifespans lengthened, the marriage age naturally rose, too. We can decide how long people are living, and the effects of this, based on story needs and general understanding of population health and resources.

Magical healing, or "laying on hands," usually means channeling a god's power through one's body as a vessel, to heal the wounded. This often means that a holy person communes with that god, first establishing a relationship through prayer so that he's not a stranger when calling on the god for this favor. Whether we call them a priest or another name doesn't matter. This can exist in either SF or fantasy but is more common in the latter; SF typically has either medicine equivalent to Earth's today or technology far in advance of us. In settings with supernatural power, we may have supernatural wounds that require supernatural healing techniques, as they may not respond to other methods. This is one justification, not that we need one, for magical healing.

Until recently on Earth, the understanding of germs was also poor, resulting in behaviors that spread illness more easily, such as people not washing their hands well or at all. The idea of invisible germs making people sick can be met with skepticism. In the early 1900s in New York, Mary Mallon, better known as Typhoid Mary, was an example of someone being a carrier, which means she showed no symptoms but can transmit that disease. She didn't believe she had it due to the lack of symptoms; she refused to change her habits and infected others continuously until health officials imprisoned her for life to stop her. While some of that is specific to her, we can apply such concepts to inventing pandemics. A fantasy setting without multiple plagues (or lesser outbreaks) in the past may be unrealistic. That a parent (or earlier generation) perished this way is useful character backstory.

Many of us have heard of bloodletting, which has an interesting theory we can incorporate into our world. Ancient physicians believed the body had four "humors" and that an excess or deficiency in any, or a poor mixture of them, resulted in illness. The four humors were blood, yellow bile, phlegm, and black bile, which is thought to be clotted blood (it appears black). Each humor was believed to have origins in specific body parts, and properties that resulted in certain illnesses. For example, yellow bile caused warm illnesses, and so on. Bloodletting attempted to cure someone by removing an excess humor to restore them to normal. People were sometimes made to consume a food or drink to counter a perceived imbalance in humors. These doctors were wrong, of course, but the practices lasted for over two thousand years, had no healing effects (unless coincidentally), and were sometimes harmful to patients. Not only can our invented world have such theories, but maybe we have species that actually work this way.

When medical ignorance abounds, quacks proliferate. Using wild claims of perfect cures, these disreputable people try to sell or otherwise profit from questionable and unproven medical remedies, then flee before the truth is discovered. Sometimes by luck, they actually helped, and not all quacks had malicious intent. They often claimed that exotic materials added to something like oil or a balm would help their foolish or desperate victims; if we've invented unique lifeforms, we can create an alternative to the "snake oil salesman" idea. These could be harmful, addictive, benign, or ease symptoms but not cure as claimed. A new, similar counterpart exists today, when conspiracy theorists claim that something proven to be beneficial, like immunization shots, are making people sick instead, in defiance of evidence to the contrary.

In SF, the exploration of new worlds can result in a flow of new discoveries, including both medical problems and solutions, and therefore, more quacks. There can also be devices, like the polygraph (lie-detector) that do not measure what they claim to. Based on the education system we've imagined, we should form an idea of the likelihood of such scams to succeed, but even today, many believe the polygraph works.

Fantasy worlds are usually akin to our past, meaning poorer health care and shorter lives, which pushes other milestones earlier. Today we consider it scandalous that a girl in her early teens might be expected to marry and give birth (especially when married off against her will), but it was practical because she might've been dead before twenty. There may also be the equivalent of medical devices to supposedly measure some aspect of a person; we have discretion to decide if they actually work or not.

SF offers a wider variety of health care quality due to lack of uniformity across the genre as to technological levels. This is especially true in planet-hopping stories, as every society on a new planet will have developed skills at different rates. Even spacecraft must get their organic medical supplies from somewhere else unless these are being synthesized. Given this wide range, how do we decide who can do what? One answer is story needs. Determine what kind of armed conflict will result, what sort of weapons exist and their damage severity and type, and then how many characters must be killed, maimed, bedridden, or healed (and to what degree) to impact our story for tension.

MENTAL

On Earth, mental health services are a recent development; they hardly existed before two hundred years ago. Before that, people were often thought to be touched by the devil, possessed, or some other nonsense. Many were either killed or confined, whether in more official places like an asylum or in the basement of a village resident assigned to care for these prisoners, who might be shackled day and night. Sometimes sane people were dealt with this way when they went against powerful people or social movements, calling for change.

We can do the same in a fantasy setting or inject our modern compassion and understanding. In SF, it's reasonable that advances in health care parallel those in other areas of technology, but it's not a rule. We've all seen seemingly dystopian SF where ships, space stations, and characters are all filthy and lawlessness seems to predominate; both physical and mental health needs may suffer, too, as the latter can almost be considered a luxury. The case can be made that the development of machinery helps provide for basics like food and shelter more easily and that "free time" is subsequently available for professions like psychology, but when people are struggling to get food, no one wants to spend time helping a disturbed person.

One reason all of this impacts characters is that people hear psychological terms, should they exist, and use them just as we do. But that depends on information flow. It's better in SF, in theory, than in fantasy, as is education. Even a dystopian society where that education system has disintegrated might still be aware of the terms, if they entered common usage before the collapse. Do we want our characters using such terms? They're optional. The term "ego" hadn't been invented in medieval times, but people were aware of it, anyway, using other words like pride.

LEGAL SYSTEMS

Most settings will have a legal system, even if it's as simple as "an eye for an eye." This section takes a high level and simplified view of these systems because most world builders will not be writing a legal drama, which is the only scenario where more detail is likely needed. Some places have a mix of the systems we'll cover, and we can do the same, though we may struggle for a reason to. In our setting, the publication of legal decisions, so that everyone can access them, is required; without this, laws are not enforced equally.

With all systems, our usage is primarily to cause trouble for our characters, who run afoul of a law, either by breaking it, encouraging others to do so, or even just speaking out against it. Any of these are more likely when traveling, due to ignorance of local laws, but there are other factors. Characters are usually on a mission and only passing through, and are therefore trying to avoid trouble, but we can have one member who tends to cause problems and another who knows the local laws and tells them what not to do. Use this as a guide. This helps us add an issue that either develops character(s) or plot.

TYPES

There are several types of legal systems. The source of laws is one of their primary differences. The system type arguably matters less than specific laws that impact our story, but they are briefly summarized next.

CIVIL LAW

One of the most widespread systems (along with common law), civil law means that a legislature creates and modifies an authoritative source that formalizes laws. That source is either a constitution (at the sovereign power or federal level) or a statute (at a lower level, such as states in the United States). Constitutional law tends to be broad and interpreted more at the statutory level, which is one reason variations can exist between states within a union. For example, as of this writing, marijuana is illegal at the federal level in the U.S. but legal in some states. To do this in our fictional world, we mostly need to know there's a sovereign power and self-governing bodies (like states or provinces) within it. A character can get themselves into trouble outside their home territory because they did not know something legal back home is illegal somewhere else. This can happen within a power, not just when traveling between them. If there's no law we've broken when brought before a judge, he has no authority and the case will be dismissed.

COMMON LAW

Common law derives its name from being common across England among the king's courts, and since Britain's empire spread far, it is now common across a third of the Earth, too, making it the other most widespread system (along with civil law). Its primary feature is that a judge will look to past cases that are like the one presented to him. If similar enough, he must abide by the past reasoning when ruling on the current case, as the precedents are considered the law; this principle is called "stare decisis" and is the main difference between this and civil law. If the case is unique, he will be the first one to rule on the matter, his decision henceforth becoming law to be considered by judges thereafter when faced with a similar case. Because of this, if there's no law, a judge can effectively make one. This contrasts with civil law, where a judge would have no authority to do anything.

Another name for this is judge-made law or judicial law.

RELIGIOUS LAW

If there's a religious document, such as the Bible or Quran, this will be the source of religious law. Either a god or a prophet (through whom they spoke) may be considered the author of the document, and this sometimes results in the ideas being named accordingly; Mosaic laws were written down by Moses, for example. Such sources are considered the word of a god about ethics and morality. A famous example may be the Ten Commandments. Variations are considerable across religions, which gives us flexibility and frees us from "getting it right." Canon law is the body of laws and regulations that a religious authority creates; these are typically named after a source, such as apostles or a church (or a group of them). As with seemingly everything in religion, these teachings can be interpreted quite differently, resulting in sects and other divisions within the religion, each adopting and applying their own laws. Past cases may or may not be considered; the interpretations of mankind are less important than the word of a god.

CONTRASTING TYPES

Both civil and common systems are unlikely among civilizations that have no written language or which are nomadic, due to the inability to codify the laws or a library in which to store them for reference. Expecting someone to memorize so much is improbable and prone to error, but maybe we have a trusted species with perfect recall or the ability to summon knowledgeable spirits from the afterlife as needed. Without such measures, only civilizations that have advanced to and beyond Roman or medieval times may reasonably be assigned either legal system. We might see elves and dwarves with such a system in fantasy, but probably not ogres and goblins.

By contrast, religious systems may be heavily dependent on fewer texts (at least in the beginning), which are readily available in churches, with the laws implied or explicitly stated in sermons and other stories that practitioners regularly hear. While not a rule, a religious system may be likely before and during more sophisticated civilizations.

A character who understands the difference between common and civil systems might have a different reaction to being accused of a crime. If he's aware there's no law and finds himself before a judge in a civil system, he might be unconcerned because the judge can't do anything to him. The case will be dismissed. But if he's in a common law system, the judge can invent the law based on this case. He might not feel so confident. In a religious system, it could go either way.

Civil judges must consider any previous cases (known as case law), but this is secondary to interpreting the source of law (constitution or statute). By contrast, in common law systems, previous cases *are* the law the judge is following, and he is highly reluctant to go against precedent.

HOW TO CREATE LAWS

Creating laws is relatively easy if we view them as having two sources: an enforcement or prohibition on values, beliefs, and morals, or to inhibit repetition of a past action, which is viewed negatively. I refer to these as moral and incident laws. While people break laws, the laws exist to inhibit or control behavior. We should keep this in mind and use it to invent ones we can use, and which our characters can break, intentionally or not. It's a good way to get them into trouble, especially in foreign lands. Sometimes a law is both moral and incidental in origin, as we'll see by some examples being reflected in both lists in this section.

What does the ruling authority want to influence? Always consider the form of government, discussed in *Creating Places (The Art of World Building, #2)* because this will impact how much control government is asserting through its legal system.

MORAL LAWS

Whether the system is religious or not, religion often influences laws as values, morals, and beliefs are promoted through restrictions on permissible behavior. Examples would be abortion or whether capital punishment is considered humane. Laws that discriminate are likely to originate in beliefs and values if not morality, as people characterize those who are different poorly. This includes gay, racial, and women's groups. We can extend this to professions such as wizardry or specific types, like witchcraft and necromancy. If we've invented species and worked out their relationships with humans and others, we can envision laws resulting from conflict with or disapproval of another race's values (or perceived values).

In chapter one, we looked at cultural ideas and vision and should leverage this while inventing laws of a moral nature. A society is a sum of its ideas, promoted in part by law, and those of the majority can inversely impact minorities through them. The simplest pronouncement of a law will not include explanation, but the reason for the law can often be inferred, at least by those living within the community. In parenthesis below, a short reason has been added, with an indication of whether it's a value, belief, or moral leading to the law.

Examples of laws based on morals, values, and beliefs:

1. Black magic is forbidden (moral: it requires dealing with unholy forces)
2. Goblins are not allowed near a treasury (belief: they're thieves)
3. Fire wizards must assist with extinguishing public fires (value: they should help)

4. Communication with alien species is prohibited without a permit and government monitoring (morals: solidarity with your species should take precedence over befriending a potential enemy of the state).

5. Wizards may not perform magic on the Holy Day (values/morals: it is reserved for godly shows of such power, as a sign of respect)

6. Ogres may not eat in public places (belief: they're believed to spread disease)

7. Children may not perform magic (belief/morals: it teaches them to rely on this)

8. Capital punishment by being drawn and quartered is forbidden (morals: too barbaric)

9. All residents must pass a biannual swimming test, especially dwarves (value: too many dwarves must be rescued during periodic flooding, hampering efforts to rescue others)

10. Those sentenced to death shall be devoured by dragon (morals/values: it's a quick death and waste not, want not)

11. A knight who flees shall be executed (value/morals: without courage, the knighthood will suffer loss of faith in it)

INCIDENT LAWS

Like the old saying, "shit happens." And sometimes, the ruling authority creates a law to inhibit it from happening again. Examples include restrictions/permits on weapons, pollution, vehicles, building and infrastructure, and many more. What they have in common is an attempt at improving safety and life quality through prohibition. If a building fell down due to an earthquake, a new law may result in better materials being used. People driving too fast or while drunk leads to accidents, injury, and death, and therefore a slew of laws. Most of those aren't particularly glamorous or useful to us and, while they'll exist, we don't need to focus on them. We should focus on what's different about our invented world (magic, tech, lifeforms) and the resulting laws we need to envision.

With technology we've invented, imagine what can go wrong and create incidents proving it. The result can be a character using a weapon that's not up to code because it was invented before a law, and possession and use of it is now illegal, either back home or where they are now. They might be upset to find it confiscated, then even destroyed by the local authority. Magic can lead to many laws, especially if we've decided that our magic system includes the ability for failed spells to still do something (see chapter six). This is a great way to invent small stories, minor characters who were involved (and for whom a law may be named, officially or colloquially), places of interest (where it happened), and some history.

Examples inspired by incidents (with explanations in parenthesis):

1. Black magic is forbidden (it leads to unsavory beings in town and the resulting problems they bring)
2. Goblins are not allowed near a treasury (they robbed several in the neighboring kingdom)
3. Children may not undertake interstellar travel unless accompanied by an adult or guardian (kidnapping risk)
4. Ogres are not allowed in public baths (they're disgusting and cause evacuation)
5. Children may not perform magic (they are too undisciplined)
6. Interstellar travel is only permissible on "Class 5" vessels or above (others are obsolete and do not work with modern docking stations)
7. All residents must pass a biannual swimming test, especially dwarves (over a hundred couldn't be rescued in the last flood and many non-dwarves also perished due to resources diverted to dwarves' rescue)
8. A federal work authorization permit from Earth is permitted to be employed on Mars (illegal immigrants are taking jobs)
9. Inciting Thor's wrath is punishable by death (Thor destroyed a city the last time someone provoked him)

TRIALS

In Earth history, a few trial types warrant mention. We don't mean the staid kind of today, where people calmly apply reason to presented evidence, but events like a trial by combat or ordeal. Some methods were thought to reveal the truth about the accused, even though they didn't. Fighting was physical, of course, but imagine how those with unique powers, like wizards, might conduct these.

A specific form of proof for murders in the medieval period was cruentation, which involved making an accused murderer touch the corpse, which might start bleeding if pressed hard. This indicated guilt and seems ripe for manipulation by the wise (don't press too hard and be exonerated!). We can leverage this to have the body react (or believed to) in different ways and for other crimes, especially with invented lifeforms, but be aware that audiences will typically scorn such beliefs as nonsense. They may feel contempt for a species or society that practices this, unless it's true. As medical knowledge rose, specifically the understanding of how and when dead bodies naturally emit fluids, this fell out of practice because people realized it was bogus.

DUELS

The goal of a duel was not to clear one's name of a crime, but to restore honor besmirched by another. These were originally fought with swords before giving way to firearms; the former continues as the sport of fencing. In both cases, the weapons were to be similar. Established rules governed the engagement. Honor was restored in part by following these rules and by showing that honor meant enough to participants that they'd risk their life over it. Killing the other person was therefore not the goal and could actually harm the honor of the survivor. Laws against duels led to their elimination, so we should decide whether they're still legal in our setting. Consider the values of each species and whether honor matters this much. They can duel in new ways or achieve "satisfaction" another way.

TRIAL BY COMBAT

Trial by combat was essentially a duel that had been officially sanctioned, except that instead of honor being the issue, the defendant had been accused of a crime by the person whom they were to fight. This happened when no witnesses or evidence could clear up the matter. The fights took place in public and on special platforms for all to see, like a boxing ring without the ropes. Some were able to decline this combat due to handicap, age (young or old), or other factors that rendered the combat unequal. They were tried by jury instead. Priests or royalty might decline as well. If fighting a woman, men were hampered on purpose to improve equality, such as one arm tied behind the back. Another option was to choose a champion, someone to fight on behalf of the accused or accuser. We could do these if two species we've invented are unmatched physically.

If the defeated didn't die in combat, he might be killed afterward, such as by hanging. In some Earth countries, depending on the crime, we could surrender when defeat was imminent, avoiding death but being dealt a harsh fate, such as slavery. World builders could extend this to include exile or, for a wizard, perhaps permanent removal of magical powers.

TRIAL BY ORDEAL

Variations on trial by ordeal exist and we can, of course, invent our own, especially if using animals or interesting places for them. Many tests were about survival, which indicated innocence, since God had saved the falsely accused. If there's a real god of justice, maybe this trial is accurate (assuming he's paying attention). This association with a deity led to these being carried out in church (maybe so he *is* paying attention!).

One version of a trial by fire was to walk several paces while holding a hot iron bar. Three days later, when the bandages were removed, an innocent person showed signs of healing while a guilty one didn't. Walking over hot coals is a variant. We can raise the drama by using volcanoes or unnatural (magic) fire, even radiation in SF.

Ordeal by water can involve binding the hands and feet and being tossed into water; the guilty floated, the innocent sank. Either might die in the process, but a rope was tied to the accused to bring them up and prevent that. A variant involved retrieving a stone from the bottom of a boiling cauldron, the depth of which corresponded to the severity of the crime; those uninjured by this were innocent. Being submerged in cold water and surviving also indicated innocence.

We can substitute supernatural or scientific elements, such as harmful substances, radiation, or dark matter. If a species is naturally resistant to an element we've devised, this can be used as a test. We can use these Earth analogues as inspiration. There's also no reason earth or air can't be used, too. Maybe those who can survive being buried alive are innocent, or those deprived of oxygen. The latter seems obvious in space, assuming people are spacefaring and yet still this barbaric.

PUNISHMENTS

Inventing punishments is a fun aspect of world building, especially if we're feeling sadistic. We have real world ideas to draw from and can create our own. We can decide later which punishments go with which crimes, but if we're feeling poetic, we can devise penalties that teach a clearer lesson about breaking a specific law. There are typically more laws and crimes than punishments; for example, jail time is used for a wide array of offenses.

We don't need to go overboard inventing punishments, especially ones we aren't going to use. If we invent some, we might benefit from one extreme, horrible, and memorable punishment and several much lesser ones. We want someone to react very seriously to being threatened with the terrible one. But lesser offenses and consequences are far more common, and our characters won't take them seriously, just as a parking ticket is an annoyance and little more. These punishments offer a chance to show the presence of the law (and making our world seem more complete) in ways that don't overtake a story.

Remember to imagine ways characters can resolve, avoid, or minimize a punishment. Sometimes we get a choice of a day in jail or paying a fine, for example. If we're nice to an officer, maybe we get a warning instead of the ticket. In corrupt places, there's always bribery. We're always looking for a way out so give the characters known ways to minimize their punishment; they'll be aware of them unless in a foreign land.

A basic decision is whether capital punishment (i.e., death) is accepted in the society. This is typically reserved for the most serious of offenses, such as murder, rape, treason, war crimes, crimes against the innocent (children), and more. When there is no feasible way to deter criminals from repeating a heinous crime, this led to the death penalty. For example, if we have a wizard who used magic to commit such a crime, and it's possible to prevent them from doing magic ever again, capital punishment is unlikely (removing their access to magic will prevent a repeat). In a nomadic tribe, death may be more common due to the lack of prisons, but an established society with cities may have less need of it.

There are many ways to kill someone in state sponsored execution. The next table lists several:

Title	Description
Boiling Alive	Immersed in boiling liquid of various kinds
Blowing from a Gun	Tied to the end of a cannon, which is then fired through the victim, blowing them to pieces
Blood Eagle	With the victim prone, the ribs are removed and placed to resemble wings
Brazen Bull	Roasted to death inside a brass bull with a fire underneath
Breaking Wheel	Tied to a wheel that slowly breaks all the bones, may slice the skin open

Title	Description
Burning at the Stake	Bound to a stake and burned alive by a fire under and around a person
Charivari	Parading an offender through the streets to mocking jeers of a crowd
Flaying	Skinning someone alive, which leads to slow death
Hung, drawn, and quartered	Dragged behind horse, hanged to near death, disemboweled (sometimes emasculated), beheaded, and finally cut into four pieces, head placed on a pike atop rampart walls
Impalement	Vertically or horizontally shoving a sharpened stake into the body and leaving the victim hanging above the ground on the stake
Keelhauling	Tied to ropes and dragged along rough/sharp bottom of ship
Mazzatello	A blow to the head knocks the victim out, the throat then slit
Sawing	Cutting someone in half with a saw
Schwedentrunk	Forcing copious amounts of foul liquid via funnel into the victim
Slow Slicing	A literal death by a thousand cuts and removal of body parts

Figure 76 Punishments

Exile is another option if value systems inhibit capital punishment.

To invent punishments, we use our imagination and the setting we've created to find uniqueness. People may be modified, such as with chemical castration for sexual crimes; a variant might be eliminating access to magic for wizards or having cybernetic implants removed (or added) in SF. If we've invented unique plants, animals, or locations, we can use them as punishment. The latter are especially useful for either banishment or temporary placement, like a jail. Merely being exposed to a phenomenon that we developed in chapter five ("The Supernatural") might be useful. A plant may be harmful. An encounter with an animal likely to produce death can be used in a trial by combat. What if there's a local monster no one can kill but they're hoping someone can and criminals get the honor of trying? Succeed and go free. Otherwise...

These are ways we can leverage other world building creations. Assigning a punishment to a crime is a matter of matching severity. Harsh governments like an absolute monarchy maybe have the punishment not fit the crime, but others generally strive for fairness, even if what they're doing makes questionable sense, as in the case of some trials by ordeal we previously examined. To people of that time, they were accepted and believed, and this will be true of most within such a society, so consider what this says (to our audience in particular) about how wise they are and their beliefs. As an example, if trial by water and sinking means innocence, the society believes it or wouldn't be following this rule of law. Do we want our readers to roll their eyes about this, or our SF characters that arrive in a less advanced world? And is the idea of God saving the innocent true or essentially superstition? A SF character could scorn this only to discover that it's true. Be sure to consider how our audience and characters will react to punishments they find in other lands.

COMMERCE

We sometimes need to understand how commerce works so we can show it with confidence. Two occasions are if we intend to show any transactions, or what characters need to do to acquire something they need. Without understanding how much an item costs, audiences have less understanding of characters' actions. Are four hours of chopping wood enough to earn a meal, or a rip off? Glossing over it is an option, but showing it adds believability. Writers can experience starting to show a transaction because it feels natural given the unfolding scene, but then hesitate to depict the amount of money being exchanged. Working out commerce solves this.

But sometimes we don't need it. We don't need details on how commerce works to show whether someone is rich, poor or in between. Audiences accept that this happens in society. It's optional to say their job is well or poorly paid, or they inherited wealth, or another factor, but not required. And if we're writing a story where everything is free, or we have a society so barbaric that even trading one thing for another doesn't happen, it won't matter. Otherwise, read on to learn how to determine commerce.

A MONETARY SYSTEM

One challenge of writing stories not taking place on Earth is that we can't say characters are paying with dollars, Euros, or bitcoins. We need a monetary system or to ignore currency altogether. It's standard in fantasy to use metal—platinum, gold, silver, copper, and iron coins—but gems and paper options exist. In SF, we can go with "credits" to keep it simple, even if we call it something else.

The money from a kingdom can and likely will have words and symbols on them, with characters reluctant to use those coins or bills at certain times if they might offend the receiver. Such items can be used to identity where they've recently been, too, though this is prone to misunderstanding; just because we have a coin from a kingdom doesn't mean we've been there; but this depends on whether the item is a unit of weight or of value, as explained next. A unit of weight, such as a measured piece of gold, can be freely traded across kingdoms so that a coin could be in circulation anywhere and we just happened to get it in our last exchange, but a unit of value is specific to a sovereign power and therefore, possessing it does suggest we've been there. An example: if I have a Canadian dollar, I've probably been there, but if I have a gold piece from Canada, the value of gold transcends borders and doesn't mean I've been there. I can't use the Canadian dollar outside Canada, but I can use that gold piece; that it was minted in Canada means nothing, unless they have a reputation for dishonesty and/or the weight is off.

UNITS OF WEIGHT OR VALUE

Money is either a unit of weight or unit of value. For example, paper money has no actual value except for the denomination printed on its surface, which spells out its value. Therefore, bills are a unit of value. On the other hand, the amount (or weight) of gold determines its value, even when fashioned into a coin. Metal is a unit of weight—but not always, because metal can have a value stamped onto it, rendering its weight irrelevant.

In media, we've seen someone handed a coin and then bite it to see if it's really made of the material that it appears to be, like gold, or whether it's only gold-plated. Alternatively, it may be placed on a scale. These matter when the coin is a unit of weight. But it could also matter with coins (of value) if two denominations are the same size. One could be stamped with the value of the other, in theory (counterfeiting). This may influence coins of different values having distinct sizes, but that is done partly to make identification and usage easier. Weighing on a scale can also lead to cheating if improper counterweights are used. These factors can contribute to units of weight falling out of favor in more advanced, established societies.

When a government collapses, so does the value of its currency when it is a unit of *value*. That $100 bill in our hand may now be worth zero if its value was backed by a now defunct government. By contrast, gold is gold.

Like other metals (or gems), its value is based on rarity in the world rather than by a sovereign power, and this seldom changes much if at all, which is why, on Earth, it's considered a safe investment—it is largely immune to the impact of a government's collapse. One reason to care about this is that a character who doesn't believe a government will last is unlikely to visit a bank, hand over his gold (a unit of weight) in exchange for bills (a unit of value), and walk away feeling safe.

Doing so seems less likely in fantasy due to the less robust governments that may exist. This robustness, or lack thereof, impacts everything, including police for those robberies, laws and courts to punish offenders, and accountability, which government provides to ensure people believe their state will take care of them and that institutions like banks and other infrastructure work. But if we have an empire, a constitutional monarchy, or a long-established state (over a hundred years), the state may insure banks (like modern ones on Earth) so that people trust them. This way, even if the bank is robbed, you'll still get your money because that bank is liable for the theft.

In SF, the advances in technology (and cooperation) that make activities like space travel possible are likely predicated on sophistication that matches or rivals that of modern-day Earth. Units of value are more likely than units of weight. A collapsing government can cause a rush on financial institutions to transfer that money to an institution in a stable, foreign country, before the value is zero. These people can be gouged by unscrupulous nations or banks who know what to do with desperate people. This can be an excellent way to create a now poor character with a backstory in wealth.

If units of weight are still in use, there's another complication in SF: the value of an ore like gold is based on its rarity. Discovering a new planet where a valuable ore is far more abundant can throw an economy into disarray as the value of that ore plummets. This is what typically happens when a new gold deposit is found: the value of all existing gold drops because greater abundance renders it less valuable. This should be a genuine fear of anyone whose fortune is in precious metals or gems. It's easy to imagine that person being opposed to space exploration – unless they think they can control how much of that ore, found on another planet, makes it to them. If that new planet has civilizations on it, both economies could be disrupted. It's unlikely that the planets have the same composition (or even extraction capabilities). It's also unlikely that a single ore will be different in rarity. While economics isn't a subject that excites, the potential financial disruption that newly discovered planets bring has been successfully overlooked by countless world builders who don't want to worry about it, and audiences accept it because they haven't thought about it, but we should. The introduction of germs and parasites between these two worlds has been featured more often.

OPTIONS

We have multiple options for currency and, just like on Earth today, more than one might exist within a single sovereign power, not to mention the world.

TRADING

Trading means providing two pigs for one chicken, for example, rather than two pigs for a unit of value or weight. It is the oldest form of exchange. While areas of our world may do this, most will be more sophisticated. Nomadic tribes and less technological cultures may not have developed currency or the means to produce it, like manipulation of ore into metal. They may not have manufactured swords, for example. Later in this chapter, we'll look at determining the value of items, but it's mostly about supply and demand.

A fictional world means imaginary supply and demand, so we can invent this and never be wrong. That said, an animal that repeatedly produces a commodity, whether wool, milk or eggs has value beyond its own body, which can be used for meat, bone, and more, so take this into account. A plant that can be duplicated (with seeds, for example) is similar. Skilled labor to produce a long-lasting or superior item is also more valuable than, for example, a ram's horn that only had to be broken off a dead ram.

If rams are common, I might need to give you five of their horns for the tanned leather hide you made from a bear. But if ram horns are used to signal in battle and few rams are around, maybe I'm giving you one horn for two hides. A word of explanation like this adds believability and can be invented in the time it takes to write the sentence. Just be consistent: don't show a hugely different number of rams existing four chapters later.

METAL

Coins have been used as money since antiquity. For fantasy worlds, this is our default currency. Long ago, metal had its value because of weight, quality, and material (like 2 oz. of 14k gold). It relied less on a trade valuation at banks and could be melted down and still have [almost] the same value. A sovereign power minted coins in a standardized process to ensure the weight, then stamped them with an official insignia to establish trust in the coin's value. One reason is that metals can be impure by accident or on purpose, whether the latter is intended to defraud the unsuspecting or to reduce the amount of precious metal used as money. This impurity can be checked by use of a touchstone, which is a stone tablet that reveals the alloy of soft metals when those are used to write on it.

In time, metal changed from being a unit of weight into one of value. In some countries, only one type of metal (like gold) was used, with different sizes denoting value. Separate regions have access to different quantities of precious metals. This could make things more realistic and more challenging when characters travel between kingdoms.

An issue with coins is their weight; no one carries around two thousand silver pieces, for example, even when they need to. Our world could have iron, copper, gold, and platinum, too. If one platinum equals a thousand silver, then they only need two coins, assuming they can find and exchange these. We may want a conversion like this example, using American money for clarity:

    1 iron piece = 10 cents
    10 iron pieces = 1 copper = $1
    10 coppers = 1 silver = $10
    10 silvers = 1 gold = $100
    10 gold = 1 platinum = $1000

Coins are typically round for several reasons. The pointed edges of a square or rectangle will wear down with use, possibly lowering weight and therefore value, while also making the now irregularly shaped coin harder to stack. In production, coins were also struck, causing the metal to push outward in a circular shape, which made this a sensible form. A lucrative business could be had shaving off flat sides of a coin, thereby reducing the weight and value, though milling was added around the edge so that it's easier to tell when the coin's edge has been shaved (the milling would be gone). The absence of these indicates a less sophisticated culture.

GEMSTONES

Any gem can be used as money, but can they be a unit of weight? Probably not. How much a gem weighs (how many carats) doesn't indicate value by itself because the quality can be so poor as to make it largely worthless. Few people have a specialized magnifier ("loupe") or the training to identify a stone's quality, making gems less viable as a unit of currency. If people can't tell the quality, they'll get manipulated during trading. Despite this, in antiquity, the naked eye was how all gems were appraised, so we can do this, too. Most gem deposits produce low quality stones that will never be fashioned into a jewel. The color and clarity are two elements that determine quality, which can be increased or decreased when the raw stone is carved into a jewel.

An underground race like dwarves would likely mine for gems and minerals, using either one as currency and easily converting values between them. Perhaps one diamond is the equivalent of one platinum piece. Would they have two currencies, or do they represent different spheres of social strata, such as royalty using gems and commoners using coins? A commoner caught with a gem coin might be assumed to be a thief. Maybe every dwarf is given a loupe at birth.

If gems are a unit of value instead, then low grade gems (like amber) can be inscribed with their denomination and function like metal coins. The gems could still be highly polished and look valuable to the naked eye. Even in antiquity, some gems were beautifully carved to show portraits of Roman emperors, including a garland of leaves with the leaf edges clearly visible. They won't need milling because shaving down a jewel doesn't produce useful shavings like it does with metal. The coins need not be round as wear on the edges is unlikely.

Compared to metal, gem coin denominations may challenge audience memories due to this being unusual in fiction and less familiarity with gem values on Earth, not to mention values in a fictitious world. By contrast, we all know gold, silver, and copper are progressively less valuable. Regardless, we can create and use a system like this one, with units of value:

Poor-Quality Stones	High-Quality Stones
1 amber = 10 cents	1 pearl = 10 cents
10 amber = 1 jade = $1	10 pearls = 1 emerald = $1
10 jade = 1 topaz = $10	10 emeralds = 1 sapphire = $10
10 topaz = 1 amethyst = $100	10 sapphires = 1 ruby = $100
10 amethysts = 1 opal = $1000	10 rubies = 1 diamond = $1000

Figure 77 Gems as Currency

BILLS

Paper money is a unit of value and therefore requires trust and the backing of a bank and/or government. Sovereign powers may be too unstable or short lived for trust to develop paper currency, however. In fantasy worlds, the machinery to mass print paper has not usually been invented, but they can be done in smaller quantities by more physical means, just like coins. Paper money can be easily destroyed in fire, water, or by being torn, but it is easier to carry around in large sums than coins, and in some cases, gems. Keep bills simple, such as ones, fives, tens, and so on. Like some Earth countries, we can change the color per denomination. Bills are typically for larger numbers (dollars) than coins (cents), but there's no reason this can't be reversed. They can also be far smaller than what we have on Earth.

CREDIT

Just like today, SF worlds of comparable or superior technology to ours might have credit as currency. This requires official banking by a trusted source, whether a sovereign power on a planet (or elsewhere), a union of powers (possibly across worlds), or an institution that regulates the currency. Today we have bitcoin and other versions of credit, and we can invent more types, but unless we intend to delve into their usage (or the rise and fall of it), we should aim for simplicity. One choice to make is how people access and exchange credit. On Earth we use cards, devices like phones, and computers. What tech might be employed in our world? An iris or face scan? Fingerprints? DNA? An implant?

CURRENCY CONVERSION

When we move between economies/powers, we must convert our money from one currency to another. Several factors influence conversion rates, including differentials in inflation and interest rates, account deficits between countries (how much they owe each other), public debt, trade terms, and economic performance. Does this sound like something an audience wants to read about, or something we want to determine for not one, but two fictional sovereign powers? Probably not. It's reasonable to desire getting it "right," but as is often the case, many details impact this and no one from our fictional world is going to show up and say we're wrong.

Do we need to show conversion and rationales in our work? Not usually. If we're doing a story with sovereign powers having just risen or fallen, or other dramatic changes within our tale, then it's obvious that currency could be disrupted, especially for units of value backed by the government, but most of us can skip it. We don't typically know why our own dollar is rising or falling and audiences certainly won't understand what's happening on a fictitious planet, especially if we don't tell them. Explaining can actually get us accused of having done research and then dropping it into our narrative.

The conversion arguably matters less with units of weight, like gold, because its size and rarity don't change. But it might be differently valued in one place. The exchange is typically transaction by transaction and decided between merchant and customer, as opposed to units of value, where the exchange rate is set by the sovereign power or other governing body and changes by the day (on Earth). A merchant must abide by it, and so do we and our characters. It's simplest to have a character express a reaction to how far their money is going and not focus on details. Being consistent matters less than other subjects because rates change daily anyway.

RELATIVE VALUE IN CURRENCY

We should strive for simplicity in our monetary system, especially in terminology.

Using the U.S. as an example, for paper money, bills come in 1, 2, 5, 10, 20, 100, and 1000. But there's only one name for all of them: "dollar." And yet "dollar" really describes "one" accurately. If I give someone a $100 bill, that's how I say it: "one hundred dollars." Unless I specify which bills I gave, you have no idea what configuration of bills I used. Now imagine that that $100 bill has a name, dellium. Then I could say, "one dellium." The problem here is that the audience has no idea that a dellium is one hundred of something else. Explaining it is a poor use of exposition, it won't be remembered, and it doesn't convey a sense of relative value to other terms we've invented and which the audience also doesn't recall. Using a specific generic term is convenient.

What about coins? Unlike with bills, each coin may have a name (penny, nickel, dime, and quarter) but they can all be referred to with the generic "cents." And that's exactly what people do. I might give someone "seventy-five cents," not say that I gave them "three quarters." Someone not familiar with the U.S. system can infer that a quarter is the one valued at 25 cents, but only because I specified that the three quarters amounted to seventy-five. By contrast, if I say I provided three nickels, do you know if that's three times one ($.03), three times five ($.15), or three times ten ($.30)?

We don't want to do this to an audience. Therefore, two generic words, such as "dollars" and "cents," one denoting whole and another for part of a whole, provide a better sense of relative value and is preferred for fictional monetary systems. Avoid inventing names for denominations (i.e., "penny," "dime"). If we really want to, we can, but use them wisely when writing. For example, "Seeing the price was fifteen cents, he pulled three nickels from a pocket." Contrast that with, "Seeing the price, he pulled three nickels from a pocket." The second tells us nothing about how much he's paying unless we know the value of the denomination; our knowledge of it is *required* to understand. The first tells us what he's paying, with a minor detail of how he did so as an *option*.

With this in mind, we can decide coins, gems, or bills have names and values but still default to generic terms like "dollars" and "cents" to indicate relative value, only rarely specifying which coins, gems, or bills someone used. Or we can just go with two generic terms and be done.

DETERMINING VALUE

It can be difficult to determine how much anything costs in a fictional world, or the wages people are paid, but this is easier than it seems. Why do we care? Because we may want to show a fantasy character, for example, paying one silver piece for a drink and then three gold pieces for a dragon, and then we wonder if that's on target or ridiculous. There's a simple trick for this: use Earth values from the country where you live, then tweak this.

For example, if I buy prepared food, I know how much things cost in the United States. Using some made-up numbers, let's say fast food is under $10, a cheap sit-down dinner is under $20, a nicer outing will set me back $30 for just myself, and something above $50 would be expensive, a meal for a rare occasion like a holiday. How does this help?

We're not going to use the words "dollars" or "cents" in a manuscript set on another planet, so let's say I'm writing fantasy and have decided that the generic "coin" is my "one dollar." A turkey leg or steak-on-a-stake (i.e., fast food) might cost me 5 coin, a sit-down meal at a tavern catering to warriors and other working types might run 20 coin, a nice inn or restaurant might set me back 30 coin, and if I'm doing the latter on the eve of a major holiday or buying the most expensive thing on the menu, I'm spending 50 coin. Notice how the numbers are the same as my U.S. analogue.

I don't have to determine value. I borrowed the economics of modern America as a starting point, at least. We can change the numbers, adding a zero so that what's five dollars here is fifty coin there. Or we can multiple or divide by three if we want less relation to our source. We can do the same with wages, products, and services. For something not in use on Earth anymore, substitute an item that *is* in use. Not sure how much a two-handed sword would be worth? Well, it's a pretty big, specialty weapon, so research big, specialty guns (still in use on Earth) and compare them to more ordinary guns to gauge a price. Plausibility is the bar to get over, not being "right."

Don't use the current price of a wagon, because who is using one aside from the Amish? Like cars, wagons come in different sizes, so create a range of values just like cars have. Note that unless a character will buy or lose the use of a wagon in our story, or express pride or dissatisfaction with one, pricing this is unnecessary world building. On the other hand, it adds believability if a farmer goes chasing after our main characters after they're stolen his best one, which cost him a year's earnings, unlike the older, more dilapidated ones. It can also make characters seem less like a jerk when they steal the latter instead.

When something is fictional, we must decide how much value it has. Even if dragons are common, one may be the equivalent of a military jet with fantastic speed, electronics, and weaponry. Those cost millions a piece. This means only a government's military likely has them, but this analogy has a flaw: it costs money to build jets, so is a naturally occurring, living possession like a dragon worth less? Undoubtedly. Training of that dragon, rarity, and possibly equipment like a saddle are the only actual costs (other than lives) of taming one. The cost also doesn't matter if they're not for sale. If you want a dragon, you might have to kill its owner, assuming the dragon lets you or allows you to take ownership. But dragons are a unique subject.

What about something less spectacular, like a flying horse? This would be the most expensive horse, so determine the value of horses (like everything, they come in a range) and raise it. Someone who trains such creatures is unique and likely earns far more, and belongs to a higher social class.

For trading systems, it can be difficult to determine that one knife is worth three cows, for example. There isn't a simple way to determine this, but we can infer that cows are naturally occurring and take no special intervention, whereas a knife, especially a well-made one, does. Therefore the knife is more valuable than a single cow? How much more? Story needs are a good way to determine this; if a character badly needs the knife and to keep the three cows, then this is a pain point for him. Do we need that? A pitfall to avoid is showing characters consuming or using items that aren't local in the absence of trade with other communities. This is a minor detail, but avoid showing an isolated place that has every item available in a city, for example.

We don't need to get value "right." Our invented world can have gold as common as rocks and therefore gold has no value. Supply and demand means we have significant leeway and only need to be consistent, which matters more when writing a long series in the same world (or region of one). To achieve that, it is best to base our system on Earth values and change the numbers in a consistent manner (such as multiplying everything by three) and using different terms. Besides, even on Earth, rates differ from one place to another. A townhouse in a nice neighborhood might get $500k in one locality, while the money buys a large single-family home with yard and pool in another. No one from our planet is going to show up and tell us we're wrong. All of this applies to SF as well, except that we have even greater leeway due to tech that has never existed here. No one can say how valued it would really be.

LABOR VALUE

We sometimes have a sense of labor's value, but with potential new jobs that exist in SF or fantasy, we may need to be creative. Being plausible is once again our goal. Local conditions will impact this and we can invent that on the fly. Maybe I'll earn a meal by chopping wood for two hours in one place, but it takes four hours in another. Why would this difference occur? The longer time means my labor has less value there. This might happen if there are plenty of potential wood choppers around. Conversely, if this is rare, maybe I'll get by with suggesting only one hour.

Chopping wood isn't unusual labor, but think of some unique jobs that might exist in a fantasy setting, given the plants, animals, and existence of magic. What if a wizard needs someone to practice casting a spell on? We'd imagine this quite lucrative, given the risks. Perhaps they need someone to assist as they prepare a potion or summon a demon.

In SF, gadgets and phenomena similarly offer opportunities. Maybe we need to test a device, whether that's dangerous or not. Cleaning radiative sludge somewhere might be needed. Imagine anything dangerous or just unpleasant, depending on how much risk we feel is needed. It's great when the experience changes our character or plot rather than being an aside, such as radiation sickness impacting a character's ability to perform like usual days later when they need to.

In both genres, there could be an animal that must be fed, or watched even though it's in a cage. Plants might need sowing, harvesting, or preparing, which doesn't sound interesting unless there's something special about this. Examples would be harvesting a man-eating plant, or cooking one which produces lethal fumes if not prepared right. Get creative when characters have no money and need something.

If they want to earn money rather than food, lodging, or transportation, we assign a value based on rarity, danger, or story impact. For example, if chopping wood will take two hours, which they have, this doesn't impact the tale (unless they hurt themselves). But if they don't have two hours to spare, this poses a problem. We can therefore choose a task and assign a value that will negatively impact them to a degree that seems appropriate to us. It can also have a positive impact. If chopping wood for a set period of time would earn me two silver pieces and I only need one, I could bargain to reduce the time or just take the extra money.

INFORMATION SYSTEMS

Even in a fantasy setting, we may need an information system. It just won't be technological like SF. Where do people get their news and other intel?

SF

We can modify any real-world technologies in SF. This includes radios, telephones, postal systems, and of course, the internet. But we can also invent new systems. The challenge of doing so is producing a result that's different from what we have. This was easier decades ago than today, when audiences may expect the equivalent of what we have – instant transfer of voice, video, and data across distances as vast as the Earth. There's still a delay across even interplanetary distances, with the speed of light being the upper limit on this. However, we've already seen depictions of seemingly real-time communication in film and TV franchises.

There's a distinction between the end result (the instant transfer mentioned previously) and the mechanism by which that is achieved. The modern mechanism is the internet, which is comprised of numerous technologies that most of us neither know nor care about. It's possible that our audience has limited interest in any replacements we devise unless their use (and breakdown) impact the story. But do we need to understand how a device works to show the reader that it's failed? Failure can take various forms, such as a battery or connection issues, both of which audiences accept without explanation because it happens now.

If we're inventing an information system and the tech by which is operates, we can approach this similarly to how we'd create items (chapter 7). We'll want new names for the components that comprise our system, basing these on current analogues. Phone systems require a phone, a contact number, and either land lines, towers, or even satellites and other data systems to carry signals, plus the companies that charge us for the privilege. Answering machines, voice dialing, and even fax transmissions are other elements. We can do this same exercise with IT systems, which may need a keyboard, mouse/touch pad, screen, and a computer with ports and wires, etc. When devising our new setup, just replace such elements. When it comes to data storage, we must also decide how much info can be taken with us in portable devices and sources of new and updated contents.

In SF, we should have characters react to the quality and availability of tech at their disposal, because that's what we'd do when confronted with something better or worse than we're used to. This is when those terms enter dialogue or narration. Show them having difficulty controlling the tech by name, jiggling it, giving it a whack, and asking if anyone has another, then show how they plug it in, turn it on, or synch it. This is how to use this without dumping exposition. All computerized tech lends itself to hacking and other compromises, so be sure to take this into account; people may have to use biometric means to access systems or otherwise be inconvenienced in ways that they gripe about, and this adds realism (and audience empathy).

FANTASY

None of this technology exists in a medieval-like setting, so what did people do on Earth? Notices were sometimes posted on the door of important buildings like a church or town hall, but we can choose any location, like a castle or tower wall. For the townspeople, this requires reading skills, so if education is lax, it may not work or the settlement may have someone, like a priest or guard, assigned to stand there and read it off to anyone who can't. With or without this, a town crier may announce the news in one of several ways, such as wandering through town as needed and repeating it as he goes, or at dawn, noon, and dusk at the town water supply. Especially important announcements might be preceded by a distinctive horn blast, guards being used to round up everyone and ensure they attend. There may be regular days when less time-sensitive addresses are made, and our ruling class may add levels of pomp and circumstance to conveying information.

We should also consider the role of messengers. Some will travel on foot, others by horse or similar, and some may fly. One that travels by land must gain entrance to the destination, with guards trained on how to deal with them. To prevent gossip, they may instruct a messenger to remain silent about news until escorted to the right person, in private. People will be watching, of course, and may relate that a messenger from a given place has arrived and their state of mind (excited, afraid, calm). Flying messengers can bypass city walls and potentially circumvent all attempts at stopping the intended recipient from getting the message. These couriers may be animals like carrier pigeons or sentient, winged species that have far more discretion in how they go about their work.

All messengers may travel through potentially dangerous lands, so are there protections afforded them, and which wearing a distinctive clothing item, like a sash, promotes? There may be penalties for detaining or interfering with one, especially a king's messenger. They might have the right to accommodations or food, free or reduced. Maybe we get kicked out of our room at a roadside inn because a king's messenger needs it. How are messengers treated where they arrive? Unless someone openly courts war, they will be treated at least decently; only a foolish ruler does otherwise because if messengers are harmed, the flow of information may stop (if from a rival). However, a king killing messengers from cities within his kingdom may not stop them from coming if he can command it, but it's the sort of abuse that leads absolute monarchs into trouble.

There may be mail systems like the Pony Express in the United States. Do ships or stagecoaches carry cargo and mail for ordinary people? They may do so for royalty, which can make them a target of pirates and thieves. As a result, many might be guarded, which could be a sign of a valuable shipment, leading to the guards pretending they aren't guards but other travelers.

Magic also provides a means of spreading information. The crystal ball or magic mirror are two physical examples, but regardless of the manifestation we choose, these can be like either phone or video calls on Earth. We don't need to restrict ourselves to one-on-one communication this way. Perhaps a shimmering image has taken the place of the town crier. Or a spell or clairaudience allows someone to communicate directly with a recipient's mind, and is this one-way or mutual? For this to be a system and not a "one off," we may want items that can be used for this.

WHERE TO START

With all systems, we need to start with our genre. Fantasy and even dystopian SF might have much poorer infrastructure than modern Earth, while other SF might have the same or greater. This and how established the government is will impact that society's ability to create a system, so consider whether it's a new sovereign power or one of several decades or more. While some systems extend throughout the society, some are more localized, so determine the scope of the system that's being invented, such as if it's a city, state, or country. These decisions are the broad strokes we need. Details such as when school starts and ends, or what kind of money is used and how it's configured, are more of a personal preference for our setting. We can decide these at any time based on what we like, more than what's likely.

CHAPTER ELEVEN

CONCLUSION

This chapter concludes *The Art of World Building* series with some final thoughts on our goals, approaches to the work, how to manage files, and ways to partner with others.

GOALS

Having a goal helps us reduce both the number of tasks and the depth of world building in which we engage. Otherwise we can spend too much time and energy on activities that don't warrant them. We should always ask ourselves what we are hoping to achieve, and this is typically an enjoyable, immersive, and unique experience for our audience. World building isn't the only way to achieve this, as good storytelling or gameplay can do the same, so world building is one trick in our arsenal – one we shouldn't do at the expense of all others. "Moderation in all things."

Decide on goals by asking yourself some questions:

1. Do I want to focus on storytelling and feel little desire to do world building?
2. Do I plan to write many books or just a few to test the waters?
3. Do I feel creative enough to invent a believable world in some detail? Will the setting be unusual enough to warrant the time spent on it?
4. Do I have the time to do extensive world building, or something less extreme?
5. Do I have the patience to stick with it for months or years?
6. How will I feel if I spend years on a setting only to have rejections from agents and publishers? Am I willing to self-publish?

7. Do I *want* to do this or do I *have* to do this?
8. Do I think it's fun and exciting or a chore and a burden?

Much of what we could do is optional, but certain elements are not. For example, we'll probably need at least one sovereign power, maybe two, plus a few settlements within each. If the characters travel, land features between origin and destination will be encountered unless it's SF and ground features can be bypassed. While we can develop only the areas to be shown in the story, we can suggest a wider world without actually creating it. Most other elements aren't universally required but are project dependent. Most chapters in this series presented a breakdown of how to assess whether or not to invent something, or to what degree, but this is a general reminder to avoid becoming overwhelmed by choosing wisely.

It's also worth mentioning that, while we often invent for a particular setting, sometimes we might not use an idea. If it's not truly integrated with the world, we can reuse it elsewhere. Always be willing to jot down ideas.

ABIDE BY RULES

Modern audiences are especially astute and often notice inconsistency. We should strive to avoid this in world building by following any rules that we've stated for our setting. There are several tricks that can assist with this by providing flexibility.

One is hedging, or using less strict language. Instead of writing that, for example, "wizards must be trained," we state that "wizards must usually be trained." There are other variants on this, such as, "No one knew how else to become skilled without it, and so wizards had to be trained," or "Wizards believed they had to be trained." With each of these, we're giving ourselves a subtle "out" that things might be different than we're saying.

One problem with this is that people don't always read carefully or remember accurately, and if characters are acting like something is an iron-clad rule, this impression can override what we technically said. In both cases, the audience can come to believe it's a bona fide rule and chide us for breaking it. That we did some narrational sleight-of-hand is something we may not have the chance to point out, and even if we do, could be accused of tricking readers. Use this wisely and not too often.

Another ploy is having characters state the supposed fact. After all, they're people, and those are fallible. It's hardly our fault a character passed bad information on to other people, including the reader (of course it's our fault)! To do this, we need either their dialogue or narration that is done in their perspective. In the former, we might put these words in someone's mouth: "Kier, why do wizards have to be trained?" or "Kier, every wizard must be trained!" If the characters to whom this is said accept it as true, so may the audience. We can use their reaction to bolster or weaken the perceived accuracy of the statements.

Whether we want to employ these practices or not, it can be wise to note any statements of absolutism that imply there's a rule. This sometimes happens in the act of storytelling. Develop a sense of this just as we do with any other aspect of writing, such as grammar mistakes. If we don't catch it on writing, hopefully we will on editing our work. When we create or find such a statement, write it down in a file about this setting, appropriately categorizing it. In the above example, it's about wizards, so it goes into the magic file, which should periodically be reviewed while writing this setting or designing games there.

TYING IT TOGETHER

Creating world building elements that stand isolated from others can make the setting seem poorly designed and lacking depth. There's no quick solution for tying everything together. It pays to have a good memory of what's been invented so far and tweak what we're inventing currently based on this.

Periodically reviewing our world building files is an excellent practice. Put a reminder on a calendar, if you keep one to organize your projects or life. What we'll do is just read through our files. That's it! It might have been months or years since gestation (or repeated refinement) led to the contents of a file. We may have invented many items since and forgotten to intertwine them. Even without that, we may have new ideas or realizations to add. We've also had time away from the invention and our fresher eyes can improve what we've done. Expect and accept that this exercise might lead to additional world building.

Another approach is what I think of as "looping." Choose a land feature, such as a forest, and describe the terrain; details and examples on what to write are discussed in *Creating Places*, but we want to discuss how dense the underbrush is, the mood of it, how many roads run through it and their condition, and what plants and animals of interest might be here, in what quantity, and in which areas. If we've invented some lifeforms, we're now merging them with this particular woodland. We can state that a given road is less traveled due to proximity to the territory of one such creature. Rare items might be here; state where they're found and how arduous the journey is. Maybe a nefarious organization has a base within.

Now start the loop. If there are multiple settlements nearby, open the file for one. The inhabitants have a relationship with this place. Describe it. Do they fear it, use it for recreation, or hunt within? How far from the walls is it? They're the one tending a road or letting it be overgrown. Do they see this terrain as protecting them from attack or as a vulnerability? Is there something nasty inside that they fear? What armed forces exist here that are present specifically to deal with such a threat? Are there raids into the woods or from things in the woods? Do knights attend those who venture into this forest? To decide this requires some imagination, and having worked out the military groups available. Are there useful plants there and major products that result? When we're done updating the settlement file, we need to revisit the one for this forest, updating our description of it to include its relationship with this settlement. We're looping from one file into another and back. If there's another settlement near this forest, we repeat the same exercise. Do it with all nearby communities.

Then choose another. Or a mountain range, a lake, a desert, or other features until there's little on a map that's not interwoven. Use the options we discussed in *Creating Places* to ensure no two are alike. While doing this, we may think of additions to non-places and should update those files, too.

For example, if we've imagined new details on our evil organization, perhaps we add a note about their base in these woods and what it's like, and how the nearby settlements impact life there. We might even say that, because a given animal is here, it's been adopted as their symbol, or they specialize in taming or killing it, even cooking it a particular way. The latter can result in a rare treat that people like but are afraid to eat in public due to its association with the group. Now we have to open our files on food and drinks of the world and update that, possibly creating occasions when something is consumed and when it's avoided, or how it's made, its reputation, and whatever else. We might decide that there's another version of it without the bad reputation, as invented by another species, and now we end up in that file jotting down a note about it but leaving the details in our food file.

The same approach is used to integrate species with each other and the world. Work on one and define it according to imagination and the guidance from *Creating Life (The Art of World Building, #1)*, using the provided template for ideas. There's a section on relationships with others. Fill out connections between, for example, your elves and dwarves while in the elven file, and then open the dwarf file and do the same there. To minimize rewrites, I will copy and paste the same text in both files, even though I generally avoid duplication in my notes. Review what's been written about both while doing this because it can trigger ideas.

When we invent an organization or military group, for example, we should define its relations with each species and location (settlements, regions, land features, and sovereign powers) where it is found. We once again want to loop back into the species and location files and update our understanding of them.

The pattern here is periodic review and update. That's the way we integrate elements in the setting. Don't expect it to all be done at once. That's not realistic. I've been updating my Llurien setting for over thirty years now, always improving and refining it. Sometimes it's been a decade since I last read a file. I'm sometimes surprised by what's in one, as I remember many grand scale inventions but often forget details of things I'm not currently using. My duration on this is extreme, but yours needn't be. We can world build many things a few minutes at a time as long as we stay organized.

APPROACHES

There are multiple approaches to world building, such as top-down and bottom-up. All are valid and have their merits and undesirable consequences, which can be mitigated.

TOP DOWN

The top down approach can be described as starting with the big picture and working our way down to smaller elements. For example, when it comes to physically designing the world, we decide how many continents it has and where they are in relation to each other. Next we focus on a single continent, deciding what nations exist and what forest, mountains, and other features exist and where, possibly drawing a map. We would repeat this on other continents. From there, we would choose a nation and decide on where its major cities and towns are and work out their relationships before moving on to other nations.

Regarding life, we would start with creating gods, the reason being that these deities presumably have attributes that affect the species, plants, and animals they created. All of those should be influenced by the land features we've already created. And they should have relationships with each other.

The species might have in turn caused supernatural disasters that left residue behind and now everyone avoids that place.

The advantage to such an approach is cohesion. The impression of randomly created pieces slapped together is less likely, as are world building holes (like plot holes). The latter would include something like a river that has no mountain source, but we can't add one because we've already decided that none of the nations near it have a mountain range and their cultures are somehow dependent on that, for example. And maybe we can't get rid of the river, either.

The disadvantage is that world building can feel like a big homework assignment. We're doing this in a specific order and may not have ideas when we need one to continue. Getting stuck can ruin momentum and enthusiasm. We can see a huge to-do list and feel overwhelmed. The process of creation is supposed to be fun; creating things in a freewheeling manner helps with that and also causes interesting ideas to develop.

Bottom Up

The bottom up approach means starting at a more localized level, such as the settlement where a story takes place. We may decide some land features are at various distances from here and any impact this causes. Later, we decide what sovereign power type exists, even if this decision changes previous work on the settlements and geography. We might decide that an adjacent sovereign power is needed and invent it, tailoring it to our current needs. We may not have decided which hemisphere this place is or the continent, which means we may not have considered climate much. This matters more with things that don't move (places) because species and animals can be relocated and found in multiple places.

An advantage of the bottom-up way is that it forces us to focus on our immediate setting needs, like a city we'll use. We may skimp on things we won't need yet, saving time. Story can also inspire our inventions. For many of us, it's also easy to envision a city that has specific features or a mood, and we may be unsure how outside factors could contribute, though hopefully this series has changed that.

One problem with this approach, for places, is that the overall picture indelibly impacts the local one. We might decide there are mountains and lush vegetation in a certain direction, then choose a hemisphere only to find out that those mountains would prevent that vegetation. Similar factors could render our work less sensible. Another disadvantage is lack of scope. When we only invent what we need and a little more, our world can seem too tightly focused and like there isn't a broader world out there. This may not matter in a short story or one where characters don't travel, beyond mentioning other places or peoples and things influenced by them, but for more epic uses, we need to at least hint at a broader world.

RANDOM

The random approach means creating individual items and worrying about how they relate to each other later. We can create a species here, a god there, a city elsewhere, doing each on the spur of the moment. There's no quota of species, cities, or gods to create, no obligations. We create whatever seems like a good idea at the time. Only later do we decide that cities are part of a nation, or a god is part of an interconnected pantheon. Or that two species live near each other and are enemies or friends, and why. We might decide a species originates from a given forest, but on later reflection, we realize they'd spread throughout the area and add them to those other regions, both in forests and settlements near. Our concept of them evolves continuously whenever we think of something.

This has the advantage of allowing us to create in an improvised style that will lend itself to rapid creation and exploration without worrying about restrictions we've imposed on ourselves. We can see if we have what it takes for more serious world building. We're focused on a single idea and making it work for its own sake. If there are elements that don't make sense yet, we can fix them later and just try to avoid boxing ourselves into a corner.

The disadvantage is a lack of global cohesion. Maybe we have too many gods, not enough, or they don't make sense as a group. If we haven't worked out how species get along and then use them in scenes together, do they interact in understandable ways?

WHICH TO DO?

If none of these approaches sounds ideal, that's because mixing them is arguably best. To do this, we need a framework, or the "top down" view on the world, establishing some basics about the physical environment, more so than individual gods, species, or other life forms. Then we can fill it in. What follows is a rough order if we're starting with a new setting; authors who already have a setting can see where they might need to backtrack to fill in some of this before forging ahead. These suggestions are just that, so if you disagree, at least it will get you thinking about how you would do this.

START WITH A CONTINENT

It might be called "world building," but many stories take place on a single continent, which is what we start with. Decide which hemisphere it's in so we know whether cold is north or south. This also helps determine whether another continent is north or south of the one we've created; if the world is Earth-like in size, there's probably only one in each hemisphere at that latitude. As discussed in *Creating Places*, this allows us to determine the prevailing winds. This matters because the combination of continent and mountain range placement will determine where vegetation is (and is not). With this done, we can decide where we'd like mountains, which will tell us many of our other land features, including deserts, grasslands, and forests. At a minimum, sketch this on a piece of paper, possibly with arrows pointing off the page to indicate other land masses.

This exercise gives us an overview of a continent with at least a high-level view of where everything lies. If we're not planning to use major areas of it, that's fine. At least we know where they are and have a rough idea of climate there. If we'd like, we can name various regions and land features. For those who want to top-down start, we have a structure we can fill in as we need.

CREATE SETTLEMENTS

Whether we have a map or not, we can start indicating where cities and towns lie. They're typically along major rivers or fresh water sources like a lake, and often where those empty into the sea. For choosing kingdom borders, we can use natural land features like mountains and rivers, even forests, which can become contested areas for resources. Before we go much further, we're going to need names, because it's time to start creating files about our world. This means settlement ones, at the least, and possibly sovereign power files and another about land features on this continent.

FREE REIN

Now that we have a framework, we can create other elements in whatever order we desire. We can fill out basic information for each location in the appropriate file. It's also recommended to create a spreadsheet that works as an overview of all locations; this allows us to determine the age of everywhere, colors, symbols, major products, and population levels. We sense where people congregate, where the oldest and newest places are, and in what direction life spread. This spreadsheet is our cheat sheet to our world.

With this done, we'll be able to work on any other element at our leisure and tie it into our setting according to the "Where to Start" suggestions that conclude nearly every chapter of *The Art of World Building* books. In no particular order, this can mean fleshing out land features, settlements, powers, species and races, plants and animals, gods, magic systems, armed forces, organizations, and ultimately, the cultures. The latter benefits from determining the cultural scope from the top down: power, region, settlement, and social group. Regardless of your decision, be sure to crisscross back and forth between files and periodically update earlier decisions.

FILE STORAGE

We need somewhere to store our ideas. An ideal scenario is to have access wherever we are, whether home, vacation, or work (we never know when an idea will strike). Or the toilet. Some smart phones are even waterproof so that we can work in the pool, a hot tub, or underwater! Depending on location, we have different devices we're likely to have with us, such as a phone, tablet, or laptop. And there's the old-fashioned pen and paper. There's no solution that will work for everyone so here we're just going to look at some options; this is not intended to be comprehensive but guidance on what to consider.

Only some of us make maps, and the programs that allow this usually require installation and a larger screen than a phone provides. Game designers may want to draw creatures that are best done in full-fledged apps as well. World builders are mostly concerned with text, including possibly a few spreadsheets for quick access to information about many places at once; this is what we're examining here. With all tools, we should consider that we may use it for months to years before changing our mind; will we be able to easily move to another working methodology?

HARD DRIVES

We can store our files on a computer hard drive. This will mean always bringing that device with us if we want to work, or taking a copy of files to another computer, which will need any app we use installed. Long ago, I used to bring mine on a writeable CD, then DVD, and finally a thumb drive as technologies changed; some of these carried a significant risk of being lost, which inspired attempts to encrypt them (another hassle). Today I bring nothing because I use Office 365, which we'll discuss later in this chapter.

Since hard drives can fail, it's wise to back up our contents to another device. We once needed a portable drive attached directly to our computer, but there are network accessible ones, some very robust. We can get one with a mirrored drive in a RAID configuration, which means it has two drives and content copied to one is automatically copied to the other. If one fails, our backup is still safe. One scenario this doesn't guard against is our home burning to the ground, destroying both backup drives *and* our laptop, for example. Due to this, it's wise to store files in two locations, such as a relative's house (if they can be trusted not to snoop, should we care) or a safety deposit box.

Hard drives offer few advantages other than a file system that can be backed up with a dragged folder. As we'll see, this can be done with other options. We can also store all types of files, not just world building ones.

WEBSITES

Websites offer the mobility we need to work from anywhere, but they carry a risk that our creative work is on someone's servers and can be compromised. This may expose us to hacking. Our devices, including a laptop (even at home), also face this risk, but it's arguably less likely that we'll be hacked than Google or Microsoft. Several niche sites dedicated to world builders also exist, and they are also less likely to be hacked because the information in them isn't personal enough and there aren't enough users to warrant the effort. However, they are probably much easier to hack. Creative people often worry about their ideas being stolen, and storing and transmitting them over the internet does expose us to more risk. The reality is that "no one" cares about stealing our ideas unless we're famous, but if it matters to you, consider it.

We should read terms of service carefully. Most of us are familiar with the idea that Facebook, for example, can sell our data to advertisers. Any website we use should explicitly state that we own our ideas, not them. I once received a job offer that stated that all work I did once hired belonged to the company, including anything I invented after hours, after I quit, and for the rest of my life. I objected and they admitted it was a mistake and changed the language to be more reasonable. It likely wouldn't have held up in court due to obscene overreach, but why take the chance?

Most sites cost money to operate, which means a potential membership fee for users, whether monthly or annually. This cost may not be necessary; what we're gaining is optional and can usually be achieved via other means. But even apps installed on a device are moving more to a subscription model, versus the old days of installing something and being able to use it indefinitely without paying again. Providers like Microsoft have seen the wisdom of making us pay all the time.

With websites, backing up our data may seem like a concern we don't have, as it's not stored locally on our device. But we should periodically download it, if possible; and if it's not possible, this is a risk. The provider is probably doing backups, but the likelihood of this depends on how professional they are. A company like Google or Microsoft almost certainly is, partly because they have businesses depending on them. But smaller sites run by a few programmers may not. Such sites might be hosted by a genuine hosting company (that does backups) or it might be on a server in the guy's basement. Some sites have already achieved a reputation for crashes that destroy data into being irretrievable. Research any such tool to see what other users are saying.

MICROSOFT OFFICE 365

While we can use installed versions of Microsoft Office, we also have the option to use the online or mobile versions. However, these typically offer a subset of features, being a less robust app. An O365 subscription includes all of them and using a browser to open a file in the desktop program takes a button click. It is fairly seamless to transfer files and folders between devices once we've synched then.

They presumably do robust backups, but if not, the files are also stored locally via Microsoft's OneDrive, which means that, provided the files are synching properly, we have the latest with our device even if we don't have an internet connection. And if we change the files, then the next time we're connected, they will synch.

There are apps included beyond just the word processor and spreadsheet programs (nearly thirty as of this writing). O365 has the advantage of being unlikely to go away anytime soon. One feature of Word that I use heavily is the "Navigation Pane," pictured next. We can use heading styles to create a hierarchy within our document, then easily collapse or expand it, and jump to a heading by clicking on it. It's only available in the full, installed version of Word, which is one reason why I work there whenever possible.

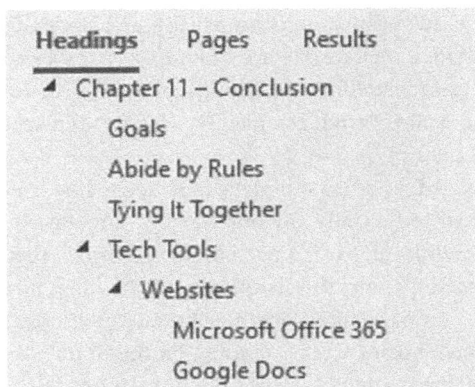

Headings	Pages	Results

◢ Chapter 11 – Conclusion

   Goals

   Abide by Rules

   Tying It Together

◢ Tech Tools

  ◢ Websites

     Microsoft Office 365

     Google Docs

Figure 78 Navigation Pane

O365 has an annual cost. Depending on what we purchase, it may include additional benefits, like the ability to have an email domain. This means that if we have a website, such as randyellefson.com, we also have an email address like mail@randyellefson.com so that we look more professional than using a Gmail one, for example; we can also add multiple addresses. If we're selling books or games, we're in business and this can be deducted as a business expense. These are not world building concerns but ones for our career.

This is what I personally use for not only world building, but for stories, email, calendars, and more. I just log in to O365 via the browser and access everything stored there; I keep many files out of O365 because they're either personal or seldom needed.

My working experience in a day can be like this:

1. Before going to work, via my laptop, I update a file, which autosaves.
2. At work, I open the file via the browser, see my morning changes, and add more.

3. While waiting in line for my lunch order, I pull up the file on the mobile app and add more notes.

4. Back at my desk during some downtime, I use the browser version again.

5. Once home, I work on my main computer and still have everything I've done.

6. Before taking my kids to an afterschool activity where I'll have no internet, I make sure files are synched to a lighter computer, then go, and while they have fun, I work disconnected.

7. At home, I ensure a synch and go back to working via my main laptop.

8. At bedtime, the kids are having trouble sleeping so I grab the lighter computer again and work beside them as they doze off.

9. I go back downstairs and resume working on the main laptop.

Aside from sometimes having to make sure a device has synched files, this is exactly what I wanted.

GOOGLE DOCS

One of Google's biggest selling points is that it's free. It offers multiple apps online and as mobile ones for a phone or tablet, including word processing and spreadsheets. We can organize our files into folders. They presumably do robust backups. We can also share a file or entire directory with someone, such as a collaborator. We can download entire folders to our computer, then store them offsite if desired, so manual backups are an option. I haven't liked the fonts and, since Microsoft Word is my main program, converting a Google file to Word produces poorer results until I manually fix it, so I stopped using this a while back.

WORLD BUILDING SITES

Multiple sites have been created to help world builders create and store their notes. As variations exist between them and we're not diving into each, only general observations are here. For the most up-to-date list, google "world building sites."

These sites are accessible from any device via login. Few if any have a mobile app and therefore, trying to use them via a small device's browser may be unappealing. We're unlikely to know their hosting practices, such as whether it's hosted in their basement or at a professional hosting company. The ability to download our data may not exist, and if it does, we'd have to investigate what format it's in. Can we easily port it to another platform?

Some sites provide writing prompts to help inspire invention. While this is good, that inspiration can come in many other ways that don't pose risks. These sites propose to help with world building, and while they offer advice, that pales in comparison to the depth that books (including this one) offer. Some provide the ability to integrate items for an interactive experience for an audience, which may become of interest if it catches on with them. Until then, no one is expecting it and it might be good to store some amount of material for our fans to enjoy but keep our main files elsewhere.

MY APPROACH

I produce and collect crazy amounts of files of many types and subjects. These include spreadsheets, word processor files, images, image editing files (i.e., Photoshop .psd files), raw and processed podcast and audiobook files, and more. There are PDFs and spreadsheets of sales reports from multiple vendors (Amazon, etc.). There are promotional images, whether final or draft book covers, advertisements, podcast episode images, and more. I run a publishing business, which results in receipts and accounting software files. It is endless. And of course, all of my world building files for each setting, including maps. Never mind all the personal stuff like photos, videos, taxes, and more.

For each book, there are character bios, an outline, random notes, and of course the manuscript. When I hire beta-readers, each returns another file to me. The same happens with an editor. I save all of these in archives, only my final manuscript being a live document on which I work. I also produce eBook files (the program I use to do it and multiple eBook formats). The publishing branch alone produces dozens of files per book.

I typically work on my laptop at home. This is where all of my files are. My fiction (and music, as I'm also a musician) files are currently sorted into four main directories:

1. (Almost) never changes: retired stuff I'll probably never touch. I rarely add to this unless I've ditched another idea or project. I not only don't need to add to this, but I don't need to look at it, but I save everything.

2. Rarely changes: previous year sales reports, published books/albums I'm unlikely to revisit, previous years taxes, old versions of websites, PDFs (they don't change). I seldom add to this and don't work in this directory.

3. Sometimes changes: frequently accessed files that don't often change, like book covers and other images I might need to repost on social media.

4. Regularly changes: my main working directory of stuff actively being worked on, and which likely changes every day. Financial transactions, current and pending book projects, sales reports, and promo materials.

What happens if my laptop's hard drive dies? I lose all of my work. I've been doing creative work for almost forty years now. Can you imagine losing all of it in a hard drive crash? I have a free backup program that runs once a week. It takes each of those directories and creates a single backup file of each, shrinking them down to take less disc space. Literally every Sunday for eons now, you can find me dragging the resulting files to a backup drive on my home network. My backup drive is a RAID setup. What this means is that there are two mirrored drives. What I copy to one gets automatically copied to the other. If one dies, the other one still exists unscathed (and there's always my laptop).

Once a month, I take my files offsite to a trusted location. I keep two identical pen drives. That way I can fill up one at home and exchange it with the other one in one trip. If I only had one drive, I'd have to go get it, come home, fill it up, and then take it back. What happens when I need a new laptop? I buy one, transfer all my files, and then I take apart the old one, get the hard drive out, get a screwdriver to open the drive, find my hammer, and have a fun few minutes destroying the disc.

I sleep like a baby.

GET ORGANIZED

If we choose to use a file system (whether online or not), we'll need to invent a way to organize our files. Otherwise we can forget entire files exist, know that they do but be unable to find them, or not remember which file we entered a note into. As some projects last years, we're going to forget all sorts of things; that's why we wrote them down in the first place, but it doesn't help us when we never see the note we left ourselves again. Knowing how we think is beneficial, so we know where we probably would've put something.

The world building websites typically have an organizational approach chosen for us. This section assumes we must decide. While there are many approaches, a rationale with examples is outlined below. Feel free to alter it to suit your sensibilities. We must always understand where we personally would have put something; I can find the sugar in my pantry faster than someone else because I know how I think. So if this organization doesn't work for you, used the guiding principles behind it to invent one that does.

FOLDER STRUCTURE

What follows is a possible folder structure, which is presented in non-alphabetic order so that it makes more sense, but a computer will often sort it alphabetically.

1. Name of World
    a. Life
        i. Animals
        ii. Plants
        iii. Monsters
        iv. Supernatural
            1. Gods
            2. Beings
        v. Species
            1. Races
    b. Armed Forces
    c. Continent Name
        i. Maps
        ii. Settlements
        iii. Sovereign Powers
    d. Continent Name
        i. Maps
        ii. Settlements
        iii. Sovereign Powers
2. Books
    a. Fiction
        i. Talon Stormbringer Series
            1. The Ever Fiend

There are different ways of doing any of this. For example, we could place settlements inside the appropriate sovereign powers folder, but this requires us to remember which one it's in when we're looking for it; also, since powers shrink and expand, it might've changed at some point. It can be easier to just list settlements by name in a single folder because their file is easier to find.

Rather than having a folder for animals with, for example, ten files (one each for ten animals), we could have a single file with all ten inside it. The same could be done with armed forces being in one file, species, races, and more. This is an approach I moved to in time to reduce the number of files and because I heavily use the Navigation Pane in MS Word to jump around.

Some of those folders have specific files in them. The "Name of World" folder might be called Llurien for my main planet, and within that are not only the folders above, but the travel and moon orbit calculator spreadsheets like the ones included in *Creating Places*, and a "Planet Llurien" file that details things like how many moons exist. My "Continent Name" folder has the folders listed and files for history, land features, and sovereign powers. If a magic system is specific to a continent, it might go there, but if it's worldwide, it goes higher in the hierarchy.

Regardless of our decision, it's easy to rearrange things in a file system.

SUGGESTED FILES

World building (and authorship) can produce many files that should be structured internally. The downloadable templates included in this series, and shown in each appendix, show ways of doing this but there are some specific instances to cover.

As just mentioned, we may want to include multiple instances in a single file instead of one per file. For example, let's say we have elves and dwarves. Do we create a file for each or one file that has both? This will depend on our use of technology. The Navigation Pane in Microsoft Word makes it easier to jump around a file. This allows us to place all of our species into one large document, which reduces file clutter and the numbers of windows we have open when working on multiple species at once, a frequent reality the farther into development we get. This happens because they've become so intertwined and updates to one often necessitate updates to another. A problem may be large file size, which can open more slowly, but this is seldom an issue.

Just as some subjects lend themselves to being in one file, others may not. For example, there could be so many settlements, such as more than fifty, that putting them in one file could make the document unwieldy. On the other hand, if we're using the plant template from *Creating Places*, this is short so that having fifty plants in one file is fine. It's all personal preference.

It's recommended to keep a spreadsheet with multiple tabs. The goal is a high-level view of many related items at once. Those fifty settlements can all be listed here, with columns for city colors, symbol, location, year founded, allies, which species founded it, population, which armed forces are here, major products, what it's famous for, and more. This is what I use when determining the age of every settlement at once, since I can see all of them in one place. Another tab can be for the world's gods, with columns for alignment (good or evil), gender, season, element, traits, symbols, which species they relate to, and more. The same can be done with species, plants, animals, and their most important attributes.

We should strive to avoid duplication in our files. With the spreadsheet just mentioned, we might place city colors on that and in a city's file. If we do this (and I do), make a mental note as to which is considered the authoritative source if they get out of sync. In my case, the spreadsheet rules because when changing something like this, I don't want it to resemble another settlement's colors and I'm therefore consulting my spreadsheet. We might also want to get into the habit of updating something everywhere, but lapses will happen.

Another issue is the rabbit hole problem. Sometimes we're busy with writing a story, for example, when we have a world building idea. We may know from experience that if we open a file to write it down more, we'll get sucked into the world building rabbit hole and stop working on our tale. My solution to this is a file with a title akin to "Llurien Changes to Make." This is my temporary location for ideas I'll flesh out and integrate with the setting later when I have time.

But what happens when we're away from that file or don't feel like looking for it? We've all heard of jotting an idea on a napkin. The technological equivalents are the notes app on our phone, or a calendar item, or emailing ourselves. This is fine but at some point, we need to take each of those and move them to that "changes to make file" for one reason: having dozens of pending ideas in a single file is far better than eight in our inbox, seven files on our phone, and the rest in calendar items that are going farther back in time, like emails, with each day. My random world building ideas flow from all of those into that pending changes file and, eventually, become integrated into the world files.

World Building Coalitions

If all of this seems like far too much work but something we still want to have, we might consider working with one or more partners. This would allow us to divide up the work and even focus on areas we excel at while leaving our weak areas for someone else to do. If all of us are authors, then all of us can write in the resulting setting. One caveat is that we'll have to be very aware of what everyone else is creating, and they might want to do some things that we don't want. One solution is to divide up continents, each of us taking certain kingdoms. One advantage here is that the gods or species can be the same across the world, but we can do different things on the smaller scale.

Tread lightly, however. More than one relationship has been destroyed by disputes over ownership, so if you embark on something like this, you should consult an attorney and draw up a legal document specifying your respective rights. This would include under what conditions someone can leave the partnership. For example, if you leave, you can no longer write books on that setting without getting approval from the remaining members in the partnership because they are still making changes and you must comply with those. This is true while you're in the partnership anyway.

What follows is a thought experiment about how multiple people can participate in a World Building Coalition (WBC). If you and others decide to enter into one, this may lend ideas on how to go about defining roles and responsibilities.

What Is It?

A world building coalition (WBC) is a collection of individuals who've agreed to build a world together, sharing the labor and fruits of that labor. While some items, such as overall world feel, gods, and many life forms will be shared, other items (like kingdoms) will belong to world building owners

(WBOs) who have ownership of them, such as say over whether proposed changes are accepted.

WHY DO IT

World building can take an enormous amount of time depending on how far someone is willing to go. By contrast, skimping on it is likely to produce mediocre results. To mitigate these problems, like-minded individuals can form a coalition, with agreed upon roles, responsibilities, and rights.

WHO DOES IT

Authors are the primary ones likely to create and participate in a WBC. However, gamers, hobbyists, or others who have no intention of ever writing a story can also form a WBC either for entertainment, or to effectively license the use of their world to authors. This can not only free some authors from the need to do world building, but allow those not given to storytelling to do creative work that results in published stories. These WBOs may have written agreements with a given author to share in the profit of any published works, though crafting those agreements lies outside the scope of this book. Interested parties should consult qualified entertainment lawyers.

THE COVENANT

Members of the WBC should agree to a covenant that lays out their rights, roles, and responsibilities, and other things to agree upon, such as terminology (are you going to call elves a species or race?). This includes "severability," meaning what happens when someone leaves the WBC and whether they retain their things or have them transferred to someone else. Or even whether they can get them back.

WORLD TYPES

There are questions to decide upon at the outset and stick to without alteration. One of these is genre. Is the world intended for fantasy, SF, steampunk, or something else? What kind of world this is should be cast in stone early on. The exception is when the WBC decides that a long history exists and what was a medieval-like fantasy setting two thousand years ago is a space-age SF one today. This allows creators to have variety and even decide that another member of the WBC can author stories in a given time period, provided that they meet the approval of the WBO of that part of the world.

Another decision is about technological level. Does the world have guns? Cars? Spaceships? How technologically advanced is the planet? Some areas can be more advanced than others, such as the Europeans being more advanced than Native Americans when Europeans discovered North America, but generally you'll want some guidelines.

ROLES

WORLD MASTER (WM)

A World Master (WM) is the overriding authority for a planet (or group of them in a solar system, for example). This can also be a called a Universe Master (UM). This person has tie-breaking authority during any voting. Responsibilities include moderating disputes, laying out rules, and general administration of everything in the WBC except what has been delegated to others for ease of management. This person is the "boss." In most instances, the WM will be the one who created the WBC, but if the original WM steps down, another member of the WBC may take his place.

WORLD MASTER BACKUP (WMB)

In the event that the WM is unavailable, such as being on vacation, a backup who has the same level of access should be appointed. The WBC will need to determine how much authority this person has, but generally, the WMB is responsible for ensuring the forward progress of the WBC can continue in the temporary absence of the WM.

WORLD BUILDING OWNER (WBO)

A World Building Owner (WBO) is every member of the WBC. Each should have voting rights, presumably equally. Each must sign the covenant and pay any dues for legal fees or hosting of shared files.

CONTINENT MASTER (CM)

While sharing a world building project is the point of a WBC, it makes sense for each member to have their own continent, with them as its Continent Master (CM). They are the owner of that continent, responsible for its name and everything on it, from land features to settlements and inhabitants. This allows each member relative freedom to do as they please on their land mass while using shared resources of the WBC/world, such as species, races, plants, animals, and gods.

A CM may carve out a period of their continent's time that belongs exclusively to themselves while allowing other members of the WBC to use or influence the events of their continent with the CM's approval, either in the past, present, or future. This might include others using or inventing history, characters, and items that originate or impact the CM's property. As the CM is the owner, he has final approval over whether such alterations are allowed. It is recommended that this approval take place prior to significant development work by another WBC member, and once approved by the CM, it cannot be rolled back. The CM becomes bound by the invention just as if imagined personally. The CM also then acquires ownership and responsibility of the item.

WBO REGENT

A regent is someone who is temporarily handling another WBO's responsibilities. This optional role must be agreed upon by others in the WBC. Any decisions made by a regent must be honored by others as if the original property owner had made them.

CREATIONS

The WBC must decide what items will be shared and what will belong to each WBO. As suggested by the Continent Master role, it is wise to let each member of the WBC own a continent. However, other divisions can be made, such as Sovereign Power Master or Settlement Master, Forest Master, or even Species Master, Plant Master, and Animal Master. What these have in common is that someone has responsibility and authority for an item and cannot be overridden by other members of the WBC (unless failing in their duties). By contrast, there are shared issues that the entire WBC must decide upon, such as by majority vote. These are often planetary-wide concerns. A potential list of shared items includes:

1. The number of and placement of continents
2. The name of world oceans and bodies of water adjacent to multiple continents
3. The number of gods and basic disposition, if the gods are real and worldwide
4. What species/races exist, especially if worldwide
5. The number and features of moons and other heavenly bodies such as rings, other solar system planets, and sun type

LIFECYCLE

World building can go on forever, but it must start somewhere. This section discusses the reality that some members of the WBC will inevitably leave the coalition. When this happens, ownership of their creations may (and probably should) fall to others. Otherwise, members of the WBC who want to use or suggest changes to the person's possessions cannot get resolution.

The WBC should agree on a rough time frame to complete shared items, such as gods, continent maps, and names of world oceans, for example. Some suggested options for a WBC to decide upon follow. Whether these options exist should be included in the WBC's Covenant.

OPTION 1 – PERPETUITY

In this option, a WBO never loses their rights. No one can alter what they've decided and codified in written world building files.

OPTION 2 – TRANSFERRED

A WBO can transfer their rights to another WBO, whether that person is an existing member of the WBC or a new, replacement one brought in for this purpose. This transfer must be approved by the WBC. The WBO must advise the WM of this request, upon which the WM will help coordinate discussion, voting, and transfer (or rejection), and any appeals or counteroffers by the WBC to the WBO. The WBC should have good, defined reason for rejecting the transfer. These include assessing the new WBO as unskilled or not a good fit personality-wise.

OPTION 3 – SUSPENDED

A WBO might be unable to participate for long periods of time, due to illness, bereavement, loss of interest, or just needing a break. The result might be inability to meet requirements, such as voting on shared resources, another WBO's request to make changes to the WBO's creations, or use them. In these cases, the WBO might intend to return and not lose stake in the WBC. The WBO will suspend their participation, but since this may negatively impact the WBC, the WBO may agree that another WBO, such as the WM, will take over responsibilities in limited fashion as a WBO Regent. Given the possibility of monthly expenses for shared hosting, an WBO might still be required to pay their share or risk expulsion.

OPTION 4 – ABANDONMENT

In the event that a WBO abandons their stake in the WBC, ownership can be assigned or taken by someone else with agreement by the remaining members of the WBC. The definition of abandonment is important and may include a timeframe upon which members are expected to reply to WBC business and failure to do such results in a declaration of abandonment. A three-month window seems plausible. A formal decision by the WBC should follow several written notices to the WBO with adequate time to reply.

OPTION 5 – QUITTING

A WBO can simply quit, permanently forfeiting all rights to their possessions, including using them in any way, such as in stories. To do this, a WBO must submit, in writing, their resignation, which becomes final upon acceptance by the WBC. However, the WBO can ask to come back at a later time at the discretion of the WBC. Another member of the WBC can take over the WBO's territory but must abide by many previous decisions so as not to impact other members of the WBC who were given rights to use material in this WBO's domain.

OPTION 6 – TERMINATED

To protect the WBC's investment of time, energy, and the integrity of the shared world, a WBO's participation in the WBC may be terminated due to violation of the covenant. Termination should be majority, not unanimous, because two WBOs can engage in collusion to violate the world's principles. The terms under which termination may occur should be explicitly stated, as with everything, in the covenant.

OPTION 7 – EXPIRATIONS

A WBC might decide in its covenant that membership in the WBC is automatically renewed annually, provided that each WBO reaffirms their continued interest in remaining.

OPTION 8 – DEATH

The death (or permanent incapacitation) of a WBO automatically transfers all WBO rights to the WBC until such time as the WBC formally votes to assign rights to another WBO. Until such time, any changes to the WBO property requires a simple majority vote of eligible WBC members.

OPTION 9 – DISBANDING

All good things must come to an end, and that can include the WBC, which should prepare for this eventuality and determine what happens. It seems obvious that future world building will not occur, but what about usage of the WBC's properties? This can be permitted for use in stories, for example, provided alteration of the world no longer occurs, unless that alteration is only to territory or items controlled by the former WBO of it.

If shared files are online and require payment for access, this can be achieved via downloading to each former WBC member's personal computers. However, if using sites that do not provide for downloading, continued access could become a problem. Consider the platform that is intended for this purpose at the outset.

COORDINATION

TRACKING

The WBC might find it helpful to keep a running list of decisions that have been made so that everyone stays aware. This will be especially useful if a new WBO joins. Maintaining this list would be the WM's responsibility.

MEETINGS

The WBC should attempt to meet periodically, such as once a month, to discuss group concerns and make decisions. This meeting can be in person or online. A possible agenda might include:

1. Members in attendance
2. Any official business, such as legal, voting, or membership changes
3. Updates of shared WBC items and progress, problems, resolutions
4. Discussion
5. Intended work to be done by next meeting
6. Incoming requests, such as those by authors wishing to write stories there
7. Membership and other dues or changes to them

TOOLS

The WBC will need to share files. This includes documents that everyone can work on, and WBO-specific documents that a WBO has rights to alter but others can only read, to make use of the WBO's work. Google Drive is free and provides both word processor and spreadsheet files. Programs that allow tracking of another's suggested changes may be useful.

LAST WORDS

Many of us will build more than one setting in our career. While this can seem intimidating due to workload, we can often reuse what we've done. For example, one absolute monarchy is much like another in its broad strokes, as is a religion, military group, or countless other elements. A god of war in one world is likely similar to another. We can tweak the details, reusing the basics. Reuse your own work whenever you can, following the Rule of Three, this time for your work instead of an analogue. Just as we don't want the audience to recognize we've modeled a power on Japan, we don't want them to realize our new book has a monarchy that's just like the one in our last book.

I hope you've enjoyed this series and found help, encouragement, and inspiration in it. I've enjoyed writing it and creating its offshoots, like the podcast that has tens of thousands of downloaded episodes. What started as a handful of articles has grown to multiple books totaling at least a quarter million words of advice. If it ever seems too much to take in, remember to do it in pieces and enjoy the process. Above all, never forget that world building is fun!

Please take a moment to review the books online. It's more important than you might think, and if you're an aspiring writer yet to publish, you'll eventually find out just how terribly difficult it is to get a book review. Established authors already know. We creatives must stick together and offer support. I hope I've found yours in the four years it's taken me to author *The Art of World Building*.

So where do you start? Where your heart lies.

Appendix 1
Culture Template

Culture Name

Naming the culture can be used within our work but is also useful for just our world building files, so we can write something like, "The Kiona culture dominates the Illiandor region." This way, we don't have to specify it everywhere, or repeat the details defined here (except when revealing them to the audience, of course).

Cultural Scope

Are we creating a culture for a sovereign power, region, settlement, species/race, or smaller sub group (such as knights, fighter pilots, royalty, etc.)?

Cultural Vision

Determine the morals, values, and beliefs of this culture. Use the government type to influence the decision.

The Body

Eye Contact

How is eye contact handled? Is deference shown? Is a gaze challenging?

Body Language

Do people move stiffly, relaxed, reserved, hunched over, sexy?

HAIR STYLES

How is hair worn by each gender, child, and professions of importance to the setting? Is hair styled a specific way on certain occasions and does this mean anything to people?

BODY MODIFICATIONS

Do people modify their bodies with piercings, tattoos, or implants? How common is this and what do they and those who don't do this think of the practice?

GESTURES

What gestures are common?

CLOTHING

How do people wear their clothes? What accessories are so common that they're part of typical dress?

GREETINGS AND FAREWELLS

Invent several expressions that are made when greeting peers and superiors. What physical behaviors accompany these?

LANGUAGE

Define the tone of conversations and invent both swear words and expressions, what they mean, their origin, and under what circumstances they tend to be used, and any responses others typically give. What languages are spoken?

Daily Life

Dining

What etiquette is followed? Do people talk with their mouth full? Is dining formal/informal? Are there multiple forks and spoons? Do people double dip? Is the mouth wiped on their sleeve, a napkin, or a tablecloth?

Bathing

How often do people bathe? Do they do alone? Is hot water an option and how often? Do they bathe in a river or a private tub? Is bath water used by multiple people?

Sleeping

Do people sleep alone? Do married people share a bed? What do people wear while asleep? What kind of beds do they have?

Employment

What is the work week like? How many hours a day, per week? Is there a siesta? Are people paid for days off? Are holidays observed and which ones?

Transportation

Is public transportation available and if so, what is it, how good is it, and what's the cost? What is its reputation?

PASTIMES

What do people do for fun?

RITUALS

How are birthdays and similar occasions celebrated? What holidays exist? What ceremonies are undertaken? Are there festivals they participate in?

FOLKLORE

What stories (and their characters or objects) exist? What lesson do they teach?

ARCHITECTURE

What impression do buildings give? What colors and materials dominate? Is there order or chaos?

APPENDIX 2
ORGANIZATION TEMPLATE

NAME

Include proper name and nicknames.

SYMBOL AND COLORS

The group may not have one in its early stages, but think of something that fits. Is anything given to new members, like a tattoo or pin with the symbol?

FAMOUS FOR

Summarize in a few sentences what people think of with this group. Details of events and traits are further down. Include legends if they exist.

THE FACTS

Are there things believed about them and which are false? Are some things true but doubted? Are some things unknown and would they change anyone's opinion of them?

TRAITS

WORLD VIEW

Are there guiding ideas that this group follows, such as the strong shall not prey upon the weak? What is the group's philosophy and how does this affect their actions?

GOALS

What does this group want to achieve?   Control objects? Control access to land or who's in control of it? Does it want power to achieve something? How close are they to achieving the goal(s)?

LOCATION

Where are they based and where do they operate? What sort of headquarters do they have, if any? Is it hidden or in plain sight? Is there anything special inside it? Is it guarded and if so, by what?

STATUS

Is the group still operating, defunct, or once gone and being resurrected?

POSSESSIONS

Does the group own any shared resources, like ships, a castle, or supernatural items? How is their usage managed?

RELATIONS

WITH SPECIES

How does this group get along with each of the species? More importantly, are they viewed differently by each species, or famous for different things? What species are in the group and in what numbers?

HUMANS

SPECIES 1

ENEMIES

Whether individuals, groups, or kingdoms, who are their enemies?

FRIENDS

WHO THEY ARE

WHO RULES

Is there one leader or a group? How is the leader(s) selected or changed?

MEMBERS

What species make up the group? What kind of people are here regarding skill set (warriors, wizards, etc.)?

IMPORTANT MEMBERS

Are any individuals especially important, besides a leader? Are any of them famous?

HISTORY

ORIGINS, DEMISE, AND IN BETWEEN

Where is the group from and based in now? What formative events made the group exist?

THE DEEDS

This is it. Tell us what this group does and how.

ARMED FORCES TEMPLATE

NAME

Include proper name and nicknames, and any slogans.

SYMBOL & COLORS

Remember to keep symbols easy for the non-artist to create in fantasy, but in SF where machines can create them, we can be more elaborate.

FAMOUS FOR

What do people think of with this group, and is it accurate?

GENERAL DESCRIPTION

The basics on what this military unit is, what it's for, and what types of sovereign powers have them go here.

LOCATION

We can leave this heading blank. Rather than listing here which places they're found, do so in a city/sovereign power file.

TERRAINS

Do they specialize or become hindered in certain terrains? Make a general statement here and tweak in the subheadings. Example: "They are effective over most terrains without vegetation to block horses."

OPEN LAND

Example: "They are especially formidable and feared in open lands, causing many to plan to lure them into other terrain or at least into hilly ground."

FORESTS

Example: "Only thicker forests slow them either with underbrush, closely packed trunks, or due to hiding opponents."

HILLS

MOUNTAINS

DESERT

Example: "The horses are slowed in sandy portions of deserts, but as most deserts are harder rock, they aren't slowed but do suffer fatigue from the hard ground and daily mileage suffers."

SWAMP

Example: "Being horsemen, they avoid swamps unless an established road exists, though these may be washed out."

SPECIAL SITES

Are there any locations they revere, fear, or where something notable happened? Do they have special buildings that cater to their needs and which are found in many locations?

LORE

Invent some famous stories involving them or their members, including an origin story if useful.

HISTORY

A generic army, for example, may not need a history, but a more specialized force like the U.S. Marines or a specific knighthood can benefit from one. If we're creating this file not for armies in general, but a specific one, we can add some details.

WORLD VIEW

PLACE IN SOCIETY

Do people respect or fear them, or take them for granted? Are they honored with holidays? Do they get special discounts at stores? Don't just say "yes." Be specific.

LANGUAGES

What languages are they required to know and to what degree? This may change by region due to the inhabitants there, but we can make general statements that they all must have a working knowledge of high-elven, for example. If we're inventing a specific army, then be specific about this one.

CUSTOMS

Use customs to add details to their behavior and expectations. Can they get a seat at a crowded bar every time because someone has to give one up for them? Do people salute? Is there a specific greeting or farewell? Using the "Cultures" chapter to flesh this out.

Relations with Regions, Cities, and Places

Is there a region (including sovereign powers), city, or place where they well received or hated? Save most details for those files, but we can note the most interesting ones below.

Regions

Cities

Places

Those Who Serve

Who Rules

Do they answer to someone outside their organization, like the Prime Minister? This may change with each army, for example, based on the sovereign power, but typically they answer to the head of state. Also decide if they unofficially answer to someone else.

Who They Are

What species or races are accepted, rejected, or in positions of power, typically?

Relation with Species/Races

For every species/race in the setting, work out how they get along and view each other.

RELATIONS WITH OTHER ARMED FORCES

How do they get along with other military groups? Are they rivals?

IMPORTANT CHARACTERS

FAMOUS MEMBERS

PAST

PRESENT

THE ROAD TO BECOMING ONE

REQUIREMENTS

What must they do before starting training? What sort skills are taught and must be mastered before full acceptance? Is there a way to bypass any of that? Are there well-known training centers or tests that cause fear and respect? Must people pass or die? All of this helps determine how elite they are.

SYMBOLS OF ACCEPTANCE

Determine what indicates membership. Is it a uniform, pin, weapons or armor no one else gets? How proud are members of these?

MEDALS, PINS...

Clothing

Arms

Weapons

Armor

In Society

Is there a day when recent graduates are announced? Do they get free drinks or food all day? How does society recognize them? Name on a digital billboard? The town crier yells it?

Ceremony

Is there a public ceremony?

Rank and Advancement

Where using standard ranks or altering them, note that here. Refer to the armed forces chapter.

Arms

The Weapons

Decide what weapons they use or never use. Much of it will be bestowed and technically owned by the military, but this isn't always true.

Required

PREFERRED

OTHER

RARE

ARMOR

What are they typically wearing and under what conditions? This detail lets us avoid showing them in the same outfit all the time. We also set scene expectations: someone not expecting battle might not be properly suited up for it.

REQUIRED

PREFERRED

OTHER

COMBAT

Invent some details on how they fight, including any back up skill like hand-to-hand fighting when disarmed. What are they not good at defending against (think a specific martial arts style)?

ON FOOT

AGAINST SPECIES

Repeat this heading for each species and how they fight them. Tactics against elves may be different from dwarves, for example.

On a Steed

Special Attacks

Special Defenses

Formal

Tournaments & Contests

Do they participate in any? Are those sanctioned or are they told to abstain?

Challenges and Duels

Do they make challenges for single combat? How and under what conditions? Do they respect challenges made by others? What happens during these and is the result highly regarded or disrespected?

War

Their Role

How are they used? In the vanguard? Are they saved for special moments and what are they?

Famous Battles

Missions

Have they been sent on any missions and what was the result? Is it famous? Did they discover anything important along the way? Unknown missions are some of the more fun to create.

Major Accomplishments

General

Inventions and Discoveries

Special, Famous, and Failed Missions

Unknown Missions

Appendix 4
Religion Template

Name

Symbols and Colors

Colors might not be important, but symbols are crucial. Use the history and a prophet's story to create simple symbols average people can draw.

Famous For

What do people] associate this religion with? A prophet? Non-violence? Aggressive missionary work? Choose the major aspects you've invented.

World View

Worship Practices

How often must they pray at home or at church? Is it formal? Are any materials or positions required (kneeling)?

Customs

Events and Holidays

Every religion will have an annual holiday and possibly events that take place regularly, such as once a week, month, or seasons.

Place in Society

How do various kinds of sovereign powers view them? Good or bad? Are they influential?

Locations and Holy Sites

Use the prophet's story to create a unique location.

Outreach

Do they perform missionary work and how aggressive are they about it.

Languages

What's the official language? What languages do they typically speak, read, and write? Do they try to be welcoming by learning them or exclusive by rejecting them?

Relations

With Species

With Military

With Other Religions

Do they have conflict with other religions? Most do.

Who They Are

FOLLOWERS

Are any refused to become practitioners?

CLERGY

Which species tend to be clergy and in what capacity?

IMPORTANT MEMBERS

Are any individuals especially important, besides a leader? Are any of them famous?

SECTS

This religion might have branches of it that believe and act differently.

HISTORY

The history should include the founding and a prophet or other legendary figure we leverage for most elements of this religion.

COMBAT

Are they allowed to fight or be in the military at all? What do they think of war?

AFTERLIFE(S)

What afterlife do they envision? Is it real? Do they help people prepare?

SUPERNATURAL ENERGY TEMPLATE

NAME

Invent a memorable name and possibly nickname (based on appearance or an event).

TYPE

Is this magic, radiation, divine power, or something else?

AVAILABILITY

How often can this force be used or encountered? Are those who harness it taxed in some way, such as with fatigue that limits usage?

PROPERTIES

APPEARANCE

This should include not only colors but whether it's invisible or can only be seen with magical sight or specific technologies. Are additional properties only visible that way?

FEEL

This includes its temperature range and whether it gives off heat, cold, or nothing. If the energy can be touched or sensed, what happens to flesh or senses? Is anything heightened or muted?

DURATION

How long does it last? Does it have phases, like a volcano?

INTENSITY

Is the intensity constant or in a state of flux?

SPECIAL

HISTORY

ORIGINS

Deciding its origins is optional as natural phenomena need no explanation, but did something cause this?

INCIDENTS

Invent a few incidents that have happened with this energy, including when it was first discovered, first contained, or first used as a weapon, especially if these went wrong or had significant impact on events of the time.

USAGE

CONTROLLING IT

Can it be controlled? By who? Is a technology needed? Is there a limit on that control? What happens when control of it is lost?

USES

Do people harness this energy for anything, or would they like to? Using it to power ship engines comes to mind. Can it be weaponized?

Appendix 6
Supernatural Land Template

Name

Decide on its name and at least one nickname, which may be derived from properties, appearance, and stories of what's taken place here.

Location

Access

How do people enter this land? Are there doorways or portals? Is magic or technology needed? Are entrances and exits guarded or available at only certain times?

Regions

Are there definable regions inside, like territories or landscape features (such as a forest)? Such regions might be named for phenomena there.

Settlements

Are there any towns inside? What are they like? Do they stay in one place or move? What is their attitude about travelers arriving?

Important Buildings

Do any buildings of note exist? What is important about them? Are some like holy ground where evil creatures cannot enter? Do they harbor bad things? Are they a trap?

INHABITANTS

THE RULER

Does anyone or anything claim to be the ruler of this land? Is that accepted or contested (and by whom)?

HORDES

Are there so many creatures of a particular type here that they amount to a horde that people associated with this place and fear? Where do they live? What attracts their attention? How can they be defeated?

MORTALS

Are there any humans (or other species) who've taken up residence here? Was that voluntarily or not? Is anyone rumored to be here but is not? Is anyone found here but no one knows they're here (i.e., presumed dead, for example)?

ANIMALS

Are there any animals that are specific to this place? Use the animal template from volume one to develop them, but indicate their presence here. There may also be animals that have wandered in or been brought here. Are they corrupted by this place in some way?

HISTORY

Have any events taken place here? Are those events known outside this land or not?

ORIGINS

Does anyone know where this land originated? Invent a reason and decide if people know or got it wrong, and how.

DEMISE

Will this place cease to exist at some point? Why and how? How soon is this to happen and what happens to everyone (and everything) still here?

LORE

Are there myths about this place? Stories true and untrue? What place does this hold in the minds of others: somewhere great or feared?

Appendix 7
Magic System Template

Name

This can be the type of magic, such as witchcraft or necromancy.

Symbols and Colors

A color is optional, but a symbol is likely. What is it?

Famous For

The practitioners will be famous for their basic skills, reputation, impact on society and events, and reputed character. State what these are.

General Description

What can practitioners do? What can't they?

Magic Source

What is the source of magic? The gods or the universe? Who made it possible?

Magic Origins

When the spellcaster is summoning power, where does it come from? People? The environment?

LAWS OF MAGIC

What laws of magic govern usage? Can people perform this type and another? Must anything happen first?

PREVALENCE

How common is the ability? How common is a fully trained practitioner?

MAGIC COST

What is the cost of performing a spell? Does it weaken them, age them, cause forgetfulness?

ARE SPELLS NEEDED?

Must practitioners use a spell and what for? What happens when a spell fails?

LOCATIONS

SPECIAL SITES

Are there any sites where magic doesn't work, or where it is augmented?

LORE

Are there any famous stories or myths about a past practitioner or all of them?

HISTORY

Invent several famous practitioners from the past and what they are famous for, such as ending or starting a war, helping royalty, saving the world, or threatening great harm. Some can be known for a smaller scale horror that occurred to them or by them.

WORLD VIEW

PLACE IN SOCIETY

How do most societies view them? Are they beneficial or harmful? Celebrated or shunned? Does family reject them or boast of them?

LANGUAGES

Is there a magic language, or another unique one, that they speak, read, and write? Can others learn it or is magic talent and training required?

CUSTOMS

How do they customarily behave in a wide variety of situations (found in chapter 1 on creating cultures)?

PRACTITIONERS

WHO RULES

Is there a governing body where wizarding practices are codified and abided by, like in the *Harry Potter* books? Who is the head of this and how is such a person chosen?

Who They Are

Is there a species, race, gender, or other characteristic that influences who becomes a practitioner? What percentage of each does this? What "walk of life" are they from?

Relations with Species/Races

Is there a uniform way they view and interact with any given species or race? And does that species view them a certain way? Have any incidents led to this relationship?

Relations with Other Groups

Are there groups, including military, with whom they have an ongoing relationship? This could be as allies or enemies.

Important Characters

Who are current and former members that have influence?

The Road to Becoming One

Requirements

How does someone acquire the talent and/or ability? Can they lose it and how? If there's a body that administers training in an official way, what must one do to be accepted into training?

Symbols of Acceptance

Are they allowed or required to wear specific clothing, pins, metals, or use an item like a staff? Is this required all the time or only at formal events?

Rank and Advancement

Are there any ranks that exist, such as starting on low magic before advancing to high magic? The ranks will have names and skill or power levels associated with them. Define them.

Training

If training is available, what form does it take, what is involved, and what limitations are imposed before graduation? What are the testing criteria, and what restrictions if any exist on those who graduate?

Arms

Are they allowed to use weapons or wear armor? What restrictions exist? Are laws of magic causing that or laws of "mankind?" In the latter case, we'll want to note that in the location's file more than here.

Combat

Are they part of any military group? If so, add them to that file. How do they behave in combat with other practitioners of this magic type or another, or physical combatants? Do they run, subdue, or kill?

SPELL TEMPLATE

NAME

What is the spell called?

MAGIC TYPE

For what type of magic is this spell or can more than one do it?

THE SPELL

Define what the spell does.

DESCRIPTION

Basic description of what the spell does, how, and under what circumstances it can be cast or be effective. What is the spell's reputation?

DIFFICULTY

How hard is the spell to cast? What skill or rank must the caster have achieved?

DURATION

For how long does the spell last? How long does it take to cast?

Range

How far from the caster does the spell take effect and for what distance or radius? How close or far must they be from the target?

Targets

Is there a species or race that is more or less affected by it? How so? Describe what they think of this being cast at them. Are they afraid or unimpressed? Are there any tactics that can be used to mitigate the effectiveness?

The Cost

What effect does this spell have on the caster? Fatigue? Memory loss? How does the caster feel about the prospect of casting it (will they be successful? Is the cost of casting it acceptable?)? Do they dread it or look forward to it?

How to Cast

Gestures

What gestures must they make to cast it? What purpose do they serve? Can the spell be done without them and if so, what impact does that have?

Ingredients

What materials are needed and in what quantity? Define how rare they are and how easy to carry or how something frequently is (such as a vial). Create this like a recipe, with instructions on the order to do everything in and how to handle something, such as rubbing it between fingers, snapping it, throwing it, etc. Be more elaborate if this is about creating a potion or item, for example, rather than a live spell done in battle where speed matters.

WORDS

Are any words needed? What are they in English? What are they in the language of magic? Are they controlling what happens, summoning power, or what?

ITEMS

Can this spell be put into an item or a potion? Are there limitations on it?

APPENDIX 9
LEGAL TEMPLATE

This template can be used to create a legal system for any jurisdiction.

SYSTEM TYPE

Is this a civil, common, or religious legal system? If the latter, what god?

THE LAWS

Create a list of laws which are specific to the setting. We can brainstorm here and then move laws to the template for the jurisdiction (city, power, etc.).

MORAL LAWS

Create laws that originate from morality.

INCIDENT LAWS

Create laws that originate from incidents. We can list the incident for our reference and understanding.

TRIALS

Who presides over the court? Who decides innocence or guilt? Are there lawyers?

DUELS

Are duels allowed? What are the rules? Where do they take place? Whether a sovereign power or settlement allows or forbids them will depend upon the location, but we can say how a government type (monarchy, federation) typically looks at them here.

TRIAL BY COMBAT

Is this allowed? What are the rules? Where do they take place?

TRIAL BY ORDEAL

Where do they take place?

PUNISHMENTS

List the available punishments that are unique to this setting, or ones common on Earth if there's something interesting about them, such as jail time in a specific jail.

APPENDIX 10
MONETARY TEMPLATE

Use this template to determine the monetary system in a sovereign power. An example is below and others are in chapter 10.

Material	Equivalent	U.S. Equivalent
1 iron	1 cent	1 penny
10 iron	1 copper	$1
10 coppers	1 silver	$10
10 silvers	1 gold	$100
10 gold	1 platinum	$1000

Figure 79 Monetary Template

UNIT

Is the currency a unit of weight or value? If a unit of value, what is backing it, a power, settlement, or another body?

FORM

Is money coins, gems, bills, or credits? Is it made from metal or gems? What does the money look and feel like? Do coins have milling around the edges?

EDUCATION TEMPLATE

SOVEREIGN POWER/SETTLEMENT

For which power or settlement is this education system being defined? Where do these schools tend to exist? Monarchies? Cities but not villages?

TYPE

What types of opportunities exist? Basic education, special education (like college or tech schools), or apprenticeships?

CURRICULUM

Don't create an entire course of study if not needed, but what subjects are taught? What languages must be understood and to what Earth grade level (3rd grade, high school). Which magic/tech subjects exist? Are there unique (and feared) tests?

RESIDENCY REQUIREMENTS

Do students live at home, in boarding school, with their master if an apprentice? For how long does this last, such as the weekdays (weekends at home), a semester, a school year, or until graduation?

FACILITIES

Are libraries, labs, and more on campus, offsite, or off world? What kinds are available and needed?

Cost

Is this a public school and there's no cost to attend aside from materials? If a private school, those are expensive. An apprenticeship might mean menial tasks while living with the master. Can students work if their family can't pay? Is a period of service required after graduation?

Student Requirements

Age

At what age must students enroll and when can they leave or graduate?

Gender

Are genders treated equally? Are classes coed? Dorms? Bathrooms?

Species/Races

Are all species allowed? Who is not and why? Are some favored?

Fame

Are there famous schools and past or current students? What caused their fame? What reputation has this given the school system?

Appendix 12
Game Template

Name

Earth Analogues

What games does it resemble? It can be more than one.

Details

Type

Is this a sport or a tabletop game? Is it only recreational or do professional versions exist?

Teams

Are there teams? How many? Can it be done without teams? How many players per team? Can they be substituted and under what conditions and how often? Can a player who leaves the game return?

Players

What skills do players need? How many positions exist and what are their roles and responsibilities? What sort of training, knowledge, or experience is required? Are species or genders (or anyone else) allowed or forbidden? What social classes play this? Do the elite only watch?

GAME PLAY

Describe how the game is played.

RULES

WHAT ARE THEY?

ITEMS

What items are needed? Balls, baskets, bats, cards, rings, dice? Is a field or court needed and how is it marked? What equipment do players wear or use?

UMPIRES/REFEREES

Do they exist? How many and how good do they tend to be?

PENALTIES

If they exist, how are penalties caused? Are there different levels of infraction? Can one be expelled over them?

SCORING

What are all the ways a point is scored?

VICTORY

How is a victor chosen? First to a score? Highest/lowest score when time runs out? Is a tie possible? Is there overtime if needed?

TOURNAMENTS

Do they exist for this game? Is this at the end of a season? Are there famous ones? What's the prize called and what is it?

ABOUT THE AUTHOR

Having written fantasy fiction since his teens, Randy Ellefson is an avid world builder whose work the Writer's of the Future contest has recognized three times. In addition to his popular world building books, he's the founder and lead instructor at World Building University, and hosts a related, popular podcast.

He has a Bachelor of Music in classical guitar but has always been more of a rocker, having released several albums and earned endorsements from music companies. A multi-instrumentalist who builds his own guitars, he's also band leader/manager, guitarist, and primary composer/lyricist for the metal band Black Halo.

A software development manager, he ran a successful consulting company for a decade before deciding to work for a comic book distributor.

Rand lives in Maryland with his son, daughter, and two cats.

Connect with him online

http://www.RandyEllefson.com
http://facebook.com/RandyEllefsonAuthor
https://linktr.ee/randyellefson

Buy books, music, and merch online at my store or others: https://www.randyellefson.com/mywork

RANDY ELLEFSON BOOKS

TALON STORMBRINGER

Talon is a sword-wielding adventurer who has been a thief, pirate, knight, king, and more in his far-ranging life.

The Ever Fiend
The Screaming Moragul

www.fiction.randyellefson.com/talonstormbringer

THE DRAGON GATE SERIES

Four unqualified Earth friends are magically summoned to complete quests on other worlds, unless they break the cycle – or die trying.

Volume 1: *The Dragon Gate*
Volume 2: *The Light Bringer*
Volume 3: *The Silver-Tongued Rogue*
Volume 4: *The Dragon Slayer*
Volume 5: *The Majestic Magus*

www.fiction.randyellefson.com/dragon-gate-series

ASCENSION QUEST

When Max awakens in a world unknown, he doesn't know how he got there or why he can't leave. And a mysterious Life Counter that no one else has is steadily descending to zero.

Death Singer

www.fiction.randyellefson.com/ascension-quest-litrpg-series

THE ART OF WORLD BUILDING

This is a multi-volume guide for authors, screenwriters, gamers, and hobbyists to build more immersive, believable worlds fans will love.

Creating Life
Creating Places
Cultures and Beyond
185 Tips on World Building
3000 World Building Prompts
The Complete Art of World Building
The Art of the World Building Workbook: Fantasy Edition
The Art of the World Building Workbook: Sci-Fi Edition
Creating Life: The Podcast Transcripts
Creating Places: The Podcast Transcripts
Cultures and Beyond: The Podcast Transcripts
The Art of World Building Podcast Transcripts Omnibus

Visit www.artofworldbuilding.com for details.

Randy Ellefson Music

Instrumental Guitar

Randy has released three albums of hard rock/metal instrumentals, one classical guitar album, and an all-acoustic album. For more information, streaming media, videos, and free mp3s: http://www.music.randyellefson.com.

2004: The Firebard
2007: Some Things Are Better Left Unsaid
2010: Serenade of Strings
2010: The Lost Art
2013: Now Weaponized!
2014: The Firebard (re-release)

Black Halo

Where classic Iron Maiden meets Metallica stands Black Halo, Randy's traditional metal band, where he is guitarist, primary songwriter, and band leader. For more, visit https://blackhalo.randyellefson.com

2024: Utopia

Bibliography

Volume 1

AAPA (1996). "AAPA statement on biological aspects of race" (PDF). *Am J Phys Anthropol*: 569–570

Apse, Will, "Types of Plants (With Pictures)," *Owlcation*. Owlcation.com, 8 JUN 2016, Retrieved 10 SEP 2016.

Arnold, Nicholas; Ovenden, Denys (2002). *Reptiles and Amphibians of Britain and Europe*. Harper Collins Publishers. pp. 13–18.

Beneski, John T. Jr. (1989). "Adaptive significance of tail autotomy in the Salamander, Ensatina". *Journal of Herpetology*. 23 (3): 322–324.

Biodiversity Institute of Ontario; Hebert, Paul D. N. (October 12, 2008). "Amphibian morphology and reproduction." *Encyclopedia of Earth*. Retrieved August 15, 2012.

Broome, Tom, "Introduction to Cycads," *Iris Online*. IrisOnline.com, Retrieved 28 DEC 2016.

Cartmill, M. (1985). "Climbing". In Hildebrand, M.; Bramble, D. M.; Liem, K. F.; Wake, D. B. *Functional Vertebrate Morphology*. Cambridge: Belknap Press. pp. 73–88.

Davis, Mark; Everson, Michael; Freytag, Asmus; Jenkins, John H. "Unicode Standard Annex #27: Unicode 3.1," Unicode.Org, 16 MAY 2001, Retrieved 15 APR 2016.

Dorit, R. L.; Walker, W. F.; Barnes, R. D. (1991). *Zoology*. Saunders College Publishing.

"Dwarfism," *WebMD.com*, WebMD, LLC, Retrieved 1 MAR 2016.

King, Gillian (1996). *Reptiles and Herbivory* (1 ed.). London: Chapman & Hall.

Garnett, S. T. (2009). "Metabolism and survival of fasting Estuarine crocodiles". *Journal of Zoology*: 493–502

Gill, Frank (1995). *Ornithology* (2nd ed.). New York: W.H. Freeman.

Hey, J., "The mind of the species problem." *Trends in Ecology and Evolution*: 326–329. 1 JUL 2001, Retrieved 12 JUN 2016.

Hildebran, M. & Goslow, G. (2001): *Analysis of Vertebrate Structure.* 5th edition. John Wiley & Sons Inc., New York.

Huey, R.B. (1982): "Temperature, physiology, and the ecology of reptiles." In Gans, C. & Pough, F.H. (red), *Biology of the Reptili* No. 12, Physiology (C). Academic Press, London.

"Long-distance Godwit sets new record". BirdLife International. 4 May 2007. Retrieved 13 December 2007.

"Introduction to Marine Mammals" and "Taxonomy," *MarineMammalCenter.org*, Marine Mammal Center, Retrieved 27 DEC 2016.

Leonard, Scott A; McClure, Michael (2004). *Myth and Knowing* (illustrated ed.). McGraw-Hill.

Mishra, S.R. (2005). *Plant Reproduction.* Discovery Publishing House.

Nelson, Joseph S. (2006). *Fishes of the World* (PDF) (4th ed.). John Wiley & Sons. Retrieved 30 APR 2013.

O'Grady, Stephen E., "Basic Farriery for the Performance Horse," *Veterinary Clinics of North America: Equine Practice*, Volume 24, Issue 1, Pages 203-218

"Plantigrade," *Wikipedia*, Wikipedia Foundation, Inc., Retrieved 8 JUL 2016.

Pitcher TJ and Parish JK (1993), "Functions of shoaling behavior in tele-osts," *Behavior of teleost fishes.* Chapman and Hall, New York, pp 363–440.

"Reptile and Amphibian Defense Systems". Teachervision.fen.com. Re-trieved March 16, 2010

Robert, Michel; McNeil, Raymond; Leduc, Alain (January 1989). "Conditions and significance of night feeding in shorebirds and other water birds in a tropical lagoon" (PDF).

"Sentience," *Merriam-Webster.com*, Merriam-Webster, Retrieved 23 DEC 2016.

Stebbins, Robert C.; Cohen, Nathan W. (1995). *A Natural History of Amphib-ians.* Princeton University Press.

Speaksman, J. R. (1996). "Energetics and the evolution of body size in small terrestrial mammals" (PDF). *Symposia of the Zoological Society of London*: 69–81.

Spearman, R. I. C. (1973). *The Integument: A Textbook of Skin Biology.* Cam-bridge University Press. p. 81.

Sullivan, Brian K. (1992). "Sexual selection and calling behavior in the Amer-ican toad (*Bufo americanus*)". Copeia.

"The Difference Between Annual Plants and Perennial Plants in the Garden," *The Garden Helper*, Retrieved 22 JUN 2008.

Thompson, Helen. "What's the Difference Between Poisonous and Venom-ous Animals?" *The Smithsonian Mag*, Smithsonian.com, Retrieved 24 JAN 2017.

Toft, Catherine A. (1981). "Feeding ecology of Panamanian litter anurans: patterns in diet and foraging mode". *Journal of Herpetology*. 15 (2): 139–144.

Toledo, L. F.; Haddad, C. F. B. (2007). "Capitulo 4". *When frogs scream! A review of anuran defensive vocalizations* (PDF) (Thesis). Instituto de Biociên-cias, São Paulo.

"Warm and Cold-Blooded," *CoolCosmos.ipac.caltech.edu*, CalTech, Retrieved 28 DEC 2016.

Willmer, P., Stone, G. & Johnston, I.A. (2000): "Environmental physiology of animals." *Blackwell Science Ltd*, London.

Womack, Mari (2005). *Symbols and Meaning: A Concise Introduction*. AltaMira Press.

"Why are most Semitic languages written from right to left, while European languages are written left to right?," *Quora*. Quora, Retrieved 12 JUN. 2016.

VOLUME 2

"Angular Speed Formula." *SoftSchools.com*, SoftSchools.com. Retrieved 03 OCT 2017

Barnes, Rory, ed. *Formation and Evolution of Exoplanets*, John Wiley & Sons 2010

Barak A. *The Judge in a Democracy*, Princeton University Press 2006

Bouvier, John; Gleason, Daniel A. (1999). *Institutes of American Law*. The Lawbook Exchange, Ltd. p. 7.

Budge, Ian. "Direct democracy". In Clarke, Paul A.B. & Foweraker, Joe. *Encyclopedia of Political Thought*. Taylor & Francis 2001

Casson, Lionel. "Speed Under Sail of Ancient Ships." *Transactions of the American Philological Association*. New York University 1951

Choi, Charles. "How Many Planets Can Fit Inside a Star's Habitable Zone?" *Space.com*, Space.com. 31 OCT 2016, Retrieved 03 OCT 2017

Culver, Henry B., *The Book of Old Ships: From Egyptian Galleys to Clipper Ships*, 2nd edition, New York: Dover, 1992

Diamond, Larry. *In Search of Democracy*. London: Routledge 2015

Diamond, Larry. "Timeline: Democracy in Recession". *The New York Times*. 15 September 2015 Retrieved 25 JAN 2016.

Gaballa, Nervana (2006). "Speed of a River." *The Physics Factbook*. Retrieved 03 OCT 2017

Hénaff, Marcel; Strong, Tracy B. *Public Space and Democracy*. University of Minnesota Press 2001

Her Majesty's Nautical Almanac Office and United States Naval Observatory (2012). "Conjunction". *Glossary, The Astronomical Almanac Online*. Retrieved 08 JUL 2012

Israel, Robert (2017). "Two moons Orbiting at Different Speeds. Formula for When They Coincide." Math.StackExchange.com, *Math.StackExchange.com*. 4 JAN 2017, Retrieved 03 OCT 2017

Jane Burbank and Frederick Cooper, *Empires in World History: Power and the Politics of Difference*, (Princeton & Oxford, Princeton University Press, 2010

Kricher JC. *A neotropical companion: an introduction to the animals, plants, and ecosystems of the New World tropics*, 2nd Edition. New Jersey: Princeton University Press. 1997

Lambeck, K. "Tidal Dissipation in the Oceans: Astronomical, Geophysical and Oceanographic Consequences". *Philosophical Transactions of the Royal Society* 1977

Lavery, Brian. *Nelson's Navy: The Ships, Men and Organisation* 1793—1815. Annapolis: Naval Institute Press 1989

Linacre   Edward   and   Geerts   Bart,HYPERLINK "https://books.google.com/books?id=10lElCT7v5wC&pg=PA363&dq=%22B ehav-iour+of+teleost+fishes%22+%22%22Functions+of+shoaling+behaviour+in+te leosts%22%22&num=50&ei=JzYKSpyWM42GkQSM992bBA" *Climates   and Weather Explained*. Routledge 1997

Lutwyche, Jayne (2013). "Why are there seven days in a week?" *BBC Religion and Ethics*. bbc.co.uk/religion. Retrieved 03 OCT 2017

"LZ-129 Hindenburg," *Airships.net*, Airships.net. Retrieved 2017-10-03

Krasner, Professor Stephen D. *Problematic Sovereignty: Contested Rules and Political Possibilities*. Columbia University Press 2001

Malanczuk, Peter. *Akehurst's Modern Introduction to International Law*. International politics/Public international law. Routledge 1997

Murray, C.D.; Dermott, Stanley F. *Solar System Dynamics*. Cambridge University Press 1999

National Oceanic and Atmospheric Administration, "Climate." Retrieved 03 OCT 2017

Núñez, Jorge Emilio. "About the Impossibility of Absolute State Sovereignty". *International Journal for the Semiotics of Law*. 24 OCT 2013, Retrieved 03 OCT 2017

O'Brian, Patrick, *Men-Of-War: Life in Nelson's Navy* 1st edition, New York: Norton, 1974

O'Callaghan, Jonathan. "Five Amazing Facts About Interstellar Space." *Space Answers*, SpaceAnswers.com, 13 SEP 2013, Retrieved 03 OCT 2017

O'Callaghan, Jonathan. "What Would Happen If We Blew up The Moon." *Space Answers*, SpaceAnswers.com, 11 MAR 2013, Retrieved 03 OCT 2017

O'Neil, Patrick H. *Essentials of Comparative Politics*. 3rd ED. W. W. Norton 2010.

Ossian, Rob. "Complete List of Sailing Vessels." *The Pirate King*. ThePirate-King.com, Retrieved 03 OCT 2017

Riemers, Bill. "Are a planet's moons and/or rings all in the same plane as the planet's orbit?" *Quora.com*. Quora.com. 26 AUG 2015, Retrieved 03 OCT 2017

Rodger, Nicholas. *The Command of the Ocean: A Naval History of Britain 1649-1815.* W. W. Norton & Company 2005

Scharringhausen, Britt. *Ask an Astronomer.* Curios.astro.cornell.edu. "Is the Moon Moving Away From The Earth? When Was This Discovered?" 18 JUL 2015, Retrieved 03 OCT 2017

Skyship Services. "FAQ." *Sky Ship Services*, SkyShipServices.com. Retrieved 03 OCT 2017

"Sloop." *The Way of the Pirates.* TheWayOfThePirates.com. Retrieved 03 OCT 2017

Touma, Jihad; Wisdom, Jack. "Evolution of the Earth-Moon system". *The Astronomical Journal* 1994

"Trigonometry." (2000) *Physics Laboratory*, Clemson Education. Retrieved 03 OCT 2017

"Types of Wetlands and Their Roles in the Watershed." *North Carolina State University*, Water.NCSU.edu. Retrieved 03 OCT 2017

Webster's Encyclopedic Unabridged Dictionary of the English Language, Portland House, New York 1989

Whipple, Addison. *Storm.* Time Life Books 1982
Whiteman, C. David. *Mountain Meteorology: Fundamentals and Applications.* Oxford University Press 2000

Wolford, Rider, Scott, Toby. "War, Peace, and Internal Sovereignty." Retrieved 19 JUN 2011. here

VOLUME 3

"11 Traditional Holiday Dishes From Around The World," *World Strides*, worldstrides.com, Retrieved 3 APR 2018

"A name given to a person at birth or at baptism, as distinguished from a surname", *American Heritage Dictionary*, Archived 11 December 2008

Anderson, Julie, Emm Barnes, and Enna Shackleton. *The Art of Medicine: Over 2, 000 Years of Images and Imagination*: The Ilex Press Limited, 2013.

Barrett, Stephen (2009-01-17). "Quackery: how should it be defined?". *quackwatch.org*. Archived from the original on 2009-02-25. Retrieved 2013-08-09.

"Bloodletting". *British Science Museum*. 2009. Retrieved 2009-07-12.

Burchfield, R. W. (1996). *The New Fowler's Modern English Usage* (3rd ed.): 512

Byron Good. *Medicine, Rationality and Experience: An Anthropological Perspective*, Cambridge University Press, 1994

Campbell, Mike. "Meaning, Origin and History of Names". *Behind the Name*. Retrieved 21 July 2008.

Carpenter, Charles E. (1917). "Court Decisions and the Common Law". *Columbia Law Review*.

"Chambers | Free English Dictionary". *Chambersharrap.co.uk*. Retrieved 10 JUL 2012.

Chauran, Alexandra (2013). *Animal Familiars for Beginners*. Jupiter Gardens Press.

"Colloquialism," *Literary Devices*, literarydevices.com, Retrieved 9 NOV 2018

Davies, Owen (1999). *Witchcraft, Magic and Culture, 1736–1951*. Manchester, England: Manchester University Press

"Death in Early America", Archived December 30, 2010, at the *Wayback Machine*.

D'Este, Madeleine, "The Origins Of 'Touch Wood': Tree Spirits, The True Cross, Or Tag?" *Folklore Thursday*, Folklorethursday.com, Retrieved 18 JUL 2019

DiGiovanna, Jessie Mooney, "Wedding Traditions: Why Is the Wedding Ring Worn on the Left Hand?" *Brides*, Brides.com, Retrieved 9 JUN 2018

"Dining Etiquette," *Etiquette Scholar*, etiquettescholar.com, Retrieved 28 FEB 2018

Faivre, Antoine; Hanegraaff, Wouter. *Western esotericism and the science of religion.* 1995.

"Feudal Japan History," *Legends and Chronicles*, http://www.legendsandchronicles.com, Retrieved 9 JUN 2018

"Fist bumps, high-fives spread fewer germs than handshakes, study says". *Los Angeles Times*. 28 July 2014. Retrieved 7 June 2015.

Forbes, Sophie, "18 gestures that can get you in trouble outside the US," *NY Post*, NYPost.com, Retrieved 15 MAY 2018

Halifax, Joan (1982). *Shaman: The Wounded Healer*. London: Thames & Hudson.

"Handshakes from Around the World," *The Connected Woman*, Theconnectedwoman.com, Retrieved 9 AUG 2019

Hasa, "Difference Between Culture and Custom," *Pediaa*, Pediaa.com, Retrieved 18 AUG 2018

Ingerman, Sandra (2004). *Shamanic Journeying: A Beginner's Guide.* Sounds True

Jackson, William A (2001). "A short guide to humoral medicine". *Trends in Pharmacological Sciences*. 22 (9): 487–489.

Janin, Hunt (2009). *Medieval Justice: Cases and Laws in France, England and Germany, 500-1500.* Jefferson, NC: McFarland.

Jouanna, Jacques (2012), "The Legacy of the Hippocratic Treatise The Nature of Man: The Theory of the Four Humours", *Greek Medicine from Hippocrates to Galen*, Brill, p. 342

Katsev, Igor. "Origin and Meaning." *MFnames.com*. 1 March 2011. Retrieved 5 January 2009.

Kehoe, Alice Beck (2000). *Shamans and religion : an anthropological exploration in critical thinking*. Prospect Heights, Ill.: Waveland Press.

Kumar, Manisha, "Difference Between Morals and Values", *DifferenceBetween.net*, DifferenceBetween.net, Retrieved 10 OCT 2019

Luck, Georg (1985). *Arcana Mundi: Magic and the Occult in the Greek and Roman Worlds; a Collection of Ancient Texts*. Baltimore, Maryland: Johns Hopkins University Press.

"Mage." *Online Etymology Dictionary*. Etymonline.com. Retrieved 10 NOV 2019

Marriott, John, Dr., "What causes people to lose their faith?" *Church Times*, Churchtimes.co.uk, Retrieved 5 MAY 2019

Melton, J. Gordo, ed. (2001). "Black Magic". *Encyclopedia of Occultism & Parapsychology*. Vol 1: A–L (Fifth ed.). Gale Research Inc.

Mircea Eliade, *Shamanism, Archaic Techniques of Ecstasy*, Bollingen Series LXXVI, Princeton University Press 1972, pp. 3–7.

Murray, M. A., *Divination by Witches' Familiars*. Man. Vol. 18 June 1918.

Nasaw, Daniel, "When did the middle finger become offensive?" *BBC*, BBC.com, Retrieved 9 DEC 2019

"Necromancy". Merriam-Webster's *Collegiate Dictionary (11th ed.)*. Springfield, MA: Merriam-Webster. April 2008.

Needham, Joseph. *Science & Civilisation in China: Chemistry and chemical technology. Spagyrical discovery and invention: magisteries of gold and immortality*. Cambridge. 1974

Neubauer, David W., and Stephen S. Meinhold. *Judicial Process: Law, Courts, and Politics in the United States*. Belmont: Thomson Wadsworth, 2007.

"Officer (armed forces)." *Wikipedia*, Wikipedia.com. Retrieved 1 SEP 2019.

Offit, Paul A. (2013). *Do you believe in magic? : the sense and nonsense of alternative medicine*. New York: HarperCollins.

Ovid. *Metamorphoses, Book IV, Fable VII*, Lines 440–464.

Palmer, Kim, "Hue Believers," *Stir*, Sherman-Williams.com, Retrieved 8 AUG 2019.

Pappas, Stephanie, "Thirteen common (but silly) superstitions to save," *Nbcnews.com*, Nbcnews.com, Retrieved 6 MAY 2019

Pereira, Michela (2018). "Alchemy". *Routledge Encyclopedia of Philosophy*. Routledge

Post, Emily (1922). *Etiquette in Society, in Business, in Politics and at Home*. New York: Funk & Wagnalls.

Rank, Scott Michael, "Crime and Medieval Punishment," Historyonthenet.com, Retrieved 6 JUL 2019

Russell, Jeffrey Burton (1972). *Witchcraft in the Middle Ages*. Ithaca, New York: Cornell University Press.

Sanderson, Brandon. "Sanderson's First Law." BrandonSanderson.com. Retrieved 8 NOV 2019.

Segal, Ph.D., Jeanne; Smith, M.A., Melinda; Robinson, Lawrence; Boose, Greg, "Nonverbal Communication," *Help Guide*, helpguide.com, Retrieved 9 FEB 2019

Seigworth, Gilbert R. (1980). "Bloodletting Over the Centuries". New York State Journal of Medicine.

Sem, Tatyana. "Shamanic Healing Rituals". Russian Museum of Ethnography.

"Significance of Tattoos in Different Cultures," *Tattoo Splendor*, Tattoosplendor.net, Retrieve 8 SEP 2018

Singh, Manvir (2018). "The cultural evolution of shamanism". *Behavioral and Brain Sciences*. 41: e66: 1–61.

Social Law Library, Common Law or Civil Code?, Boston Mass.

Thomas, Keith (1997). *Religion and the Decline of Magic*. Oxford, England: Oxford University Press.

Twin, Alexandra, "6 Factors That influence Exchange Rates." *Investopedia*, Investopedia.com. Retrieved 20 MAY 2019.

"What is social class?" udel.edu, Retrieved 8 APR 2019

"Why do some countries drive on the left and others on the right?" *World Standards*, Worldstandards.eu, Retrieved 10 JAN 2018

"Why fair tests are needed". jameslindlibrary.org. 2009. Retrieved January 8, 2017.

Wilbert, Johannes; Vidal, Silvia M. (2004). Whitehead, Neil L.; Wright, Robin (eds.). *In Darkness and Secrecy: The Anthropology of Assault Sorcery and Witchcraft in Amazonia*. Durham, NC: Duke University Press.

www.ingramcontent.com/pod-product-compliance
Lightning Source LLC
Chambersburg PA
CBHW031114020426
42333CB00012B/85